LONG LOAN

Items must be returned by the last date
stamped below or immediately if recalled.
To renew telephone 01792 295178.

BENTHYCIAD HIR

Dylid dychwelyd eitemau cyn y dyddiad a
stampiwyd olaf isod, neu ar unwaith os
gofynnir amdanynt yn ôl.
I adnewyddu ffôn 01792 295178.

English Prose
of the
Nineteenth Century

Hilary Fraser
with
Daniel Brown

Longman

London and New York

Addison Wesley Longman
Edinburgh Gate
Harlow
Essex CM20 2JE
England
and Associated Companies throughout the world.

Published in the United States of America
by Addison Wesley Longman Inc., New York.

First published 1997

ISBN 0 582 05137 1 CSD
ISBN 0 582 05136 3 PPR

British Library Cataloguing-in-Publication Data

A catalogue record for this book is
available from the British Library

Library of Congress Cataloging-in-Publication Data

A catalog entry for this title is
available from the Library of Congress

Set by 35 in 9½ on 11pt Bembo
Produced by Longman Singapore Publishers (Pte) Ltd.
Printed in Singapore

Contents

Editors' Preface

The multi-volume Longman Literature in English Series provides students of literature with a critical introduction to the major genres in their historical and cultural context. Each volume gives a coherent account of a clearly defined area, and the series, when complete, will offer a practical and comprehensive guide to literature written in English from Anglo-Saxon times to the present. The aim of the series as a whole is to show that the most valuable and stimulating approach to the study of literature is that based upon awareness of the relations between literary forms and their historical contexts. Thus the areas covered by most of the separate volumes are defined by period and genre. Each volume offers new and informed ways of reading literary works, and provides guidance for further reading in an extensive reference section.

In recent years, the nature of English studies has been questioned in a number of increasingly radical ways. The very terms employed to define a series of this kind – period, genre, history, context, canon – have become the focus of extensive critical debate, which has necessarily influenced in varying degrees the successive volumes published since 1985. But however fierce the debate, it rages around the traditional terms and concepts.

As well as studies on all periods of English and American literature, the series includes books on criticism and literary theory and on the intellectual and cultural context. A comprehensive series of this kind must of course include other literatures written in English, and therefore a group of volumes deals with Irish and Scottish literature, and the literature of India, Africa, the Caribbean, Australia and Canada. The forty-seven volumes of the series cover the following areas: Pre-Renaissance English Literature, English Poetry, English Drama, English Fiction, English Prose, Criticism and Literary Theory, Intellectual and Cultural Context, American Literature, Other Literatures in English.

David Carroll
Michael Wheeler

Preface

I wish first of all to thank Michael Wheeler and David Carroll not only for inviting me to contribute to the Longman Literature in English Series but also for their help and encouragement throughout the writing of this book. I have been fortunate indeed in having two such eminent Victorianists as my general editors. I am particularly grateful to them for their qualities of patience and understanding. Since agreeing to write this volume I have had three children, each of whom has brought forth warm congratulations from Michael and David, even though they must have wondered when the book would ever appear.

It was partly because of such new pressures upon my time, but mainly because of the truly illuminating comments Daniel Brown had made in our many discussions of the project while it was still in its early stages, that I decided to ask him to make a more formal and substantial contribution to its writing. Daniel wrote the Introduction and the section on 'Intellectual Formations' on pages 226–67. I am extremely grateful to him for taking time away from his own work on Hopkins and nineteenth-century philosophical and scientific thought, and lending this book an expertise on the complex and interconnecting intellectual currents of the age which it otherwise would have lacked.

Even with Daniel's contribution it has of course been impossible to include an adequate discussion of any (let alone all) of the nineteenth-century non-fiction prose genres and prose writers. In every chapter I have been obliged to select for detailed discussion a small number of writers and areas that, whilst not in themselves in any simple sense 'representative' of their age or their discipline, have been chosen for the purposes of this study to illustrate aspects of the discursive practices of the period. Thus it is that, in the chapter on science, works by Davy and Darwin are examined in some detail as particularly rich and accessible examples of nineteenth-century scientific writing, the rest of which is only sketched in; in that on exploration and travel literature I confine myself to a few writers on Africa, the United States, and Italy, as a way of gesturing towards the wider field; and so on through the volume.

The book does not aim at comprehensiveness, but it does attempt to suggest something of the extraordinary range of nineteenth-century prose by including discussion of texts by writers typically neglected in studies which concentrate upon canonical sage-writing. As well as the kinds of prose which have always had a place in literary studies it looks at prose genres which have until recently often been regarded as sub-literary or extra-literary – such as domestic manuals, social reportage, and scientific treatises. Alongside the monumental figures of the period – Coleridge, Newman, Arnold, Ruskin – appear an array of more modest but nonetheless important writers – women, working-class authors, and writers who have simply been cast into the shadows by the conventional literary historical practice of highlighting a 'great tradition'. This has meant, regrettably, that the monumental figures have had to be squeezed into a smaller space, or even, in some cases, excluded altogether. It is hoped that the resulting selective account of the century's prose writing is at least no guiltier of distortion and partiality than more traditional studies, and that it offers a glimpse of the astonishing richness and diversity of Romantic and Victorian prose discourse.

One of the great pleasures of writing this book has been the opportunity afforded to read widely in recent nineteenth-century critical scholarship. In the last two decades the critical analysis of non-fiction prose, more than perhaps any other area of writing, has undergone a revolution. The boundaries that once seemed so important between non-fiction and fiction, between different non-fiction prose genres, indeed between 'literature' as a category and other kinds of writing, seem increasingly irrelevant in the current revisionary critical context. The most innovative and important recent work in nineteenth-century studies has, rather, attended to the discursive play between and within disciplines, to the ideological forces and rhetorical habits that govern all forms of cultural discourse, demonstrating, in a way that is quite distinct from earlier scholarship, the irreducible historicity of the text and the strategies of culture. Such research has tended to contest the very concept of canonicity, and has led to the critical rehabilitation of a great body of non-fiction prose that previously only had the status of background material. I hope that my survey of the field reflects something of the vigour and originality of this new historicist interdisciplinary scholarship. Where my own arguments represent a distillation of the work of others, the debt has been acknowledged in endnotes, and I have included the critical texts upon which I have drawn in the bibliographies at the end of the book.

The project has been generously supported by the Australian Research Council and The University of Western Australia, to whom I am greatly indebted and wish to record my thanks. The award of an ARC grant funded some research assistance and enabled me to consult material in the Bodleian Library and the British Library; a UWA research award relieved me of teaching responsibilities for six months, giving me a period in which to write without interruption. I have completed the book whilst on study leave at The University of Lancaster, where the English Department, and particularly its Head, Keith Hanley, has given me a warm welcome and a good deal of practical support.

The University of Western Australia, like Lancaster, has provided a stimulating intellectual environment within which to prepare such a book, and I owe a great deal to the friends and colleagues who have been so generous with their help. Bob White has been a sympathetic and inspirational Head of Department and a good friend; he has also shared with me his extensive library and his own enthusiasm for and expertise on Clare and Hazlitt, in particular. My former and much-missed colleague, Tim Dolin, was an enormous help in the early stages of the project, as always enabling me to see things in new and interesting ways. Other nineteenth-century colleagues who have contributed to my understanding of the prose of the period are Dorothy Collin, Kieran Dolin, Ray Forsyth, Judith Johnston, and, in the History Department, Iain Brash and Jane Long. I thank them all, as I do the members of my Honours class on ninetenth-century women's prose writing who taught me so much – especially Victoria Burrows and Melanie Cariss – and my graduate students, past and present – particularly Lucy Dougan and Sally Scott. A book such as this has meant exploring unfamiliar territories, and I am grateful to Robyn Owens for our long talks about scientific writing and to Deirdre Coleman for sharing so generously her rich and various knowledge of early nineteenth-century writing. These women, together with Gail Jones, Sue Midalia, Prue Kerr, Patricia Crawford, Philippa Maddern, and Delys Bird, as well as having the kind of intellectual qualities to which I aspire, have been very important to me in more personal ways. I thank them for their friendship and affirmation. For their invaluable and meticulous help at the editing stage, my thanks to Bruce McClintock (again) and Tony Hughes d'Aeth.

Most of all, I thank Rob, for making the juggling act possible by shouldering more than his fair share of the domestic responsibilities, and for sustaining me on a day-to-day basis. And finally, but with all my heart, I thank Matthew, Clair, and Adam, who, when the prose threatened to take over, have filled my life with poetry.

Hilary Fraser
1996

Longman Literature in English Series

General Editors: David Carroll and Michael Wheeler
University of Lancaster

Pre-Renaissance English Literature

* ⋆ English Literature before Chaucer *Michael Swanton*
* English Literature in the Age of Chaucer
* ⋆ English Medieval Romance *W. R. J. Barron*

English Poetry

* ⋆ English Poetry of the Sixteenth Century *Gary Waller (Second Edition)*
* ⋆ English Poetry of the Seventeenth Century *George Parfitt (Second Edition)*
* English Poetry of the Eighteenth Century, 1700–1789
* ⋆ English Poetry of the Romantic Period, 1789–1830 *J. R. Watson (Second Edition)*
* ⋆ English Poetry of the Victorian Period, 1830–1890 *Bernard Richards*
* English Poetry of the Early Modern Period, 1890–1940
* ⋆ English Poetry since 1940 *Neil Corcoran*

English Drama

* English Drama before Shakespeare
* ⋆ English Drama: Shakespeare to the Restoration, 1590–1660 *Alexander Leggatt*
* ⋆ English Drama: Restoration and Eighteenth Century, 1660–1789 *Richard W. Bevis*
* English Drama: Romantic and Victorian, 1789–1890
* ⋆ English Drama of the Early Modern Period, 1890–1940 *Jean Chothia*
* English Drama since 1940

English Fiction

* ⋆ English Fiction of the Eighteenth Century, 1700–1789 *Clive T. Probyn*
* ⋆ English Fiction of the Romantic Period, 1789–1830 *Gary Kelly*
* ⋆ English Fiction of the Victorian Period, 1830–1890 *Michael Wheeler (Second Edition)*
* ⋆ English Fiction of the Early Modern Period, 1890–1940 *Douglas Hewitt*
* English Fiction since 1940

English Prose

* English Prose of the Seventeenth Century, 1590–1700 *Roger Pooley*
  English Prose of the Eighteenth Century
* English Prose of the Nineteenth Century *Hilary Fraser with Daniel Brown*

Criticism and Literary Theory

Criticism and Literary Theory from Sidney to Johnson
Criticism and Literary Theory from Wordsworth to Arnold
* Criticism and Literary Theory, 1890 to the Present *Chris Baldick*

The Intellectual and Cultural Context

The Sixteenth Century
* The Seventeenth Century, 1603–1700 *Graham Parry*
* The Eighteenth Century, 1700–1789 *James Sambrook (Second Edition)*
* The Romantic Period, 1789–1830 *J. R. Watson*
* The Victorian Period, 1830–1890 *Robin Gilmour*
  The Twentieth Century: 1890 to the Present

American Literature

American Literature before 1880
* American Poetry of the Twentieth Century *Richard Gray*
* American Drama of the Twentieth Century *Gerald M. Berkowitz*
* American Fiction, 1865–1940 *Brian Lee*
* American Fiction since 1940 *Tony Hilfer*
* Twentieth-Century America *Douglas Tallack*

Other Literatures

Irish Literature since 1800
Scottish Literature since 1700
Australian Literature
* Indian Literature in English *William Walsh*
  African Literature in English: East and West
* Southern African Literatures *Michael Chapman*
  Caribbean Literature in English
* Canadian Literature in English *W. J. Keith*

* *Already published*

For
Rob Matthew, Clair, and Adam

And for
Porraig and Jonah

Introduction

History and genre: the periodical essay

> On the eve of the nineteenth century began in Europe the
> great modern revolution. The thinking public and the human
> mind changed, and underneath these two collisions a new
> literature sprang up.
>
> (Taine)[1]

> . . . [T]he great and peculiar change which was begun at the
> end of the last century, and dominates our own; that sudden
> increase of the width, the depth, the complexity of intellectual
> interest, which has many times torn and distorted literary style,
> even with those best able to comprehend its laws.
>
> (Pater)[2]

Both Taine and Pater locate the writing of their century firmly within
its history, a history they describe in transitive verbs as accelerated and
as violent. Furthermore these passages indicate the importance of historical contexts for understanding even the briefest pieces of writing.
Each of these short extracts draws not only upon their contemporary
readers' general knowledge, but also upon codes of rhetoric that would
have been familiar to them. Rather than regarding their age as part of a
steady, gradually unfolding narrative of history, Taine and Pater see it
as marking a radical break with such a pattern. In a century when knowledge of the Bible was inseparable from literacy, this view of history
was often cast in millenarian rhetoric, and such calamitarian overtones can
be discerned in Taine and Pater. Both look back to 'the eve of the nineteenth century' as the moment at which a fundamental change occurred.
For Pater this change is 'peculiar' (that is, unique), 'great', and 'sudden'.
Taine similarly equates the nineteenth century with 'the great modern
revolution'.

While such violent and rapid change was familiar to a nineteenth-
century readership from the events of the French Revolution of 1789
and the dislocations of the Industrial Revolution, the imagery of violence used by Taine and Pater is more abstract than that associated with

bloody social revolution and dark satanic mills. Instead it suggests another source of imagery that was often drawn upon in millenarian rhetoric, namely, Catastrophism, the hypothesis of geological revolutions which maintains that the earth has been formed not gradually but abruptly, by massive volcanic and other geological upheavals that occurred throughout its history. The theory had a general currency for most of the nineteenth century, probably because it sees in nature a clear parallel to recent history and the dynamic experiences of modernity. All those things which had traditionally seemed to be most secure and which were accordingly referred to by analogy with geological phenomena, such as the 'strata' of society and the 'rock' of the Church, were from the late eighteenth century increasingly called into doubt. By seeing the most apparently inert and foundational matter, the very earth beneath our feet, as in fact dynamic, Catastrophism was hugely successful in expressing this new sense of radical uncertainty. While neither Taine nor Pater refers explicitly to this geological theory, their imagery invokes analogies drawn from it.

It is presumably to the new middle-class demography of the 'thinking public' (which became entrenched as a result of the class conflicts of the French Revolution and the Industrial Revolution), and the attendant upheaval, in ideas and belief, in 'the human mind', that Taine refers in his passage and these which he sees as comprising the 'two collisions'. The metaphor suggests the collision of massive historical entities analogous to huge bodies of rock forced against one another by seismic pressures: the struggle for power between two strata of society, the rising mercantile classes and the traditional feudal aristocracy; or the conflict between the rock of Church doctrine and rationalist thought. Such 'collisions', Taine suggests, provided the conditions for the rapid and strong growth of 'a new literature', much as the turning over of soil, or, more radically, the upheaval of rich volcanic matter to the surface of the earth, promote the growth of plants.

A geological metaphor is also discernible in Pater's description of modern intellectual life, the terms of which suggest the opening of a huge fissure, a 'sudden increase of . . . width' and 'depth', an abyss of bewildering 'complexity' into which the modern thinker has been hurled. Furthermore, the violence of this upheaval inflects modern writing. The macrocosmic ripping apart of the earth beneath our feet which opens up the abyss of modern intellectual history registers at the microcosmic level of 'literary style', 'which has [been] many times torn and distorted'.

The passages from Taine and Pater are remarkable for their brevity and lack of specific detail. The suggestive pair of sentences from Taine constitute in its entirety the opening paragraph of Book Four of his popular *History of English Literature*, while Pater makes his similar observations in passing in a newspaper review on 'English Literature'. To a large extent both extracts depend for their meaning upon the knowledge that a contemporary general readership could be trusted to bring to them. Such vague references as Taine's to 'two collisions' and Pater's to 'the great and peculiar change' evidently provided their original readers with sufficient cues to allow them to be understood. It is with such relations between nineteenth-century non-fiction prose and its historical contexts, relations which Taine and Pater regard as fundamental to understanding the literature of the period, that the following book is concerned.

The present, introductory chapter continues the discussion prompted by the extracts from Taine and Pater by asking a few general questions about the relations between history and literary form in nineteenth-century England. Before dividing up the formidable field of nineteenth-century non-fiction prose into the more manageable categories specified by the headings of the other chapters in this book, it is useful to have some sense of what draws them all together – to have an overview of some of the historical circumstances and forms of writing that are common to most of them. This chapter addresses the fundamental question of why this time and place produced such a vast torrent of non-fiction prose, of why such a plethora of new (and old) ideas, information and opinions churned out of the printing presses, engendering new areas of study and speculation (as well as complicating established ones) with constant streams of controversy. This issue is related to the question of form, of why some genres of prose, and one in particular – the period-ical essay – proved to be so central to the intellectual life of nineteenth-century England. The concern with genre is an abiding one for this book, with particular genres associated with specific areas of inquiry discussed more fully in the relevant chapters. However, as the great overarching non-fiction genre of the nineteenth century, the periodical essay warrants separate and preliminary attention. It accordingly provides the main focus for the present chapter.

When we think of nineteenth-century non-fiction prose it is prob-ably of the row upon row of heavy volumes that make up the collected works of writers such as Coleridge, Ruskin, Carlyle, Newman and Matthew Arnold, or of the multi-volume lives and letters of Victorian worthies, or of the massive sociological surveys of Mayhew and Booth. The overwhelming impression most people have of the prose of the last century is that it was weighty and expansive. And yet within the col-lected library editions may be found multiple works, many of which were in their origins occasional pieces, written for a journal in reaction to a controversial publication; numerous biographies were written, like Thomas de Quincey's of Coleridge, for instance, for a periodical, on an impulse, upon news of the subject's death; and many a study of the urban poor originated, like Mayhew's, as a piece of journalism. Over against the familiar perception of the monumental nature of nineteenth-century prose, and of the predominance of the book, it must be recalled that non-fiction prose found other forms of publication and methods of circulation: in the tract, the pamphlet, the published lecture or sermon, and above all the periodical essay and review.

While the essay was often regarded at the turn of the nineteenth century as lightweight and belle-lettristic, the fortunes and status of the genre were greatly enhanced with the advent of the mandarin quarterly reviews, the *Edinburgh* (1802) and the *Quarterly* (1809). Reviews and magazines became big business in the nineteenth century and contributors were often paid well and promptly. They consequently enabled many people, including women and men of lower-class origins, to be professional writers and intellectuals. Subjects that could be explored in the essay, and the ways in which they could be treated, ranged very widely indeed. This factor again made the genre truly democratic, and open to those who were denied formal educations, including women of all classes. Perhaps most importantly, anonymous publication was an option, and indeed often a requisite, in periodical publication throughout the century, a factor that shielded women writers from the censure they attracted in writing on subjects deemed inappropriate to their gender.

According to J. Don Vann and Rosemary T. Van Arsdel the 'circulation of periodicals and newspapers was larger and more influential in the nineteenth century than printed books, and served a more varied constituency in all walks of life'.[3] This is saying a great deal, given that printed books were read widely and in unprecedented numbers. For the first half of the century books were expensive and available to middle-class people mainly through paying subscriptions to lending-libraries, which became profitable businesses, with some boasting a million volumes. While the need for circulating libraries continued during the second half of the century, new books became more affordable for many as incomes rose and printing costs continued to fall. From the 1850s some free lending libraries began to appear.[4]

While the newspaper had its beginnings early in the eighteenth century, and reviews such as *The Monthly Review* (1749–1825) and the *Critical Review* (1756–1817) had a role in the literary culture of the second half of the century, these forms can be said to belong more properly to the nineteenth century. Walter E. Houghton estimates that the Victorians published over 25,000 journals and guesses that the number of magazines was in the hundreds. He quotes George Saintsbury who, reviewing the century's literature at its close, wrote summarily, 'perhaps there is no single feature . . . not even the enormous popularization and multiplication of the novel, which is so distinctive and characteristic as the development in it of periodical literature.'[5] Saintsbury is rather more bold in describing the importance of the periodical essay during the first thirty years of the century. He writes in his *Short History of English Literature* (1898) that 'the chief special feature in prose of the first thirty years of the nineteenth century' belonged not to the novels of Austen and Scott, but 'rather to the new developments of the essay, which was fostered, and indeed rendered possible, by the increased demand for periodical literature'.[6] Periodicals were available, from early in the century, to all classes of people. Cheap subsidised Evangelical papers were affordable for many of the poor, while more expensive periodicals, such as Cobbett's radical *Political Register*, were also available to them, even to the illiterate, through readings in public bars. Such readings, along with rentals (which for newspapers were often by the hour), and systems of shared subscriptions, meant that the readership of periodicals tended greatly to exceed their print runs.[7]

From the point of view of the kind of literary and intellectual work focused upon in this book, the most important innovation of the early part of the nineteenth century was the advent of the quarterly reviews. Margaret Oliphant, writing in 1882, looked back to the *Edinburgh Review* as 'the beginning of the great and popular school of periodical writing'.[8] Issued four times a year, the *Edinburgh* and the *Quarterly* were thick magazines of 250 to 300 pages,[9] consisting of a large group of unsigned articles which commented upon specific contemporary non-fiction works. They were very expensive to buy, costing as much as six shillings,[10] and were available only to the affluent. Their print runs were about 12,000 each in 1818,[11] with a readership estimated at three times this figure. Nevertheless, this readership, considered as a proportion of those literate at the time, gave them an influence that has not been matched by any periodicals since.[12] The power of the reviews is indicated by the fact that the death of Keats in 1819 was widely attributed to the effects of a bad review of his poems in the *Quarterly*.

By the early 1840s the circulation of the two principal quarterlies was waning,[13] largely due to the success of new monthly magazines such as the influential *Blackwood's Edinburgh Magazine*, which began in 1817.[14] The monthly magazines were less monumental than the reviews. They had fewer pages and lighter entertainment, including short stories, serialised novels, poetry, general essays, satire, 'light' articles, and often pictures too. Joanne Shattock observes that '. . . quarterlies had *gravitas* and solidity', while 'monthly magazines were measured by their entertainment value.'[15] This dichotomy holds throughout the century, but much less straightforwardly from the 1850s and 1860s, as magazines began to assume the critical role that the quarterly reviews had fulfilled during the first half of the century.[16] They had also become hugely popular. The circulation of weekly and monthly magazines was estimated at about 250,000 in 1831, while it was calculated at 6,094,950 in 1864.[17] It is at this time, in the 1860s, that the practice of signing reviews and other essays (though often only with initials) began.[18]

Periodicals are urban forms, and their popularity and form in nineteenth-century England correlates with the demographic movement to the cities.

'We exist in the bustle of the world,' Hazlitt writes in an essay on
'The Periodical Press' (1823), 'and cannot escape from the notice of our
contemporaries.'[19] Periodicals pander to urban preoccupations with
entertainment and gossip. They furnish material for conversation and
information for 'the merchant in the railway', the figure that Walter
Bagehot, writing in 1855, casts as the type for contemporary readers of
magazines and reviews. Periodicals convey new information and ideas
quickly, in convenient and portable forms that, as Bagehot notes, kept
up with changes in the pace of middle-class life: 'Disraeli once compared the great Quarterly Reviews . . . to the old mail coaches, which
are capital things in their way, but when they tried to start in the
present day found that all the travellers had gone on by the train. A
quicker mode of travelling has come in, a hastier mode of reading, and
a scrappier mode of writing.'[20]

The great success of the reviews early in the century indicates that a
need was felt for an agency to mediate between the reading public and
the increasing diversity and quantity of ideas and information that was
being published. Hazlitt comments in the May 1823 issue of the *Edinburgh Review*:

> Who is there that can read all those [books] with which the
> modern press teems, and which, did they not daily disappear
> and turn to dust, the world would not be able to contain
> them? Are we to blame for despatching the most worthless of
> these from time to time, or for abridging the process of
> getting at the marrow of others . . . ?[21]

At the beginning of the century the material printed in the great
quarterlies was meant to be strictly reviews, essays addressed to the
exposition and evaluation of recently published books. This model of
the periodical essay did not, however, remain static. According to Walter
Bagehot, 'Hazlitt started the question, whether it would not be as well
to review works which did not appear.'[22] As the century progressed
there was a tendency for essays to be related more tenuously to the
books they were meant to review, to the point where they became
autonomous and asserted their primacy as the main vehicle for directly
communicating new ideas in nineteenth-century Britain. Gladstone's
monumental twenty-two-page review of Mrs Humphry Ward's *Robert
Elsmere* (1888) in the *Nineteenth Century*, for example, which was reprinted in pamphlet form and very widely read, is not so much a detailed
literary analysis of the novel as a vigorous refutation of its hero's (and
author's) religious position.[23] While in the early part of the century the
essay depended for its existence upon the books it reviewed, as the century progressed the contrary was more often the case, with books emerging as collections of essays which had first appeared in periodicals. Mark

Pattison, for example, observed in 1877 that 'books now are largely made up of republished review articles'.[24]

The changing function and importance of the essay form in the nineteenth century can be explained as a consequence of the proliferation of ideas and information that occurred at this time. While the powerful quarterlies of the first third of the century mediated the increase in the amount and range of material being published in book form, the progressive autonomy of the essay from its original reviewing function meant that the short form of the essay itself came to supersede the book as the main means of directly communicating new ideas to the public.[25] The dominance that the short and relatively ephemeral medium of the periodical essay assumed as the vehicle for presenting ideas and information indicates that such works had become not only greater in quantity and in range, but also impermanent, liable to revision and contestation. Bagehot, writing in the first volume of the *National Review* (which he founded and edited), vividly describes the place of periodical literature in modern experience and reflects upon its materiality:

> In truth review-writing but exemplifies the casual character of modern literature. Everything about it is temporary and fragmentary. Look at a railway stall; you see books of every colour, blue, yellow, crimson, 'ring-streaked, speckled, and spotted,' on every subject, in every style, of every opinion with every conceivable difference, celestial or sublunary, maleficent, beneficent – but all small. People take their literature in morsels, as they take sandwiches on a journey. The volumes at least, you can see clearly, are not intended to be everlasting. It may be all very well for a pure essence like poetry to be immortal in a perishable world; it has no feeling; but paper cannot endure it, paste cannot bear it, string has no heart for it. The race has made up its mind to be fugitive, as well as minute. What a change from the ancient volume![26]

Compared with the treatise, the traditional form of publishing new ideas – typically produced in small numbers, usually by subscription, as a magisterial letter-press book of thick rag paper and sturdy leather binding – the flimsy magazine and the cloth-bound book (which was used widely from 1825)[27] are ephemeral forms which anticipate their imminent supersession by other ideas and information which would be conveyed in the same forms. 'Modern literature . . .', writes Hazlitt in his 1823 essay on 'The Periodical Press', 'is a gay Coquette, fluttering fickle vain . . . [it] trifles with all sorts of arts and sciences . . . glitters, flutters, buzzes, spawns, dies, – and is forgotten!' Ideas change like fashion and like insects breed prolifically, buzz around noisily, offer a passing jewel-like appearance that suggests permanence, but soon disappear, superseded by another ephemeral generation. 'But', Hazlitt continues, 'the very variety and superficial polish [of modern literature] show the extent and height to which knowledge has been accumulated, and the general interest taken in letters.'[28] The question arises as to why so much was published in the nineteenth century. What are the conditions that facilitated this vast productivity?

One obvious but important condition is the rise of the mechanical presses and other factors springing from the Industrial Revolution which enabled the cheap mass-production and distribution of printed material. But the mere fact of supply does not guarantee consumption. Nor does the rise in literacy rates over the century in itself account for the restless production of new ideas that fuelled much of nineteenth-century non-fiction publishing.[29] It may well be the case that, just as the earlier achievements of the Industrial Revolution in the mechanical production of huge quantities of cheap fabric necessitated means such as advertising and fashion to ensure their continued consumption,[30] novelty and newness were also needed to guarantee that the increased capacities for production of the printing machines could be sold. The brief extract from Hazlitt which describes '[m]odern literature' as 'a gay Coquette' and 'the directress of fashion'[31] invokes this parallel. Indeed, the ephemeral form of the periodical, the average life of each issue being at this time four to six weeks, fits the requirements of this new capacity for mass-production, with new ideas often being introduced in periodical essays and only later being repackaged for sale again in book-form.

But it seems trivialising – and inadequate – to argue that the range and rapid succession of ideas published in new books and periodicals was driven purely by a need to be able to reap a profit from the huge productivity of the new printing machines; to assert that such ideas are a matter of fashion, a parallel to the constantly changing width of men's coat lapels and colours of women's dresses that maximised the amount of machine-made cloth that could be sold. While this materialist consideration is an interesting and important factor, it is only part of a much larger cultural context, the nature of which was introduced earlier in Taine's and Pater's brief comments on modern history and the production of ideas and literature.

Taine and Pater characterise their age as one of overwhelming change, a perception that was common amongst thinkers of the nineteenth century. Thomas Carlyle, writing in the *Edinburgh Review* in 1831, states what he sees to be the central fact of modern experience, a 'discovery' which 'belongs wholly to these latter days': 'Nevertheless so much has become evident to everyone, that this wondrous Mankind is advancing somewhither; that at least all human things are, have been and forever will be, in Movement and Change.'[32] Radical instability and change in social relations and in ideas was a new thing, which was promoted by the French and Industrial Revolutions.

The revolution in France, and the Industrial Revolution, which began in England, together impelled the upheaval in European society in which the middle classes displaced the aristocracy as the most powerful group in society. Traditional English society, which for much of the eighteenth century was still fixed along essentially feudal lines, was transformed by the social ascendancy of the middle classes that occurred as a result of their mercantile success in the Industrial Revolution and the pressure for democracy that sprang up with the French Revolution.[33] Political suffrage was ceded to middle-class men with property in the Reform Bills of 1832 and 1867. Writing towards the end of the century, Edward Dowden, like Taine and Pater, uses a calamitarian metaphor to convey a sense of the impact of the social changes that had occurred: 'Society, founded on the old feudal doctrines, had gone to wreck in the storms that have blown over Europe during the last hundred years. A new industrial and democratic period has been inaugurated; already the interregnum of government by the middle classes has proved its provisional character.'[34]

The class mobility exemplified by Charles Dickens's fictional orphans, and indeed Dickens himself, moving from humble beginnings to worldly success, was a popular story in the nineteenth century, celebrated not only in novels but in biographies and autobiographies. It may be described as the great Victorian middle-class narrative, and its popularity can be attributed, at least in part, to the optimistic resolution it furnished to anxieties about the security of the individual's social position; for a society that allowed one to rise from poverty to wealth and position in a generation could as easily make it a round trip back to the poorhouse, especially in old age. The newness and fluidity of this dynamic capitalist society engendered much documentation of its miserable consequences, such as poverty and disease, and speculation about the social and political engineering needed to manage such problems. It also fuelled the cult for 'self-improvement'. Demand for the 'Classics', for example, was more widespread in the nineteenth century than ever before. Such canonical works, traditionally the preserve of the upper classes, were from the 1840s onwards translated into English and made available to a new mass market, members of the autodidactic lower and middle classes anxious to realise the goals of 'self-improvement'.

Not only knowledge of the Classics but also familiarity with modern concepts and discussions, such as those of Utilitarianism, mesmerism and Darwinian evolution, also came to be regarded as a type of cultural capital which helped individuals to move up the social ladder, or to consolidate middle-class status after the advent of commercially achieved wealth. Periodicals served to fulfil this function. A critic wrote in the 1860s that 'though review reading will never produce a scholar . . . it may make an intelligent and well-informed man.'[35] John Henry Newman attests in *The Idea of a University* (1856) to the fact that 'periodical literature and occasional lectures . . . diffuse through the community' a 'superficial acquaintance with chemistry, and geology, and astronomy, and political economy, and modern history, and biography, and other branches of knowledge', conferring upon the consumer 'a graceful accomplishment, nay, in this day a necessary accomplishment, in the case of educated men'.[36] These extracts testify to the way in which non-fiction literature was in fact partly responsible for the very formation of the new middle classes. The new and sizeable mercantile class of the nineteenth century had at first little of their own cultural identity. Some of their members were preoccupied with emulating the aristocracy, while others repudiated this model, and worked against it to define their own cultural styles. As Klancher observes, conservatives of the early nineteenth century, especially Coleridge (following the abandonment of his youthful radical politics), saw the formation of the new powerful classes as an urgent and very important task.[37] To this end literature, and especially periodical literature, was critical.

Nineteenth-century England was a dynamic society, an unprecedented experiment in social mobility and middle-class social and political power. The nature of this society provides one of the central factors which contribute to the radical experience of change and sense of instability which impelled the production of new ideas and documentation, and hence new publications, over the century. The other main factor is the intellectual uncertainty of the period. 'Our own age . . .', Dowden writes in 1887, 'has been pre-eminently an age of intellectual and moral trial, difficulty and danger; of bitter farewells to things of the past, of ardent welcomes to things as yet but dimly discerned in the coming years.'[38] A root cause of this uncertainty was the moribund state of the Church in the early decades of the century, and its progressive loss of authority under pressure from rationalism and scientism throughout the period.

As early as 1831 Carlyle observed that Church doctrine no longer functioned as the cultural foundation of English society and the basis of personal moral and cosmological certainty: 'But now the ancient "ground-plan of the All" belies itself when brought into contact with reality; Mother Church has, to the most, become a superannuated Stepmother.'[39] Without faith, the traditional anchor of the Absolute, values and perceptions of the world became *relative*, much as in society the rigid feudal hierarchy of aristocracy and peasant had become fluid with the rise of the middle classes and industrial capitalism. In the modern world, where relativist values replace the objective and absolute conceptions of Truth and moral good that traditionally provided the foundations for intellectual discourses, 'the Thinker must,' according to Carlyle, 'in all senses, wander homeless, too often aimless, looking up to a Heaven which is dead for him.' The restlessness promoted by the intellectual and social uncertainties of the age both impelled the continual production of new ideas and ensured that there was always a readership for them anxious either to find new certainties, to re-enshrine the old ones, or to acquire what Keats called 'negative capability', the capacity to live with radical uncertainty.

Walter Bagehot, writing in 1855, comments that in the present 'times of miscellaneous revolution' in which relativism has usurped the authority of 'ancient assumptions' it is very difficult to fulfil the desire for a complete and encompassing 'theory':

> Such a want it is difficult to satisfy in an age of confusion and tumult, when old habits are shaken, old views overthrown, ancient assumptions rudely questioned, ancient inferences utterly denied, when each man has a different view from his neighbour, when an intellectual change has set father and son at variance, when a man's own household are the special foes of his favourite and self-adopted creed.[40]

Coleridge's prose writings exemplified this dilemma early in the century, for while he envisaged the production of a grand, totalising theory, the work towards it which survives is remarkably fragmentary and dissipated, consisting mainly of notes and scattered journal entries. Coleridge can be regarded rather ironically as one of the pioneers of the genre of the literary fragment.

In trying to establish an all-encompassing system of science, morals and metaphysics Coleridge was following the model of the German Romantic philosophers. Of these philosophers, Hegel, who worked during the first thirty years of the nineteenth century, was the last of the great systematic philosophers,[41] a tradition which had begun with Descartes in the seventeenth century. Coleridge's failure to establish his over-arching theory of the world signals a new intellectual environment in which fragmentary forms able to express the diversity and changing nature of knowledge came to supersede the imposing systematic edifices, the 'grand narratives,' which discerned a unity of purpose to all things, an ultimate *objective* Truth.

In an intellectual milieu in which there is no radical consensus, but rather, as Carlyle puts it, only a 'stunning hubbub, a true Babel-like confusion of tongues',[42] the possibility of establishing over-arching systems of thought retreats and traditional forms such as the treatise lose their authority. The protean form of the essay is better adapted for representing the diverse range of tentative and fragmentary perceptions and speculations thrown up by a modern world of constant change. Montaigne, an originator of this genre, sees it to be predicated upon instability and uncertainty: 'If my mind could gain a firm footing, I would not make essays, I would make decisions.'[43] The essay is a very free mode of discourse. It presupposes no specific types of content or attitudes, and ranges in subject matter and point of view from formal expositions of new scientific theories to private musings on Indian jugglers and the fear of death. It may follow a rigid path dictated by logic or its own playful belle-lettristic wanderings. It has a peculiarly fluid potential. Because of the 'freedom from generic limits' it allows, the essay has been aptly described by John Snyder as the '*nongenre*'.[44] All that is required of essays is that they be relatively short and use words to discuss a subject or subjects in a way that maintains the interest of the reader (or even just the writer writing them), for one of their main functions has been to entertain.

The protean mode of the essay naturally lent itself to the service of a time that many saw to be characterised by intellectual anarchy. Indeed, so apt was it to its age, so intertwined, that there was controversy throughout the century as to whether the essay simply expressed the spirit of the time or was responsible for it. In an essay on 'Periodicalism' written at mid-century, the geologist Hugh Miller accused the phenomenon of destroying literature. Periodical essays dissipated the talents of writers by imposing 'the necessity . . . of taking up subject after subject in the desultory, disconnected form in which they chance to arise'.[45] Conversely, he wrote, 'it is surely natural to infer that the exclusive reading of such works must have a dissipating effect also'. A corollary of the dilettantish variety exhibited by modern essays is seen to be their superficial treatment of their subject matter. Just as readers are corrupted, dissipated, by the fragmentary outpourings of the periodical press, so similarly, according to Miller, it is 'from the closets of over-toiled *littérateurs* [that] an excited superficiality creeps out upon the age'.[46]

While contemporary commentators like Miller saw periodicalism as a Pandora's box of dissipation and superficiality loosed upon society, others made the case that the great success of the essay was due to its historical aptness, to the fact that it lent itself to the expression of the perceptions and needs of the times. Hazlitt's review of 'The Periodical Press', which was written for the *Edinburgh Review* in 1823, naturally focuses upon the definitive critical nature of periodical essays at the time. Hazlitt, writing in response to the 'often . . . asked' question as to '*Whether Periodical Criticism is, upon the whole, beneficial to the cause of literature?*',[47] argues that it fulfils an historical need and is accordingly not simply beneficial but necessary: 'If literature in our day has taken this decided turn into a critical channel, is it not a presumptive proof that it ought to do so?'[48] While commentators such as Miller hold periodical writing responsible for dissipating literary genius, Hazlitt, unperturbed by this possibility, observes drolly that 'Literary immortality is now let on short leases'.[49]

The observations, often made accusingly, that periodical essays were self-conscious, overly critical, ideological, subjective, and superficial, that they presented ideas and perceptions as dissipated and disconnected, can all be related back to historical factors, especially to the expansion of intellectual relativism. In order to appreciate this more fully it is necessary to look further at the beginnings of the nineteenth-century periodical essay in the great reviews.

The genre of the nineteenth-century essay was, of course, established in the reviews as a form not only of exposition but also of *criticism*. Indeed, not only did essays in the influential reviews decide the worth of particular books, but more radically they challenged the privileged status accorded to the very form of the book itself. It is not surprising to find this tendency to question the authority traditionally given to the book extending later in the century to the authority of *the* Book, the Bible, as an ahistorical text. This was done most notably and controversially by Benjamin Jowett, Mark Pattison and others in their significantly titled book, *Essays and Reviews* (1860).

The institution of the quarterly review reflects a time of growing uncertainty and relativism in which traditional presuppositions of Truth, of cosmological and social order, could no longer be taken for granted. The intellectual impetus of the period is devoted not so much to reinstating ultimate notions of Truth and other traditional certainties, but to being sceptical of the very enterprise of seeking such absolutes, to being critical and self-conscious: "Our whole relations to the Universe and to our fellow-man', wrote Carlyle in 'Characteristics' (1831), 'have become an Inquiry, a Doubt; nothing will go on of its own accord, and do its function quietly; but all things must be probed into, the whole of man's world be anatomically studied.'[50]

Critical inquiry remained central to English culture throughout the nineteenth century. Indeed its status became such that, writing toward the close of the century, Oscar Wilde could argue for 'The Critic as Artist'. The main intellectual achievements of the epoch are described in this dialogue as the work of two critics: 'The nineteenth century is a turning point in history simply on account of the work of two men, Darwin and Renan, the one the critic of the Book of Nature, the other the critic of the books of God.'[51] The light and playful manner in which Wilde deals with the critical spirit is an index of the way in which English culture became acclimatised to the critical attitude as the century progressed. Earlier in the century, however, it was more often regarded as a matter of serious concern.

Carlyle pathologises the compulsive modern habit of inquiry in 'Characteristics' as a disease of self-consciousness: 'the world "listens to itself," and struggles and writhes, everywhere externally and internally, like a thing in pain.'[52] The implicit presupposition of Carlyle's argument is an optimistic Romantic trust in nature. All that is naturally good is seen to occur *unconsciously*, much as the flower opens itself to the sun, or the healthy body functions spontaneously as a whole.[53] The new modern city, according to Romantic ideology, provides the antithetical principle to nature. The quarterly reviews which were so important to urban culture during the first third of the century are accordingly found to be at the heart of the malady. Symptomatic of its age, 'the diseased self-conscious state of Literature' was seen by Carlyle to be 'disclosed in this one fact, which lies so near us here [he is writing in the *Edinburgh Review*], the prevalence of Reviewing! . . . all Literature has become one boundless self-devouring Review.'[54]

Writing almost a quarter of a century after 'Characteristics', Bagehot is much more at ease with the self-consciousness of the times and the other corollaries of relativism that so troubled Carlyle and many of his generation. In his essay on 'The First Edinburgh Reviewers' (1855), Bagehot, like Wilde after him, enjoys the range of possibilities opened up by contemporary experience and literature. He distinguishes 'modern' writing from all that went before it. What he refers to as 'ancient writing' is described as 'profound' and 'systematic', and he likens it to 'the lecture of a professor':

> There is exactly the difference between books of this age, and those of a more laborious age, that we feel between the lecture of a professor and the talk of the man of the world – the former profound, systematic, suggesting all arguments, analysing all difficulties, discussing all doubts, – very admirable, a little tedious, slowly winding an elaborate way, the characteristic effort of one who has hived wisdom during many studious years, agreeable to such as he is, anything but agreeable to such as he is not – the latter, the talk of the manifold talker, glancing lightly from topic to topic, suggesting deep things in jest, unfolding unanswerable arguments in an absurd illustration, expounding nothing, completing nothing, exhausting nothing, yet really suggesting the results of a more finely tested philosophy, passing with a more Shakespearian transition, connecting topics with a more subtle link, refining on them with an acuter perception, and what is more to the purpose, pleasing all that hear him, charming high and low, in season and out of season, with a word of illustration for each and a touch of humour intelligible to all, – fragmentary yet imparting what he says, allusive yet explaining what he intends, disconnected yet impressing what maintains. This is the very model of our modern writing. The man of the modern world is used to speak what the modern world will hear; the writer of the modern world must write what that world will indulgently and pleasantly peruse.
>
> In this transition from ancient writing to modern, the review-like essay and the essay-like review fill a large space.[55]

'[T]he very model of our modern writing' is represented as purely discursive, corresponding 'exactly' to 'the talk of the man of the world'.[56] It is no wonder that the review essay is seen to have played a large part in determining the change from 'ancient' literature to 'modern' writing, for, as was discussed earlier, the 'nongenre' of the essay is, beyond other forms of writing, characterised by its potential for free discursivity.

Bagehot's 'man of the world' suggests Baudelaire's figure of the *flâneur*, the nineteenth-century stroller of city streets whom Walter Benjamin sees as the prototype for the modern intellectual.[57] The social type that Bagehot invokes is, like the *flâneur*, 'of the world', and contrasted to the traditional figure of the academic professor, whose reflective work occurs in detachment from the outside world and in economic security. The *flâneur* and the historically self-conscious periodical essayist work in the economic marketplace, both studying and commenting upon this modern world and deriving their livelihood from it. Hence, 'the writer of the modern world must write what that world will indulgently and pleasantly peruse'. The professional periodical essayist, like the *flâneur*, and unlike the professor, was a non-specialist, a 'manifold talker'. This is, it may be recalled, one of Hugh Miller's main complaints; that in order to make a living the modern writer is forced continually to turn his attention from one disparate topic to another. Such writing parallels 'the talk of the manifold talker'. It tends to be 'fragmentary', 'allusive', and 'disconnected'. In contrast to the 'systematic' professor 'slowly winding an elaborate way', 'the talk of the man of the world' wanders in the manner of the *flâneur*, 'glancing lightly from topic to topic'.

By 'suggesting deep things in jest, unfolding unanswerable arguments in an absurd illustration, expounding nothing, completing nothing, [and] exhausting nothing . . .', 'the talk of the man of the world' mocks the 'systematic' exhaustiveness and 'slowly winding' elaboration of the professor's discourse. The man of the world's talk implicitly criticises a subject position that has become outdated. The professor, having 'hived wisdom during many studious years', represents a more or less unanimous body of learning. He speaks from the objectivist perspective of an intellectual world that is assured of certain traditional absolutes. With the breakdown of this consensus and its replacement by relativism, the 'profound, systematic' discourse of the professorial lecture becomes outmoded, an object of mockery for the new individual voice represented here by 'the man of the world'.

In the place of the third-person voice adopted by the professor, with its absolutist faith in objective truth, are a multitude of individual voices speaking from self-consciously subjective positions. Bagehot documents the fact that for many in the nineteenth century the studied abstract knowledge of the professor lost much of its intellectual authority to the 'wider experience' of the individual free-lance thinker and writer, 'the man of the world'. As the impact and implications of relativism became absorbed by nineteenth-century English culture the model of knowledge shifted from being purely objectivist to being subjectivist. Wilde brings this tendency into strong relief in 'The Critic as Artist', where he argues that criticism cannot claim scientific objectivity but must recognise its basis in acts of interpretation and hence in personal sensibility:

> Gilbert: . . . it has been said . . . that the proper aim of Criticism is to see the object as in itself it really is. But this is a very serious error . . . Criticism's most perfect form . . . is in its essence purely subjective, and seeks to reveal its own secret.[58]

This new model which regards knowledge as subjectivist, as contingent upon individual experience, means that modern thought and literature are relatively *superficial*. It involves the loss of the conception of knowledge of the outside world as depth, as an objective truth that can be uncovered. What is left after the abandonment of such secure conceptions of meaning are simply types of personal experience and conventions for making sense of them and for communicating them. We can recall Hugh Miller's portrayal of a febrile contemporary culture that is coming into being as 'an excited superficiality creeps out upon the age.' This is the sort of earnestly made observation that is ironised by Wilde later in the century in Lady Bracknell's comment, 'We live, I regret to say, in an age of surfaces', and in his 'Phrases and Philosophies for the Use of the Young'; 'It is only the superficial qualities that last. Man's deeper nature is soon found out.'[59] The work of Wilde, while frequently noting ironically that the quality of superficiality, of depthlessness, is often spoken of disapprovingly, ultimately makes the point that there is no longer any possibility (as there is in Miller's polemic) that it can be expunged from the age for it *defines* the age. This corollary of relativism is still prominent in our own time, most notoriously in Baudrillard's postmodernist conception of 'simulacra'.

The loss of an absolute and impartial notion of Truth has interesting implications for the way in which we think of literature. For one thing it problematises and blurs the basic distinction we make between fiction and non-fiction.[60] The difference between historical novels and novelistic histories, such as those of Carlyle and Macaulay, is merely relative. English literature of the nineteenth century is full of strange hybrid works like Landor's *Imaginary Conversations* and Pater's *Studies in the History of the Renaissance* in which personal imagination not only interprets but also enhances the historical evidence. It is precisely this relativist treatment of the traditional categories of fiction and non-fiction that Wilde notes in another of Pater's works, the *Imaginary Portraits*. He writes that in this book fiction has become a 'fanciful guise' for the presentation of insights that are traditionally presented as non-fiction: '*Imaginary Portraits* . . . presents to us, under the fanciful guise of fiction, some fine and exquisite piece of criticism, one on the painter Watteau, another on the philosophy of Spinoza.'[61]

Another important consequence of the new subjectivism and self-consciousness promoted by relativism was the proliferation of ideologies. Indeed, the term 'ideology' originates in the early nineteenth century as a relativistic concept of ideas determined by, and imbricated in, specific power interests within society:[62] a suspicious attitude to ideas that contrasts radically with absolutist notions of ultimate ideas, such as God or Truth. The concept of ideology insists that groups of ideas be understood in relation to their social and temporal contexts; it historicises ideas. Similarly, the periodical's ephemeral mode of presentation presupposes that ideas are temporal (even temporary) and polemical. Hence, periodical literature foregrounds the range and importance of the ideological perspectives which competed for power in nineteenth-century society. Right from the start, the two great original reviews, the *Edinburgh* and the *Quarterly*, established their respective identities along political lines as Whig and Tory. William Cobbett's *Political Register* was the leading journal of radical politics in the late 1810s. The *Westminster Review* was started in 1824 by followers of Jeremy Bentham in order to promote his Utilitarian ideology and agenda of reforms. Similarly, the *National Review* was published in 1883 simply 'to supply the demand for an exclusively Conservative review'.[63] Because they are a flexible and temporal form in which particular perspectives can be promptly aired and criticised, periodicals, rather than books, provide the main arena for ideological battles in nineteenth-century England.

What was at stake in these ideological battles? Broadly speaking, it was an entity that was often discussed from early in the century, the rising 'reading public', the new and ever-expanding middle classes. The 'reading public' was not only a new and expanding market for literature, it was also, as Jon Klancher argues, a new historical power that was shaped and given an identity through literature. In particular, periodical literature acted to form what Coleridge refers to as the 'luxuriant misgrowth' of the middle-class reading public, encouraging it to recognise and act upon its power.[64]

'The modern man must', Bagehot maintains, 'be told what to think, – shortly no doubt, – but he *must* be told it.'[65] Indeed, this and similar sentiments were given the authority of an editorial policy by being published in the first volume of the *National Review*, the magazine Bagehot began in 1855. Periodical essays provide the means for instructing the 'modern man . . . shortly', that is, in a suitably concise form. Indeed, Bagehot looks back to the *Edinburgh Review* as the first to provide this service, by giving 'suitable views for sensible persons'.[66] Bagehot, like so many writers and intellectuals of his century, has his own views as to what ideology such persons should embrace: 'The exact mind which of all others dislikes the stupid adherence to the status quo, is the keen, quiet, improving Whig mind; the exact kind of writing most adapted to express that dislike is the cool, pungent, didactic essay.' The very style of writing addresses and confirms, *interpellates*, the identity of the modern man as a member of a cultural class that is at once 'elite' and 'common', between the aristocracy and the 'lower orders', that is, middle-class: 'that species of writing . . . addresses the *elite* of common men . . . men of cool, clear, and practical understandings'.[67] It is significant that the focus of Bagehot's essay, the *Edinburgh Review*, and indeed all such reviews and magazines until the 1860s, published their essays anonymously, thereby generating an author function that could be regarded as a single anonymous voice, a collective cultured middle-class identity with which the reader could identify.

While Carlyle is nostalgic for the old objectivist certainties, Bagehot finds the pervasively self-conscious voice of modern relativism playful and 'charming'. He seems to be in agreement with Hazlitt: 'Instead of solemn testimonies from the learned, we require the smiles of the fair and the polite . . . let Reviews flourish – let Magazines increase and multiply.'[68] The absolutist certainties of an ultimate or objective truth no longer provide the bases for evaluating intellectual discourse. In their place rather more utilitarian or hedonistic criteria were often invoked. Although Bagehot defends the capacity of 'the man of the world' for making subtle intellectual connections and refinements, 'what is more to the purpose' than such intellectual astuteness is the purely utilitarian consideration of the value of his discourse as entertainment, his capacity for 'pleasing all that hear him, charming high and low'. While this value is consistent with the loss of absolutes and the rise of intellectual relativism, it is also closely related to the commercial exigencies that drove the literary market, which was directed mainly at the leisured middle classes: 'the writer of the modern world must write what that world will indulgently and pleasantly peruse.'

The amusing possibilities of the essay flow from its discursivity. As Bagehot's analogy with 'the talk of the man of the world' makes clear, the periodical essay can draw upon all of the devices and possibilities of the conversationalist. Bagehot, commenting upon the contributions of one of the founders and first editor of the *Edinburgh Review*, Sydney Smith, writes that 'There is little trace of labour in his composition; it is poured forth like an unceasing torrent, rejoicing daily to run its course.' The breakdown of traditional structures of thought and belief may have engendered anxiety and foreboding, but it also encouraged such qualities of exuberance and fluidity as Bagehot finds in the work of Smith. Indeed, the loss of fixed structures liberated the essay, allowing the full exploration of the almost formless potential of this 'nongenre'.

Metaphors of fluidity, such as that of the river used by Bagehot in his comments on Smith, are especially appropriate to the essay genre. The use of the metaphor of the river to represent change is as least as ancient as the pre-Socratic philosopher Heraclitus. In applying this metaphor to the essay form, Bagehot highlights the genre's peculiar appositeness for the nineteenth century, an age – as such contemporary observers as Carlyle and Pater never tired of noting – of unprecedented change. Attributes of flow and of pace are as integral to the essay form as they are to a river. The essay, like the river, follows its own course, and often involves wanderings from one region of knowledge to another, or may be regarded as the peculiar flow of an individual consciousness. It allows a freedom of movement, to take surprising turns and pursue divergent points of view and arguments much as a river may divide at certain points or expand and contract at others. And of course, while rivers and streams may have a certain depth to them, it is their superficies that are most easily apparent to us and most attractive; the sparkling qualities of moving water and the play of light on it. So also, as Hazlitt notes in his analogy of '[m]odern literature' to 'a gay Coquette', the essay often delights in superficies.

The freedom and suppleness of form enjoyed by the nineteenth-century English essay is parallelled by the other great literary form of the period, the novel. The following extract from an apology for the novel made in *A New Spirit of the Age* (1844) draws upon analogies with liquidity:

> Very grave people, who set up to be thought wiser than their neighbours, are no longer ashamed to be caught reading a novel. The reason of this is plain enough . . . It is no longer a mere fantasy of the imagination, a dreamy pageant of unintelligible sentiments and impossible incidents; but a sensible book, insinuating in an exceedingly agreeable form . . . a great deal of useful knowledge, historical, social, and moral. Most people are too lazy to go to the spring-head, and are well content to drink from any of the numerous little rills that happen to ripple close at hand.[69]

The form of the novel specified here is akin to that of the essay, appropriate to the fluidity and diversity of its subject matter: 'it is really a channel for conveying actual information, the direct result of observation and research, put together with more or less artistic ingenuity.'[70] It, like the review essay, offers an easy alternative to an acquaintance with ideas and information gained from their original sources, their 'spring-head[s]'.

The apologetic strategy of the extract is to assert the respectability of the novel by arguing that it is in effect reconstituted non-fiction, 'a sensible book', which like the essay presents 'useful knowledge' in an 'agreeable form'. It accordingly sketches the criteria by which the early Victorians judged non-fiction to be superior to fiction, and, by finding such qualities embodied in the modern novel, argues for its 'respectability'. Values of common sense, of being 'sensible' and 'useful', are appealed to here, with the impression being given that the modern novel was commissioned by the Society for the Diffusion of Useful Knowledge.

The 'very grave people, who set up to be thought wiser than their neighbours' belong to the earnest new middle classes. Baudelaire dedicates his review of 'The Salon of 1846' 'To the Bourgeois', the powerful majority in contemporary society: 'Some of you are "learned"; others are the "haves". A glorious day will dawn when the learned will be "haves", and the "haves" will be learned. Then your power will be complete and nobody will challenge it.'[71] Non-fiction prose provided the main avenue for such personal and social empowerment, working to establish middle-class cultural hegemony and social progress. Such functions valorised the Utilitarian and didactic impetus of Victorian non-fiction.

The categories of 'useful knowledge' given in the passage from *A New Spirit of the Age* derive from the public sphere of political and moral action. The implication here is that the respectability of novels can be argued only once they repudiate the irrational female-gendered attributes of fantasy, dream, and sentiment in favour of the 'sensible' and 'useful' masculine-gendered realms of the 'historical, social, and moral'. In accordance with what were regarded as the masculine prerogatives of rationality and Truth and the feminine qualities of the fancy, sentimentality, and interests in the ornamental and the domestic, the gender divide in nineteenth-century literature is in large part demarcated from early in the century by the line separating non-fiction from fiction.

In one of his 'Lectures on the Principles of Judgement, Culture, and European Literature', delivered to the London Philosophical Society in 1818, Coleridge remarks of women that 'they rarely or never thoroughly distinguish between fact and fiction'.[72] In keeping with this common presupposition of the time, men were entrusted to write in areas concerned with fact and Truth (which meant not only areas like science but, especially for the Romantics, the privileged genre of poetry), while the novel, which was often seen as a sub-literary form of fanciful lies and gossip, was mainly the sphere of women writers and readers. While this basic distinction is most clearly evident early in the century, it provided the ground rules for the practice of writing well beyond this time. Most of the subject areas that comprise nineteenth-century non-fiction writing (and are consequently discussed in this book) were regarded as masculine discourses. For the whole of the century disciplines such as history, Classics, science, philosophy and theology were mainly the preserve of men, while women were allocated such areas as fiction, belles-lettres, and domestic writing. Nevertheless, the century's endemic propensity for intellectual relativism did exert an influence upon the gender politics of literary genres. If at the beginning of the century Coleridge's presupposition that 'Women . . . rarely or never thoroughly distinguish between fact and fiction' was tenable, much literature produced as the century progressed, such as that by Pater and Landor, could be described by the words in which Coleridge described the feminine form of the modern novel, as a 'jumble of the two'.

Many women, by working within the genres conventionally allowed them, explored areas that were largely forbidden to them. Historical novels are an important case in point. Gary Kelly cites Elizabeth Hamilton's *Memoirs of the Life of Agrippina, the Wife of Germanicus* (1804) as an example of 'a historical quasi-novel' in which the author ventures into what were at the time the masculine preserves of historiography and classical studies. It is also, as Kelly goes on to note, an early example of a female biography, a genre that developed in the nineteenth century as an important area of feminist enquiry.[73] More generally biography provided nineteenth-century women writers with a way of discreetly practising history. Women could also write on science without provoking public censure by restricting themselves to popular expositions or to works for children, as Jane Marcet did.[74] Similarly, Mary Shelley finds a medium for writing on contemporary science in *Frankenstein; or, The Modern Prometheus* (1818). Travel writing, originally a belle-lettristic genre, allowed women to write on art and history, and, as the British empire expanded over the century and opportunities for travel increased, it came to include very unladylike excursions into such areas as ethnography, geography, science, and adventure writing. Although most of the categories of writing introduced in the following chapters were considered primarily masculine territories, they were as the century progressed increasingly impinged upon by women writers. And it was the periodical essay, with its convention of anonymity, which, arguably more than any other genre, even the novel, was the Trojan horse that allowed women writers to enter the male preserve of professional writing.

Notes

1. Hippolyte Taine, *History of English Literature*, 5th edn, trans. H. Van Laun, 4 vols (Edinburgh, 1874), II, p. 223.

2. Walter Pater, 'English Literature', in *Essays from 'The Guardian'* (London, 1903), p. 12.

3. J. Don Vann and Rosemary T. Van Arsdel, eds, *Victorian Periodicals and Victorian Society* (Aldershot, 1994), p. 3.

4. Richard D. Altick, *Victorian People and Ideas* (New York, 1973), pp. 61–5. See also Altick's *The English Common Reader: A Social History of the Mass Reading Public 1800–1900* (Chicago, 1957), ch. 10.

5. Walter E. Houghton, 'Periodical literature and the articulate classes', in Joanne Shattock and Michael Wolff, eds, *The Victorian Periodical Press: Samplings and Soundings* (Leicester, 1982), pp. 3–27 (p. 3).

6. George Saintsbury, *Short History of English Literature* (London, 1913; 7th printing), p. 690. See p. 795 also.

7. Altick, *The English Common Reader*, ch. 11.

8. Many other literary histories and reminiscences from the later part of the century agree with her in stressing the momentousness of the reviews. H. R. Tedder, writing in the article on 'Periodicals' for the ninth edition of the *Encyclopaedia Britannica*, writes that the *Edinburgh* created 'a new era in periodical criticism, and assumed from the commencement a wider range and more elevated tone than any of its predecessors' ((Edinburgh, 1885), XVIII, 536).

9. Joanne Shattock, *Politics and Reviewers: The* Edinburgh *and The* Quarterly *in the Early Victorian Age* (London, 1989), p. 11.

10. Ibid, p. 12.

11. Altick, *The English Common Reader*, p. 392.

12. Altick, *Victorian People and Ideas*, p. 66.

13. Shattock, *Politics and Reviewers*, p. 12.

14. Weekly reviews were also established at this time, with the *Literary Gazette* first published in 1817 and the *Athenaeum* in 1828.

15. Shattock, *Politics and Reviewers*, p. 6.

16. See Shattock, *Politics and Reviewers*, p. 20, and Houghton, 'Periodical literature and the articulate classes', p. 19. Such weekly magazines as the *Saturday Review* (1855) and the *Academy* (1869) and such monthly magazines as the *Fortnightly Review* (1865) and the *Contemporary Review* (1866) all began at this time.

17. Tedder, 'Periodicals', *Encyclopaedia Britannica*, 9th edn, XVIII, 538.

18. This innovation was at the time a matter of discussion and some controversy. See, for example, John Morley's 'Memorials of a Man of Letters', in his *Nineteenth-Century Essays*, edited by Peter Stansky (Chicago, 1970), pp. 267–69.

19. William Hazlitt, 'The Periodical Press', in *The Complete Works of William Hazlitt*, edited by P. P. Howe, 21 vols (London and Toronto, 1930–4), XVI, 211–39 (p. 220).

20. Walter Bagehot, 'Senior's Journals', in *Collected Works*, edited by N. St John Stevas, 15 vols (London, 1965–86), II, 374–86 (p. 376). Apropos of this Hazlitt refers in passing to the current 'rage for conveying information in an easy and portable form' (*Works*, XVI, 221). Bagehot's essay on 'The First Edinburgh Reviewers' develops further the relationship between the new magazines and rail travel.

21. Hazlitt, 'The Periodical Press', *Works*, XVI, 213–14.

22. Bagehot, 'The First Edinburgh Reviewers', *Collected Works*, I, 308–41 (p. 309).

23. William E. Gladstone, '"Robert Elsmere" and the Battle of Belief', *Nineteenth Century*, 23 (May 1888), 766–88.

24. Quoted by Houghton, 'Periodical literature and the articulate classes', p. 21. Shattock, in *Politics and Reviewers* (p. 9), quotes Leslie Stephen's opinion that 'much of the most solid and original work of the time first appears in periodicals.'

25. The fact that Hazlitt comments upon the juxtaposition of entirely different discourses within the reviews indicates the novelty of this arrangement for a contemporary readership: 'A Whig or Tory tirade on a political question . . . now stands side by side . . . with a disquisition on ancient coins' (Hazlitt, 'The Periodical Press', *Works*, XVI, 221).

26. Bagehot, 'The First Edinburgh Reviewers', *Collected Works*, I, 310.

27. Altick, *The English Common Reader*, p. 379.

28. Hazlitt, 'The Periodical Press', *Works*, XVI, 219. In an 1814 review of Fanny Burney's *The Wanderer* John Wilson Croker describes the novel as 'an old coquette'. For further discussion of the gendering of texts by nineteenth-century reviewers and critics see chapter 9.

29. Altick notes that the marriage records show that in 1841 sixty-seven per cent of men and fifty-one per cent of women could at least write their own name, a figure which rose to approximately ninety-seven per cent for both sexes in 1900. (Many of these would, however, only have been able to trace their own name, not read it.) (Altick, *Victorian People and Ideas*, p. 60.)

30. Colin Campbell, *The Romantic Ethic and the Spirit of Modern Consumerism* (Oxford, 1987), ch. 2.

31. Hazlitt, 'The Periodical Press', *Works*, XVI, 219.

32. Thomas Carlyle, 'Characteristics', *Critical and Miscellaneous Essays*, 3 vols (London, 1887), II, 191–227 (p. 222).

33. Note, though, Andrew Blake's observation that 'after [the] ostensible "triumph of the middle classes" between 1832 and 1851, the process of the transfer of power at least slowed down considerably, and perhaps went into reverse' (*Reading Victorian Fiction: The Cultural Context and Ideological Content of the Nineteenth-century Novel* (Basingstoke and London, 1989), p. 45).

34. Edward Dowden, *Studies in Literature, 1789–1877* (London, 1889), p. 159.

35. Quoted by Houghton, 'Periodical literature and the articulate classes', p. 8.

36. Ibid.

37. Jon Klancher, 'Reading the social text: power, signs, and audience in early nineteenth-century prose', *Studies in Romanticism*, 23 (1984), 183–204 (pp. 183–4).

38. Dowden, *Studies in Literature, 1789–1877*, p. 154. The publisher, editor and author John Morley makes a similar observation: 'It was the age of science, new knowledge, searching criticism, followed by multiplied doubts and shaken beliefs' (John Morley, *Recollections*, 2 vols (London, 1917), I, 100).

39. Carlyle, 'Characteristics', *Critical and Miscellaneous Essays*, II, 216.

40. Bagehot, 'The First Edinburgh Reviewers', *Collected Works*, I, 316–17.

41. It is significant that Hegel's system unified the phenomena of the world through the principle of change, of becoming.

42. Carlyle, 'Characteristics', *Critical and Miscellaneous Essays*, II, 219.

43. *Essays*, 3.2B. Quoted in John Snyder, *Prospects of Power: Tragedy, Satire, the Essay, and the Theory of Genre* (Kentucky, 1991), p. 151. Snyder (p. 16) cites another saying of Montaigne's which similarly illuminates the aptness of the genre for the fluctuous nineteenth century: 'I do not portray being: I portray passing' (*Essays*, 3.2B).

44. Ibid, p. 12. The platonic dialogue is another genre that suited the relativist mood of the time. It, like the similarly discursive essay, accommodates a plurality of voices and points of view: 'Dialogue . . . that wonderful literary form which, from Plato to . . . Bruno . . . the creative critics of the world have always employed, can never lose for the thinker its attraction as a mode of expression. By its means he can both reveal and conceal himself, and give form to every fancy, and reality to every mood. By its means he can exhibit the object from each point of view and show it to us in the round, as a sculptor shows us things' (Wilde, 'The Critic as Artist', in *Intentions* (London, 1934), p. 187).

45. Hugh Miller, 'Periodicalism', in *Leading Articles on Various Subjects* (Edinburgh, 1870), p. 213.

46. Ibid, p. 210.

47. Hazlitt, 'The Periodical Press', *Works*, XVI, 211.

48. Hazlitt elaborates this argument further: '*Periodical criticism is favourable – to periodical criticism* . . . its cultivation proves not only that it suits the spirit of the times, but advances it. It certainly never flourished more than at present . . . If there is a preponderance of criticism at any one period, this can only be because there are subjects, and because it is the time for it' (ibid, p. 212).

49. Ibid, p. 220.

50. Carlyle, 'Characteristics', *Critical and Miscellaneous Essays*, II, 208.

51. Wilde, 'The Critic as Artist', in *Complete Works of Oscar Wilde*, edited by Vyvyan Holland (London and Glasgow, 1966), pp. 1009–59 (p. 1058).

52. Carlyle, 'Characteristics', *Critical and Miscellaneous Essays*, II, 218.

53. Ibid, p. 194.

54. Ibid, p. 212. As well as the ascription of cannibalism, modern literature is diagnosed here as a vicious self-inflicted wasting disease.

55. Bagehot, 'The First Edinburgh Reviewers', *Collected Works*, I, 311–12.

56. The way in which social discourse parallelled that of periodical criticism was observed in 1823 by Hazlitt in his essay on 'The Periodical Press': 'The style of our common conversation has undergone a total change from the personal and the *piquant* to the critical and the didactic; and, instead of aiming at elegant raillery or pointed repartee, the most polished circles now discuss general topics, or analyze abstruse problems' (Hazlitt, *Works*, XVI, 216).

57. Charles Baudelaire, 'The Painter of Modern Life', in *The Painter of Modern Life and other essays*, trans. Jonathan Mayne (London, 1964), pp. 1–40, especially p. 9; Walter Benjamin, *Charles Baudelaire: A Lyric Poet in The Era Of High Capitalism*, trans. Harry Zohn (London, 1983).

58. Wilde, 'The Critic as Artist', p. 1028.

59. Wilde, *The Importance of Being Earnest*, in *Complete Works*, ed. Holland, pp. 321–84 (p. 374); 'Phrases and Philosophies for the Use of the Young', ibid, pp. 1205–06 (p. 1206).

60. This is apparent from the subjective, indeed idiosyncratic, voices of 'professional' essayists such as Hazlitt, Bagehot and Pater, who freely treat issues of fact in a personal way.

61. Wilde, 'The Critic as Artist', p. 1046.

62. Terry Eagleton offers an historical discussion of the rise of the concept in the third chapter of his *Ideology: An Introduction* (London, 1991), pp. 63–91.

63. *Encyclopaedia Britannica*, XVIII, 536.

64. Quoted in Klancher, 'Reading the social text', p. 183.

65. Bagehot, 'The First Edinburgh Reviewers', *Collected Works*, I, 313. He comments earlier in this essay that 'It is, indeed, a peculiarity of our times, that we must instruct so many persons' (p. 311).

66. Ibid, p. 313.

67. Ibid, p. 322.

68. Hazlitt, 'The Periodical Press', *Works*, XVI, 220.

69. 'G. P. R. James,—Mrs. Gore,—Captain Marryatt, and Mrs. Trollope' in Richard Hengist Horne, ed., *A New Spirit of the Age*, 2nd edn, 2 vols (London, 1844), I, 213–44 (pp. 215–16). Horne (known also by the pseudonyms Sir Lucius O'Trigger and Mrs Fairstair) probably wrote (as well as edited) these essays.

70. Ibid, p. 216.

71. Charles Baudelaire, 'The Salon of 1846', in *Strangeness and Beauty: An Anthology of Aesthetic Criticism 1840–1910, Vol. 1; Ruskin to Swinburne*, edited by Eric Warner and Graham Hough (Cambridge, 1983), pp. 173–82 (p. 173).

72. Samuel Taylor Coleridge, *Lectures 1808–1819 On Literature*, edited by R. A. Foackes, 2 vols (Princeton and London, 1987), II, 193.

73. Gary Kelly, 'Revolutionary and Romantic Feminism: Women, Writing and Cultural Revolution', in *Revolution and English Romanticism*, edited by Keith Hanley and Raman Selden (Hemel Hempstead, 1990), pp. 107–30 (p. 123).

74. See, for example, her *Conversations on Chemistry* (1806), *Conversations on Natural Philosophy* (1819), and *Conversations on Vegetable Physiology* (2 vols, 1829).

Chapter 1
Prose of Discovery

'Farewell, Walton! Seek happiness in tranquillity, and avoid
ambition, even if it be only the apparently innocent one of
distinguishing yourself in science and discoveries. Yet why do I
say this? I have myself been blasted in these hopes, yet another
may succeed.'

(Mary Shelley, *Frankenstein*)[1]

Mary Shelley's *Frankenstein; or, The Modern Prometheus* (1818) is a novel
which somewhat equivocally critiques the Promethean ambitions of its
twinned protagonists, the scientist Victor Frankenstein and the explorer
Robert Walton, both of whom are represented as obsessively driven in
their pursuit of distinction in 'science and discoveries' and in their
masculinist determination 'to penetrate the secrets of nature'.[2] A key
text of Romanticism, it exposes the dark other side of the heroic quest
for knowledge as a ruthless disregard for those who are the unacknowledged victims or by-products of that personal quest. It is not insignificant
that the nameless Creature and his Creator have become conflated under
the single name Frankenstein in the popular imagination, that they are
perceived to share a common identity, much as Kurtz, the would-be
civiliser of the African interior, is identified with the monstrous heart
of darkness he has 'penetrated' in Conrad's novel written at the height
of imperialism. Although its politics are contradictory, and it has
been variously interpreted, *Frankenstein* is indubitably a product of the
post-French Revolutionary years, when a newly-awakened egalitarian
conscience about the suffering masses sat uneasily alongside a fear of the
monstrous power of the oppressed and socially outcast.[3] The heart of
this book, by the daughter of two of the most prominent supporters of
the Revolution, Mary Wollstonecraft and William Godwin, is given to
the Creature's narrative of his own personal history, in which he tells
of his education in the class system ('I heard of the division of property,
of immense wealth and squalid poverty; of rank, descent, and noble
birth')[4] and his own social condition. It is also a product of the new age
of Romantic science. Just before she wrote *Frankenstein*, Mary Shelley had
been reading Humphry Davy, who had represented the scientist as having

'penetrated into [the earth's] bosom . . . for the purpose of allaying the restlessness of his desires, or of extending and increasing his power', and proclaimed that science

> has bestowed upon [man] powers which may be almost called creative; which have enabled him to modify and change the beings surrounding him, and by his experiments to interrogate nature with power, not simply as a scholar, passive and seeking only to understand her operations, but rather as a master, active with his own instruments . . . who would not be ambitious of becoming acquainted with the most profound secrets of nature, of ascertaining her hidden operations, and of exhibiting to men that system of knowledge which relates so intimately to their own physical and moral constitution?[5]

She was also living with Percy Shelley, who had a passionate interest in chemistry, in particular electricity and galvanism,[6] and so she had first-hand experience of the fascination exercised by science on the modern Promethean mind. Moreover, she was herself a discoverer of sorts, being a great traveller and travel writer, and therefore not immune to the attraction of exploring wild unknown places which is Walton's obsession. Indeed, as Percy Shelley points out in his anonymous Preface, 'this story was begun in the majestic region where the scene is principally laid.'[7] And Mary Shelley too felt that she had arrogated to herself creative powers by giving birth to her own 'hideous progeny',[8] *Frankenstein* itself. In short, *Frankenstein* is a novel which condemns the ambitions of its seekers after knowledge, but which nevertheless appears partly to endorse the human aspiration to discover which Victor Frankenstein maintains to the end: 'yet another may succeed.'

Frankenstein is, of course, a fictional text, and yet it gives voice to a particular historical moment when there was great interest in uncovering the secrets of the universe, and an unprecedented confidence in the human potential for knowledge. There was a voracious appetite among the English middle classes for information about the latest scientific, geographical, anthropological and sociological discoveries, a desire for intellectual and arguably other kinds of mastery of foreign territories, whether the African continent or London's East End or their own pre-history. A whole body of English prose in the nineteenth century was dedicated to the project of articulating and deciphering the meaning of an expanding world. The section that follows draws parallels between scientific writing, travel and exploration literature, and social reportage as different, but related, instances of discovery narrative.

It must be acknowledged from the outset, of course, that what we are concerned with here is the expanding consciousness of white and, for the most part, middle-class English men of the world they inhabited, and the strategies of representation by which that world, and their own mastery of it, were produced. European travel and exploration writing constituted not so much the 'discovery' as the production of other parts of the world. White explorers typically hired local inhabitants to take them to the sites that they would then duly 'discover' for European consumption. The discourse of exploration depended upon the translation and appropriation of indigenous knowledges and discourses.[9] A similar point might be made about those nineteenth-century social explorers who 'discovered' for the middle classes the living conditions of the urban poor of which those who lived in poverty were all too aware. E. P. Thompson has remarked of Henry Mayhew, for instance, that it would be 'ludicrous' to suggest that he 'discovered Victorian poverty', for 'the poor had long before discovered themselves'.[10] Discovery frequently involves not only the shock of the new but the reconfiguration of the familiar.[11] The claims to objectivity of both travel writing and social reportage were underpinned by an appeal to science, but of course scientific discovery was itself a construction, as George Eliot recognised when she wrote as her opening epigraph to *Daniel Deronda*, 'Men can do nothing without the make-believe of a beginning. Even Science, the strict measurer, is obliged to start with a make-believe unit, and must fix on a point in the stars' unceasing journey when his sidereal clock shall pretend that time is at Nought.' Eliot here challenges the naive view that the scientist simply records a pre-given world, replacing the notion of science as transparent empirical transcription with the idea that it traffics, like fiction, in the 'make-believe'.[12]

In her epigraph to *Daniel Deronda*, Eliot represents science and writing as comparable practices, and it is upon the rhetorical and discursive strategies of nineteenth-century scientific prose, on science *as writing*, that more recent literary criticism and history of science have tended to focus. This will be the emphasis of my own account of nineteenth-century scientific prose, and I shall additionally be examining ways in which it can be seen to share certain of the rhetorical devices of the travel and exploration writing and social reportage of the period. In a way, this is not surprising, for there were many significant points of connection between these activities and their literatures, which burgeoned in response to the historical imperatives of the Industrial Revolution, economic expansion, and imperialism. From the middle of the eighteenth century onwards, travellers to uncharted regions were often part of a scientific expedition, and, as Mary Louise Pratt points out, 'Journalism and narrative travel accounts . . . were essential mediators between the scientific network and a larger European public. They were central agents in legitimating scientific authority and its global project.'[13] Explorers were frequently themselves scientists, as in the case of David Livingstone, whilst other travellers made their journeys in the cause of science, as Charles Lyell did when he visited America, or used their travels as an opportunity to reflect upon their lives as scientists, as Humphry Davy did in his last book *Consolations in Travel*.

Similarly, many of the best-known social explorers and theorists of the day, such as William Cobbett, Charles Dickens, Harriet Martineau, Anna Jameson, and Flora Tristan, also wrote travel books, in which they generally commented on the social, political and cultural aspects of the countries they visited. Conversely, the travel writer Frances Trollope wrote novels about factory workers and the victims of the 1834 New Poor Law, basing her work closely on contemporary social reportage. And the social explorer Henry Mayhew, who had run away from school to become a seaman and travel to India, adapted his childhood ambition to be an experimental chemist, resolving as an urban sociologist 'to deal with human nature as a natural philosopher or a chemist deals with any material object'.[14]

There were numerous ways in which science, exploration and the social condition of England impinged upon each other. New regions were explored as potential colonial sites to which England's urban poor were encouraged to go to seek a better, richer life. Developments in science and technology made a great practical impact on travel and exploration as well as on the economic and social life of England. Steam trains and steam ships revolutionised travel, and scientific instruments were an important component of the explorer's baggage, while techno-logical discoveries were responsible for the industrialisation and urban-isation of Britain, the attendant social problems of which were the subject of so many blue books and philanthropical reports. Science, like travel and exploration, was harnessed for political and commercial ends, often at great human cost. Comparisons were commonly made between new scientific discoveries that had not yet been applied and recently explored territories that had not yet been exploited.[15]

It is hardly surprising, then, given the immensely complex involve-ment of science, travel and social issues in the nineteenth century, that there should be so many rhetorical similarities between their literatures. Pratt has argued compellingly for the impact of the discourse of natural history on travel writing, for instance noting 'The emergence of a new version of . . . Europe's "planetary consciousness," a version marked by an orientation towards interior exploration and the construction of global-scale meaning through the descriptive apparatuses of natural history.'[16] Moreover, as physical anthropology, 'ethnology' and pre-history developed as scientific disciplines they shaped representations of class and race in social reportage and travel writing alike: explicit or implied correlations were made between the working-class and the colonial subject, each of whom was perceived to be at a primitive stage in the evolution of civilisation.

The narratives of science, exploration and social reportage were fre-quently emplotted in similar ways. And so, for instance, the quest motif is a trope in the writings of scientists such as Humphry Davy and Charles Darwin as well as in those of explorers such as David Livingstone and social explorers such as William Booth. The very metaphors these writers use to define their enterprise suggest how they appropriate each others' discourses. While Henry Stanley takes the armchair explorer into 'Darkest Africa', William Booth leads us into 'Darkest England' (and finds 'The Way Out').[17] Humphry Davy, like many of his Romantic scientific counterparts, similarly sees himself as a traveller on a quest, making a chemical journey of discovery: 'there is now before us a boundless prospect and novelty in science, a country unexplored but noble and fertile in aspect; a land of promise in electricity.'[18]

In what follows I shall look at some examples of what may be collectively termed prose of discovery, from the genres of scientific writing, travel and exploration literature, and social reportage, in terms of their language, structures, tropes and rhetorical devices, and show how it is, like Frankenstein's ambition to seek distinction in science and discoveries, only 'apparently innocent'.

Scientific writing

One of the greatest benefits conferred by experimental sciences is, that they have given the true progression to the mind; they have appeared as a work begun, but not perfected. There is no spirit or feeling of imitation in them, which uniformly cramps the best energies of the mind; but one desire for extending them: and *discovery* is the great stimulus to exertion, is the highest stimulus to inquiry; and the title of *discoverer* is the most honourable that can be bestowed on a scientific man.

(Humphry Davy)[19]

The nineteenth century has been identified by historians of science such as David Knight as 'the age of science'.[20] A full survey of the range of scientific literature produced in the period would properly encompass not only chemistry, physics, biology, astronomy, mathematics, geology, palaeontology, the medical sciences and other mainstream scientific disciplines, but also areas, such as phrenology and psychical research, which have since been discredited as fields of academic enquiry. As it is clearly impossible in a short chapter to do justice either to the range and diversity of scientific disciplines in the nineteenth century or to the plethora of distinguished scientific practitioners writing in the period – which includes such eminent figures as Charles Lyell, John Herschel, Charles Babbage, William Whewell, Michael Faraday, James Clerk Maxwell, John Tyndall and T. H. Huxley – this chapter will focus on the work of two scientists, the Romantic chemist Humphry Davy and the Victorian evolutionary biologist Charles Darwin, as a way of exploring some of the general issues raised by scientific writing.

As Knight points out, the word 'scientist' did not come into the language before the 1830s, when it was coined by analogy with 'artist': 'Before that time, scientific men called themselves "natural philosophers", or "natural historians"; and indeed the word "science" meant any organized body of knowledge, down to about the same date.'[21] Not only did the nineteenth century witness a rapid expansion of the scientific enterprise, and the development of new fields of inquiry and new methodologies; it also saw the transformation of British science from an amateur to a professional standing. Despite Babbage's view in 1830 that science in England was in decline,[22] the most revolutionary research for which the period was renowned – Darwin's development of evolutionary theory, Faraday's work on electricity and magnetism, William Thomson's on thermodynamics, Maxwell's introduction of statistical methods into physical science – was still to be done. Yet Babbage's attack on the British scientific establishment in *Reflections on the Decline of Science in England* does highlight the generally impoverished state of science in the early decades of the century, and in particular the gross neglect of science in most areas of the English education system, and the atrophy of the Royal Society, which conspicuously failed to provide adequate professional leadership. Ironically, it is precisely because of the amateur status of science in the first half of the century that so much brilliant scientific writing was produced. In the absence of a specialist professional audience, scientists were forced to make themselves understood to a lay public; more, to inform, to persuade, to excite their non-scientific but literate audience, to bring their abstruse knowledge into the realm of public discourse, to represent the significance of their material discoveries in as compelling a way as possible.

This goes a long way towards explaining the extraordinary rhetorical complexity of so much nineteenth-century scientific literature which makes it such a good subject for modern literary critics and historians of science interested in science as discourse. Nineteenth-century scientific writing flagrantly refuses to conform to the conventional view of scientific language as, in Roland Barthes' words, 'simply an instrument, which it profits to make as transparent and neutral as possible . . . subordinate to the matter of science (workings, hypotheses, results) which, so it is said, exists outside language and precedes it'.[23] It is now widely accepted, among literary critics at least, and within many other disciplines too, that language is never transparent and neutral, and that the text serves a constituting function. This is particularly evident in nineteenth-century scientific prose because of its need to appeal to the unscientific imagination of a non-professional audience, for whom the text before them is the only reality.

The requirement to communicate effectively in an extrascientific realm also makes it the more obvious in nineteenth-century scientific writing that science is always implicated in its social, political, and economic milieu, and to some extent shaped by that milieu. Against the conventional view that science is no more nor less than the objective and disinterested pursuit of the truth, unaffected by commercial or political pressures, students of the nineteenth century are now exposing the cultural subtext of the scientific text, and investigating the infiltration of contemporary ideologies into scientific writing, finding in it a play of discourses, rather than a detached and aloof presentation of laboratory experiments and results.[24] As Gillian Beer points out, 'all description draws, often unknowingly, upon shared cultural assumptions which underwrite its neutral and authoritative status and conceal the embedded designs upon which describing depends'.[25]

Not only does nineteenth-century scientific writing have 'embedded designs' upon its readers, and often tends to confirm teleological patterns like the Argument from Design itself, but it is also shaped by the rhetorical design of the generic forms available to it. Because, once again, of the amateur status of science through the first half of the nineteenth century, there is a much greater diversity in styles and modes of communication than in the later professionalised disciplines. Although the beginning of the nineteenth century saw a significant expansion in the number of professional scientific journals, most scientists communicated their ideas and discoveries through other media as well. Scientists seeking to capture the public imagination expressed their ideas in many different forms – children's books and lectures, articles in the periodical press, official reports, exhibition catalogues, diaries, 'lay sermons' – and their writing was 'designed' accordingly. A particularly popular and effective mode for both educating the populace and generating enthusiasm and public support for scientific research was the public lecture, which was often illustrated by spectacular demonstrations. Depending on the genre chosen, then, the scientist might assume the persona of story-teller, educator, prophet, hero, genius, magician or showman.

A scientist who at one time or another in his writing adopts all of these stances is Humphry Davy. A close friend of Coleridge, Wordsworth and other prominent literary figures of his day, and a poet himself, Davy was not only a brilliant scientist but also a particularly literary one. Firm in his belief that chemistry was the science 'the most capable of all others of being expressed by Language', Davy developed, as Trevor H. Levere has demonstrated, a Romantic view of the relations among thought, language and chemical science which paralleled Coleridge's. He wrote, for instance,

> [We] use Words for Ideas as we use signs for collections of
> units in algebra . . . if we were accurately to examine the

> progress of intellect we shall find that . . . the Laws of the
> universe have owed their origin more to the combination of
> terms and propositions than to the perpetual consideration of
> ideas representing facts.[26]

Levere mounts a persuasive case for the mutual inspiration of Davy,
Coleridge and Wordsworth, and it is evident that Coleridge makes
significant use of chemical metaphors in his theoretical writings while,
conversely, Davy's vision for chemistry arguably draws upon Wordsworth's account of poetry in the Preface to *Lyrical Ballads*, which Davy
proofread in July 1800.[27] Davy saw chemistry as a creative pursuit which,
like other branches of the study of nature, 'must be always more or less
connected with the love of the beautiful and sublime' and is 'eminently
calculated to gratify and keep alive the more powerful passions and
ambitions of the soul'.[28] It is, indeed, often made the subject of his
poetry, which is typically highly Romantic in its eulogy of the natural
world and its subjective preoccupation with the feelings.

Davy's posthumously published *Consolations in Travel; or The Last
Days of a Philosopher* (1830) contains a description of 'the chemical philosopher' which might have been spoken by Frankenstein. In it, Davy
arrogates to the scientist a god-like power which parallels Coleridge's
and Wordsworth's shared belief in the divine power of the poet's
creative imagination:

> It is a sublime occupation to investigate the cause of the
> tempest and the volcano, and to point out their use in the
> economy of things, – to bring the lightning from the clouds
> and make it subservient to our experiments, – to produce as it
> were a microcosm in the laboratory of art, and to measure and
> weigh those invisible atoms, which, by their motions and
> changes according to laws impressed upon them by the Divine
> Intelligence, constitute the universe of things. The true
> chemical philosopher . . . sees man an atom amidst atoms fixed
> upon a point in space; and yet modifying the laws that are
> around him by understanding them; and gaining, as it were, a
> kind of dominion over time, and an empire in material space,
> and exerting on a scale infinitely small a power seeming a sort
> of shadow or reflection of a creative energy, and which entitles
> him to the distinction of being made in the image of God and
> animated by a spark of the divine mind.[29]

It is interesting to find, a few pages on from this highly rhetorical and
metaphor-laden account of the scientist's work, advice on the kind of
language the 'chemical philosopher' should use to communicate his ideas:

> In detailing the results of experiments, and in giving them to the world, the chemical philosopher should adopt the simplest style and manner; he will avoid all ornaments, as something injurious to his subject, and should bear in mind the saying of the first King of Great Britain respecting a sermon which was excellent in doctrine, but overcharged with poetical allusions and figurative language, "that the tropes and metaphors of the speaker were like the brilliant wild flowers in a field of corn, very pretty, but which did very much hurt the corn." In announcing even the greatest and most important discoveries, the true philosopher will communicate his details with modesty and reserve; he will rather be a useful servant of the public, bringing forth a light from under his cloak when it is needed in darkness, than a charlatan exhibiting fireworks and having a trumpeter to announce their magnificence.[30]

Language should, it seems, like nature itself, be subservient to the imperatives of science. And yet the tropes and metaphors which are so firmly repudiated in the early part of this passage come back to haunt him at the end, and the stark 'laboratory of art' becomes crowded with servants, charlatans and trumpeters. The emotive and metaphorical discourse undermines the argument, exploding the myth that language can be simple, objective and unadorned as spectacularly as the charlatan's fireworks. And so although Davy sometimes represents the scientist/genius as transcending language ('The man of true genius . . . in the search of discovery . . . will rather pursue the plans of his own mind than be limited by the artificial divisions of language'),[31] he is as firmly enmeshed in it as the preacher straining for rhetorical effect in his anecdote.

But if the scientist finds it difficult to keep his language in order, the objective truth of his discoveries is borne out by the scientific method itself. As David Locke points out,

> the scientist . . . often will divide the enterprise of the scientist into two portions, the phase of generation, in which the ideas are born, and the phase of justification, or verification, in which they are tested. . . . Now the contaminated idea is tested in the crucible of the scientific method. The fire of scientific scrutiny burns away from the idea – the hypothesis or the theory – the stain of its origin. In this way, one can acknowledge the humanity of the scientist and yet maintain the ultimate objectivity of the endeavour.[32]

Such a division of labour is frequently apparent in Davy's work. So, for instance, at the beginning of his second Bakerian Lecture, he explains that he proposes to support what he put forward in his previous lecture as merely conjecture, 'sanctioned only by strong analogies', with 'some conclusive facts', for, 'In the course of a laborious experimental application of the powers of electro-chemical analysis, to bodies which have appeared simple when examined by common chemical agents, or which at least have never been decomposed, it has been my good fortune to obtain new and singular results.'[33] He emphasises that 'when general facts are mentioned, they are such only as have been deduced from processes carefully performed and often repeated'. Davy then goes on to describe the experimental process whereby he isolated the two metals potassium and sodium, using the new method of electrolysis to break down the alkalis potash and soda. At a stroke, Davy establishes himself as the discoverer of both the metals and the method, and as the founder of a new discipline, electrochemistry. And the experiments themselves, while legitimating the speculations of genius, make by no means dull reading. Potassium and sodium are amongst the most reactive of all metals and Davy records dramatic results and 'brilliant phenomena':

> Under these circumstances a vivid action was soon observed to take place. The potash began to fuse at both its points of electrization. There was a violent effervescence at the upper surface; at the lower, or negative surface, there was no liberation of elastic fluid; but small globules having a high metallic lustre, and being precisely similar in visible characteristics to quick-silver, appeared, some of which burnt with explosion and bright flame, as soon as they were formed, and others remained, and were merely tarnished, and finally covered by a white film which formed on their surfaces.[34]

Soda exhibits an analogous result, and when more power is used, 'the globules often burnt at the moment of their formation, and sometimes violently exploded and separated into smaller globules, which flew with great velocity through the air in a state of vivid combustion, producing a beautiful effect of continued jets of fire'. Davy may here be writing as 'a useful servant of the public bringing forth a light from under his cloak', but the dynamic nature of his material is indeed as breathtaking as the charlatan's fireworks. As he was to write elsewhere, 'the business of the laboratory is often a service of danger, and the elements, like the refractory spirits of romance, though the obedient slave of the magician, yet sometimes escape the influence of his talisman, and endanger his person'.[35]

Davy's descriptions of his laboratory experimentation make compelling reading, but his earlier accounts of his personal experiments with the respiration of nitrous oxide, published in 1800, precisely detailed though they are, take us still further from the idea that the presentation of scientific results must take an impersonal and objective form. He freely admits, and indeed makes a virtue of the fact, that scientific method is not an infallible conduit to the 'truth': 'Fortunately for the active and progressive nature of the human mind, even experimental research is only a method of approximation to truth.'[36] It is in his research on nitrous oxide that Davy is perhaps at his most Romantic. His decision to inhale the gas about which so little was known in order to determine whether it was a common stimulant was extremely courageous, and he entered into a lengthy period of personal experimentation with an extraordinary degree of commitment, in the full knowledge that he might do himself great damage. Inevitably, the scientist figures as the hero of his own story, braving death as surely as the explorer did amidst the wild animals, deadly fevers, and marauding tribes in the African jungle, especially when he attempted to compare the physiological actions of other gases 'which are sooner or later fatal to life when respired', such as the highly dangerous nitric oxide (nitrous gas), with the effects produced by respiration of nitrous oxide:

> . . . during a fit of enthusiasm produced by the respiration of nitrous oxide, I resolved to endeavour to breathe nitrous gas.
>
> 114 cubic inches of nitrous gas were introduced into the large mercurial air-holder; two small silk bags of the capacity of seven quarts were filled with nitrous oxide.
>
> After a forced exhaustion of my lungs, my nose being accurately closed, I made three inspirations and expirations of nitrous oxide in one of the bags, to free my lungs as much as possible from atmospheric oxygen; then, after a full expiration of the nitrous oxide, I transferred my mouth from the mouthpiece of the bag to that of the air-holder, and turning the stop-cock, attempted to inspire the nitrous gas. In passing through my mouth and fauces, it tasted astringent and highly disagreeable; it occasioned a sense of burning in the throat, and produced a spasm of the epiglottis so painful as to oblige me to desist instantly from attempts to inspire it. After moving my lips from the mouth-piece, when I opened them to inspire common air, aeriform nitrous acid was instantly formed in my mouth, which burnt the tongue and palate, injured the teeth, and produced an inflammation of the mucous membrane which lasted some hours.
>
> As after the respiration of nitrous oxide in the experiments in the last Research, a small portion of the residual atmospheric air remained in the lungs, mingled with the gas, after forced expiration; it is most probable that a minute portion of nitrous acid was formed in this experiment, when the nitrous gas was taken into the mouth and fauces, which might produce its stimulating properties. If so, perhaps I owe my life to the

circumstance; for supposing I had taken an inspiration of nitrous gas, and even that it had produced no positive effects, it is highly improbable, that by breathing nitrous oxide, I should have freed my lungs from it, so as to have prevented the formation of nitrous acid when I again inspired common air. I never design again to attempt so rash an experiment.[37]

Inevitably too, given the circumstances, experiment is written as experience, and Davy dwells in minute detail upon his own feelings and sensations:

A thrilling, extending from the chest to the extremities, was almost immediately produced. I felt a sense of tangible extension highly pleasurable in every limb; my visible impressions were dazzling, and apparently magnified, I heard distinctly every sound in the room, and was perfectly aware of my situation. By degrees, as the pleasurable sensations increased, I lost all connection with external things; trains of vivid visible images rapidly passed through my mind, and were connected with words in such a manner, as to produce perceptions perfectly novel. I existed in a world of newly connected and newly modified ideas. I theorised – I imagined that I made discoveries. When I was awakened from this semi-delirious trance by Dr. Kinglake, who took the bag from my mouth, indignation and pride were the first feelings produced by the sight of the persons about me. My emotions were enthusiastic and sublime; and for a minute I walked round the room, perfectly regardless of what was said to me. As I recovered my former state of mind, I felt an inclination to communicate the discoveries I had made during the experiment. I endeavoured to recall the ideas, they were feeble and indistinct; one collection of terms, however, presented itself: and with the most intense belief and prophetic manner, I exclaimed to Dr. Kinglake, 'Nothing exists but thoughts! – the universe is composed of impressions, ideas, pleasures and pains!'[38]

At the close of the section of this work devoted to his personal experimentation with nitrous oxide and other gases Davy notes the imperfections of his account, arising from 'the nature of the language of feeling', and explains that he has tried to be as accurate as possible 'by making use of terms standing for the most similar common feelings'. In trying to articulate his experiences he suffers in a particularly acute form – because of the subjective nature of the experiments, because he needs to talk about feelings and sensations rather than, say, atoms or currents

– a problem faced by other scientific discoverers: how to find a language for the new. It is a major dilemma for a Romantic scientist, especially one so closely involved with the development of Wordsworthian and Coleridgean poetics:

> We are incapable of recollecting pleasures and pains of sense. It is impossible to reason concerning them, except by means of terms which have been associated with them at the moment of their existence, and which are afterwards called up amidst trains of concomitant ideas.
>
> When pleasures or pains are new or connected with new ideas, they can never be intelligibly detailed unless associated during their existence with terms standing for analogous feelings.
>
> I have sometimes experienced from nitrous oxide, sensations similar to no others, and they have consequently been indescribable.[39]

Davy's account of his own experiences with breathing nitrous oxide is followed by a series of detailed first-person descriptions of the effects produced by its respiration upon a number of other individuals, one of whom was Coleridge. Interestingly, Coleridge employs analogy to describe his first experience of the gas: 'I felt a highly pleasurable sensation of warmth over my whole frame, resembling that which I remember once to have experienced after returning from a walk in the snow into a warm room.' But his final experience is indescribable: 'my sensations were highly pleasurable . . . of more unmingled pleasure than I had ever before experienced'.[40]

It has been plausibly argued by L. Pearce Williams that it was through Coleridge that Davy became acquainted with the ideas of Immanuel Kant,[41] and it is in his researches into nitrous oxide and his second Bakerian Lecture that his Kantian leanings may be felt most strongly. In the former, Kant's intellectual presence makes itself felt in the transcendentalist language in which he describes his experiences of breathing nitrous oxide: 'I have often felt very great pleasure when breathing it alone, in darkness and silence, occupied only by ideal existence.'[42] In the second Bakerian Lecture, Kant's intellectual influence is more fundamental. In *The Critique of Pure Reason* (1781) Kant had written: 'We know substance in space only through the forces which work in this space, either by drawing others to it (attraction) or by preventing penetration (repulsion and impenetrability); we know no other quality pertaining to the concept of substance existing in space which we call matter.'[43] Five years later he published a treatise on the *Metaphysical Foundations of Natural Science*, in which he tried to show how a new dynamic physics, based on the idea of forces, might be developed.

Williams describes the framework Kant's system of dynamic physics provided for early nineteenth-century scientists such as Davy:

> Every point in space was . . . associated with attractive and repulsive forces whose 'conflict' produced all the phenomena of the observable world. Forces gave Kant the plenum required by his epistemological conclusions; they also provided a continuity in nature which the older atomic theory violated so flagrantly by its insistence upon the dichotomy between matter and space . . . The reduction of all physical phenomena to attractive and repulsive forces acting upon one another was seductively simple. The different *kinds* of attraction and repulsion – electrical, magnetic, etc. – were the results of different conditions under which the two basic forces manifested themselves. Behind these differences lay the essential *unity* of all forces. From this it followed logically that all the forces of nature were convertible into one another; one need only find the proper conditions for accomplishing the conversion.[44]

Davy's earliest poetry reveals him to have had a strong sense of the divinity and unity of nature, and his conviction of the interconnectedness of phenomena would have been strengthened by the discovery of galvanism and of the electric current. It is clear why Kant's ideas on forces would have appealed, and they do seem to inform his own theory of electrochemical action developed in the Bakerian Lectures of 1806 and 1807, a new dynamic chemistry that corresponded with Kant's ideas for a dynamic physics.

As Christopher Lawrence, David Knight and others have argued, Davy's work had a Romantic core: 'Davy used chemistry to ask and answer questions about the material and spiritual constituents of the universe and thus about the nature of life and mind . . . Romanticism was not a hindrance to chemistry, nor yet something that enabled Davy to discover truths about nature. Rather, the nature that Davy discovered was itself Romantic.'[45] Scientific theories and methodologies are inevitably developed and practised in a specific historical context, and it is therefore not surprising that Davy's writings should share the preoccupations of other Romantic writers. His interest in Idealist philosophy, his intense love of nature, which he perceived as an organic unity, his conviction of his own genius, his distrust of abstraction and rationalism, and his faith in the subjective life of the feelings, mark him out as a Romantic, and so does his oft-professed commitment to the idea that science should be directed to the betterment of the human lot. His research did, of course, have significant practical outcomes: although it was not immediately applied, his work on nitrous oxide led eventually to its use as an anaesthetic, and his research on gaseous combustion led to his invention of a safety lamp for miners. Whether the Davy lamp should in the event be seen as improving the working condition of miners is, though, a matter of some debate. To the extent that it saved lives it was undoubtedly a benefit, but the fact that its invention made possible the mining of deeper and more dangerous seams led to further loss of life. Christopher Lawrence sees the Davy lamp as epitomising Davy's work and his socio-political stance, and indeed as symbolising 'the new web of social relations which were generated during the Industrial Revolution', for 'On the one hand it was, apparently, a practical demonstration of his lifelong rhetoric that natural science could be used for the relief of man's estate. On the other hand, it demonstrates his continual enslavement to the industrial and aristocratic interests which he served so well.' For Davy's move to the political right was something else he had in common with Coleridge and Wordsworth. Lawrence argues that

> Davy's lectures on matter, life and mind were . . . political practices which can only be understood in the context of the dangerous years of the French Wars, the years of conservative reaction. . . . During the first two decades of the new century any account of life or mind which so much as hinted that they were merely the products of corporeal organization was condemned as atheistical and politically subversive, which usually meant French-inspired. Conversely vitalism of the sort espoused by Davy and Coleridge was used to underwrite the existing social order. This was achieved by the identification of the vital power with the Creator worshipped by the Church of England.[46]

It is important to recognise that science always is embedded not only in a wider intellectual and cultural context, but also in social relationships and in particular economic and political conditions. It is crucial to acknowledge, too, that the history of science does not consist of a one-way traffic in ideas, whereby scientists make discoveries and pass on the fruits of their esoteric learning to the community at large. Scientific discovery in the nineteenth century everywhere demonstrates the essential reciprocity of knowledge. Davy may have invented a lamp for miners, but the knowledge and practical expertise of miners and quarrymen were immensely valuable to geologists and made a major contribution to the development of the earth sciences. Darwin's theory of the origin of species depended in part upon the specialist knowledge of animal and plant breeders, upon 'generations of horticulturalists, beekeepers, cattle and sheep breeders, pigeon fanciers and nurserymen', as well as on his reading of political economy and literature. Science constitutes what

James A. Secord has called 'a pattern of interchange' between scientific practitioners and the broader milieu,[47] and in the nineteenth century, as at other times in history, the intellectual generation of scientific discoveries is inseparable from the social, economic and ideological issues of the day.

If Davy's work was thus inevitably ideologically charged, so was that of other nineteenth-century scientists, and this despite a continuing and increasing emphasis on the objective, value-free, and strictly factual nature of science. John Herschel's influential *Preliminary Discourse on the Study of Natural Theology* (1830) grounds scientific knowledge in a commitment by scientists 'to stand and fall by the result of a direct appeal to facts in the first instance, and of strict logical deduction from them afterwards', while in his presidential address to the British Association for the Advancement of Science in 1859 Prince Albert describes the domain of the inductive sciences as the domain of facts 'which are "objective" and belong to everybody'.[48] And yet many early nineteenth-century scientists subscribed to a Paleyan natural theology which Basil Willey has described as 'Cosmic Toryism' because of its endorsement, indeed consecration, of the concept of a fixed natural order.[49] As Tess Cosslett reminds us, there was a historical connection between natural theology and empirical science, both of which grew out of the literal-mindedness of late seventeenth-century Puritanism, and so it is not altogether surprising to find scientists committed to natural theology as firmly as they are to the inductive method.[50] The respected astronomer John Herschel and the equally eminent thermodynamicist William Thomson (Lord Kelvin) were only two of many professional scientists who publicly rejected Darwin's theory of natural selection on the grounds that it ran counter to the Argument from Design.

As the century progressed, the association of science with Britain's material aspirations became more explicit. The Great Exhibition of 1851, for instance, celebrated the links between science and technology and the commercial and imperial ambitions of the British. For if the advocacy of a static view of nature can be seen to have implications for the social order, if the Argument from Design is ideological, then dynamic theories of nature have their own ideological baggage. And so both thermodynamics and evolution have respectively been identified as the science of imperialism. The literature of thermodynamics is freighted with the moral and political preoccupations of High Victorian imperial Britain. For instance, the contemporary moral connotations of the second law of thermodynamics are vividly present in William Thomson's language as he describes, in 1852, the effects and the implications of entropy. He writes that 'There is at present in the material world a universal tendency to the dissipation of mechanical energy', placing entropic heat loss, as N. Katherine Hayles points out, 'in the same semantic category as deplorable personal habits'. He goes on to predict that 'any restoration of mechanical energy, without more than an equivalent of dissipation, is impossible . . . and is probably never effected by means of organized matter, either endowed with vegetable life or subjected to the will of an animated creature,' so that 'within a finite period of time . . . the earth must again be unfit for the habitation of man as at present constituted'. For Hayles, and other commentators such as Crosbie Smith, the cultural subtext of Kelvin's conclusions, and those of his fellow thermodynamicists, is palpable in their rhetoric: 'entropy represented the tendency of the universe to run down, despite the best efforts of British rectitude to prevent it. In Kelvin's prose, the rhetoric of imperialism confronts the inevitability of failure.'[51]

Darwin's theory of evolution may seem to offer a scenario diametrically opposed to the tragic vision of nineteenth-century thermodynamics, but it too has been closely, and more notoriously, implicated in imperialism. Patrick Brantlinger observes that 'Evolutionary thought seems almost calculated to legitimize imperialism', whilst Walter F. Cannon identifies Darwin's 'most original rhetoric, at the heart of his theory' as 'the rhetoric of the British colonial empire'.[52] Indeed, Cannon goes so far as to say that 'In order to invent the theory of descent with modification by natural selection, it was probably necessary to be English in the middle of the nineteenth century.'[53] John C. Greene similarly situates the theory of natural selection within its time and place, noting that its proponents in the first half of the nineteenth century were mostly British; however, he explains this 'curious fact' by reference not specifically to imperialism but to the ascendancy of the capitalist political economy and the competitive ethos in the first industrial nation, which predisposed British naturalists to see the world in terms of competitive struggle.[54]

It is clear that Darwin's work not only made history but also, like all writing and all theory, was the product of a particular historical moment: a particular scientific moment (he was able to consolidate the evolutionary researches of scientists such as Lyell and Lamarck); a particular cultural moment (his writing and his perception of the world were informed by Romantic aesthetic ideals and also by contemporary fictional practices); but also a particular social, political and economic moment. Darwin himself acknowledged the influence of Malthus on his ideas, describing the 'struggle for existence' he observes in the natural world as 'the doctrine of Malthus applied with manifold force to the whole animal and vegetable kingdoms',[55] and among contemporary commentators Marx and Engels both drew attention to the social constitution of Darwin's theory:

> It is remarkable how Darwin recognizes among beasts and
> plants his English society with its division of labour,
> competition, opening-up of new markets, 'inventions', and the

Malthusian 'struggle for existence'. It is Hobbes's *bellum omnium contra omnes*, and one is reminded of Hegel's *Phenomenology*, where civil society is described as a 'spirited animal kingdom', while in Darwin the animal kingdom figures as civil society.

Engels was later to reflect: 'Darwin did not know what a bitter satire he wrote on mankind, and especially on his countrymen, when he showed that free competition, the struggle for existence, which the economists celebrate as the highest historical achievement, is the normal state of the *animal kingdom*.'[56] Even to his contemporaries, Darwin's theory had the quality of a fable, a fact that has not been lost on later interpreters. For instance, with her usual sense of mid-nineteenth-century obsessions and the densely interwoven texture of Victorian intellectual and social life, A. S. Byatt wittily explores the parallels between insect and human society in relation to Darwinian theories of breeding and sexuality in her brilliant novella *Morpho Eugenia* (1992).

The appropriation of Darwin's *On the Origin of Species, by means of Natural Selection* (1859), almost from its first publication, by propagandists of both the right and the left is testimony both to the social and political resonances of this work of science and to its ideological flexibility. Darwin has been invoked in support of theories of progress and theories of degeneration. His work has been used by some to legitimate a conservative vision of social order and by others to countenance change. So-called 'Social Darwinism' took many forms, and different aspects of Darwin's work were used to endorse wildly different ideologies. While phrases such as 'the struggle for existence', 'natural selection', and 'survival of the fittest' were used by some to justify poverty and exploitation under industrial capitalism, the concepts of 'adaptation', 'mutual aid', and 'struggle for the life of others' were enlisted by reformers in the cause of industrial regulation and social welfare. It is well known that in late nineteenth-century England Darwinism was appropriated to underwrite the imperialist project.[57] But as early as the 1860s scientists with reputations for being advanced thinkers, such as Thomas Henry Huxley and John Tyndall, were bringing Darwinian biology and anthropology to the aid of the ascendant liberal bourgeoisie, providing from science authoritative but ideologically motivated arguments against equality and democracy. In his essay 'On the Natural Inequality of Man', for instance, Huxley wielded his considerable scientific clout on behalf of the elitist cause, in opposition to democratic government and socialistic reform, invoking evolutionary theory in support of the conservative argument that there were natural limits controlling social change, and that the inferior could not compete on equal terms.[58] And, although Darwin's emphasis upon competition and individualism was anathema to thorough-going socialists, the evolutionary principle did also appeal strongly to many of those who wanted an escalated programme of reform, because most were anxious to avoid revolution at all costs. The idea of continuity without 'cataclysm' and of biological progress towards a 'secure future' was reassuring to those who feared the consequences of more interventionist and insurrectionary social and political strategies.[59]

Recent commentators have, indeed, questioned the legitimacy of the traditional historiographic distinction between Darwinism and Social Darwinism, perceiving 'Social Darwinism' as the 'artifact of a professional discourse that increasingly pretended to divorce science from ideology'.[60] There is no doubt that, despite Darwin's deliberate eschewal of anthropomorphism, as Gillian Beer compellingly argues, 'Man is a determining absence in the argument of *The Origin of Species*', for the simple reason that the only language available to Darwin was one that was permeated with natural theological assumptions: 'Presumptions about creation and design had constantly to be contested, yet this contest must, as it were, be dramatized, enacted, within a received language weighted towards that which he seeks to controvert.'[61] The problem is encapsulated in the very title of his most famous work, *The Origin of Species*, in which he in fact challenges the prevailing belief in absolute origins and an originary first cause with a theory of natural law and adaptation, and undermines the whole notion of fixed species.

Darwin was, then, severely constrained by the language available to him and obliged to exploit all the rhetorical and linguistic resources at his disposal to their fullest extent in order to articulate a theory and its implications which were, in a sense, beyond language as it was currently constituted. It is its complex and eloquent narrative organisation, its at once evocative and levelling language, its accomplished use of classical rhetoric, its literary and biblical allusiveness, its engagingly personal style, and above all its metaphorical density which make *The Origin of Species* such a brilliant work of literature.[62] But it is precisely those literary qualities which resist closure, which guarantee its multivocality and render it so hermeneutically vulnerable.

Like many other scientists writing in the early to mid-nineteenth century, Darwin was keen to develop a scientific discourse which approximated to popular discourse so that he might reach a wider, non-specialist audience. *The Origin of Species* therefore encompasses a great discursive range, from the technical to the vernacular. To complement this linguistic attempt to communicate new scientific discoveries to a lay audience, Darwin made significant use of metaphor, as a way of presenting the unfamiliar in familiar form. Most notably, he develops the metaphor of 'Natural Selection', by analogy with the methods of plant and animal breeders, and the metaphor of the 'Struggle for Existence'. Such resonant metaphors were crucial to the impact of *The Origin*, not only because they gave concrete realisation to abstract and essentially speculative ideas, but because they were so suggestive and open-ended, and because they could accommodate contradictions. The charms of what Beer has called his 'generous semantic practice' are self-evident, but the pitfalls soon became clear, as such metaphors came to take on a life of their own. 'Darwin was much beset by the tendency of metaphor to become more concrete than was intended,' observes Beer, as she analyses the famous passage in *The Origin* which concludes 'The face of Nature may be compared to a yielding surface, with ten thousand sharp wedges packed close together and driven inwards by incessant blows, sometimes one wedge being struck, and then another with greater force.' As such passages indicate, 'Darwin's writing profoundly unsettled the received relationships between fiction, metaphor, and the material world.'[63]

It has frequently been noted that Darwin's use of personification in such metaphors as 'Natural Selection' militates against the whole thrust of his argument, which was to remove humanity from centre stage, and to remove altogether the idea of selection, of an intelligent choice. However, the implied analogies between nature and humanity (and, by extension, a benign creator) which personification encourages, the oblique references through metaphor to a more familiar world-view by which human beings hold a more assured and cherished place, do soften the implications of Darwin's theory. Natural Selection might be seen as a set of divinely-ordained processes designed to bring about adaptation and improvement, as Charles Kingsley believed. Darwin identifies Natural Selection as 'the principle of preservation'; indeed, the sub-title of the book, in its first edition, stresses 'the preservation of favoured races'. And the persistent gendering of Nature as a nurturing female, who selects 'only for [the good] of the being which she tends', ascribes what Beer terms a 'benign surveillance' to the natural world.[64]

But if there are certain very obvious respects in which Darwin's use of metaphor may be seen to run counter to or compromise his thesis, in other regards the metaphorical abundance of *The Origin* provides the perfect linguistic enactment of his theory. Darwin's awareness of his own linguistic practices was extremely sophisticated. 'I use the term Struggle for Existence,' he readily acknowledges, 'in a large and metaphorical sense.'[65] Moreover, he was alert to the ways in which his own language and tropes were implicated in the theory he was delineating. 'A breed, like a dialect of a language', he notes, 'can hardly be said to have had a definite origin':

> A man preserves and breeds from an individual with some slight deviation of structure, or takes more care than usual in matching his best animals and thus improves them, and the improved individuals slowly spread in the immediate neighbourhood. But as yet they will hardly have a distinct

name, and from being only slightly valued, their history will be disregarded. When further improved by the same slow and gradual process, they will spread more widely, and will get recognized as something distinct and valuable, and will then probably first receive a provincial name. In semi-civilised countries, with little free communication, the spreading and knowledge of any new sub-breed will be a slow process.[66]

The breed comes into being with its naming (ironically recalling Adamic tradition), and is not until then clearly delineated. The effect of metaphor is to suggest the common roots of things, rather than distinct and absolute origins, to suggest interaction and kinship, precisely that 'propinquity of descent' and that 'web of complex relations' which binds together things 'most remote in the scale of nature' upon which Darwin's theory insists.[67]

Similarly, the narrative structure of *The Origin of Species* realises in textual form Darwin's theory of descent. His description of the process of becoming does not constitute a steady and unswerving development plot. Its structure is not linear and teleological, but determined by observation (it begins with the words 'When we look') and expressive of variability.[68] The theory's emphasis on variation is there in the individuation and diversity, in the sheer abundance that characterises Darwin's descriptions of the natural world; its vast compass of space and time is there in the text's own geographical range, its juxtapositions of different worlds, its time-travelling. The idea of 'un-design' is brilliantly rendered in the text's radical subversion of conventional narrative strategies, in its profusion of examples of the diversity of species, in its cavalier disregard for the rules of spatial and temporal unity.

In his chapter 'On the Imperfection of the Geological Record' Darwin explains the difficulty of communicating the time-scale involved for the effecting of organic change. 'It is hardly possible for me even to recall to the reader, who may not be a practical geologist, the facts leading the mind feebly to comprehend the lapse of time,' he complains, warning that it is not enough to read learned accounts and 'to mark how each author attempts to give an inadequate idea of the duration of each formation or even each stratum'. Inspiring a whole generation of amateur fanatics, he exhorts:

> A man must for years examine for himself great piles of superimposed strata, and watch the sea at work grinding down old rocks and making fresh sediment, before he can hope to comprehend anything of the lapse of time, the monuments of which we see around us.

And yet it is crucial that he persuade his readers 'What an infinite number of generations, which the mind cannot grasp, must have succeeded each

other in the long roll of years!'[69] He does so by making use of an extraordinary technique whereby present and past geological formations
are represented as coexisting atemporally in the reader's visual field.[70]
Through an evolutionary lens he looks, for instance, at the denudation
of the Weald:

> ... it is an admirable lesson to stand on the North Downs and
> to look at the distant South Downs; for, remembering that at
> no great distance to the west the northern and southern
> escarpments meet and close, one can safely picture to oneself
> the great dome of rocks which must have covered up the
> Weald within so limited a period as since the latter part of the
> Chalk formation.[71]

Only having made this imaginative leap can the reader be expected to
enter into the complicated geological calculations which conclude with
the announcement that the denudation of the Weald must have taken
place over a period of three hundred million years.

An even more awesome task facing Darwin was to convey the
concept of forms that were ever in a state of mutation, never fixed or
hardedged, for with evolutionary vision, 'the whole organisation
becomes in some degree plastic.' Aptly enough, his discussion of the
eye provides a good example of what he requires his reader to envisage:

> ... we ought in imagination to take a thick layer of
> transparent tissue, with a nerve sensitive to light beneath, and
> then suppose every part of this layer to be continually
> changing slowly in density, so as to separate into layers of
> different densities and thicknesses, placed at different distances
> from each other, and with the surfaces of each layer slowly
> changing in form.[72]

It has often been observed, particularly by his detractors, that Darwin
has a habit of 'looking at an apparently rigid structure and "seeing" it
flow into another apparently quite different form'.[73] Ruskin, in his 'Lecture on Snakes', professedly a 'spiritual version of the development of
species', ridicules Huxley for doing the same, when he suggests that a
serpent is not only 'as Professor Huxley showed you, a lizard that has
dropped his legs off', but 'a duck that has dropped her wings off ... a
fish that has dropped his fins off ... And ... a honeysuckle, with a
head put on'.[74] Darwin does indeed bring before us a startling array of
organic forms which he shows to be related: 'The framework of bones
... in the hand of a man, wing of a bat, fin of the porpoise, and leg
of the horse – the same number of vertebrae forming the neck of the
giraffe and of the elephant ... The similarity of pattern in the wing and

leg of a bat, though used for such different purposes – in the jaws and legs of a crab – in the petals, stamens, and pistils of a flower', and so on. The sheer accumulation of these juxtapositions insists upon the morphological relationship he is proposing. And, as always, he shows a sophisticated understanding of metaphor, and of that grey area between fictiveness and fact in scientific language, when he discusses nature in metamorphosis:

> Naturalists frequently speak of the skull as formed of metamorphosed vertebrae: the jaws of crabs as metamorphosed legs; the stamens and pistils of flowers as metamorphosed leaves . . . Naturalists, however, use such language only in a metaphorical sense. They are far from meaning that during a long course of descent, primordial organs of any kind – vertebrae in the one case and legs in the other – have actually been modified into skulls or jaws. Yet so strong is the appearance of a modification of this nature having occurred that naturalists can hardly avoid employing language having this plain signification. On my view these terms may be used literally; and the wonderful fact of the jaws, for instance, of a crab retaining numerous characters, which they would probably have retained through inheritance, if they had really been metamorphosed during a long course of descent from true legs, or from some simple appendage, is explained.[75]

At a key point in his metaphor-driven text, then, Darwin achieves a powerful effect by insisting on the literal signification of what might be taken as purely metaphorical.

Darwin's language, in short, makes actual his thesis that the natural world is dynamic and evolving, containing the memory of its past, the very process of its becoming, within its present form; that natural organisms are not discrete but structurally and genealogically related:

> When we look at the plants and bushes clothing an entangled bank, we are tempted to attribute their proportional numbers and kinds to what we call chance. But how false a view is this! Every one has heard that when an American forest is cut down, a very different vegetation springs up; but it has been observed that the trees now growing on the ancient Indian mounds, in the Southern United States, display the same beautiful diversity and proportion of kinds as in the surrounding virgin forests. What a struggle between the several kinds of trees must here have gone on during long centuries, each annually scattering its seeds by the thousand; what war between insect and insect – between insects, snails, and other

animals with birds and beasts of prey – all striving to increase, and all feeding on each other or on the trees or their seeds and seedlings, or on the other plants which first clothed the ground and thus checked the growth of the trees! Throw up a handful of feathers, and all must fall to the ground according to definite laws; but how simple is this problem compared to the action and reaction of the innumerable plants and animals which have determined, in the course of centuries, the proportional numbers and kinds of trees now growing on the old Indian ruins![76]

In this famous passage on the struggle for existence in the natural world, human struggles for supremacy are not forgotten. The 'ancient Indian mounds' and 'old Indian ruins' are testimony to the lost tribes which have been extinguished as surely as the fossilised remains of ammonites, for instance, tell us of 'the extermination of whole groups of beings.'[77] Darwin has a notable tendency to use a vocabulary which has a technical meaning in the discourse of natural history but which has more general connotations which it is hard for the non-specialist reader to ignore. In the following passages, for example, the spectre of imperialism haunts the naturalist's language of 'native inhabitants' and 'foreigners', of 'immigration' and 'improvement':

> . . . in the case of an island, or of a country partly surrounded by barriers, into which new and better adapted forms could not freely enter, we should then have places in the economy of nature which would assuredly be better filled up, if some of the original inhabitants were in some manner modified; for, had the area been open to immigration, these same places would have been seized on by intruders. In such case, every slight modification, which in the course of ages chanced to arise, and which in any way favoured the individuals of any of the species, by better adapting them to their altered conditions, would tend to be preserved; and natural selection would thus have free scope for the work of improvement.

> . . . No country can be named in which all the native inhabitants are now so perfectly adapted to each other and to the physical conditions under which they live, that none of them could anyhow be improved; for in all countries the natives have been so far conquered by naturalised productions, that they have allowed foreigners to take firm possession of the land. And as foreigners have thus everywhere beaten some of the natives, we may safely conclude that the natives might have been modified with advantage, so as to have better resisted such intruders.[78]

The text is full of such passages which remind the reader that *The Origin of Species* was written in the heyday of imperialist exploration. We are told, disconcertingly, that 'Probably no region is as yet fully stocked, for at the Cape of Good Hope, where more species of plants are crowded together than in any other quarter of the world, some foreign plants have become naturalised, without causing, as far as we know, the extinction of any natives.' He explains the close relationships which exist between different 'inhabitants' of an archipelago according to 'the view of colonisation from the nearest and readiest source, together with the subsequent modification and better adaptation of the colonists to their new homes'.[79]

But it was of course the fact that it appealed so deliberately to a set of social and cultural assumptions, to a shared value system, that made *The Origin* so popular, and now makes it seem at once so original and so representative. We have seen, for instance, that an ideology of gender is inscribed in Darwin's principal analogy between natural and human selection whereby Nature is associated with the feminine and Culture with the masculine. It is a cultural dualism which he articulates more explicitly in *The Descent of Man*:

> Woman seems to differ from man in mental disposition, chiefly in her greater tenderness and less selfishness . . . Woman, owing to her maternal instincts, displays these qualities towards her infants in an eminent degree; therefore it is likely that she would often extend them towards her fellow-creatures. Man is the rival of other men; he delights in competition, and this leads to ambition which passes too easily into selfishness . . . It is generally admitted that with women the powers of intuition, of rapid perception, and perhaps of imitation, are more strongly marked than in man.[80]

Moreover, Darwin typically writes, like most scientists of his day, as a man speaking to men. Nature may be female, but the scientist and his implied readers are unequivocally male.

Throughout much of the nineteenth century scientists pondered on the question of how to communicate their discoveries to the non-specialist reader. Rarely were questions of gender articulated, yet assumptions about science as a male pursuit were frequently embedded in the language used by scientists. In 1855, James Clerk Maxwell, for instance, as a student at Cambridge, declared to his all-male audience in an essay for the Apostles' Club, 'By all means let us have technical terms belonging to every science and mystery practised by men, but let us not have mere freemasonry or Ziph language by which men of the same cult can secretly combine.' While he objects to a linguistic cliquishness between men of different cults, it is perfectly acceptable for men to practise 'science and mystery' from which women, presumably, are excluded.[81] More than twenty years later, in a review of 'Tait's *Thermodynamics*' for *Nature*, he returns to the problem of science and its communication, mounting a scathing attack on contemporary scientific writing practice and exposing the inadequacies of both the popular and the technical treatise:

> In the popular treatise, whatever shreds of the science are allowed to appear, are exhibited in an exceedingly diffuse and attenuated form, apparently with the hope that the mental faculties of the reader, though they would reject any stronger food, may insensibly become saturated with scientific phraseology, provided it is diluted with a sufficient quantity of more familiar language. In this way, by simple reading, the student may become possessed of the phrases of the science without having been put to the trouble of thinking a single thought about it. The loss implied in such an acquisition can be estimated only by those who have been compelled to unlearn a science that they might at length begin to learn it.
>
> The technical treatises do less harm, for no one ever reads them except under compulsion. From the establishment of the general equations to the end of the book, every page is full of symbols with indices and suffixes, so that there is not a paragraph of plain English on which the eye may rest.

After this, Professor Tait must have been relieved to read that he himself was guilty of neither scientific nor literary abomination:

> He serves up his strong meat for grown men at the beginning of the book, without thinking it necessary to employ the language either of the nursery or of the school; while for younger students he has carefully boiled down the mathematical elements into the most concentrated form, and has placed the result at the end as a *bonne bouche*, so that the beginner may take it in all at once, and ruminate upon it at his leisure.[82]

Maxwell's metaphors are a graphic reminder that the scientist had always to keep the consumer in mind, and they also make it plain that his intelligent reader is, like his articulate scientist, gendered male. Given the popular association of middle-class women with invalidism in the period,[83] the implied reader of that bland nourishment, the popular scientific treatise, is a woman, who would reject stronger food. And of course the preparer of invalid food (to which Isabella Beeton's *Book of Household Management* devotes a whole chapter) is always a woman, so the whole project of popular science is feminised. The matter of the technical treatise is as indigestible as the food at a boys' public school. But the admirable Tait serves up 'his strong meat for grown men' as the provedore of a good gentleman's club should. And so, by appropriating for male scientists the traditionally female role of preparer and server of nourishment, Maxwell succeeds in excluding women altogether from the all-male club of professional science.

Maxwell's prose here provides a precise metaphorical counterpart to the gender apartheid which operated in the nineteenth-century scientific community, and which debarred women from membership of many professional societies and even from attendance at some 'public' lectures. In a personal letter to Edward Perceval Wright, who had invited him to address the Dublin University Association, Huxley explicitly identifies the gender dimension which Maxwell only alludes to in his representation of the problems of scientific communication: 'I perceive I misunderstood the tenor of your former note – and that Ladies *are* to come – More's the pity – I shall have to emasculate my discourse or else be unintelligible – I think I prefer the latter alternative.'[84] Huxley conducted a protracted campaign against women's membership of learned scientific societies, despite his reputation as a supporter of the women's cause.[85] Two years previously, in 1860, he had privately objected to Lyell's suggestion that women be admitted to the Geological Society on the grounds that their (necessarily) amateur presence would emasculate serious scientific discussion and threaten the professional status of the Society: 'five sixths of women will stop in the doll stage of evolution, to be the stronghold of parsondom, the drag on civilization, the degradation of every important pursuit with which they mix themselves – "intrigues" in politics and "friponnes" in science.'[86] Huxley was more circumspect in his public utterances on the subject, but he continued to bring Darwinian evolution to the aid of misogyny by arguing in his 1864 Hunterian Lectures that women (and 'the lower races') had simpler brain structures than men, and following up with his essay of 1865, 'Emancipation – Black and White,' in which he avers 'in every excellent character, whether mental or physical, the average women is inferior to the average man, in the sense of having that character less in quantity and lower in quality,' and therefore men have nothing to fear from their emancipation as they cannot possibly compete.[87]

Given their virtual exclusion from the professional scientific confraternity, it is most extraordinary that there were any female scientists of note, and not at all extraordinary that those who achieved public recognition did so because they wrote for a popular readership. The most famous of early nineteenth-century popularisers of science was Jane Marcet, a student of Humphry Davy whose 'Conversations' on Chemistry, Botany, Vegetable Physiology and Natural Philosophy, as well as on Language, the History of England and Political Economy, went into many editions and were widely plagiarised. Her books were designedly elementary guides for young people, and seemed particularly directed at girls. Indeed, *Conversations on Chemistry*, published in 1805, is designated as *intended more especially for the Female Sex*. The 'Conversations' took the form of a dialogue between the teacher, Mrs Bryan, and one or more of her students, who are mostly female. Such dialogues, Marcet explains, 'gave her an opportunity of introducing objections, and placing in various points of view questions and answers as they had actually occurred to her own mind, a plan which would not have suited a more didactic composition'.[88] Marcet makes no claim to scientific originality, but her success in the market (aptly enough) leaves no doubt as to her creative skills as an author and explicator, and tradition has it that the great chemist Michael Faraday, then an apprentice to a bookbinder, was first introduced to chemistry when given the task of binding Marcet's *Conversations on Chemistry*.[89]

Conversations on Chemistry was published anonymously and, despite the fact that Marcet identified herself as a woman in the preface, was assumed for the next three decades to have been written by a man. Questions of language, gender and authorship, familiar to us from the famous experiences of women novelists who published pseudonymously or anonymously, were relevant to the world of scientific writing too. Essentialist notions of male and female writing prevailed, but did not go unquestioned. While preparing her notes on Charles Babbage's analytical engine, her most important published work, the mathematician Ada Lovelace wrote to Babbage, 'I am quite thunderstruck by the *power* of the writing. It is especially unlike a *woman's* style surely; but neither can I compare it with any man's exactly.'[90] Lovelace was unusually confident about her abilities as a scientist: 'The more I study the more irresistible do I feel my genius for it to be.' Perhaps, though, as the daughter of Byron, she felt she had genius in her blood; indeed, she claimed 'I do *not* believe that my father was (or ever could have been) such a poet as I shall be an *Analyst* & Metaphysician, for with me the two go together indissolubly.'[91] Far more common was a tendency for female scientists to feel that their writing was second-rate and derivative. Even Mary Somerville, a leading scientific writer for some four decades, saw herself, as many male historians of science have since seen her, as suffering from that peculiarly female affliction – lack of originality:

> . . . although I had recorded in a clear point of view some of the most refined and difficult analytical processes and astronomical discoveries, I was conscious that I had never made a discovery myself, that I had no originality. I have perseverance and intelligence but no genius, that spark from heaven is not granted to the sex, we are of the earth, earthy, whether higher powers may be allotted to us in another

existence God knows, original genius in science at least is hopeless in this.[92]

The Romantic idea of genius is, of course, like that of the discoverer, gendered male, and Somerville, like most of her female contemporaries, therefore had great difficulty in positioning herself as an 'original genius in science'. Her ambitions were altogether more modest. In the dedication to Queen Adelaide which prefaces her second book, *On the Connexion of the Physical Sciences* (1834), Somerville wrote that she had tried 'to make the laws by which the material world is governed more familiar to my countrywomen'.

Somerville was, though, acclaimed by her contemporaries, somewhat patronisingly, as 'The Queen of Nineteenth-Century Science', and her bust was hung in the Great Hall of the Royal Society as 'a proud tribute to the powers of the female mind'.[93] One is reminded of the painting by Johann Zoffany of *The Academicians of the Royal Academy* (1771–2), in which the two women who were among the founding members of the Royal Academy, Angelica Kauffmann and Mary Moser, appear only as painted busts hanging on the wall, as objects of aesthetic contemplation rather than professional artists. For, as a woman, Mary Somerville was debarred from membership of the Royal Society which so honoured her. If literature was judged to be not 'the business of a woman's life'[94] then how much more decisively outside the designated sphere of womanly activities was science. Indeed, about the only career one can think of that is more uncompromisingly gendered than that of the scientist-discoverer in the nineteenth century is that of the explorer-discoverer, the subject of the next section.

Travel and exploration literature

We see the full meaning of the wonderful fact, which must
have struck every traveller, namely, that on the same
continent, under the most diverse conditions, under heat and
cold, on mountain and lowland, on deserts and marshes, most
of the inhabitants within each great class are plainly related; for
they will generally be descendants of the same progenitors and
early colonists.

(Charles Darwin)[95]

Darwin's *On the Origin of Species* has been compared to a travel book. Like his first and most enduringly popular book *The Voyage of the Beagle* (1839), it travels the world companionably with the reader and, like that book too, it fashions a vast amount of empirical material into an absorbing quest narrative.[96] The reader and fellow-traveller is constantly invited to participate in the process of discovery which is enacted before them. Darwin appeals to our experience. We have seen the evidence for his theory with our own eyes; we have, after a fashion, contributed to its discovery.

Like some of the best Victorian novels, Darwin's writing depends a good deal for its effect upon the rapport he establishes with his reader, upon direct appeals to implied common interests and shared experiences, and, as in most nineteenth-century scientific writing, the relationship between narrator and reader is gendered male. The same may be said of much of the travel and exploration literature of the period, even though women were enthusiastic readers of the genre. It was, typically, men who, accompanied by male companions and servants, voyaged into the unknown in search of new discoveries, and they wrote of their experiences to and for other men. And yet despite the very real disincentives for women to travel there were in fact many female travellers and explorers in the nineteenth century (among them, interestingly, Ada Lovelace's daughter, Lady Anne Blunt, the first Western woman to explore the central regions of Saudi Arabia), providing a radical counterpoint to the prevailing ideology that an Englishwoman's place was in the home, and that she should be content with the adventures life offered within the domestic space.[97] The wives, daughters and sisters of British men serving their country and their own careers overseas observed the new worlds which were opened up to them, often noticing rather different things from their husbands, fathers and brothers, while female missionaries, tourists, and explorers, travelling in their own right, similarly offered an alternative vision of the rest of the world to that of their male counterparts. Moreover, many of them wrote about what they saw and experienced, whether as professional travel writers, or privately in journals and letters, or both. They wrote guidebooks and adventure stories, they collected and sketched and described native flora and fauna, and they attempted to record and interpret the cultural beliefs and practices of indigenous peoples which were so foreign to their own.

Some of the numerous women travellers who wrote in the period are included in this section which, like others in this book, is necessarily highly selective in its coverage of what is a vast and various body of writing. Of the many destinations represented in the extensive travel literature of the period, I have chosen to focus upon Africa, Europe (mainly Italy), and North America, looking at a small sample of writers on each as a way of suggesting some of the general characteristics and preoccupations of nineteenth-century exploration and travel writing. One common factor, for instance, among both male and female travellers, is that, relatively free of the constricting conventions of life at home, they had an opportunity to view their own country and its customs afresh in the light of their exposure to other cultures. Sometimes their experiences abroad tended to confirm their previous ideas and prejudices about British culture and society; sometimes they radically challenged them. But whatever effect their travels had on their perception of their own national characteristics, British explorers and travel writers typically made use of their journeys to reflect upon the country whose shores they had left and for whose citizens they were writing.

And so amidst the detailed factual descriptions of what they saw and experienced in foreign parts come reminders of the relevance of all this information for the reader back home. Climates and terrains are described for the would-be settler; forms of government are explained for purposes of comparison with the Westminster system; pagan customs and beliefs are detailed in order to reveal the degradation of the native peoples and their need for civilisation; adventures are recounted which underline the natural superiority of the white man, or which assert the courage and capacity of women to endure all the hardships that men can.

Such references to the interests of the reader at home are often merely implied, but frequently travellers explicitly drew attention to the connections between their activities abroad and pressing local and domestic issues. The American explorer Fanny Bullock Workman had herself photographed on a Himalayan mountain holding a 'Votes for Women' poster. David Livingstone prefaced his *Missionary Travels* (1857) with a comment which reveals an eye for more than just the landscape prospects of the African interior: 'The prospects there disclosed are fairer than I anticipated, and the capabilities of the new region lead me to hope, that, by the production of the raw materials of our manufactures, African and English interests will become more closely linked than heretofore.'[98]

It was the expanding prospects of a world newly opened up not only geographically but also politically, commercially and socially that made the genres of exploration and travel literature so successful. In the first few months after its publication *Missionary Travels* sold 70,000 copies, making Livingstone a national hero. Stanley's *In Darkest Africa* (1890) sold 150,000 copies in English, and many other writings by explorers were immediate bestsellers. Although standard literary histories tend to exclude such exploration narratives, they were hugely influential cultural texts.[99]

Exploration literature appealed not only to lovers of adventure stories and of descriptive scientific writing about the natural wonders of the world, but to investors, entrepreneurs, and potential colonists. Travel writing offered vicarious pleasures for the armchair explorer who enjoyed the evocation of exotic scenes and foreign customs for their own sake, but also practical information for the would-be traveller. Following the fall of Napoleon in 1814–15, Europe was once again opened up to British tourists, and as the century wore on, with the wider distribution of wealth and the advent of the railway, it became increasingly accessible.

Continental Europe had always been a popular destination for English Romantic writers: Byron had memorialised his journeyings in his poetry; Keats and Shelley had lived and died in Italy; Hazlitt had published a personal account of his Continental travels; Leigh Hunt, Landor, and Samuel Rogers had lived in and written extensively about Italy. By the middle of the century, the European tour was no longer the exclusive preserve of the aristocracy and literati, and was taken up enthusiastically by prosperous middle-class men and women keen to expand their cultural horizons along with their bank balances. Thomas Cook organized his first excursion to Italy in July 1864. Such a rapid expansion of the travel market created an unprecedented demand for guidebooks, which series like the Murray's 'Handbooks', the first of which appeared in 1836, hastened to meet.

The increasing ease of travel had an even greater impact on the popularity of America as a destination for British travellers. The first steamship made its initial voyage across the Atlantic in 1819, reducing what had been a journey of several months' duration and severe hardship to a comparatively quick and easy crossing.

In the early decades of the century, the perilous voyage out from England is often at least as significant a part of the narrative as its faraway destination. Anna Maria Falconbridge, for instance, entitled her epistolary account of her experiences and impressions of the Sierra Leone settlement *Narrative of Two Voyages to the River Sierra Leone, during the years 1791–2–3*,[100] and it is indeed the voyages themselves which produce some of the book's most exciting and evocative scenes. Her summary of the first stage of her first journey home gives some sense of the hardships she and her fellow travellers endured:

> we have been fifty-eight days in a deck'd boat . . . continued rains almost all the while – three weeks a quarter of a pound of beef, and about half the quantity of flour our allowance – eighteen days more baffled by calms and contrary winds, or beat about by merciless storms, fed upon mean disagreeable food, and scarcely enough of that to keep soul and body together; and, what was worse than all, the apprehension of being left morseless of any kind of nourishment; which certainly must have been the case, had we not arrived at Fayal when we did.[101]

Such experiences do not merely provide the material for a gripping adventure story, though. They tie in with the theme of transportation which is such a striking motif of her account, and link the author herself with the experiences of those whose journeys provide the real occasion of her book.

Anna Maria Falconbridge had sailed to West Africa in 1791 as the new wife of a slave-ship-physician-turned-abolitionist, Alexander Falconbridge, who was employed by the Sierra Leone Company, set up by abolitionists to found and administer colonies in Sierra Leone for former slaves transported from North America. She left England as, at best, a half-hearted opponent of slavery, and returned three years later, via Jamaica, as an outspoken opponent of abolitionism. The rights and wrongs of slavery are a major theme of her book, one which she addresses both directly and obliquely, making full use of the metaphorical associations of her own shipboard experiences to explore the dimensions of her topic which go beyond the slave trade itself into related questions pertaining to domination and the curtailment of personal liberty. From the outset, it seems, their enterprise is compromised. As they prepare to set sail in Portsmouth, Falconbridge observes that 'The gentlemen whom Mr. Falconbridge is employed by are for abolishing the slave trade: the owners of this vessel are of that trade, and consequently the Captain and Mr. Falconbridge must be very opposite in their sentiments.'[102] She comments that the only thing to have captured her notice in the harbour is 'the fleet with the convicts for Botany Bay, which are wind bound as well as ourselves'. Continuing the association between the convict ship and their own, she comments that 'The destiny of such numbers of my fellow creatures has made what I expect to encounter, set lighter upon my mind than it ever did before . . . the sight of those unfortunate beings, and the thoughts of what they are to endure, have worked more forcibly on my feelings than all the accounts I ever read or heard of wretchedness before.'[103] It is a most suggestive passage, with its implied indictment of the government which professed to oppose slavery but which could subject its convicts to such misery, and its allusions to her own fears of the horrors she must encounter in the journey ahead on this her maiden voyage, a prisoner to the whims of the Company and of her husband.

That such fears are well founded is confirmed when the image of the slave ship/convict ship is again invoked shortly after their arrival in Africa, when her husband insists that she remain on board ship rather than associate with the European slave-traders on shore, confining her in 'this tub of a vessel, which in point of size and cleanliness, comes nigher a hog-trough than any thing else you can imagine'. Describing herself as 'confined' and 'imprisoned' in 'a place so disgusting' there was every likelihood of it 'endangering [her] health', she begs her correspondent

> Conceive yourself pent up in a floating cage, without room either to walk about, stand erect, or even to lay at length; exposed to the inclemency of the weather, having your eyes

and ears momently offended by acts of indecency, and language too horrible to relate – add to this a complication of filth, the stench from which was continually assailing your nose, and then you will have a faint notion of the Lapwing Cutter.[104]

Falconbridge's description of her 'floating prison'[105] deliberately recalls gruesome abolitionist descriptions of slave ships, such as her own husband included in his *Account of the Slave Trade on the Coast of Africa* (1788).[106]

Comparisons between the plight of enslaved Africans and disenfranchised women were a commonplace of 1790s' English women's protest writing[107] and indeed continued to be drawn throughout the nineteenth century. The analogy between the sexual exploitation of women and the racial exploitation of black Africans is one that is frequently implied in Falconbridge's letters to her friend. Just before her own incarceration in the Lapwing Cutter, Falconbridge has been shocked to discover that the European slave-traders all had black mistresses: 'I then understood that every gentleman on the island had his *lady*.'[108] She is later outraged to learn that upwards of a hundred London prostitutes had been kidnapped, 'intoxicated with liquor, then inveigled on board of ship, and married to *Black men*, whom they had never seen before', before being shipped out to service the settlers. She encounters seven such women, 'decrepid with disease, and so disguised with filth and dirt, that I should never have supposed they were born white'.[109] The identification of the sexually exploited Englishwoman and the enslaved African is complete. Falconbridge comments, 'I cannot altogether reconcile myself to believe it; for it is scarcely possible that the British Government, at this advanced and enlightened age, envied and admired as it is by the universe, could be capable of exercising or countenancing such a Gothic infringement on human Liberty.' Nevertheless, when later a Portuguese lady in Fayal says to her, 'the women of your country must surely be very happy: they have so much more liberty than we have, or I believe, than the women of any other country, I wish I was an English woman!' she assures her that her countrywomen 'had their share of thorns and thistles, as well as those of other countries'.[110]

The thorn in her own side, Alexander Falconbridge, did the right thing and drank himself to death, to her undisguised relief, leaving her free to remarry and abandon altogether her lukewarm commitment to the abolitionist ideals of the Sierra Leone Company. She travelled home to England on a slave ship, remarking all the while on the comfort and happiness of the slaves: 'I never saw more signs of content and satisfaction, among any set of people, in their or any other country.' By contrast with the misery of the free settlers in Sierra Leone, 'they experienced the utmost kindness and care.' And as for the slaves in Jamaica, they not only seemed much happier than the blacks she had seen in Africa, but rather better off than 'our labouring poor' in England.[111]

Travel writing quite often provides the context for discussion of the problem of slavery and its alternatives in the nineteenth century. Following the abolition of the slave trade in the British Empire in 1807 and emancipation of the slaves in 1833, attention shifted to America. Travellers to America in the 1830s, such as Harriet Martineau, eloquently exposed the 'moral evils, the unspeakable vices and woes of slavery',[112] calling for universal emancipation. The English actress Fanny Kemble had the misfortune to marry a Southern planter and slave-owner, and she wrote movingly of her experiences and the conditions of the slaves on her husband's estates in her *Journal of a Residence on a Georgian Plantation in 1838–9*, which was eventually published in 1863, a timely book to appear in the midst of the American Civil War.

British commentators on American slavery were generally condemnatory, but some there were still among mid-nineteenth-century travellers in Africa who spoke out strongly against anti-slavery 'do-gooders' from the point of view of their own political agenda. Harriet Ward, the first woman journalist in the Cape Colony, was one. The wife of Captain Ward of the Ninety-First Regiment, she accompanied her husband on his mission to the Cape Colony in 1842, and from there contributed articles to *The United Service Magazine*. She also wrote a journal, upon which she drew for her two-volume account of her residence there, *Five Years in Kaffirland; with Sketches of the Late War in that Country, to the Conclusion of Peace*, which was published in 1848, and appeared in an abridged form as *The Cape and the Kaffirs* in 1852. She was highly critical of the anti-slavery movement, commenting that 'how to set about the remedy should have been considered'. Taking authority from the fact that her account of the Cape and its indigenous inhabitants was 'Written on the Spot', she proclaims,

> From the far plains of Southern Africa . . . let the voice of Truth be heard! Ye philanthropists – fallacious reasoners on subjects of which ye know nothing certain, who romanticise about savages and slavery till ye get entangled in a web of metaphysics of your own weaving, from which ye have neither the power nor the courage to extricate yourselves – who would leave the savage in undisturbed possession of a vast tract of country as much in need of population as England is of the reverse; who would take the yoke from the slave's neck and send him forth – free, indeed, in body, but trammelled in mind with sin and sorrow, since he knows not how to live, or to earn a living, – hear the voice of Truth![113]

Throughout her account Harriet Ward insists upon the objective truth and accuracy of her description of the history of the Cape Colony, the current political situation, and of the Kaffirs themselves. Hers is, she says, 'a simple narration of facts'.[114] She includes quotation from dispatches to authenticate her accounts of events which she did not personally witness, claiming to 'offer such particulars only as I ascertained to be perfectly correct'.[115] But despite her self-assessment as a disinterested observer, Harriet Ward is deeply implicated in her husband's militaristic project and the whole colonialist enterprise of which that was a part. Her class affiliations, her assumption of racial superiority and her colonial ambitions inform her writing at every point, so that, far from being the neutral 'narration of facts' she insists upon, her work is clearly ideologically positioned.[116]

The reader encounters rabid racism in virtually every description of 'the Kaffir', who is generally discussed in terms of racial type. Ward offers a totalising account of 'the Kaffir' as a savage, characterised by a natural ingratitude, indolence, and low cunning: 'He is a liar, a thief, and a beggar.'[117] She frequently compares so-called 'Kaffirs' to vermin, insects, and wild beasts, sometimes putting forth pseudo-scientific evidence in support of her assertion. And so we are informed,

> A Kaffir will not raise his hand to remove a fly from his face; and, as he rubs his skin with clay and grease to protect it from the effects of the sun, these attract the flies, and I have known a savage sit for hours in the sun with his cheeks and brow covered by these tormenting and fidgetty insects, without attempting to remove them. It must be allowed, though, that a Kaffir skin more resembles the hide of some powerful animal than the skin of a human being. In the early part of this war, some person procured the entire skin of a Kaffir, and had it braded in the same way that leather is first prepared for tanning. I am told that the texture is at least three times the thickness of a white man's, and I see no reason for doubting the assertion.[118]

The horrendous image of the flaying, then measuring and calculation of the thickness of the skin of another human being seems not to strike Harriet Ward, and here and elsewhere in her account the savagery might seem to be all on the white person's side. For instance, shortly after she makes the comment, '"I beseech you by the meekness and gentleness of Christ," is an appeal which the South African savage, in his present state, cannot be brought to understand,' she offers the view, 'If we had not the heart to shoot the Kaffirs into subjection, they might have been starved into humility.'[119] Such unintentionally ironic juxtapositions abound in Ward's narrative. She looks forward to the day, for instance, when 'By God's help, and by severe sacrifices and privation on the part of the troops, we shall be enabled to establish our rights to the hunting-ground of the idle, thieving Kaffir,' clearly with no perception of colonial appropriation as itself a form of thieving, albeit one legitimated by imperialist ideology and sanctified by the suffering of the troops in the service of the Christian redemption of benighted Africa.[120]

Harriet Ward's judgement on the future of the Cape Colony is unequivocal: 'The peace of the Colony will never be fairly established until we take the Kaffirs under British rule.'[121] 'Under another system,' she urges, 'affording protection to the settler, this country will offer a refuge to the starving population of Ireland,' as well as 'the labourer, the mechanic, the servant without work':

> It is singular that, while our fellow creatures in Great Britain, in 1847, were suffering from the failure of their crops, the gardens of corn, pumpkin, etc., in Kaffirland, are more than usually productive.
>
> The miserable mechanics from our crowded manufacturing districts may here earn six shillings a-day with ease; the ruined tradesman of England, with a gaol staring him in the face, will meet with a welcome here, where a position in trade is required, to promote industry, honesty, and civility; and the youths of Ireland, instead of arming themselves for rebellious purposes, may, in this Colony, serve their Queen more honourably, by protecting their fellow-creatures from the aggressions of the savage, and laying the foundations of peace, comfort, and prosperity, throughout the hitherto distracted dependency of England, and even beyond its borders.[122]

In 1848, amidst renewed Chartist agitation in England, and revolutionary uproar throughout Europe, it would have been an appealing idea to middle- and upper-class readers to ship off all those troublesome mechanics and Irish youths full of 'rebellious purposes' to vent their anger upon 'Kaffir savages' in an honourable patriotic cause. Yet the benefits of colonisation are presented as accruing solely to the working-class settler – and, of course, to the 'savage' who is to be civilised. According to Ward, 'no other country but England would have treated a savage foe with such lenity, forbearance, and humanity as we have done. Had we not been guided by these truly British attributes, we might have conquered our enemy by annihilating him.' But 'the Kaffir' is 'a noble animal' and, if brought 'under wholesome restraint', there is some prospect of improving, even civilising him.[123]

Whereas the 'rebellious' voices of Chartists, trade unionists and other agents of 'anarchy' could be heard competing against the rhetoric of 'culture' at home, imperialist discourse, the engine of 'civilisation', effectively silences the discourses of the dominated, who are in every sense dispossessed. Yet, paradoxically, the roots of the colonial project

in Africa may be traced back to turn-of-the-century abolitionism.[124]
Moreover, slavery remained a persistent theme in mid-century exploration literature. For David Livingstone, the missionary of humble Scottish origins who was to become Britain's most famous explorer,[125]
the continuing prevalence of slavery in Africa provided the principal
argument for the joint expansion of missionary work and commercial
activity in the region, and he describes the atrocities of the slave trade
at great length in his *Missionary Travels* (1857). Livingstone focuses
particularly on the activities of the Boers of the Cashan Mountains
who, despite the supposed emancipation of their 'Hottentot' slaves,
'determined to erect themselves into a republic, in which they might
pursue without molestation the "proper treatment of the blacks", whom
they regarded as '"black property" or "creatures"''. He also, though,
describes the slave trade among black tribes who sold children for arms.[126]
What he saw of slavery in the region strengthened his resolve to combat
the slave trade by the promotion of commerce:

> the idea was suggested that, if the slave-market were supplied
> with articles of European manufacture by legitimate commerce,
> the trade in slaves would become impossible. It seemed more
> feasible to give the goods, for which the people now part with
> their servants, in exchange for ivory and other products of the
> country, and thus prevent the trade at the beginning, than try
> to put a stop to it at any of the subsequent steps. This could
> only be effected by establishing a highway from the coast into
> the centre of the country.[127]

Thus it was that the unholy alliance between Christianity and commerce
came to be formed out of the desire to supplant slavery with something
more acceptable to the conscience of the Western world. Livingstone
certainly sees his mission as a trade mission as well as a Christian one,
unequivocally linking 'civilisation' with capitalism as well as with
Christianity:

> Sending the Gospel to the heathen must . . . include much
> more than is implied in the usual picture of a missionary,
> namely, a man going about with a Bible under his arm. The
> promotion of commerce ought to be specially attended to, as
> this, more speedily than anything else, demolishes that sense of
> isolation which heathenism engenders, and makes the tribes feel
> themselves mutually dependent on, and mutually beneficial to,
> each other . . . My observations on this subject make me
> extremely desirous to promote the preparation of the raw
> materials of European manufactures in Africa, for by that
> means we may not only put a stop to the slave-trade, but

introduce the negro family into the body corporate of nations, no one member of which can suffer without the others suffering with it. Success in this, in both Eastern and Western Africa, would lead, in the course of time, to a much larger diffusion of the blessings of civilization than efforts exclusively spiritual and educational confined to any one small tribe. These, however, it would be extremely desirable to carry on at the same time at large central and healthy stations, for neither civilization nor Christianity can be promoted alone. In fact, they are inseparable.[128]

Livingstone's view of the Christian mission in Africa is, then, built firmly upon capitalist and colonialist ideology, and this determines the way in which *Missionary Travels* is written. Most of the commercial transactions he describes are informed by what Mary Louise Pratt has identified as a myth of reciprocity.[129] He tells, for instance, of the induction of the Bakuena people into Western ways in a manner which insists upon a scrupulous concern that the natives be properly recompensed for their land, but reveals a businesslike concern to protect an investment, and a sharp eye for future profit:

A small piece of land, sufficient for a garden, was purchased when we first went to live with them, though that was scarcely necessary in a country where the idea of buying land was quite new. It was expected that a request for a suitable spot would have been made, and that we would have proceeded to occupy it, as any other member of the tribe would. But we explained to them that we wished to avoid any cause of future dispute when land had become more valuable; or when a foolish chief began to reign, and we had erected large or expensive buildings, he might wish to claim the whole. These reasons were considered satisfactory. About £5 worth of goods were given for a piece of land, and an arrangement was come to that a similar piece should be allotted to any other missionary, at any other place to which the tribe might remove. The particulars of the sale sounded strangely in the ears of the tribe, but were nevertheless readily agreed to.[130]

Livingstone felt it was inexpedient for missionaries to trade, but he bartered his way across the African continent and did his best to facilitate trade, occasionally dabbling himself, though never, it is stressed, for profit:

Presents were always given to the chiefs whom we visited, and nothing accepted in return; but when Sebituane (in 1851) offered some ivory, I took it, and was able by its sale to present his son with a number of really useful articles of a higher value than I had ever been able to give before to any chief. In doing this, of course, I appeared to trade, but, feeling I had a right to do so, I felt perfectly easy in my mind.[131]

The transactions described are always presented as being of pecuniary benefit to the natives, but they are, in fact, always on the white man's terms; it is he who determines what is valuable and useful, or what is just payment to the black man. Livingstone is prepared, for instance, to pay the equivalent of £5 for a piece of land, but notes that 'Englishmen have always very properly avoided giving the idea to the native mind which we shall hereafter find troublesome, that payment ought to be made for passage through a country.'[132] The English middle-class value systems according to which he operates are interestingly displayed in a discussion of the desire of Boer colonists to expand their territory:

> Nor does it seem much of an evil for men who cultivate the soil to claim a right to appropriate lands for tillage which other men only hunt over, provided some compensation for the loss of sustenance be awarded. The original idea of a title seems to have been that 'subduing' or cultivating gave that right. But this rather Chartist principle must be received with limitations; for its recognition in England would lead to the seizure of all our broad ancestral acres by those who are willing to cultivate them. And, in the case under consideration, the encroachments lead at once to less land being put under the plough than is subjected to the native hoe, for it is a fact that the Basutos and Zulus, or Caffres of Natal, cultivate largely, and undersell our farmers wherever they have a fair field and no favour.[133]

Here considerations of natural justice do battle with concerns about landed property rights in England and trade figures, and the deep contradictions of the colonial project are laid bare.

The myths of free exchange and independent choice are revealed as strategic and Eurocentric in other telling passages. When living among the Makololo, for instance, Livingstone notes that 'in the very spot where we had been engaged in acts of devotion, half an hour after, a dance would be got up,' and that 'these habits cannot be at first opposed without the appearance of assuming too much authority over them.' He is of the view that 'It is always unwise to hurt their feelings of independence. Much greater influence will be gained by studying how you may induce them to act aright, with the impression that they are doing it of their own free will.' He might be speaking of the entire colonial enterprise. Moreover, everything is commodified in this free market barter economy, even medical knowledge. Dr Livingstone knows the value of his professional training, and makes sure to exact a fee:

> The plan of showing kindness to the natives in their bodily ailments secures their friendship; this is not the case to the same degree in old missions, where the people have learned to look upon relief as a right, a state of things that sometimes happens among ourselves at home. Medical aid is therefore most valuable in young missions, though at all stages it is an extremely valuable adjunct to other operations.[134]

Even medical relief is a matter for negotiation. For all his squeamishness about missionaries trading, Livingstone represents himself as the very type of the disinterested entrepreneur.[135]

At numerous points in Livingstone's narrative the great explorer and discoverer reveals himself as a commercial traveller. Travelling up river towards Lake Ngami, he received the first confirmation that the country beyond was not a desert plain:

> The prospect of a highway capable of being traversed by boats to an entirely unexplored and very populous region, grew from that time forward stronger and stronger in my mind; so much so, that, when we actually came to the lake, this idea occupied such a large portion of my mental vision that the actual discovery seemed of but little importance.[136]

Frequently, 'the magnificent prospects of the new country' displaced the prospects which he literally beheld. Of course, it was his lyrical descriptions of the exotic scenes – the dense and mysterious forests, the cascading waterfalls, the vast rivers and lakes – through which he passed on his journey which captivated Victorian readers. His description of what he named the Victoria Falls, on the Zambesi River, is just one among many examples of writing that feasts upon the natural wonders he witnesses as the first European to explore the African interior:

> After twenty minutes' sail from Kalai, we came in sight, for the first time, of the columns of vapour, appropriately called 'smoke', rising at a distance of five or six miles, exactly as when large tracts of grass are burned in Africa. Five columns now arose, and bending in the direction of the wind, they seemed placed against a low ridge covered with trees; the tops of the columns at this distance appeared to mingle with the clouds. They were white below and higher up became dark, so as to simulate smoke very closely. The whole scene was extremely beautiful; the banks and islands dotted over the river

are adorned with sylvan vegetation of great variety of colour
and form. At the period of our visit several trees were
spangled over with blossoms. There, towering over all, stands
the great burly baobab, each of whose enormous arms would
form the trunk of a large tree, beside groups of graceful palms,
which, with their feathery-shaped leaves depicted on the sky,
lend their beauty to the scene. As a hieroglyphic, they always
mean 'far from home', for one can never get over their foreign
air in a picture or landscape.[137]

The beauty and foreignness of this African landscape so 'far from
home' are everywhere evoked in Livingstone's lush prose. Yet the scenes
before him are evaluated not only aesthetically but also with an eye to
how the land might be improved. The country of the Cape Colony is
'prosperous and capable of great improvement'. The Barotse valley 'is
not put to the tithe of the use it might be'. Although the Chobe River
is 'broad enough to allow a steamer to ply upon it, the suddenness of
the bendings would prevent navigation, but, should the country ever
become civilised, the Chobe would be a convenient natural canal'. Indulg-
ing in a little 'speculation' of his own, Livingstone expresses confidence
in 'the success of artesian wells in extensive tracts of Africa now un-
peopled solely on account of the want of surface water':

> We may be allowed to speculate a little at least on the fact of
> much greater vegetation, which, from whatever source it
> comes, presents for South Africa prospects of future greatness
> which we cannot hope for in Central Australia. As the interior
> districts of the Cape colony are daily becoming of higher
> value, offering to honest industry a fair remuneration for
> capital, and having a climate unequalled in salubrity for
> consumptive patients, I should unhesitatingly recommend any
> farmer at all afraid of that complaint in his family to try this
> colony. With the means of education already possessed, and
> the onward and upward movement of the Cape population,
> he need entertain no apprehensions of his family sinking into
> barbarism.[138]

The barbarism of the land is consistently linked, through metaphor, to
the supposed barbarism of its native inhabitants, and their need of cultivation. Livingstone describes, for instance, the baptism of the Bakuena
chief Semele, and the inability of his people to accept his conversion to
Christianity, commenting, 'It was trying, after all we had done, to see
our labours so little appreciated; but we had sown the good seed, and
have no doubt but it will yet spring up, though we may not live to see
the fruits.' Immediately after thus deploying the familiar metaphor of

sowing seeds and reaping harvests, he describes his cultivation of a garden. Later in his journey, he follows a description of the vegetation of the Kuruman district with a discussion of 'Christianity among the natives' in which he proclaims 'let the good seed be widely sown, and, no matter to what sect the converts may belong, the harvest will be glorious.'[139]

Livingstone is outraged by the racism of the Boers, and frequently expresses his respect and affection for the black Africans whom he meets on his travels. But it is necessary, for his project to convert Africa to Christianity and commerce, to convey to his readers that the native population and native culture are inferior to white people and Western civilisation, and yet are capable of cultivation. Many are the occasions when the indigenous people are described in ways which suggest they are lower in the scale of evolutionary development. He complains that English ideas about the appearance of the Bushmen are distorted by the fact that 'the specimens brought to Europe have been selected, like costermongers' dogs, on account of their extreme ugliness.' Neverthe-less, he comments 'That they are like baboons is in some degree true, just as these and other simiae are in some points frightfully human.'[140] To convey the fact of their primitiveness, he describes the native inhab-itants variously as being like animals, like children, or like lunatics. He vents his disgust at the degradation and depravity of heathenism, in particular. Of the Makololo dance, which 'consists of the men standing nearly naked in a circle, with clubs or small battle-axes in their hands, and each roaring at the loudest pitch of his voice, while they simulta-neously lift one leg, stamp heavily twice with it, then lift the other and give one stamp with that', we are told, 'If the scene were witnessed in a lunatic asylum it would be nothing out of the way.'[141] Livingstone readily condemns the benighted African for his savage customs and primitive behaviour but, crucially, stresses those qualities which indicate him to be redeemable by white civilisation. Of the Bakuena, for inst-ance, he notes, 'They might be called stupid in matters which had not come within the sphere of their observation, but in other things they showed more intelligence than is to be met with in our own uneducated peasantry.'[142] Elsewhere, he represents the native population as intellec-tually lazy, but not stupid. He discovers, for example, that for genera-tions the Bechuanas have been aware of electricity in the atmosphere:

> Nothing came of that, however, for they viewed the sight
> as if with the eyes of an ox. The human mind has remained
> here as stagnant to the present day, in reference to the
> physical operations of the universe, as it once did in England.
> No science has been developed, and few questions are ever
> discussed except those which have an intimate connection with
> the wants of the stomach.[143]

Such people can be improved, indeed have been, immeasurably so, Livingstone argues, through the influence of Christianity. He compares Griqua and Bechuana converts with their unconverted brethren, and asserts that 'if the question were examined in the most rigidly scientific way, the change effected by the great missionary movement would be considered unquestionably great.'[144] He admits, though, that he was disappointed when he first encountered the native converts, expecting them to be like his image of the primitive disciples. However, he argues,

> We cannot compare these poor people with ourselves, who have an atmosphere of Christianity and enlightened public opinion, the growth of centuries, around us, to influence our deportment; but let any one from the natural and proper point of view behold the public morality of Griqua Town, Kuruman, Likatlong, and other villages, and remember what even London was a century ago, and he must confess that the Christian mode of treating aborigines is incomparably the best.[145]

In the light of 'the natural and proper point of view' and 'the most rigidly scientific' methodology, the natural superiority of the white man is unquestionable, as he demonstrates at a number of points in his narrative. And so writing of the Bushmen's expertise in hunting elephants, he remarks,

> In this case the uncivilized have the advantage over us, but I believe that with half their training Englishmen would beat the bushmen. Our present form of civilization does not necessarily produce effeminacy, though it unquestionably increases the beauty, courage, and physical powers of the race.

He goes on to explain how he had recently taken notes of the different numbers of elephants killed, and the manner of their killing, by parties of Griquas, Bechuanas, Boers and Englishmen, respectively, and concludes on the basis of this scientific evidence 'that our more barbarous neighbours do not possess half the courage of the civilized sportsman'.[146]

Livingstone was himself the great exemplar of the courageous hero, not emasculated by Christianity and civilisation but rather made fearless. Only pages into his narrative he tells how he is ravaged by a lion – 'Besides crunching the bone into splinters, he left eleven teeth wounds on the upper part of my arm' – and rescued by a man whose life *he* had saved after he had been tossed by a buffalo.[147] This is but the first of his encounters with local wildlife ranging from tsetse fly to marauding hippos. As he sets off on the most dangerous leg of his mission, he reflects on what lies before him:

The prospect of passing away from this fair and beautiful
world thus came before me in a pretty plain matter-of-fact
form, and it did seem a serious thing to leave wife and
children – to break up all connection with earth, and enter on
an untried state of existence; and I find myself in my journal
pondering over that fearful migration which lands us in
eternity; wondering whether an angel will soothe the fluttering
soul, sadly flurried as it must be on entering the spirit world;
and hoping that Jesus might speak but one word of peace, for
that would establish in the bosom an everlasting calm. But as I
had always believed that, if we serve God at all, it ought to be
done in a manly way, I wrote to my brother, commending
our little girl to his care, as I was determined to 'succeed or
perish' in the attempt to open up this part of Africa.[148]

This is no namby-pamby preacher, but a muscular Christian of the first
order.

The great popular success of *Missionary Travels* was due to the fact
that Livingstone was not only a famous explorer-adventurer but also a
great raconteur. Despite his professed lack of literary accomplishments
and his claim that he would 'rather cross the African continent again
than undertake to write another book',[149] Livingstone tells his story
with style. From the very first page the reader is made aware of the
importance of story, as Livingstone remembers his childhood:

Our grandfather was intimately acquainted with all the
traditionary legends which [Scott] has since made use of in the
Tales of a grandfather and other works. As a boy I remember
listening to him with delight, for his memory was stored with
a never-ending stock of stories, many of which were
wonderfully like those I have since heard while sitting by the
African evening fires. Our grandmother, too, used to sing
Gaelic songs, some of which, as she believed, had been
composed by captive islanders languishing hopelessly among
the Turks.[150]

He recalls how, when his grandfather died, 'I was at the time on
my way below Zumbo, expecting no greater pleasure in this country
than sitting by our cottage fire and telling him my travels.'[151] Immediately the connection is made between exotic faraway places and home,
between the adventure and its telling. The emphasis is on the oral tradition of story-telling, in both Scotland and Africa, but from an early
age he used to love reading travel books, he tells us, and learns from
them in writing his own book. He cuts himself off, for instance, in an

account of a fever he has contracted, saying 'as I am already getting tired of quoting my fevers, and never liked to read travels myself, where much was said about the illnesses of the traveller, I shall henceforth endeavour to say little about them.'[152]

Missionary Travels is full of stories within stories, so that Livingstone's own great over-arching quest is punctuated and informed by other people's adventures too. Sometimes these stories within stories provide a counterpoint or embellishment of his own, sometimes they remind us of its place in a history of quest and conquest narratives, as when, having included the great warrior chief Sebituane's narration of his life story, Livingstone tells us, 'His narrative resembled closely the "Commentaries of Caesar," and the history of the British in India.'[153] For all his disclaimers, Livingstone was a highly accomplished writer who came from an impressive Scottish lineage. As a teller of tales he inherits Scott and anticipates Stevenson. And his book has a strong sense of its own status as a literary artefact. It is an adventure story, like those his grandfather told round the fire in Scotland; it is a travel book, like those he loved as a child; it is an autobiography and spiritual journey; it is a picaresque tale; a quest narrative; an heroic epic; not the mission impossible it must at first have seemed, but one which brought the light of Christianity to darkest Africa and held the reciprocal promise of bright commercial returns for England.

The books that the naturalist and ethnologist Mary Kingsley wrote about her African expeditions in the 1890s, *Travels in West Africa* (1897) and *West African Studies* (1899), are very different in kind from Livingstone's, though similarly entertaining. Their differences have something to do with the forty years which separate them, and the loss of innocence associated with the accomplishment of the imperialist partitioning of Africa by the end of the century. Having spent a sequestered youth in Cambridge, nursing her invalid mother, Kingsley had become free to travel with the death of both her parents in 1893, by which time the scramble for Africa was underway and the civilising mission was open to critique by writers such as Conrad and Gide.[154] Equally important were the gender differences between Livingstone's and Kingsley's writing, for Kingsley seems often to be consciously positioning herself against the heroic style of exploration literature epitomised by *Missionary Travels*.

Kingsley does not mince words when voicing her hostility to mission work in West Africa. In her text we find discussion of the problems confronting missionary work referred to by Livingstone, but her tone and treatment of the same issues is very different. Livingstone talks about the practice of polygamy, for instance, as a barrier to conversion, and so does Kingsley, but she does so with more sympathy towards the perspectives of those who are asked to give up a traditional custom, and, at the same time, with a greater sense of humour about the subject. She makes the serious point, for instance, that many men who would otherwise make good Christians 'hesitate about turning off from their homes women who have lived and worked for them for years, and not only for them, but often for their fathers before them'. But she also gives an amusing 'explanation' for the prevalence of polygamy: 'that it enabled a man to get enough to eat'. She adds, 'This sounds sinister from a notoriously cannibal tribe; but the explanation is that the Fans are an exceedingly hungry tribe, and require a great deal of providing for.'[155] Two of the great indicators of African 'savagery' – polygamy and cannibalism – are joked about in a manner that would have been inconceivable in high Victorian writing on Africa and its moral and cultural depravity.

Conscious of her subversive appropriation of the masculine role of the fearless explorer/discoverer, Kingsley constantly undercuts her own capacity for heroics. Livingstone's famous encounter with the lion was part of the myth of the hero/saint which grew up around him, but Kingsley, at the end of the century, confesses her terror when she sees big game, and admits, 'Whenever I have come across an awful animal in the forest and I know it has seen me I take Jerome's advice, and instead of relying on the power of the human eye rely upon that of the human leg, and effect a masterly retreat in the face of the enemy.'[156] Likewise she makes little of her role as discoverer, preferring a humorous, debunking mode when describing journeys that were clearly hazardous and uncomfortable in the extreme, as in her account of the ascent of the great Peak of Cameroon, which degenerates into farce as she and her men scramble in a muddy and undignified fashion up the waterlogged mountain.

Mary Kingsley is really much more interested in describing the people and their customs and tribal differences. She makes a point of explaining the historical and cultural origins of customs that seem cruel or simply strange to Europeans, in an attempt to counter the 'want of interest or . . . sense of inability on the part of most white people to make head or tail out of what seems to them a horrid pagan practice or a farrago of nonsense'.[157] She insists upon the need for Europeans to learn about native laws, religion, institutions and government, and criticises the inability of white people to view indigenous people from the latter's own standpoint.[158]

Reciprocal vision there is in this text, but it is of a markedly different kind from Livingstone's. 'I was never tired of going and watching those Igalwa villagers, nor were, I think, the Igalwa villagers ever tired of observing me.'[159] She was particularly conscious of the spectacle she represented as a female European explorer. The indigenous people are not rendered passive and silent in Kingsley's narrative. They question her ('"Where be your husband, ma?" . . . "no got one, ma?" . . . "Why you no got one?"')[160] and the women in particular befriend her ('I own I like African women; we have always got on together').[161]

As might be expected, she focuses on the role of women in African culture much more than her male counterparts, and indeed sardonically alludes to the way 'the African woman . . . has imposed on the male explorer, and caused him to give the idea that the African woman is the down-trodden fool of Creation who is treated anyhow.'[162] Kingsley, by contrast, argues that it is the women who offer most resistance to the incursions of white 'civilisation', and emphasises the power invested in women by *Mutterrecht* (the accounting of family relationships only through the mother), although she also acknowledges the traditional means by which women are kept down, in this as in other cultures; how they are excluded from membership of the secret societies, and how they are 'whacked' by their husbands.[163] She writes very deliberately as a woman, giving serious attention to the varieties of the native women's dress and the styling of their hair, and alluding, self-parodically, to the difficulty of maintaining a proper womanly gentility in the wilds of Africa. For instance, she begins her ascent of the waterlogged Cameroons holding an umbrella, 'knowing that though hopeless it is the proper thing to do'. She comments on the interior design of one of the huts she and her party stay in *en route*: 'There is a new idea in decoration along the separating wall. Mr. Morris might have made something out of it for a dado. It is composed of an arrangement in line of stretched out singlets.' Upon arrival at a station in the charge of a German officer, she refuses a bath ('How in the world is any one going to take a bath in a house with no doors, and only very sketchy wooden window shutters?'), but manages to clean herself up somehow to 'appear as a reasonable being before society'.[164]

And yet despite drawing attention to her sex in such scenes, there are other points in her narrative of the ascent of the mountain when she assumes an explicitly male persona. As she contemplates the mountain for the first time, she ponders,

> I feel quite sure that no white man has ever looked on the
> great Peak of Cameroon without a desire arising in his mind to
> ascend it . . . I have given in to the temptation and am the
> third Englishman to ascend the Peak and the first to have
> ascended it from the south-east face.[165]

In West Africa the fact that Kingsley was white tended to outweigh the fact that she was a woman. Her assumption of racial superiority, as a member of a colonising country, gave her a freedom denied her in England because of her gender. She herself perceived parallels between racial and gender difference, observing that 'the mental difference between the two races is very similar to that between men and women among ourselves. A great woman, either mentally or physically, will excel an indifferent man, but no woman ever equals a really great man.'[166]

Kingsley certainly has decided views on what she calls 'the superiority of my race' or, 'In philosophic moments', racial 'difference', and arguably, as Birkett and Wheelwright maintain, 'Her freedom as a white traveller was predicated on emphasising difference, not struggling to overcome it.'[167] Nevertheless she does forcefully critique the ideology of the civilising mission, commenting in her usual outspoken way, 'I think that a good many of the West African wars of the past ten years have been the result of the humbug of the previous sixty, during which we have proclaimed that we are only in Africa for peaceful reasons of commerce, and religion, and education, not with any desire for the African's land or property.'[168] She is sympathetic to the Africans' hostility towards white culture, ascribing it to 'the reasonable dislike to being dispossessed alike of power and property in what they regard as their own country'.[169] And she exposes 'one of those strange things that are in men's minds almost without their knowing they are there, yet which, nevertheless, rule them', namely 'the idea that those Africans are, as one party would say, steeped in sin, or, as another party would say, a lower or degraded race'.[170]

She gives numerous instances of the patronising, wholly inappropriate and often ludicrous attempts of European Christians to 'civilise the natives'. One such is her description of the Hubbard, 'a female garment patronised by the whole set of missions from Sierra Leone to Congo Belge':

> These garments are usually made at working parties in Europe; and what idea the pious ladies in England, Germany, Scotland, and France can have of the African figure I cannot think, but evidently part of their opinion is that it is very like a tub . . . There is nothing like measurements in ethnology, so I measured and found one that with a depth of thirty inches had a breadth of beam of forty-two inches; one with a depth of thirty-six inches had a breadth of sixty inches. It is not in nature for people to be made to fit these things. So I suggested that a few stuffed negroes should be sent home for distribution in working-party centres, and then the ladies could try the things on.[171]

So-called civilisation is, Kingsley recognises, an ill-fitting garment for Africa, one that should be rejected and sent back to the makers.

Kingsley's perceptions about the covert ideology underpinning the colonial enterprise in Africa are acute, and her outspoken attacks on the mealy-mouthed proponents of the civilising mission refreshing, but she was still a child of her time, and despite her relatively sympathetic attitude towards the colonised nation nevertheless believed it to be culturally backward. In terms of its cultural evolution, Africa was in her view some six hundred years behind England, arrested at a stage of development somewhat like England's in the thirteenth century:

The destruction of what is good in the thirteenth century culture level, and the fact that when the nineteenth century has had its way the main result is seedy demoralised natives, is the thing that must make all thinking men wonder if, after all, such work is from a high moral point of view worth the nineteenth century doing. I so often think when I hear the progress of civilisation, our duty towards the lower races, &c., talked of, as if those words were in themselves Ju Ju, of that improving fable of the kind-hearted she-elephant, who, while out walking one day, inadvertently trod upon a partridge and killed it, and observing close at hand the bird's nest full of callow fledglings, dropped a tear, and saying 'I have the feelings of a mother myself,' sat down upon the brood. This is precisely what England representing the nineteenth century is doing in thirteenth century West Africa.[172]

Kingsley bases her own assessment of British attempts to drag the thirteenth-century culture of West Africa into the nineteenth century upon H. Clifford's sympathetic view of the natives of the Malay Peninsula who, under white imperialism, 'are suddenly and violently translated from the point to which they have attained in the natural development of their race, and are required to live up to the standard of a people who are six centuries in advance of them in national progress'.[173] Kingsley's and Clifford's works, both published in the late 1890s, reflect their times, not only in their uneasiness about imperialist expansionism, which could no longer be regarded in the idealistic light which had bathed earlier nineteenth-century exploration literature, but also in their acceptance of an evolutionary model of society. Herbert Spencer had published *The Principles of Sociology* in 1876, followed by *The Study of Sociology* in 1889 and *First Principles* in 1893, in all of which he put forward the argument that human societies are organisms which evolve like other living bodies from simple primitive forms to complex higher structures. Late nineteenth-century evolutionists applied the Spencerian concept not only to political and economic institutions, and social structures in general, but also to religion, morals and family structures. Whilst *Travels in West Africa* and *West African Studies* contain much which indicates that Kingsley had reservations about some of these extensions of evolutionism into different aspects of culture, her consignment of West Africa to the thirteenth century, and her evident belief that the thirteenth century represented a lower stage in the evolution of European society and culture than the present, place her as a late nineteenth-century writer.

Interestingly enough, for some influential cultural critics writing earlier in the century, the relative status of the Middle Ages and the nineteenth century had been precisely the reverse. A. W. Pugin, for instance, in *Contrasts* (first published in 1836, then, in a considerably expanded version, in 1841), presents a series of comparative illustrations of architectural subjects designed to demonstrate the spiritual degradation of nineteenth-century England by contrast with its medieval past. From a similar point of view, in 1843, after visiting the ruined abbey at Bury St Edmunds, Thomas Carlyle wrote *Past and Present*, in which he analyses the condition of his own society, comparing it unfavourably with that of the medieval monastic community memorialised by the abbey. Also in the 1840s, the most powerful Victorian spokesperson for the Middle Ages began writing books which revealed his own passionate interest in Gothic architecture as well as in early Italian painting. With the early writings of John Ruskin, produced at the same time as Livingstone was taking the light of British civilisation into benighted Africa and Harriet Ward was measuring herself so complacently against the indigenous peoples of the Cape, comes a reversal whereby a degenerate and benighted industrial England is invited to seek civilisation amidst the monuments of thirteenth-century Italy.

For Ruskin, 'all great European art is rooted in the thirteenth century,'[174] and his first independent journey to Italy was dedicated to seeing as much of that art as possible, in particular the fresco painting which seemed to be deteriorating before his very eyes. There was little doubt in his mind which represented the more advanced state of culture, thirteenth-century Italy or nineteenth-century England. He compares, for instance, the experiences of entering the still intact gates of medieval Siena and contemporary London:

> recollect always the inscription over the north gate of Siena: 'Cor magis tibi Sena pandit.' 'More than her gates, Siena opens her heart to you.'
>
> When next you enter London by any of the great lines, I should like you to consider, as you approach the city, what the feelings of the heart of London are likely to be on your approach, and at what part of the railroad station an inscription, explaining such state of her heart, might be most fitly inscribed. Or you would still better understand the difference between ancient and modern principles of architecture by taking a cab to the Elephant and Castle, and thence walking to London Bridge by what is in fact the great southern entrance to London. The only gate receiving you is, however, the arch thrown over the road to carry the South-Eastern Railway itself; and the only exhibition either of Salvation or Praise is in the cheap clothes' shops on each side; and especially in one colossal haberdasher's shop, over which you may see the British flag waving (in imitation of Windsor Castle) when the master of the shop is at home.[175]

Ruskin famously drew upon his Italian journeys to make comparisons with his own country's spiritual, cultural, social and economic condition, holding up medieval Pisa as an example to Victorian Bradford, and suggesting to his Sheffield readers 'suppose you set your wits to work for once in a Florentine or Venetian manner, and ask, as a merchant of Venice would have asked, or a "good man" of the trades of Florence, *how much money there is in the town*, – who has got it, and what is becoming of it.' He tells them to 'Elect a doge' and build a Ducal Palace.[176]

But if contemporary England suffers by comparison with medieval Italy, the contrast between past glories and present degeneration presents itself even more sharply to Ruskin in Italy itself. In Venice, where the people have their magnificent Ducal Palace, he is horrified to see men urinating against its walls. He is no less appalled to see ancient frescoes being wilfully destroyed; to see batteries of guns before Corinthian porticoes; people selling toys and chickens and religious artefacts at the door of St Mark's; an abbot's palace now inhabited by a vendor of marine stores; other beautiful palaces turned barracks and coal warehouses, 'a crane out of the gothic balconies'; and, most outrageous of all, 'the church tower with the smoke coming out of the top. The Italians admire steam engines as much as we do, but cannot afford to build chimneys – it is cheaper to use old church steeples.'[177] In short, 'the modern work has set its plague spot everywhere – the moment you begin to feel, some gaspipe business forces itself on the eye, and you are thrust into the nineteenth century.'[178] Ironically alluding to the notion of England as the source of civilisation, the purveyor of light to the rest of the world, Ruskin traces the source of the modern infection to the leading industrial nation. The romance of Venice is destroyed by the advent of *'gas lamps! . . . in grand new iron posts of the last Birmingham fashion'*, by the 'iron station' and new patent iron railings on the bridges, by the 'omnibus gondolas', and worst of all by the monstrous new bridge, uglier than the Greenwich railway, built across the lagoon, reducing it to a city 'as nearly as possible like Liverpool'.[179]

For Charles Dickens, as for Ruskin, modern Italy's likeness to England is depressing. While the outskirts of Venice recall to Ruskin in 1849/1850 'the kind of place in the outskirts of London which are the shrines of Warren's blacking and Parr's pills', Dickens, who knew such areas all too personally, had in 1846 pictured Rome as a macabre London slum, with its 'narrow streets, devoid of footways, and choked, in every obscure corner, by heaps of dunghill-rubbish', a fit setting for the Dead Cart carrying the corpses of the poor to their communal grave.[180] Dickens' first view of the Eternal City was not encouraging:

it looked like – I am half afraid to write the word – like LONDON!!! There it lay, under a thick cloud, with

> innumerable towers, and steeples, and roofs of houses, rising
> up into the sky, and high above them all, one Dome. I swear,
> that keenly as I felt the absurdity of the comparison, it was so
> like London, at that distance, that if you could have shewn it
> me, in a glass, I should have taken it for nothing else.[181]

Dickens was without doubt much more interested in the Italian people,
their life and their customs, than he was in their buildings, their art and
their history. He was not uncritical of them, of their Romish supersti-
tions as well as their squalid living conditions, but his affection seems
genuine, and his criticisms were tempered by a sympathy for the contemporary Italian situation which Ruskin manifestly lacked. Whereas
Ruskin's generally acute sense of the political, economic, and social
determinants of culture seemed to fail him in the face of modern Italy,
and he was strongly opposed to 'Red Republicanism' in the revolutionary late 1840s, Dickens was from the mid-1840s until his death in 1870
an avid supporter of the Risorgimento cause. Although he makes little
mention of Italy's political situation in *Pictures from Italy*, his allegiances
are clear in his journalistic writing, and both *Household Words* and *All
the Year Round* were openly supportive of Italian nationalism under his
editorship.

If Dickens was more sensitive than Ruskin to the social and cultural
effects upon Italian life of oppression by a foreign power, he was also
more keenly aware of the oppression of the past, of the great weight of
history carried by modern Italy. His approach to the first Neapolitan
town he encounters provides almost as stark a contrast to Ruskin's
entrance into Siena as London does:

> Take note of Fondi, in the name of all that is wretched and
> beggarly.
>   A filthy channel of mud and refuse meanders down the
> centre of the miscrable street: fed by obscene rivulcts that
> trickle from the abject houses. There is not a door, a window,
> or a shutter; not a roof, a wall, a post, or a pillar, in all Fondi,
> but is decayed and crazy, and rotting away. The wretched
> history of the rown, with all its sieges and pillages by
> Barbarossa and the rest, might have been acted last year.[182]

The macabre imagery running through the sections on Naples and Rome
in particular suggest that Dickens perceived the whole of Italy as a vast
graveyard of the past. It is impossible to escape a sense of the layers and
layers of history which constitute modern Italy:

> whether, in this ride, you pass by obelisks, or columns: ancient
> temples, theatres, houses, porticoes, or forums: it is strange to

see, how every fragment, whenever it is possible, has been blended into some modern structure, and made to serve some modern purpose – a wall, a dwelling-place, a granary, a stable – some use for which it never was designed, and associated with which it cannot otherwise than lamely assort. It is stranger still, to see how many ruins of the old mythology: how many fragments of obsolete legend and observance: have been incorporated into the worship of Christian altars here; and how, in numberless respects, the false faith and the true are fused into a monstrous union.[183]

Whether, like Dickens, one felt oppressed by a sense of the stranglehold of the past in Europe, conscious above all of the ingrained historical and economic injustices as legacies deforming young nationhood, or, like Ruskin, one saw in Europe's glorious history and monuments a source of inspiration for a spiritually degenerate age, English travellers typically found Continental Europe evocative of the historical past in a way that industrial England no longer was. Ruskin, for instance, finds in France 'that agedness in the midst of active life which binds the old and the new into harmony', noting that 'on the Continent, the links are unbroken between the past and the present,' unlike England, where 'Everything is perpetually altered and renewed by the activity of invention and improvement.'[184] Whether the tenacity of the European past was celebrated or deplored, there was no question that it was of continuing significance, and, moreover, that in it were to be found the origins and achievements, as well as the atrocities and the downfalls, of Western civilisation. Travellers to the New World – particularly, in the nineteenth century, to America – encountered a society either disabled or blessed (depending on one's political stance) by the fact of its lack of white, European history, by the absence of the virtues (or constraints) of 'civilisation'.

The nineteenth-century writer who most infamously pilloried Americans for their lack of culture was Frances Trollope. She published her acidulous and highly prejudiced *Domestic Manners of the Americans* in 1832 following a failed business venture in the frontier city of Cincinnati. From what she clearly regarded as the unimpeachable position of being British, and having cultured European taste, she patronisingly catalogued the American people's want of civilisation in everything from their dress, their food and their manners, to their art and literature and their system of government. This general want of elegance and taste is always, and often explicitly, attributed to their fatal newness as a nation, and their lack of exposure to classical European civilisation. Hence, an 'obvious cause of inferiority in the national literature, is the very slight acquaintance with the best models of composition, which is thought necessary for persons called well educated', namely the classical authors.[185] Her description of a visit to the Antique Statue Gallery at the Pennsylvania academy of the fine arts links the misplaced delicacy, the vulgarity masquerading as prudery, which she finds so much a part of the American character, specifically with their ignorance of classical civilisation:

> The door was open, but just within it was a screen, which prevented any objects in the room being seen from without. Upon my pausing to read this inscription, an old woman who appeared to officiate as guardian of the gallery, bustled up, and addressing me with an air of much mystery, said, 'Now, ma'am, now: this is just the time for you – nobody can see you – make haste.'
>
> I stared at her with unfeigned surprise, and disengaging my arm, which she had taken apparently to hasten my movements, I very gravely asked her meaning.
>
> 'Only, ma'am, that the ladies like to go into that room by themselves, when there be no gentlemen watching them.'
>
> On entering this mysterious apartment, the first thing I remarked, was a written paper, deprecating the disgusting depravity which had led some of the visitors to mark and deface the casts in a most indecent and shameless manner. This abomination has unquestionably been occasioned by the coarse-minded custom which sends alternate groups of males and females into the room. Were the gallery open to mixed parties of ladies and gentlemen, it would soon cease. Till America has reached the degree of refinement which permits of this, the antique casts should not be exhibited to ladies at all. I never felt my delicacy shocked at the Louvre, but I was strangely tempted to resent as an affront the hint I received, that I might steal a glance at what was deemed indecent. Perhaps the arrangements for the exhibition of this room, the feelings which have led to them, and the result they have produced, furnish as good a specimen of the kind of delicacy on which the Americans pride themselves, and of the peculiarities arising from it, as can be found.[186]

This account is accompanied by an illustration showing a group of prurient, tittering ladies, furtively viewing the rude casts, carrying the caption 'Antique Statue Gallery'. The antique casts themselves are point-edly absent from the scene, as being of little relevance to these women. Earlier, Trollope had expressed the view that 'I certainly believe the women of America to be the handsomest in the world, but as surely do I believe that they are the least attractive.'[187]

Throughout the book, Europe and America are dichotomised in terms of civilisation and its lack in the old and the new cultures. The pathologically supercilious and status-conscious Trollope puts the sneer on the American's face, and the chip on his shoulder, in the following passage:

> the favourite, the constant, the universal sneer that met me everywhere, was on our old-fashioned attachments to things obsolete. Had they a little wit among them, I am certain they would have given us the cognomen of 'My Grandmother, the British,' for that is the tone they take, and it is thus they reconcile themselves to the crude newness of every thing around them.
>
> 'I wonder you are not sick of kings, chancellors, and archbishops, and all your fustian of wigs and gowns,' said a very clever gentleman to me once, with an affected yawn; 'I protest, the very sound almost sets me to sleep.'
>
> It is amusing to observe how soothing the idea seems, that they are more modern, more advanced than England. Our classic literature, our princely dignities, our noble institutions, are all gone-by relics of the dark ages.[188]

Trollope despises the modernity of American culture precisely because of its much-vaunted egalitarianism and its social mobility. She condescendingly disparages the Americans' obsession with making money with all the *hauteur* of an English aristocrat's contempt for 'trade', despite the fact that she herself had gone to America to restore the family fortunes by opening a bazaar for the sale of fancy goods.

A nation which in place of the cherished institutions of the Monarchy, the Established Church and the law of primogeniture put its faith in Republicanism, freedom of worship and meritocracy provided a dangerous example for England in 1832. For readers of the Tory press, such as the *Quarterly Review* and *Blackwood's Edinburgh Magazine* which had waged a vitriolic campaign against America for several decades, Trollope's book confirmed all their prejudices about what would become of England under democracy. Appearing in the very year of the Reform Act, amidst increasing Chartist agitation, a book which so vituperatively decried the very exemplum of the modern liberal democratic government found a ready readership among Britain's beleaguered Tories, and sold very well. Trollope poured scorn on Thomas Jefferson and his works, claiming that 'his hot-headed democracy has done a fearful injury to his country':

> Hollow and unsound as his doctrines are, they are but too palatable to a people, each individual of whom would rather derive his importance from believing that none are above him, than from the consciousness that in his station he makes part of

> a noble whole. The social system of Mr. Jefferson, if carried
> into effect, would make of mankind an unamalgamated mass of
> grating atoms, where the darling 'I'm as good as you,' would
> soon take place of the law and the Gospel. As it is, his
> principles, though happily not fully put in action, have yet
> produced most lamentable results. The assumption of equality,
> however empty, is sufficient to tincture the manners of the
> poor with brutal insolence, and subjects the rich to the paltry
> expediency of sanctioning the falsehood, however deep their
> conviction that it is such.[189]

She concludes her book on the Americans and their domestic unmanner-
liness with the generous promise that 'if refinement once creeps in among
them, if they once learn to cling to the graces, the honours, the chivalry
of life, then we shall say farewell to American equality, and welcome
to European fellowship one of the finest countries on the earth.'[190]

Another female traveller to America in the 1830s, Harriet Martineau,
was also angry with its leading theorist of democracy, Thomas Jefferson,
but for different reasons from those of her compatriot. In her *Society in
America* of 1837, Martineau attacks Jefferson for his exclusion of women
from political power on the unreasonable grounds that 'to prevent dep-
ravation of morals, and ambiguity of issue, [they] could not mix
promiscuously in the public meetings of men,' a fallacy, she contends,
'as disgraceful as any advocate of despotism has adduced':

> Woman's lack of will and of property, is more like the true
> cause of her exclusion from the representation, than that which
> is actually set down against her. As if there could be no means
> of conducting public affairs but by promiscuous meetings! As
> if there would be more danger in promiscuous meetings for
> political business than in such meetings for worship, for
> oratory, for music, for dramatic entertainments, – for any of
> the thousand transactions of civilized life![191]

Martineau's object, like Alexis de Tocqueville's in *Democracy in America*
(1835), was to examine American society in the light of the democratic principle upon which it claimed to be founded, but unlike the
Frenchman she paid proper attention to the social conditions and political and legal status of women. Beginning her argument with a reference
to the fact that 'One of the fundamental principles announced in the
Declaration of Independence is, that governments derive their just
powers from the consent of the governed,' she bluntly poses the question
'How can the political condition of women be reconciled with this?'
Martineau traces the severely circumscribed nature of American women's
lives, which Trollope merely describes and deplores, to their true political

origin. The political status of women in America is, she avers, no higher than that of slaves, and for Martineau, by this time a noted abolitionist, America's conspicuous failure to extend the egalitarian principles upon which it was supposedly founded to women or slaves seriously compromised its claims to being a democracy, and was profoundly disappointing.

Interestingly, although they are otherwise such different writers, Martineau, like Trollope, invokes 'civilisation' in support of her argument:

> If a test of civilisation be sought, none can be so sure as the condition of that half of society over which the other half has power, – from the exercise of the right of the strongest. Tried by this test, the American civilisation appears to be of a lower order than might have been expected from some other symptoms of its social state. The Americans have, in the treatment of women, fallen below, not only their own democratic principles, but the practice of some parts of the Old World.
>
> The unconsciousness of both parties as to the injuries suffered by women at the hands of those who hold the power is a sufficient proof of the low degree of civilisation in this important particular at which they rest. While woman's intellect is confined, her morals crushed, her health ruined, her weaknesses encouraged, and her strength punished, she is told that her lot is cast in the paradise of women: and there is no country in the world where there is so much boasting of the 'chivalrous' treatment she enjoys.[192]

In the 1830s, coming hard on the heels of Trollope's and other books denouncing American manners and morals, Martineau's identification of the political non-existence of women in America as a sign of its lack of civilisation would have carried particular force, although John Stuart Mill was later to level at England the charge of failure to behave in a civilised way towards women, in *The Subjection of Women* (1861). It is worth noting that in his *North America*, published in 1862 following a nine-month visit to the United States during the Civil War, Anthony Trollope did much to counteract his mother's earlier hostile account, but his criticisms of American women showed him to be no supporter of Martineau's or Mill's position. He was totally unsympathetic to women's demands for equal economic and political rights, contending, 'The best right a woman has is the right to a husband, and that is the right to which I would recommend every young women . . . to turn her best attention.'[193]

Despite the fact that the Republic survived the Civil War unscathed and continued to gain international respect, English readers did not apparently tire of hearing how uncivilised their transatlantic cousins were, and continued to enjoy the opportunity to congratulate themselves on their own superior taste and conduct. At a time when the middle classes were anxiously trying to establish their own social credentials and class identity, and to redefine what it meant to be a 'gentleman' in England's rapidly changing economic, political and social structure,[194] it was satisfying to be able to point a finger at people more *nouveau* than themselves. Having cringed for years under Matthew Arnold's depiction of them as Philistines, they must have enjoyed reading his account of a whole nation of surely more thorough-going Philistines in *Discourses in America* (1885) and *Civilization in the United States* (1888). Travelling to the United States on a lecture tour two decades after the Civil War, Arnold was impressed by its strengths as a nation – its Constitution, its legal and federal system, its rich natural resources and its vigorous industry – but for all its success and prosperity it lacked tradition, it lacked culture, in short, and he felt bound to raise questions 'as to the character and worth of American civilization'. His conclusion is that 'a great void exists in the civilisation over there: a want of what is elevated and beautiful, of what is interesting', a want felt to be the graver 'because it is so little recognised by the mass of Americans'.[195]

Given its fatal flaw of being 'uninteresting', 'America is not a comfortable place of abode', Arnold points out, for educated, moneyed Englishmen:

> for all that large number of men, so prominent in this country and who make their voice so much heard, men who have been at the public schools and universities, men of the professional and official class, men who do the most part of our literature and our journalism . . . A man of this sort has in England everything in his favour; society appears organised expressly for his advantage.

But, he observes, 'for that immense class of people, the great bulk of the community, the class of people whose income is less than three or four hundred a year', a nation which has constituted itself in a modern democratic age has more to offer.[196] This is something that a different tradition of British writers on America had recognised from the beginning of the century, when, driven by dissatisfaction with the poverty and the political, economic, and social injustices so manifest in England, they had travelled there to assess its potential for investment and settlement. America had always been represented as an alternative society for both radical thinkers and those persecuted in England for their political or religious views, and this is how it was perceived by Romantic writers and turn-of-the-century political thinkers. It was the site of Coleridge's and Southey's imagined utopian Pantisocracy, and the place where Joseph Priestley sought refuge when driven from England in 1794.

When the journalist and pamphleteer William Cobbett first went to live in America, from 1792 until 1800, he was an outspoken opponent of Priestley and his Republican supporters, and an ardent defender of his native England. During this period he wrote a devastating satire on Jefferson and the egalitarian principles he espoused. However, upon his return to England Cobbett became increasingly committed to the radical cause, and by 1817, when he went back to the United States to farm and to write a guide for would-be emigrant farmers, he had suffered harsh fines and two years' imprisonment for his subversive views, and his earlier allegiances had changed so much that he was to take the bones of Thomas Paine back to England with him on his return there in 1819.[197]

Cobbett's *A Year's Residence in the United States* (1818) provides an admirably clear description of early nineteenth-century American farming and American society and, by implication, of the inequities of the agricultural economy, and, indeed, of the whole social system, in England at the same time. For Cobbett, 'This America, this scene of happiness under a free government, is the beam in the eye, the thorn in the side, the worm in the vitals, of every despot upon the face of the earth.' The dignity and integrity of American farm labourers which he observes and describes 'arises from free institutions of government. A man has a voice *because he is a man*, and not because he is the *possessor of money*.' He appeals to his reader (he has already explained that he is addressing himself to English farmers), 'And, shall I *never* see our English labourers in this happy state?'

> Let those English farmers, who love to see a poor wretched labourer stand trembling before them with his hat off, and who think no more of him than of a dog, remain where they are; or, go off, on the cavalry horses, to the devil at once, if they wish to avoid the tax-gatherer; for, they would, here, meet with so many mortifications that they would, to a certainty, hang themselves in a month.[198]

His description of the housing in the Pennsylvanian town of Lancaster, 'No *fine* buildings; but no *mean* ones', causes him to reflect upon the cruel contrast between the living conditions of the rich and the poor in England. Of urban dwellings, he writes,

> Here are none of those poor, wretched habitations, which sicken the sight at the *outskirts* of cities and towns in England; those abodes of the poor creatures, who have been reduced to beggary by the cruel extortions of the rich and powerful

and of rural:

> What a contrast with the farm-houses in England! There the
> *little* farm-houses are falling into ruins, or, are actually become
> cattle-sheds, or, at best, *cottages*, as they are called, to contain a
> miserable labourer, who ought to have been a farmer, as his
> grandfather was. Five or six farms are there *now* levelled into
> one, in defiance of *the law*; for, there is a law to prevent it.
> The *farmer* has, indeed, a *fine house*; but, what a life do his
> labourers lead![199]

He blames the depopulation of rural England on

> The Funding and Manufacturing and Commercial and Taxing
> System [which] has, by drawing wealth into great masses,
> drawn men also into great masses. London, the manufacturing
> places, Bath, and other places of dissipation, have, indeed,
> wonderfully increased in population. Country seats, Parks,
> Pleasure-gardens, have, in like degree, increased in number and
> extent. And, in just the same proportion has been the increase
> of Poor-houses, Mad-houses, and Jails. But, *the people of
> England*, such as FORTESCUE described them, have been
> *swept away* by the ruthless hand of the Aristocracy, who,
> making their approaches by slow degrees, have, at last, got
> into their grasp the substance of the whole country.[200]

Charles Dickens, in his *American Notes* (1842), is more circumspect in
his comments on the respective social conditions of the working classes
in the United States and England, and he even suggests that in terms of
its public health system it could take a few lessons from England, claiming that 'There is no local Legislature in America which may not study
Mr. Chadwick's excellent Report upon the Sanitary Condition of our
Labouring Classes, with immense advantage.'[201] Nevertheless, following
a very positive description of factory workers in Lowell, he comments
that it 'cannot fail to afford [gratification] to any foreigner to whom the
condition of such people at home is a subject of interest and anxious
speculation', adding that he has 'carefully abstained from drawing a
comparison between these factories and those of our own land', for

> The contrast would be a strong one, for it would be between
> the Good and Evil, the living light and deepest shadow. I
> abstain from it, because I deem it just to do so. But I only the
> more earnestly adjure all those whose eyes may rest on these
> pages, to pause and reflect upon the difference between this
> town and those great haunts of desperate misery: to call to
> mind, if they can in the midst of party strife and squabble, the
> efforts that must be made to purge them of their suffering and

danger: and last, and foremost, to remember how the precious Time is rushing by.[202]

Like Cobbett on the American farm labourer, Dickens attributes the dignity and culture of the young female factory workers to the fact that they live under a less rigidly defined class system. After noting that the young women play the piano, subscribe to circulating libraries, and even produce their own periodical, he alludes to the fact that this might seem preposterous to English readers, who would consider such activities to be above the station of factory workers, but asks 'Are we quite sure that we in England have not formed our ideas of the "station" of working people, from accustoming ourselves to the contemplation of that class as they are, and not as they might be?'[203] However, America is not immune from Dickens' biting satire. Like Martineau and other travellers to the United States of the period, he was sickened by the continuance of slavery in a country which proclaimed itself to be a democracy. He describes the recent trial in Washington of an elderly man 'charged with having dared to assert the infamy of that traffic, which has for its accursed merchandise men and women, and their unborn children':

> Yes. And publicly exhibited in the same city all the while; gilded, framed and glazed; hung up for general admiration; shown to strangers not with shame, but pride; its face not turned towards the wall, itself not taken down and burned; is the Unanimous Declaration of the Thirteen United States of America, which solemnly declares that All Men are created Equal; and are endowed by their Creator with the Inalienable Rights of Life, Liberty, and the Pursuit of Happiness![204]

Here one recognises the savage anger against the hypocrisy of governments and institutions that one finds in later novels such as *Bleak House* (1851–53), but his representation of Mrs Jellyby and her misplaced philanthropic efforts on behalf of the Borrioboola-Gha mission in that novel reminds us that, for all his sympathy for American slaves, Dickens believed that charity should begin at home. In an essay he wrote on the ill-fated Niger Exhibition in 1848, in which he expressed the view that 'Between the civilized European and the barbarous African there is a great gulf set', making the 'railroad Christianisation' and civilisation of Africa a doomed project, he asserted: 'The work at home must be completed thoroughly, or there is no hope abroad.'[205] Thomas Carlyle shared his view, as is clear from his essay of 1849 on 'The Nigger Question' and his later writing on the rebellion in Jamaica in 1865. Both Carlyle and Dickens perceived anti-slavery and missionary activities as distractions from more urgent problems associated with poverty and misgovernment in Britain, and there were many like them whose sympathies for the poor at home outweighed their concern for the exploited abroad.[206] As the next section will demonstrate, the social explorers saw it as their duty to keep their nineteenth-century readers at least as well informed about the dark secrets of unknown England, and the customs and morals of that foreign tribe the urban proletariat, as they were about the dark continent of Africa or the domestic manners of Americans.

Social reportage

But O Cook, O Thomas Cook & Son, path-finders and trail-clearers, living sign-posts to all the world and bestowers of first aid to bewildered travellers – unhesitatingly and instantly, with ease and celerity, could you send me to Darkest Africa or Innermost Thibet, but to the East End of London, barely a stone's throw distant from Ludgate Circus, you know not the way!

(Jack London)[207]

In his preface to the first cheap edition of *Oliver Twist*, published in 1850, Dickens directs the reader's attention to his description, in chapter 50 of the novel, of the squalid riverside slum known as 'Jacob's Island', an area, he says, which is 'wholly unknown, even by name, to the great mass of [London's] inhabitants'. He describes how it was mentioned in a recent speech by the Bishop of London, who wished to reform living conditions in the area. Dickens notes that an opponent of such reform, Sir Peter Laurie, Master of the Saddler's Company and former Lord Mayor, responded a few days later with the assertion that Jacob's Island did not exist, saying that 'The Bishop of London, poor soul, in his simplicity, thought there really was such a place, which he had been describing so minutely, *whereas it turned out that it* ONLY *existed in a work of fiction, written by Mr. Charles Dickens ten years ago* [roars of laughter].'[208] Dickens's purpose is to underline the point made again and again in his fiction and journalism that the Victorian upper classes and bourgeoisie had contrived a kind of cultural apartheid which meant that the poor never actually crossed their field of vision or entered their consciousness. Like Jacob's Island, in Sir Peter Laurie's formulation, they did not exist.

Jacob's Island did, of course, exist, as did its inhabitants, together with many more thousands living in penury and misery at whom the moneyed classes did not find it comfortable to look. However, in the period since the first publication of *Oliver Twist* (1837–39) they had increasingly been obliged to look. The extreme poverty and distress of the Hungry Forties, the controversy generated by the Repeal of the Corn Laws in 1846, mounting Chartist agitation culminating in the 1848 uprising, ensured that by the middle of the century the Condition of England Question dominated economic, political, and social debate, and had become a major literary theme for both poets and novelists. The most influential Victorian social problem fiction – Disraeli's *Coningsby* (1844) and *Sybil* (1845), Kingsley's *Yeast* (1848), Gaskell's *Mary Barton* (1848) and *North and South* (1854–55), Dickens's *Hard Times* (1854) – appeared in the middle decade of the century.[209] Moreover, since the 1830s both government bodies and concerned individuals had taken upon themselves the task of looking at the lives of the poor, indeed of examining, measuring, and classifying them in painstaking detail, and forcing them upon the attention of their deliberately impercipient social superiors.

Shortly before Sir Peter Laurie proclaimed the non-existence of Jacob's Island, Henry Mayhew had been commissioned by the *Morning Chronicle* to prepare a piece on the South London area of Bermondsey, which appeared under the title 'A Visit to the Cholera Districts of Bermondsey' on 24 September, 1849. The article culminates with a horrifyingly detailed description of the very area – Jacob's Island – whose existence was to be so firmly denied. Following a graphic account of the disgustingly polluted 'tidal sewer' which runs in front of the houses, its murky waters 'covered with a scum almost like a cobweb, and prismatic with grease', and full of 'swollen carcasses of dead animals, almost bursting with the gases of putrefaction', and its banks piled high with 'heaps of indescribable filth', Mayhew reveals the most shocking detail of all:

> yet we were assured this was the only water the wretched inhabitants had to drink. As we gazed in horror at it, we saw drains and sewers emptying their filthy contents into it; we saw a whole tier of doorless privies in the open road, common to men and women, built over it; we heard bucket after bucket of filth splash into it; and the limbs of the vagrant boys bathing in it seemed, by pure force of contrast, white as Parian marble. And yet, as we stood doubting the fearful statement, we saw a little child, from one of the galleries opposite, lower a tin can with a rope to fill a large bucket that stood beside her. In each of the balconies that hung over the stream the self-same tub was to be seen in which the inhabitants put the mucky liquid to stand, so that they may, after it has rested for a day or two, skim the fluid from the solid particles of filth, pollution, and disease.[210]

He saw, he heard, he doubted what he was told, but he again *saw* the impossible truth of the 'indescribable' conditions under which these slum-dwellers lived. Much as Sir Peter Laurie and his ilk might have preferred it to be merely fictional, Jacob's Island and its wretched inhabitants continued to exist long after Sykes met his novelistic end there.

Mayhew's article created a considerable stir, not only because the facts he uncovered touched the conscience of London's more privileged citizens, but also because they were struck by the piquancy of the idea that this alien underclass passed their very different lives in such close proximity to themselves, indeed under their very fastidious noses, and yet were as foreign as the primitive tribes described by explorers of the African interior. As Thackeray wrote in response to Mayhew's article, 'We had but to go a hundred yards off and see for ourselves, but we never did'; or, as George Sims was later ironically to put it, this was a voyage of discovery 'into a dark continent that is within easy walking distance of the General Post Office'.[211] Back in 1842 Edwin Chadwick had commented of the facts disclosed in his *Report on the Sanitary Condition of the Labouring Population of Great Britain* that they were 'as strange as if they related to foreigners or the natives of an unknown land', adding, by way of illustration, 'We have found that the inhabitants of the front houses in many of the main streets of those towns and of the metropolis, have never entered the adjoining courts, or seen the interiors of any of the tenements, situate at the back of their own houses, in which their own workpeople reside.'[212] A decade later, despite all the blue books and parliamentary speeches, the wealthy classes apparently still remained unaware of what went on in their own backyards, and needed a guide to take them over the fence and into foreign territory.

In his preface to the first volume of the massive work of urban sociology upon which he embarked following the success of the *Morning Chronicle* article, *London Labour and the London Poor*, Mayhew describes himself as 'supplying information concerning a large body of persons, of whom the public had less knowledge than of the most distant tribes of the earth . . . and as adducing facts so extraordinary, that the traveller in the undiscovered country of the poor must . . . be content to lie under the imputation of telling such tales, as travellers are generally supposed to delight in.'[213] The imagery of exploration became a classic motif of Victorian social reportage, a device used to expose not only the manifest inequalities in English society but also the reader's blindness to and ignorance of the social world they inhabit. As in Disraeli's image of the 'two nations', exploration metaphor reinforces the idea that the poor dwell in a separate, and quite strange and exotic, country, an alien territory yet to be discovered by the wealthy.[214] Whilst the use of such metaphor encouraged the idea that, armed as it were with a temporary visa, the rich could cross class boundaries as easily as they could cross the borders which separated their own privileged enclaves from the regions

inhabited by the poor, it also reinforced the notion of irreducible difference, of the otherness of this alien underworld.[215] There was only one
class of travellers, and they always held return tickets; diplomatic relations did not extend to allowing the poor to penetrate the country of
the rich.

The invocation of exploration narratives undoubtedly drew attention
to the divisions within English society in an effective way and evoked
a compassionate response. But, in the context of contemporary evolutionism and developing imperialist ideology, the deployment of a
discourse of colonialism to articulate domestic social problems inevitably
tended to reinforce and consolidate notions of hierarchies of power.[216]
There was clearly a close connection between the domestic and the
colonial spheres of otherness in the nineteenth-century imagination, a
connection which is particularly exemplified in representations of Irish
migrants and slum communities, in which the Irish poor, at once colonial subjects and working-class subjects, are likened to shiftless heathen
savages. James P. Kay, for instance, writing on Manchester in 1832,
wrote of the Irish,

> Debased alike by ignorance and pauperism, they have
> discovered, with the savage, what is the minimum of the
> means of life, upon which existence may be prolonged. The
> paucity of the amount of means and comforts *necessary for the
> mere support of life* is not known by a more civilized population,
> and this secret has been taught the labourers of this country
> by the Irish . . . The contagious example of ignorance and
> barbarous disregard of forethought and economy, exhibited by
> the Irish, spread.[217]

The imagery of contagion and invasion underlines the threat that Irish
'savagery' represents to the much-vaunted civilisation of England. For
Thomas Carlyle, writing on Chartism in 1839, the Irishman is similarly
'the sorest evil this country has to strive with':

> In his rags and laughing savagery, he is there to undertake all
> work that can be done by mere strength of hand and back;
> for wages that will purchase him potatoes. He needs only
> salt for condiment; he lodges to his mind in any pighutch or
> doghutch, roosts in outhouses; and wears a suit of tatters, the
> getting off and on of which is said to be a difficult operation,
> transacted only in festivals and the hightides of the calendar.
> The Saxon man if he cannot work on these terms, finds no
> work . . . the uncivilised Irishman, not by his strength, but by
> the opposite of strength, drives out the Saxon native, takes
> possession in his room. There abides he, in his squalor and

unreason, in his falsity and drunken violence, as the ready-made nucleus of degradation and disorder.[218]

In *The Condition of the Working Class in England* (1845), Engels distances himself from Carlyle's 'exaggerated and one-sided condemnation of the Irish national character', but quotes him at length on the subject, and indulges in his own vituperative characterisation of the 'savagery' of the Irish, describing 'The southern facile character of the Irishman, his crudity, which places him but little above the savage', indeed 'upon the lowest plane possible in a civilized country'.[219]

But it is not only the Irish poor who are likened to savages striking at the very heart of British civilisation. For all his sympathetic understanding of the conditions of the working-class population of Manchester, Engels resorts to racial analogies to articulate their difference, calling the urban poor 'a race wholly apart from the English bourgeoisie'.[220] Such language is ubiquitous in nineteenth-century social reportage. Mayhew famously describes the London street people as a 'nomad race'. The opening sentence of his first chapter, entitled 'Of Wandering Tribes in General', explains that humankind had always comprised 'two distinct and broadly marked races, viz., the wanderers and the settlers – the vagabond and the citizen – the nomadic and the civilized tribes'. He goes on to point out that the street-folk of the English metropolis, like the African Bushmen and the Arabian Bedouins, manifested certain physical and moral characteristics – a 'greater development of the animal than of the intellectual or moral nature of man . . . high cheek-bones and protruding jaws . . . their use of a slang language . . . their lax ideas of property . . . their general improvidence – their repugnance to continuous labour – their disregard of female honour – their love of cruelty – their pugnacity – and their utter want of religion' – which distinguished them from 'civilized man'.[221] Indeed, they are represented as not so much another class as another species.[222]

Mayhew's racial characterisation of the street-folk of London was later echoed by the social theorist John McLennan, who wrote of them in 1869 as 'predatory bands, leading the life of the lowest nomads'.[223] More sensationalist use is made of exploration metaphor by James Greenwood, who collected a number of his own newspaper articles and republished them in 1874 as a book with the title *The Wilds of London*. Greenwood saw himself as a 'volunteer explorer in the depths of social mysteries',[224] and the first of the articles in the volume tells of his 'exploration' of an area in London known as 'Tiger Bay', where sailors are 'shamefully used by ruffianly men and women'. He locates it with some difficulty: it is so densely foggy that he, tellingly, cannot read the street names, and a passing policeman claims not to know of it. Again, it seems to be a place more familiar in print, through newspaper reportage, than in reality. The article opens,

Everybody addicted to the perusal of police reports, as
faithfully chronicled by the daily press, has read of Tiger Bay,
and of the horrors perpetrated there – of unwary mariners
betrayed to that craggy and hideous shore by means of false
beacons, and mercilessly wrecked and stripped and plundered –
of the sanguinary fights of white men and plug-lipped Malays
and ear-ringed Africans, with the tigresses who swarm in the
'Bay,' giving it a name.

It continues in the same vein, equating the 'ruffianly' Londoners with
their Malay and African victims, and the women in particular with savage beasts of the jungle, describing them as 'tigresses' 'out hunting',
'growling', 'showing their claws', even biting men's ears off.[225] As in
the pornography of the period, such women are represented as dangerous, forbidden fruit. Like Irishmen, lower-class women were commonly
seen to share certain characteristics with 'savages': they were represented
as governed by impulse and instinct, lascivious, lacking in foresight.
And, like Mayhew's street-folk, they share a characteristically 'primitive' physiognomy:

Take fifty of them, and, setting aside trifling variations as
regards complexion and colour of hair and eyes, they would
pass as children of the same parents. The same short, bull-like
throats, the same high cheek-bones and deep-set eyes, the same
low, retreating foreheads and straight wide mouths, and
capacious nostrils, the same tremendous muscular development
stamps one and all.[226]

Predatory, sub-human, monstrously sexual, in Greenwood's article as
in other writing of the period, they seem to embody middle-class male
fears of, and subliminal attraction to, both female sexuality and working-
class power, which must equally be severely curtailed and contained.[227]
The exploration metaphor is most famously and laboriously unpacked
in the first chapter of General William Booth's In Darkest England and
the Way Out (1890), and is the informing idea of the book. Booth, who
with his wife Catherine founded the Salvation Army, rhetorically asks
'Why "darkest England"?' and goes on to explain how he has just been
reading the book that has arrested the attention of 'the civilised world',
Stanley's In Darkest Africa:

It is a terrible picture, and one that has engraved itself deep on
the heart of civilisation. But while brooding over the awful
presentation of life as it exists in the vast African forest, it
seemed to me only too vivid a picture of many parts of our
own land. As there is a darkest Africa is there not also a

darkest England? Civilisation, which can breed its own
barbarians, does it not also breed its own pygmies? May we
not find a parallel at our own door, and discover within a
stone's throw of our cathedrals and palaces similar horrors to
those which Stanley has found existing in the great Equatorial
forests?[228]

After pursuing the analogy for some pages he exclaims, after the fashion
of Dickens, 'What a satire it is upon our Christianity and our civilisation, that the existence of these colonies of heathens and savages in the
heart of our capital should attract so little attention!'[229] Booth maps
'darkest England', 'this great lost land', as the three circles of hell:

The outer and widest circle is inhabited by the starving and the
homeless, but honest, Poor. The second by those who live by
Vice; and the third and innermost region at the centre is
peopled by those who exist by Crime. The whole of the three
circles is sodden with Drink. Darkest England has many more
public-houses than the Forest of the Aruwimi has rivers,
of which Mr. Stanley sometimes had to cross three in
half-an-hour.[230]

The solution Booth proposes, his 'scheme', is similarly three-fold, and
in keeping with the imperialist ideology of the book that inspired him,
in that it involves the formation of three levels of 'colony' – the 'City
Colony', the 'Farm Colony' and the 'Over-Sea Colony' – each function-
ing as 'a kind of co-operative society, or patriarchal family', within
which the destitute can exercise self-help and start their lives afresh.[231]
    Just as parallels are drawn between the urban proletariat of 'outcast'
London and savage foreign tribes, comparisons are made between the
perilous journeys of the social explorer and the intrepid explorers of
distant lands on their 'civilising' imperial missions into the 'terra incognita' of urban poverty. Invoking Stanley, who 'in his own [masculinist]
phrase, "marched, tore, ploughed, and cut his way for one hundred and
sixty days through this inner womb of the true tropical forest"', Booth
urges his army of Christian soldiers to hack through 'the endless tangle
of monotonous undergrowth' that is 'the Forest of the Shadow of Death
at our doors'.[232] Middle-class philanthropists such as Edward Denison
went to live and work in the East End much in the way that missionaries were to live and work in Africa; 'missions' were established by the
churches to bring civilisation to the heart of the big cities; and in the
1880s and 1890s the settlement movement, inspired by Ruskin, Arnold
Toynbee, and Samuel Barnett, was responsible for encouraging middle-
class men and women to 'settle' in impoverished areas to bring 'culture'
to the working-class community. The novelist Mary Ward, for instance,

with her philanthropical associates founded a settlement for Bible teaching and social purposes at University Hall in Gordon Square in 1890, and in 1897 opened the Passmore Edwards Settlement in Tavistock Square.

In accounts which draw upon the conventions of travel literature as well as upon anthropology, social explorers penetrate the foreign territory of the urban poor, giving the armchair traveller an opportunity to learn about their exotic and bizarre customs, rituals and taboos, and vicariously to experience the colourful scenes, thrills, and dangers of a voyage into the unknown. Like their heroic counterparts, social explorers took their lives in their hands, it is suggested, when they ventured into the nether regions of the industrial city, risking disease, violent assault, and the ever-present danger of losing caste, of 'going native'. George Sims begins his 'book of travel', *How the Poor Live* (1883), first published in the *Pictorial World*, with the modest disclaimer, 'I have no shipwrecks, no battles, no moving adventures by flood and field, to record. Such perils as I and my fellow-traveller have encountered on our journey are not of the order which lend themselves to stirring narrative.' His quotation from *Othello* evokes the exotic, and reminds us of the orientalism of Victorian accounts of other worlds than their own, whether Arabia Deserta and the Holy Land or the stewpits of Stepney and the Isle of Dogs. And of course perils, albeit second-order perils, there were, as he is quick to remind us:

> It is unpleasant to be mistaken, in underground cellars where the vilest outcasts hide from the light of day, for detectives in search of their prey – it is dangerous to breathe for some hours at a stretch an atmosphere charged with infection and poisoned with indescribable effluvia – it is hazardous to be hemmed in down a blind alley by a crowd of roughs who have had hereditarily transmitted to them the maxim of John Leech, that half-bricks were specially designed for the benefits of 'strangers' . . .[233]

Frequently, like travellers elsewhere, social explorers considered it practical or politic to modify their dress and bearing, or even to adopt a disguise; often they used native guides to help them find their way. Moreover, in their transcription of their adventures, a rhetoric of difference is constructed around working-class people and their culture. The 'otherness' of, for instance, the East End of London, was measured against the implied norm of metropolitan, middle-class culture. Through rhetorical means, such as the phonetic representation of working-class dialect which seems unnatural compared with the 'norm' of the middle-class narrative voice, the urban poor are represented as foreigners speaking a strange tongue.[234] And so although it is a more democratic way of writing about the poor to make use of interviews and direct speech, giving working-class individuals a voice, and enabling them to speak for themselves 'in their own "unvarnished" language', as Mayhew put it,[235] the linguistic difference between the investigator and his subject ironically underlines the social distance between them.

In short, although the new social reportage was finally forcing the existence of the urban poor into the consciousness of the moneyed classes, their culture and the way in which they lived were still mediated by middle-class writers. Even though urban sociologists such as Mayhew and Charles Booth were doing their best to bring the facts of the matter into the public realm, theirs was still a *representation* of working-class life, a construction. Charles Booth wrote: 'East London lay hidden from view behind a curtain on which were painted terrible pictures: starving children, suffering women, overworked men; horrors of drunkenness and vice; monsters and demons of inhumanity; giants of disease and despair.' He asks 'Did these pictures truly represent what lay behind . . . ?' and explains, 'This curtain we have tried to lift.' Booth, like Mayhew, Gaskell and others, did get behind the veil and witness the scenes beyond. But although arguably more realistic than the sensational depiction of the poor on the curtain (just as realist novels attempted to be more 'truthful' than gothic romances), his own representation is no more 'real', no more innocent of ideology, than that which it seeks to modify. Moreover, Booth's image of the curtain being raised on the lives of the poor not only contains more than a suggestion of voyeurism and peepshows, but also conveys something of the theatricality which informs some of the best-known examples of Victorian social reportage. Henry Mayhew, for instance, like Dickens, was closely involved with the theatre of his day, having written farces and taken part in professional productions in his youth, and he brought his experience to the service of his social writing, where he makes masterly use of dialogue, dramatic entrances, and other theatrical devices. And Greenwood's description of the 'spectacle' he encountered on his visit to the 'Globe and Pigeons' at 'Tiger Bay' ('It was like being "behind the scenes" at a theatre during the pantomime season') reminds us that parties of young men used to go to pubs such as this and 'Paddy's Goose' to watch the sailors and prostitutes perform.[236] Mayhew's writing is clearly of a different order from the popular London low-life genre of which Greenwood's work is an example,[237] but it is nevertheless shaped and informed by the human drama he finds in London's streets, by what Booth describes as 'this excitement of life which can accept murder as a dramatic incident, and drunkenness as the buffoonery of the stage'. As Booth tellingly exclaims, 'looked at in this way, what a drama it is!'[238]

We now know a great deal about the use made by Victorian novelists of blue books and other social reportage.[239] But it is misleading to view such literary appropriations as the transposition of simple 'fact' into 'fiction'. It is not at all clear, for instance, whether Dickens was inspired by earlier newspaper accounts of cholera-stricken Jacob's Island or whether Mayhew, in writing his account of the epidemic, was inspired by Dickens. Moreover, Mayhew was a skilful professional writer, who had tried his hand at writing novels. He wanted to reach a wide popular readership, and therefore presented his material in as lively a way as possible, selecting the most interesting stories, creating dramatic juxtapositions, and generally bringing fictional techniques to the service of the 'factual' survey.[240] Furthermore, as several recent critics have pointed out, the factual information in the social commentary of writers such as Mayhew and Booth is so ideologically charged as to become fantasy and myth.[241] Thus East London, for example, became not merely a geographical location to be 'discovered', or a social map to be plotted, but a signifier of the 'condition of England' problem to be solved.[242] The fact that working-class slum districts were known to most members of the moneyed classes only through their literary incarnation in the writings of social investigators and novelists meant that they could be imaginatively conquered and controlled. Not only did the mass of statistical evidence, the detailed enumeration of the conditions in which the poor lived, create a reassuring sense of the working classes as being under surveillance, it also made wonders seem familiar. The investigator's very methodology meant that the strange and the terrible could be experienced vicariously and emotionally assimilated.[243] Working-class life is, then, discovered and demythologised in these texts, and reconfigured as the knowable.

The increasing dependence of nineteenth-century social reportage upon statistical methods and information, its status indeed as social science, points to the fact that it was at least as closely related to the scientific writing as it was to the exploration literature of the period. Mayhew, Booth and other social investigators were obsessive about the 'scientific' classification of the working-class population into categories and subcategories. Mayhew, for instance, explained his view that one of the 'most important' ways to order a body of information was through 'a correct grouping of objects into genera, and species, orders and varieties'.[244] Moreover, if their classificatory methods were borrowed from biology, their view of society was Darwinian. Darwin's indebtedness to Malthus in the development of his idea of the struggle for existence is well known; but there are also direct parallels between Mayhew's 'feeling of awe' in the face of 'the struggle for life partaking of the sublime' he witnesses as he watches 'thousands of men struggling for only one day's hire' at the dockyards, Booth's excitement at the 'clash of contest, man against man, and men against fate – the absorbing interest of a battle-field' that he finds in the East End, and Darwin's view of the war of nature.[245] Sociology has been described as a kind of 'third culture', between the natural sciences on the one hand and the humanities on the other,[246] a status it shares with statistics itself, which similarly occupies a marginal position between scientific and non-scientific disciplines.[247] A discipline developed in the early decades of the nineteenth century, statistics is a mixed form of representation in which discursive narratives and numerical formulations are juxtaposed. In nineteenth-century social writing, because of its claims to be an objective, empirical science, statistics was frequently deployed as a way of legitimating recommendations about social policy and legislation.[248]

The Victorians' well known obsession with numbers and 'facts', so memorably satirised in Dickens' *Hard Times* (1854), had its roots in the early decades of the century. T. R. Malthus's *Essay on the Principle of Population* (1798) stimulated a great interest in population theories, which in turn created a demand for accurate statistical information. The first English census was taken in 1801, and as the century progressed ever more elaborate machinery was developed for the collection of statistical data. From the outset, social analysts brought statistical methodologies to the aid of non-statistical ideologies: numbers were gathered by some for purposes of legislation and reform, and by others for purposes of social control; they were collected by government commissioners and by chambers of commerce, and made use of by novelists, preachers, and industrialists; they were designed to induce a range of responses, from shame and fear to religious conversion and self-congratulation. It was because statistical information was so often very obviously made to serve a political agenda that the discipline of statistics was looked upon with suspicion by 'pure' scientists, who prided themselves on their Newtonian objectivity and disinterestedness. But despite such reservations, the Board of Trade set up a Statistical Office in 1832, the British Association for the Advancement of Science reluctantly established a statistical section in 1833, the Manchester Statistical Society was founded in the same year, and the Statistical Society of London the following year, so that by the beginning of Victoria's reign statistics had found its footing in the intellectual establishment, and was there to be made use of by social commentators of all persuasions.[249]

Nevertheless, as is clear from Dickens's famous denunciation of Gradgrindian 'facts', and from the determined resistance of writers such as Ruskin and Carlyle to the lure of statistics, numerical methods were spurned by some, who preferred to rely on their own impressions and responses to individual felt experiences. One such was William Cobbett, who in *Rural Rides* (1830) dismisses the government's population statistics with magnificent contempt, preferring the evidence of his own eyes when he visits the village of East Meon near the Hampshire/Surrey border:

> I am sure that East-Meon has been a *large place*. The church
> has a *Saxon Tower* pretty nearly equal, as far as I recollect, to

that of the Cathedral at Winchester. The rest of the church has
been rebuilt, and, perhaps, several times; but the *tower* is
complete; it has had a *steeple* put upon it; but, it retains all its
beauty, and it shows that the church (which is still large) must,
at first, have been a very large building. Let those who talk so
glibly of the *increase of the population* in England, go over the
country from Highclere to Hambledon. Let them look at the
size of the churches, and let them observe those *numerous small
enclosures* on every side of every village, which had, to a
certainty, *each its house* in former times. But, let them go to
East-Meon, and account for that church. Where did the hands
come from to make it? Look, however, at the downs, the
many square miles of downs near this village, *all bearing the
marks of the plough*, and yet all out of tillage for many many
years; yet, not one single inch of them but what is vastly
superior in quality to any of those great 'improvements' on the
miserable heaths of Hounslow, Bagshot, and Windsor Forest.
It is the destructive, the murderous paper-system [i.e. paper
money], that has transferred the fruit of the labour, and the
people along with it, from the different parts of the country to
the neighbourhood of the all-devouring *Wen*. I do not believe
one word of what is said of the *increase of* the population. All
observation and all *reason* is against the fact; and, as to the
parliamentary returns, what need we more than this: that *they*
assert, that the population of Great Britain has *increased* from
ten to *fourteen* millions in the last *twenty years!* That is enough!
A man that can suck that in will believe, literally believe, that
the *moon is made of green cheese*. Such a thing is too monstrous
to be swallowed by any body but Englishmen, and by any
Englishmen not brutified by a Pitt-system.[250]

This passage, which is preceded by a description of the singular beauty
of the village and its location, manifests Cobbett's characteristic preoccupations as he travels – literally, on horseback – into a country familiar
to him from his youth but vastly changed in the intervening period by
the enclosure of what had been open common land, by the depopulation of the villages. Reading the politics of the rural landscape which
surrounds him, Cobbett finds in the grand remains of the Saxon church
a rebuke to the corrupt church of his own day, in the small enclosures
and degraded land evidence of the deracinated condition of agricultural
labour. He moves from lyrical description into a tirade against the evils
of the funding system and paper money which have left their mark on
the landscape as unequivocally as the turnpike roads which serve the
great Wen, that metropolitan tumour which feeds on and inexorably
depletes rural England. He turns on its head the notion that statistics

convey empirically verifiable truth: if one actually *looks* at the country-side, one can see the truth.

Cobbett rode his horse through the southern counties, avoiding the evil turnpike roads, preferring the 'stern way' of the ancient lanes and bridlepaths, at a crucial time in England's agricultural history. He witnessed the effects of the late eighteenth-century agrarian revolution – the enclosure of common land, the proletarianisation of the farm labourer, the displacement of traditional landowners by capitalist farmers – in the decade which culminated in 1830 with the Labourers' Revolt.[251] The censuses about which he was so disparaging showed that, whereas two-thirds of the population lived in the countryside in 1801, the number and size of towns and cities was rapidly increasing, there was a massive redistribution of population between the country and the city, and with each new census a dramatic increase in the relative proportion of urban dwellers to the whole population. There was plenty of rural poverty for the social investigator to explore and expose, but by the 1830s and 1840s attention had shifted to the city as the primary locus of modern society. Charles Booth, making use of a by now familiar metaphor, was later to explain its draw for him:

> It is not in country but in town that 'terra incognita' needs to be written on our social map. In the country the machinery of human life is plainly to be seen and easily recognized: personal relations bind the whole together. The equipoise on which existing order rests, whether satisfactory or not, is palpable and evident. It is far otherwise with cities, where as to these questions we live in darkness, with doubting hearts and ignorant unnecessary fears, or place our trust with rather dangerous consequences in the teachings of empiric economic law.[252]

A more pragmatic reason for focusing attention on the northern industrial worker in the 1830s and 1840s, and from the 1860s onwards on working-class Londoners, among whom all householders were enfranchised by the 1867 Reform Act, was the threat of class warfare. In the early Victorian period revolutions across Europe fanned fears among the middle and upper classes of the revolutionary potential of their own massive working-class population. The Irish potato famine, the financial crisis, mass unemployment, the devastating cholera epidemics made already poor conditions intolerable, and, driven by desperation and anger, the English proletariat became politically organised and mobilised, first of all under the auspices of Chartism in the 1830s and 1840s, and later with the foundation of the Trades Union Council in 1868. Annie Besant led a strike by Bryant and May matchgirls in 1888, and, shortly afterwards, industrial action by the gas workers and the London dock strike consolidated the idea that working-class people were not prepared to accept such poor conditions. In the political sphere, the Communist League was founded in 1847, the Reform League was established in 1865 to increase working-class representation in Parliament, and the 1860s also saw the beginning of a powerful campaign for the enfranchisement of women. The Fabian Society was formed in 1884, and the Independent Labour Party founded in 1887. That British society was inexorably moving towards mass democracy must have been clear to all, and the danger of ignoring the plight of the poor, especially the urban poor, who were in a much stronger position to take effective mass action, created a politically compelling reason for governments, private organisations and individuals to try to ascertain the extent of their grievances and alleviate the worst of their suffering. As Peter Gaskell points out in *The Manufacturing Population of England* (1833):

> Much should be done – and done vigorously and resolutely. Like other great revolutions in the social arrangement of kingdoms, it is to be feared that the explosion will be permitted to take place, undirected by the guiding hand of any patriotic and sagacious spirit, and its fragments be again huddled together in hurry and confusion; and finally to undergo a series of painful gradations, from which the imagination turns with sickening terror.[253]

Such fears of working-class revolution and mass violence are deep and enduring. Ten years after Gaskell wrote, W. Cooke Taylor offered an even more graphic warning to his middle-class readers:

> It would be absurd to speak of factories as mere abstractions, and consider them apart from the manufacturing population. That population is a stern reality, and cannot be neglected with impunity. As a stranger passes through the masses of human beings which have accumulated round the mills and print-works in Manchester and the neighbouring towns, he cannot contemplate these 'crowded lives' without feelings of anxiety and apprehension almost amounting to dismay. The population, like the system to which it belongs, is NEW; but it is hourly increasing in breadth and strength. It is an aggregate of masses, our conceptions of which clothe themselves in terms that express something portentous and fearful. We speak not of them indeed as of sudden convulsions, tempestuous seas, or furious hurricanes, but as of the slow rising and gradual swelling of an ocean which must, at some future and no distant time, bear all the elements of society aloft upon its bosom, and float them – Heaven knows whither.

There are mighty energies slumbering in those masses. Had
our ancestors witnessed the assemblage of such a multitude as
it is poured forth every evening from the mills of Union-
street, magistrates would have assembled, special constables
would have been sworn, the riot act read, the military called
out, and most probably some fatal collision would have taken
place. The crowd now scarcely attracts the notice of a passing
policeman, but it is, nevertheless, a crowd, and therefore
susceptible of the passions which may animate a multitude.[254]

While most social investigators of the period were, like Peter Gaskell
and W. Cooke Taylor, fearful of organised Labour movements and
their potential to incite the masses to revolution, one commentator was
notably in favour of the proletariat rising up against their oppressors,
and welcomed the inevitability of revolution. Frederick Engels was only
twenty-four when he wrote *The Condition of the Working Class in England* (1845), and a newcomer to Manchester, but he had an acute sense
of the social relations and the social geography of the city. Like other
commentators on English urban life, he remarks upon the fact that the
wealthy contrive not to see the misery of the poor, but unlike them he
shows their ignorance to be entirely calculated, and to be a function of
the very design of the city:

The town itself is peculiarly built, so that a person may live in
it for years, and go in and out daily without coming into
contact with a working-people's quarter or even with workers,
that is, so long as he confines himself to his business or to
pleasure walks. This arises chiefly from the fact, that by
unconscious tacit agreement, as well as with out-spoken
conscious determination, the working-people's quarters are
sharply separated from the sections of the city reserved for the
middle-class.

The upper and middle bourgeoisie, he explains, are able to travel into
the central commercial area of the city from their comfortable homes in
the healthy and unpolluted outer suburbs along thoroughfares lined
with shops held by the middle and lower bourgeoisie 'without ever seeing that they are in the midst of the grimy misery that lurks to the right
and left', for the shops 'conceal from the eyes of the wealthy men and
women of strong stomachs and weak nerves the misery and grime
which form the complement of their wealth', and 'one is seldom in a
position to catch from the street a glimpse of the real labouring districts.' The very urban design of Manchester, as of other great cities,
then, is a 'hypocritical plan': 'I have never seen', he writes, 'so systematic
a shutting out of the working-class from the thoroughfares, so tender

a concealment of everything which might confront the eye and the nerves of the bourgeoisie, as in Manchester.' 'I cannot help feeling', he concludes, 'that the liberal manufacturers, the "Big Wigs" of Manchester, are not so innocent after all, in the matter of this sensitive method of construction.'[255]

By contrast with this 'hypocritical plan', the 'planless, knotted chaos' of working-class housing points to a civic carelessness when it comes to the needs of the poor. Imagery of labyrinthine confusion characterises Engels' descriptions of these districts. 'He who turns to the left here from the main street', he tells us, 'is lost,' and there is more than a suggestion that the hellish underground cellars, holes, and closed-in courts are the dwellings of the lost, the regions of the damned. Engels is as much like Aeneas entering the underworld as he is like Livingstone penetrating the interior:

> Immediately under the railway bridge there stands a court, the filth and horrors of which surpass all the others by far, just because it was hitherto so shut off, so secluded that the way to it could not be found without a good deal of trouble. I should never have discovered it myself, without the breaks made by the railway, though I thought I knew this whole region thoroughly. Passing along a rough bank, among stakes and washing-lines, one penetrates into this chaos of small, one-storied, one-roomed huts, in most of which there is no artificial floor; kitchen, living and sleeping-room all in one. In such a hole, scarcely five feet long by six broad, I found two beds – and such bedsteads and beds! – which, with a staircase and chimney-place, exactly filled the room. In several others I found absolutely nothing, while the door stood open, and the inhabitants leaned against it. Everywhere before the doors refuse and offal; that any sort of pavement lay underneath could not be seen but only felt, here and there, with the feet. This whole collection of cattle-sheds for human beings was surrounded on two sides by houses and a factory, and on the third by the river, and besides the narrow stair up the bank, a narrow doorway alone led out into another almost equally ill-built, ill-kept labyrinth of buildings.[256]

'And such a district,' he exlaims, 'exists in the heart of the second city of England, the first manufacturing city of the world.' It is a heart of darkness, indeed, one in which human beings 'in any degree civilised' should not be expected to live. And its existence should not be condoned, either, by people who consider themselves civilised. The airless, foetid hovels of Engels' description recall the horrors of the middle passage, and their inhabitants are referred to as 'these helots of modern society', as the victims of the 'slavery' of the modern industrial epoch who, 'scarcely freed from feudal servitude could be used as mere material, a mere chattel', to create 'the highest possible profit' for their 'owners'.[257]

The trope of slavery is one which can be found throughout the literature of social investigation, particularly in the 1830s and 1840s. Lord Ashley's famous speech to the House of Commons on 7 June 1842, introducing his bill to exclude women and children from working in the mines, and summarising the findings of the Commission on the Employment of Children in Mines and Factories, contained descriptions of women and children in chains and ropes like beasts of burden or slaves in a chaingang:

> Now, it appears that the practice prevails to a lamentable extent of making young persons and children of a tender age draw loads by means of the girdle and chain. The child, it appears, [has] a girdle bound round its waist, to which is attached a chain, which passes under the legs, and is attached to the cart. The child is obliged to pass on all fours, and the chain passes under what, therefore, in that posture, might be called the hind legs; and thus they have to pass through avenues not so good as a common sewer, quite as wet, and oftentimes more contracted. This kind of labour they have to continue during several hours, in a temperature described as perfectly intolerable. By the testimony of the people themselves, it appears that the labour is exceedingly severe; that the girdle blisters their sides and causes great pain. 'Sir,' (says an old miner), 'I can only say what the mothers say, it is barbarity – absolute barbarity.' Robert North says, 'I went into the pit at seven years of age. When I drew by the girdle and chain, the skin was broken, and the blood ran down. If we said anything, they would beat us. I have seen many draw at six. They must do it or be beat. They cannot straighten their backs during the day. I have sometimes pulled till my hips have hurt me so that I have not known what to do with myself.'[258]

As the sub-commissioner is reported to have commented, such practices are 'a cruel slaving . . . revolting to humanity'.[259] And the children were not the only ones to suffer. Ashley's speech quotes the evidence of women forced to do such work when they were in an advanced state of pregnancy:

> 'I have a belt around my waist,' (says Betty Harris), 'and a chain passing between my legs, and I go on my hands and feet. The road is very steep, and we have to hold by a rope, and where there is no rope, by anything that we can catch

hold of. It is very hard work for a woman. . . . The pit is very wet. . . . I have seen water up to my thighs. My clothes are wet through almost all day long. . . . I have drawn till I have had the skin off me. The belt and chain is worse when we are in the family way.' . . . 'I have had,' (says a witness), 'three or four children born the same day that I have been at work, and have gone back to my work nine or ten days after: four out of eight were still-born.'[260]

Ashley appeals to the House as a gathering of civilised men who will surely not condone such slavery in their own midst:

Is it not enough to announce these things to an assembly of Christian men and British Gentlemen? For twenty millions of money you purchased the liberation of the negro; and it was a blessed deed. You may, this night, by a cheap and harmless vote, invigorate the hearts of thousands of your countrypeople, enable them to walk erect in newness of life, to enter on the enjoyment of their inherited freedom, and avail themselves (if they will accept them) of the opportunities of virtue, of morality, and religion.[261]

Ashley spoke the language of Evangelicalism and Tory paternalism, and also the language of imperialism. He notes that 'the sufferings of these people, so destructive to themselves, are altogether needless to the prosperity of the empire.' He does not fear revolution among the working population, he says, but he does fear 'the progress of a cancer, a perilous, and, if we much longer delay, an incurable cancer, which has seized upon the body, social, moral, and political', and he predicts that one day 'the strength of the empire will be found prostrate, for the fatal disorder will have reached its vitals.'[262]

Ashley knew the effect of incorporating into his own speeches the first-hand accounts by coal-mining and factory operatives of their working conditions, which were published in newspapers and blue books and reached a wide circulation. Their testimony had a horrifying immediacy and authority which no amount of middle-class rhetoric could achieve. Working-class autobiographies of the period had a similarly powerful appeal. William Dodd, for instance, wrote about the enslaved condition of industrial workers from their own perspective in his autobiographical *Narrative of the Experience and Sufferings of William Dodd, Factory Cripple* (1841). Dodd's account is naturally quite different in tone and mode from both Ashley's Evangelical paternalism and Engels's analysis of post-industrial capitalism, yet like Engels he clearly perceives that the wealth of the profit-driven industrialist and the deprivation of the worker are inversely related under capitalism:

for while I and hundreds of work-people were toiling and
sweating day after day for the bare necessaries of life –
struggling, as it were, against wind and tide, and still hoping
that some favourable turn would afford a resting-place for our
wearied and emaciated frames – the manufacturers were
amassing immense wealth, and thus converting what ought to
have been a national blessing into a national curse – 'adding
field to field, and house to house', and rolling about in their
carriages, surrounded by every luxury that this world can give,
and looking upon us poor factory slaves as if we had been a
different race of beings, created only to be worked to death for
their gain.[263]

Dodd writes with anger and compassion of the low value placed
upon the lives and limbs of factory workers from a position of particular authority and poignancy, but the subject of industrial accidents caused
by the failure of factory owners to fence off dangerous machinery was
one which lent itself to reformist journalism. Henry Morley, for instance,
in his unsigned article 'Ground in the Mill', published in *Household Words*
in 1854, draws up a grotesque account sheet, measuring and costing out
'the blood of the operatives' against 'the gold of the mill-owners':

Mercy debtor to justice, of poor men, women, and children,
one hundred and six lives, one hundred and forty-two hands
or arms, one thousand two hundred and eighty-seven (or, in
bulk, how many bushels of) fingers, for the breaking of one
thousand three hundred and forty bones, for five hundred and
fifty-nine damaged heads, and for eight thousand two hundred
and eighty-two miscellaneous injuries. It remains to be settled
how much cash saved to the purses of the manufacturers is a
satisfactory and proper off-set to this expenditure of life and
limb and this crushing of bone in the persons of their
workpeople.[264]

In this grim depiction of a society governed by the cash nexus, the
grisly catalogue of dismembered limbs suggests the status and condition
of the factory operatives. Already reduced to metonymic 'hands', they
are still further deformed and diminished, their torn-off fingers pointing the blame unequivocally at the mill owners and those 'kind-hearted
interpreters of the law' who protect their interests rather than those of
the workers the laws were designed to protect. The careful enumeration
of mangled bodies, broken bones and severed limbs, like corpses piled
up in a mass grave, graphically and ironically draws attention to the
fact that, under the present system, industrial workers are not treated as
individual human beings who are of value to society, but are deprived

of integrity and identity, even by the statistical methods which are employed to expose their misery. Later in the article the satirical point is
reinforced when the author asks, 'and what great harm is done, if A,
putting a strap on a driving pulley, is caught by the legs and whirled
round at the rate of ninety revolutions in a minute? – what if B, adjusting gear, gets one arm and two thighs broken, an elbow dislocated and
a temple cracked?' and so on through the alphabet.[265] But in Morley's
argument, interwoven with the dehumanising statistics of mass mutila-
tion, are stories of individual lives; of the 'gamesome youth' who says
to his fellow 'Watch me do a trick!' and is paid for his childish sense
of fun with death; of the factory girl 'who has not the whole spirit of
play spun out of her for want of meadows, [who] gambols upon bags
of wool, a little too near the exposed machinery that is to work it up,
and is immediately seized, and punished by the merciless machine that
digs its shaft into her pinafore and hoists her up, tears out her left arm
at the shoulder joint, breaks her right arm, and beats her on the head.'[266]
Such vignettes provide a stark contrast to the tersely noted compensa-
tion manufacturers are obliged to pay for their 'annual of horrors': 'For
severe injury to a young person caused by gross and cognisable neglect
to fence or shaft, the punishment awarded to a wealthy firm is a fine of
ten pounds twelve shillings costs. For killing a woman by the same act
of indifference to life and limb, another large firm is fined ten pounds,
and has to pay one guinea costs . . . Ten pounds was the expense of
picking a man's wife, a child's mother, limb from limb.'[267]

    Household Words, under Dickens's editorship, published a number of
similarly powerful articles on social and industrial conditions in the Northern manufacturing towns in the 1850s, including some by Dickens
himself, in which he brings his skills as a novelist to bear on his journalism. A characteristic example is an unsigned article on the Preston
strike in 1854 with the title 'On Strike'.[268] The piece begins with a debate
between the narrator and a man he putatively meets on the train to
Preston, to whom he refers as Mr Snapper, who is of the view that 'the
hands' 'want to be ground . . . to bring 'em to their senses'.[269] Their
discussion enables Dickens to represent the manufacturers' position on
the strike, and to recount something of its history in a lively, dramatic
and humorous way. Upon his arrival in Preston, the narrator is immediately confronted with the opposing view of the strike, in the form of
placards, one of which, addressed to 'Friends and Fellow Operatives',
is reproduced. And so the article continues, in a dramatic play of voices,
to render different perspectives on the strike. The narrative of the 'foreigner's' impressions of what he sees is interpolated with songs, poems,
hymns, texts, publicly posted threats and promises, balance sheets, and
political speeches in regional dialect, with the result that the reader (also,
probably, a 'foreigner') is encouraged to imagine experiencing first hand,
along with the narrator, the personal and political dynamics of a northern

town in the grip of industrial action. The style of the article is recognisably Dickensian, with its mixture of humour and pathos, its appeals to sentiment, its theatricality, and its deployment of repetition for accumulated rhetorical effect:

> In any aspect in which it can be viewed, this strike and lockout is a deplorable calamity. In its waste of time, in its waste of a great people's energy, in its waste of wages, in its waste of wealth that seeks to be employed, in its encroachment on the means of many thousands who are laboring from day to day, in the gulf of separation it hourly deepens between those whose interests must be understood to be identical or must be destroyed, it is a great national affliction.[270]

It is also highly characteristic of Dickens's political position as we know it from his fiction. In his discussion with Mr Snapper on the train, the narrator describes himself as a friend to neither the strike nor the lockout, rather as 'a friend to both [the Masters and the Hands]'.[271] He refuses either to condemn the political and industrial action of the operatives or to attribute blame to the manufacturers:

> Masters right, or men right; masters wrong, or men wrong; both right, or both wrong; there is certain ruin to both in the continuance or frequent revival of this breach. And from the ever-widening circle of their decay, what drop in the social ocean shall be free![272]

Retreating from the actual specifics of the Preston lockout and strike which he has so carefully conjured (but which, as in his other writing on the North, he does not imaginatively enter) into a generalised plea for good sense and reconciliation, Dickens tries to impose the kind of fictional resolution he generally endorses in his novels upon this real-life drama. Rather than emphasising insurmountable class divisions, he invokes the shared humanitarian instincts which supposedly unite people of all classes and interest groups, urging that 'political economy is a mere skeleton unless it has a little human covering and filling out, a little human bloom upon it, and a little human warmth in it.'[273]

Certainly the bare bones of political economy were fleshed out in the middle decades of the century, if not by 'a little human covering', then by the vast number of investigations into the condition of the poor which were undertaken during the period. Royal Commissions and Select Committees were established to gather empirical evidence on the administration of the Poor Laws, the health of towns, and industrial conditions in the factories, mines and agriculture, for the purpose of formulating new social policy and instituting reform. Alongside the official investigations of government bodies and the information-gathering exercises of voluntary statistical societies, there was a burgeoning of journalistic social reportage in the newspaper and periodical press. The power of journalism in this regard is incalculable, for it was in periodicals such as *Household Words* and newspapers such as the *Morning Chronicle* that the general reading public would encounter, amidst the poems, short stories, news reports, recipes, and other pieces that make up these mixed literary forms, polemical articles on the 'condition of England' question and hard information on the living and working conditions of the poor. These decades were also notable for the publication of numerous specialist studies of particular social problems – such as public health and sanitation, housing, juvenile delinquency – related to the professionalisation of medicine, architecture, law, and the social sciences.[274]

Mayhew's was, though, the first attempt to conduct an empirical survey into poverty itself. Like Dickens, Mayhew was hostile towards the laissez-faire doctrines of the political economists, which he saw as buttressing the interests of the moneyed classes. He represents political economy not as skeletal but rather as grossly battening upon society:

> economists . . . have shown the same aversion to collect facts as mad dogs have to touch water. It is so much easier to ensconce themselves in some smug corner and there remain all day, like big-bottomed spiders, spinning cobweb theories amid heaps of *rubbish*.[275]

Mayhew made it his task to 'collect facts', and his work contained prodigious quantities of statistics, calculations, tables, classifications and maps, as well as minutely observed social details. But Mayhew saw his vocation as being 'to collect facts *and* register opinions' (my emphasis).[276] The opinions to which he refers here are the opinions of the poor, and his work is notable for the space it gives to recording his subjects' own perception of their lot, their aspirations and expectations, in a form which suggests the direct transcription of their answers.[277] But of course also registered in his empirical investigation were his *own* opinions, the exercise of which severely compromised the claims of his work to scientific objectivity.

Mayhew's classification system for criminal behaviour, for example, translates the problem of urban poverty into sexual terms.[278] In volume 4 of *London Labour and the London Poor*, in which Mayhew proposes to survey 'those that *will not* work' (having already dealt with 'those that *will* work' and 'those that *cannot* work' in previous volumes), after mapping out the various kinds of crime against property to be found in London, the text suddenly identifies prostitution as the type of criminal behaviour.[279] And so we are told

> Prostitution, professionally resorted to, . . . consists, when
> adopted as a means of subsistence without labour, in inducing
> others, by the performance of some immoral act, to render up
> a portion of their possessions. Literally construed, prostitution
> is the putting of anything to a vile use; in this sense perjury is
> a species of prostitution, being an unworthy use of the faculty
> of speech; so, again, bribery is a prostitution of the right of
> voting; while prostitution, specially so called, is the using of
> her charms by a woman for immoral purposes. This, of
> course, may be done either from mercenary or voluptuous
> motives; be the cause, however, what it may, the act remains
> the same, and consists in the base perversion of a woman's
> charms – the surrendering of her virtue to criminal
> indulgence.[280]

By Mayhew's account, not only is the criminality of prostitution all the
woman's, but it also becomes a trope for and, implicitly, the source of
crime in all its forms, expanding as a category to such an extent that it
comprises half the entire volume.[281]

There was, of course, a long and eminent tradition in English writing
from Thomas Malthus onwards of translating social issues into sexual
terms. And so, for instance, Joseph Adshead, in his report on *Distress in
Manchester* of 1842, is disproportionately concerned about the sleeping
arrangements of Manchester's cellar-dwelling population:

> Frequently, different families occupy *opposite corners of the same
> room*, the sexes being no further separated than by the few feet
> of space which lie between their respective beds of straw . . .
> six or eight persons have I witnessed inhabiting a damp cellar,
> males and females congregated together, with a line hung
> along the hovel for the use of the inmates, upon which were
> suspended, indiscriminately, their torn and dirty apparel; with
> other scenes of a nature too disgusting for recital . . .
>   It would be impossible to over-state the moral and social
> evils arising from this state of things. The domestic decencies
> must be utterly unknown where habits like these prevail; and
> every barrier against profligacy in its coarsest form must be
> broken down.[282]

More famously, Lord Ashley, who concerned himself professedly with
'the moral statistics of a country', was at least as appalled by the moral
dangers of work in the collieries as he was by the physical conditions
under which people had to labour. He comments, for instance,

> The girls are of all ages, from seven to twenty-one. They
> commonly work quite naked down to the waist, and are
> dressed – as far as they are dressed at all – in a loose pair of

trousers. These are seldom whole on either sex. In many of the
collieries the adult colliers, whom these girls serve, work
perfectly naked.[283]

For Ashley, social reform constituted moral reform, and it was particularly crucial to protect women from moral temptation and corruption:

> In the male the moral effects of the system are very sad,
> but in the female they are infinitely worse, not alone upon
> themselves, but upon their families, upon society, and, I may
> add, upon the country itself. It is bad enough if you corrupt
> the man, but if you corrupt the woman, you poison the waters
> of life at the very fountain.[284]

In Mayhew's work, it is just such a corrupt woman who is the very
fountain of urban criminal culture. 'Thousands of our felons', we are
told, 'are trained from their infancy in the bosom of crime . . . Many
of them are often carried to the beer shop or gin palace on the breast of
worthless drunken mothers, while others, clothed in rags, run at their
heels or hang by the skirts of their petticoats.'[285] In this revealing passage,
the bad mother, gin-soaked and signified by her heels and petticoats, is
equated with a prostitute; her breast, not nurturing but sexualised, sites
her at 'the bosom of crime', the very source of urban crime, poverty,
and social disorder.[286]

Mayhew's was but one among many views of prostitution as both
symptom and effect of urban poverty and immorality that were expressed in a range of public forums from the mid-1850s onwards. The
Times saw prostitution as the 'Greatest of our Social Evils', while for
W. R. Greg it was 'The Great Sin of Great Cities'.[287] Periodicals such
as the *Westminster Review* and professional journals such as the *Lancet* ran
series of articles on the subject, while there was a proliferation of books
and pamphlets written from every possible perspective, from the evangelical moralist to the medical to the feminist. Discussion of prostitution was often connected to discussion of disease. Two of the most
important books on prostitution were written by doctors with extensive experience in the study and treatment of venereal disease: William
Tait's *Magdalenism. An Inquiry into the Extent, Causes and Consequences
of Prostitution in Edinburgh* (1840) and William Acton's *Prostitution . . .*
(1857). The passing of the Contagious Diseases Act of 1864 and of
subsequent acts attempting to regulate prostitution polarised the debate
and led to a spate of publication both in support of and opposing the
legislation. Feminists such as Harriet Martineau, Josephine Butler and
Florence Nightingale campaigned vigorously for its repeal, outraged
by its blatant enactment of a double standard of morality for men and
women, and for the moneyed and the poor.

As both the legislation and the debates which surrounded it reveal,
not only were there different rules for men and women and the rich and

the poor, there was a tendency for middle-class men to construct prostitutes, and indeed all working-class women, as constituting what one writer called 'a multitudinous amazonian army [of] the devil', preying on innocent young men and luring them into debauchery (and, to voice another fear, miscegenation).[288] One reason why the prostitute became the representative figure for urban criminal activity was that the working classes were as a species constructed as liberated from the constraints of civilisation, and enjoying a sexual freedom and licence denied to the middle-class investigator and his reader. This was undoubtedly a symbolic act of displacement onto a class of 'other' Victorians on the part of the dominant class of their own repressed sexual desire.[289]

Also a crucial part of the contemporary image of poverty was the image of unutterable filth and contamination. Mayhew's fascination with dirt may be seen as an example of a broader Victorian phobic aversion that was arguably the root-cause of the systematic mistreatment of the poor. His representation of filth in London Labour is deeply equivocal, for while, on the one hand, his detailed evocation of the dirt and excrement amidst which the poor live is charged with compassion and indignation, and is rhetorically effective in forcing the realities of poverty upon his polite readership, on the other hand so potent is it that the poor themselves seem to be morally polluted by the physical conditions that surround them.[290] Mayhew's obsession with and repugnance towards the filthy carnality and moral contamination of the poor[291] may be seen in his account of the street-finders or collectors, who made their living as bone-grubbers, rat-catchers, scavengers, dredgermen, and 'pure-finders' (collectors of dog's dung). Here there are disturbing parallels between the 'sanitary condition' described by Chadwick in his 1842 Sanitary Report and the human condition of those whose very existence depends on excrement and debris. It is a correspondence which is reinforced by the fact that, in the period, both the lowest class of dirt and the lowest class of society were referred to by the word 'residuum'.[292]

Whilst it is clear that, for all its claims to systematic empirical objectivity, London Labour and the London Poor is a representation of poverty informed by ideology, Mayhew's attempt to document the lives of the metropolitan poor is nevertheless a significant milestone in the history of sociology. His sympathetic exploration of the moral condition of those who live in poverty (for instance, the development of his early insight that 'regularity of habits [is] incompatible with irregularity of income'),[293] his recognition of the irrelevance of the complacent middle-class ideology of self-help to many among the poor, and of the culpable irresponsibility of laissez-faire economics, set him apart from many of his contemporaries. Moreover, he was the first in the history of English social investigation to attempt to define a poverty line, an undertaking which Charles Booth and Seebohm Rowntree were subsequently to refine.[294]

The work of these later social explorers carried on the investigation into poverty initiated by Mayhew, and like his their writings make a major contribution in terms of the information they provided about the urban poor. Booth's seventeen-year-long and seventeen-volume study of poverty in London, for instance, beginning with his *Life and Labour of the People* (1889), a vast compendium of statistical tables, maps, charts, and descriptions of people's lives derived from a house-to-house survey of each individual street in a district, provided incontrovertible evidence of the extent of the problem. Booth undermined comfortable Victorian notions about the 'deserving' and 'undeserving' poor, for his figures showed that the poor generally had no control over their destiny. 'Habit', so-called, was responsible for only fifteen percent of poverty, according to his statistics; for the vast majority of those living in poverty, the idea that they could improve their lives by the exercise of self-help was a patronising and irrelevant piety. It seems ironically appropriate that the second volume of Booth's work had to appear under the title *Labour and Life of the People*, rather than *Life and Labour*, because Samuel Smiles himself had laid claim to the original title with his book *Life and Labour, or Characterizations of Men of Industry, Culture and Genius*, published in 1887. Booth's emphasis on the industry, culture and genius of a different class of citizens was, like Mayhew's, radical and groundbreaking, but inevitably his work was similarly informed by the prejudices of his class in ways which modern readers find unacceptable. His method of classification of the poor into those who were more-or-less self-sufficient (classes C and D) and the hopeless poor (classes A and B) and, worse, his recommended solution to the problem of poverty (the extirpation of class B, through the establishment of compulsory labour camps, to prevent the contamination of civilised society)[295] reveal the class interests which his work ultimately served.

Booth's colleague Beatrice Webb clearly had her fellow-worker in mind when, in her autobiography *My Apprenticeship*, she made her famous diagnosis of the tremendous proliferation of protest literature in the 1880s:

> The origin of the ferment is to be discovered in a new sense of sin among men of intellect and men of property . . . The consciousness of sin was a collective or class consciousness; a growing uneasiness, amounting to conviction, that the industrial organization, which had yielded rent, interest and profits on a stupendous scale, had failed to provide a decent livelihood and tolerable conditions for a majority of the inhabitants of Great Britain.[296]

As the foregoing discussion will have indicated, more recent readers of nineteenth-century investigative writing have supplemented Webb's insight into the politics and psychology of Victorian social reportage, postulating other and equally compelling forms of class consciousness. As in their anthropological and ethnographical discovery of other cultures, and in their scientific discovery of the laws of the physical world, in their discovery of working-class culture nineteenth-century writers figured their own social, political and moral values and their own collective obsessions. Nineteenth-century prose of discovery is also a prose of invention; moreover, it is a prose of appropriation, and of the consolidation of power, as Nietzsche understood when he wrote,

> The spirit's power to appropriate the foreign stands revealed in its inclination to assimilate the new to the old, to simplify the manifold, and to overlook or repulse whatever is totally contradictory – just as it involuntarily emphasizes certain features and lines in what is foreign, in every piece of the 'external world', retouching and falsifying the whole to suit itself. Its intent in all this is to incorporate new 'experiences', to file new things in old files – growth, in a word – or, more precisely, the feeling of growth, the feeling of increased power.[297]

But if nineteenth-century writers were driven by a desire to discover and appropriate the other, they were equally concerned to discover and lay bare the *terra incognita* of the self. The next section of this book will look at the life stories the nineteenth century told about itself, at the prose forms used for the exploration of the world within.

Notes

1. Mary Shelley, *Frankenstein: or, The Modern Prometheus*, edited by Maurice Hindle (London, 1992), p. 210.

2. Ibid, p. 39.

3. Chris Baldick, *In Frankenstein's Shadow: Myth, Monstrosity, and Nineteenth-Century Writing* (Oxford, 1987), pp. 54–55.

4. Shelley, *Frankenstein*, p. 116.

5. Humphry Davy, *A Discourse, Introductory to a Course of Lectures on Chemistry, Delivered in the Theatre of the Royal Institution on the 21st of January, 1802*, in *The Collected Works of Sir Humphry Davy*, edited by John Davy, 9 vols (London, 1839–40), II, 311–26 (pp. 318, 319–20).

6. See Thomas Jefferson Hogg, *The Life of Shelley*, 2 vols (London, 1858), I, 33, 70–71.

7. Shelley, *Frankenstein*, p. 12.

8. Ibid, p. 10.

9. See Mary Louise Pratt, *Imperial Eyes: Travel Writing and Transculturation* (London and New York, 1992), pp. 5, 202.

10. E. P. Thompson, 'The Political Education of Henry Mayhew', *Victorian Studies*, 11 (1967), 43–62.

11. See Gillian Beer, 'Problems of Description in the Language of Discovery', in *One Culture: Essays in Science and Literature*, edited by George Levine (Madison, Wisconsin, 1987), p. 35.

12. See Sally Shuttleworth, *George Eliot and Nineteenth-Century Science: The Make-Believe of a Beginning* (Cambridge, 1984), p. 1.

13. Pratt, *Imperial Eyes*, p. 29.

14. Quoted in George Woodcock, 'Henry Mayhew and the Undiscovered Country of the Poor', *Sewanee Review*, 92 (1984), 556–73 (p. 565).

15. David M. Knight, *Natural Science Books in English 1600–1900* (London, 1972), p. 107.

16. Pratt, *Imperial Eyes*, p. 15.

17. See Henry M. Stanley, *In Darkest Africa; or, the Quest Rescue and Retreat of Emin, Governor of Equatoria* (London, 1890); and William Booth, *In Darkest England and the Way Out* (London, 1890).

18. Quoted in Colin A. Russell, *Sir Humphry Davy* (Bletchley, 1972), p. 56. For other Romantic scientists and their quests, see *Romanticism and the Sciences*, edited by Andrew Cunningham and Nicholas Jardine (Cambridge, 1990), especially the introduction.

19. *Works of Davy*, I, 154.

20. David Knight, *The Age of Science: The Scientific World-View in the Nineteenth Century* (Oxford, 1986). See, in particular, chapter 1.

21. Knight, *Natural Science Books in English 1600–1900*, p. 1. The word 'scientist' first appeared in a review of Mary Somerville's *On the Connexion of the Physical Sciences* (1834), in the *Quarterly Review* (ibid, p. 202).

22. Charles Babbage, *Reflections On the Decline of Science in England, and On Some of Its Causes* (London, 1830).

23. Roland Barthes, 'Science versus Literature', in *Structuralism: A Reader*, edited by Michael Lane (London, 1970), p. 411.

24. See, for instance, Crosbie Smith, 'Natural Philosophy and Thermodynamics: William Thomson and the "Dynamical Theory of Heat"', *British Journal of the Philosophy of Science*, 1 (1976), 293–319; James Paradis and Thomas Postlewait, eds, *Victorian Science and Victorian Values: Literary Perspectives* (New Brunswick, N.J., 1985); Peter Alan Dale, *In Pursuit of a Scientific Culture: Science, Art, and Society in the Victorian Age* (Madison, Wisconsin, 1989); Andrew Cunningham and Nicholas Jardine, eds, *Romanticism and the Sciences* (Cambridge, 1990).

25. Beer, 'Problems of Description in the Language of Discovery', p. 35.

26. Royal Institution, Davy Papers, MS 20c; Victoria College Library, University of Toronto S MS 29 1, f38. Quoted in Trevor H. Levere, *Poetry Realised in Nature: Samuel Taylor Coleridge and Early Nineteenth-Century Science* (Cambridge, 1981), p. 29.

27. See Christopher Lawrence, 'The Power and the Glory: Humphry Davy and Romanticism', in Cunningham and Jardine, pp. 220–21.

28. *Works of Davy*, II, 325.

29. *Works of Davy*, IX, 361.

30. Ibid, pp. 366–67.

31. Ibid, II, 315.

32. Locke, *Science as Writing*, p. 17.

33. Davy, 'The Bakerian Lecture, On Some New Phenomena of Chemical Changes Produced by Electricity, Particularly the Decomposition of Fixed Alkalies, and the Exhibition of the New Substances which Constitute their Bases; and on the General Nature of Alkaline Bodies', in *Works of Davy*, V, 57–58.

34. Ibid, pp. 59, 60–61.

35. *Works of Davy*, IX, 365–66.

36. *Works of Davy*, III, 2.

37. Ibid, pp. 276, 282–83.

38. Ibid, pp. 289–90.

39. Ibid, pp. 293–94.

40. Ibid, pp. 306, 307.

41. See L. Pearce Williams, *Michael Faraday: A Biography* (New York, 1971), pp. 66–71. My own brief account of the influence of Kantian ideas on early nineteenth-century science is indebted to Williams's full and convincingly argued discussion, pp. 59–71, 137–38.

42. *Works of Davy*, III, 291.

43. Quoted in Williams, p. 61.

44. Ibid, p. 62.

45. Christopher Lawrence, 'The Power and the Glory: Humphry Davy and Romanticism', p. 222. See also David M. Knight, *Atoms and Elements. A Study of Theories of Matter in England in the Nineteenth Century* (London, 1967).

46. Lawrence, p. 223.

47. James A. Secord, 'Darwin and the Breeders: A Social History', in *The Darwinian Heritage*, edited by David Kohn (Princeton, 1985), pp. 519–42 (p. 521).

48. See Donald R. Benson, 'Facts and Constructs: Victorian Humanists and Scientific Theorists on Scientific Knowledge', in Paradis and Postlewait, pp. 299–318 (pp. 299, 302).

49. See Basil Willey, *The Eighteenth Century Background: Studies on the Idea of Nature in the Thought of the Period* (London, 1965), chapter 3.

50. See Tess Cosslett, ed., *Science and Religion in the Nineteenth Century* (Cambridge, 1984), p. 2.

51. Sir William Thomson (Lord Kelvin), *Mathematical and Physical Papers . . . Collected from Different Scientific Periodicals from May, 1841, to the Present Time*, 6 vols (Cambridge, 1882–1911), I, 514; N. Katherine Hayles, 'Self-Reflexive Metaphors in Maxwell's Demon and Shannon's Choice', in *Literature and Science: Theory and Practice*, edited by Stuart Peterfreund (Boston, 1990), pp. 209–37

(pp. 215–16). See also Crosbie Smith, 'Natural Philosophy and Thermodynamics: William Thomson and the "Dynamical Theory of Heat"', *British Journal of the Philosophy of Science*, 1 (1976), 293–319.

52. Patrick Brantlinger, 'Victorians and Africans: The Genealogy of the Myth of the Dark Continent', in *'Race', Writing and Difference*, edited by Henry Louis Gates (Chicago and London, 1986), pp. 185–221 (p. 203); Walter F. Cannon, 'Darwin's Vision in *The Origin of Species*', in *The Art of Victorian Prose*, edited by George Levine and William Madden (New York, 1968), pp. 154–76 (p. 163).

53. Cannon, p. 164.

54. See the 'Introductory Conversation' between John C. Greene and James R. Moore in *History, Humanity and Evolution: Essays for John C. Greene*, edited by James R. Moore (Cambridge, 1989), pp. 1–38 (p. 6).

55. Charles Darwin, *The Origin of Species by Means of Natural Selection, or The Preservation of Favoured Races in the Struggle for Life*, edited by J. W. Burrow (Harmondsworth, 1968), p. 117. (This volume reprints the text of the first edition, 1859.)

56. Karl Marx and Frederick Engels, *Selected Correspondence* (Moscow, 1965), p. 128; Frederick Engels, *The Dialectics of Nature* (Moscow, 1964), pp. 35–36. More recent commentators have elaborated upon the question of the influence of Malthus's principle of population on Darwin's theory, and identified Adam Smith's principle of the division of labour as a central component in Darwin's theory of the divergence of character. See, for instance, Robert M. Young, 'Darwin and the Genre of Biography', in *One Culture: Essays in Science and Literature*, edited by George Levine (Madison, Wisconsin, 1987), pp. 203–24; and S. S. Schweber, 'Scientists as Intellectuals: The Early Victorians', in Paradis and Postlewait.

57. See Robert C. Bannister, *Social Darwinism: Science and Myth in Anglo-American Social Thought* (Philadelphia, 1979), pp. 3–4.

58. See, for instance, Adrian Desmond, *Archetypes and Ancestors: Palaeontology in Victorian London, 1850–1875* (London, 1982), pp. 158–64; Michael Helfand, 'T. H. Huxley's "Evolution and Ethics": The Politics of Evolution and the Evolution of Politics', *Victorian Studies*, 20 (1977), 157–77; and Eric J. Hobsbawm, *The Age of Capital, 1848–1875* (London, 1975), p. 268.

59. See Hayden White, 'The Fictions of Factual Representation', in *The Literature of Fact*, edited by Angus Fletcher (New York, 1976); rpt. in Hayden White, *Tropics of Discourse: Essays in Cultural Criticism* (Baltimore, 1978), p. 132.

60. James Moore, 'Socializing Darwinism: Historiography and the Fortunes of a Phrase', in *Science as Politics*, edited by Les Davidov (London, 1986), pp. 38–80 (p. 39). Robert M. Young, for example, has argued that 'Darwinism *is* Social', maintaining that 'the extrapolations from Darwinism to either humanity or society are not separable from Darwin's own views, nor are they chronologically subsequent. They are integral' (Robert M. Young, 'Darwinism *is* Social', in *The Darwinian Heritage*, edited by David Kohn, pp. 609–38 (p. 609)). They are indeed integral, despite the fact that, as Gillian Beer has emphasised, 'Darwin . . . did take considerable pains – not always successfully – to avoid legitimating current social order by naturalizing it' (Gillian Beer, '"The Face of Nature": Anthropomorphic Elements in the Language of *The Origin of Species*', in *Languages of Nature: Critical Essays on Science and Literature*, edited by L. J. Jordanova (London, 1986), pp. 207–43 (p. 215)).

61. Beer, '"The Face of Nature"', pp. 212, 221. My own discussion of Darwin is deeply indebted to Gillian Beer's brilliant revisionary account in this and other studies of his work.

62. See Gillian Beer, *Darwin's Plots: Evolutionary Narrative in Darwin, George Eliot and Nineteenth-Century Fiction* (London, 1983); Linda S. Bergmann, 'Reshaping the Roles of Man, God, and Nature: Darwin's Rhetoric in *The Origin of Species*', in *Beyond the Two Cultures: Essays on Science, Technology, and Literature*, edited by Joseph W. Slade and Judith Yaross Lee (Ames, Iowa, 1990); A. Dwight Culler, 'The Darwinian Revolution and Literary Form', in Levine and Madden, pp. 224–46; James Krasner, 'A Chaos of Delight: Perception and Illusion in Darwin's Scientific Writing', *Representations*, 31 (1990), 118–41; David Locke, *Science as Writing*, pp. 87–9; Michael Spindler, '*The Origin of Species* as Rhetoric', *Nineteenth-Century Prose*, 19 (1991), 26–34.

63. Beer, '"The Face of Nature"', pp. 236–37; Gillian Beer, 'Darwin's Reading and the Fictions of Development', in *The Darwinian Heritage*, edited by David Kohn, pp. 543–88 (pp. 543, 562).

64. Darwin, *Origin*, pp. 170, 132; Beer, *Darwin's Plots*, p. 71.

65. Darwin, *Origin*, p. 116.

66. Ibid, p. 97.

67. Ibid, pp. 399, 124–25.

68. See Beer, 'Darwin's Reading', pp. 575–76.

69. Darwin, *Origin*, pp. 293–94, 297.

70. See James Krasner, 'A Chaos of Delight: Perception and Illusion in Darwin's Scientific Writing', *Representations*, 31 (1990), 118–41 (p. 31).

71. Darwin, *Origin*, p. 296.

72. Ibid, pp. 130, 219.

73. Walter F. Cannon, 'Darwin's Vision in *The Origin of Species*', in Levine and Madden, pp. 154–76 (pp. 160–62).

74. *The Works of John Ruskin*, edited by E. T. Cook and Alexander Wedderburn, Library Edition, 39 vols (London, 1903–12), XXVI, 306.

75. Darwin, *Origin*, pp. 451, 419.

76. Ibid, pp. 125–26.

77. Ibid, p. 322.

78. Ibid, pp. 131–32. For conflicting interpretations of the politics of these passages and of Darwin's attitude towards imperialism see Cannon, 'Darwin's Vision', and Beer, 'Darwin's Reading', pp. 563–69.

79. Darwin, *Origin*, pp. 154, 392.

80. Charles Darwin, *The Descent of Man*, 2 vols (London, 1871), II, 326. Discussed in James Eli Adams, 'Woman Red in Tooth and Claw: Nature and the Feminine in Tennyson and Darwin', *Victorian Studies*, 33 (1989), 7–27 (p. 11).

81. Lewis Campbell and William Garnett, *The Life of James Clerk Maxwell, with selections from his correspondence and occasional writings* (London, 1894), p. 347.

82. Reprinted from *Nature*, 17, in *The Scientific Papers of James Clerk Maxwell*, edited by W. D. Niven, 2 vols (Cambridge, 1890), II, 660–61.

83. See Bram Dijkstra, *Idols of Perversity: Fantasies of Feminine Evil in Fin de Siècle Culture* (New York and Oxford, 1986), chapter 2, for a full discussion of the cult of invalidism.

84. T. H. Huxley to E. P. Wright, 8 March, 1862 (Imperial College London Archives, Huxley Papers, 29, 115). Quoted in Evelleen Richards, 'Huxley and Woman's Place in Science: The "Woman Question" and the Control of Victorian Anthropology', in Moore, *History Humanity and Revolution*, pp. 253–84 (p. 259). NB. some public speakers, such as John Ruskin, repeated their lectures for women audiences.

85. See Richards, 'Huxley and Woman's Place in Science'.

86. T. H. Huxley to Lyell, 17 March, 1860 (Huxley Papers, 30, 34). Quoted ibid, p. 256.

87. Quoted ibid, p. 260.

88. Jane Marcet, *Conversations on Political Economy; in which the elements of that science are familiarly explained* (London, 1816), pp. viii–ix. NB. some male writers, such as Ruskin in *Ethics of the Dust*, also wrote dialogue texts.

89. See Margaret Alic, *Hypatia's Heritage: A History of Women in Science from Antiquity to the Late Nineteenth Century* (London, 1986), pp. 176–78.

90. Quoted in Doris Langley Moore, *Ada Countess of Lovelace: Byron's Legitimate Daughter* (London, 1977), p. 157. For a more recent biographical study see Dorothy Stein, *Ada: A Life and a Legacy* (Cambridge, Massachusetts, and London, 1985). See also Joan Baum, *The Calculating Passion of Ada Byron* (Hamden, Connecticut, 1986).

91. Quoted in Alic, p. 160, from Maboth Moseley, *Irascible Genius: The Life of Charles Babbage* (London, 1964; rpt. Chicago, 1970), p. 182.

92. From a draft of her autobiography in the Somerville Collection, quoted in Alic, pp. 184–85.

93. See Alic, p. 182.

94. Robert Southey to Charlotte Brontë, quoted in Elizabeth Gaskell, *The Life of Charlotte Brontë*, edited by Alan Shelston (Harmondsworth, 1975), p. 173.

95. Darwin, *Origin*, p. 449.

96. See Beer, '"The Face of Nature"', p. 225; and John Tallmadge, 'From Chronicle to Quest: The Shaping of Darwin's *Voyage of the Beagle*', *Victorian Studies*, 23 (1980), 325–45.

97. New editions of texts by nineteenth-century women travellers have been recently republished in the Virago Travellers series, in the Century Travellers series, and by Beacon Press, and there is a significant secondary literature on Victorian women's travel writing (see General Bibliography).

98. David Livingstone, *Missionary Travels* (London, 1910), p. ix.

99. See Brantlinger, 'Victorians and Africans', p. 195.

100. The second edition of her narrative (first published in 1794) was published in 1802 in London by L. I. Higham under the title, *Narrative of Two Voyages to the River Sierra Leone, during the years 1791–2–3, performed by A. M. Falconbridge. With a Succinct account of the Distresses and proceedings of that Settlement; a description of the Manners, Diversions, Arts, Commerce, Cultivation, Custom, Punishments, &c. And Every interesting Particular relating to the Sierra Leone Company. Also The*

present State of the Slave Trade in the West Indies, and the improbability of its total Abolition. It was reprinted by Cass in facsimile in 1967.

101. Ibid, p. 119.

102. Ibid, pp. 15–16.

103. Ibid, pp. 16–17.

104. Ibid, pp. 23–24.

105. Ibid, p. 33.

106. Pratt, *Imperial Eyes*, p. 103.

107. See Deirdre Coleman, 'Conspicuous Consumption: White Abolitionism and English Women's Protest Writing in the 1890s', *ELH*, 61 (1994), 341–62. See also her 'Sierra Leone, Slavery, and Sexual Politics: Anna Maria Falconbridge and the "swarthy daughter" of late 18th century abolitionism', *Women's Writing*, 2 (1995), 3–23, which first brought Falconbridge to my attention.

108. A. M. Falconbridge, *Two Voyages*, p. 22.

109. Ibid, pp. 64–65.

110. Ibid, pp. 64, 121–22.

111. Ibid, pp. 233, 236–38.

112. Harriet Martineau, *Society in America*, edited and abridged by Seymour Martin Lipset (New York, 1962), pp. 206–7.

113. Harriet Ward, *Five Years in Kaffirland; with Sketches of the Late War in that Country, to the Conclusion of Peace, 'Written on the Spot'*, 2 vols (London, 1848), I, 34–35, 27–28.

114. Ibid, I, 204.

115. Ibid, II, 281.

116. I am indebted to an unpublished paper on Harriet Ward by Jenny de Rueck, of Murdoch University, delivered at The University of Western Australia in 1993.

117. Ward, *Five Years in Kaffirland*, II, 111. See also, for his other so-called qualities, II, 33, 45, 179.

118. Ibid, II, 127–28.

119. Ibid, II, 129, 139.

120. Ibid, II, 234.

121. Ibid, II, 36.

122. Ibid, II, 192–94.

123. Ibid, II, 233–34.

124. See Brantlinger, 'Victorians and Africans', pp. 185–86; and Coleman, 'Conspicuous Consumption', p. 341.

125. See John Mackenzie's inaugural lecture on the role of the Scots as builders of Empire, *Scotland and the Empire* (University of Lancaster, 1992).

126. Livingstone, *Missionary Travels*, pp. 25–34, 79.

127. Ibid, pp. 79–80.

128. Ibid, p. 24.

129. See Pratt, *Imperial Eyes*, pp. 84, 82.

130. Livingstone, *Missionary Travels*, pp. 16–17.

131. Ibid, p. 166.

132. Ibid, p. 128.

133. Ibid, p. 90.

134. Ibid, pp. 163–64.

135. Pratt makes a similar point about Mungo Park, in *Imperial Eyes*, p. 81.

136. Livingstone, *Missionary Travels*, p. 56.

137. Ibid, pp. 444–45.

138. Ibid, pp. 56, 90, 187, 203, 85.

139. Ibid, pp. 16, 104.

140. Ibid, pp. 42–43.

141. Ibid, p. 196.

142. Ibid, p. 17.

143. Ibid, p. 109.

144. Ibid, p. 94.

145. Ibid, p. 94.

146. Ibid, pp. 144–45.

147. Ibid, p. 11.

148. Ibid, p. 200.

149. Ibid, p. 7.

150. Ibid, p. 1.

151. Ibid, p. 3.

152. Ibid, p. 215.

153. Ibid, p. 74.

154. See Pratt, *Imperial Eyes*, p. 215.

155. Mary H. Kingsley, *Travels in West Africa: Congo Français, Corisco and Camaroons*, 3rd edn, introduction by John E. Flint (London, 1965), pp. 213, 211.

156. Ibid, p. 544.

157. Ibid, p. 534.

158. Mary H. Kingsley, *West African Studies*, 3rd edn, introduction by John E. Flint (London, 1964), pp. 324–27.

159. Kingsley, *Travels in West Africa*, p. 219.

160. Ibid, p. 216.

161. Kingsley, *West African Studies*, p. 387.

162. Ibid, p. 390.

163. Ibid, pp. 321, 322; Kingsley, *Travels in West Africa*, pp. 224, 225, 526.

164. Kingsley, *Travels in West Africa*, pp. 554–64.

165. Ibid, p. 550.

166. Kingsley, *Travels in West Africa*, p. 659, quoted in Dea Birkett and Julie Wheelwright, '"How could she?" Unpalatable Facts and Feminists' Heroines', *Gender and History*, 2 (1990), 49–57 (p. 55), upon which I draw here.

167. *West African Studies*, p. 330; Birkett and Wheelwright, '"How could she?"', p. 55.

168. Kingsley, *West African Studies*, p. 315.

169. Ibid, p. 320.

170. Ibid, p. 327.

171. Kingsley, *Travels in West Africa*, pp. 221–22.

172. Kingsley, *West African Studies*, p. 326.

173. Quoted ibid, p. 325, from H. Clifford *East Coast Etchings* (Singapore, 1896).

174. *Works of Ruskin*, X, 400–1.

175. Ibid, XXIII, 27–28.

176. Ibid, XXIX, 18, 33, 21.

177. See *Ruskin's Letters from Venice, 1851–1852*, edited by John Lewis Bradley (New Haven, Connecticut, 1955), pp. 31–32; *Ruskin in Italy: Letters to his Parents, 1845*, edited by Harold I. Shapiro (Oxford, 1972), pp. 52, 61, 76, 128–29; Bodl. MS. Eng. Lett. C.33, fos. 31–35, quoted in Jeanne Clegg, *Ruskin and Venice* (London, 1981), pp. 81–84.

178. *Ruskin in Italy*, pp. 201–2.

179. Ibid, pp. 198–99.

180. *Works of Ruskin*, IX, xxx; Charles Dickens, *Pictures from Italy*, edited by David Paroissien (London, 1973), pp. 200–1.

181. Dickens, *Pictures from Italy*, pp. 160–61.

182. Ibid, p. 215.

183. Ibid, p. 201. On Dickens's horror of the past, see Steven Marcus, *Dickens: From Pickwick to Dombey* (London, 1965), p. 304.

184. *Works of Ruskin*, VI, 11–12; I, 14–15.

185. Frances Trollope, *Domestic Manners of the Americans*, edited by Donald Smalley (New York, 1949), p. 312.

186. Ibid, pp. 268–69.

187. Ibid, pp. 267.

188. Ibid, pp. 160–61.

189. Ibid, p. 316.

190. Ibid, p. 409.

191. Martineau, *Society in America*, p. 126.

192. Ibid, p. 291.

193. Quoted from Anthony Trollope, *North America* (London, 1862), in *America through British Eyes*, edited by Allan Nevins (New York, 1948), p. 222.

194. See Robin Gilmour, *The Idea of the Gentleman in the Victorian Novel* (London, 1981).

195. Matthew Arnold, *Civilization in the United States*, in *The Last Word, The Complete Prose Works of Matthew Arnold*, edited by R. H. Super, 11 vols (Ann Arbor, Michigan, 1960–77), XI, 350–69 (p. 363).

196. Ibid, p. 353.

197. See Allan Nevins' editorial introduction to the extract from Cobbett's *A Year's Residence in the United States of America*, in *America Through British Eyes*, pp. 62–64.

198. William Cobbett, *A Year's Residence in the United States of America*, introduced by J. E. Morpurgo (Fontwell, Sussex, 1964), pp. 180–81.

199. Ibid, pp. 47–48.

200. Ibid, pp. 49–50.

201. Charles Dickens, *American Notes, and Pictures from Italy*, introduced by Sacheverell Sitwell (London, 1957), p. 252.

202. Dickens, *American Notes, and Pictures from Italy*, pp. 69–70.

203. Ibid, p. 68. Elizabeth Gaskell, in her fiction, frequently makes a similar point.

204. Ibid, p. 119.

205. *The Works of Charles Dickens*, 20 vols (New York, 1903), XVIII, 64, 63.

206. See Brantlinger, 'Victorians and Africans', p. 193.

207. Jack London, *The People of the Abyss* (London, 1903), pp. 2–3.

208. Charles Dickens, *Oliver Twist*, edited by Kathleen Tillotson (Oxford and New York, 1982), pp. 320, 352. The preface to the 1850 edition is reprinted as an appendix, pp. 351–53. For a full account of the meeting of the Metropolitan Sanitary Association at which the Bishop of London made his speech, and Dickens himself was the principal speaker, see *The Speeches of Charles Dickens*, ed. K. J. Fielding (Oxford, 1960), pp. 104–10.

209. By which time there had been an improvement in the economy.

210. Henry Mayhew, *The 'Morning Chronicle' Survey of Labour and the Poor: The Metropolitan Districts*, 6 vols (1849–50; reprinted, Firle, 1980–82), I, 31–39 (pp. 32–33, 37). For another contemporary account of the area, see Thomas Beames, *The Rookeries of London* (London, 1850), p. 81.

211. W. M. Thackeray, 'Waiting at the Station', *Punch*, 18 (1850), 93; George Sims, *How the Poor Live* (London, 1889; reprinted New York, 1984), p. 1. Quoted in *Into Unknown England 1866–1913: Selections from the Social Explorers*, edited by Peter Keating (Manchester, 1976), p. 15.

212. Edwin Chadwick, *Report on the Sanitary Condition of the Labouring Population of Great Britain*, edited by M. W. Flinn (Edinburgh, 1965), p. 397. See Gertrude Himmelfarb, *The Idea of Poverty: England in the Early Industrial Age* (London, 1984), pp. 356–57.

213. Henry Mayhew, *London Labour and the London Poor: A Cyclopaedia of the Condition and Earnings of Those that Will Work, Those that Cannot Work, and Those that Will Not Work*, 4 vols (1861–62, reprinted London, 1967), I, iii.

214. See the introduction to Keating, pp. 11–32, for a full discussion of the language of exploration and its uses in Victorian social reportage.

215. See Himmelfarb, pp. 404–5.

216. See *The Victorian Novelist: Social Problems and Social Change*, edited by Kate Flint (London, 1987), p. 8.

217. J[ames] P[hillips] Kay, *The Moral and Physical Condition of the Working Classes employed in the Cotton Manufacture in Manchester*, 2nd edn (London, 1932), p. 21. Quoted in Lynn H. Lees, 'Patterns of Lower-Class Life: Irish Slum Communities in Nineteenth-Century London', in *Nineteenth-Century Cities: Essays in the New Urban History*, edited by Stephan Thernstrom and Richard Sennett (New Haven, Connecticut, 1969), pp. 359–85 (p. 360).

218. Thomas Carlyle, 'Chartism', in *Critical and Miscellaneous Essays*, 3 vols (London, 1888), III, 271–72.

219. Frederick Engels, *The Condition of the Working Class in England, From Personal Observation and Authentic Sources*, edited by Eric Hobsbawm (St Albans, 1969), pp. 124–25.

220. Ibid, p. 154.

221. Mayhew, *London Labour*, I, 1–3.

222. See Gertrude Himmelfarb, 'The Culture of Poverty', in *The Victorian City: Images and Realities*, edited by H. J. Dyos and Michael Wolff, 2 vols (London, 1973), II, 707–36 (p. 712).

223. John McLennan, 'The Early History of Man', *North British Review*, 50 (1868), 272–90 (pp. 286–88).

224. James Greenwood, *The Seven Curses of London* (London, 1869), p. 47. Quoted in Keating, p. 17.

225. James Greenwood, 'A Visit to "Tiger Bay"', in *The Wilds of London* (London, 1874; reprinted New York, 1985), pp. 1–11.

226. Ibid, p. 7.

227. See, for instance, Mary Poovey on Mayhew, in *Uneven Developments: The Ideological Work of Gender in Mid-Victorian England* (Chicago, 1988), pp. 15, 131; Nancy Armstrong on Mayhew, in *Desire and Domestic Fiction: A Political History of the Novel* (New York, 1987), p. 182; Gill Davies on working-class fiction, in 'Foreign Bodies: Images of the London Working Class at the end of the 19th Century', *Literature and History*, 14 (1988), 64–80 (75–76).

228. General William Booth, *In Darkest England and the Way Out*, 6th edition (London, 1970), pp. 9, 11–12.

229. Ibid, p. 16.

230. Ibid, p. 24.

231. Ibid, pp. 90–93.

232. Ibid, pp. 9, 13, 15.

233. George R. Sims, *How the Poor Live* and *Horrible London* (London, 1889; reprinted New York, 1984), pp. 1–2.

234. See Gill Davies, 'Foreign Bodies: Images of the London Working Class at the end of the Nineteenth Century', *Literature and History*, 14 (1988), 64–80.

235. Mayhew, *London Labour*, I, iii.

236. See the accounts of such outings by George R. Sims in *Glances Back* (London, 1917) and Captain Donald Shaw, in *London in the Sixties by One of the Old Brigade* (London, 1908).

237. See Eileen Yeo, 'Mayhew as a Social Investigator', in *The Unknown Mayhew: Selections from the* Morning Chronicle *1849–1850*, edited by E. P. Thompson and Eileen Yeo (London, 1971), pp. 66–67.

238. Quoted in the introduction to *Charles Booth's London: A Portrait of the Poor at the Turn of the Century drawn from his* Life and Labour of the People in London, edited by Albert Fried and Richard Elman (Harmondsworth, 1971), p. 21.

239. See, for example, Sheila Smith, 'Willenhall and Wodgate: Disraeli's Use of Blue Book Evidence', *Review of English Studies*, N.S.2 (1962), 368–84; Sheila Smith, 'Blue Books and Victorian Novelists', *Review of English Studies*, 21 (1970), 23–40; Martin Fido, 'The Treatment of Rural Distress in Disraeli's *Sybil*', *The Yearbook of English Studies*, 5 (1975), 153–63; Martin Fido, '"From His Own Observation": Sources of Working-class Passages in Disraeli's *Sybil*', *Modern Languages Review*, 72 (1977), 268–84; Anne Humphreys, *Travels into the Poor Man's Country: The Work of Henry Mayhew* (London, 1977).

240. See Himmelfarb, 'The Culture of Poverty', pp. 708, 727, 714. Both Himmelfarb and Brantlinger remark on the frequency with which the adage 'truth is stranger than fiction' was invoked in contemporary critical commentary on blue books and other social reportage.

241. See, for example, Christopher Herbert, 'Rat Worship and Taboo in Mayhew's London', *Representations*, 23 (1988), 1–24; Gill Davies, 'Foreign Bodies'.

242. See Davies, 'Foreign Bodies,' p. 64.

243. See Flint, p. 2.

244. Mayhew, *London Labour*, III, 4, quoted in Yeo, 'Mayhew as a Social Investigator', p. 69.

245. See Himmelfarb, 'The Culture of Poverty', pp. 724–25, 735n.

246. See Wolf Lepenies, *Between Literature and Science: the Rise of Sociology*, trans. R. J. Hollingdale (Cambridge, 1988), p. 7.

247. Theodore M. Porter, *The Rise of Statistical Thinking 1820–1900* (Princeton, N.J., 1986), p. 9.

248. See Mary Poovey, 'Figures of Arithmetic, Figures of Speech: The Discourse of Statistics in the 1830s', *Critical Inquiry* 19 (1993), 256–76 (pp. 258–59). According to Poovey, the hybrid nature of statistical discourse has to do partly with the historical circumstances in which statistics was institutionalised as a discipline (and reflects the competing claims of Newtonian 'truth' and the imperative of social reform associated with Britain's industrialisation and urbanisation), partly with the inherent contradiction between 'the ambitions of the discourse to "map" the world and the peculiar limitations statisticians imposed on this form of representation'.

249. On the development of statistics in the nineteenth century, see Asa Briggs, 'The Human Aggregate', in *The Victorian City: Images and Realities*, edited by H. J. Dyos and Michael Wolff, I, 83–104; see also Porter, op. cit., and Poovey, op. cit.

250. William Cobbett, *Rural Rides*, edited by George Woodcock (Harmondsworth, 1967), pp. 80–81.

251. Ibid, pp. 17–18.

252. Charles Booth, *Life and Labour of the People in London*, 2nd series: *Industry* (1903), I, 18. Quoted in Briggs, 'The Human Aggregate', p. 93.

253. Peter Gaskell, *The Manufacturing Population of England, its Moral, Social, and Physical Conditions, and the Changes which have arisen from the Use of Steam Machinery, with an Examination of Infant Labour* (London, 1833), p. 341.

254. W. Cooke Taylor, *The Handbook of Silk, Cotton, and Woollen Manufacturers* (London, 1843), p. 201.

255. Engels, *The Condition of the Working Class in England*, pp. 78–81.

256. Ibid, pp. 84–85.

257. Ibid, pp. 84, 85, 87.

258. Lord Ashley, 'Employment of Women and Children in Mines and Collieries' (June 7, 1842), Hansard, 63, 1320–64, (pp. 1326–27).

259. Ibid, 1328.

260. Ibid, 1329.

261. Ibid, 1352.

262. Ibid, 1350–51.

263. William, Dodd, *Narrative of the Experience and Sufferings of William Dodd, Factory Cripple* (London, 1841), p. 27.

264. [Henry Morley], 'Ground in the Mill', *Household Words*, 9 (22 April 1854), 224–27; reprinted in *The Victorian Novelist: Social Problems and Social Change*, edited by Kate Flint, pp. 86–92 (pp. 87–88).

265. Ibid, p. 88.

266. Ibid, p. 86.

267. Ibid, p. 90.

268. [Charles Dickens], 'On Strike', *Household Words*, 8 (11 February, 1854), 553–59; reprinted in *The Victorian Novelist*, edited by Flint, pp. 59–73.

269. Ibid, p. 60.

270. Ibid, p. 73.

271. Ibid, p. 61.

272. Ibid, p. 73.

273. Ibid, p. 73.

274. See Yeo, 'Mayhew as a Social Investigator', pp. 52–53, 64–65, 88–89 for a discussion of the range of social reportage in the period.

275. Henry Mayhew, 'Answers to Correspondents', No. 34 (2 August), quoted in Yeo, 'Mayhew as a Social Investigator', p. 74.

276. *The Unknown Mayhew*, Letter II, p. 605. Quoted in Yeo, 'Mayhew as a Social Investigator', p. 57.

277. See Yeo, 'Mayhew as a Social Investigator', p. 57.

278. See Nancy Armstrong, *Desire and Domestic Fiction: A Political History of the Novel* (New York and Oxford, 1987), p. 180.

279. Ibid, p. 181.

280. Mayhew, *London Labour*, IV, 35.

281. See Armstrong, p. 181.

282. Joseph Adshead, *Distress in Manchester: Evidence (Tabular and Otherwise) of The State of the Labouring Classes in 1840–42* (London, 1842), pp. 15–16.

283. Ashley, 'Employment of Women and Children in Mines and Collieries', Hansard, 63, 1327.

284. Ibid, 1335.

285. Mayhew, *London Labour*, IV, 273.

286. See Poovey, *Uneven Developments*, p. 15.

287. The *Times*, 6 May, 1857; [W. R. Greg] *The Great Sin of Great Cities*, 1853. See also the *Lancet*, 20 January, 1855. Quoted in the introduction to *Prostitution in the Victorian Age: Debates on the Issue from 19th Century Critical Journals*, edited by Keith Nield (Farnborough, 1973), pp. 1–2. (This is a useful collection of reprints of articles on prostitution from the *Westminster Review*.)

288. Quoted ibid, p. 3.

289. See Himmelfarb, 'The Culture of Poverty,' p. 731.

290. See Herbert, 'Rat Worship and Taboo', pp. 10–12.

291. See Catherine Gallagher, 'The Body Versus the Social Body in the Works of Thomas Malthus and Henry Mayhew', *Representations*, 14 (1986), 83–106; Himmelfarb, 'The Culture of Poverty'.

292. See Himmelfarb, 'The Culture of Poverty', p. 719.

293. *Morning Chronicle*, Letter IV (30 October, 1849).

294. For a full assessment of Mayhew's contribution to the history of social investigation see Yeo, 'Mayhew as a Social Investigator', in *The Unknown Mayhew: Selections from the* Morning Chronicle *1849–1850*, pp. 51–95.

295. See the introduction to *Charles Booth's London*, edited by Albert Fried and Richard M. Elman, pp. 31–32, for a discussion of the gap between his radical work as an investigator and his conservative evaluation of and solutions to the problem of poverty.

296. Beatrice Webb, *My Apprenticeship* (London, 1926), pp. 173–74.

297. Friedrich Nietzsche, *Beyond Good and Evil*, trans. Walter Kaufmann (New York, 1966), p. 160.

Chapter 2
Life Stories

How inexpressibly comfortable to know our fellow-creature; to
see into him, understand his goings-forth, decipher the whole
heart of his mystery: nay, not only to see into him, but even
to see out of him, to view the world altogether as he views it;
so that we can theoretically construe him, and could almost
practically personate him; and do now thoroughly discern both
what manner of man he is, and what manner of thing he has
got to work on and live on!

(Thomas Carlyle)[1]

It is no mere coincidence that the new emphasis placed upon the significance of the self and the importance of individual experience by the
German transcendentalist philosophers (whom Carlyle so admired) and
by the English Romantic poets was accompanied by a voracious appetite for reading and writing life stories which prevailed throughout the
nineteenth century. In an age famous equally for its nurture and refinement of the cult of personality and for its investigative fervour, life
narratives flourished in an unprecedented way. Alongside that proliferation of published lives which has seemed to some later commentators,
such as Lytton Strachey, to typify the period – biographies, memoirs,
reminiscences, autobiographies – there existed a vigorous culture of
private life-writing, in the form of letters, journals, and diaries, some of
which, nevertheless, became available for public consumption, if not in
their day then in our own.

It is not always easy to distinguish between public and private utterance in the domain of life-writing, as Oscar Wilde brilliantly suggests
in *The Importance of Being Earnest* (1895) when he has Cecily respond to
Algernon's request to look at her diary by covering it with her hand
and saying 'Oh, no. You see, it is simply a young girl's record of her
own thoughts and impressions, and consequently meant for publication. When it appears in volume form I hope you will order a copy.'[2]
Moreover, in formal terms, the various sub-genres of life-writing
frequently converge. This occurs most notably in the predominant Victorian biographical mode, the 'Life and Letters', in which the biography

is bolstered and validated by the documentary evidence of selected letters, but there are also numerous individual examples of publications which draw upon more than one genre in the project of writing the self. The boundaries between autobiography and biography are not always strictly observed.[3] Thomas De Quincey's biographical 'Lake Papers' on Wordsworth and Coleridge, for instance, first published in Tait's *Edinburgh Magazine* in the 1830s, appeared in 1854 under the title 'Autobiographic Sketches', and constitute an intriguing generic mixture of biography, autobiography, political and philosophical discussion, literary criticism, gossip, and farce. Another text which is hard to classify is *Sartor Resartus: The life and opinions of Herr Teufelsdrockh* (1833–34). It has conventionally been regarded as the ironically displaced spiritual autobiography of Carlyle, but both the sub-title and the discourse suggest an intertextual reworking of Boswell's *Life of Johnson*, the new edition of which, edited by John Wilson Croker, Carlyle had reviewed in 1831.[4] Other examples of generic ambiguity abound. A famous instance of an autobiography masquerading as a biography is the *Life of Hardy* (1928–30), which was ostensibly by his second wife, but was in fact mainly dictated to her by the novelist himself. Another work which is part autobiography and part biography is John Forster's *Life of Charles Dickens* (1872–74). Not only are the most memorable passages of this life extracts from Dickens's own autobiographical recollections, but the biographical enterprise of writing his friend's life involved Forster himself in an act of autobiography. Indeed, Wilkie Collins described the work as 'The Life of John Forster with occasional anecdotes of Charles Dickens.'[5]

For women writing their own or others' biographical narratives, there were particular and complex reasons, to do with the ideological delineation of the female sphere as private and secluded, for circumspection in the matter of life-writing, and for operating across and between conventional generic boundaries. Biography enabled an individual to gain access to recorded history through the life of a more celebrated figure. Women, in particular, often seized the opportunity of entering the sphere of public discourse by inscribing their own lives surreptitiously into the biographies of their famous male relatives or associates.[6] Women adopted various strategies in order to justify publication in a genre generally considered inappropriate for women. Susanna Winkforth, for example, when asked 'by many friends' to write a memorial of her sister's life, seized the opportunity to write her own life too, and produced *Memorials of Two Sisters, Susanna and Catherine Winkworth*.[7] Mother and daughter conspire in playing down the autobiographical pretensions of Mary Somerville's account of her life, for the title-page reads '*Personal Recollections from early life to old age, of Mary Somerville*, with Selections from her Correspondence, by her daughter Martha Somerville', and the introductory chapter opens with the reassuring apology:

The life of a woman entirely devoted to her family duties and to scientific pursuits affords little scope for a biography. There are in it neither stirring events nor brilliant deeds to record; and as my Mother was strongly averse to gossip, and to revelations of private life or of intimate correspondence, nothing of the kind will be found in the following pages. It has been only after very great hesitation, and on the recommendation of valued friends, who think that some account of so remarkable and beautiful a character cannot fail to interest the public, that I have resolved to publish some detached Recollections of past times, noted down by my mother during the last years of her life, together with a few letters from eminent men and women, referring almost exclusively to her scientific works. A still smaller number of her own letters have been added, either as illustrating her opinions on events she witnessed, or else as affording some slight idea of her simple and loving disposition.[8]

No one could accuse this 'biography', based on 'detached Recollections' and 'letters from eminent men and women', and published only under pressure from valued friends, of being so hubristic as to consider itself an autobiography.

Many women of the period felt excluded from the masculine genre of formal autobiography, and displaced their impulse to write about themselves into letters and journals, and therefore it is appropriate to consider these more private genres as constituting women's autobiography.[9] By contrast, polemical feminist texts on contemporary social issues pertaining to the 'woman question', such as Florence Nightingale's *Cassandra* and Caroline Norton's *English Laws for Women*, drawing as they so powerfully do upon the personal experiences of their authors, may also be classified as autobiographies. And both men and women of the period were in the habit of introducing personal recollections into their writings on no matter what subject, from literary criticism to the theological treatise to the domestic manual.[10]

Just as the different sub-genres of life-writing converge and intersect in interesting ways in the nineteenth century, so do they interrelate with other kinds of writing. If we are tempted to categorise life stories as belonging to a personal, subjective mode of writing, it is salutary to recall that nineteenth-century biographers and even autobiographers like Mary Somerville often made a practice of expunging 'revelations of private life' from their texts, and regarded thorough research and factual accuracy as more essential to their task. To this extent, biography, in particular, is closely aligned to the scientific and empirical spirit of the age in its project to represent the objective 'truth' of an individual's life, even though the commemorative impulse often meant that, where the facts of a person's private life undermined or compromised their public persona, the truth was actually suppressed in the interests of discretion.[11]

Carlyle was properly sceptical for other reasons about the perception of life-writing as a mere compilation of factual information: 'What are your historical Facts; still more your biographical?' he demanded in 1834. 'Wilt thou know a Man, above all a Mankind, by stringing together beadrolls of what thou namest Facts?'[12] Nevertheless, he distinguishes between fictional and biographical writing in ways which suggest the importance of a concept of 'truth' to his definition of life-writing, arguing that fiction, by contrast, 'partakes, more than we suspect, of the nature of *lying*'.[13] For Carlyle, as for many other biographers of the period, life stories were closely related to another prominent nineteenth-century discourse, historical writing. 'Of History,' he exclaims, 'the most honoured, if not honourable species of composition, is not the whole purport Biographic?' In his view, history should be 'the essence of innumerable Biographies'.[14] John Robert Seeley, who was appointed to the Regius Chair of History at Cambridge University in 1869, whilst a quite different kind of historian and biographer from Carlyle, similarly found important connections between historiography and life-writing, if only for the reason that, in his view, 'The mass of mankind, those who will have little leisure for reading, and no motive for it but amusement, will not read any more about states and governments than can be presented to them in the biographies of famous men.'[15] The fact that the characteristic Victorian biography was in the 'Life and Times' mode in itself suggests the powerful relation between life-writing and history in the period.

But if the great efflorescence of biographical and autobiographical writing in the nineteenth century can be related to the new reverence for 'facts' engendered by contemporary developments in scientific and historiographical method, then it can just as clearly be associated with popular styles of fiction writing in the period. The project of Realist fiction was, like that of biography, to delineate the lives of representative individuals in the context of the contemporary social conditions which shaped and constrained them, and which they helped to produce. Like the *Bildungsroman*, biography and autobiography typically follow conventional chronology and an archetypal developmental plot; often the hero (the protagonists of both fiction and non-fiction genres are generally male) struggles against the odds to achieve success through his own efforts, affirming the ideology of 'self-help'. This is the pattern of, say, John Forster's *Life of Dickens*, which manifests clear formal parallels with Dickens's 'autobiographical' *Bildungsroman, David Copperfield*. Moreover, as Virginia Woolf points out, 'The biographer's imagination is always being stimulated to use the novelist's art of arrangement, suggestion, dramatic effect to expound the private life.'[16] In short, for all their claims to rest upon fact, life narratives of all kinds, whether biographies, autobiographies, letters or journals, depend to a greater or lesser degree upon fictional conventions for their effect. Insofar as they can be said to give us the fact of a person's life, it is what Woolf calls 'the creative fact; the fertile fact; the fact that suggests and engenders'.[17]

Biography

Those two fat volumes, with which it is our custom to commemorate the dead – who does not know them, with their ill-digested masses of material, their slipshod style, their tone of tedious panegyric, their lamentable lack of selection, of detachment, of design? They are as familiar as the *cortège* of the undertaker, and wear the same air of slow, funereal barbarism. One is tempted to suppose, of some of them, that they were composed by that functionary, as the final item of his job.

(Lytton Strachey)[18]

Lytton Strachey's witty characterisation of the Standard Victorian Biography in *Eminent Victorians* (1918) reminds us that biographies – Strachey's own iconoclastic brief lives, no less than the weighty and ponderous 'two fat volumes' of the Victorians – are fundamentally shaped by the historical moment of their production, and embedded in its cultural language and ideologies. For the biographers of the new century, the cumbersome *Lives* of the old were as aesthetically offensive as was that 'loose, baggy monster', the Victorian novel, to the refined sensibility of Henry James, and Strachey offers instead a series of 'haphazard visions' of his 'eminent Victorians', preserving a 'becoming brevity – a brevity which excludes everything that is redundant and nothing that is significant'.[19] The high moral tone of the earlier generation was no less antithetical to modern tastes. Virginia Woolf complained that 'the Victorian biographer was dominated by the idea of goodness. Noble, upright, chaste, severe; it is thus that the Victorian worthies are presented to us.'[20] In his 'new biography', Strachey countered the 'tedious panegyric' favoured by his predecessors with the promise 'to lay bare the facts . . . as I understand them, dispassionately, impartially, and without ulterior intentions'.[21]

Strachey's caricature of nineteenth-century biography was extravagant and totalising but, like all good caricatures, a recognisable exaggeration of the truth. There were, first of all, an enormous number of biographies produced in the nineteenth century. Oscar Wilde's Ernest and Gilbert, discussing biography in 'The Critic as Artist' (1891), describe 'our industrious compilers of Lives and Recollections' as 'the pest of the age':

> Every great man nowadays has his disciples, and it is always
> Judas who writes the biography . . . Formerly we used to
> canonise our heroes. The modern method is to vulgarise them.
> Cheap editions of great books may be delightful, but cheap
> editions of great men are absolutely detestable . . . We are
> overrun by a set of people who, when poet or painter passes
> away, arrive at the house along with the undertaker, and forget
> that their one duty is to behave as mutes . . . They are the
> mere body-snatchers of literature. The dust is given to one,
> and the ashes to another, and the soul is out of their reach.[22]

That most prolific of biographers, Leslie Stephen, himself commented in 1898 of another famous Victorian biographer, J. A. Froude, that he was 'perhaps the most eminent man of letters of his generation who has not become the victim of a biography'.[23] H. Paul's *Life of Froude*, published in 1905, was soon to remedy this omission, but even those who were destined never to become the victims of a full-blown biography generally escaped the fate of 'England's forgotten worthies' memorialised by Froude in an article of 1852, and found inclusion in one of the many collections of brief lives which enjoyed a vogue in the period, culminating with that great late Victorian cultural project, *The Dictionary of National Biography* (1885–1900).

While the massive multi-volume study – one thinks, for example, of Lockhart's seven-volume *Life of Sir Walter Scott* (1837–38), Froude's four-volume *Life of Carlyle* (1882–84), and John Morley's three-volume *Life of Gladstone* (1903) – remained the standard form of the nineteenth-century biography, Strachey's objections to its inclusiveness and general bulk were anticipated by many a Victorian reviewer. For example, in a review of Carlyle's *Life of John Sterling* (1851), George Eliot remarks:

> We have often wished that genius would incline itself more
> frequently to the task of the biographer, – that when some
> great or good personage dies, instead of the dreary three or
> five volumed compilation of letter, and diary, and detail, little
> to the purpose, which two thirds of the reading public have
> not the chance, nor the other third the inclination, to read, we
> could have a real 'Life', setting forth briefly and vividly the
> man's inward and outward struggles, aims, and achievements,
> so as to make clear the meaning which his experience has for
> his fellows.[24]

Carlyle had himself regretted, in 1838, that Lockhart had not published his *Life of Sir Walter Scott* in one volume instead of seven, commenting: 'There is a great discovery still to be made in Literature, that of paying literary men by the quantity they *do not* write.'[25]

Carlyle laments the fact that Lockhart's seven-volume 'compilation' of 'all such letters, documents and notices about Scott as he found lying suitable', 'intelligibly bound together by order of time, and by some requisite intercalary exposition', was not, rather, a one-volume 'composition', but concedes that 'the public so required it'.[26] This was certainly true when Carlyle made the observation in 1838. Like the 'triple-decker' novel, which was the staple form for nineteenth-century fiction, the multivolume biography of an exemplary figure, the real-life *Bildungsroman*, was immensely popular in a period when the reading aloud of improving and uplifting literature was a significant middle-class family leisure activity, and such monumental lives sold very well to both individuals and circulating libraries. Their properties of expansiveness and weightiness were part and parcel of their dual role as morally instructive entertainment. However, as the century wore on, more and more reviewers and readers demanded briefer and more shaped interpretative biographies, after the manner of Plutarch's *Lives* or Johnson's *Lives of the Poets*. As one reviewer put it, 'We want to see a portrait, not an inventory of the features possessed by the subject.'[27]

Such demands led to something of a fashion for collective lives, which offered a quite different kind of biographical narrative from the compendious, multi-volumed accumulation of material represented by the standard nineteenth-century biography. The periodical press had always offered scope for the brief life, and continued to do so throughout the century, giving writers such as Thomas De Quincey, George Eliot, and Harriet Martineau a suitable forum for their witty and learned biographical sketches. But increasingly popular were biographical dictionaries and biographies in series.

Some, like the early nineteenth-century *Universal Biographical Dictionary*, edited by John Watkins, and the aborted *Biographical Dictionary* (began in 1842 and abandoned in 1846) produced by the Society for the Diffusion of Useful Knowledge, were devoted exclusively to biographical entries; other publications, such as *The Penny Cyclopedia*, which was aimed at a working-class readership, and Lardner's encyclopaedias, to which Mary Shelley contributed some thirty-five biographies of eminent Europeans in the 1830s, were of a more general nature but gave a great deal of space to exemplary lives. Others again looked at particular categories of lives: Jane Williams published *Literary Women of England* (1861); Charlotte M. Yonge edited a volume of *Biographies of Good Women* (1862); W. H. Davenport Adams a compilation of the *Child-Life and Girlhood of Remarkable Women* (1883); Samuel Smiles numerous collective biographies, the most famous and influential of which was his *Lives of the Engineers* (1861–62); Julia Kavanagh and Gertrude Mayer volumes of *Women of Letters* (in 1862 and 1894 respectively); and John Morley the series entitled *Twelve English Statesmen* in the late 1880s and the *English Men of Letters Series*, which began appearing in 1878 and continued over the next four decades.

The biographical subjects might be contemporary figures, as in Hazlitt's *Spirit of the Age: or Contemporary Portraits*, or historical figures, as in Thackeray's *English Humorists of the 18th Century*; heroic successes, as in *Heroes of Industry* (1866), *Heroes of the Telegraph* (1891), and Carlyle's more famous *On Heroes and Hero Worship* (1841), or ignominious failures, as in a volume entitled *Wrecked Lives; or, Men Who Have Failed.*[28]

But it was the publication of the *Dictionary of National Biography* under the editorship first of Leslie Stephen and later of Sidney Lee that marked the triumph of the collective biographical project. The *Dictionary of National Biography* bore witness to the importance of the fact in an age whose values and methodologies were shaped by the developing disciplines of science and history.[29] It also reflected the professionalisation of biography which had been effected in the course of the nineteenth century, that saw the emergence of more detached, accurate, and selective life studies in place of the inclusive hagiographic memoirs which had predominated in the high Victorian period. It established a style and approach to life-writing, in short, which set the scene for Strachey himself.

Just as it is important to recognise that, in purely formal terms, nineteenth-century biography does not, as Strachey implies, constitute a single tradition, so it must be conceded that the moral tone so deplored by the Modernist generation as being fundamental to Victorian life-writing was not universally condoned in its day. Carlyle, for instance, who favoured in his own biographical enterprises the shaped interpretative life in the Romantic mode, was hotly critical of the contemporary demand for reticence in biography. Of Lockhart's *Life of Sir Walter Scott*, for example, he writes,

> One thing we hear greatly blamed in Mr. Lockhart: that he has been too communicative, indiscreet, and has recorded much that ought to have lain suppressed. Persons are mentioned, and circumstances, not always of an ornamental sort. It would appear there is far less reticence than was looked for! Various persons, name and surname, have 'received pain:' nay, the very Hero of the Biography is rendered unheroic; unornamental facts of him, and of those he had to do with, being set forth in plain English: hence 'personality,' 'indiscretion,' or worse, 'sanctities of private life,' &c. &c. How delicate, decent is English Biography, bless its mealy mouth! A Damocles' sword of *Respectability* hangs forever over the poor English Life-writer (as it does over poor English Life in general), and reduces him to the verge of paralysis.

In Carlyle's view biography proper has been supplanted in England by 'some vague ghost of a biography, white, stainless; without feature or substance; *vacuum*, as we say, and wind and shadow, – which indeed the material of it was'.[30] Despite his own propensity for heroes and hero worship, Carlyle provided something of a corrective to this impoverished notion of the life in his own biographical writing, and indeed was to become, as we shall see, the subject of a more robust and controversial form of biography after his death. Another practitioner of biography, Harriet Martineau, warns in the preface to the second edition of her collected *Biographical Sketches* that she is committed to 'the true principle of Biographical delineation', the purpose and character of which 'a large proportion of readers fail to apprehend':

> Some expect in it a solace to mourners, – such a solace as is afforded by those 'filial biographies' which were the despair of Jeffrey in his connexion with the *Edinburgh Review*. Some think that faults and foibles should be hidden, in charity, or as a matter of taste. Some believe that the love of goodness is best cherished by presenting goodness unmixed and unshadowed. Some are blinded to moral considerations by the lustre of intellectual ability. To none of these can thoroughly honest portraiture be acceptable; and they had better resort to private memorials, and to fiction, for the solace of their affections, and the fulfilment of their ideal.

Martineau promises, by contrast, 'to tell, in the spirit of justice, the whole truth about the characters of persons important enough to have their lives publicly treated at all'.[31]

It has to be said, though, that for the most part, as both Carlyle and Martineau suggest, the demand for discretion seems to have been paramount. In an essay on 'The Ethics of Biography' published in the *Contemporary Review* in 1883, Margaret Oliphant, herself a prolific writer of lives – others' as well as her own – explained the peculiarly demanding ethical responsibilities of the biographer as follows:

> The question of how far the world should be allowed to penetrate into those sanctuaries, and to invade the privacy which every soul has a right to guard for itself, is one in which the delicacy of his perceptions and that good taste of the heart, which no artificial standard can supply, will be severely tested.[32]

Such respect for the sanctity of private life is everywhere apparent in nineteenth-century biography. In the case of Fanny Kingsley's life of her husband, for instance, it manifests itself in the complete suppression of details of their personal relationship, as in her extraordinarily dispassionate reference to the birth of her own child: 'His youngest daughter, Mary St Leger, was born in June, and the day following he resumes his letters to Mr Ludlow . . .'[33] Fanny Kingsley's reticence in the matter of relating her childbirth experience is in the spirit of Gaskell's refusal to enter into the details of Charlotte Brontë's married life ('henceforward the sacred doors of home are closed upon her married life')[34] and Hallam Tennyson's silence on the subject of his father's forty-year relationship with his mother Emily Sellwood, and is typical of a tendency in the period to mark off the private from the public, to give a limited glimpse of family life only as part of the picture of the public person. But there were other kinds of omission in Victorian biography which were designed rather to avoid embarrassment and the sullying of the departed hero's name. For the commemorative biographer, it was essential above all to maintain a consistent vision of the heroism of the protagonist and to avoid at all costs including any matter which might compromise that vision; hence the censorship of anything which might offend against general standards of moral behaviour.

The practice of excluding reference to sexual irregularities, alcohol and drug dependence, mental instability and other such skeletons in the cupboard of the life under investigation was in the interests not only of the biographical subject and his surviving family and associates but also of the reading public. For biography was considered to be of value chiefly because of its moral and pedagogic uses, as its promotion by organisations such as the Society for the Diffusion of Useful Knowledge and individuals such as Samuel Smiles indicates. Biography, from medieval Lives of the Saints onwards, always had the potential to be a source of moral instruction and example, but in the context of nineteenth-century England, where the Protestant ethos and the ideology of self-help reigned supreme, the moral imperative driving the genre was particularly powerful. The exemplary life, even one which shamelessly deployed the sensationalist conventions of popular fiction, constituted a legitimate form of improving reading to those Evangelical readers who shunned and denounced the novel.[35]

The various biographical initiatives developed in the nineteenth century for pedagogic purposes, from the SDUK's *Biographical Dictionary* to the *DNB*, were all ideologically, if differently, motivated.[36] Through its focus upon upper- and middle-class male public figures as suitable subjects and its virtual exclusion of women and the under-privileged, biography as a genre effectively reinforced the values of the dominant society.[37] Nineteenth-century biography valorises precisely those experiences which were denied to women, the poor, and the working class: self-determination and self-development, personal heroism of a kind that gains public recognition, a significant destiny considered worthy of the recording. There was a place for women and working-class protagonists whose ambitions were thwarted in the more socially critical fiction of the period – one thinks, for instance, of Eliot's Dorothea Brooke and Maggie Tulliver, of Hardy's Jude Fawley and Sue Bridehead – and a still more assured place for those, like Brontë's *Jane Eyre* and Disraeli's *Sybil*, who were miraculously able to escape the constraints of their gender and class positions via the marriage plot and the romance ending. But biography, dealing as it professed to do with the historical 'truth' and the 'facts' in a more rigorous way than even the most realist of fiction, and jealously guarding the criteria for membership of this most exclusive of clubs, remained the domain of middle- and upper-class statesmen, churchmen, captains of industry, scientists and men of letters throughout the nineteenth century.

One man who became the subject of a major mid-nineteenth-century biography was none of these, but could be said to have made the mould for many of the eminent Victorians to be thus memorialised. The *Life of Thomas Arnold, D. D., Head-Master of Rugby* was published by his star pupil A. P. Stanley in 1844, and there is perhaps no better example of the pedagogic impulse of nineteenth-century biography than this panegyric to the life of the most influential schoolmaster of the period. Indeed, in 1904 it was prescribed as part of the curriculum to be followed in the preparation of candidates for the Teacher's Certificate, on the grounds that it demonstrates 'the relation between the discipline and the studies of a school on the one hand, and on the other, the claims of citizenship, of professional or industrial work, of the family, of the social organism and of Christian manhood', and 'shows how the career of a schoolmaster may connect itself with the politics, the religious interests, the literature and the corporate life of the community'.[38] Stanley's *Life of Arnold* demonstrates its imbrication with the social and political values of its time at every turn. Stanley commemorates the life of a man who became headmaster of Rugby in 1828 and, in the words of Dr Hawkins, the Provost of Oriel, 'changed the face of education all through the public schools of England',[39] inculcating in the upper- and middle-class boys in his charge the ideals of duty, moral virtue, industry, discipline, teamsmanship, Christian manliness, and empire celebrated by Thomas Hughes in *Tom Brown's Schooldays*, and by English style public schools across the world ever since. 'He governed the school precisely on the same principles as he would have governed a great empire,' writes Stanley,[40] and to the extent that a good number of his pupils went on to become colonial administrators Rugby values did indeed determine the principles according to which the British empire was governed.

Stanley is a brilliant stylist, and his prose vibrates with the passion of his own emotional attachment to his former headmaster as he writes of Arnold's extraordinary ability to inspire his students, who felt, when they left school, 'that they had been in an atmosphere unlike that of the world about them':

> Pupils with characters most different from each other's, and
> from his own – often with opinions diverging more and more

widely from his as they advanced in life – looked upon him with a love and reverence which made his gratification one of the brightest rewards of their academical studies – his good or evil fame, a constant source of interest and anxiety to them – his approbation and censure, amongst their most practical motives of action – his example, one of their most habitual rules of life. To him they turned for advice in every emergency of life, not so much for the sake of the advice itself, as because they felt that no important step ought to be taken without consulting him. An additional zest was imparted to whatever work they were engaged in by a consciousness of the interest which he felt in the progress of their undertaking, and the importance which he attached to its result.[41]

Yet for all his benevolent paternalism, Arnold also had for Stanley a 'youthfulness of temperament' which meant that 'All the new influences which so strongly divide the students of the nineteenth century from those of the last, had hardly less interest for himself than for [his former pupils].' His house was 'always open' to his former students, 'his advice and sympathy ready':

> His very presence seemed to create a new spring of health and vigour within them, and to give to life an interest and an elevation which remained with them long after they had left him again, and dwelt so habitually in their thoughts, as a living image, that, when death had taken him away, the bond appeared to be still unbroken, and the sense of separation almost lost in the still deeper sense of a life and an union indestructible.[42]

This is arguably the effect of the biography itself also, and the reason for its enduring popularity. Through the words of his pupil, who was to become a leader of the Broad Church Movement, like his master, and later Dean of Westminster, Arnold remains present 'as a living image'. The qualities of toleration and judgement for which he was famed are articulated in the expansiveness and the balanced rhythms of Stanley's prose. His sympathetic understanding and generosity of spirit are reproduced in his biographer's own emotional and intellectual capacity, in his ability to enter into the feelings of the small boys who heard their headmaster preach, or to express the shocked grief of his five children awaiting their father's arrival at Fox How, 'fondly preparing to celebrate [his birthday] with its usual pleasures', but instead being greeted by the news of his sudden death.[43]

It is easy to understand why Stanley's *Life of Arnold* captured the hearts of Victorian readers. But it is not difficult to see also that it constitutes the cultural legitimation of the interests of a certain class of men. The ideological status of numerous other biographies of the period may be similarly identified. Another biography of particular interest in this regard is G. O. Trevelyan's *Life and Letters of Lord Macaulay* (1876). Like Arnold, Macaulay is celebrated for his moral probity, although in his case it is the product of his rigorous Clapham Sect upbringing, which, according to Trevelyan, encouraged him always to frame 'his decisions in accordance with the dictates of honour and humanity, of ardent public spirit and lofty public virtue'.[44] Macaulay was one who had the opportunity to take the kind of principles espoused by Arnold to the empire when he served as a member of the Supreme Council of India from 1834 to 1838. 'Fired by the prospect of the responsibility of a law-giver', he set off for India where he immediately set about the cultural and intellectual colonisation of the indigenous cultures. In his 'Minute on Indian Higher Education' of January 1835 he made what was to be a decisive intervention in the debate about whether Indians should continue to be educated in the great Hindu classics or be given the benefit of the intellectual heritage of Homer, Thucydides and Aristotle. Macaulay was so contemptuous of Hindu astronomy that he considered it 'would move laughter in the girls at an English boarding school' – his lowest example of intellectual credulity. Hindu history, he wrote, abounded with 'kings thirty feet high, and reigns thirty thousand years long – and geography made up of seas of treacle and seas of butter', and he lent his voice to the cause of replacing such absurd instances of so-called Indian culture by the European classics. Arnold would have heartily approved of Macaulay's endorsement of the kind of classical education he himself promoted in the British public school system, and of the decision of the Committee of Public Instruction that 'the great object of the British Government ought to be the promotion of European literature and science among the natives of India.'[45]

Just as the life of an influential schoolmaster may be seen to be specially relevant to the study of nineteenth-century biography, given the pedagogic nature of the genre in the period, so the life of an eminent historian – one, moreover, written by another similarly eminent historian, his nephew – seems to offer a particularly notable instance of a form which, as we have seen, was frequently closely associated with historiography. On the face of it, Trevelyan's training appears to show itself in his generous inclusion of sources, most obviously the documentary evidence provided by Macaulay's letters, and his tendency to let them speak for themselves. But the life does not, for all that, follow the biographical practice professed by Lockhart in his *Life of Scott* of letting 'the character develop itself'. For Trevelyan was a Whig historian, with an intellectual and political investment in representing his subject as one, and was carefully selective in the use he made of Macaulay's letters and journal to reinforce the idea of his uncle's ideological orthodoxy.[46]

Trevelyan's Whig interpretation of history as progress also inevitably affected the way in which he manipulated his uncle's life and times into a coherent and shapely developmental narrative. His life of his uncle was manifestly not the raw 'truth' but a construction, as all biography must be – a construction whose shape and whose ideology are determined by the particular and inevitably partial perspective of the biographer. Like Trevelyan's *Life of Macaulay*, John Morley's *Life of William Ewart Gladstone* (1903) unfolds with a sense of its subject's inevitable destiny, in this case because it is a uniformly retrospective account, and one that is informed by a resolutely evolutionary way of thinking.[47] Morley insists, moreover, upon the extent to which Gladstone is exemplary of his times in being shaped by 'an agitated and expectant age' whilst at the same time 'propelling, restraining, guiding his country at many decisive moments'.[48] In Hazlitt's earlier *Life of Napoleon Buonaparte* (1828–30), that dialectical relationship between the great national leader and his age is similarly stressed. As Hazlitt's son, who edited a revised edition of the life, observes, 'Buonaparte as the creature of circumstances, is one thing; as their creator, another; and it is curious to contemplate him under both views.'[49]

Unlike the lives of Arnold, Macaulay, and Gladstone, which unquestioningly conformed to the dominant nationalist ideology, Hazlitt's *Life of Napoleon* was politically oppositional in its praise of Napoleon and its condemnation of Britain's role in the quashing of liberty in France and, in particular, of its own national hero, the Duke of Wellington. Hazlitt's son directly addresses the question of his father's unconcealed partisanship in his preface to the life, reminding us that, then as now, it was the practice to find bias only on the radical side in politics:

> The author may be accused of partiality when the very original views he takes are submitted to the judgement of prejudice and preconception. But let it be remembered, that wealth and genius have been lavished to give a false color to many transactions which are here related in their simple nakedness, and the charge of partisanship may be retorted on the accuser.

As both he and his father freely admit, 'The political bias of Hazlitt's mind was to popular right and the sovereignty of the people.'[50] Hazlitt confesses, 'I am a Revolutionist,'[51] and accordingly constructs Napoleon's life as the triumph and tragic fall of a great man who brought liberty to an oppressed people. He was the 'sword-arm' of the revolution, and 'its fate became in a manner bound up with him.'[52]

Biographers typically divide up their subjects' lives into chapters, creating moments of triumph, crucial turning points, crises and catastrophes. Hazlitt is no exception, and interestingly, given Napoleon's high military and political profile, such moments are by no means always battles, political victories or losses, or other public events. His account of the birth of the young Napoleon, for instance, marks a climax in his representation of his hero's humanity. Buonaparte is constructed as a new-age man, at his wife Josephine's bedside as she endures a hard labour, comforting and holding her in her agony. Mother and child might not both survive, and asked, if it were necessary that one should be sacrificed, who should be saved, he replies 'The mother, certainly, . . . it is her right.' In the event, 'The child was apparently dead when born, but by friction and other means it was restored to life.'[53] To this powerful demonstration of Napoleon's tender humanity is added a suggestion of supernatural powers over life and mortality. But this high point in Napoleon's moral life is to be followed by a dramatic fall, as he succumbs to political pressure, and has his true-love marriage to Josephine annulled in order that he can make a powerful alliance by marriage to Marie Louise, Archduchess of Austria. In the unfolding drama of Napoleon's life, this decision, 'a mere state manoeuvre', a marriage of convenience, marks a fatal turning-point: 'It was an evil hour that Josephine was cast away, for after it, the star of Napoleon gradually, but surely, declined.'[54] By contrast with the standard Victorian biography, which typically eulogises the hero's life as progressing forward to ever higher states of being, Napoleon's life is cast as a tragedy, the hero fatally flawed.

Another key moment in the determination of Napoleon's, and European, destiny is dwelt on in great detail, and that is Marshal Grouchy's failure to go to Buonaparte's assistance in the Battle of Waterloo. Hazlitt's treatment of this disastrous lapse offers a fine example of Barthes's theory of how 'l'effet du réel' is achieved in history writing by the dramatic inclusion of insignificant details and purely fictional speculation about the inner motives of the historical actors. And so we are told how, while General Excelmans and Count Gerard urged Grouchy to march to the scene of the action between the British and French armies,

> Still nothing would move him; he remained as if spell-bound. The very fear of what might happen, the magnitude of the people, took away the power to avert it. He saw the sun shining above his head, that was no more to behold his country's independence or the face of freedom; he saw the triumphs, the struggles, the sacrifices of the last five-and-twenty years about to be annulled and made of no account, which it required but one more effort to sanction and confirm for ever; the blood that had flowed turn into laughter and scorn; an imbecile monarch forced back on an hereditary throne, like some foul Eastern idol, borne in defiance over the bleeding bodies and the prostrate necks of an abused people; liberty bound hand and foot, afraid to breathe or move, its

name henceforth to become a reproach, reviled, suspected, hunted down, and trod into the earth under the hoofs of kings: he saw this done by an English general, vaunting the rights, the glory, and the generosity of his own country; he saw the greatest reputation in modern times about to become a prey to the most shallow and worthless; –

> – 'Saw where an eagle in his pride of place
> Was by a mousing owl hawk'd at and killed –'

He saw or should have seen all this, and could not be prevailed upon to stir a step to prevent it.[55]

In his representation of Napoleon, particularly in his moment of defeat at Waterloo (which he attributes entirely to Grouchy's unaccountable absence from the scene and to the English soldiers' 'inherent stubbornness of character and daring resistance to the enemy', rather than to Wellington's leadership), Hazlitt deliberately offers an alternative account to the conventional British condemnation of Buonaparte and celebration of the glorious victory at Waterloo. In so doing he makes clear his awareness that biography, like history, is not a matter of the objective accumulation of facts, but the subjective and selective interpretation of a body of material which might equally be seen from a quite different perspective.

Carlyle revealed a similar awareness when he undertook to write the life of his friend John Sterling in 1851, only three years after Archdeacon Hare had published a collection of Sterling's writings accompanied by a biographical account. Sterling had been a restless intellectual figure who had taken orders in 1834, but resigned his curacy only eight months later, professedly on the grounds of ill health. He then went on to make his career as a reviewer with the periodical press. He was not a particularly distinguished public or intellectual figure and, as George Eliot comments in her review of Carlyle's life, 'The public . . . since it is content to do without biographies of much more remarkable men, cannot be supposed to have felt any pressing demand even for a single life of Sterling; still less, it might be thought, when so distinguished a writer as Archdeacon Hare had furnished this, could there be any need for another.' But, she concludes, she agrees with Carlyle that 'the first life is properly the justification of the second.'[56] Carlyle believed that Archdeacon Hare's account of Sterling's life was coloured by his clerical position, and that he accordingly put undue emphasis on his 'transient conformity' rather than his 'ultimate alienation from the Church'. Carlyle's aim, in a work which, like so much Victorian prose, was written in reaction to another piece of writing and accordingly has an occasional quality, was to correct what he saw as a complete misrepresentation of Sterling's decision to enter the Church. Eliot explains their divergence of opinion thus:

> [Archdeacon Hare] holds that had Sterling's health permitted him to remain in the Church, he would have escaped those aberrations from orthodoxy, which, in the clerical view, are to be regarded as the failure and shipwreck of his career, apparently thinking, like that friend of Arnold's who recommended a curacy as the best means of clearing up Trinitarian difficulties, that 'orders' are a sort of spiritual backboard, which, by dint of obliging a man to look as if he were strait, end by making him so. According to Carlyle, on the contrary, the real 'aberration' of Sterling was his choice of the clerical profession, which was simply a mistake as to his true vocation.[57]

Carlyle attributes Sterling's decision to take orders to Coleridge's influence – in particular to his metaphysical reformulation of the role of the Established Church, which was founded, in Carlyle's view, upon 'a fatal delusion' – and indeed Hare's biography includes letters by Sterling which testify to his belief in Coleridge's intellectual ascendancy. Sterling's praise for the 'oceanic ebb and flow' of Coleridgean philosophical conversation is nicely parodied by Carlyle as he elaborates upon the watery metaphor:

> To sit as a passive bucket and be pumped into, whether you consent to or not, can in the long run be exhilarating to no creature; how eloquent soever the flood of utterance that is descending. But if it be withal a confused unintelligible flood of utterance, threatening to submerge all known landmarks and thought and drown the world and you! – ... He began anywhere: you put some question to him, made some suggestive observation: instead of answering this, or decidedly setting out towards answer of it, he would accumulate formidable apparatus, logical swim-bladders, transcendental life-preservers and other precautionary and vehiculatory gear, for setting out.[58]

Carlyle's view of Coleridge's conversation was that 'it was talk not flowing anywhither like a river, but spreading everywhither in extricable currents and regurgitations like a lake or sea ... So that, most times, you felt logically lost; swamped near to drowning in this tide of ingenious vocables, spreading out boundless as if to submerge the world.'[59]

Fundamental, then, to Carlyle's revisionary life of Sterling is his demolition of Coleridge. He is derisive of Coleridge's intellectual irresolution, to which he gives brilliant figurative expression:

> He hung loosely on his limbs, with knees bent, and stooping
> attitude; in walking, he rather shuffled than decisively stept;
> and a lady once remarked, he never could fix which side of the
> garden walk would suit him best, but continually shifted, in
> corkscrew fashion, and kept trying both.

The passage offers a wonderful sidelight on the Platonic mind. Carlyle
is similarly impatient with Coleridge's preaching tone and his excessive
dependence on Kantian terminology:

> His voice, naturally soft and good, had contracted itself into
> a plaintive snuffle and singsong; he spoke as if preaching, –
> you would have said, preaching earnestly and also hopelesssly
> the weightiest things. I still recollect his 'object' and 'subject,'
> terms of continual recurrence in the Kantian province; and
> how he sang and snuffled them into 'om-m-mject' and
> 'sum-m-mject,' with a kind of solemn shake or quaver, as
> he rolled along.

And yet, of course, the qualities he most despises in Coleridge – the
preacherly style, the interest in German transcendentalist philosophy,
the distinction drawn between the material and the spiritual – are traits
we might well associate with Carlyle himself. Perhaps what we are witnessing in his witty denunciation of his illustrious predecessor is an
Oedipal slaying of the father.

Coleridge was one of those figures who lived semi-public private
lives, whose milieu was the salon and whose table talk and correspondence were published, and he seems to have been particularly susceptible to having his life and characteristics dissected by other writers
who shared his own personal and intellectual propensities. And so De
Quincey, like Coleridge an opium addict, financially precarious, notoriously unreliable in his habits, includes in his biography descriptions of
his erstwhile hero which have all the elements of self-portrait:

> Nobody who ever knew him ever thought of depending
> on any appointment he might make: spite of his uniformly
> honourable intentions, nobody attached any weight to his *in re
> futura*: those who asked him to dinner or any other party as a
> matter of course, sent a carriage for him, and went personally
> or by proxy to fetch him; and, as to letters, unless the address
> were in some female hand that commanded his affectionate
> esteem, he tossed them all into one general *deadletter bureau*,
> and rarely, I believe, opened them at all.[60]

Perhaps it is not, in the end, surprising that it is those who are most in sympathy with a person's failings, as well as their strengths, who are able to write most perceptively about their lives. The very style of De Quincey's essay on Coleridge, indeed, speaks of the chaotic habits that the biographer shares with his subject, as he himself disarmingly confesses:

> the whole of this article upon Mr Coleridge, though carried through at intervals, and (as it has unexpectedly happened) with time sufficient to have made it a very careful one, has, in fact, been written in a desultory and unpremeditated style.

He explains that the essay was originally undertaken 'on the sudden but profound impulse communicated to the writer's feelings, by the unexpected news of this great man's death', partly to relieve 'his own deep sentiments of reverential affection to his memory', and partly in response to public curiosity about a man who figured in the public imagination as one of the great intellectuals of his day. Both purposes, he explains, 'required that it should be written almost *extempore*':

> the greater part was really and unaffectedly written in that way, and under circumstances of such extreme haste, as would justify the writer in pleading the very amplest privilege of licence and indulgent construction which custom concedes to such cases. Hence it had occurred to the writer as a judicious principle, to create a sort of merit out of his own necessity; and rather to seek after the graces which belong to the epistolary form, or to other modes of composition professedly careless, than after those which grow out of preconceived biographies, which, having originally settled their plan upon a regular foundation, are able to pursue a course of orderly development, such as *his* slight sketch had voluntarily renounced from the beginning. That mode of composition having been once adopted, it seemed proper to sustain it, even after delays and interruption had allowed time for throwing the narrative into a more orderly movement, and modulating, as it were, into a key of the usual solemnity.[61]

The contrast with John Stuart Mill's later retrospective essay on Coleridge is telling. Mill's is a highly schematised account of the complementary influences of Bentham and Coleridge upon subsequent generations, and his own sympathies, although not unqualifiedly Benthamite, are more clearly in accord with the utilitarian position than with Coleridge's. Nevertheless he shows a tolerance for Coleridge, and indeed for Carlyle, whom he clearly casts in the same mould, which is quite absent from the latter's account of Coleridge. Of Carlyle's writings, Mill wrote in his *Autobiography* (1873), 'They seemed a haze of poetry and German metaphysics, in which almost the only clear thing was a strong animosity to most of the opinions which were the basis of my mode of thought.' Nevertheless, he adds, 'I did not seek and cultivate Carlyle less on account of the fundamental differences in our philosophy.'[62]

Carlyle was to say, in turn, of Mill's *Autobiography*, 'I have never read a more uninteresting book, nor I should say a sillier, by a man of sense, integrity, and seriousness of mind.'[63] His own *Reminiscences* were published just three weeks after his death in 1881 by the person whom he entrusted with the responsibility of publishing his collected letters, J. A. Froude, who followed Carlyle's autobiographical account over the next three years with his own four-volume life of Carlyle. Nobody judged Carlyle's *Reminiscences* as uninteresting, but many there were who considered them shocking in their revelations about his personal life, and in particular the miseries of his marriage with Jane Welsh Carlyle, for which he assumed responsibility. The first two volumes of Froude's biography were published in the following year, and his judgement was questioned for bringing before the public yet further details of the private life of this revered man of letters. As Frederic Harrison, himself a biographer, remarked,

> The biographies and autobiographies, the unroofing of his home and the unveiling of his hearth, the letters, journals, and recorded sayings are intensely interesting. But they have told us things we would rather not have heard. Those who loved him and those who loved her have been shocked, amazed, ashamed, in turn. Those who love good men and good women, those who honour great intellects, those who reverence human nature, have been wounded to the heart. Foul odours, as from a charnel house, have been suddenly opened on us.[64]

Froude offended against the great imperatives of Victorian biography, reticence and discretion, citing as his authority for so doing Carlyle himself, whose review of Lockhart's *Life of Sir Walter Scott* is invoked and copiously quoted. Froude celebrated Carlyle's greatness as a writer and a sage, but did not pretend that his character was wholly unblemished. Like other nineteenth-century biographies, his *Life of Carlyle* shaped the facts of his subject's life into a literary structure. It is not, however, the formula of the *Bildungsroman* that we find in this work, for all that Carlyle's rise out of childhood poverty into successful and virtuous manhood through sheer determination and industry could have been perfectly adapted to such a treatment, but that of Greek tragedy. Froude figures himself throughout the biography as a Greek Chorus commenting on a fateful series of events in which the chief actors are the tragically flawed Carlyle and his sacrificial victim Jane Welsh.[65]

Jane Welsh is a crucial character in Froude's biography, but her life is subsumed in her husband's, as it was in reality, and she herself was to receive no full biography until the twentieth century. Even in his memoir of her life in *Reminiscences*, Carlyle structures his representation of her around his own publications:

> 'Cromwell' was by much the worst book-time, till this of 'Friedrich,' which indeed was infinitely worse; in the dregs of our strength too; – and lasted for about thirteen years. She was generally in quite weak health, too, and was often, for long weeks or months, miserably ill . . . 'Latter-Day Pamphlet' time, and especially the time that preceded it (1848 etc.) must have been very sore and heavy . . . On the back of 'Latter-Day Pamphlets' followed 'Life of Sterling'; . . . What now will please me best in it, and alone will, was then an accidental quality, the authentic light, under the due conditions, that is thrown by it on her.[66]

Thomas Carlyle was allegedly impotent, and Jane Welsh was denied the experience of motherhood which gave structure to many women's lives; as he remorsefully points out, his books were destined to be her only children:

> I said long since, I never saw so beautiful a childhood. Her little bit of a first chair, its wee wee arms etc., visible to me in the closet at this moment, is still here, and always was. I have looked at it hundreds of times; from of old, with many thoughts. No daughter or son of hers was to sit there; so it had been appointed us, my darling. I have no book a thousandth-part so beautiful as thou; but these were our only 'children,' – and, in a true sense, these were verily ours.[67]

That's as may be, but it was Thomas Carlyle whose life was celebrated in a major biography, and Jane Welsh's name is not to be found on the title-pages of his books. Indeed, as she frequently felt the need to point out, in a phrase which sounds the keynote of her married life, 'I too am here'.[68]

Whilst it is true that Thomas Carlyle was widely regarded as the most influential writer of the age, and Jane Welsh clearly did not command such a degree of public recognition, her fate, to be the appendage of her husband even in her commemoration, was a common one for even the most exceptional of nineteenth-century women. She appeared in the autobiographical reminiscences of writers such as Harriet Martineau and Anne Thackeray Ritchie, but was the subject of only two commemorative articles in her own right, one by Margaret Oliphant in the *Contemporary Review* and the other unsigned in the *Temple Bar Magazine*. Both appeared in 1883, after the death of Thomas Carlyle, and after the publication of his *Reminiscences* and the first part of Froude's life.

For all but a very few women, such as Charlotte Brontë and George Eliot, the brief life was felt to be an adequate memorial, and more often than not such portrait sketches were written by other women. Harriet Martineau is a case in point. Between 1852 and 1868 she published numerous biographical sketches of female royalty, socialites, and women writers in the pages of the *Daily News*.[69] But even she wrote memoirs of rather more men than women, and this was the pattern for the few women of the period who made a living as professional biographers.

Some women undertook to write the biographies of lost loved ones; perhaps the most famous instance of a widow's panegyric is Mary Kingsley's life of her husband. But it is instructive to consider too the *absence* of biographies of famous men by the women who knew them best. For example, Mary Shelley fought for the right to write the lives of both her father, William Godwin, and her husband, Percy Bysshe Shelley, but although she was permitted to publish a brief 'Memoir of the Author' together with the 1831 reissue of Godwin's *Caleb Williams*, and although she published a volume of Percy Bysshe's poems with biographical notes in 1839, she was never given the opportunity to publish full-scale biographies of either.[70] Despite the fact that Mary Shelley was the obvious person to write the 'official' biographies of both her husband and her father, and that she, moreover, wrote some thirty-five biographies of other individuals for Lardner's encyclopaedias in the decade which opened with the brief memoir of the one and closed with fragmentary notes on the other, Godwin's and Percy Shelley's lives were to fall to more 'important' men to write.[71]

Women were the subjects of full-scale biographies even less frequently than they were the authors of such works. Female writers were the women most likely to be commemorated, and often by other admiring writers or by friends. And so the poet Mathilde Blind published a life of George Eliot in 1883, and Anna Stoddart wrote a biography of the travel writer Isabella Bird in 1906. But the first, and the most important and personal biography of one woman writer by another was Elizabeth Gaskell's *Life of Charlotte Brontë*, which appeared in 1857. When Gaskell was commissioned to write the biography by her friend's father, Patrick Brontë, she was already a novelist of some reputation, having published *Mary Barton* in 1848, *Ruth* in 1853, *North and South* in 1854–55 and *Cranford* in 1855, and she was to bring both her personal and professional experiences as a woman writer and her fictional skills to the writing of her fellow novelist's life.

The epigraph from Elizabeth Barrett Browning's *Aurora Leigh* that Gaskell chooses for the biography signals the emphasis she is to take:

> Oh my God,
> ——Thou hast knowledge, only Thou,
> How dreary 'tis for women to sit still
> On winter nights by solitary fires
> And hear the nations praising them far off.

Gaskell's heartfelt portrayal of Charlotte Brontë stresses precisely that disjunction between the public figure of the acclaimed author and the private suffering woman which Barrett Browning represents as the condition of the female writer in the nineteenth century. In a particularly powerful and personal section of the life, Gaskell describes how, after the publication of *Jane Eyre*, 'Charlotte Brontë's existence becomes divided into two parallel currents – her life as Currer Bell, the author; her life as Charlotte Brontë, the woman.' She goes on to explain this divided state further, and to identify it as something which only women writers experience:

> There were separate duties belonging to each character – not opposing each other, but difficult to be reconciled. When a man becomes an author, it is probably merely a change of employment to him. He takes a portion of that time which has hitherto been devoted to some other study or pursuit; he gives up something of the legal or medical profession, in which he has hitherto endeavoured to serve others, or relinquishes part of the trade or business by which he has been striving to gain a livelihood; and another merchant or lawyer, or doctor, steps into his vacant place, and probably does as well as he. But no other can take up the quiet, regular duties of the daughter, the wife, or the mother, as well as she whom God has appointed to fill that particular place: a woman's principal work in life is hardly left to her own choice; nor can she drop the domestic charges devolving on her as an individual, for the exercise of the most splendid talents that were ever bestowed. And yet she must not shrink from the extra responsibility implied by the very fact of her possessing such talents. She must not hide her gift in a napkin; it was meant for the use and service of others. In an humble and faithful spirit must she labour to do what is not impossible, or God would not have set her to do it.[72]

The successful novelist and mother of five knew what she was talking about, and whilst she herself had a relatively supportive environment in which to work, her isolated friend had had to nurture her talent against formidable odds, as she graphically illustrates. We are told how all the family's efforts were directed towards the male child of the family, Branwell Brontë: 'all his home kindred were thinking how they could best forward his views, and how help him up to the pinnacle where he desired to be.' And so Charlotte resolves to be a governess, so that her brother may enrol at the Royal Academy. As Gaskell wryly comments, 'These are not the first sisters who have laid their lives as a sacrifice before their brother's idolized wish.'[73] But she leaves no doubt that they are perhaps the most talented sisters who have thus denied their own needs and desires for a brother who proves particularly unworthy of their sacrifices. Neither do Charlotte and her sisters get much support for their writing from their father. Gaskell narrates the episode where Charlotte tells him that she has written a book. He at first refuses to look at it because it would try his eyes too much, but she explains that it is in print, for it has been published. He then worries about the costs this must incur. And Charlotte's eventual marriage did not promise much better. Gaskell ominously remarks that, shortly before her marriage to her father's curate, the Reverend Arthur Bell Nicholls, she wrote a letter to Mr Dobell 'which develops the intellectual side of her character, before we lose all thought of the authoress in the timid and conscientious woman about to become a wife, and in the too short, almost perfect, happiness of her nine months of wedded life.'[74] In Gaskell's view, the Reverend Nicholls clearly expected his wife to suspend her literary activities upon her marriage to him.

Gaskell's careful inclusion of Charlotte's hesitant and apologetic correspondence with various famous literary men is also designed to emphasise the gendering of professional literary work in the period. Immediately following Charlotte's resolution to write to Robert Southey, the Poet Laureate, for advice on her writing, Gaskell places Branwell's confident letter to Wordsworth asking him to comment on his poem. She then quotes Southey's infamous reply to his sister, in which he opines:

> Literature cannot be the business of a woman's life, and it ought not to be. The more she is engaged in her proper duties, the less leisure will she have for it, even as an accomplishment and a recreation. To those duties you have not yet been called, and when you are, you will be less eager for celebrity. You will not seek in imagination for excitement, of which the vicissitudes of this life, and the anxieties from which you must not hope to be exempted, be your state what it may, will bring with them but too much.[75]

A female writer of the next generation, the Victorian poet and essayist Alice Meynell, remarks acutely of the critical comments that Charlotte Brontë had to endure, not only from male writers and critics but from some women too,

> Mistress of some of the best prose of her century, Charlotte Brontë was subject to a Lewes, a Chorley, a Miss Martineau:

that is, she suffered what in Italian is called *Suggezione* in their presence. When she had met six minor contemporary writers – by-products of literature – at dinner, she had a headache and a sleepless night. She writes to her friend that these contributors to the quarterly Press are greatly feared in literary London, and there is in her letter a sense of tremor and exhaustion. And what nights did the heads of the critics undergo after the meeting? Lewes, whose own romances are all condoned, all forgiven by time and oblivion, who gave her lessons, who told her to study Jane Austen? The others, whose reviews doubtless did their proportionate part in still further hunting and harrying the tired English of their day? And before Harriet Martineau she bore herself reverently. Harriet Martineau, albeit a woman of masculine understanding (we may imagine we hear her contemporaries give her the title), could not thread her way safely in and out of two or three negatives, but wrote – about this very Charlotte Brontë: 'I did not consider the book a coarse one, though I could not answer for it that there were no traits which, on a second leisurely reading, I might not dislike.' Mrs Gaskell quotes the passage with no consciousness of anything amiss.[76]

However, although Gaskell often quotes such passages without comment, it seems unlikely that she does so without consciousness that there is anything amiss. The very fact that she selects the quotations she does implies a critical view, and supports her general representation of the lot of the woman writer. And so she chooses to quote Charlotte's reply to Southey's patronising letter, in which she tells the Laureate,

> Following my father's advice – who from my childhood had counselled me just in the wise and friendly tone of your letter – I have endeavoured not only attentively to observe all the duties a woman ought to fulfil, but to feel deeply interested in them. I don't always succeed, for sometimes when I am teaching or sewing I would rather be reading or writing; but I try to deny myself; and my father's approbation amply rewarded me for the privation.[77]

In relation to subsequent correspondence with male writers, Gaskell generally comments on the gender issues raised, and sometimes, as in the case of a letter she quotes from Charlotte Brontë to Wordsworth, refers explicitly to her previous correspondence with Southey:

> There are two or three things noticeable in the letter from which these extracts are taken. The first is the initials with

which she had evidently signed the former one to which she alludes. About this time, to her more familiar correspondents, she occasionally calls herself 'Charles Thunder,' making a kind of pseudonym for herself out of her Christian name, and the meaning of her Greek surname. In the next place, there is a touch of assumed smartness, very different from the simple, womanly, dignified letter which she had written to Southey, under nearly similar circumstances, three years before. I imagine the cause of this difference to be twofold. Southey, in his reply to her first letter, had appealed to the higher parts of her nature, in calling her to consider whether literature was, or was not, the best course for a woman to pursue. But the person to whom she addressed this one had evidently confined himself to purely literary criticisms; besides which, her sense of humour was tickled by the perplexity which her correspondent felt as to whether he was addressing a man or a woman. She rather wished to encourage the former idea; and, in consequence, possibly, assumed something of the flippancy which was likely to exist in her brother's style of conversation, from whom she would derive her notions of young manhood.[78]

Later, anxieties over reading and writing as gendered activities surface again, this time in relation to her decision to adopt a male pseudonym as a published writer. In a letter to G. H. Lewes, who had written to her to say that he intended reviewing *Shirley* for the *Edinburgh Review*, 'C. Bell' writes, 'I wish you did not think me a woman. I wish all reviewers believed "Currer Bell" to be a man; they would be more just to him. You will, I know, keep measuring me by some standard of what you deem becoming to my sex; where I am not what you consider graceful, you will condemn me.' Gaskell goes on to elaborate upon Brontë's reasons for hoping that 'there were fewer traces of the female pen' in *Shirley* than in *Jane Eyre*, and her disappointment when the earliest reviews asserted that Currer Bell must be a woman: 'She especially disliked the lowering of the standard by which to judge a work of fiction, if it proceeded from a feminine pen; and praise mingled with pseudo-gallant allusions to her sex, mortified her far more than actual blame.'[79] Again, as a woman writer who had received her fair share of pseudo-gallantry, Gaskell speaks from a position of authority.

Alice Meynell, a mother of eight, implies that Gaskell also fails to comment critically enough upon the Brontës' loveless childhood. She writes,

'Mr. Brontë', says Mrs. Gaskell, in perfect good faith, 'was not naturally fond of children, and felt their frequent appearance on the scene both as a drag on his wife's strength and as an interruption to the comfort of the household.' Nor was the mother, in her long, last illness, 'anxious to see much of her children'.[80]

Meynell seems as shocked by Gaskell's disregard for Charlotte's neglected childhood as by her parents' apparent lack of affection for their children, but here again she seems unjust to the biographer who had, after all, been commissioned by Patrick Brontë to write his daughter's life, and was therefore compelled to be somewhat circumspect regarding their relationship. Moreover, Gaskell dwells in particular upon her subject's emotional deprivation, both as a child and as an adult, seeing her as an exemplification of the very qualities of fortitude and endurance that characterise her own fictional heroines. Like Margaret Hale and Mary Barton, Gaskell's Brontë practises self-denial, cares for a difficult widowed father, is exposed to extreme psychological suffering, to sickness and death.[81] When Gaskell and Brontë first met, Arthur Bell Nicholls was not yet on the scene to supply the conventional marriage plot, but the standard alternative ending was anticipated by Gaskell, who wrote to a friend, 'There seems little doubt she herself is already tainted with consumption.'[82] In the event, Brontë's biography was brought to a close, almost simultaneously, by her marriage and her death.

From beginning to end, Gaskell's *Life of Brontë* has the imaginative power and structure of the best of nineteenth-century novels. The opening scene, which introduces the reader to the unfamiliar northern region from which this extraordinary young woman writer emerged, is somewhat reminiscent of the opening chapter of Froude's later *Life of Carlyle*, in which we learn how the wild country and beliefs and traditions amidst which Carlyle grew up would determine the manner of his later writing, but we are reminded more forcefully still of Gaskell's representation of the northern settings of her own novels. Her biographical heroine was brought up in the wild and isolated village of Haworth, to be sure, but Gaskell emphasises from the outset that the rapidly expanding industrial town of Keighley, which is served by the Leeds and Bradford railway, and in which 'Nearly every dwelling seems devoted to some branch of commerce', is only a short distance away.[83] Her first chapter also anticipates the arresting opening of Dickens's *Great Expectations* (1860–61) by entering the narrative of her protagonist's life via the graveyard and the memorial tablet. Such novelistic strategies abound in this biography, whose characters and characterisation, themes, dramatic conflicts, plotting and narrative voice often sharply recall the fiction not only of the author but of the biographical subject.[84]

Gaskell's skilful characterisation, her exploitation of dramatic incident, and above all her formal control, bespeak her considerable talents as a fiction writer, and render *The Life of Charlotte Brontë* a very different kind of biography from that pilloried by Strachey in *Eminent Victorians*. But its uniqueness among Victorian biographies is due not only to its literary qualities, but to its subject. As Meynell explains,

> Charlotte Brontë's history, her work, her sorrows, take the imagination of man, woman, and child; and with the ambition, the day-dream, the self-consciousness, and the anger of women born to obscurity her great example wrought. To the unnumbered ranks of girls in the generation following her own, destined, most unjustly, to one inevitable career of teaching, the fame of the governess, poor, born in mediocrity, perhaps ill-favoured, but with a fiery heart, was a single message of hope and suggestion of glory. Many a woman out of reach of envy towards the fortunate and the brilliant was touched to the quick by the renown of the unfortunate author of *Jane Eyre*. It seemed a possible, a not improbable, an accessible splendour; something golden lurking in the dullest of all dull worlds, and discoverable haply yet once again.[85]

Amidst all those nineteenth-century biographies commemorating the glittering lives and achievements of eminent men, Gaskell's life of a plain and impoverished governess-become-novelist does indeed stand out. But *The Life of Charlotte Brontë* was to remain the only biography of its kind, for such women were typically denied status as subjects of history. Indeed, as Charlotte M. Yonge wrote in her *Biographies of Good Women* (1862), 'Nearly all women, who have been renowned enough to come under the notice of history, (even of those more quiet histories which dwell the least on political changes, and the most on domestic life,) have been so by the sacrifice of something more or less womanly.'[86] Those obscure young women whom Meynell imagines being inspired by Brontë's example were destined to have to write their own life stories, for nobody else was going to write them for them in a century when biography remained overwhelmingly the preserve of 'great men'.

Autobiography

Nobody ever wrote a dull autobiography. If one may make such a bull, the very dulness would be interesting. The autobiographer has *ex officio* two qualifications of supreme importance in all literary work. He is writing about a topic in which he is keenly interested, and about a topic upon which he

is the highest living authority. It may be reckoned, too, as
a special felicity that an autobiography, alone of all books,
may be more valuable in proportion to the amount of
misrepresentation which it contains. We do not wonder when
a man gives a false character to his neighbour, but it is always
curious to see how a man contrives to give a false testimonial
to himself. It is pleasant to be admitted behind the scenes and
trace the growth of that singular phantom which, like the
Spectre of the Brocken, is the man's own shadow cast upon
the coloured and distorting mists of memory.

(Leslie Stephen)[87]

The word 'autobiography' was an early nineteenth-century coinage,
first used by Robert Southey, who, in an 1809 article in the *Quarterly
Review*, predicted an 'epidemical rage for auto-biography'. It was a
prediction which was to be amply fulfilled in the century that followed.
For whilst only those who had attained celebrity status could expect to
have their lives commemorated in a biography, any literate, or even semi-
literate person could, theoretically at least, write their own life. Within
two decades of Southey's prophecy, the *Quarterly* carried an unsigned
article by its editor, James Lockhart, commenting on the recent spate
of autobiographical writings by decidedly undistinguished practitioners
of the genre:

> The classics of the *papier maché* age of our drama have taken
> up the salutary belief that England expects every driveller to
> do his Memorabilia. Modern print-makers must needs leave
> *confessions* behind them, as if they were so many Rousseaus.
> Our weakest mob-orators think it a hard case if they cannot
> spout to posterity. Cabin-boys and drummers are busy with
> their commentaries *de bello Gallico*; the John Gilpins of 'the
> nineteenth century' are the historians of their own *anabases*,
> and, thanks to 'the march of intellect', we are already rich
> in the autobiography of pickpockets.[88]

As this dismissive account of the degenerate condition of modern self-
writing makes clear, the practice of writing autobiography was by no
means a nineteenth-century invention; indeed, numerous recent critics
have focused attention on the various autobiographical traditions, particularly that of spiritual autobiography, from which the nineteenth-
century forms emerged, and traced their intertextual relations to St
Augustine, Bunyan, Rousseau, and other seminal figures.[89] Nevertheless, the genre was named, assumed a formal identity, and flourished in
the period, and does seem to be symptomatic of a quite unprecedented
fascination with the self and subjectivity in nineteenth-century writing.
In Gerard Manley Hopkins's memorable formulation,

when I consider my selfbeing, my consciousness and feeling
of myself, that taste of myself, of *I* and *me* above and in all
things, which is more distinctive than the taste of ale or alum,
more distinctive than the smell of walnutleaf or camphor, and
is incommunicable by any means to another man (as when
I was a child I used to ask myself: What must it be to be
someone else?). Nothing else in nature comes near this
unspeakable stress of pitch, distinctiveness, and selving, this
selfbeing of my own. Nothing explains it or resembles it . . .
searching nature I taste *self* but at one tankard, that of my own
being. The development, refinement, condensation of nothing
shews any sign of being able to match this to me or give me
another taste of it, a taste even resembling it.[90]

Such a powerful need to articulate the uniqueness of the individual's
sense of self sounds a very different note from that found in the writing
of an earlier period, and marks Hopkins's work, so often perceived as
out of step with the age in which he wrote, as highly characteristic of
the subjective sensibility of the nineteenth century.

It is perhaps not surprising to find the autobiographical impulse
evident in so much of the literature of a century in which the leading
intellectual currents are so notably concerned with the self: a century
which began with Wordsworth's 'egotistical sublime' and Coleridge's 'I
am', moved through Pater's solipsistic 'hard, gem-like flame' and Wilde's
claims for the absolute subjectivity of all artistic creation and criticism,
and closed with Freud; one which embraced the ideologies of laissez-
faire economics, self-help, and the bourgeois subject, and which beat to
the Evangelical religion of the heart; one which had to come to terms
equally with Kant, with Darwin, and with Nietzsche. But the flowering
of autobiography in the nineteenth century cannot be attributed unprob-
lematically to the influence of Romanticism, and cannot be associated
with an uncomplicated desire for introspection and self-revelation.[91] For
all Hopkins' joy in selfhood, in the sense that all of creation cries out,
'What I do is me, for that I came', he also experiences a profound self-
loathing: 'Self-yeast of spirit a dull dough sours.' For all George Eliot's
realist affirmation of the bourgeois subject, she has her narrator in
Middlemarch admit: 'I know no speck so troublesome as self.'[92]

Few are more equivocal about the literary practice of introspection than autobiographers themselves. The author of some of the most
unrestrained 'confessions' of the period, Thomas De Quincey, declared:
'Nothing . . . is more revolting to English feelings, than the spectacle
of a human being obtruding on our notice his moral ulcers or scars,
and tearing away that "decent drapery", which time, or indulgence to
human frailty, may have drawn over them';[93] while Anthony Trollope
frankly admits in his *Autobiography* (1883), 'That I, or any man, should

tell everything of himself, I hold to be impossible.'[94] And for Wilde, for whom 'autobiography is irresistible', but who abhors 'that dreadful universal thing called human nature', telling the truth about oneself is not only impossible but uninteresting: 'What is interesting about people in good society . . . is the mask that each one of them wears, not the reality that lies behind the mask. It is a humiliating confession, but we are all of us made out of the same stuff.'[95]

In fact nineteenth-century autobiographical writing more often leaves an impression of the elusiveness of the self, even of the deliberate avoidance of introspection, than it does of genuine self-exploration. Memories of things past can be notoriously unreliable. Trollope makes the point that 'A man does, in truth, remember that which it interests him to remember.'[96] Some autobiographers freely admit to having lost touch with their own past selves. Herbert Spencer's account of his reaction to the appearance of *The Origin of Species*, for example, is an extraordinary confession of the fact that a crucial episode in the autobiographer's life has clearly been lost to him:

> That reading it gave me great satisfaction may be safely
> inferred. Whether there was any setoff to this great satisfaction,
> I cannot now say; for I have quite forgotten the ideas and
> feelings I had . . . Whether proof that what I had supposed
> to be the sole cause, could be at best but a part cause, gave
> me any annoyance, I cannot remember; nor can I remember
> whether I was vexed by the thought that in 1852 I had failed
> to carry further the idea, then expressed, that among human
> beings the survival of those who are the select of their
> generation is a cause of development.[97]

Darwin himself is more unreliable still as an authority on his own interior life. Some three years after he wrote his *Recollections of the Development of my Mind and Character* (1876) he admitted in a note to Francis Galton: 'I have never tried looking into my own mind.'[98] Another prominent autobiographer, John Stuart Mill, made a similarly astonishing confession to Harriet Taylor in 1855 when he conceded: 'I know how deficient I am in self-consciousness & self observation.'[99] Ruskin is conscious of significant lapses of memory in *Praeterita*, noting with amazement: 'Certainly the most curious failure of memory – among the many I find – is that I don't know when I *saw* my first [Turner]!'[100] Ruskin's decision, because of the precarious state of his mental health, to exclude anything 'disagreeable or querulous' (such as his six-year marriage to Effie Gray) from *Praeterita* is well known,[101] and entirely consistent with his general stance of eschewing subjectivism – although, as in so much of his writing, for all his desire to expunge the personal from his work, *Praeterita* is in fact infinitely more self-revelatory than a good deal of

Victorian literature. And Carlyle, too, hedges about his autobiographical reflections in *Sartor Resartus* with a fictional framework involving an
imaginary protagonist and an equally imaginary editor in such a way as
effectively to displace the personal.

The milieu of nineteenth-century England was not conducive to the
writing of confessional autobiography after the manner of Rousseau.[102]
The curiously un-self-conscious self-writing of the period may be related
to the fact that Victorians were scrutinising and narrating their lives
at a crucial historical juncture, after Romanticism had foregrounded the
whole question of human consciousness, but before Freud's radical reformulation of the self.[103] Self-representation, and the forms it takes, is
closely associated with, if not determined by, the cultural imperatives of
the historical moment of its production. The transcendental philosophy
of Kant and Schelling upon which Romantic writers such as Coleridge
and Wordsworth based their own positions claimed the act of self-
consciousness to be the source and principle of all human knowledge.
By the end of the nineteenth century Freud was arguing that the real
meanings of our words and actions are utterly beyond the reach of the
conscious mind.

All this is to say that the genre of autobiography, like other literary forms, is subject to historical shifts, which means that not only is
nineteenth-century English autobiography qualitatively different from
Rousseau's eighteenth-century French confessions, but late nineteenth-
century English autobiography is quite different in kind from early. It
is salutary to remind ourselves that, while both Wordsworth and Pater
were indeed profoundly interested in the self and the development and
articulation of subjective experience, whereas the former asserted the
existence of a sense of individual identity, both unique and at the same
time representative of 'the mind of man', that is organically unified,
endures over time, and is self-aware and self-motivating ('I had a world
about me; 'twas my own,/ I made it'),[104] the latter's sense of self, in
a world newly defined by relativism, is radically reduced. In the Conclusion to *Studies in the History of the Renaissance* (1873) Pater asserts
the contingent and discontinuous nature of physical reality: 'That
clear perpetual outline of face and limb is but an image of ours . . . a
design in a web, the actual threads of which pass out beyond it.' Turning to 'the inward world of thought and feeling', he finds 'the whirlpool
is still more rapid, the flame more eager and devouring'. Perceptions of
external objects are 'loosed into a group of impressions', until ultimately
'the whole scope of observation is dwarfed into the narrow chamber
of the individual mind', 'the individual in his isolation'.[105] This disturbing reduction of consciousness to a random collection of momentary
impressions undermines the substantiality of the human mind itself;
Wordsworth's heroically liberating self, his achievement of 'Man free,
man working for himself, with choice/ Of time, and place, and object',

has been displaced by a self perceived as a prison from which the spirit may only perhaps be set free 'for a moment', by 'the individual in his isolation, each mind keeping as a solitary prisoner in his own dream of a world'.[106] One recalls the frontispiece to Freud's *Introductory Lectures on Psychoanalysis*, which represents a man lying asleep in a dungeon and dreaming of freedom, as is suggested by the gnomes sawing at the bars on his window. It is, significantly, in his prison autobiography *De Profundis*, begun in 1896, that Wilde bleakly confesses 'The soul of man is unknowable,' 'the final mystery is one's self.'[107]

Late nineteenth-century autobiography is, then, typically very different in style from Romantic autobiography, because it arises out of radically altered theories of human identity. Earlier in the century, when an altogether more confident vision of the Romantic subject had prevailed, it had seemed altogether appropriate for Coleridge to present his great philosophical and literary treatise in the form of an autobiography, the *Biographia Literaria* (1817). As he wrote in his notebook, 'Seem to have made up my mind to write my metaphysical works as *my* Life, & *in* my Life – intermixed with all the other events or history of the mind & fortunes of S. T. Coleridge.'[108] Although an equally eccentric and selective and, ironically, fragmentary work, De Quincey's *Confessions of an English Opium-Eater* (1821) articulates a similar faith in the organic unity of the individual life in its portrayal of the imaginative development of a dreamer and philosopher into full artistic consciousness. Like Wordsworth's representation of the growth of the poet's mind in *The Prelude*, the *Confessions* traces those events and experiences of his life which contributed to the unfolding of a unique and unitary Romantic consciousness.

The autobiographical writings of Coleridge, De Quincey, and Wordsworth are, then, indubitably, for all their uniqueness, the products of a particular time and milieu, a particular sensibility. But they are also the products of literary men, of prominent intellectuals, and therefore while they may be seen as representative of Romantic sensibility, they do not, of course, represent all the kinds of autobiography that were being written at this time. As Lockhart's previously quoted anonymous review in the *Quarterly* indicates, autobiography was already by the 1820s a rapidly expanding genre, one that was no longer the exclusive domain of the male intelligentsia. The emergence of class-consciousness in the 1790s, along with a new awareness of women's issues inaugurated by writers such as Mary Wollstonecraft, encouraged more extensive exploration of working-class and female identity. Working-class and women's self-writing were coming into their own. At about the same time that Coleridge and De Quincey brought their autobiographies before the world, a very young Elizabeth Barrett Browning was writing pieces on 'My own character' and 'Glimpses into my own life . . .', and the peasant poet John Clare was writing *Sketches in the Life of John Clare* and a series of autobiographical fragments. Many autobiographies by working-class men and both middle- and lower-class women were written and published in the course of the nineteenth century.[109] Lest we adopt too monolithic a view of nineteenth-century autobiography, it is important to recall that in the middle of the century not only did Newman write the *Apologia*, but Florence Nightingale wrote *Cassandra*, the governess Elizabeth Ham wrote *Elizabeth Ham, by herself, 1783–1820*, and the 'Victorian maidservant' Hannah Cullwick wrote her autobiographical 'Hannah's Places'; that 1873 saw the publication not only of Mill's *Autobiography* but also of Sara Coleridge's *Recollections of the Early Life* and Mary Somerville's *Personal Recollections*; that the Fenian political prisoner Michael Davitt published his *Leaves from a Prison Diary* in the same year, 1885, that Ruskin began to publish *Praeterita*.

Generations of critics have excluded from the autobiographical canon works, and authors, that have not conformed to a very rigidly circumscribed and prescriptive definition of the genre,[110] and it has only been in the last decade or so that such non-standard autobiographies have begun to be rediscovered. Not only was the period rich in women's and working-class autobiography, but it also produced a flourishing genre of prison autobiographies and confessions by criminals. A more generous sampling of nineteenth-century autobiography reveals, in addition to the familiar introspective personal journeys, the deployment of a personal life story for polemical purposes, as in the case of Caroline Norton's pamphlets demanding legal reform. Although most Victorian autobiographies are remarkable for their discreet avoidance of all things sexual, even in accounts of the most proper heterosexual marriage, some Victorians, such as J. A. Symonds, wrote frankly about their homosexuality, while others wrote erotic, even pornographic autobiography (often hyperbolic or fantasising), such as the eleven-volume sexual adventures of a Victorian gentleman who identifies himself only as 'Walter', entitled *My Secret Life* (1890).

The paradigm of autobiography, codified as male and middle-class, which critics have traditionally recognised and used to determine 'the undisputed masterpieces of Victorian self-writing',[111] is clearly inadequate, and it is crucial that the diversity of nineteenth-century autobiography be recognised, that definitions of the genre be broadened, and that non-standard examples of self-writing be rehabilitated and admitted to the canon. It is nevertheless significant that such a paradigm existed in the nineteenth century itself, and that it was one which effectively excluded would-be practitioners of self-writing who were not middle-class males of some intellectual standing. Hence Lockhart's article in the *Quarterly* reports on the new forms that autobiography is taking, but does not accept the lives of print-makers and cabin-boys and pickpockets as legitimate examples of the genre, rather dismisses them as risible pastiches of a noble form. The classic realist autobiography typically includes elements which would have been quite alien to many working-class writers: recollections of childhood and early familial relations, an account of the subject's formal education, at home, or more usually at a public school, and a progressive narrative of self whereby the individual surmounts any obstacles in his way to develop into a successful, fulfilled and respected member of society. Moreover, the bourgeois model of autobiography relies upon crisis, climax, and resolution in an active and reactive world, and upon the subject's economic and social self-determination. It is not hard to see why most working people simply could not mould their experiences, or square their sense of disempowerment, to such a narrative.[112]

There were, of course, some notable exceptions. The peasant poet John Clare, for instance, wrote his *Sketches in the Life of John Clare* (1821) after the type of bourgeois autobiography, describing his birth, his early education, the awakening of his poetic genius, the overcoming of personal and financial crises; but ironically such structural conformity to the classical model only serves to mark how different were the life experiences of one of his class from those of his middle-class contemporaries. He records his lineage, for instance: 'my father was one of fates chance-lings who drop into the world without the honour of matrimony ... Both my parents was illiterate to the last degree.'[113] Despite, or rather because of, his parents' lack of education, they were keen that their son should have schooling, but again Clare's experiences were a long way removed from those recounted in other autobiographies of the period:

> my mothers hopfull ambition ran high of being able to make me a good scholar, as she said she expirenced enough in her own case to avoid bringing up her children in ignorance, but god help her, her hopfull and tender kindness was often crossd with difficultys, for there was often enough to do to keep cart upon wheels, as the saying is, without incuring an extra expence of putting me to school, though she never lost the opportunity when she was able to send me nor woud my father interfere with her kind intentions till downright nessesity from poverty forced him to check her kind intentions ... as to my schooling, I think never a year passd me till I was 11 or 12 but 3 months or more at the worst of times was luckily spared for my improvement, first with an old woman in the village and latterly with a master at a distance from it[114]

Clare's account of his reading as a child similarly marks his class difference even as it invokes the practice of contemporaries who fondly recalled in their autobiographies the books that shaped their childhood imagination and introduced them to adult learning. The opportunities available to the young Clare were pitifully few. Apart from sixpenny romances and chapbooks, his reading material was confined to books he could beg or borrow for a brief period. He remembers how reading a borrowed copy of Thomson's *Seasons* for the first time at the age of thirteen 'made my heart twitter with joy', and how he 'resolved to posses one my self', and the difficulty of realising that desire.[115] He also recalls reading *Robinson Crusoe* for the first time:

> twas in the winter and I borrowd it of a boy at s[c]hool who said it was his uncles and seemed very loath to lend it me, but pressing him with anxious persuasions and assuring him of its safety while in my hands he lent it me that day to be returned in the morning when I came to school, but in the night a great snow fell which made it impossible to keep my promise as I coud not get, Glinton being 2 miles from our village were I went to school, so I had the pleasure of this delightful companion for a week[116]

Like other writers, he tells of his developing recognition and nurturing of his poetical talents. He notes his difference from his companions, his preference for solitude, his perception of the natural world; he fondly recalls his early employer Francis Gregory, and how he provided 'the Nursery for fostering my rustic Song'.[117] And he describes how he used to try out his first attempts at writing poetry on his parents, all the while pretending that he had copied the poems from the works of an established poet:

> their remarks was very useful to me at somethings they woud laugh here I distinguishd Affectation and consiet [conceit] from nature some verses they woud desire me to repeat again as they said they coud not understand them here I discoverd obscurity from common sense and always benefited by making it as much like the latter as I coud, for I thought if they coud not understand me my taste shoud be wrong founded and not agreeable to nature, so I always strove to shun it for the future and wrote my pieces according to their critisisms, little thinking when they heard me read them that I was the author[118]

As far as paid work was concerned at this point in his life, Clare's preference was for hard labour in the fields rather than for gardening or service, and he explains how his parents became less enthusiastic about his book-learning when they felt that he was not going to make use of it to better his lot in the world. But ultimately he was to make use of his education in ways that they had never imagined. Like many women writers of the period, Clare first turned to the idea of professional writing out of economic necessity. His own and his father's illnesses had reduced the family to poverty and debt, and he decided to try to publish his poetry as a way of rescuing them from their dire situation. Once again, it is the contrast between his own experiences and those of his better placed contemporaries that is striking. The first printer he approaches tries to take advantage of him, although he shortly afterwards meets with happier experiences. But, more significantly, he has to cope with the idea of communicating with a public. He has never had any difficulty in pouring forth his songs, but the proposition that he must write an 'Address to the Public' ('which I knew little about addressing') to accompany a prospectus of the volume – an address, in other words, to potential middle-class subscribers and readers – is a daunting one.[119]

As will be clear from the above extracts from his writing, Clare's class and regional origins are manifestly evident in his robust and forthright language, which is liberally sprinkled with dialect words and popular expressions. His punctuation, spelling and grammar are highly idiosyncratic; as he confessed, 'Grammer I never read a page of in my Life.'[120] He did once try to read the 'Universal Spelling Book', he explains,

> but finding a jumble of words classed under this name and that name and this such a figure of speech and that another hard worded figure I turned from further notice of it in instant disgust for as I knew I coud talk to be understood I thought by the same method my writing might be made out as easy and as proper, so in the teeth of grammer I pursued my literary journey as warm as usual[121]

His is language which comes out of a rich oral tradition, and deserves to be read aloud with gusto if its rhythms and accents are to be fully appreciated. Nevertheless, it would be a mistake to regard *Sketches in the Life of John Clare* as the spontaneous outpourings of an untutored rustic. As its modern editor points out, this is as much a shaped life as are the more mainstream autobiographies of the period; moreover, 'Clare had literary models, at least in part, for the kind of life that he wanted to write,' even if those models included *Jack and the Beanstalk* and *Robinson Crusoe* as well as *Pilgrim's Progress*.[122] More significantly still, Clare was writing his life for a very specific audience, and was conscious of the need to present a particular image of himself. *Sketches in the Life of John Clare* was 'addressed to his friend John Taylor Esqr' and, as Eric Robinson points out, 'the poet wishes to present himself to his evangelical publisher and to his patrons, Lord Radstock and Mrs Emmerson, as a very proper object for their support. He therefore puts himself forward as Hogarth's Industrious Apprentice.'[123] Clare also makes a point of reassuring his publisher and patrons that he is no radical:

In politics I never dabbled to understand them thoroughly
with the old dish that was served to my forefathers I am
content. but I believe the reading a small pamphlet on the
Murder of the french King many years ago with other
inhuman butcheries cured me very early from thinking
favourably of radicalism the words 'revolution and reform'
so much in fashion with sneering arch infidels thrills me
with terror when ever I see them[124]

Historians and critics of working-class autobiography have drawn
attention to the ambiguities of the genre for its proletarian practitioners.
On the one hand, that men and women of the labouring classes were
writing their lives indicated a new pride in their identity, their history
and their experiences, and a determination to distinguish themselves as
individuals from totalising representations of the proletariat as a homogeneous mass. But, on the other hand, autobiography is so closely associated with the emergence and promotion of middle-class ideologies of
individualism and self-determination, with a subjectivist aesthetic, that
for working-class people to engage in self-writing involves a kind of
embourgeoisement, a complicity with, and capitulation to, middle-class
values. In short, although from one perspective working-class autobiographies are a sign of empowerment and emancipation, from another
they signify the potential for the culture of the labouring classes to become assimilated and subjugated by the dominant culture.[125]
    That there were ideologically determined formal parameters around
what we might be tempted to think of as the most personal and individual form of public utterance is, of course, indisputable. Autobiography
is not simply raw, unmediated personal experience but carefully and
artfully constructed life narrative which refers to, draws upon, or sometimes writes against, common figures, tropes, structures and traditions
of life writing. Far from being the ultimate autonomous expression of
self-being, it is fundamentally intertextual. This is in large part because
the autobiographer is required to negotiate a difficult path in order to
justify the enterprise. The life that is narrated must seem exceptional
enough to be worth the telling, and yet in some ways representative;
the decision to devote a whole book to oneself must appear to arise
not out of mere egotism but out of the desire to teach something of
value to the world at large. Hence the appeals by even the most unlikely
of autobiographers to common experience and the widespread tendency to claim for their works an ostensible moral purpose. Even 'Walter'
prefaces his eleven-volume account of his sodomising, 'fist-fucking',
'minetting', 'gamahuching', and general whoremongering, with the disclaimer, 'Whatever society may say, it is but a narrative of human life,
perhaps the every day life of thousands, if the confession could be had.'
And although he says at one point that the autobiography is 'written by

myself and for *myself*', and counts among the main pleasures of writing it that 'in doing so I almost had my sexual treats over again', he concludes a chapter 'On copulation, and the copulative organs' with a tongue-in-cheek statement as to its educational and moral usefulness:

> This is a description of the organs employed, and the object, art, and manner of using them, which is called fucking – together with its results. It is written in this simple, homely, yet classical manner; so as to enable the dullest, simplest, and most unsophisticated to understand it. It is specially suitable for ignorant boys and girls from twelve to fifteen years of age, – at which period they begin to think of such matters, and when they may study it with most advantage, because and at that age the world tries its best to obscure the consideration, and to hinder all real knowledge about it getting to them. It may be read usefully after evening family prayers also, by older members of the family, to whom at times, it may serve as an aphrodisiac, and it will spare many young, but full grown people, trouble and loss of time in searching for knowledge which ought to be known to all, but which owing to a false morality, is a subject put aside as improper.[126]

If 'Walter' could thus justify his autobiography as having a didactic purpose it is not hard to imagine how more upstanding citizens were able to lend a moral to their life stories.

John Henry Newman's *Apologia Pro Vita Sua* (1864) has little in common with 'Walter's' *My Secret Life* (indeed, Newman is said to have felt queasy when he thought of married clergy), but in the case of this most celebrated of Victorian autobiographies too the author's professed purpose in writing his life is not what most readers, either then or now, find most compelling about the book. The *Apologia* is another major Victorian text that originated as a reaction to a piece of contemporary journalism. Newman wrote it, he explains in the lengthy prefatory chapters, in response to Charles Kingsley's 'accusations against the Catholic Church', made in the course of a review in *Macmillan's Magazine*; specifically, his public statement that 'Truth, for its own sake, had never been a virtue with the Roman clergy. Father Newman informs us that it need not, and on the whole ought not to be.'[127] Although Newman argues that he aims 'to be simply personal and historical', and not to engage in 'expounding Catholic doctrine', he confesses he has only been able to overcome his repugnance at exposing his life to public scrutiny 'for the sake of the Religion which I profess, and of the Priesthood in which I am unworthily included, and of my friends and of my foes, and of that general public which consists of neither one nor the other'.[128] And yet for generations of readers it has been not the religion he professed but the romance of his life which has attracted them to the *Apologia*. As Wilde's Gilbert exclaims in his encomium to autobiography in 'The Critic as Artist',

> The mode of thought that Cardinal Newman represented –
> if that can be called a mode of thought which seeks to solve
> intellectual problems by a denial of the supremacy of the
> intellect – may not, cannot, I think, survive. But the world
> will never weary of watching that troubled soul in its progress
> from darkness to darkness. The lonely church at Littlemore,
> where 'the breath of the morning is damp, and worshippers
> are few,' will always be dear to it, and whenever men see the
> yellow snapdragon blossoming on the wall of Trinity they will
> think of that gracious undergraduate who saw in the flower's
> sure recurrence a prophecy that he would abide for ever with
> the Benign Mother of his days – a prophecy that Faith, in her
> wisdom or her folly, suffered not to be fulfilled.[129]

For some modern readers, the intellectual moment which the *Apologia* articulates most compellingly is not so much the crisis in the Anglican Church precipitated by the Oxford Movement and ultimately by Newman's conversion to Rome in 1845, but the crisis precipitated by Darwin in 1859, whereby the natural world which had for so long seemed to provide proof of God's existence now seemed to speak of His absence. Newman poignantly records his acute sense of the aboriginal calamity of original sin:

> I look out of myself into the world of men, and there I see a
> sight which fills me with unspeakable distress. The world
> seems simply to give the lie to that great truth, of which my
> being is so full; and the effect upon me is, in consequence, as
> a matter of necessity, as confusing as if it denied that I am in
> existence myself. If I looked into a mirror, and did not see my
> face, I should have the sort of feeling which actually comes
> upon me, when I look into the living busy world, and see no
> reflection of its Creator.[130]

The natural world having failed him, the only solution, for Newman and others like him, was to turn to the world within, to his inner sense of God's presence, and it was precisely this strategy which made the *Apologia*'s highly personal account of an individual's inner spiritual journey so very eloquent of its time:

> Were it not for this voice, speaking so clearly in my conscience
> and my heart, I should be an atheist, or a pantheist, or a

polytheist when I looked into the world. I am speaking for myself only; and I am far from denying the real force of the arguments in proof of a God, drawn from the general facts of human society, but these do not warm me or enlighten me; they do not take away the winter of my desolation, or make the buds unfold and the leaves grow within me, and my moral being rejoice. The sight of the world is nothing else than the prophet's scroll, full of 'lamentations, and mourning, and woe.'[131]

The only thing that sustains him is his inner conviction of God's existence, 'this absolute primary truth', the grounds of which he nevertheless finds difficult to put 'into logical shape'. By contrast, he has no difficulty at all in articulating the reason for his sense of the chaos of the world before him. Although Darwinian evolution is nowhere explicitly mentioned, it pervades every aspect of his language, from the metaphors and vocabulary to the sentence structure:

To consider the world in its length and breadth, its various history, the many races of man, their starts, their fortunes, their mutual alienation, their conflicts; and then their ways, habits, governments, forms of worship; their enterprises, their aimless courses, their random achievements and acquirements, the impotent conclusions of long-standing facts, the tokens so faint and broken, of a superintending design, the blind evolution of what turn out to be great powers or truths, the progress of things, as if from unreasoning elements, not towards final causes, the greatness and littleness of man, his far-reaching aims, his short duration, the curtain hung over his futurity, the disappointments of life, the defeat of good, the success of evil, physical pain, mental anguish, the prevalence and intensity of sin, the pervading idolatries, the corruptions, the dreary hopeless irreligion, that condition of the whole race so fearfully yet exactly described in the Apostle's words, 'having no hope and without God in the world,' – all this is a vision to dizzy and appal; and inflicts upon the mind the sense of a profound mystery, which is absolutely beyond human solution.[132]

In this powerful rhetorical evocation of evolution's devastating path of destruction through the world, Newman suggests, in a single, monumentally long sentence, the huge vistas of time opened up by the new geology. The reader is 'dizzied' and 'appalled' by the vertiginous perspective that is opened up, by the almost unbearable accumulation of phrases which are in themselves so eloquently expressive of the evolutionary variousness, aimlessness and randomness of the world's history, the absence of a 'superintending design'. The very rhythms and cadences conjure the 'starts' and 'impotent conclusions' of an evolutionary world-view; the short clauses within a seemingly never-ending sentence the paradoxical 'greatness and littleness of man, his far-reaching aims, his short duration'. Faith is pitted against 'blind evolution' in the very texture of the prose, the post-lapsarian state signified metaphorically in a terrifying vision of post-Darwinian degeneration.

Another writer in whose autobiography may be found side by side biblical mythology and contemporary scientific ideas is Ruskin. In the early chapters of *Praeterita*, he figures his childhood self in the garden of the family home at Herne Hill as being like Adam in the Garden of Eden:

> The differences of primal importance which I observed between the nature of this garden, and that of Eden, as I had imagined it, were, that, in this one, *all* the fruit was forbidden; and there were no companionable beasts: in other respects the little domain answered every purpose of Paradise to me.[133]

And yet later in the narrative he represents that same child as a primitive form of life on the evolutionary scale:

> I was simply a little floppy and soppy tadpole, – little more than a stomach with a tail to it, flattening and wriggling itself up the crystal ripples and in the pure sands of the spring-head of youth.[134]

Like Darwin and Spencer, about whose theories he was so scathing elsewhere in his writing, Ruskin wrote about himself in his autobiography in terms which suggest the objective scientific method of the natural historian. He examines himself as a child as if he were another species, and attempts to describe 'the effect on my own mind of meeting myself, by turning back, face to face'.[135] Ruskin was the child of deeply Evangelical parents who brought him up in circumstances which meant that 'what powers of imagination I possessed, either fastened themselves on inanimate things – the sky, the leaves, and pebbles, observable within the walls of Eden – or caught at any opportunity of flight into regions of romance, compatible with the objective realities of existence in the nineteenth century, within a mile and a quarter of Camberwell Green.'[136] It seemed no less natural for him to invoke scriptural models alongside scientific ones, in the tradition of the Bridgewater Treatises, than it was, from his earliest childhood compositions onwards, to draw upon scientific as well as aesthetic sources in his writing. As he notes of a small volume written when he was seven years old on the subject of an electrical storm, the adaptation of materials for my story out of Joyce's *Scientific Dialogues* and *Manfred*, is an extremely perfect type of the interwoven temper of my mind, at the beginning of days just as much as at their end – which has always made foolish scientific readers doubt my books because there was love of beauty in them, and foolish aesthetic readers doubt my books because there was love of science in them.[137]

Ruskin was a precocious child, and in *Praeterita* the writer in his sixties goes into some detail about the virtues and inadequacies of his education and general upbringing, using his own experiences as a benchmark for the kind of education that should be offered by the St George's schools which he was instrumental in founding. To modern readers, his life as a child seems rigidly over-disciplined to the point of cruelty. He was permitted no toys by his Evangelical parents, had throughout his childhood 'been steadily whipped' if he was 'troublesome', and was from his birth 'bred for "the Church" ', despite the fact that 'the horror of Sunday used even to cast its prescient gloom as far back in the week as Friday – and all the glory of Monday, with church seven days removed again, was no equivalent for it.'[138] Ruskin counts among the blessings of his childhood 'Peace, obedience, faith', the cultivation of 'the habit of fixed attention with both eyes and mind', and the development of all his bodily senses. But against these he weighs 'the equally dominant calamities', the chief of which was that he 'had nothing to love'.[139]

John Stuart Mill's was not an Evangelical childhood – indeed, he was able to describe himself as 'one of the very few examples, in this country, of one who has not thrown off religious belief, but never had it' – and yet there are remarkable parallels between his own upbringing and Ruskin's. Like Ruskin, he was provided with an education which equipped him for a distinguished intellectual career, but, like him too, he was deprived of playthings, companionship and love. In the *Autobiography* (1873), paradoxically a work of passionate feeling, he makes much of his emotional starvation under the direction of a father who 'professed the greatest contempt' for 'passionate emotions of all sorts, and for everything which has been said or written in exaltation of them'.[140] In an earlier draft, he wrote more explicitly, 'mine was not an education of love but of fear.'[141]

Nevertheless, he makes that education one of the primary justifications for presenting 'such a memorial of so uneventful a life as mine' to the world, explaining in the opening paragraph of the *Autobiography*,

> I have thought that in an age in which education, and its improvement, are the subject of more, if not of profounder study than at any former period of English history, it may be

useful that there should be some record of an education which was unusual and remarkable, and which, whatever else it may have done, has proved how much more than is commonly supposed may be taught, and well taught, in those early years which, in the common modes of what is called instruction, are little better than wasted.[142]

It was indeed an unusual and remarkable education. Personally supervised by his father, the Utilitarian James Mill, he began to learn Greek at the age of three, before moving on to arithmetic, Latin at the age of seven, logic at twelve, and political economy at thirteen. By the age of five he was engaged in a regular private reading programme, comprising chiefly histories, such as Robertson's, Hume's, and Gibbon's, and by his eighth year was an avid reader of books on experimental science, including Ruskin's favourite, Joyce's *Scientific Dialogues*. Mill acknowledges the extraordinary nature of this educational experiment, but claims that his own natural talents were no more, indeed rather less than the ordinary:

> In the course of instruction which I have partially retraced, the point most superficially apparent is the effort to give, during the years of childhood, an amount of knowledge in what are considered the higher branches of education, which is seldom acquired (if acquired at all) until the age of manhood. The result of the experiment shews the ease with which this may be done, and places in a strong light the wretched waste of so many precious years as are spent in acquiring the modicum of Latin and Greek commonly taught to schoolboys; . . . If I had been by nature quick of apprehension, or had possessed a very accurate and retentive memory, or were of a remarkably active and energetic character, the trial would not be conclusive; but in all these natural gifts I am rather below than above par. What I could do, could assuredly be done by any boy or girl of average capacity and healthy physical constitution: and if I have accomplished anything, I owe it, among other fortunate circumstances, to the fact that through the early training bestowed on me by my father, I started, I may fairly say, with an advantage of a quarter of a century over my contemporaries.[143]

Like so many other autobiographers of his generation, Mill portrays himself here as at once exceptional and representative of the ordinary run of humanity. The representative quality of his mind is insisted upon from the outset, and proffered as another justification for the autobiography:

in an age of transition in opinions, there may be somewhat both of interest and of benefit in noting the successive phases of any mind which was always pressing forward, equally ready to learn and to unlearn either from its own thoughts or from those of others.[144]

In tracing his own intellectual development, and the transition in his own opinions, from the narrowly sectarian Benthamism in which he was immersed in his youth to a new respect for the imagination and the feelings learned in his twenties, Mill believed he traced that of his age. Elsewhere Mill identifies Jeremy Bentham and Samuel Taylor Coleridge as 'the two great seminal minds of England in their age', arguing that their country is indebted to them 'not only for the greater part of the important ideas which have been thrown into circulation among its thinking men in their time, but for a revolution in its general modes of thought and investigation';[145] but in the *Autobiography* the tribute goes to James Mill and Wordsworth as the major formative influences on his own mind and the intellectual revolution of his times. In common, again, with numerous contemporary autobiographers, novelists and poets,[146] Mill describes 'a crisis in my mental history', making it the focal point of his life narrative. At the age of twenty this extraordinarily well-educated but emotionally starved young man was overcome by despair: 'I seemed to have nothing left to live for.'[147] He was saved by reading Wordsworth's poems, which he describes, employing a common trope of his day, as 'a medicine for my state of mind', in that they 'seemed to be the very culture of the feelings, which I was in quest of'.[148]

Wordsworth's long autobiographical poem *The Prelude* had been published in 1850, strengthening his status as the great poet of the feelings, and providing a mid-century paradigm for Victorian autobiographers such as Mill. But if it was Wordsworth who provided redemption from Mill's youthful intellectual crisis, it is Harriet Taylor who is honoured in the *Autobiography* as 'the source of a great part of all that I have attempted to do, or hope to effect hereafter, for human improvement'. In his wife he found the perfect union of the speculative intellect embodied by his father and the poetry exemplified by Wordsworth, and he took advantage of the opportunity of writing his autobiography to acknowledge the level of the contribution she had made to his published writings, which were, he said, 'not the work of one mind, but of the fusion of two', 'as much her work as mine'.[149] Such open recognition of his wife's intellect was not at all well-received in his own day, and neither has it been in our own. Leslie Stephen, for instance, sceptically notes, 'It may be true that Mrs. Mill was more of a poet than Carlyle, and more of a thinker than Mill himself; that she was like Shelley, but that Shelley was but a child to what she ultimately became;

that her wisdom was "all but unrivalled," and much more to the same
purpose,' but, he asks, how can it be proved or disproved of 'a person
of whom the world knows so little'? Thus he turns Mill's attempt
to introduce to the public 'one whom the world had no opportunity of
knowing' back upon itself. Stephen's own view is that 'these extravagant expressions of admiration may have been lavished upon a living
echo – an echo, it is true, skilful enough to anticipate as well as to
repeat, but still essentially an echo.'[150] Modern critics have been similarly hostile to the notion that one of the great male thinkers of the
century might have owed so much to a woman. Jack Stillinger, for
instance, remarks in 1961 that Harriet 'may have aided Mill by ordinary
wifely discussion and debate', but asserts that she 'was no originator of
ideas'; he concludes, 'It is unfortunate that Mill did not simply thank
his wife for encouragement, perhaps also for transcribing a manuscript
or making an index, and let it go at that,' as, he might have added, male
academics have been in the habit of doing for years.[151]

The enlightened author of *The Subjection of Women* (1869) was acutely
aware of the inequitable position of women in Victorian society, and
his praise for Harriet Taylor's role in his life's work constitutes not
only a personal acknowledgement to his wife, but also a more general acknowledgement of women's unwritten and unrecognised lives.
Nineteenth-century women were taught to think of themselves not as
individuals but, in the words of the highly influential writer of conduct
books, Sarah Ellis, as 'relative creatures':

> Women considered in their distinct and abstract nature, as
> isolated beings, must lose more than half their worth. They
> are, in fact, from their own constitution, and from the station
> they occupy in the world, strictly speaking, relative creatures.
> If, therefore, they are endowed only with such faculties as
> render them striking and distinguished in themselves, without
> the faculty of instrumentality, they are only as dead letters in
> the volume of human life, filling what would otherwise be a
> blank space, but doing nothing more.[152]

Women encouraged to view themselves in this way would hardly think
it appropriate to engage in such an egocentric activity as writing an
autobiography. The dominant ideology which positioned women firmly
in the home and shackled them with the entire burden of familial and
domestic responsibilities helps explain why most Victorian women, even
those who indulged in some form of self-writing, felt obliged to oper-
ate outside the formal parameters of autobiography.[153]

Women autobiographers found themselves in a similarly parlous position to that of working-class autobiographers in the nineteenth century,
caught between a sense of exclusion from a genre traditionally defined

as male and the necessity of collusion with its masculinist assumptions and imperatives if they were to tell their own life stories. It is easy to see why most female autobiographers would have been obliged to deviate from the paradigmatic form of bourgeois male self-writing, for many middle-class Victorian women were, like working-class men and women, denied agency and the opportunities enjoyed by their male counterparts to achieve recognition in the public sphere. Early feminist attempts to characterise the differences between female and male autobiography stressed the fact that women's definitions of their identity tend to depend upon relationships with others as opposed to men's assertion of their individualism; suggested that women's life-writing is more personal and intimate than that of men, who tend to project a more public persona; and pointed to formal differences between the discontinuities and fragmentariness of women's lives and life narratives compared with the coherent linearity of men's life stories.[154] However, more recent feminist critics of autobiography have pointed out the limitations of such a model of difference, which often cannot be sustained in individual cases, and which tends to elide differences between women and their diverse rhetorical strategies.[155] Ahistorical, totalising and essentialist accounts of female self-writing are now giving way to analyses grounded in a recognition of the specific historical and cultural circumstances which produced particular autobiographical texts.

One woman whose autobiographical writings were closely linked to, even determined by, the particular legal disabilities suffered by women in the middle of the nineteenth century, and who wrote her life for polemical reformist purposes, was Caroline Norton. Norton was a well-connected writer who gained prominence for herself in the highest political and literary circles in London in the 1830s. A close friend of Lord Melbourne and other senior members of Lord Grey's reform ministry, she was establishing herself as a successful poet and novelist when fame turned to notoriety in 1836. Unlike Mill, she did not have the good fortune to marry a compatible partner, and after several years of unhappy marriage, in which she suffered continual violence and abuse, she was forced to undergo the further indignity of being publicly accused by her husband of adultery with Lord Melbourne, who was by then Prime Minister. George Norton's action was clearly politically and financially motivated, and his accusations did not stand up in court, but the episode marked the beginning of a long publicly-waged battle on Caroline Norton's behalf to regain access to her children, over whom her husband exercised exclusive legal custody rights, and subsequently to maintain control over her own income.

From the outset, and in the numerous pamphlets and letters she wrote in the pursuit of justice and the reform of English law, she drew upon her autobiographical experiences in constructing her case, and couched her argument in a passionately personal style. She anticipated the disapproval with which such a strategy would meet, and defends herself accordingly. She opens her pamphlet on *English Laws for Women* (1854), for example, by acknowledging that 'To publish comments on my own case for the sake of obtaining sympathy; to prove merely that my husband has been unjust, and my fate a hard one, would be a very poor and barren ambition.' The real purpose of her appeal is more far-reaching: 'I desire to prove, not my suffering or his injustices, but that the present law of England cannot prevent any such suffering, or control any such injustice.' 'I write,' she affirms, 'in the hope that the law may be amended.'[156] She is fully aware of how society at large will view the 'interference with such a subject' by a mere woman, 'and a woman personally interested' at that. Moreover, she notes, 'In arguing my case from my own example, I am not ignorant that there are persons who think such argument blameable on other grounds; who deem a husband's right so indefeasible, and his title so sacred, that even a wronged wife should keep silence.' But she determines to speak nevertheless, and in speaking up for herself to articulate the misery of the multitudes of other unhappily married women who have no legal existence and therefore enjoy no protection from the law. She is, then, a representative women, yet one who feels compelled to tell her own life story as a way of bringing about reform:

> oppression is brought to a halt not by a multitude of instances, but by some single example; which example may be neither more nor less important than others, though it be made the argument and opportunity for change.[157]

She duly begins the central section of her argument with the words 'I shall now give a narrative of my own case, as an example of what can be done under the English law of 1853.'[158] And once again, and most powerfully, at the end of the pamphlet, she vigorously defends her decision to make use of her own autobiography as she has, to bring the domestic misery which, in the view of many, should have remained private, into the interdicted public domain:

> Ah! how often, in the course of this session, in the course of this year, will *the same men*, who read this appeal with a strong adverse prejudice, – be roused by some thought in a favourite author; struck by some noble anecdote; touched by some beautiful pageant of human feeling, seen among glittering lights from a side-box; chaunted perhaps in a foreign tongue. And yet I have an advantage over these, for *my history is real* . . . Let that thought haunt you, through the music of your Sonnambulas and Desdemonas, and be with you in your readings of histories and romances, and your criticism of the jurisprudence of countries less free than our own. I *really* wept

and suffered in my early youth, – for wrong done, not *by* me, but *to* me, – and the ghost of whose scandal is raised against me this day. I *really* suffered the extremity of earthly shame without deserving it . . . I *really* lost my young children – craved for them, struggled for them, was barred from them, – and came too late to see one who had died a painful and convulsive death, except in his coffin. I *really* have gone through much, that if it were invented, would move you.[159]

Curiously, Caroline Norton has never been popular with feminists, either in her own day or since. This is partly because of her reputation as a socialite, and partly because of her avowed anti-feminism, and her stated view that men are superior to women and that she sought justice for women rather than equality, despite the fact that such attitudes may have been articulated strategically rather than been genuinely held. But oddly enough one of the reasons why feminists of her own time viewed her with suspicion was precisely the strongly autobiographical element in her writing. Contemporary feminists such as Harriet Martineau accused her of thinking only of herself, and of only concerning herself with the legal disabilities of women in general when her own circumstances brought her face to face with the fact of her own legal non-existence, as if it were outrageously inappropriate for a woman to make the personal political, to make the catastrophe that befell her and the personal opprobrium she incurred the catalyst for a fight not only for her own rights but for the rights of all women.[160]

Martineau preferred the perceived style of a woman like Florence Nightingale, whom she characterises in her obituary as 'the lady with the lamp', and praises for having self-effacingly 'effected two great things: a mighty reform in the care of the sick and an opening for her sex into the region of serious business, in proportion to their ability to maintain a place in it'.[161] Martineau was a great friend and supporter of Nightingale, and knew enough about her early life to be aware that the domestic pursuits that a young middle-class lady of the time was expected to engage in were uncongenial to her. She notes of Florence and her sister Parthenope,

> The sisters grew up unspoiled, and thoroughly exercised in the best parts of middle-class education, while living in an atmosphere of accomplishment, such as belongs to a station and a family connection like theirs . . . yet, as we have all seen, Florence had as familiar an acquaintance with the world's daily work as any farmer's or shopkeeper's daughter. She was never quite happy, in fact, till she had escaped from the region of factitious interests and superficial pursuits and devoted herself to stern, practical toil, appropriated to a benevolent end.[162]

But the blandness of her tone here, and her later assertion that Night-ingale 'was no declaimer, but a housewifely woman',[163] makes it clear that she had not read her friend's enraged account of her early life in her brilliant autobiographical fragment *Cassandra*.[164] Had she done so, she would have been aware that Nightingale's contribution to the improvement of the position of women was no less personally motivated than was Norton's.

Nightingale makes *Cassandra* the vehicle of other women's stories. As she notes,

> if they were strong, all of them, they would not need to
> have their story told, for all the world would read it in the
> missions they have fulfilled. It is for common place, every-day
> characters that we tell our tale – because it is the sample of
> hundreds of lives (or rather deaths) of persons who cannot
> fight with society, or who, unsupported by the sympathies
> about them, give up their own destiny as not worth the fierce
> and continued struggle necessary to accomplish it.[165]

But, as in Norton's representations, the real story is her own, and the most impassioned cries against the constraints imposed upon middle-class women are in the first person:

> We fast mentally, scourge ourselves morally, use the
> intellectual hair-shirt, in order to subdue that perpetual day-
> dreaming, which is so dangerous. We resolve 'this day month
> I will be free from it'; twice a day with prayer and written
> record of the times when we have indulged in it, we
> endeavour to combat it. Never, with the slightest success. By
> mortifying vanity we do ourselves no good. It is the want of
> interest in our life which produces it; by filling up that want
> of interest in our life we can alone remedy it. And, did we
> even see this, how can we make the difference? How obtain
> the interest which society declares *she* does not want, and *we*
> cannot want?[166]

In place of such self-martyrdom she calls for real pain:

> Give us back our suffering, we cry to Heaven in our hearts –
> suffering rather than indifferentism . . . Better have pain than
> paralysis![167]

Tropes of suffering, torture, starvation and forced feeding pervade this woman's text, as in Nightingale's account of the degrading denial of autonomy implied by the practice of women being 'read aloud to':

> If we do attempt to do anything in company, what is the
> system of literary exercise which we pursue? Everybody
> reads aloud out of their own book or newspaper – or, every
> five minutes, something is said. And what is it to be 'read
> aloud to'? The most miserable exercise of the human intellect.
> Or rather, is it any exercise at all? It is like lying on one's
> back, with one's hands tied and having liquid poured down
> one's throat. Worse than that, because suffocation would
> immediately ensue and put a stop to this operation. But no
> suffocation would stop the other.[168]

Against such violent invocations of forced feeding are placed similarly
shocking images of intellectual and moral starvation:

> To have no food for our heads, no food for our hearts, no
> food for our activity, is that nothing? If we have no food for
> the body, how do we cry out, how all the world hears of it,
> how all the newspapers talk of it, with a paragraph headed in
> great capital letters, DEATH FROM STARVATION! But
> suppose one were to put a paragraph in the *Times*, Death of
> Thought from Starvation, or Death of Moral Activity from
> Starvation, how people would stare, how they would laugh
> and wonder![169]

As part of her indictment of the malnourished condition of women,
Nightingale sternly critiques the institution of marriage as it is constituted in the nineteenth century, although without the personal rage of
Caroline Norton. Her own focus is somewhat different. In the artifi-
cially constrained world in which they now live, she asks, how can a
man and a woman come to learn enough of each other to know whether
or not they can live happily together? Almost the only way in which
this is possible under present circumstances, namely where 'accident or
relationship has thrown them together in their childhood, and acquaintance has grown up naturally and unconsciously', is one which is unde-
sirable for biological reasons:

> in novels, it is generally cousins who marry; and *now* it seems
> the only natural thing – the only possible way of making any
> intimacy. And yet, we know that intermarriage between
> relations is in direct contravention of the laws of nature for
> the well-being of the race; witness the Quakers, the Spanish
> Grandees, the royal races, the secluded valleys of mountainous
> countries, where madness, degeneration of race, defective
> organisation and cretinism flourish and multiply.[170]

In language newly informed by contemporary ideas about heredity, natural selection, and racial evolution, Nightingale exposes the unnatural tendencies of even the most 'natural' of current courtship practices.

There are other ways in which this polemical text is rendered less personal than Norton's. For example, through her subversive references to classical mythology (in her choice as persona of Cassandra, the prophetess doomed never to be believed) and to the Scriptures (hers is 'The voice of one crying in the "crowd" ') Nightingale brilliantly carves out for herself the position of a female John the Baptist heralding the coming of a female Christ. Such strategies also have the effect of displacing the personal onto a more universalised, mythologised, cultural plane. By deploying a pagan/Christian prophetic voice, she rises above the anguished tones which characterise the most poignantly personal parts of her text:

> Why cannot we *make use* of the noble rising heroisms of our own day, instead of leaving them to rust?
> They have nothing to do.[171]

And yet such passages are at the heart of this extraordinary piece of writing, making it as autobiographically centred a work of polemic as Norton's own.

It is, interestingly, though, as difficult to determine the generic classification of *Cassandra* as it is to classify much of Caroline Norton's work. Originally intended as a novel, but eventually included in a long meditation on religious and philosophical matters, this autobiographical-fragment-cum-political-tract does not fit into conventional, male-defined generic categories.[172] As a feminist intervention into the historically male genre of sage-writing, *Cassandra* raises important questions about gender and genre in the nineteenth century, and about ways in which women writers accommodated themselves to and appropriated masculine discourse.[173] The generic imperative, fundamental to both autobiography and sage-writing in the nineteenth century, that the private and the personal be articulated in a public voice, posed particular problems for women, whose right to speak in public was severely circumscribed.[174] Nightingale was certainly all too aware of the interdiction on women's meaningful speech ('Men . . . say . . . "Why don't you talk in society?" I can pursue a connected conversation, or I can be silent; but to drop a remark, as it is called every two minutes, how wearisome it is') and of the cruel trick of teaching women to be proud of the very role of keeper of the 'domestic hearth' which disables them from participating in life beyond the domestic sphere.[175] She herself, of course, eventually broke out of that sphere, although the popular representation of her as 'the lady with the lamp' ensured that her activities were viewed as exceptional but not inappropriate to an angel in the house who took her heavenly attributes to the battlefield. But it is significant that *Cassandra*, which makes such potentially incendiary public and political use of private experience, had none of the public status enjoyed by the works of the other, male Victorian sages; that it did not in fact become a public document until 1928.

At about the same time as Harriet Martineau wrote her celebrated obituary of Florence Nightingale, she also wrote her own. Both women believed themselves to be close to death in 1855, although in fact Martineau lived until 1876 and Nightingale until 1910. The relationship between these two invalids, who corresponded regularly for many years, is a fascinating one. Whether their illnesses were psychoneurotic or strategic (Nightingale notes in *Cassandra* that 'A married woman was heard to wish that she could break a limb that she might have a little time to herself. Many take advantage of the fear of "infection" to do the same'),[176] both women exercised enormous influence in the most 'masculine' departments of the public sphere from their invalid couches. Nightingale's life story was much more to Martineau's taste than that of a woman whom she saw as 'violating all good taste by her obtrusiveness in society, and oppressing every body about her by her epicurean selfishness every day, while raising in print an eloquent cry on behalf of the oppressed.'[177] Here was a single woman, like herself, who had withdrawn from the world, and shown what a woman could accomplish of real significance if she worked hard enough.

To write one's own obituary smacks of the kind of egotism that Ruskin detected in those Renaissance dignitaries who commissioned their own funerary monuments, or that Browning created in the Bishop ordering his tomb, but it is perhaps understandable that a woman who had so remarkably taken control of her life at a time when women were universally encouraged to do otherwise, and who had spoken out on all subjects where women were meant to be silent, should have wanted to take control of her written life, to give voice to her own experiences too. She wrote the obituary in the same year as she wrote her autobiography, which was also intended for publication after her death, and in both texts she presents herself in an oddly contradictory way. In the obituary, for example, written in the third person, she appears complicit with the idea that women are incapable of originality and genius, and can only be the popularisers of the ideas of great men:

> Her original power was nothing more than was due to earnestness and intellectual clearness within a certain range. With small imaginative and suggestive powers, and therefore nothing approaching to genius, she could see clearly what she did see, and give a clear expression to what she had to say. In short, she could popularize, while she could neither discover nor invent.[178]

And yet she was also anxious to establish the fact publicly that she had been the initiator of her tremendously successful series of 'Illustrations of Political Economy', which had 'met with uniform discouragement, except in her own home, where her own confidence that the book would succeed, because it was wanted, commanded the sympathy of her family', and that she had had to fight hard to get it published 'in any manner and on any terms'.[179]

In both the obituary and the autobiography Martineau consistently asserts her independence and autonomy, and insists on her ability to shape her own destiny, and to establish a successful career in public life, in a manner which gestures towards the paradigmatic male self-writing of the period.[180] And yet she deliberately challenges the gendering of the genre of autobiography as masculine by using it to articulate her experiences as a woman.[181] If in formal terms the *Autobiography* may be seen as a text which appropriates and reconfigures a historically masculine genre for a woman's life,[182] questions of gender are also central thematic concerns. A distinctive motif of the *Autobiography* is the gendered opposition of domestic and professional life, figured in the text as the needle and the pen.[183] Martineau is keen to point out that she is as proficient and as capable of earning a living through domestic as through literary labour:

> I could make shirts and puddings, and iron and mend, and get my bread by my needle, if necessary, – (as it once was necessary, for a few months,) before I won a better place and occupation with my pen.[184]

Although she reports that her eldest brother urged her, upon publication of her first work, 'Now, dear, leave it to other women to make shirts and darn stockings; and do you devote yourself to this', she supported herself, for a while, with her needle by day, while she plied her pen by night.[185] But as she became more confident of her prospects as a writer, she resolved to live by her pen alone, despite the advice of a male cousin that she abandon her literary ambitions and 'eke out my earnings by my needle'.[186] Symbolic of, respectively, her feminine and her masculine identity, of her ambitions to fulfil a 'daughter's duty' to her mother as well as becoming 'as much a citizen of the world as any professional *son* of yours could be', the demands of the needle and the pen are finally reconciled in the life she leads in the 'house of her own' she builds at Ambleside, where she writes for two or three hours a day and 'always had some piece of fancy-work on hand'.[187]

Martineau arrogated to herself 'that power of public speech'[188] which was constructed as the preserve of men in the nineteenth century, and although she used that public voice to discuss women's issues, from her volume on *Household Education* (1848) to her writings in support of the campaign to repeal the Contagious Diseases Act, her status as a transgressive woman rendered her position quite different from that of most other women of her period. Her public status made it acceptable for her to voice her most private experiences in an autobiography, as men such as Mill and Ruskin were able to do. Like them, she could express her sense of a loveless childhood: 'I really think, if I had once conceived that any body cared for me, nearly all the sins and sorrows of my anxious childhood would have been spared me.'[189] She could tell of her 'special trial', when the man to whom she was engaged became ill, and died; and she could confess that 'it was happiest for us both that our union was prevented by any means. I am, in truth, very thankful for not having married at all.'[190] All the requisite experiences for the nineteenth-century genius – unhappy childhood, deracination, alienation – are here. More significantly still, Martineau's active involvement in public life meant that, like male autobiographers such as Newman and Mill, she could situate her own intellectual development in relation to the major cultural issues of her day, and provide, at the same time as an account of her life, an account of her times.

Most of the other women who wrote formal autobiographies in the period were also women who had gained fame, or notoriety, in the public sphere. The feminist and philanthropist Frances Power Cobbe, for instance, made use of her autobiography to reiterate the key issues pertaining to the 'woman question', and to outline the main achievements of the women's movement to which she had contributed so indefatigably. In her preface, she writes,

> I have tried to make it the true and complete history of a
> woman's existence *as seen from within*; a real LIFE, which he
> who reads may take as representing fairly the joys, sorrows
> and interests, the powers and limitations, of one of my sex and
> class in the era which is now drawing to a close. The world
> when I entered it was a very different place from the world I
> must shortly quit, most markedly so as regards the position of
> women and of persons like myself holding heterodox opinions,
> and my experience practically bridges the gulf which divides
> the English *ancien regime* from the new.[191]

She devotes chapter 19 to a discussion of 'The Claims of Women', the causes for which she has fought, and the great many articles on women's concerns she has written over the years. Although single herself, and one of those 'happily circumstanced women' who 'have had no immediate wrongs of our own to gall us', she worked for the reform of the Married Women's Property laws, and for 'the mothers whose children were torn from them at the bidding of a dead or living father', and fought 'to obtain protection for unhappy wives, beaten, mangled,

mutilated or trampled on by brutal husbands'.[192] But her own autobiographical account of the public struggle for the political and civil emancipation of women is, like Martineau's, of a very different order from
those of women who were more personally imbricated in the kinds
of domestic tragedies they sought to ameliorate, such as Annie Besant
and Margaret Oliphant. Such women were public figures too, but their
autobiographies reveal an altogether more problematical relationship
between their public personae and their private lives, and tensions which
are more difficult to resolve within the constraints of a masculinist generic
form than those of successful single women like Harriet Martineau and
Frances Power Cobbe.

In her *Autobiographical Sketches* (1885), the reformer and free-thought
lecturer and journalist Annie Besant describes how one of her early
lectures, on 'The true basis of morality', delivered at a Unitarian chapel,
gave 'great offence to some of the congregation, especially to Miss
Frances Power Cobbe, who declared that she would have left the chapel
had not the speaker been a woman'. Besant goes on to explain that 'The
ground of complaint was that the suggested "basis" was Utilitarian
and human instead of Intuitional and Theistic.'[193] The younger woman
was a reader of Cobbe's theological works, but this episode reveals an
important distinction between her own 'Utilitarian and human' approach
to moral issues and Cobbe's more intellectual engagement, a distinction
which manifests itself clearly in their very different autobiographical
styles. After a cheerful and humorous account of her idyllic childhood
and her youthful religiosity, Besant charts the decline which set in
after her marriage to the Rev. Frank Besant. Like contemporary 'New
Woman' fiction writers, such as George Egerton, she draws attention
to the fact that she was fatally unprepared for her new condition:

> My ignorance of all that marriage meant was as profound as
> though I had been a child of four, and my knowledge of the
> world was absolutely *nil*. My darling mother meant all that
> was happiest for me when she shielded me from all knowledge
> of sorrow and of sin, when she guarded me from the smallest
> idea of the marriage relation, keeping me ignorant as a baby
> till I left her home a wife. But looking back now on all, I
> deliberately say that no more fatal blunder can be made than to
> train a girl to womanhood in ignorance of all life's duties and
> burdens, and then to let her face them for the first time away
> from all the old associations, the old helps, the old refuge on
> the mother's breast.[194]

Not only does she quickly become aware of their marital incompatibil-
ity, but she also comes to realise her legal disabilities as a married woman.

Her sense of new-found independence upon earning money for her first piece of professional writing is, she discovers, misplaced: 'I had not realised then the beauty of the English law, and the dignified position in which it placed the married woman; I did not understand that all a married woman earned by law belonged to her owner, and that she could have nothing that belonged to her of right.'[195] When she subsequently, after a long struggle, lost her faith, and found her position as the wife of an intractable clergyman untenable, she gained legal separation from him. It was only then that she experienced, as Caroline Norton had before her, 'The worst stigma attached to marriage by the law of England', namely the 'ignoring of any right of the married mother to her child'.[196] Robbed of her children 'by legal violence', she describes how 'the theft was successfully carried out by due process of law.'[197]

In Besant's autobiography, there is no possibility of accommodation between her public and her private lives. Her 'unwomanly' activities in the public sphere – her lectures and writings promoting atheism, and her involvement in the controversial publication of a pamphlet on contraception – were cited as the very grounds for taking her daughter Mabel from her. The law effected a split between her professional persona and her role as a mother which no amount of negotiation could heal and which could not be papered over within the bounds of conventional autobiography. This was perhaps why her autobiography was not received as warmly as either Cobbe's or Martineau's. Another woman who, despite the fact that she was a well-known writer, found it difficult to reconcile her professional and domestic roles, both in her life and in her autobiography, was the prolific popular novelist Margaret Oliphant. Significantly, Oliphant did not approve of Martineau's *Autobiography* precisely because of its cavalier disregard for the proper boundary between public and private life. In a hostile review, she accuses Martineau of unwomanliness in offending against 'good taste, as well as against all family loyalty and the needful and graceful restraints of private life', by bringing individuals and incidents which properly belong to that private life into the public eye.[198] When her own autobiography was published posthumously some twenty-two years later in 1899 it was clear that the question of the relationship between the private woman and the public artist remained a major and unresolved preoccupation.

As in Martineau's autobiography, a recurring motif of Oliphant's is the opposition between domestic labour (defined as female) and professional work, which is represented as essentially unwomanly. Oliphant interestingly places herself, in her youth at least, in the male corner of this gendered antithesis. Describing how she occupied herself while nursing her sick mother for a period, for instance, she explains, 'I had no liking then for needlework, a taste which developed afterwards, so I took to writing.'[199] As her writing came to assume more importance in her life, she depicts the conditions in which she worked:

> I had no table even to myself, much less a room to work in,
> but sat at the corner of the family table with my writing-book,
> with everything going on as if I had been making a shirt
> instead of writing a book ... My mother sat always at needle-
> work of some kind, and talked to whoever might be present,
> and I took my share in the conversation, going on all the
> same with my story ... up to this date, 1888, I have never
> been shut up in a separate room, or hedged off with any
> observances. My study, all the study I have ever attained to,
> is the little second drawing-room of my house, with a wide
> opening into the other drawing-room where all the (feminine)
> life of the house goes on; and I don't think I have ever had
> two hours undisturbed (except at night, when everybody is
> in bed) during my whole literary life.[200]

She represents herself here, as a woman writer, as occupying an uneasy
position between the conventional young lady 'doing her embroidery'
and the professional writer sequestered away from domestic disturbances
in a room of his own. For a briefly happy period of her life, she was
able to hold the domestic and professional demands of her life in balance, in much the same way as Martineau did at Ambleside. She recalls
a time when her husband was alive and her children were young, when
she used to write all morning, then play with the children, then enjoy
'the moment after dinner when I used to run up-stairs to see that all was
well in the nursery ... before I took up my evening work, which was
generally needlework, something to make for the children'.[201] But after
her husband and, one by one, her children tragically died, and the burden
of supporting the rest of her own and her brother's family fell solely
to her, she increasingly felt a conflict of interest between her literary and
domestic activities. Forced to write quickly for money, she compared
herself as a hack writer to unshackled female novelists like George Eliot,
who were in a position to devote themselves properly to their work.
And if she felt her lack of success as a writer most acutely, she was
forced to recognise that, despite all her efforts, her home life was no
more satisfactory. As she poignantly writes in the autobiography, 'All
failure, failure everything, and I am thought a successful woman, but
everything I touch seems to go wrong.'[202]

Margaret Oliphant's *Autobiography* demonstrates how damaging it
is for the writing subject who has imagined her narrative conforming
to the great middle-class success story (famous novelist, perfect Victorian mother, worthy descendant of a noble family) to discover that
the myth is not realised in her life.[203] It is not, perhaps, surprising that
one of the aspects of Martineau's autobiography that most irritated
Oliphant was her tendency to dwell on her successes, her constant 'self-
applauses'.[204] Whereas Martineau was able to write her life in such a way

as to position herself at the intersection of the private and public spheres as a self-determining, authoritative subject, and thus conform to the male paradigm of autobiography, Oliphant is everywhere conscious of both her difficulties as a woman and the problematics of articulating those difficulties within a male genre.[205] Her *Autobiography*, indeed, began as a private journal, a narrative of her life intended only for the eyes of her sons, and it was only when they both met with premature deaths that Oliphant envisaged a wider audience. The *Autobiography* retains the marks of its origins. As Oliphant comments, 'All my recollections are like pictures, not continuous, only a scene detached and conspicuous here and there.'[206] This makes her *Autobiography* a very different kind of self-writing from the dominant male form to which Martineau and Cobbe accommodate themselves, a kind of self-writing that is, it has been suggested, ineluctably female in its preference for the fragmentary and the disjointed, in its privileging of the domestic and the personal, of 'unconsidered moments of happiness'. Viewed as an experimental self-narrative, it may be seen as a textual analogue of the pattern of a woman's life, an affirmation of difference.[207] Margaret Oliphant's *Autobiography* is distinctive, and perhaps unique, in constituting within a single text a convergence of the private journal and the public autobiography. But its hybrid form declares, albeit obliquely, that Oliphant was like many other women of her period in finding the journal a more congenial medium of self-expression and self-analysis than formal autobiography. The next section will explore the opportunities afforded both women and men by both journals and letters for a less rigidly structured and gendered, an altogether less historically and publicly determined form of self-writing than conventional autobiography offered.

Journals and letters

'God bless you my boy! write to your mother soon, and remember your Journal.'

(Benjamin Disraeli, *Vivian Grey*)[208]

Horace Grey's exhortation to his son Vivian, as he packs him off to school, to fulfil his epistolary and journalistic duties, suggests both how important these literary activities were in a middle-class upbringing and, to some extent, why they were so important. It was common practice for middle- and upper-class boys to be sent away from home for their schooling, and subsequently to take up positions in far-flung outposts of the empire. Meanwhile their mothers (and sisters, and lovers) remained at home, dependent upon what the mails would bring for news of their loved ones. Working-class families were divided for different reasons, often through economic necessity and the need to find employment, and the desire to keep in touch was often an incentive for the acquisition of literacy. Margaret Aitken Carlyle, for instance, taught herself to write so that she could remain in contact with her son when he left home.[209] The fact that urban industrial and colonial expansion caused dislocation among all classes of people, together with the relative difficulty of travel, accounts in no small measure for the potency of letter writing as a genre during the nineteenth century. Enforced separation from loved ones also created the conditions for an expansion of the significance of journal writing, for capturing all the details of daily life at home or in a strange place, perhaps to be shared one day, and for pouring out feelings which could not be shared personally. In an age before the telephone (invented in 1876) was widely available, but when the postal service was well established and efficient (the Penny Post was introduced in 1840), family and friends who lived more than a carriage or train journey apart depended upon letters for their communication. Moreover, in the absence of television and radio, writing and reading letters provided not only a major form of entertainment but also a forum for dramatic dialogue and for the exchange of news and ideas.

Letter writing also provided opportunities for the development of individualism and personality, and for self-analysis and self-understanding. The diary offered even more scope for the exploration and articulation of the inner life, especially for women, who, in the nineteenth century, were not encouraged to think of themselves as individuals or to voice their views in public. Forbidden to be outspoken, women spoke to themselves, and sometimes to their intimates, through their diaries. Diaries and letters were perceived as private forms of writing, and as such suitable for women. It is no accident that a number of women of the period entering the professional world of letters for the first time couched their early works in the form of letters or diaries, after the manner of their eighteenth-century predecessors. One thinks, for example, of Anna Maria Falconbridge's epistolary *Narrative of Two Voyages to the River Sierra Leone*; and of Anna Jameson's *Diary of an Ennuyée* (1826), which purports to be an authentic diary of the European travels of a young lady disappointed in love. 'Now if my poor little Diary should ever be seen!' the heroine exclaims. 'I tremble but to think of it! what egotism and vanity, what discontent, – repining, – caprice – should I be accused of . . . but I think I have taken sufficient precautions against the possibility of such an exposure.' Modesty and propriety are preserved by an elaborate framing device which places the responsibility for publication entirely with a male editor, who, we are told, collected the young lady's random private thoughts, 'written down at the moment', and placed them into a narrative order to present 'a real picture of natural and feminine feeling'.[210]

Such were some of the general conditions which fostered the arts of letter and journal writing and governed the literary use of epistolary and diary forms, but, as always, individual circumstances also played an important role in the development of these genres. Poets such as Keats and Hopkins (or, as in the case of Dorothy Wordsworth, their sisters) made use of their journals to record experiences which would become the basis of published poems, and developed their theories about poetry in letters. Some letters between writers, such as those of Edith Somerville and Violet Martin (Somerville and Ross), trace a long-term literary collaboration; others, such as those between Elizabeth Barrett and Robert Browning, are the record of a more passionate poetic and romantic encounter. Elizabeth Barrett's letters acquire a certain poignancy and intensity from the fact that they were penned from her lonely invalid couch, while for Florence Nightingale letters were a crucial means of developing and communicating her reformist ideas and of exercising power after she took to her sick bed. Both letters and journals were written across gender, class, and other social and intellectual boundaries. Hannah Cullwick wrote a journal of her life as a servant for the perusal of her middle-class lover, later husband, Arthur Munby, while Hopkins, a member of a Roman Catholic religious order, maintained contact with the literary world through his correspondence with very differently circumstanced writers such as Robert Bridges and Coventry Patmore. The most 'private' of prose sub-genres, in that they are, ostensibly at least, not intended for publication and are directed at a very limited readership, journals and letters are less rigidly governed by the formal demands which determine the shape, style, and content of other genres of prose writing, and therefore exhibit a greater degree of variety.[211] They are also not the sole province of those who think of themselves as professional writers or intellectuals, and therefore open up different perspectives on a century which has, until relatively recently, been defined according to the views of those who have a place in the canon.

Dorothy Wordsworth was one who rejected the notion of herself as a writer, indeed claimed to 'detest the idea of setting myself up as an Author' when asked to publish her account of the tragic history of a local family.[212] And yet she was, throughout her life, the author of letters and journals which, whilst not conforming, as works of prose, to Romantic ideological formulations of imaginative literature,[213] are now being accorded the status they deserve as a major corpus of Romantic writing. She is now dignified as a writer with a distinctly separate authorial voice from that of her brother, and her journals are read not just for what they tell us about William's daily life and creative processes but as autonomous literary artefacts.

Dorothy Wordsworth's journal writing spans a period of over three decades, from 1798, when she began keeping a journal at Alfoxden House in Somerset, where she and William lived for a year, to 1833, when she made her last entry in the journal she kept while living at Rydal Mount. Over this time her writing took a number of forms, from the descriptive sketchbook style of the early diaries to the travel journals of the 1820s.[214] It is, though, in the journal she kept between 14 May 1800 and 16 January 1803 recording the life she and William led at Grasmere that she achieved a style of writing distinctively her own. The journal begins with a characteristic directness, noting the facts, and providing the small domestic detail: 'Wm. and John set off into York-shire after dinner at 1/2 past 2 o'clock, cold pork in their pockets.' This first entry exhibits a number of the stylistic features that are typical of her writing. Her feelings are no sooner expressed than they are checked and diverted to the natural world:

> I sate a long time upon a stone at the margin of the lake, and after a flood of tears my heart was easier. The lake looked to me, I know not why, dull and melancholy, and the weltering on the shores seemed a heavy sound. I walked as long as I could amongst the stones of the shore. The wood rich in flowers; a beautiful yellow, palish yellow, flower, that looked thick, round, and double, and smelt very sweet – I supposed it was a ranunculus. Crowfoot, the grassy-leaved rabbit-toothed white flower, strawberries, geranium, scentless violets, anemones two kinds, orchises, primroses. The heckberry very beautiful, the crab coming out as a low shrub.[215]

With characteristic precision and attention to the particular she dis-tinguishes minutely between varieties of anemone and violet, registers tactile qualities, sounds and scents as well as the appearance of things. She records the people she met on her way: the 'blind man, driving a very large beautiful Bull, and a cow – he walked with two sticks', and the Rydal woman, 'stout and well dressed', who 'begged a half-penny; she had never she said done it before, but these hard times!' She records her state of physical health – 'Arrived at home with a bad headache' – as she does of all her household and visitors throughout the journal. And, most characteristically of all, this first entry is shot through with thoughts of her brother, who is referred to at three separate points after the initial description of his departure (for three weeks, let it be noted): 'My heart was so full that I could hardly speak to W. when I gave him a farewell kiss . . . I resolved to write a journal of the time till W. and J. return, and I set about keeping my resolve, because I will not quarrel with myself, and because I shall give Wm. pleasure by it when he comes home again . . . Oh! that I had a letter from William!'

As this opening entry reveals, she embarks on the Grasmere journal for William, but also for her own peace of mind, 'because I will not quarrel with myself'. Eschewing that 'dialogue of the mind with itself' which Arnold was to characterise as the besetting flaw of his own times, Dorothy Wordsworth seeks through her writing to order and calm her mind, so clearly susceptible to agitation. Out of the fragmentary record that it is in the nature of a journal to be emerges the narrative of a life with a readily discernible emotional structure, emplotted around her relationship with her brother. Her patient and precise recording of the weather, of what she sees on her long daily walks in the country-side surrounding Grasmere, of her day-to-day household chores and the comings and goings of those in her immediate social circle, honours and affirms the rhythms of everyday life. Indeed, her journal-keeping, like her letter writing, becomes itself an important part of her domestic routine, which she can no more neglect than the linen or the garden.[216] In the georgic tradition, art and labour converge in her writing.[217] It is, moreover, a mode of writing which formally enacts Dorothy Words-worth's involvement with the community within which she has made her home. Not only is her journal populated by colourful locals and enlivened by neighbourhood stories, but it frequently incorporates the dialect words and regional idiom and accents of those among whom she dwells, demonstrating an ear for the poetry of everyday language that eluded her brother.

Dorothy Wordsworth's journals have traditionally been read as offer-ing a chronicle of the daily lives of writers of far greater significance than herself, rather as William Michael Rossetti's are read for what they say about the activities of more interesting members of the Pre-Raphaelite Brotherhood, and William Allingham's for their references to Tennyson and Browning and others who had a place in the literary charmed cir-cle upon which he was only an onlooker. And yet her writings do not read like marginal texts, but rather seem the still centre upon which the poetry of her brother and Coleridge turns. To the extent that they assert a powerfully independent voice, and engage vigorously and creatively with the aesthetic issues of the day, they resemble more the journals of a writer such as Gerard Manley Hopkins than, say, those of the contemporary diarist Henry Crabb Robinson. Indeed, the similarities between the preoccupations and style of Dorothy Wordsworth's journal and the journal writing of Hopkins, who, in his own day, had no public identity as a writer and who spent much of his life on the cultural and geographical margins, are quite striking. Both writers, for instance, are committed to capturing the changing appearances of a nature that is always in flux: effects of the weather, tricks of light, cloudscapes and seascapes, the particular stage of development of a bud or a leaf, the juncture of seasons. Both have a striking respect for and command of the particular, and take great efforts in their writing to articulate the unique nature of the composition or the colours or the drama of the scene before them, and of their emotional response to what they see. Both are capable of finding beauty in the ordinary and the everyday, and conversely both make use of familiar domestic images and language to describe extraordinary and spectacular sights.[218]

Here is Dorothy Wordsworth, for instance, in the Alfoxden journal on a Welsh landscape:

> The Welsh hills capped by a huge range of tumultuous white clouds. The sea, spotted with white, of a bluish grey in general, and streaked with darker lines. The near shores clear; scattered farm houses, half-concealed by green mossy orchards, fresh straw lying at the doors; hay-stacks in the fields. Brown fallows, the springing wheat, like a shade of green over the brown earth, and the choice meadow plots, full of sheep and lambs, of a soft and vivid green; a few wreaths of blue smoke, spreading along the ground; the oaks and beeches in the hedges retaining their yellow leaves; the distant prospect on the land side, islanded with sunshine; the sea, like a basin full to the margin; the dark fresh-ploughed fields; the turnips of a lively rough green. Returned through the wood.[219]

And here is Hopkins, nearly eighty years later, on another Welsh scene:

> It was a leaden sky, braided or roped with cloud, and the earth in dead colours, grave but distinct. The heights by Snowdon were hidden by the clouds but not from distance or dimness. The nearer hills, the other side of the valley, shewed a hard and beautifully detached and glimmering brim against the light, which was lifting there. All the length of the valley the skyline of hills was flowingly written all along upon the sky. A blue bloom, a sort of meal, seemed to have spread upon the distant south, enclosed by a basin of hills. Looking all round but most in looking far up the valley I felt an instress and charm of Wales.[220]

Like Dorothy Wordsworth, Hopkins's description negotiates between the foreground and the distance, and discriminates carefully between the various effects of light and colour he notes. And like her he readily makes use of domestic images where they capture the essence of what he sees: a 'braided' sky, 'a sort of meal', and, uncannily echoing Dorothy's comparison of the sea to 'a basin full to the margin', 'a basin of hills'. If we are tempted to make the essentialist assumption that such homely images are peculiarly a feature of women's writing, a glance at Hopkins's descriptive prose shows that deployment of the domestic is not gender-specific. 'Scum in standing milk',[221] for example, is noteworthy; and the figurative use of ordinary images in bizarre contexts creates striking effects. Thus the fall of the Gelmer is likened to 'milk chasing round blocks of coal; or a girdle or long purse of white weighted with irregular black rubies, carelessly thrown aside and lying in jutty bends, with a black clasp of the same stone at the top'.[222] Clouds are described as being 'like seams of red candle-wax'; garden mould is 'meshed over with a lace-work of needles'; the boughs of apple trees 'made an embroidery'; the West Country had 'soft maroon or rosy cocoa-dust-coloured handkerchiefs of ploughfields'.[223]

Dorothy Wordsworth's interest in regional dialects and idioms is echoed in Hopkins's journals, which reveal a delight in local words and usages consistent with his more general fascination with the etymological derivation and the sounds and meanings of words. Throughout his journals there are lengthy entries on particular words, such as '*Horn*', and linguistic groupings, such as '*Grind, gride, gird, grit, groat, grate, greet* . . . etc.*', '*Crook, crank, kranke, crick, cranky*', '*slip, slipper, slop, slabby* (muddy), *slide*, perhaps *slope*', '*Drill, trill, thrill, nostril, nese-thirl* (Wiclef etc.)', '*Flick, fillip, flip, fleck, flake*'.[224] Such lists probably fulfilled various functions for the poet: the writing of them was a verbal exercise; once noted, they became a database upon which he could later draw; like his nature notes and sketches, they served as memoranda of inscapes, 'catching' (to use his word) the quiddity of language, as the former 'catch' the instress of nature's inscapes.

Often in his descriptive passages Hopkins seems at least as interested in the complex rhyming of sound and meaning and the figurative play of metaphorical associations as in the object under survey, or rather he draws on all the resources of his language to try to convey every facet of his perceptual experience:

> Drops of rain hanging on rails etc seen with only the lower
> rim lighted like nails (of fingers). Screws of brooks and twines.
> Soft chalky look with more shadowy middles of the globes of
> cloud on a night with a moon faint or concealed. Mealy clouds
> with a not brilliant moon. Blunt buds of the anh. Pinil luoly
> ol tlu beech. Lobes ol the trees. Cups of the eyes. Gathering
> back the lightly hinged eyelids. Bows of the eyelids. Pencil of
> eyelashes. Juices of the eyeball. Eyelids like leaves, petals, caps,
> tufted hats, handkerchiefs, sleeves, gloves. Also of the bones
> sleeved in flesh. Juices of the sunrise. Joins and veins of the
> same. Vermilion look of the hand held against a candle with
> the darker parts as the middles of the fingers and especially
> the knuckles covered with ash.[225]

Such passages of extraordinary beauty abound in Hopkins's journals, which, in their linguistic density, their expression of the chromatic modulations of both language and the natural objects it represents, their command of prose rhythms, and their sheer lyrical power, clearly constitute much more than the mere quarry for his poems. They are, rather, prose poems that rank with his very best sonnets and odes.

Living as he did for so much of his life in relative intellectual isolation, away from the centres of learning, Hopkins relied a good deal on letters for both intellectual and emotional sustenance. The correspondence between the then obscure poet and other more famous poets, such as Coventry Patmore and Robert Bridges, is fascinating, not least because their roles have been reversed and it is now Hopkins's poetry that is celebrated, and theirs that is neglected, if not derided. His friendship with these established writers afforded opportunities which he would otherwise have lacked for critical debate about literature. Hopkins's views on other writers, as expressed in his letters, are often acute and illuminating. Bridges, Patmore, and a former teacher, the minor Pre-Raphaelite poet and clergyman Richard Watson Dixon, also provided Hopkins, who was adamant that it was not appropriate for a religious to seek publication, with a select audience for his own poetry. His more conservative correspondents clearly found Hopkins's radical poetic experimentation not to their taste; some of his work appears to have met with blank incomprehension. In a number of his letters he is obliged to defend himself vigorously against charges that his poetic style, and in particular his use of 'sprung rhythm', is perverse and obscure:

> Why do I employ sprung rhythm at all? Because it is the nearest to the rhythm of prose, that is the native and natural rhythm of speech, the least forced, the most rhetorical and emphatic of all possible rhythms, combining, as it seems to me, opposite and, one wd. have thought, incompatible excellences, markedness of rhythm – that is rhythm's self – and naturalness of expression – for why, if it is forcible in prose to say 'lashed. rod', am I obliged to weaken this in verse, which ought to be stronger, not weaker, into 'lashed birch-rod' or something?
>
> My verse is less to be read than heard, as I have told you before; it is oratorical, that is the rhythm is so. I think if you will study what I have here said you will be much more pleased with it and may I say? converted to it.
>
> You ask may you call it 'presumptious jugglery'. No, but only for this reason, that *presumptious* is not English.
>
> I cannot think of altering anything. Why shd. I? I do not write for the public. You are my public and I hope to convert you.[226]

His choice of metaphor in this final sentence is an interesting one, not only because it suggests the close connection between the religious and the aesthetic in his thought, but because it reminds us of the fact that

Hopkins's conversion to Roman Catholicism created a permanent division between himself and the Protestant Bridges, to whom the letter is addressed. In numerous letters to his friend, Hopkins patiently, and often with good humour and wit, explains his work, and suggests how it might best be approached, even though Bridges' lack of sympathy for what he was trying to do must have been hurtful, at times devastating. For instance, he writes of 'The Wreck of the Deutschland',

> You say you wd. not for any money read my poem again. Nevertheless I beg you will. Besides money, you know, there is love. If it is obscure do not bother yourself with the meaning but pay attention to the best and most intelligible stanzas, the two last of each part and the narrative of the wreck. If you had done this you wd. have liked it better and sent me some serviceable criticisms, but now your criticism is of no use, being only a protest memorialising me against my whole policy and proceedings.[227]

Some nine months later, he wrote to Bridges again, saying that he was sorry his friend had never read 'The Wreck of the Deutschland' again. He acknowledged that the poem was difficult and obscure, but explained that it was deliberately so, adding:

> Besides you would have got more weathered to the style and its features – not really odd. Now they say that vessels sailing from the port of London will take (perhaps it should be / used once to take) Thames water for the voyage: it was foul and stunk at first as the ship worked but by degrees casting its filth was in a few days very pure and sweet and wholesomer and better than any water in the world. However that maybe, it is true to my purpose. When a new thing, such as my ventures in the Deutschland are, is presented us our first criticisms are not our truest, best, most homefelt, or most lasting but what comes easiest on the instant. They are barbarous and like what the ignorant and the ruck say. This was so with you. The Deutschland on her first run worked very much and unsettled you, thickening and clouding your mind with vulgar mudbottom and common sewage (I see that I am going it with the image) and just then unhappily you *drew off* your criticisms all stinking (a necessity now of the image) and bilgy, whereas if you had let your thoughts cast themselves they would have been clearer in themselves and more to my taste too. I did not heed them therefore, perceiving they were a first drawing-off.[228]

Hopkins's conceit is, indeed, perfect for his 'purpose', not only because of its appropriateness to the subject of the poem in question, but because it enables him in an amusing way to express both his sorrow at Bridges' failure to honour their friendship and his contempt for his poor critical judgement (it is bilgewater). It also allows him to articulate a theory of reading that is adequate to poetry, like his own, that is truly radical in its linguistic and metrical experimentation. Hopkins's witty elaboration of the bilgewater metaphor notwithstanding, he is clearly disappointed by his friend's unwillingness even to take the first steps towards being 'converted'.

In short, one suspects that, whilst Hopkins's correspondence with Bridges, Patmore and Dixon in some respects sustained him as a writer both intellectually and emotionally, their fundamental lack of sympathy with his radical, revisionary poetics meant that in practice he was defining himself as a poet *against* their own more conservative stance. His letters record the forging of an oppositional poetic identity. Whilst Matthew Arnold had a quite different literary agenda from Hopkins's, his own letters to his friend Arthur Hugh Clough similarly carve out a poetic persona defined as the antithesis of his correspondent's. Arnold's uneasy relationship with Clough is intimately bound up with his personal struggle to define his own moral, intellectual and aesthetic standpoint, and his own views on the nature and function of literature. Arnold seems to have thought of Clough as his *alter ego*, and his letters read like attempts to bolster up his resolve not to fall into the sorry state of vacillation and subjectivism which he saw as his fellow poet's ruin: 'you poor subjective, you', as he referred to him. He clearly felt vulnerable to the very weaknesses that he saw manifested in Clough, and resented him as a bad influence, and a dangerous threat to his own poetic ambitions:

> You certainly do not seem to me sufficiently to desire and earnestly strive towards – assured knowledge – activity – happiness. You are too content to *fluctuate* – to be ever learning, never coming to the knowledge of the truth. This is why, with you, I feel it necessary to stiffen myself – and hold fast my rudder.[229]

He virtually accuses Clough of deliberate subversion, when he has evidently been persuaded by him to read Keats's letters:

> What a brute you were to tell me to read Keats' Letters. However it is over now: and reflexion resumes her power over agitation.
> What harm he has done in English Poetry. As Browning is a man with a moderate gift passionately desiring movement and fulness, and obtaining but a confused multitudinousness, so

> Keats with a very high gift, is yet also consumed by this
> desire: and cannot produce the truly living and moving, as
> his conscience keeps telling him. They will not be patient
> neither understand that they must begin with an Idea of
> the world in order not to be prevailed over by the world's
> multitudinousness.[230]

Such a powerful response to reading Keats's letters suggests how susceptible Arnold himself was to the 'multitudinousness' the Romantic poet embraced and developed in the theory of 'Negative Capability' that he worked out in his letters. Given Arnold's own critical predilections – for living and writing according to an ideal of Hellenic reason, for 'seeing the object as it really is' – it is not hard to see why he found some of Keats's pronouncements unacceptable. For instance, Keats argues in a letter to his brothers George and Thomas that '*Negative Capability*, that is, when a man is capable of being in uncertainties, mysteries, doubts, without any irritable reaching after fact and reason', is a quality fundamental in the formation of 'a Man of Achievement, especially in Literature'.[231] In a later letter to George and his wife Georgiana he contends that 'The only means of strengthening one's intellect is to make up ones [sic] mind about nothing – to let the mind be a thoroughfare for all thoughts.'[232] And in another letter to the same he dismisses one more of what were to become Arnold's sacred critical precepts when he maintains that 'Very few men have ever arrived at a complete disinterestedness of Mind':

> I perceive how far I am from any humble standard of
> disinterestedness – Yet this feeling ought to be carried to its
> highest pitch as there is no fear of its ever injuring Society
> – which it would do I fear pushed to an extremity – For in
> wild nature the Hawk would loose his Breakfast of Robins
> and the Robin his of Worms – the Lion must starve as well
> as the swallow. The greater part of Men make their way with
> the same instinctiveness, the same unwandering eye from their
> purposes, the same animal eagerness as the Hawk . . . This it
> is that makes the Amusement of Life to a speculative Mind.
> I go among the Fields and catch a glimpse of a Stoat or a
> fieldmouse peeping out of the withered grass – the creature
> hath a purpose and its eyes are bright with it. I go amongst
> the buildings of a city and I see a Man hurrying along – to
> what? the Creature has a purpose and his eyes are bright with
> it.[233]

Keats's defence in his letters of his own and humanity's fundamental enslavement to self-interest would have been anathema to Arnold. What a brute indeed – a brute with a purpose – was Clough to make him read them!

The letters of poets, then, often function as a vehicle for the formulation of the ideas upon which their poetry is founded and from which they derive their critical bearings. But they frequently amount to much more than a theoretical discourse of secondary importance to the writer's poetic praxis. In the letters of poets may sometimes be found the genius of a prose stylist to complement the poetry for which they are more widely acclaimed. Such is the case with Byron, whose letters and journals exhibit a range and diversity of style and tone and a command of language comparable with his greatest poems. That Byron was a brilliant prose writer is insisted upon by no less a stylist than Ruskin, who quotes an excerpt from Byron's defence of Sheridan in a letter written to Thomas Moore from Venice as an example of the perfection of his prose:

> The Whigs abuse him; however, he never left them, and such blunderers deserve neither credit nor compassion. – As for his creditors, – remember, Sheridan *never had* a shilling, and was thrown, with great powers and passions, into the thick of the world, and placed upon the pinnacle of success, with no other external means to support him in his elevation. Did Fox — *pay his* debts? or did Sheridan take a subscription? Was the —'s drunkenness more excusable than his? Were his intrigues more notorious than those of all his contemporaries? and is his memory to be blasted and theirs respected? Don't let yourself be led away by clamour, but compare him with the coalitioner Fox, and the pensioner Burke, as a man of principle, and with ten hundred thousand in personal views, and with none in talent, for he beat them all *out* and *out*. Without means, without connexion, without character, (which might be false at first, and drive him mad afterwards from desperation,) he beat them all, in all he ever attempted. But, alas, poor human nature! Good night or rather, morning. It is four, and the dawn gleams over the Grand Canal, and unshadows the Rialto.[234]

Ignoring the final sentence of the letter ('I must to bed; up all night – but as George Philpot says, "it's life, though, damme it's life!" '), Ruskin enthusiastically analyses Byron's prose style:

> Now, observe, that passage is noble . . . But it is more than noble, it is *perfect*, because the quantity [of thoughts] it holds is not artificially or intricately concentrated, but with the serene swiftness of a smith's hammer-strokes on hot iron; and with

choice of terms which, each in its place, will convey far more
than they mean in the dictionary. Thus, 'however' is used
instead of 'yet,' because it stands for 'howsoever,' or, in full,
for 'yet whatever they did.' 'Thick' of society, because it
means, not merely the crowd, but the *fog* of it; 'ten hundred
thousand' instead of 'a million,' or 'a thousand thousand,' to
take the sublimity out of the number, and make us feel that
it is a number of nobodies. Then the sentence in parenthesis,
'which might be false,' etc., is indeed obscure, because it was
impossible to clarify it without a regular pause, and much loss
of time; and the reader's sense is therefore left to expand it for
himself into 'it was, perhaps, falsely said of him at first, that
he had no character,' etc. Finally, the dawn 'unshadows' –
lessens the shadow on – the Rialto, but does not *gleam* on that,
as on the broad water.[235]

Although in some respects as unlike as two men could be, Ruskin
shared Byron's passion for justice, and respected him for his integrity.
Such qualities are everywhere apparent in Byron's letters, from his
championing of individuals such as Sheridan to his championing of
social causes, such as that of the frame-breakers, whose plight was the
subject of his inaugural speech before the House of Lords on 27 February 1812. He wrote to Lord Holland two days before he was to speak
against the Frame-Work Bill in terms that would have won Ruskin's
approval, anticipating both the kind of argument and the language of
his own later social writings:

> For my own part, I consider the manufacturers as a much
> injured body of men, sacrificed to the views of certain
> individuals who have enriched themselves by those practices
> which have deprived the frame-workers of employment. For
> instance, – by the adoption of a certain kind of frame, one
> man performs the work of seven – six are thus thrown out of
> business. But it is to be observed that the work thus done is
> far inferior in quality, hardly marketable at home, and hurried
> over with a view to exportation. Surely, my Lord, however
> we may rejoice in any improvement in the arts which may
> be beneficial to mankind, we must not allow mankind to be
> sacrificed to improvements in mechanism. The maintenance
> and well-doing of the industrious poor is an object of greater
> consequence to the community than the enrichment of a few
> monopolists by any improvement in the implements of trade,
> which deprives the workman of his bread, and renders the
> labourer 'unworthy of his hire'.
> My own motive for opposing the bill is founded on its

palpable injustice, and its certain inefficacy. I have seen the state of these miserable men, and it is a disgrace to a civilised country. Their excesses may be condemned, but cannot be the subject of wonder. The effect of the present bill would be to drive them into actual rebellion.[236]

Byron finishes his letter with a characteristic postscript: 'P.S. I am a little apprehensive that your Lordship will think me too lenient towards these men, and half a *frame-breaker myself.*'[237]

Ruskin also shared Byron's passion for Venice, but their experiences of the city could hardly have been more different. Whereas for Ruskin it became the backdrop against which his disastrous marriage to Effie Gray was played out, and the symbol of her sexual 'fall', for Byron it was the opportunities Venice afforded for engaging in an orgy of sexual liaisons that made his sojourn there, in exile from a more prudish England where 'the state of Cuckoldom was not quite so flourishing',[238] so enjoyable. In his letters Byron describes his libidinous escapades with the verve, wit, and theatricality of Browning's Fra Lippo Lippi, as in the following to John Murray:

> I wrote to you in haste and at past two in the morning having besides had an accident. In going, about an hour and a half ago, to a rendezvous with a Venetian girl (unmarried and the daughter of one of their nobles), I tumbled into the Grand Canal, and, not choosing to miss my appointment by the delays of changing, I have been perched in a balcony with my wet clothes on ever since, till this minute that on my return I have slipped into my dressing-gown. My foot slipped in getting into my Gondola to set out (owing to the cursed slippery steps of their palaces), and in I flounced like a Carp, and went dripping like a Triton to my Sea nymph and had to scramble up to a grated window: –
>
> Fenced with iron within and without
> Lest the lover get in or the Lady get out.

He goes on to describe her parents' efforts to put a stop to their meetings:

> they sent a priest to me, and a Commissary of police, and they locked the Girl up, and gave her prayers and bread and water, and our connection was cut off for some time; but the father hath lately been laid up, and the brother is at Milan, and the mother falls asleep, and the Servants are naturally on the wrong side of the question, and there is no Moon at Midnight just now . . .

And then he gleefully recounts the young woman's suggestion regarding his wife, 'But . . . can't you get rid of her?':

> 'Not more than is done already (I answered): You would
> not have me *poison her*?' Would you believe it? She made me
> *no answer*. Is not that a true and odd national trait? It spoke
> more than a thousand words, and yet this is a little, pretty,
> sweet-tempered, quiet feminine being as ever you saw, but
> the Passions of a Sunny Soil are paramount to all other
> considerations.[239]

The control of pace, the perfect timing, and the brilliant use of dialogue in the letter from which these passages are exerpted show Byron to be as consummate a dramatic writer in prose as in poetry.

The high comedy of letters such as this contrasts with the urgency and pain of his love letters to his half-sister Augusta. A letter written just the day before the one previously quoted shows that the philanderer was also capable of the deepest feelings for a woman, even though his relationship with Augusta was of a kind even more offensive to society than his more transient liaisons:

> I have never ceased nor can cease to feel for a moment that
> perfect and boundless attachment which bound and binds me
> to you – which renders me utterly incapable of *real* love for
> any other human being – for what could they be to me after
> *you*? My own – we may have been wrong – but I repent of
> nothing except that cursed marriage – and your refusing to
> continue to love me as you had loved me – I can neither forget
> nor *quite forgive* you for that precious piece of reformation. –
> but I can never be other than I have been . . . It is heart-
> breaking to think of our long Separation – and I am sure more
> than punishment enough for all our sins – Dante is more
> humane in his 'Hell' for he places his unfortunate lovers
> (Francesca of Rimini and Paolo whose case fell a good deal
> short of *ours* – though sufficiently naughty) in company – and
> though they suffer – it is at least together.[240]

If his amorous adventures recall Don Juan, then Byron's incestuous love for his half-sister recalls the passion of Manfred for his sister-bride Astarte. As in *Manfred*, this passion is perceived as destructive:

> They say absence destroys weak passions – and confirms
> strong ones – Alas! *mine* for you is the union of all passions
> and of all affections – Has strengthened itself but will destroy
> me – I do not speak of *physical* destruction – for I have

endured and can endure much – but of the annihilation of all thoughts, feelings or hopes – which have not more or less reference to you and to *our recollections*.[241]

Incest is, of course, a trope of Romanticism, and is symptomatic of a characteristic tendency for the male lover to efface the female into a projection of himself.[242] Just as Manfred chose Astarte because she 'was like me in lineaments – her eyes, / Her hair, her features, all, to the very tone / Even of her voice, they said were like to mine; / But soften'd all, and temper'd into beauty,'[243] Byron sees himself as bound to Augusta in a 'boundless attachment', whereby her identity as an independent Other is assimilated into his own.

Love affairs that are forbidden are conducted with a special urgency, and the love letters that are their literary manifestation typically dwell upon the pain and frustration of separation. Byron declares himself to be 'grieved and tortured with *your new resolution*', recalls to Augusta the anguish of their parting ('and *what tears*! do you remember *our* parting?'), and claims to see 'nothing in England but the country which holds *you* – or around it but the sea which divides us'.[244] The nature of the obstacles to the early love affair of Elizabeth Barrett and Robert Browning was quite different – her father's implacable opposition to the marriage of any of his children, and her own tubercular condition which confined her to her room – but the fire of their mutual passion was similarly fuelled by their enforced separation. In his first letter to Elizabeth, Robert describes how tantalisingly close he had once come to 'seeing – really seeing you':

> Mr. Kenyon said to me one morning 'would you like to see Miss Barrett?' – then he went to announce me, – then he returned . . . you were too unwell – and now it is years ago – and I feel as at some untoward passage in my travels – as if I had been close, so close, to some world's-wonder in chapel or crypt, . . . only a screen to push and I might have entered, but there was some slight . . . so it now seems . . . slight and just-sufficient bar to admission; and the half-opened door shut, and I went home my thousands of miles, and the sight was never to be![245]

As in Byron's searing letter to Augusta, quoted above, the use of dashes instead of more formal punctuation suggests the urgency and agitation of the writer's feelings in this first letter of 10 January 1845. As time goes on, and Robert presses for that long-denied meeting to take place, it is the continuing cold weather that creates a barrier. Robert declares that he 'will joyfully wait for the delight of your friendship, and the spring, and my Chapel-sight after all!' and his letter of February 26th opens with the premature announcement 'Wednesday morning – Spring! Real warm Spring, dear Miss Barrett, and the birds know it; and in Spring I shall see you, surely see you.'[246] However, Elizabeth's response the next day is more realistic:

> Yes, but, dear Mr. Browning, I want the spring according to the new 'style' (mine), & not the old one of you & the rest of the poets. To me unhappily, the snowdrop is much the same as the snow – it feels as cold underfoot – and I have grown sceptical about 'the voice of the turtle,' the east winds blow so loud. April is a Parthian with a dart, & May (at least the early part of it) a spy in the camp. *That* is my idea of what you call spring; mine, in the *new style!*[247]

Come March, and Elizabeth is still confined to her room by 'This implacable weather!' and promising to meet him 'when the warm weather has revived me a little'.[248] In the event, the east wind prevents them from meeting until 20 May.

For all that Elizabeth Barrett resists submitting to the old style of Browning '& the rest of the poets' in the matter of heralding spring, and Robert Browning disclaims the idea that he is 'attitudinizing à la Byron, and giving you to understand unutterable somethings, longings for Lethe and all that', their story, as told in their letters, does 'reenact an archetypal myth'.[249] Just as Byron mythologises his forbidden and doomed love affair with his half-sister by comparing it with that of Dante's Paolo and Francesca, so Robert mythologises his 'rescue' of Elizabeth Barrett from her entombment in her father's house at Wimpole Street by reference to the legend of Perseus's rescue of Andromeda.[250] The contrast between her sequestered existence and his full engagement with life threads through their letters from the beginning. Elizabeth writes, for instance, invoking another mythic figure with whom Robert identifies,

> You are Paracelsus, and I am a recluse, with nerves that have been all broken on the rack, & now hang loosely, . . . quivering at a step and breath.
> And what you say of society draws me on to many comparative thoughts of your life & mine. You seem to have drunken of the cup of life full, with the sun shining on it. I have lived only inwardly, – or with *sorrow*, for a strong emotion. Before this seclusion of my illness, I was secluded still . . . It was a lonely life – growing green like the grass around it. Books and dreams were what I lived in – & domestic life only seemed to buzz gently around, like the bees about the grass. And so time passed, and passed – and

afterwards, when my illness came & I seemed to stand at the
edge of the world with all done, & no prospect (as appeared at
one time) of ever passing the threshold of one room again, –
why then, I turned to thinking with some bitterness . . . that
I had stood blind in this temple I was about to leave . . . that
I had seen no Human nature, that my brothers & sisters of
the earth were *names* to me, . . . that I had beheld no great
mountain or river – nothing in fact. I was as a man dying
who had not read Shakespeare . . . & it was too late! – Do
you understand? And do you also know what a disadvantage
this ignorance is to my art – Why, if I live on & yet do not
escape from this seclusion, do you not perceive that I labour
under signal disadvantages . . . that I am, in a manner, as a
blind poet?[251]

Their respective attitudes to letter writing owe much to their very different situations. The gregarious Robert represents himself as, generally,
a very reluctant correspondent: 'See how I go on and on to you,' he
writes, 'I who, whenever now and then pulled, by the head and hair,
into letter-writing, get sorrowfully on for a line or two, as the cognate
creature urged on by stick and string, and then come down "flop" upon
the sweet haven of page one, line last, as serene as the sleep of the
virtuous!'[252] Elizabeth, by contrast, depends upon letters for her 'social
pleasure', having 'done most of my talking by post of late years – as
people shut up in dungeons, take up with scrawling mottos on the
walls'. She writes affectionately of how letters from friends such as
Mary Russell Mitford have brought joy into her secluded life: 'she has
filled a large drawer in this room with delightful letters, heart-warm
& soul-warm, . . . driftings of nature (if sunshine cd drift like snow) –
& which, if they shd ever fall the way of all writing, into print, wd
assume the folio shape as a matter of course, & take rank on the lowest
shelves of libraries, with Benedictine editions of the Fathers.'[253]

One letter writer whose correspondence would fill several folio volumes were it ever to be published in a collected edition is Florence
Nightingale. The more than ten thousand surviving letters by her, most
of which are neither heart-warm nor soul-warm, reveal her to have
found different uses for the genre from those of either the Brownings
or Miss Mitford. Although she took to her invalid bed following her
return from the Crimea, her experiences there had given her more
knowledge of the world than most of her male contemporaries would
ever have, and after her retirement to her room she made use of that
knowledge to become the driving force behind the much needed reform
of the army and the War Office and later of the profession of nursing and the hospital system. Whereas Elizabeth Barrett felt her work to
be handicapped by her sequestered invalid condition, the editors of a

discriminating selection of her letters point out that Nightingale used her 'self-enforced isolation' to her advantage, and that 'As an invalid Nightingale was freed from the stresses of the working world to which her collaborators were subject.'[254] They describe how

> Both her collaborators and those who wished to influence her were kept waiting downstairs in the living room, while she exchanged notes with them from her bedroom. Anyone who seriously wished to capture her attention quickly realized that the most effective mode was via paper. Her chief assistant, Dr John Sutherland, sometimes exchanged half a dozen notes with her in a day. For many years Henry Bonham Carter, a cousin who became Secretary of the Nightingale [Nursing] Fund, received a letter from her almost every morning at breakfast. Her messenger then waited for a response . . . Only after communicating in this manner for fourteen years did he persuade Nightingale that they could more efficiently settle some problems if she would admit him to her room. Her brother-in-law, Sir Harry Verney, who lived only a few doors away when Parliament was in session, looked forward to a daily letter on the breakfast tray from Nightingale.[255]

Such practices reveal a particularly acute consciousness of the authority, even tyranny, of the written word, an authority which she was reluctant to relinquish even with those to whom she was closest. Her letters show what a consummate strategist she was. Both in her private correspondence and in her professional communications she is always the skilled tactician, modulating her tone to appeal to her correspondent, and making her letters *work* for her. Although throughout her life she wrote private notes which recall *Cassandra* in their passion and intensity – notes which record her grief over the suffering of the soldiers ('my 18,000 children') who died in the Crimea, and her rage at the studied indolence of her mother and sister[256] – her letters in the main display a controlled purposefulness appropriate to the lofty work of which they were the instrument.

Clearly letter writing played a crucial role in the maintenance of Nightingale's public persona and in the conduct of her professional life, and for other women in the period too their correspondence was closely related to their work. For instance, the Anglo-Irish writers Edith Somerville and Violet Martin, who wrote as Somerville and Ross, exchanged hundreds of letters over three decades, some of which contain stories which later become the basis for their published fiction, and all of which teem with the brilliantly observed characters and reverberate with the richly idiomatic language that is the hallmark of their work. As Gifford Lewis observes, they 'wrote about aspects of Irish life previously unseen or unnoticed by the centre-stage male; they enjoyed laundries, kitchens, boot cupboards, ashpits – in short, places frequented by servants, most of whom were women'.[257]

Jane Welsh Carlyle writes in her letters about life below stairs with great verve and wit as well, although her emphasis is upon the trials and tribulations of running a home and of finding, and keeping, good servants. She too was a prolific and gifted letter writer: 'I never sit down at night, beside a good fire, *alone*,' she writes, 'without feeling a need of talking a little, on paper, to somebody that I like well enough, and that likes *me* well enough, to make it of no moment – whether I talk sense or nonsense, and with or without regard to the rules of grammar.'[258] However, in her case, sinking as she was under the demanding task of playing supporting role to 'my Man of Genius', letter writing was not, as it was for Somerville and Ross, the private and informal literary activity of a professional writer, but rather a substitute for a professional career. The characters and stories and incidents which fill Jane Welsh Carlyle's letters were not written for publication, neither did they provide the quarry for later published work, but, like her oral story-telling and her reputedly brilliant conversation, were reserved for a private audience.

'My dear,' asked her good friend the novelist Geraldine Jewsbury, 'how is that women who don't write books write always so much nicer letters than those who do?' 'Because they do not write in the "Valley of the shadow" of their future biographer, but write what they have to say frankly and naturally,' retorted Jane, in line with her maxim that letters should be written 'off-hand, as one speaks',[259] even though

> One cannot in writing eke out one's words with tones of the voice – looks – gestures – an occasional *groan* – an occasional kiss! and speech reduced to bare words is so inadequate for certain '*beings*' – like *me*! – Besides *talking comes natural* to every woman   *writing* is an *acquirement* – and between the exercise of one's natural and one's acquired faculties there is no comparison in point of ease![260]

Florence Nightingale wrote disparagingly, as a young woman of twenty-five in a letter to her father, of the average woman's '*habit* . . . of never interesting herself much, in any conversation, printed or spoken, which is not personal, of making herself & her own feelings the subject of speculation – (& what is the good of studying our own individuality, save as the reflection of the generality) – of making all she says autobiographical, & being always is [sic] a moral tête-à-tête, of considering her own experiences as the principal part of her life.'[261] Behind Nightingale's words to her father lie, of course, her personal frustration and her ambition for 'higher things',[262] but it is nevertheless interesting to consider

Jane Carlyle's epistolary practice in the light of her contemporary's criticism of the circumscription of women's concerns. Her letters contain little in the way of serious criticism of the arts, and scant mention of religion, science, politics or public affairs.[263] She does not dwell immoderately upon 'her own feelings', but she does indeed write in her letters about 'her own experiences as the principal part of her life', creating a discursive space for herself as an individual to compensate, one suspects, for the fact that her marriage to a 'great man' required her to suppress her own ambitions and identity in deference to his.

Her letters contain many brilliant sketches of the literary and intellectual circle in which the Carlyles moved; however, her greatest talent as a letter writer is in her stories of the ordinary people she encounters within her domestic circle, and the everyday experiences of a Victorian housewife responsible for maintaining her middle-class home.

She created brilliantly mock-heroic domestic drama out of the details of her own daily life that was the antithesis to her husband's heroic vision.[264] The difficulties of hiring and retaining good servants, the business of decorating and cleaning an old house, and all without upsetting her temperamental husband, these are the things that preoccupy Jane Carlyle and which she makes the subject of her own writing. As she wrote in 1862, 'when one has so little communication with the outer-world – above all with the outer *air* it is difficult to avoid occupying oneself morbidly with the affairs within doors.'[265]

A succession of servants dust and polish their way through the Carlyles' residences during their forty-year marriage, and most are memorialised in Jane's letters. Like Somerville and Ross, she had a flair for writing about life below stairs, that predominantly female domain so foreign to most male writers of the period. In a letter of 1843 to her Liverpool cousin Jeannie Welsh, she describes the importance of servants in her life:

> as if '*the servants*' were not a most important – a most fearful item in our female existence! I think, talk, and write about my own servants as much as Geraldine does about her lovers – and make myself sure that everybody that cares for me will sympathise with me in the matter.[266]

Such comments mark this as a nineteenth-century document. By the beginning of the century, the middle classes were defining themselves in part by their ability to maintain large and well-ordered homes. As the century wore on there was increasing pressure for middle-class households to employ domestic servants to undertake the heavier domestic duties. The responsibility for the management and maintenance of the home fell to the lady of the house, and it was in this context that the servants came to be such a 'fearful item in our female existence'. By the middle of the century about 750,000 women were employed in residential domestic service. Many of these were young, unmarried, and far from home, and their relationship with their mistresses was often a complex and difficult one as a consequence of the radical social division between them coupled with the fact that they lived in such close domestic proximity.

As her letters testify, Jane Carlyle became very attached to some of her servants, and immersed herself in their problems. Helen Mitchell came to work for the Carlyles in 1837, and was to stay with them for about eleven years. But by 1840 Jane was writing to her mother about 'My poor little Helen [who] has been gradually getting more and more into the habit of tippling', and her subsequent letters record the ups and downs in Helen's unequal struggle with 'the perdition of strong liquors'.[267] Her letters reveal her consciousness of the hardships and tragedies of her servants' lives, her affection for their eccentricities, and her enjoyment of their conversation. She records, for instance, in a letter to her Liverpool cousin Jeannie Welsh, Helen's comments, 'while clearing away the breakfast things', on some people's speedy recovery, and often remarriage, after the death of their loved ones: ' ". . . But I do think", she resumed after some interruption of dusting, "that Mr Carlyle *will be* (admire the tense) a very *desultory widow*! He is so *easily put about* – and seems to take no pleasure *in new females*"! . . .'[268]

Many of her letters reveal an intriguing fascination with the servant's attitude and relationship to her employers. And so she writes about her discovery of the perfidious behaviour of one of her housemaids, Mary, during one of her illnesses; of how she was informed,

'Well, ma'am . . . it is known to all the neighbours round here – you will be told some day, and if I don't tell you now, you will blame me for having let you be so deceived. Mary is the worst of girls! She had an illegitimate child in your house on the 29th of last July. It was her *second* child – and all the things you have been missing have been spent on her man and her friends. There has been constant company kept in your kitchen since there was no fear of your seeing it; and whenever Helen threatened to tell you, she frightened her into silence by threats of poisoning *her* and cutting her own throat!!'

Now, my Dear, if you had seen the creature Mary you would just as soon have suspected the Virgin Mary of such things! But I have investigated, and find it all true. For two years I have been cheated and made a fool of, and laughed at for my softness, by this half-idiotic-looking woman; and while she was crying up in my room, moaning out: 'What would become of her when I died?' and witnessing in me as sad a spectacle of human agony as could have been anywhere seen;

> she was giving suppers to men and women downstairs;
> laughing and swearing – oh I can't go on. It is too disgusting!
> I shall only say that while she was in labour in the small
> room at the end of the dining room, Mr Carlyle was taking
> tea in the dining room with Miss Jewsbury talking to him!!!
> Just a thin small door between them! The child was not born
> till two in the morning when Mr C. was still reading in the
> Drawingroom.[269]

It is in the very fact that the middle-class ladies and gentlemen sipping tea were separated by 'just a thin small door' from the more primitive, physical lives of those 'in labour' that the piquancy of the relationship between the bourgeois householders and their servants resides.

One wonders what Jane Carlyle would have made of Hannah Cullwick, and, indeed, what that intelligent and forthright member of the servant classes would have made of the Carlyles. Hannah Cullwick was in her day a lowly and obscure maidservant who has achieved fame in the twentieth century not only through her extensive diaries, which provide a uniquely detailed personal account of the working life of a Victorian lower-class woman in service, but also because of her unusual relationship with the upper-middle-class poet and barrister Arthur Munby, who moved in similar circles to the Carlyles. Hannah was born in Shropshire in 1833, and went into domestic service in 1841 at the age of eight. In 1854 she went to London, where she met Munby, who encouraged her to keep a diary for his benefit recording all the details of her daily drudgery. Thence began an extraordinary eighteen-year secret courtship leading to an equally secret marriage which lasted for a further thirty-six years, although for much of that time they did not live together. Munby's 'secret life' had something in common with 'Walter's', whose 'earliest recollection of things sexual' revolve around 'an erotic nursemaid', and whose 'first fuck' was his near-rape of one of the family servants, a seventeen year-old virgin named Charlotte.[270] Munby's diaries and photographs reveal him to have been fascinated, indeed obsessed, by working-class women, particularly those engaged in hard labour, but whereas 'Walter' unashamedly exploited the economic subservience of the lower class for his own sexual gratification, Munby's relationships with such women were apparently highly respectable, his attitude towards them typically chivalrous and protective. Nevertheless, as Liz Stanley points out, 'chivalry depends upon and derives from inequalities in power, privilege and material possessions and resulting images of the social groups involved. It is an important way of oppressing people, because at the same time it denies the existence of oppression under the appearance of service to the oppressed class.'[271]

Questions of power and subordination are clearly crucial in determining the nature of these diaries written by a lower domestic servant for the voyeuristic pleasure of her upper-class lover. We know that Munby gave her what he called a 'training and teaching' in servitude and humility.[272] He held the key to a padlock and chain which she used to wear around her neck, and was referred to by her as 'Massa'. To signify her enslavement to him, she would black her face and body; he photographed her in the guise of a black slave. Her diaries represent their relationship as a text-book case of the intersection of class, gender and race. She washed his feet and licked his boots, and performed degrading acts of domestic drudgery before him. She pandered to his desire to see her 'in her dirt', occasionally going a bit too far, so that 'he was, I think, disgusted:' 'My face was dirty (I'd been cleaning the dirty scullery out) & my arms black'd & my *hands* look'd swell'd & red, & begrimed with dirt – *grener'd* as we say in Shropshire . . . It seems he began to think I *was too low* & degraded.'[273] She describes her degradation with, it seems, a clear awareness of what it signifies about her class position and with a consciousness too of how her journalistic account, reiterating the details of her 'poor & black' drudgery, would rekindle her 'Massa's' desire:

> I was now a regular drudge & my hands were grimed with dirt, & big & red wi' the frost, & M. told me to come to him in my dirt. I did once or twice & walk'd up the Strand with dirty frock & striped apron & my old bonnet & hands & arms & face begrimed with dirt, so that once I think he really pitied me, & never wish'd me to come out so again. As I was cleaning the hall on my hands & knees one morning a gentleman came down to go out, & I let him step over me as he was in a hurry. Of course he never thought anything of it, neither did I, only of the difference 'twixt him & me. Massa used to pass close by on his way to Westminster daily, & he came once or twice to see me shake the mats against the lamp post in the street, & I think I look'd as poor & black a drudge as any in the street.[274]

If she colludes with Munby's designation of her to a position of such lowly servitude, such passages reveal her acute appreciation of the performative in their relationship. She describes, for instance, one occasion when, while she was working at a respectable lodging house in Margate, Munby came to stay there as a guest:

> I made him a curtsy & said, 'Yes, sir,' pretty loud & then put the door to but of course didn't shut it. Then I *think* I went up & he kiss'd me quickly & then spoke louder about his dinner . . . after the dinner was over, & Missis was safe upstairs at reading as she always did with her sister of an evening, & so *then* I went in & had a petting with Massa &

talk'd about things. It was delightfully amusing altogether, for our having such a grand lodger at Margate was quite a new thing that even the Missis seem'd pleas'd, for she said, 'He's *quite* a gentleman,' & I thought, 'Yes, ma'am, *I* could tell you that.'[275]

Needless to say, Munby's holiday in Margate provides all sorts of delicious opportunities for Hannah to perform dirty tasks for him, like cleaning the grate and making up a fire in his room and cleaning his boots, and to wait on him hand and foot.

Clearly Hannah enjoyed the necessity for subterfuge involved in the conduct of their improbable illicit affair. In particular, she is amused by the idea of what people would think of their liaison. How would the gentleman who steps over her as she cleans the hallway react to the idea that she commanded the heart of one such as he? What would her mistress who is thrown into such a maidenly flutter by Munby's arrival make of the fact that her maid of all work was petting with him in his bedroom? When she goes out 'in her dirt' to buy 'Massa' a Valentine, choosing one showing 'a dog with a chain round his neck' which she thought 'fit for me', she comments to the shop assistant, 'I dare say you wonder why I want one at all.'[276]

For all that she appears to embrace the subordinate role that Munby assigns to her, her diaries give the impression of a woman who is strong-willed and independent, proud of her physical strength (as well she might be, with her thirteen- to eighteen-inch biceps) and of her capacity for hard work. Although her pride in her work is clearly attributable in part to her internalisation of the middle-class ideology of work in general and Munby's 'training' in particular, there is no doubt that she derives a sense of personal dignity from the fact that she does her job well and is able to make a living. There are, for instance, several points in her diary where she writes of feeling empowered by her strength and domestic knowledge in a way that is denied to a 'lady'. Of her employer Miss Knight, for example, she wrote,

> She told me she would try to do with no servants in winter – only for the errands & for cleaning the front door steps. She says, 'I *cannot* do them' – and I feel so sorry for her. I can do them & always do everywhere I like, but she seem'd to think it very degrading, & of course it would be to her.
>
> Miss K. thought me very strong, & so I am, 4 times stronger nor she is I should say, for she couldn't draw a cork, nor lift a saucepan. She could not *sew* well either, therefore a poor drudge like me is more use in a lodging house than her being a brought-up lady, as couldn't boil a 'tatoe when she first came, as she said. She told me lots o' things I didn't know, about the sun & moon & planets, & about France that I

never had heard. I liked to hear her talk, still I thought it would be better if she was stronger & more used to work, for all that learning wouldn't get her a living in a lodging house.[277]

Her sense of her own identity and personal integrity and, ironically given the poor conditions under which servants worked, of her freedom, is closely bound up with her work and her class affiliations, and she refuses to relinquish that identity for Munby. Hannah clearly viewed the kind of work she did as 'unsexing', as releasing her from the constraints placed by gender ideology upon the middle-class lady; indeed, she described herself as 'not a woman' because of the 'unfeminine' nature of her appearance and habits.[278] It was partly her transgressive sexual identity which seems to have appealed to Munby, who photographed her with her hair cut short and wearing men's clothes.[279] However, he also photographed her as a middle-class lady, and as an angel, roles which Hannah was not so willing to play in life. While she was prepared to exaggerate her lowly position in life and accede to Munby's fantasies in the early years of their relationship, she was not prepared to become a lady at his bidding, and even after their marriage she continued to act as his servant.

Although her diaries were written at Munby's instigation, over her twenty years as a diarist Hannah learned to make use of the form for her own purposes too. Liz Stanley points out that 'she used them to express things, in complex and subtle ways, that she didn't feel able to talk about,' and moreover that 'she increasingly used the diaries to gain greater influence within and over their relationship.'[280] Hannah's diaries become a voice for herself and her class. Telling her story her own way, articulating her self in her own accents, itself constitutes an act of resistance. Her diaries not only give us her side of the story of her intriguing relationship with Munby, they also describe the life of a Victorian maidservant from the servant's point of view, which is inevitably very different from that of an Edith Somerville or a Jane Carlyle.

Of course it is the flexibility of the journal form which enables Hannah thus to write herself, and which enabled so many others in the period who did not think of themselves as authors to commit their thoughts and experiences to paper. Like letters, journals and diaries are relatively private forms of writing, and tend to be less rigidly structured, less polished, more informal than other prose genres discussed in this book. In most nineteenth-century letters and diaries, the rules of grammar are relaxed, balanced sentences and formal syntax are abandoned in favour of a style which captures the rhythms of everyday speech, thoughts in the making, the immediacy of the moment, the contingency and open-endedness of life itself.

Both letters and diaries are forms which refuse closure. In an exuberant description of the letter-writing practices of her Victorian great-aunt, the photographer Julia Margaret Cameron, Virginia Woolf gives an entertaining illustration of this feature of the genre:

> She wrote letters till the postman left, and then she began her postscripts. She sent the gardener after the postman, the gardener's boy after the gardener, the donkey galloping all the way to Yarmouth after the gardener's boy. Sitting at Wandsworth Station she wrote page after page to Alfred Tennyson until 'as I was folding your letter came the screams of the train, and then the yells of the porters with the threat that the train would not wait for me,' so that she had to thrust the document into strange hands and run down the steps. Every day she wrote to Henry Taylor, and every day he answered her.[281]

Letter writing had not always been so undisciplined. The informality, the promiscuous disregard for propriety, the sheer abundance of the form in Victorian England was historically conditioned, as all literary genres are. Whistling trains that 'would not wait' had superseded the old mail-coaches and set a new epistolary pace. There were servants aplenty to wait upon the postscripts of the rich, but even the poor had access to the Penny Post and, thus democratised, the letter lost something of its dignity. As Woolf points out:

> The Victorian age killed the art of letter writing by kindness: it was only too easy to catch the post. A lady sitting down at her desk a hundred years before had not only certain ideals of logic and restraint before her, but the knowledge that a letter which cost so much money to send and excited so much interest to receive was worth time and trouble. With Ruskin and Carlyle in power, a penny post to stimulate, a gardener, a gardener's boy, and a galloping donkey to catch up the overflow of inspiration, restraint was unnecessary and emotion more to a lady's credit, perhaps, than common sense. Thus to dip into the private letters of the Victorian age is to be immersed in the joys and sorrows of enormous families, to share their whooping coughs and colds and misadventures, day by day, indeed hour by hour. The standard of family affection was very high. Illness elicited showers of enquiries and kindnesses. The weather was watched anxiously to see whether Richard would be wet at Cheltenham, or Jane catch cold at Broadstairs. Grave misdemeanours on the part of governesses, cooks, and doctors . . . were detailed profusely, and the least departure from family morality was vigilantly pounced upon and volubly imparted.[282]

Woolf's affectionate and witty account of the epistolary activities of her great-aunt and her contemporaries not only evokes the pleasure of reading Victorian letters, it also reminds us of how important letters are in revealing the lived culture of a period, that of the governesses and cooks and gardeners' boys as well as that of the Victorian lady who employs them and writes about them. The private life of nineteenth-century England is laid bare in its letters as it is in its journals and diaries. It is here that we discover the diversity of nineteenth-century culture. The power of a diary such as Hannah Cullwick's reminds the twentieth-century reader, who might have imagined that culture, in the nineteenth century, was the exclusive property of the middle-class men who wrote about it in books, that there were formidable alternative cultures, against which the dominant culture defined itself. Just as Arthur Munby, that 'man of culture', was parasitical upon 'other women',[283] so the cultural identity of the middle classes was constructed upon a concept of difference, upon a set of dichotomies – dominance and sub-ordination, autonomy and dependence, masculine and feminine – by which the world could be categorised.[284] The following chapter will explore some of these dichotomies as they relate to questions of cultural definition and the contest for cultural authority in nineteenth-century England.

Notes

1. Thomas Carlyle, 'Biography', in *Critical and Miscellaneous Essays*, 3 vols (London, 1887), II, 245–60 (p. 247). Reprinted from a review of Croker's 1831 edition of Boswell's *Life of Johnson*, in *Fraser's Magazine*, no. 27 (April, 1832).

2. *Complete Works of Oscar Wilde*, Introduction by Vyvyan Holland (London and Glasgow, 1973), p. 357. Cited by Judy Simons, *Diaries and Journals of Literary Women from Fanny Burney to Virginia Woolf* (London, 1990), p. 1.

3. See Introduction, *Revealing Lives: Autobiography, Biography, and Gender*, edited by Susan Groag Bell and Marilyn Yalom (Albany, N.Y., 1990), p. 3.

4. See David Amigoni, *Victorian Biography: Intellectuals and the Ordering of Discourse* (New York, London, etc., 1993), pp. 52–61.

5. Quoted in Kenneth Robinson, *Wilkie Collins* (London, 1951), p. 260, and cited in Ira Bruce Nadel, *Biography: Fiction, Fact and Form* (London, 1984), p. 87.

6. See Introduction, Bell and Yalom, pp. 4, 9.

7. Cited, with other examples, in Valerie Sanders, *The Private Lives of Victorian Women: Autobiography in Nineteenth-Century England* (New York, London, etc., 1989), p. 15.

8. *Personal Recollections from early life to old age of Mary Somerville, with Selections from her Correspondence*, by her daughter Martha Somerville (London, 1874), pp. 1–2.

9. As critics such as Valerie Sanders, Judy Simons and Mary Jean Corbett have argued.

10. See Sanders, pp. 14–15.

11. See Richard D. Altick, *Lives and Letters* (New York, 1969), p. 151.

12. Thomas Carlyle, *Sartor Resartus*, edited by C. F. Harrold (New York, 1937), p. 203.

13. Carlyle, 'Biography', p. 251.

14. Ibid, p. 249.

15. J. R. Seeley, 'Introduction', *The Life and Adventures of E. M. Arndt* (London, 1879), pp. v–vi. Quoted in Amigoni, p. 98.

16. Virginia Woolf, 'The New Biography', in *Collected Essays*, 4 vols (London, 1967), IV, 229–35 (p. 234).

17. Virginia Woolf, 'The Art of Biography', in *Collected Essays*, IV, 221–28 (p. 228).

18. Lytton Strachey, *Eminent Victorians* (Harmondsworth, 1948), p. 10.

19. Strachey, pp. 9–10.

20. Woolf, 'The New Biography', p. 231.

21. Strachey, p. 10.

22. *Complete Works of Oscar Wilde*, p. 1010.

23. Leslie Stephen, *Studies of a Biographer*, 4 vols (London, 1898), III, 220.

24. George Eliot, 'Thomas Carlyle's *Life of John Sterling*', *Westminster Review* (January, 1852), reprinted in *George Eliot: Selected Essays, Poems and Other Writings*, edited by A. S. Byatt and Nicholas Warren (Harmondsworth, 1990), pp. 297–301 (p. 299).

25. Thomas Carlyle, 'Sir Walter Scott', *Westminster Review*, 28 (1838). Reprinted in *Critical and Miscellaneous Essays*, III, 165–224 (pp. 170–71).

26. Ibid, pp. 171–72.

27. [Anon.], 'Contemporary Literature', *Westminster and Foreign Quarterly Review* 66 (1857) 581 Quoted in Nadel, p. 15. Nadel discusses the importance of Plutarch for the development of English biography in chapter 1 of his study. David Amigoni also contests the idea that Victorian biographical writing should be perceived as a singular tradition and draws attention to the significance of compendia of brief lives, in *Victorian Biography*.

28. These and other examples of the collective biography are discussed in Nadel, chapter 1.

29. See Nadel, pp. 47, 53.

30. Carlyle, 'Sir Walter Scott', pp. 172–73.

31. Harriet Martineau, *Biographical Sketches. 1852–1868*, 2nd edn (London, 1869), pp. v–vi.

32. Cited in J. L. Clifford, *Biography as an Art* (London, 1962), p. 100.

33. Frances E. Kingsley, ed., *Charles Kingsley: His Letters and Memories of his Life* (London, 1884), p. 135.

34. Elizabeth Gaskell, *The Life of Charlotte Brontë*, edited by Alan Shelston (Harmondsworth, 1975), p. 519.

35. See Richard D. Altick, *The English Common Reader: A social history of the mass reading public 1800–1900* (Chicago, 1963), pp. 122–23.

36. See Amigoni, p. 21.

37. See Phyllis Rose, 'Fact and fiction in biography', in *Nineteenth-Century Lives*, edited by Laurence S. Lockridge, John Maynard, and Donald D. Stone (Cambridge, 1989), pp. 188–202 (pp. 191–92).

38. Quoted from the Preface, by Sir Joshua Fitch, LL.D., to the Teachers' Edition of the *Life of Thomas Arnold, D.D., Head-Master of Rugby*, by Arthur Penrhyn Stanley (London, 1904), p. vi.

39. Quoted ibid, p. vi.

40. Arthur Penrhyn Stanley, *The Life and Correspondence of Thomas Arnold, D. D.* 7th edn (London, 1852), p. 79.

41. Ibid, pp. 140, 141–42.

42. Ibid, p. 142.

43. Ibid, p. 622.

44. G. O. Trevelyan, *Life and Letters of Lord Macaulay* (London, 1909), p. 52.

45. The foregoing quotations and discussion of Macaulay's impact on higher education in India are derived from A. O. J. Cockshut, *Truth to Life: The Art of Biography in the Nineteenth Century* (London, 1974), p. 128.

46. See Owen Dudley Edwards, *Macaulay* (London, 1988), p. 151.

47. Again see Cockshut's discussion of the formal quality of Morley's *Life of Gladstone*, in *Truth to Life*, pp. 175–92.

48. John Morley, *The Life of Gladstone*, 3 vols (London, 1903), I, 4.

49. See Preface to William Hazlitt, *The Life of Napoleon Buonaparte*, 2nd edn, revised by his son, 4 vols (London, 1852).

50. Ibid.

51. Ibid, III, 3.

52. Ibid, I, 58.

53. Ibid, III, 202–3.

54. Ibid, IV, 335–36.

55. Ibid, IV, 175–76.

56. George Eliot, 'Thomas Carlyle's *Life of John Sterling*', *Westminster Review* (January, 1852). Reprinted in Byatt and Warren, pp. 297–301 (p. 298).

57. Ibid, pp. 298, 300.

58. See Amigoni, pp. 30–31.

59. Thomas Carlyle, *The Life of John Sterling* (1851), in *The Centenary Edition of the Works of Thomas Carlyle*, edited by H. D. Traill, 30 vols (London, 1896–99), XI, 55.

60. Thomas De Quincey, 'Samuel Taylor Coleridge', in *Recollections of the Lakes and the Lake Poets*, edited by David Wright (Harmondsworth, 1970), pp. 33–111 (pp. 42–43).

61. Ibid, pp. 99–100.

62. John Stuart Mill, *Autobiography*, edited by Jack Stillinger (London, 1971), p. 105.

63. James Anthony Froude, *Thomas Carlyle, A History of his Life in London, 1834–1881*, 2 vols (London, 1891), II, 449.

64. Frederic Harrison, *The Choice of Books* (London, 1886), p. 175.

65. See the Introduction to *Froude's Life of Carlyle*, abridged and edited by John Clubbe (London, 1979), pp. 8–27.

66. Thomas Carlyle, *Reminiscences*, edited by James Anthony Froude, 2 vols (London, 1881), II, 227–30.

67. Ibid, p. 237.

68. From a letter to John Sterling, 15 June, 1835, quoted in the Introduction to *I too am here: Selections from the letters of Jane Welsh Carlyle*, edited by Alan and Mary McQueen Simpson (Cambridge, 1977), p. 7.

69. On female biographers of the period see Rohan Maitzen, '"This Feminine Preserve": Historical Biographies by Victorian Women', *Victorian Studies*, 38 (1995), 371–93.

70. See Judith Barbour, 'Among the Dead Men: Mary Wollstonecraft Shelley's writings in the biographical genre', in *Australasian Victorian Studies Association Conference Papers, 1989*, edited by Catherine Waters and Helen Yardley (Sydney, 1989), pp.10–28 (p. 11).

71. See ibid, p. 10; and see, for instance, T. Medwin's two-volume *Life of Shelley* (1847); T. H. Hogg's two-volume *Life of Shelley* (1858); E. J. Trelawny's *Recollections of the Last Days of Shelley and Byron* (1858); T. L. Peacock's 'Memoirs of Shelley', *Fraser's Magazine* (June 1858, Jan. and March 1860, March 1862).

72. Gaskell, *Life of Brontë*, p. 334.

73. Ibid, p. 156.

74. Ibid, pp. 511–12.

75. Ibid, pp. 167–69, 173.

76. Alice Meynell, 'The Brontës', in *Essays of Today and Yesterday* (1926) Reprinted in *Alice Meynell: Prose and Poetry*, edited by P. P., V. M., O. S., and F. M., with a biographical and critical introduction by V. Sackville-West (London, 1947), pp. 97–108 (p. 100).

77. Gaskell, *Life of Brontë*, p. 175.

78. Ibid, p. 202.

79. Ibid, pp. 386–87.

80. Alice Meynell, 'The Brontës', pp. 98–99.

81. See Shelston, Introduction to Gaskell, *Life of Brontë*, pp. 13, 15.

82. Quoted ibid, p. 15. See also Appendix B to Shelston's edition.

83. Gaskell, *Life of Brontë*, pp. 53–54.

84. See Shelston, Introduction to Gaskell, *Life of Brontë*, p. 29.

85. Meynell, 'The Brontës', p. 97.

86. Quoted in Sanders, p. 8.

87. Leslie Stephen, 'Autobiography', in *Hours in a Library* 3rd edn, 4 vols (London, 1907), IV, 185.

88. *Quarterly Review*, 35 (28 December, 1826), 149. Quoted in David Vincent, *Bread, Knowledge and Freedom: A Study of Nineteenth-Century Working Class Autobiography* (London, 1981), p. 30.

89. See, for instance, Linda H. Peterson, *Victorian Autobiography: The Tradition of Self-Interpretation* (New Haven, Connecticut, and London, 1986); Heather Henderson, *The Victorian Self: Autobiography and Biblical Narrative* (Ithaca, N.Y., and London, 1989); Avrom Fleishman, *Figures of Autobiography: The Language of Self-Writing in Victorian and Modern England* (Berkeley, California, and London, 1983); Susanna Egan, *Patterns of Experience in Autobiography* (Chapel Hill N.C., and London, 1984).

90. *The Sermons and Devotional Writings of Gerard Manley Hopkins*, edited by Christopher Devlin (London, 1959), p. 123.

91. See, for instance, Fleishman in *Figures of Autobiography*, and George P. Landow, ed., *Approaches to Victorian Autobiography* (Athens, Ohio, 1979), especially the introduction and essays by Phyllis Grosskurth, Howard Helsinger and Elizabeth Helsinger.

92. *The Poems of Gerard Manley Hopkins*, edited by W. H. Gardner and N. H. Mackenzie, 4th edn (London, New York, Toronto, 1967), no. 67, p. 101; George Eliot, *Middlemarch: A Study of Provincial Life*, edited by Bert G. Hornback (New York, 1977), p. 289.

93. Thomas De Quincey, *Confessions of an English Opium-Eater and Selections from the Autobiography*, edited by Edward Sackville-West (London, 1950), 'To the Reader', p. 253.

94. Anthony Trollope, *An Autobiography*, vol. I of 'The Shakespeare Head Trollope' (Oxford, 1929), p. 1.

95. *Complete Works of Oscar Wilde*, pp. 1010, 975.

96. Trollope, *An Autobiography*, p. 111.

97. Herbert Spencer, *An Autobiography*, 2 vols (New York, 1904), II, 57. Quoted as part of an interesting discussion of Spencer's autobiography in Landow's introduction to *Approaches to Victorian Autobiography*, p. xxxii.

98. Letter of November, 1879, *The Life and Letters of Charles Darwin*, edited by F. Darwin, 3 vols (New York, 1896), II, 414. Quoted in John D. Rosenberg, 'Mr. Darwin collects himself', in *Nineteenth-Century Lives*, edited by Laurence S. Lockridge, John Maynard, and Donald D. Stone (Cambridge, 1989), pp. 82–111 (p. 102).

99. *The Later Letters of John Stuart Mill, 1849–1873*, edited by Francis E. Mineka (Toronto, 1972), p. 476. Quoted in Howard Helsinger, 'Credence and Credibility: The Concern for Honesty in Victorian Autobiography', in Landow, pp. 39–63 (p. 53).

100. *The Works of John Ruskin*, XXXV, 252–53.

101. Ibid, p. 49.

102. See Phyllis Grosskurth, 'Where was Rousseau?', in Landow, pp. 26–38 (p. 37).

103. See Landow, Introduction, *Approaches to Victorian Autobiography*, p. xv.

104. William Wordsworth, *The Prelude*, XIII, l. 446; 1805 edn, III, ll. 142–43.

105. Walter Pater, *The Renaissance* (London, 1910), pp. 234–35.

106. Wordsworth, *The Prelude*, VIII, ll. 152–53; Pater, *The Renaissance*, p. 235.

107. *Complete Works of Oscar Wilde*, p. 934.

108. Quoted in Introduction to Samuel Taylor Coleridge, *Biographia Literaria: or Biographical Sketches of my Literary Life and Opinions*, edited by George Watson (London, 1956), pp. xi–xii. Interestingly, Ruskin's *Fors Clavigera* (1871–84) is a similarly mixed form, mingling the treatise on contemporary society and thought with personal confession in a manner more in keeping with Romantic organic subjectivity than with late Victorian theories of the self.

109. For example, 804 texts are indexed in John Burnett, David Vincent, and John Mayall's bibliography, *The Autobiography of the Working Class* (1984). For full discussions of the development of working-class and woman's autobiography in the period, see David Vincent, *Bread, Knowledge, and Freedom: A Study of Nineteenth-Century Working Class Autobiography* (London, 1981); Valerie Sanders, *The Private Lives of Victorian Women: Autobiography in Nineteenth-Century England* (New York, London, 1989); Julia Swindells, *Victorian Writing and Working Women: The Other Side of Silence* (London, 1985).

110. Jerome H. Buckley, for instance, notes 'the virtual absence of women' from his general argument, explaining their exclusion by the fact that 'there have been remarkably few women autobiographers devoted intensely, like Wordsworth or Ruskin . . . to the projection of their inner lives'. The *Turning Key: Autobiography and the Subjective Impulse since 1800* (Cambridge, Massachusetts, 1984), p. ix.

111. Fleishman, p. 111. It is only fair to note that Fleishman himself comments on the variety of Victorian autobiography; indeed, he is the only critic to note 'an equine item', *Black Beauty: The Autobiography of a Horse*.

112. See Regenia Gagnier, 'The Literary Standard, Working-Class Autobiography, and Gender', in Bell and Yalom, pp. 93–114 (pp. 103–4).

113. 'Sketches in the Life of John Clare', in *John Clare's Autobiographical Writings*, edited by Eric Robinson (Oxford, 1986), pp. 1–26 (p. 2).

114. Ibid, pp. 3–4.

115. Ibid, p. 9.

116. Ibid, p. 13.

117. Ibid, p. 10.

118. Ibid, p. 12.

119. Ibid, pp. 18–19.

120. 'More Hints in the Life etc', in *John Clare's Autobiographical Writings*, p. 28.

121. 'Sketches in the Life of John Clare', p. 15.

122. Robinson, Introduction, *John Clare's Autobiographical Writings*, p. viii.

123. Ibid, p. xiii.

124. 'Sketches in the Life of John Clare', p. 26. It should be noted that in the more extensive 'Autobiographical Fragments' Clare is considerably more critical of the middle classes and of the inequities of a social system which countenances the oppression of the rural poor.

125. See Vincent, *Bread, Knowledge and Freedom*, p. 37. See also Regenia Gagnier's account of the gap between middle-class gender ideology and experience in some examples of working-class autobiography, in 'The Literary Standard, Working-Class Autobiography, and Gender', pp. 106–14.

126. 'Walter', *My Secret Life*, vols 5–8, Introduction by Donald Thomas (London, 1994), pp. xxvi, 564–65, 107.

127. John Henry Newman, *Apologia Pro Vita Sua* (London, 1959), pp. 11, 14.

128. Ibid, pp. 95, 93.

129. *Complete Works of Oscar Wilde*, pp. 1009–10.

130. Newman, *Apologia*, pp. 277–78.

131. Ibid, p. 278.

132. Ibid, p. 278.

133. *The Works of John Ruskin*, XXXV, 36.

134. Ibid, pp. 279–80.

135. Ibid, p. 279.

136. Ibid, p. 37.

137. Ibid, p. 56.

138. Ibid, pp. 20, 22, 24, 25.

139. Ibid, p. 44. It should be noted that *Praeterita* was begun in 1885, after Ruskin had experienced major mental breakdowns in 1878 and the early 1880s, and that as an accurate account of his life it is unreliable.

140. Mill, *Autobiography*, pp. 27–28, 31.

141. *The Early Draft of John Stuart Mill's 'Autobiography'*, edited by Jack Stillinger (Urbana, Illinois, 1961), p. 66.

142. Mill, *Autobiography*, p. 3.

143. Ibid, pp. 19–20.

144. Ibid, p. 3.

145. *Mill on Bentham and Coleridge*, edited by F. R. Leavis (Cambridge, 1980), pp. 39–40.

146. See, for example, Carlyle's *Sartor Resartus*, Robert Browning's 'Christmas Eve and Easter Day', and the *Autobiography of Mark Rutherford*.

147. Mill, *Autobiography*, p. 81.

148. Ibid, p. 89.

149. Ibid, pp. 111, 114, 145.

150. Stephen, 'Autobiography', in *Hours in a Library*, pp. 221–22; Mill, *Autobiography*, p. 3.

151. Mill, *Autobiography*, Introduction, pp. xvii, xix. For a more sympathetic account of Mill's acknowledgement of his wife's contribution to his work see Susan Groag Bell, 'The Feminization of John Stuart Mill', in Bell and Yalom, pp. 81–92.

152. Sarah Ellis, *The Women of England* (London, 1839), p. 155.

153. See Sanders, p. 5.

154. See, for instance, Mary G. Mason, 'The Other Voice: Autobiographies of Women Writers', in *Autobiography: Essays Theoretical and Critical*, edited by James Olney (Princeton, N.J., 1980), pp. 207–35; and Estelle C. Jelinek, ed., *Women's Autobiography: Essays in Criticism* (Bloomington, Indiana, 1980).

155. Shirley Neuman gives a useful overview in 'Autobiography and Questions of Gender: An Introduction', *Prose Studies*, 14, 2 (1991), 1–11; see also Domna C. Stanton, 'Autogynography: Is the Subject Different?', in *The Female Autograph: Theory and Practice of Autobiography from the Tenth to the Twentieth Century*, edited by Domna C. Stanton (New York, 1984); and Sidonie Smith, *A Poetics of Women's Autobiography: Marginality and the Fictions of Self-Representation* (Bloomington, Indiana, 1987).

156. Caroline Norton, *English Laws for Women in the Nineteenth Century*, in *Selected Writings of Caroline Norton*, edited by James O. Hoge and Jane Marcus (New York, 1978), p. 1.

157. Ibid, pp. 1–3.

158. Ibid, p. 22.

159. Ibid, p. 173.

160. See Margaret Forster, *Significant Sisters: The Grassroots of Active Feminism 1839–1939* (New York, 1984), chapter 1; and Mary Poovey, *Uneven Developments: The Ideological Work of Gender in Mid-Victorian England* (Chicago, 1988; London, 1989), chapter 3, both excellent on Norton's feminism.

161. 'Florence Nightingale', in *Harriet Martineau on Women*, edited by Gayle Graham Yates (New Brunswick, N.J., 1985), pp. 196–202 (p. 196). This was written when Nightingale was believed to be dying after the Crimean War, but not published until she actually died in 1910.

162. Ibid, p. 198.

163. Ibid, p. 202.

164. Written in 1852, as part of the second volume of Nightingale's three-volume *Suggestions for Thought to Searchers after Religious Truth*, which was revised and privately printed in 1860 after Nightingale's return from the Crimea, *Cassandra* was finally published for the first time as an Appendix to Ray Strachey, 'The Cause', A Short History of the Women's Movement in Great Britain (London, 1928).

165. Florence Nightingale, *Cassandra and Other Selections from Suggestions for Thought*, edited by Mary Poovey (London, 1991), p. 218.

166. Ibid, p. 207.

167. Ibid, p. 208.

168. Ibid, p. 213.

169. Ibid, p. 220. I am indebted to Victoria Burrows for her original and insightful feminist reading of *Cassandra* in '*Cassandra*: Florence Nightingale's "shriek of agony"', Honours thesis, The University of Western Australia (1994).

170. Nightingale, *Cassandra*, p. 225. Interestingly Harriet Martineau also spoke out publicly against marriages between cousins, in the Liberal newspaper the *Daily News*, at about the same time. See *Harriet Martineau on Women*, p. 31.

171. Nightingale, *Cassandra*, p. 215.

172. See Elaine Showalter, 'Florence Nightingale's Feminist Complaint: Women, Religion, and *Suggestions for Thought*', *Signs: Journal of Women in Culture and Society*, 6, 3 (1981), 395–412.

173. See George P. Landow, 'Aggressive (Re)interpretations of the Female Sage: Florence Nightingale's *Cassandra*', in *Victorian Sages and Cultural Discourse: Renegotiating Gender and Power*, edited by Thais E. Morgan (New Brunswick, N.J., 1990), pp. 32–45 (pp. 32–33).

174. See ibid, p. 38.

175. Nightingale, *Cassandra*, pp. 220, 229.

176. Ibid, p. 213.

177. Harriet Martineau, *Autobiography*, with Memorials by Maria Weston Chapman, 2nd edn, 3 vols (London, 1877), I, 400–1.

178. Ibid, III, 469.

179. Ibid, III, 461.

180. See Mary Jean Corbett, *Representing Femininity: Middle-Class Subjectivity in Victorian and Edwardian Women's Autobiographies* (New York, 1992), p. 7.

181. See Linda Peterson, *Victorian Autobiography* (New Haven, Connecticut, 1986), p. 124; Mitzi Myers, 'Harriet Martineau's *Autobiography*: The Making of a Female Philosopher', in *Women's Autobiographies: Essays in Criticism*, edited by Estelle C. Jelinek (Bloomington, Indiana, 1980), pp. 53–70 (p. 59).

182. I am indebted to Melanie Cariss for her fine study, 'Harriet Martineau's *Autobiography* in the context of women's autobiography in the nineteenth century', unpublished manuscript, English Department, The University of Western Australia (1993). On this point see p. 21.

183. See ibid, pp. 23–30. See also Corbett, pp. 84, 91–93; Sanders, pp. 132–34; and Sanders's *Reason Over Passion: Harriet Martineau and the Victorian Novel* (Hemel Hempstead, 1986), chapter 6.

184. Martineau, *Autobiography*, I, 27.

185. Ibid, I, 120, 146 47.

186. Ibid, I, 168.

187. Ibid, III, 91; II, 414–15. It is interesting to note that Florence Nightingale also referred to herself as being a 'son' to her mother.

188. Ibid, I, 147.

189. Ibid, I, 29.

190. Ibid, I, 130–31.

191. *Life of Frances Power Cobbe. By Herself*, 2nd edn, 2 vols (London, 1894), I, iv–v.

192. Ibid, II, 210, 218.

193. Annie Besant, *Autobiographical Sketches* (London, 1885), pp. 95–96. Besant published her *Autobiography*, an extension of the *Sketches*, in 1893, the year before the publication of Cobbe's.

194. Ibid, p. 39. Compare, for instance, Egerton's story 'Virgin Soil', in *Keynotes and Discords*, first published in 1894.

195. Ibid, p. 46.

196. Ibid, p. 167.

197. Ibid, p. 107.

198. Margaret Oliphant, 'Harriet Martineau', *Blackwood's*, 121 (April, 1877). Quoted in Corbett, p. 93.

199. *The Autobiography of Margaret Oliphant*, edited by Elisabeth Jay (Oxford, 1990), p. 24.

200. Ibid, p. 30.

201. Ibid, p. 63.

202. Ibid, p. 81.

203. See Corbett, p. 104.

204. Oliphant, 'Harriet Martineau', *Blackwood's*, 121 (April, 1877), 495. Quoted in Sanders, *The Private Lives of Victorian Women*, p. 79.

205. Sanders, *Private Lives*, p. 88.

206. *The Autobiography of Margaret Oliphant*, p. 42.

207. See Elisabeth Jay, Introduction, *The Autobiography of Margaret Oliphant*, pp. xii, xiv.

208. The Earl of Beaconsfield (Benjamin Disraeli), *Vivian Grey*, Hughenden Edition (London, 1900), p. 4.

209. See Ian Campbell, 'Letters from Home: The Carlyle Family Correspondence', *Prose Studies*, 10 (1987), 307–17.

210. [Anna Jameson] *Diary of an Ennuyée* (Boston, 1833), pp. 137–38, 1. See Dorothy Mermin, *Godiva's Ride: Women of Letters in England, 1830–1880* (Bloomington and Indianapolis, 1993), pp. xiii–xiv, for further discussion of Jameson's use of the diary as a fictive device.

211. Thomas Mallon, in *A Book of One's Own: People and their Diaries* (New York, 1984), classifies his diarists, for instance, into chroniclers, travellers, pilgrims, creators, apologists, confessors, and prisoners.

212. *The Letters of William and Dorothy Wordsworth*, edited by E. de Selincourt, revised by Chester L. Shaver, Mary Moorman and Alan G. Hill, 7 vols (Oxford, 1967–93), II, 454.

213. See Paul Hamilton, Introduction to *Dorothy Wordsworth: Selections from the Journals* (London, 1992), p. xxii.

214. She wrote a *Journal of a Tour on The Continent* in 1820, a *Journal of My Second Tour in Scotland* in 1822, and *Journal of a Tour in the Isle of Man* in 1828.

215. *Dorothy Wordsworth: Selections from the Journals*, p. 19.

216. See, for instance, ibid, p. 41.

217. See Hamilton, Introduction, ibid, p. xxvii.

218. Such qualities may also be found in Ruskin's diaries. Indeed, Ruskin probably influenced Hopkins's way of looking at nature.

219. Ibid, pp. 9–10.

220. *The Journals and Papers of Gerard Manley Hopkins*, edited by Humphry House (London, 1959), p. 258.

221. Ibid, p. 162.

222. Ibid, p. 178.

223. Ibid, pp. 201, 250.

224. Ibid, pp. 4, 5, 9, 10, 11.

225. Ibid, p. 72.

226. *The Letters of Gerard Manley Hopkins to Robert Bridges*, edited by Claude Colleer Abbott, 2nd imp. rev. (London, 1955), p. 46.

227. Ibid, pp. 46–47.

228. Ibid, pp. 50–51.

229. *The Letters of Matthew Arnold to Arthur Hugh Clough*, edited by Howard Foster Lowry (London, 1932), p. 146.

230. Ibid, pp. 96–97.

231. *The Letters of John Keats*, edited by Maurice Buxton Forman, 3rd edn (London, 1947), p. 72.

232. Ibid, p. 426.

233. Ibid, p. 316.

234. *Byron: Selected Prose*, edited by Peter Gunn (Harmondsworth, 1972), pp. 283–84.

235. *The Works of John Ruskin*, XXXV, 146.

236. *Byron: Selected Prose*, p. 105.

237. Ibid, p. 106.

238. Ibid, p. 298.

239. Ibid, pp. 297–98.

240. Ibid, pp. 296–97.

241. Ibid, p. 297.

242. See Anne K. Mellor, *Romanticism and Gender* (New York, 1993), p. 25.

243. *Manfred*, Act II, sc. ii, ll. 106–9.

244. *Byron: Selected Prose*, p. 297.

245. *The Letters of Robert Browning and Elizabeth Barrett Barrett: 1845–1846*, edited by Elvan Kintner, 2 vols (Cambridge, Massachusetts, 1969), I, 3–4.

246. Ibid, pp. 7, 25.

247. Ibid, p. 29.

248. Ibid, pp. 40–41.

249. Ibid, pp. 75, xxi.

250. See William C. DeVane, 'The Virgin and the Dragon', *Yale Review*, N. S. 37 (September, 1947), 33–46, and, for a more recent feminist inflection, Adrienne Munich, *Andromeda's Chains: Gender and Interpretation in Victorian Criticism and Art* (New York and Oxford, 1989).

251. *The Letters of Robert Browning and Elizabeth Barrett Barrett*, p. 41.

252. Ibid, p. 7.

253. Ibid, pp. 12–13.

254. *Ever yours, Florence Nightingale: Selected Letters*, edited by Martha Vicinus and Bea Nergaard (London, 1989), p. 5.

255. Ibid, pp. 6–7.

256. See, for example, ibid, pp. 46–48, 171–72, 177–82.

257. *The Selected Letters of Somerville and Ross*, edited by Gifford Lewis (London, 1989), p. xxv.

258. Quoted in *I too am here: Selections from the letters of Jane Welsh Carlyle*, edited by Alan and Mary McQueen Simpson (Cambridge, 1977), p. 21.

259. Quoted ibid, pp. 24, 23.

260. Letter to Jeannie Welsh, 12 November, 1843, in *Jane Welsh Carlyle. Letters to her Family, 1839–1863*, edited by Leonard Huxley (London, 1924), p. 159. Quoted in Aileen Christianson, 'Jane Welsh Carlyle and Her Friendships with Women in the 1840's', *Prose Studies*, 10 (1987), 283–95 (p. 286).

261. *Ever yours, Florence Nightingale*, pp. 30–31.

262. Ibid, p. 31.

263. See *I too am here*, p. 23.

264. See Christianson, p. 283.

265. Quoted in *I too am here*, p. 129.

266. Letter of 8 April, 1843, in *Jane Welsh Carlyle. Letters to her Family*, p. 104. Quoted in Christianson, p. 285.

267. *I too am here*, p. 130.

268. Ibid, p. 132.

269. Ibid, p. 156.

270. *My Secret Life I* (Volumes 1–4), edited by Donald Thomas (London, 1994), pp. 51–59.

271. *The Diaries of Hannah Cullwick, Victorian Maidservant*, edited by Liz Stanley (London, 1984), p. 11.

272. Quoted ibid, p. 12.

273. Ibid, pp. 61–62.

274. Ibid, p. 57.

275. Ibid, pp. 68–69.

276. Ibid, p. 57.

277. Ibid, p. 78.

278. See Stanley's argument, ibid, pp. 4–5.

279. See Leonore Davidoff, 'Class and Gender in Victorian England: The Diaries of Arthur J. Munby and Hannah Cullwick', *Feminist Studies*, 5, 1 (1979), 86–141 (pp. 118–19).

280. *The Diaries of Hannah Cullwick*, p. 9.

281. *Victorian Photographs of Famous Men and Fair Women*, by Julia Margaret Cameron, with Introductions by Virginia Woolf and Roger Fry, edited by Tristram Powell (London, 1973), p. 16.

282. Ibid.

283. See Anita Levy, *Other Women: The Writing of Class, Race, and Gender, 1832–1898* (Princeton, N.J., 1991).

284. See Davidoff, 'Class and Gender in Victorian England', 111.

Chapter 3
Discourses of Culture

Romanticism, reacting in part to the universalism of the Enlightenment, as well as to the war with France, was a strongly nationalistic movement. Such cultural properties as Gothic architecture, Shakespeare's plays, and the rural landscape are instated as definitively English around the turn of the nineteenth century. A new self-consciousness about national identity originated with the Romantics at this time, a self-consciousness which was foundational for Victorian culture. George Cruikshank's cover for *Ainsworth's Magazine*, a monthly periodical which began in 1842 and was edited by the popular historical novelist William Harrison Ainsworth, serves to illustrate this point. The top part of the cover features two medallions attended by angels, who are embellishing them with flowers. The medallion on the left is of the young Queen Victoria in profile. She is depicted looking forward, as if towards the future, and faces the profile of an older Queen Elizabeth I in the other medallion. The parity given to the English Renaissance and the incipient age of Victoria in this image indicates the great cultural optimism and confidence of the early Victorians.

While Victoria functioned throughout her long reign as the transcendental signifier of national cultural unity, as the parallel to Elizabeth and incarnation of Britannia, the society over which she presided was diverse and dynamic, containing masses of competing and developing factional interests. 'Culture', which had long been regarded as an exclusively aristocratic prerogative, was identified by the Romantics with the rural poor. Wordsworth and Coleridge announce this new direction in their 'Preface' to the *Lyrical Ballads* (1802):

> The principal object, then, which I proposed to myself in these
> Poems was to chuse incidents and situations from common life
> . . . Low and rustic life was generally chosen, because in that
> condition, the essential passions of the heart find a better soil
> in which they can attain their maturity, are less under restraint,
> and speak a plainer and more emphatic language; . . . because
> the manners of rural life germinate from those elementary
> feelings; and from the necessary character of rural occupations
> are more easily comprehended; and are more durable; and

lastly, because in that condition the passions of men are
incorporated with the beautiful and permanent forms of
nature.[1]

The classical principle of culture as the disciplining and refinement
of nature (which is nicely emblematised by the geometrical planning
and use of topiary in the French garden of the seventeenth and eighteenth century) is entirely contradicted here. The horticultural metaphor
of culture is short-circuited, literalised, as human nature is entrusted to
external nature for its cultivation: 'the passions of men are incorporated
with the beautiful and permanent forms of nature.' The aristocratic
value of 'restraint' is rejected in favour of what is regarded as the free
and natural growth in the 'better soil' of rustic life. Civilised society is
seen not to refine human manners and language but to corrupt them,
generating 'social vanity' and 'arbitrary and capricious habits of expression, in order to furnish food for fickle tastes'.[2] Classical aristocratic
'culture' is equated here with decadence.

The Wordsworthian effort to draw society together through a vision
of an indigenous rustic culture was a fraught one. Even as Wordsworth
and Coleridge were celebrating the English countryside and its traditional
inhabitants, this culture was becoming anachronistic. Industrialisation
was both invading the countryside, establishing new manufacturing and
mining towns and connecting them with railways, and draining it of its
inhabitants, who became the new masses of urban workers, many of
whom, as the century progressed, would join the new middle classes.
The cultural models of the Gothic and of rustic life provided by Romanticism were, and remain, a nostalgic, indeed imaginary, focus for national
unity, an 'imagined community'[3] for what was fast becoming at the time
the most urbanised country in the world.

The Wordsworthian demotic conception of culture has provided a
liberating precedent and a justification for subsequent popular culture.
But alongside the rural working class the other half of the feudal
equation, the gentry, also functioned as a model in the shaping of
middle-class cultural identity. While the young Wordsworth looks back
to the rural poor, the older, politically conservative, Coleridge develops
his principle of a cultural 'clerisy', an intellectual and spiritual aristocracy
to rule over and guide the rising middle classes. But the middle classes,
by definition caught between the lower and upper classes, tended to be
an odd hybrid of each of these more established castes. This is illustrated
by the cacophony of styles, and kitsch, of much of what passes for Victorian taste. It is also testified to by the popular genre of books offering
hints about manners and household management, such as the bestselling
compendium, *Enquire Within Upon Everything*, first published in 1856
and copiously reprinted during the remainder of the century.

Enquire Within Upon Everything describes itself as a vast 'store of useful information'.[4] It is in its preoccupation with 'useful knowledge' representative of a great deal of non-fiction writing during the nineteenth century. The main use of this very popular category would seem to be social improvement, to furnish the means by which families could negotiate the transition from working-class to middle-class 'respectability'. This is the world of Pip and his great expectations, of Samuel Smiles and his prescriptions for self-help. As well as thousands of entries on inexpensive ways of 'keeping up appearances', such as making clothes, removing various stains, and economising in the use of tea and coffee by adulterating them with cheaper substances, it also contains elaborate 'Rules of Conduct' and instructions about 'correct' speaking aimed to facilitate the elimination of tell-tale signs of working-class and regional origins. The section entitled 'Error in Speaking' castigates the use of 'provincialisms' which brand the urban middle-class aspirant with the mark of their rural working-class origins, reinforcing its lesson by making it clear that such regionalisms are an object of ridicule: 'The Following Examples of provincial dialects will be found very amusing . . .'[5] There are also, as the section on 'Conversation' makes clear, important protocols about laughter: 'Tell your jokes, and laugh afterwards.' The art of conversation (interspersed with appropriate forms of laughter) is presented primarily as a female requisite:

> The Woman who wishes her conversation to be agreeable will avoid conceit or affectation, and laughter which is not natural and spontaneous. Her language will be easy and unstudied, marked by a graceful carelessness, which, at the same time, never oversteps the limits of propriety. Her lips will yield to a pleasant smile; she will not love to hear herself talk; her tones will bear the impress of sincerity, and her eyes kindle with animation as she speaks. The art of pleasing is, in truth, the very soul of good breeding; for the precise object of the latter is to render us agreeable to all with whom we associate – to make us, at the same time, esteemed and loved.[6]

The aristocratic criterion of 'good breeding' is invoked here to shape the compliant identity of the middle-class 'Angel in the House', the main function of whom is to be 'agreeable'. The didactic impetus of the passage is to prescribe this aristocratic ideology, to insist paradoxically that the behaviour to be learnt should be 'natural and spontaneous' and 'unstudied'. The middle-class reader, giving no indication of her other efforts 'To have Vegetables delicately clean', restore rancid butter and make 'A very Nice and Cheap Cake',[7] is required to perform naturally the role of woman of leisure, the adjunct to and proof of the husband's wealth and social position. *Enquire Within Upon Everything* provides a manual to enable the average middle-class woman to fulfil the functions of both lady and servant.

The preliminary advertisement to the sixty-third edition of *Enquire Within Upon Everything* lists two 'Companion Work[s]' which indicate nicely the stereotypical gender divide in Victorian culture:

> 'Daily Wants, The Dictionary of,' a Cyclopaedia embracing nearly 1,200 pages of sound Information upon all matters of Practical and Domestic Unility. . . .

> 'Useful Knowledge, The Dictionary of,' a Book of Reference upon History, Geography, Science, Statistics, &c. A Companion Work to the 'Dictionary of Daily Wants.'

Enquire Within Upon Everything draws from and unites these 'Companion[s]', these mutually exclusive categories, in a union that thereby logically encompasses '*Everything*'. The union is consummated accordingly as they 'embrace the very essence of demonstrative Truth and inductive Reasoning.'[8] These positivist criteria are exhaustively satisfied by the useful hints and instructions that are packed in over 400 pages of tightly printed columns. But above the double columns of each page, beside the page numbers, are a random series of 'useful' and instructive sayings and statements which highlight aspects of middle-class ideology and taste: 'Use a book as a bee does a flower'; 'A cow consumes 100 lbs. of green food daily'; 'A chair unsound soon finds the ground'; 'Hide thy domestic wounds'; 'A blunt knife shows a dull wife'; 'A lady in America made a quilt in 55,555 pieces'; 'Knowledge is the wing whereby we fly to heaven'; 'Auctions commenced in Britain A.D. 1779'; 'Eggs badly boiled are good things spoiled'; 'At open doors dogs come in'; 'Morning is welcome to the industrious'; 'Every man is the architect of his own fortune'; 'A bird's-nest is a natural egg-cup'.[9]

While *Enquire Within Upon Everything* presents a self-contained and complete cultural universe, like a Victorian emporium of the mind, or a literary version of the Crystal Palace, its popular ideologics were much contested throughout the Victorian period. Feminist retaliations against the gender ideology perpetrated by such popular compendiums arc, as earlier sections of the book have indicated, found in a range of non-fiction prose texts. The present section focuses upon the often passionate polemic over issues of gender, belief, class, and national cultural identity enacted in writings on history, politics, domestic culture, and literary and aesthetic criticism.

Intellectual formations

The spirit of philosophy in England, like that of religion, is still rootedly sectarian.

(J. S. Mill)[10]

The Romantics, writing during the early part of the nineteenth century, asserted their aesthetic ontology of holism against the increasing tendency in artistic and intellectual pursuits toward specialisation, the division of intellectual labour into discrete disciplines such as those represented by modern university departments.[11] Samuel Taylor Coleridge, who wrote extensively on history, politics, science, aesthetics, philosophy, religion, and literary criticism, is the pre-eminent English example of this effort to unify intellectual endeavours. The historian Thomas Carlyle, who like Coleridge was greatly influenced by German Romantic philosophy and poetry, is similarly wide-ranging in his interests. History is presented in his 1830 essay 'On History' as a great Romantic category that embraces the divisions between different intellectual and creative areas: 'Poetry, Divinity, Politics, Physics, have each their adherents and adversaries; each little guild supporting a defensive and offensive war for its own special domain; while the domain of History is a Free Emporium, where all these belligerents peaceably meet and furnish themselves.'[12] Carlyle implicitly rejects the Romantic yearning for a medieval past, and instead aligns history with both Romantic metaphysical holism *and* the laissez-faire capitalism of Adam Smith and the new industrial economy.[13] Just as the mass economy and middle-class society brought about by the Industrial Revolution was superseding the traditional feudal division of labour (the small 'guild[s]' of artisans), so the study of history is seen by Carlyle to be the overarching principle which, like the free enterprise money economy, facilitates the free exchange of all ideas.

The radical upheavals caused by the French Revolution and the advent of industrial capitalism in England during the second half of the eighteenth century made it increasingly difficult adequately to describe social relations in static terms of universal truth. Human experience and society came to be theorised and described as dynamic – as changing, progressive, developmental, *historical*. The German philosopher Hegel, writing early in the nineteenth century, produced a massive system of thought which effectively historicises the metaphysical Idea (which since Plato had been regarded as static and transcendent), making it a developmental principle meant to embrace all phenomena, including those of art, science, philosophical theory, and politics. The German biblical critics and their English followers, who wrote in the decades after Hegel's death in 1831, theorised the great traditional constant of Christian revelation as a historical construction, while the other great basis for Christian belief, nature or the Creation, was similarly established as a primarily historical phenomenon by Darwinian biology.

The brief extract from Carlyle aligns history with the industrial middle classes: his metaphor for the encompassing power of history is mercantile, the free market to which the optimistic new middle classes entrusted their personal and national futures. History is largely written and re-written in the nineteenth century by and for the new middle classes, the new mass-reading classes, of Victorian England. It is basic to the project of achieving a cultural identity of their own, which is manifest in the surge of nationalism that attended their rise from early in the century. History, as Benedict Anderson has recently reminded us in *Imagined Communities*, provides groups of people with a narrative myth of origin. It is integral to the sense of identity that galvanises such groups in their struggle for power and self-determination, and was fundamental to the struggle of the new English middle classes to gain access to such powerful social institutions as parliament and education.

History, politics, philosophy, and religion (along with science, with which they all dealt) can claim to be the most powerful public discourses for mediating change and the cultural aspirations of the middle classes in the nineteenth century. While the four broad subject areas discussed in this section fall naturally into two groups, according to the affinities of history and politics on the one side, and religion and philosophy on the other, all of these groups were, as Carlyle's view of history serves to highlight, treated by nineteenth-century writers as interrelated.

Christian belief, which had, from the middle ages, provided the core of European intellectual and social culture, was notoriously in decline during the nineteenth century. This, however, did not mean a decline in interest in religious questions, but rather a preoccupation with them, as the Oxford lecturer and liberal theologian Mark Pattison observed in 1860: 'When an age is found occupied in proving its creed, this is but a token that the age has ceased to have a proper belief in it.'[14] The great personal and cultural anxiety over belief that Pattison finds in his age accounts in large part for the predominantly polemical nature of both religious and philosophical writing in the nineteenth century. Philosophy during this period can be characterised by its often duplicitous relation to religion, for some strains of philosophy asserted their radical independence of it in favour of modern science, while others, remaining faithful to their traditional ally, redoubled their efforts to defend religion in its time of crisis.

Western philosophy has for most of its history been founded upon theological considerations. The preoccupation of early Greek philosophy with *logos*, which can be variously translated as 'reason', 'order' or 'word', is adopted and inflected by Christianity as 'the Word'. Friedrich Max Müller, the first Oxford Professor of Sanskrit, argues in *An Essay on Comparative Mythology* (1856) and subsequent writings that the ancient religions expressed in the Greek myths inform the pre-Socratic beginnings of philosophy. Plato develops such proto-theological pre-Socratic ideas as Parmenides' One and the Pythagorean principles of harmony and number, while Aristotle's ontology, with its principle of the 'Unmoved Mover', provides the basis for medieval scholasticism. It is only with the humanism of the Renaissance and the scientific revolution of the seventeenth century that philosophers (and natural philosophers or 'scientists' as they became known in the nineteenth century) began to assert their independence from Christian teaching and theology. While Francis Bacon (1561–1626) addresses his philosophical writings to questions of scientific method arising from the new experimental science of the seventeenth-century scientific revolution, Descartes (1596–1650) famously begins his metaphysical investigations not from the premise of an ultimate being or of His creation, but from the imperative sense of personal consciousness, 'I think, therefore I am.'

Although the grounds for asserting the radical independence of philosophical and theological speculation had been established, mutual relations between them were for the most part insistently maintained by thinkers throughout the seventeenth and eighteenth centuries. The new science's paradigm of clockwork mechanism provided the analogy for the Deist conception of a cosmos created upon the Newtonian principle of law by a perfectly rational God. Similarly, the close empirical observations made by the natural sciences were frequently seen to testify to the moral nature and creative power of an original first principle.

Such rationalist and empiricist approaches were integrated in the Argument from Design, which is recapitulated in one of the earliest and most popular religious works of the nineteenth century, William Paley's *Natural Theology or, Evidences of the Existence and Attributes of the Deity, Collected from the Appearances of Nature* (1802). The book opens with Paley's famous statement of the Argument from Design. If we were to find a watch we would naturally think that such a sophisticated object could not have come about through chance, but must necessarily presuppose a maker. So, Paley reasons by analogy (Bishop Butler's bequest to natural theology), the more complex phenomena of nature must be regarded accordingly as evidence of a correspondingly more powerful creator:

> The marks of design are too strong to be gotten over. Design must have a designer. That designer must have been a person. That person is GOD.[15]

For Paley everything in nature comes with this designer label attached. Most of the *Natural Theology* is dedicated to demonstrating the premise of this argument by piling up detailed examples of the wonderful mechanisms of nature: 'The hinges in the wings of an earwig, and the joints of its antennae, are as highly wrought, as if the Creator had nothing else to finish.'[16] God was evidently working to a deadline, and His acts of Creation are accordingly discussed in the past tense: the 'designer must have been . . .' One of the criticisms levelled at Paley, principally by Coleridge, was that the God he infers from nature is not the loving personal God of the New Testament, but impersonal and detached, the supreme mechanist who need not have any interest in his creations once the mechanism had been wound up. There is no need for God to be personally interested in each of his creatures, for their welfare was provided for before the beginning of history, at the time of Creation. Paley, as if to compensate for this awkward situation, stresses the supreme goodness of Creation, from which it is easy to infer the benign and providential moral nature of its Creator:

> It is a happy world after all. The air, the earth, the water, teem with delighted existence. In a spring noon, or a summer evening, on whichever side I turn my eyes, myriads of happy beings crowd upon my view. 'The insect youth are on the wing.' Swarms of new born *flies* are trying their pinions in the air. Their sportive motions, their wanton mazes, their gratuitous activity, their continual change of place without use or purpose, testify to their joy, and the exultation which they feel in their lately discovered faculties . . . The *whole winged* insect tribe, it is probable, are equally intent upon their proper enjoyments, and, under every variety of constitution, gratified, and perhaps equally gratified, by the offices which the Author of their nature has assigned to them . . . Other species are *running about*, with an alacrity in their motions, which carries with it every mark of pleasure . . . If we look to what the *waters* produce, shoals of the fry of fish frequent the margins of rivers, of lakes, and the sea itself. These are so happy, that they know not what to do with themselves . . . what a sum, collectively, of gratification and pleasure have we here before our view.[17]

By the time that James Joyce makes a casual reference to 'playful insects' in *Ulysses*[18] 120 years later, this anthropomorphic and anthropocentric view of nature had come to be seen as an amusing, but thoroughly fanciful, conceit. How could we ever know that insects and young fish were happy (or, for that matter, 'in one of their moods')? The evidence is, according to Paley, simply 'here before our view'. It is, he writes, directly available 'on whichever side I turn my eyes', wherever 'we look'. The whole of Paley's book is based upon the close observation of natural phenomena, the *empiricist* premise that sense experience conveys to us directly the truth of the outside world. Such empiriXcism characterises the mind as passive and receptive to sense data from the outside world, which it examines analytically: 'Now it is by frequent or continued meditation upon a subject, by placing a subject in different points of view, by induction of particulars, by variety of examples, by applying principles to the solution of phaenomena, by dwelling upon proofs and consequences, that mental exercise is drawn into any particular channel.'[19] This statement of method, from Paley's concluding chapter, describes the central empiricist activity of induction, that is, of generalising from particulars, and the subsequent analysis of such observations and generalisations. Thought, or 'mental exercise', is itself regarded not in the manner of the idealists, as a formal principle, but as protean matter: like water it can be 'drawn into any particular channel'. According to Locke's famous metaphor the mind receives the impress of sense data as sealing wax takes the impression of the seal. Thought is, in this theory, formed from without by sense data, so that it is, in other words, always contingent upon matter and is itself seen to have a material nature.

We can, perhaps rather mischievously, apply Paley's own empiricist criteria to the passage quoted above. In this case it is not an analytical act of *induction*, but a synthetic act of *imagination*, that appears, at least to the post-Darwinian mind, to be at work here. In the guise of simply looking, Paley is actively imposing his own preconceptions upon the sensory evidence. This is one of the main idealist criticisms of empiricism, that for sense experience to make any sense at all and not to be a chaotic mass of unnameable and undifferentiated *stuff*, the mind must have some *a priori* formal means of anticipating and processing such matter. Passages such as the one above highlight the problematic coexistence of empiricism and rationalism in Paley and other eighteenth-century thinkers. Rationalism gives priority to the existence of rational structures in the mind's workings or as the foundation of objective reality, or both. Paley's argument is founded upon a rationalist presupposition, the watch analogy,[20] which he justifies empirically by scrutinising the phenomena of nature.

As long as Paley's argument is granted and presupposed from the start, it all works out very cosily. One of his main examples in the *Natural Theology* is the eye, which, he argues, is naturally preadapted and formed to perceive Creation.[21] In other words, as long as God has organised the world in such a rational way, the organ of sight naturally allows us to directly grasp ultimate Truth. It is a self-enclosed, tautologous argument. The evidence of the passage quoted above suggests that the method consists of a fanciful imposition upon nature perpetrated in the guise of unmediated sense experience.

Another important observation that can be made about Paley from the above extract is the value he gives to the criterion of *happiness*. This consideration is at the heart of his moral philosophy, which is a theological version of Utilitarianism, a doctrine which equates moral value with the quantity of happiness produced, and which, while it has its roots in the Enlightenment, comes to great prominence in the first half of the nineteenth century in the secular philosophies of Jeremy Bentham, James Mill and his son John Stuart Mill. Utilitarianism extends empiricist psychology to morality. The empiricists reject the *a priori* capacities that many rationalists attribute to the mind, including notions of an innate moral sense such as conscience or Kant's Categorical Imperative. Instead they privilege sense experience, and, as a corollary of this, make the states of pleasure and pain the criteria for their ethics. For theological Utilitarians like Bishop Butler and Paley, who see human nature as fundamentally egoistic, threats of pain, such as that of eternal punishment in hell, and promises of pleasure, an afterlife in heaven, encourage people to obey God's will.[22] In Paley's *Natural Theology* the world is judged to be morally good because of the providential opportunities it affords for sensory pleasures, both 'the capacity of our senses to receive pleasure, and the supply of external objects fitted to produce it'. Paley writes further to this point that 'looking to the average of sensations, the plurality and the preponderancy is in favour of happiness by a vast excess.'[23] This draws attention to a commonly observed problem with Utilitarianism; how can states of mind be quantified in the scientific way proposed by the Utilitarians? How are we to go about calculating 'the average of sensations'?

Natural Theology received a further lease of life in the 1830s through the series of eight *Bridgewater Treatises*, which argue for 'the Power, Wisdom, and Goodness of God, as manifested in the Creation'. It was also in this decade that Natural Theology's ultimate nemesis, Charles Darwin, developed an admiration for Paley whilst studying his *Evidences of Christianity* at Cambridge.[24] Instead of becoming a clergyman after completing his B.A., as he and his family had anticipated, he of course became a scientist. Darwin's *Origin of Species* follows Paley's model of close and attentive observation of a huge quantity and range of phenomena, only to derive from his inductions a hypothesis, the principle of natural selection, which led many to a conclusion that was the precise opposite to the doctrine of the *Natural Theology*.

While Paley's book casts a vast and powerful shadow of eighteenth-century thought over most of the nineteenth century, the work of the historian and politician Thomas Babington Macaulay marks more of a transition between these periods. Macaulay, who like Paley wrote one of the biggest non-fiction bestsellers of the century, came into prominence in the 1820s as a writer of essays for the *Edinburgh Review* and then, from 1830–34, as an actively reformist Whig politician. He was the Member of Parliament for Edinburgh from 1839 to 1847 and 1852 to 1856. The first volumes of his *History of England from the Accession of James II*, the work which made him '[i]n his own day . . . the most honoured of all English authors',[25] appeared in 1848, with the two subsequent volumes being published in 1855 and the last, posthumously, in 1861. An essay on 'History' written for the *Edinburgh Review* in 1828 codifies the practice of writing that would make his *History of England* so successful. The political nature of Macaulay's imagination is evident from the very start of his discussion of history in the essay:

> This province of literature is a debatable land. It lies on the confines of two distinct territories. It is under the jurisdiction of two hostile powers; and, like other districts similarly situated, it is ill defined, ill cultivated, and ill regulated. Instead of being equally shared between its two rulers, the Reason and the Imagination, it falls alternately under the sole and absolute dominion of each. It is sometimes fiction. It is sometimes theory.[26]

History is presented as a land which itself has a history. The discipline needs, according to Macaulay, to be brought to a condition of nationhood analogous to that which England had arrived at by 1830, the date at which he intended his *History of England* to finish. History needs to overcome its internal divisions, and become 'defined' as a distinctive discipline with a code of laws by which its practice can be 'regulated' and 'cultivated'.

Macaulay's work as both a barrister and a politician appears to have shaped his adversarial representation of the plight of history in this essay, while the plea he makes for reconciling the principles of 'the Reason and the Imagination' offers an interesting parallel to his political stance as a moderate. Rosemary Jann, following the work of Joseph Hamburger, observes that Macaulay was 'less a Whig than a trimmer. He favored not a consistent party line, but rather those forces that stabilized opposing political interests in order to achieve the balance necessary for prosperity and progress.'[27] Macaulay desires a resolution in the field of historical studies to the opposition of the Imagination and the Reason, and presents as parallels the respective practices of history writing to which he sees these principles to give rise: 'It is sometimes fiction. It is sometimes theory.' The syntactic symmetry of these brief sentences enacts Macaulay's belief that rather than alternately pulling history in different directions the two principles would work well together. They can be linked grammatically to form one of the balanced syntactic structures which he borrows from Augustan writing and which are a hallmark of his writing and oratorical style. The essay concludes, after a lengthy critical history of history writing, by presenting the balance of principles he advocates in the form of such apt syntactic structures: 'The instruction derived from history thus written would be of a vivid and practical character. It would be received by the imagination as well as by the reason. It would be not merely traced on the mind, but branded into it.'[28] Such oratorical writing is a reflection of the more emphatic rhetorical effect of, for instance, his 1839 Edinburgh election speech:

> I entered public life a Whig; and a Whig I am determined to remain. I use that word, and I wish you to understand that I use it, in no narrow sense. I mean by a Whig, not one who

subscribes implicitly to the contents of any book, though that book may have been written by Locke; not one who approves the whole conduct of any statesman, though that statesman may have been Fox; not one who adopts the opinions in fashion in any circle, though that circle may be composed of the finest and noblest spirits of the age. But it seems to me that, when I look back on our history, I can discern a great party which has, through many generations, preserved its identity; a party often depressed, never extinguished; a party which, though often tainted with the faults of the age, has always been in advance of the age; a party which, though guilty of many errors and some crimes, has the glory of having established our civil and religious liberties on a firm foundation; and of that party I am proud to be a member.[29]

The speech continues for another page to cast, neatly and impressively, in antitheses and other balanced syntactic forms further details of the Whig party's historical achievements. The genre of the political speech was at this time an object of connoisseurship, 'a notable [Parliamentary] orator "up" and going well was like a *diva* in fine voice.'[30] Macaulay's style here is classical and literary, indebted to the writing of the Augustan age that he devoted so much of his life to studying and writing on, and of which he is often described as the last representative before the ascendancy of the Victorian rhetoric of the platform and the pulpit, with its direct and practical appeals to a more democratically constituted audience.

G. H. Francis, a journalist and parliamentary reporter contemporary with Macaulay, commented of him that 'His speeches read like essays, as his essays read like speeches.'[31] The aristocratic Augustan values of his style are, however, blended with characteristics that can be identified with the more democratic age of the Victorian period: Augustan 'Reason' is fused with the nineteenth-century demotic 'Imagination'. The latter principle is elaborated upon in the 'History' essay, where it is interestingly identified with Herodotus:

> The faults of Herodotus are the faults of a simple and imaginative mind. Children and servants are remarkably Herodotean in their style of narration. They tell everything dramatically. Their *says hes* and *says shes* are proverbial. Every person who has to settle their disputes knows that, even when they have no intention to deceive, their reports of conversation always require to be carefully sifted.[32]

Macaulay writes elsewhere of his appreciation of Herodotus's writing. Indeed, picturesque, dramatic, and other appeals to the reader's imagination, such as he identifies with the ancient historian, are integral to his own practice of history writing. The principle of imagination is, however, regarded by Macaulay as rudimentary, belonging to the childhood of Western civilisation. The story-telling of children and servants, the uncultivated, are represented here as a sort of recapitulation of history writing as it begins with Herodotus. Seen as lacking in judgement, self-discipline, and maturity, their behaviour accordingly needs to be supervised and their words interpreted and judged, 'carefully sifted', by the responsible head of the household, the parent or master. While Macaulay insists upon the importance of imagination for history writing, and like Carlyle reasserts it against the prevailing practice, the implication of his analogy is that the reason must, in the manner of the head of the household, maintain ultimate control. It implies the classical doctrine of the 'sovereign Reason' and represents the coalescence of the Imagination and the Reason he advocates in the essay as a coalition of paternalistic traditional rulers with the uneducated 'lower orders'. The resultant of this coalition can be identified with the new middle classes, the members of which at this time usually rose from the rural and urban working classes and often aspired to the values represented by the other traditional class, the aristocracy. Macaulay was instrumental in the early Victorian forging of a middle-class identity, of providing this class with a common 'myth of origin', a history of its own.

Macaulay's *History of England* celebrates the achievement of Victorian middle-class society, presenting the previous 150 years as a clearly-focused progression toward this state, thereby providing a reassuring sense of continuity for an age of great change. His project was meant to cover the whole period from 1688 to 1830, 'between the Revolution which brought the crown into harmony with the Parliament, and the Revolution which brought the Parliament into harmony with the nation [i.e., the 1832 Parliamentary Reform Act].'[33] He worked in his history writing, as in his parliamentary life, to represent this new constituency. His writing accordingly discusses not only the lives of the aristocracy but people of all classes, especially the rising middle classes: '[The Historian] must mingle in the crowds of the exchange and the coffee-house.'[34]

Macaulay endeavours to overcome the traditional aristocratic biases of history, which he refers to dismissively as 'the majesty of history',[35] by treating 'ordinary' life equally with 'high' life and doing so in a vivid and dramatic manner: 'In Covent Garden a filthy and noisy market was held close to the dwellings of the great. Fruit women screamed, carters fought, cabbage stalks and rotten apples accumulated in heaps at the thresholds of the Countess of Berkshire and of the Bishop of Durham.'[36] Such writing is, in line with middle-class propensities for positivism and materialism, attentive to concrete empirical details. It is also, in its quest to entertain, in open competition with fiction and other popular writing of the time. The early essay on 'History' asserts the popular middle-class genres of the biography (for which, he observes, '[t]he writers of history seem to entertain an aristocratical contempt') and the novel as models for history writing; '. . . a truly great historian would reclaim those materials which the novelist has appropriated.'[37] Such novelistic values as 'the art of narration, the art of interesting the affections and presenting pictures to the imagination'[38] are incorporated as definitive characteristics of Maculay's style of history writing. The *History of England* is a sort of first cousin to another group of very popular imaginative histories, the historical novels of such writers as Scott, Dickens, and Thackeray.

Macaulay regards 'the science of government' as an 'experimental science', which like other such sciences is 'generally in a state of progression.'[39] History is conceived of by Macaulay in the definitive manner of the Whig historian as fundamentally *progressive*. His *History of England* is a celebration of the progress which led to the Victorian age. He recapitulates upon this progress at the close of chapter 3 and looks forward to the future:

> We shall, in our turn, be outstripped . . . It may well be, in the twentieth century, that the peasant of Dorsetshire may think himself miserably paid with twenty shillings a week; that the carpenter at Greenwich may receive ten shillings a day; that labouring men may be as little used to dine without meat as they now are to eat rye bread; that sanitary police and medical discoveries may have added several more years to the average length of human life; that numerous comforts and luxuries which are now unknown, or confined to a few, may be within the reach of every diligent and thrifty working man.

The passage highlights the materialist and utilitarian criteria for progress that informs Macaulay's history: food, comfort, health. While both his and Paley's forms of Utilitarianism and empiricism, and characteristics of their writing styles, can be traced to eighteenth-century rationalism, their secular use in Macaulay proved to be especially attractive to a Victorian readership which was becoming increasingly preoccupied with issues of progress and science.

The Victorian ideology of historical progress was expressed in the complementary philosophical terms of Hegelian idealism mentioned earlier and scientistic positivism, the extreme form of empiricism. Apart from the mainly academic interest in Hegel generated by Benjamin Jowett, Thomas Hill Green, and the British Idealist school of philosophy during the last third of the century, Victorians looked to the Positivism of Auguste Comte and his English followers for an agreeable narrative of progress by which to organise the history of philosophy. George Henry

Lewes, best known to readers of Victorian fiction as George Eliot's partner, was also the prime British exponent of Comte's progressive doctrine of Positivism. Lewes's *Biographical History of Philosophy* (1845) carefully recounts the history of philosophy from the pre-Socratic 'Physiologists' (as he refers to such early philosophers of the elements as Thales) to the apotheosis of philosophical exploration in Comte: 'It is the object of the present work to show how and by what steps Philosophy became Positivist Science; in other words, by what Methods the Human Mind was enabled to conquer for itself, in the long struggle of centuries, its present modicum of certain knowledge.'[40] The *History of Philosophy*, like Macaulay's *History of England*, assumes a direct 'filiation' between the past and the present, a narrative of progress which Lewes's metaphors suggest is conceived of as a sort of colonising adventure.

Positivism had from the late eighteenth century been coming up with the goods: it was proving itself spectacularly successful in adding to the sum of knowledge of the physical world and producing the technology which drove the Industrial Revolution. For Positivists and Utilitarians like Bentham, J. S. Mill and Lewes modern science indicated the direction in which philosophy must proceed. They saw the role of philosophy to be the theorising of methods that were proving to be successful in science and the extrapolation from them of a theory of mind and, in accordance with the practical ethics of Utilitarianism, the grounds for the social sciences. Empiricism by definition rejects any form of *a priori* foundation for science, such as the grounds of rationalism and revelation that Paley invokes in his *Natural Theology*. Paley's optimistic conviction that empiricist science is a natural ally of religion was questioned and placed under threat well before Darwin's book resolutely overturned the grounds of the Argument from Design.

Philosophical writings in the nineteenth century can be broadly categorised by whether they embrace or resist scientistic positivism and its consequences. John Stuart Mill famously allocates contemporary thinkers to two classes according to their affiliation with the thought of the empiricist Bentham or of the idealist Coleridge: 'Whoever could master the premises and combine the methods of both, would possess the entire English philosophy of his age . . . every Englishman of the present day is by implication either a Benthamite or a Coleridgian.'[41] The Benthamite tradition includes Alexander Bain, James and John Stuart Mill, and later 'agnostics' such as T. H. Huxley and Herbert Spencer, all of whom championed positivist epistemologies, theories which, following the success of modern scientific method, see knowledge as building strictly from the aggregation of sense experience, and regard philosophy as akin to modern science in its autonomy from theology. In opposition to such positivists, thinkers like Coleridge, J. H. Newman, J. F. Ferrier, William Hamilton, Benjamin Jowett, T. H. Green, John Grote and F. H. Bradley were all anxious to maintain some form of the traditional alliance of philosophy and religion. While some of these figures subscribe to aspects of the British empiricist tradition that inform the positivism of Bentham and Mill,[42] their various positions can be defined by their adoption of forms of metaphysical idealism, their insistence upon the necessity in thought of *a priori* factors, elements which precede or transcend experience. These can be described by two broad categories: objectively existent forms or essences, which are seen to provide the ultimate ontological substratum of things, and subjective qualities of mind, such as innate ideas, radical belief or emotional conviction.

Lewes distinguishes between idealism and empiricism by placing them in a perspective determined by his positivism: 'the one proceeds from *a priori* axioms – that is, from axioms taken up without having undergone the laborious but indispensable process of previous verification; the other proceeds from axioms which have been rigidly verified.'[43] While Lewes endeavours in the main body of the book to be scrupulous in his accounts of idealist philosophies, his attitudes to the two classes he distinguishes are put clearly in his introduction, where he suggests the terms to be adopted for each: 'In order to prevent confusion, and at the same time to avoid the introduction of words so distasteful as metaphysics and ontology, we shall throughout speak of Philosophy in its earlier and more restricted sense; and shall designate by the term *Positive Science* that field of speculation commonly known as Inductive, or Baconian, Philosophy.' One form of thought is designated by 'uncouth'[44] and 'distasteful' terms, the other attributed with the authoritative title of '*Positive Science*'.

Mill provides a useful summary of the criticisms that the two broad schools of positivism and idealism directed at one another:

> Sensualism is the common term of abuse for the one philosophy, mysticism for the other. The one doctrine is accused of making men beasts, the other lunatics. It is the unaffected belief of numbers on one side of the controversy, that their adversaries are actuated by a desire to break loose from moral and religious obligation; and of numbers on the other that their opponents are either men fit for Bedlam, or who cunningly pander to the interests of hierarchies and aristocracies, by manufacturing superfine new arguments in favour of old prejudices.[45]

The positivists, by presupposing the irrelevance of religion for their thought, and hence of such concepts as a soul and an innate abstract moral sense or conscience, were charged by their critics with characterising humankind as bestial and encouraging cynical moral opportunism. Conversely, by arguing from *a priori* premises (such as the existence of a moral imperative), premises which cannot be established on any objective basis, metaphysical idealism and theology were seen to be arbitrary and fundamentally irrational, as either delusional, 'lunacy', or as ways of mystifying certain phenomena which the positivists believed could be examined scientifically. In writing his criticism of idealism at the end of the extract Mill probably had in mind Coleridge's conservative doctrine of the 'clerisy', which offered a way of renewing the traditional elitist social order in the guise of the new middle-class society. Bentham is described by Mill in contrast to such alleged apologists for 'old prejudices' as 'the great questioner of things established'.[46] However, while idealist philosophies have the most obvious capacity to reify, to give illegitimate substance and authority to inventions of the mind, to mere ideology, empiricist schemes are also often ideologically driven, and their purported empiricist or 'commonsense' methods can serve to import specific ideological agendas covertly. Paley provides a case in point.

Interestingly, while Paley's empiricist psychology precludes him from treating certain ideas as innate and so 'natural' to the human mind, he manages as best he can to naturalise property ownership as 'the first of our abstract ideas'. In doing so he also defends the stratified society upon which it is based, which is represented in the following passage by the feudal examples of the peasant and the landholder:

> I do not know whether our attachment to *property* be not something more than the mere dictate of reason, or even than the mere effect of association. Property communicates a charm to whatever is the object of it. It is the first of our abstract ideas; it cleaves to us the closest and longest. It endears to the child its plaything, to the peasant his cottage, to the landholder his estate.

Furthermore, while Kant had argued in *The Critique of Judgement* (1790) that our senses of beauty and of the sublime were directly traceable to the relation to certain perceptions of our peculiar *a priori* faculty psychology, Paley traces much of our aesthetic enjoyment to 'our attachment to *property*': 'It supplies the place of prospect and scenery . . . It gives boldness and grandeur to plains and fens, tinge and colouring to clays and fallows.'[47] This is a politically conservative strategy, a way of naturalising the social *status quo*, which was at the time threatened by the spread of revolutionary ferment across the English Channel from France. Paley argues in a similar vein against David Hume's criticism of idleness, saying that it too evidences divine beneficence: 'In the civil world, as well as in the material, it is the *vis inertiae* which keeps things in their places.'[48]

Paley's model of language follows the 'commonsense' British empiricist model in which words directly reflect things, a corollary of his faith in the preadaptation of human capacities, such as the eye, to perceive and understand the nature (and ultimate meaning) of Creation. The purer and more self-conscious empiricism of Jeremy Bentham and his follower John Stuart Mill lead them to be critical about the nature of language. According to Bentham the 'illusions' pursued by idealism can be traced to their most rudimentary reification in language. If a word does not precisely mirror a fact, it is for Bentham immediately suspect: 'Words', Mill writes of Bentham, 'he thought were perverted from their proper office when they were employed in uttering anything but precise logical truth.'[49] Such 'truth' requires a direct and strict relation to empirical 'facts'. The function of words is for him simply to reflect 'facts'. Language is accordingly regarded as a tool, which needs to be kept in working order and used properly to ensure that it functions in a serviceable manner: 'Language is,' Mill writes in his *System of Logic*, 'evidently, and by the admission of all philosophers, one of the principal instruments or helps of thought; and any imperfection in the instrument, or in the mode of employing it, is confessedly liable, still more than in almost any other art, to confuse and impede the process, and destroy all ground of confidence in the result.'[50] Just as the positivist scientist has certain instruments that facilitate his probings of nature, so in an analogous fashion the positivist theorist depends upon precise language and an ability to use it.

Mill's account of language as a tool of the trade implies a claim that philosophy be established as a profession, akin to other professional roles which were established in the middle-class society of nineteenth-century Britain through the transformation of such traditionally privileged and elitist preserves as politics, law, and university teaching. Bentham's first published work criticises the institution of government and throughout his life he attacked this institution and that of the law and argued for their reform. It is largely because of his distrust of such traditional social institutions that Bentham insists upon his criterion that words always be used to reflect facts precisely: 'Proceeding on this principle,' writes Mill, 'Bentham makes short work with the ordinary modes of moral and political reasoning. These, it appeared to him, when hunted to their source, for the most part terminated in [mere] *phrases*.' Such ciphers without concrete references are seen to provide the basis for discussions in politics, law, ethics, and metaphysics, where according to Bentham they enjoy an undeservedly privileged status. Mill refers to them in a revealing and descriptive metaphor as 'sacramental expressions'.[51] Their traditional usages in established discourses effectively *consecrate* them, place them beyond questioning. They are, Mill seems to be suggesting, the intellectual equivalents of ancient religious rituals, endowed with authority on the irrational basis of little more than tradition, faith, prejudice or superstition. Of course, Mill's phrase, like most analogies, works in two directions, serving also to indicate his attitude to religion.

Typical of a growing number of intellectuals in the nineteenth century, he is prepared to respect religious belief but insists upon its radical distinction from the scientific pursuit of truth.

While Mill resorts to metaphor in his discussion of Bentham's views of language, Bentham himself was suspicious of such figurative language. His literalism led him to dismiss the foremost and most prestigious literary genre of his age: 'All poetry', he writes, 'is misrepresentation.'[52] Bentham's position is extreme and accordingly criticised by his disciple, who observes that his later style, far from precisely conveying 'facts', is instead 'intricate and involved'[53] and very difficult to understand: 'We regard it as a *reductio ad absurdum* of his objection to poetry . . . he could stop nowhere short of utter unreadableness.'[54]

The empiricists' insistence that words accurately represent 'facts', and their consequent distrust of figurative language, springs from their fundamental epistemological conviction that all knowledge arises through induction, by generalising from the observation of particulars: 'Bentham's method', Mill writes, 'may be shortly described as the method of detail; of treating wholes by separating them into their parts, abstractions by resolving them into Things . . .'[55] If a term or phrase could not be seen to stand in for an actual experiential 'fact', but was instead founded on an analogy to such direct experience, its meaning was often seen to be diminished. Hence, the idea of 'good taste', of a capacity for aesthetic discrimination, is an analogy which, according to Bentham, borrows its authority illegitimately from the physical reality of the sense of taste. However, for many of the idealists, such as the philosopher of science William Whewell, analogy is one of the criteria which indicate the truth of a hypothesis. Whewell argues that separate sciences may progress in parallel and that their discoveries often draw them together in what he calls a 'consilience':

> The Consilience of Inductions takes place when an Induction
> obtained from one class of facts, coincides with an Induction,
> obtained from another different class. This Consilience is a
> test of the truth of the Theory in which it occurs.[56]

While we are used to thinking of coincidences as contingent, a matter of chance, for Whewell the fact that one discovery 'coincides' with another is considered natural. This attitude flows from his idealist conviction that reality comprises a rational unity, a whole which precedes its parts. It is on the basis of this presupposition that the analogy of a discovery in one branch of science to that of another can constitute 'a test of the truth of the Theory'.

Idealists like Whewell see ideas as having priority over observable facts. Knowledge proceeds, in the words of the young Gerard Manley Hopkins, 'from the whole downwards to the parts'.[57] This furnishes a theory of induction that is radically opposed to the empiricist 'method of detail', which aggregates particulars as generalisations. Whewell was engaged in a longstanding public debate with Mill over the nature of induction, which occurred in the successive editions of their respective works *The Philosophy of the Inductive Sciences* (1840) and *A System of Logic* (1843). Whewell saw Mill's model of induction as begging the question as to how it is that particular aggregates of facts should be taken to exemplify some theoretical conclusions and not others. For Whewell what is important here is not so much the 'facts' but what the mind does with them, how it makes sense of them. So, rather than seeing the mind as passively receiving observed 'facts' which become associated together, in Whewell's account of induction the mind actively '*superinduces*' a hypothesis upon the observable facts: 'Facts are bound together by the aid of suitable Conceptions . . . by an act of the intellect, we establish a precise connexion among the phenomena which are presented to our senses.'[58] In contrast to the objective bias of the positivist epistemology, in which we passively receive sense data from the external world, idealist epistemologies all emphasise the role of the subjective mind in perception.

The public controversy between Whewell and Mill over the nature of induction was just one manifestation of the nineteenth-century battle between metaphysical idealism and scientistic positivism, which was most clearly drawn and intensely fought around the middle of the century. Gerard Manley Hopkins, writing as a student at Oxford during the 1860s, bears testimony to the anxiety and emotion that came to be invested in this conflict. His undergraduate essay on 'The Probable Future of Metaphysics' opens on a note of prophetic apprehension: 'The Positivists foretell and many other people begin to fear, the end of all metaphysics is at hand. Purely material psychology is the *triakter* [i.e., 'conqueror'] foretold and feared.'[59] Modern psychology, which Hopkins effectively equates here with the beast of Revelation, was one of the most determined aggressors against idealist metaphysics. The work of Mill's friend Alexander Bain and others during the 1850s endeavoured to supplant the traditional metaphysical conception of the theory of mind with physiological reductionism, which regards perception as merely the physical affect of external stimuli upon the organ of the brain.

Bain's psychology is one amongst many efforts made around mid-century to lend the prestige and authority of contemporary science to positivist theory. Henry Thomas Buckle offers such a scientific foundation for history in his massive but incomplete project of constructing a *History of Civilization*, the first and only volumes of which appeared in 1857 and 1861. The object of great controversy, the notoriety of the first volume was only eclipsed by the appearance of Darwin's *Origin of Species* in 1859.[60] Buckle argues that history, like physical science, has as its task the establishment of the laws of objective phenomena: 'history deals with the actions of men, and since their actions are merely the product of a collision between internal and external phenomena, it becomes necessary to examine the relative importance of those phenomena, to inquire into the extent to which their laws are known, and to ascertain the resources for future discovery possessed by these two great classes, the students of the mind and the students of nature.'[61] Human actions are theorised here in reductionist terms as 'merely the product of a collision between internal and external phenomena', as if what were involved were simply the mechanical interaction of atomic particles, such as those of gas, where the individual atom may act in an irregular manner whilst contributing to a mass which manifests a regular behaviour.

Buckle contrasts the success of philosophy (both idealist and empiricist) in explaining the 'internal' phenomena of individual psychology, with that of positivist science in the analysis of the physical world: 'Everything we at present know has been ascertained by studying phenomena, from which all casual disturbances having been removed, the law remains as a conspicuous residue. And this can only be done by observations so numerous as to eliminate the disturbances, or else by experiments so delicate as to isolate the phenomena. One of these conditions is essential to all inductive science: but neither of them does the metaphysician obey.'[62] Science has, according to Buckle, progressed by making observations of phenomena *en masse*, and it is accordingly upon this positivist 'inductive' approach that Buckle wishes to establish a science of history. The study of the individual mind, upon which both sensationalist and idealist philosophical psychologies dwell, is seen by him to focus upon the aberrant or eccentric rather than upon the mass of mental phenomena as they become manifest in human actions. He accordingly regards it as unprogressive.

The mass of human actions, the interactions of subjective mind with the material world, of 'internal and external phenomena', is for Buckle the subject matter of history. His concern with 'induction' is accordingly grounded in statistics, and he notoriously confuses the understanding of laws as statistical regularities with laws as objective causal forces, arguing, for instance, from the regularity of recent annual statistics for suicide that 'a certain number of persons must put an end to their own life' each year. This 'law is', he maintains, 'so irresistible, that neither the love of life nor the fear of another world can avail anything towards even checking its operation.'[63] He also cites the recent annual statistics for the number of unaddressed letters that collected in the London and Paris post offices: 'Year after year the same proportion of letter-writers forget this simple act; so that for each successive period we can actually foretell the number of persons whose memory will fail them in regard to this trifling and, as it might appear, accidental occurrence.'[64] It is only a small step from these observations to the parody of them by Wilde in *The Importance of Being Earnest*, where Lady Bracknell, on hearing of

Algernon and Cecily's plan to marry, comments that 'the number of engagements that go on seems to me considerably above the proper average that statistics have laid down for our guidance.'[65] Buckle's approach to social phenomena, regarded by many as a precursor of modern sociology, presents in effect a *reductio ad absurdum* of the modern attempt to establish a science of society.

The mechanistic metaphor implicit in Buckle's definition of human actions as 'the product of a collision between internal and external phenomena' is made explicit early in the book, where, after his discussion of the statistical 'law' of suicide, classical Newtonian mechanics is invoked to describe the relation of apparently irregular phenomena to lawful phenomena: 'Such aberrations proceed . . . from minor laws which at particular points meet the larger laws, and thus alter their normal action. Of this, the science of mechanics affords a good example in the instance of that beautiful theory called the parallelogram of forces; according to which the forces are to each other in the same proportion as is the diagonal of their respective parallelograms.'[66] Newton's first corollary to his laws of motion represents two forces by the two converging sides of the parallelogram, and their product by the diagonal which bisects their angle. Buckle uses the analogy to describe the way in which apparently eccentric individual phenomena form a synthetic mass that instances a specific law.

Buckle's invocation of the Newtonian 'parallelogram of forces', and indeed his enthusiastic reference to it as 'that beautiful theory', points to the source of his method in the revolutionary scientific practice of the seventeenth century. This method, based upon the criteria of induction and physical experimentation which Buckle refers to in one of the passages quoted above, was first theorised by Francis Bacon. Buckle, like Bacon, presupposes that humanity is at war with nature, and that science is the fundamental means by which we combat it and establish 'civilisation':

> If . . . we take the largest possible view of the history of Europe, and confine ourselves entirely to the primary cause of its superiority over other parts of the world, we must resolve it into the encroachment of the mind of man upon the organic and inorganic forces of Nature . . . The first essential was, to limit the interference of these physical phenomena; and that was most likely to be accomplished where the phenomena were feeblest and least imposing. This was the case with Europe; it is accordingly in Europe alone that man has really succeeded in taming the energies of nature, bending them to his own will, turning them aside from their ordinary course, and compelling them to minister to his happiness, and subserve the general purposes of human life.[67]

Tropes of force and enslavement such as Buckle uses here in his talk of 'compelling' nature to act as the servant of humankind are comparable to those found in Bacon, who, for instance, assures us that 'Nature betrays her secrets more fully when in the grip and under the pressure of art than when in enjoyment of her natural liberty.'[68] Buckle continues triumphantly from the point at which the above extract finishes: 'All around us are the traces of this glorious and successful struggle.'[69]

History emerges in Buckle's formulation as a celebration of the European domination of nature. His *History of Civilization* naturalises the Victorian conception of 'progress' by making it the very pattern, the scientific formula, for history, and in doing so presents a rationale not only for the free exploitation of nature but also for colonialism. The 'superiority' of European civilisation is contrasted by Buckle with that of the rest of the world: 'Hence it is that, looking at the history of the world as a whole, the tendency has been, in Europe, to subordinate nature to man; out of Europe, to subordinate man to nature ... The great division, therefore, between European civilization and non-European civilization, is the basis of the philosophy of history.' The example he gives for this principle is the jewel in the Victorian colonial crown, 'the history of India'. The strong implication of Buckle's writing is that European colonialism effects the liberation of our fellows in 'barbarous countries'.[70]

Buckle's ambitious attempt at constructing a scientific history of European civilisation reflects both the ascendancy of positivist method and the Victorian optimism about social progress that it engendered through its successes in science. While the legacy of the French Revolution encouraged historical narratives of cultural pessimism[71] earlier in the century, the idea of progress provided the main narrative for history generally at this time, as well as for other genres such as biography and autobiography, and the *Bildungsroman*. Walter Bagehot, for example, uses the analogy of the arch-Victorian embodiment of this narrative, the self-made man (the 'successful merchant'), to describe the economic and cultural progress of his country: 'England is a success in the world; her career has had many faults, but still it has been a fine and winning career upon the whole.'[72]

Bagehot provides an interesting exploration of the Victorian idea of progress as it relates to politics and science. Ideologies of progress received a fillip from Darwinism, with the hypothesis of natural selection being popularly understood not so much as a mechanism responsive to arbitrary changes in the natural environment but as describing a tendency within biological nature for improvement over time. The application of Darwinism, and of contemporary scientism in general, to political theory and history is well exemplified by Bagehot in the book from which the earlier extract was taken, *Physics and Politics: Or Thoughts on the Application of the Principles of 'Natural Selection' and 'Inheritance' to*

Political Society, a group of essays first published between 1867 and 1872 in the *Fortnightly Review*.

Bagehot's book begins with the observation that 'One peculiarity of this age is the sudden acquisition of much physical knowledge.'[73] This provides the premise for his work, and that of many others who are trying at this time to establish the social sciences on a firm footing. The new progressive science is seen to entail that all other knowledge 'is made "an antiquity."'[74] Bagehot tries to save 'politics and political economy' from such obsolescence. He, like Buckle and Herbert Spencer, rejects metaphysics and Christian doctrine in favour of accepting contemporary science as the first principle for political and social theory.

Bagehot, like Buckle, adopts a physiological reductionist view of the mind and nervous system, and sees such factors as determining human actions. Furthermore, he identifies this physical causal principle with a principle of 'force' which, while comparable to Buckle's principle of force, is theorised according to a synthesis of energy physics and Darwinian biology. Each organism is conceived of as similar to an electric battery which passes on its power (a version of the 'divine spark' of life rendered in a new mechanistic guise) to the next generation: 'Power that has been laboriously acquired and stored up as statical in one generation manifestly in such cases becomes the inborn faculty of the next; and the development takes place in accordance with that law of increasing speciality and complexity of adaptation to external nature which is traceable through the animal kingdom.'[75] Bagehot asserts that only 'this notion of a transmitted nerve element' or 'force' permits an understanding of '"the connective tissue" of civilisation . . . There is, by this doctrine, a physical cause of improvement from generation to generation.'[76] His scientistic position is, as he acknowledges, aligned with that of Buckle.[77]

The improvements in the 'nerve force' transmitted over the generations is theorised by Bagehot in Darwinian terms as incremental and a matter of random changes that become selected and somehow inherited by succeeding generations (the genetic mechanism by which evolutionary changes become heritable had not yet been discovered at the time that he was writing). The stimulus which necessitates such improvement in human beings is for Bagehot *political*. It is a natural consequence of human beings grouping together and, having overcome stages dominated by superstition, inflexible tribal law, and tyrannical government, adopting a social organisation in which *discussion* is permitted and promoted. This is an argument for a limited democracy; not one involving a universal suffrage, which would, according to Bagehot, mean that discussion would become swamped by the voice of the working-class majority, but rather one such as that of the classical Greeks or the early Victorians, in which a range of voices are represented and allowed to speak.

The values of Bagehot's conception of 'discussion', which he sees as symptomatic of a breakdown of rigid central authority and as an index of social tolerance for a number of points of view, is fundamental to his style of writing. It is what he refers to in 'The First Edinburgh Reviewers' as 'the talk of the manifold talker'[78] which is so well suited to the genre of the review essay and was discussed in the introductory essay to this book. This ironic way of writing is interestingly exemplified in the letters that Bagehot wrote in response to the French *coup d'état* of 1851. While the later essay from *Physics and Politics* makes direct statements which trace the formation of 'English originality' to the fact that its 'government by discussion quickens and enlivens thought all through society',[79] the earlier letter accounts for a distinctively English character in quite different terms:

> I fear you will laugh when I tell you what I conceive to
> be about the most essential mental quality for a free people,
> whose liberty is to be progressive, permanent, and on a large
> scale; it is much *stupidity* . . . I need not say that, in real sound
> stupidity, the English are unrivalled. You'll hear more wit, and
> better wit, in an Irish street row than would keep Westminster
> Hall in humour for five weeks. Or take Sir Robert Peel – our
> last great statesman, the greatest member of parliament that
> ever lived, an absolutely perfect transacter of public business,
> – the type of the nineteenth-century Englishman . . . Can any
> one, without horror, foresee the reading of his memoirs? . . .
> Whose company [is] so soporific? His talk is of truisms and
> bullocks; his head replete with rustic visions of mutton
> and turnips, and a cerebral edition of Burns' 'Justice!'
> Notwithstanding, he is the salt of the earth, the best of the
> English breed. Who is like him for sound sense? But I must
> restrain my enthusiasm.[80]

Bagehot, in defending his conception of a steady and moderate English character, employs the very wit that he identifies with the rebellious Irish character and the volatile French character ('*esprit* is his essence, wit is to him as water, *bon-mots* as *bon-bons*')[81] which he sees as having lent itself naturally to the cause and spread of revolution. The teasing irony of his style reproduces in a single voice the dynamic of discussion, of contrasting points of view. The dynamic tension it sets up between 'restrain[t]' and 'enthusiasm', of criticism and praise, radically ironises each of its terms.

Buckle and Bagehot base their respective social theories upon physiological reductionist conceptions of mind, the most famous and influential of which for the mid-Victorians was elaborated by Alexander Bain in such books as *The Senses and the Intellect* (1855). Bain theorises the empiricist conception of sense data or perception as physiological 'feeling', remarking that 'the presence of Feeling is the foremost and most unmistakable mark of mind.'[82] 'Feeling' is a key word in the distinction between positivism and idealism, and provides a touchstone by which much of the religious and philosophical thought of the nineteenth century can be compared. For Mill, 'Feeling, in the proper sense of the term, is a genus, of which Sensation, Emotion, and Thought, are subordinate species.'[83] The claim to scientific status implied by Mill's taxonomic language underlines the objective nature of his notion of feeling which he proceeds to elaborate here as a 'mental image'.

While the objective bias of empiricism understands feeling as the registration in the brain of a phenomenal fact, such as sensations derived from sensory experience or the feelings of pleasure and pain upon which its utilitarian ethic is based, forms of idealism emphasise its subjective nature. In the midst of the scientific positivist onslaught upon faith Tennyson declares defiantly: '*I have felt.*'[84] Coleridge similarly argues against Paley: 'Evidences of Christianity! I am weary of the word. Make a man feel the want of it; rouse him, if you can, to the self-knowledge of his need of it; and you may safely trust it to its own Evidence.'[85] Against the external evidences of nature Coleridge invokes an intrinsic subjective moral and emotional nature. This is the realm of Romantic poetry, in which the writer gives authority to his subjectivity.

For Newman too, even as he argues for the importance of reason as the 'stay' of belief, 'the imagination and affections' are declared to be 'the life of religion'.[86] He theorises the imagination in *An Essay in Aid of a Grammar of Assent* (1870) as an ontological power able to represent the ideal 'real' principle of God. He sees it as providing the criterion for his famous distinction of a 'real' assent to God from a 'notional' assent in which belief is registered through the reasoning mind. It is an echo of the 'primary imagination' which Coleridge describes as 'the living Power and prime Agent of all human Perception, and as a representation in the finite mind of the eternal act of creation in the infinite I AM' of God.[87] A real assent to God is that which 'is discerned, rested in, and appropriated as a reality, by the religious imagination' (while a notional assent entails that 'it is held as a truth, by the theological intellect').[88] However, unlike the more metaphysical Coleridge, who was directly influenced by Schelling and other German idealists, Newman conceives of the workings of the imagination and its authority by analogy with empirical experience. The 'more vivid assent to the Being of God' does not so much participate in the original principle of creativity via the creative imagination, as is the case in Coleridge's theory of imaginative activity, but is rather an ideal means of bearing witness; 'an imaginative apprehension' by which 'I believe as if I saw'.[89] In his rhetoric, at least, Newman offers a concession to the 'commonsense' British empiricist dictum that 'seeing is believing'. He is part of a great Victorian tradition

which worked to domesticate the Continental Romantic idealism introduced earlier in the century by Coleridge and Carlyle.

While the positivist conceptions of feeling are phenomenal and contingent, the idealists often insist that feeling belongs to a deeper realm
of noumena, of an essential moral self or soul, and see it as betokening
a unity of personal consciousness that has its ultimate parallels in
the unity of Creation and of the divine mind. The trust, and indeed
prestige, which idealists often vest in personal feeling means that they do
not necessarily see it as inappropriate to express their private emotional
experience in works of philosophy. In the following extract from Part
One of his *Exploratio Philosophica* (1865), John Grote[90] provides a good
insight into the nature of Victorian idealism and its attitudes to contemporary empiricism, which he refers to here as 'phenomenalism':

> To me there is something in the simply phenomenalist spirit,
> so far as one has a tendency to sink (as I should say) into it,
> inexpressibly depressing and desolate. We are supposed to
> wake into a world (for even a world or universe is something
> for the imagination to lay hold of, a unity, a something added
> to what we wake into from ourselves) but into circumstances
> to which we ourselves are accidental, and our knowing which
> or knowing anything as to which, is quite an accident in
> regard to them: as if we were thrown on an uninhabited island
> where everything, in a manner which to our actual human
> experience is impossible, was strange and out of relation to us.
> And as we go on in our island, in this view, the state of things
> does not alter. Without the links to bind them together which
> our mind must supply, one thing is as strange to another as
> each thing is to us – though here I am using wrong language,
> as it is impossible to avoid doing, for unless our mind
> proceeded otherwise than phenomenally at first there would
> not be even things to us, we should separate and distinguish
> nothing. The progress of knowledge, so far as we can be true
> to this manner of thought, is the passing on unmeaningly, we
> might almost say the falling helplessly, from one view to a
> fresh one in a course which is not advance towards an end but
> the getting further and further into a hopeless infinity.
>
> I am aware that it will be said that . . . what we do is mount
> up from particular facts to general laws . . . But what do we
> mean by 'laws'? Why do we thus take pleasure, and find our
> minds exalted, in the seeing in the universe these uniformities,
> and recurrences, and order? It is because we recognise a
> likeness to what we should do ourselves, and *do* do, that is,
> we trace mind, and here we are going quite beyond the
> phenomena. When we view things in this way, knowledge is

not accidental to the universe, or to fact, but so far as either is to be postponed to the other, the universe is accidental to knowledge, we are brought into relation with the knowledge of which it is a result and an example. This is what I meant by our feeling ourselves, as to knowledge, at home in the universe. And this is something quite beside phenomenalism.[91]

Grote, who was Whewell's successor to the Chair of Moral Philosophy at Cambridge, echoes his precursor's idealist account of mind in the reference to 'the links to bind them [i.e., particulars] together which our mind must supply'. Whilst positivists like Bentham argue that the conceptions of the idealists are illusory, because they lack the tangible nature of empirical 'fact', Grote argues that on the contrary positivism is a theory that, unlike idealism, does not admit to being a theory. Grote presents the theoretical world of phenomenalism metaphorically as an island which is reminiscent of one of Lemuel Gulliver's ports of call, a place 'where everything . . . was strange and out of relation to us'. The 'commonsense' empiricist paradigm of knowledge, the concrete, tangible fact, is on the contrary meaningless, because it bears no relation to anything else, it has no context within which it can be understood. What is required is the over-arching *a priori* context of the unity of the world which we conceptualise and grasp through the synthetic imagination; 'a world or universe is something for the imagination to lay hold of, a unity.' Paradoxically, the phenomenalist 'fact' cannot be grasped by the means allowed by positivist theory: we can only 'lay hold of' it through an act of mind.

According to Grote phenomenalism and idealism present us with an existential choice between being radically alienated and constrained on an *island* or the more comfortable and expansive alternative of 'feeling ourselves . . . at home in the universe'. Phenomenalism constructs us as passive, so that knowledge is 'accidental', a matter of 'falling helplessly'. In contrast to this creed, which Grote personally finds 'inexpressibly depressing and desolate', a principal consequence of idealism is seen to be 'pleasure, . . . [we] find our minds exalted'. The reason for this is that our minds, our ideas, are, according to a fundamental idealist presupposition, in fact *analogous* to the ultimate unity of the universe: 'we recognise a likeness to what we should do ourselves, and *do* do, that is, we trace mind.'

Because of the precedence it gives to the whole over the part, the organic idea over the empirical 'fact', the principles of context and analogy are central to idealism's approach to knowledge, and also to its theory and practice of language. Language is not viewed by idealists in its smallest units, atomistic words (as it is by positivists), but rather meaning is seen to inhere through relations within larger wholes, such as sentences, poems, and ultimately the whole of language itself.[92] Words and experience are typically subordinated by idealism to their larger context, to greater wholes.[93] Hence, stylistically idealist writing typically draws upon ways of unifying experience and language, such as forms of analogy, which highlight a unity shared by ostensibly disparate things, and metonymic devices of symbolism, in which a thing announces that it is incomplete and needs to be referred to a larger, transcendent whole in order to be understood. Indeed Coleridge distinguishes analogy from metaphor by identifying it with this symbolist function. As the 'material' or 'base' of the symbol, analogy presents a comprehensible thing or experience as a way of referring to a higher or greater truth that is less easy for us to comprehend. This general function suggests the requirement of religious faith to communicate the transcendent principle of God. Whereas metaphors are seen to be merely illustrative, 'analogies are used in aid of *Conviction*.'

> The language is analogous, wherever a thing, power, or principle in a higher dignity is expressed by the same thing, power, or principle in a lower but more known form. Such for instance, is the language of John iii.6. *That which is born of the Flesh, is Flesh; that which is born of the Spirit, is Spirit.* The latter half of the verse contains the fact *asserted*; the former half the *analogous* fact, by which it is rendered intelligible.

Analogies are described as 'expressing the *same* subject but with a *difference*', whereas metaphors and similitudes express 'a *different* subject but with a resemblance'.[94] Analogy, to a far greater extent than metaphor, stresses similarity, indeed more than that, identity, for unlike metaphor the difference expressed is one of degree rather than of kind. The tendency of analogy is accordingly to unify experience in a larger whole, to make the ineffable comprehensible. Indeed, the effect of this conception of analogy, which is shared by idealist philosophers and poets throughout the nineteenth century, is to try to draw together everything, including words, into a single principle: all things in Creation provide analogies for one another and ultimately for the supreme principle of God; all words struggle through analogy to express the Word.[95]

The Romantic idealist principle of *logos*, of the Word, is also fundamental to Carlyle's history, as the close of *The French Revolution* (1837) serves to highlight:

> And so here, O Reader, has the time come for us two to part. Toilsome was our journeying together; not without offence; but it is done. To me thou wert as a beloved shade, the disembodied or not yet embodied spirit of a Brother. To thee I was but as a Voice. Yet was our relation a kind of sacred one; doubt not that! For whatsoever once sacred things become

hollow jargons, yet while the Voice of Man speaks with
Man, hast thou not there the living fountain out of which all
sacredness sprang, and will yet spring? Man, by the nature of
him, is definable as 'an incarnated Word.' Ill stands it with me
if I have spoken falsely: thine also it was to hear truly.
Farewell.[96]

The tone of this passage is diametrically opposed to the scientistic
objectivity of Buckle's history, and indeed of professional history in our
own century. It is personal, directly addressing the reader as kin, and
claims its authority not from an appeal to the methodological standards
and findings of professional science but rather from a spiritual principle
of community, 'Man . . . as ". . . incarnated Word"'. But even so, the
analogy here is secularised. The principle of brotherhood appealed to
here, at the end of a history of the French Revolution, resonates with the
final term of the revolutionary slogan 'Liberty, Equality, Fraternity'.
The reader and the author are brought *into relation* with one another, not
as father and child, as is the case with the author of the Bible and its
reader, but as equals. Carlyle, despite his authorial omniscience, does
not identify himself with an aloof God-like author-function that tran-
scends history, but rather with the reader as a fellow journeyman through
recent history.

Carlyle's closing paragraph is, in its self-conscious play with the principles of the real and the illusory, reminiscent of Prospero's speech at the
end of Shakespeare's *The Tempest*. Carlyle describes himself as simply
'a Voice', the substance of which is granted by the reader in reading,
while the reader himself is regarded as another ghostly principle;
'beloved shade, the disembodied or not yet embodied spirit of a Brother'.
The principle of 'relation' is regarded here in accordance with Romantic
doctrine as 'sacred', because it draws together discrete objects into unity.
This relation, the interaction of reader and writer in the text, is conceived of as an active process in which the text can be sacralised as true
experience: 'Ill stands it with me if I have spoken falsely: thine also it
was to hear truly.' Through such interaction his history is either lent
the substance of real human experience, so as to become 'an incarnated
Word', or else rendered meaningless, insubstantial; 'hollow jargons'.

History is for Carlyle, as his journeyman-brother metaphor highlights, a cultural product that all (men) participate in and produce. It is
for him our mode of Being-in-the-world, and its narrative is conceived
of in radical terms reminiscent of the Kantian synthetic *a priori*: 'Cut us
off from Narrative, how would the stream of conversation, even among
the wisest, languish into detached handfuls, and among the foolish utterly
evaporate! Thus, as we do nothing but enact History, we say little but
recite it nay, rather, in that widest sense, our whole spiritual life is built
thereon . . .'[97] Carlyle's essay 'On History' ends with the prayer that

history develop in such a way 'that increased division of labour do not here, as elsewhere, aggravate our already strong Mechanical tendencies, so that in the manual dexterity for parts we lose all command over the whole'.[98]

History, which for Carlyle sacralises experience into relation and meaning, is conceived of as 'a real Prophetic Manuscript, and can be fully interpreted by no man'.[99] The narrative of 'Universal History' that Carlyle gives 'Voice' to in *The French Revolution*, is, like the Bible, a complex and various text demanding endless acts of interpretation. The analogy of reading accordingly figures prominently throughout the work: 'What, then, is this Thing called *La Revolution*, which, like an Angel of Death, hangs on France . . . *La Revolution* is but so many Alphabetic Letters.'[100] The historian gives 'Voice' to and tries to organise the letters, the disparate phenomena of history, in relations which yield meaning.

Certain names are invested with great significance by the historian's narrative. Mirabeau, for example, is given the full Romantic mythic treatment: 'The fierce wear and tear of such an existence has wasted out the giant oaken strength of Mirabeau. A fret and fever that keeps heart and brain on fire: excess of effort, of excitement; excess of all kinds . . . Cannot Mirabeau stop; cannot he fly, and save himself alive? No! there is a Nessus-Shirt on this Hercules; he must storm and burn there . . . til he be consumed . . . While he tosses and storms, straining every nerve, in that sea of ambition and confusion, there comes, sombre and still, an intuition that for him the issue of it will be swift death.'[101] Carlyle's Mirabeau is the Romantic archetype of the Promethean overreacher. A sublime elemental collocation of fire and ocean he 'dies a gigantic Heathen and Titan; stumbling blindly, undismayed, down to his rest . . . as a tower falls'.[102]

Mirabeau, however, lives on beyond his physical death: '. . . For three days there is a low wide moan; weeping in the National Assembly itself . . . The bourne-stone orators speak as it is given them; the Sanscullottic People, with its rude soul, listens eager, – as men will to any Sermon, or Sermo, when it is a spoken Word meaning a Thing, and not a Babblement meaning No-thing.'[103] This takes us back to Carlyle's definition of 'man . . . as "an incarnated Word"': words are understood by him reciprocally as at best living principles of meaning, as extensions, or the eternal after-life, of the historical person they designate. They are invested with an ontological force which is recognisable even to the 'rude soul' of the *sansculottes*. 'Mirabeau' is for Carlyle an ontologically charged signifier. His semi-divine status as '"an incarnated Word"' perseveres beyond his death through the voice of 'Universal History', the prophetic 'Voice' of Carlyle's book. The authenticity of his existence contrasts with the category of those who are 'in good part, manufactured Formalities, not Facts but Hearsays!' Mirabeau 'is a Reality and no Simulacrum; a living Son of Nature . . . not a hollow Artifice, and mechanism of

Conventionalities, son of nothing, *brother* to nothing.'[104] Carlyle's Romantic conception of language is juxtaposed with that of the empty sign without a signified, a principle which looks forward to the Baudrillardian 'simulacrum'. For Carlyle, however, the 'Simulacrum' is defined in binary opposition to nature. It is attributed with all the corrupting values of artificiality, convention and mechanistic and atomistic contingency that Romantics in the Rousseauian and Wordsworthian tradition identify with urban society: Romantic 'Non-being'. The people who are identified with 'hollow artifice' suggest the alienated urban inhabitants, the 'hollow men' of T. S. Eliot's *The Wasteland* who 'can connect / Nothing with nothing'; those who are deprived of the Romantic principle of relation to others, 'son of nothing, *brother* to nothing', and who act mechanistically and by mere convention.

Coleridge discusses the Romantic principle of unity directly in terms of Christian belief in the posthumously published *Confessions of an Inquiring Spirit* (1840): 'Revealed Religion . . . is in its highest contemplation the unity, that is, the identity or co-inherence, of Subjective and Objective . . . [of] inward Life and Truth, and outward Fact and Luminary . . .'[105] Romantics such as Coleridge and Carlyle assume that unity is an ultimate reality, though not one that is always apparent to the human perceiver. This leads to their anxieties about perception and interpretation, evident for example in Carlyle's acknowledgement of his dependence upon the journeyman-reader: 'thine [responsibility] also it was to hear truly'. Coleridge similarly discusses the importance of the reader in understanding the Bible correctly: 'Is it necessary, or expedient, to insist on the belief of the divine origin and authority of all, and every part of, the Canonical Books as the condition, or first principle, of Christian Faith? . . . Or, may not the due appreciation of the Scriptures collectively be more safely relied on as the result and consequence of the belief in Christ; – the gradual increase, – in respect of particular passages – of our spiritual discernment of their truth and authority supplying a test and measure of our own growth and progress as individual believers, without servile fear that prevents or overclouds the free honor which cometh from love?'[106] Coleridge argues for the necessity of a dynamic faith which continuously reinvigorates the Scriptures according to the felt experience and needs of their historical readers. In arguing against the imposition of fixed and prescriptive interpretations of the Bible Coleridge maintains that the humble believer in Christ would read the Scriptures in the manner that they were meant to be read. He, like Carlyle, puts his trust in the natural good will of the reader. As Welch notes, Coleridge feels that 'the notion of the dictation of the Scriptures by an infallible intelligence violates the living character of revelation and faith.'[107]

The whole question of how to interpret the Bible rose to great prominence in the nineteenth century. This occurred in England most notably and notoriously in the immensely controversial *Essays and*

Reviews (1860), the work of seven Church of England liberals. Of these Benjamin Jowett's contribution, 'On the Interpretation of the Scriptures', the most controversial of them, is also the most apposite for the present discussion.

Jowett, along with his fellow contributors to *Essays and Reviews*, was in fact working within an intellectual tradition of biblical criticism that, like the very different thought of Marx and Engels, sprang from the so-called 'Left Hegelians' of 1830s Germany. One work in particular, David Strauss's *Life of Jesus* (1835), is of special importance to English writing in the nineteenth century, not only because of the early date of its publication in English eleven years after the German original, but because its translator was the young George Eliot. Whilst Hegel historicised his ultimate (and theological) principle of the Idea or Spirit, seeing it as becoming manifest through changing phenomena, Strauss inverted this theory. Giving priority to history rather than to an idealist principle of Spirit, he argued that the Bible, the supposed revelation of God, was itself historically specific, the product of particular human cultures and individual writers. The Gospels, for example, were identified by him as records of Jewish mythology and the existence of an historical Jesus was questioned. While the *Essays and Reviews* are not as extreme as their German forebears, they nevertheless apply the same basic approach of regarding the Bible as an historical document. Jowett, for example, following Coleridge, urges his readers to 'Interpret the Scripture like any other book.'[108]

The question of the methodological grounds for interpreting the Scriptures, which is the central problem of German biblical criticism, and of the *Essays and Reviews* in general and Jowett's contribution in particular, marks the beginning of hermeneutics, the science of interpretation, which is foundational for the academic study of English literature and for semiotics. Like Mark Pattison, who in his contribution argues for the importance of the period 1688–1750 to the formation of contemporary religious English culture, Jowett, in his complementary essay on 'Interpretation', argues that the Bible has long been construed as the indeterminacies of language allow and historical vagaries have demanded: 'If words have more than one meaning, they may have any meaning . . . The unchangeable word of God, in the name of which we repose, is changed by each age and each generation in accordance with its passing fancy.' Rather like Marx, who privileges his understanding of society as scientific while dismissing those with which it competes as mere ideologies, Jowett juxtaposes his scientific hermeneutics with mystificatory and empty readings of the Bible: 'Where there is no critical interpretation of Scripture, there will be a mystical or rhetorical one . . . The book in which we believe all religious truth to be contained, is the most uncertain of all books, because interpreted by arbitrary and uncertain methods.'[109] Jowett observes that interpretations of the Gospels are often the result of overtly ideological pressures: 'false and miserable applications of them are often made, and the kingdom of God becomes the tool of the kingdoms of the world.'[110]

In arguing for the possibility of determining finally the significance of the Bible, Jowett first of all demonstrates its semantic instability by drawing attention to the historical uses to which the Scriptures have been put. Indeed, his science will not be able to reinstate the comforting certainties of traditional mystical and ideological construals of the Bible, for it puts finite and fluctuous human history in their place. Biblical criticism seemed to assert that revelation, rather than being the great cultural anchor, was only a life-boat, and that it was only the rope attaching it to such man-made structures as language, ideology, and interpretative commentaries, that stopped it from drifting away into the mists of history or becoming swamped in the seas of relativism.

While Jowett was, as a consequence of his contribution to the *Essays and Reviews*, generally charged, and indeed tried within the University of Oxford, with undermining Christian culture, he saw his essay to be in fact devoted to the exploration and strengthening of this culture. Furthermore, although he regarded religion very self-consciously, he was, perhaps inevitably, not himself above ideology. This is apparent from the following passage, in which Jowett reminds us of the importance and ubiquity of Biblical language in nineteenth-century England:

> It supplies a common language to the educated and the uneducated, in which the best and highest thoughts of both are expressed; it is a medium between the abstract notions of one and the simple feelings of the other. To the poor especially, it conveys in the form which they are most capable of receiving, the lesson of history and life. The beauty and power of speech and writing would be greatly impaired, if the Scriptures ceased to be known or used among us. The orator seems to catch from them a sort of inspiration; in the simple words of Scripture which he stamps anew, the philosopher often finds his most pregnant expressions. If modern times have been richer in the wealth of abstract thought, the contribution of earlier ages to the mind of the world has not been less, but, perhaps greater, in supplying the poetry of Language. There is no such treasury of instruments and materials as Scripture. The loss of Homer, or the loss of Shakespear, would have affected the whole series of Greek or English authors who follow. But the disappearance of the Bible from the books which the world contains, would produce results far greater; we can scarcely conceive the degree in which it would alter literature and language – the ideas of the educated and philosophical, as well as the feelings and habits of mind of the poor.[111]

This passage highlights some of the issues which were at stake in the various battles to preserve the authority of the Bible and of Christian culture generally in nineteenth-century England. Christian culture during the nineteenth century, a time of great cultural change and class tensions in England, represented continuity with the past and, bridging differences in education and class, a basis for social cohesion. Jowett parallels the Bible to the works of Homer, the national poet of ancient Greece, and those of Shakespeare, who with the rise of nationalism early in the nineteenth century was promoted as the symbol of a unified British culture. Shakespeare was at the heart of the new study of 'English Literature' in the Working Men's Colleges during the second half of the century, which, by emphasising a national cultural heritage that workers shared with their employers and rulers, helped to defuse working-class unrest. In the passage from Jowett a similarly ideologically-driven mode of instruction seems to be offered to the poor in the Bible's 'lesson of history and life', a mysterious phrase that suggests the ideological uses of religion which had been critiqued earlier by the thinkers of the French Enlightenment and Romantic writers such as William Blake, as well as by Feuerbach, Engels and Marx in the first half of the nineteenth century. Christian culture, like the education in the 'national literature' offered by the Working Men's Colleges, often functioned to disguise the reality of exploitative and unjust class relations. This at least is the case that Marx makes with the use of a couple of orientalist metaphors in his *Introduction to a Critique of Hegel's Philosophy of Right*. Building upon Christianity's ancient associations with the pungent and intoxicating scent of incense (which he presents as an olfactory parallel to the whited sepulchre) Marx famously extends this suggestion of oriental languor to more intoxicating effects: 'that [exploitative] world whose spiritual aroma is religion . . . Religion is the opium of the people'.[112]

Jowett, who became Regius Professor of Greek at Oxford from 1855 and Master of Balliol College from 1870 to 1893, distinguishes two social castes· his own, 'the educated and philosophical', and 'the poor'. It was indeed the case that in Victorian England Classics and philosophy graduates from the principal universities dominated national politics, the civil service and the administration of the British empire. However, while the division that Jowett presents here is fair as a general representation of contemporary society, his contrasting characterisation of each group is curious and reveals his biased attitudes to them.

Each of Jowett's broad classes is defined by the criterion of how he sees their minds to work. The poor have simply a 'capa[city] of receiving' the 'form' of the Biblical 'lesson'. Like the subjects postulated by the (for Jowett inadequate and 'dangerous') doctrines of empiricism, the minds of the poor are passive receptacles for 'simple feelings'. They lack the powers of independent reason which Jowett championed throughout his writings and teaching, subsisting instead on their simple 'habits of mind'. In direct contrast to the mental passivity and fundamental irrationality of the poor, Jowett's superior caste are intellectually active and reasonable. Whereas Locke pictured the mind passively as analogous to sealing wax upon which sensory input is impressed like the imprint of a signet ring, Jowett inverts this metaphor in his representation of the philosopher as actively making his mark upon external matter: 'the simple words of Scripture which he stamps anew'. Whilst the Scriptures provide the appropriate 'form' for the 'simple', receptive minds of the poor, the contrary case describes the mind of Jowett's intellectual aristocrat, in which the Scriptures themselves become the 'simple' matter which receives the form. Jowett's own educated class, like Coleridge's 'clerisy', are seen to have shaped their epoch ('modern times have been richer in the wealth of abstract thought') and, unlike the mob of the poor, are represented as individuals, 'the Orator' and 'the philosopher'. Furthermore the philosopher and the orator are gendered male, a characterisation that aligns with the prevalent stereotyped associations of activity and rationality with masculinity, whilst the amorphous 'they' of 'the poor' are implicitly attributed with its binary opposite, a 'feminine' passivity.

Apart from his sermons Jowett, understandably, did not write again on theological matters, but instead channelled all of his intellectual liberalism into his teaching at Oxford and the long introductory essays to his translations of Plato, which were first published in 1871. Jowett re-introduced the study of Plato to Oxford and, a keen student of Kant and Hegel, was also instrumental in introducing German idealist thought to the Oxford Classics course, an effect of which was to set in motion the neo-Hegelian British Idealist movement of the last third of the century, the leading lights of which, T. H. Green, Edward Caird, William Wallace, R. L. Nettleship and F. H. Bradley, were all taught by him. Amongst his other students were Arthur Symonds, Walter Pater, and Gerard Manley Hopkins.

The attack upon the foundations of Victorian Christian belief, which was commonly identified with Jowett and Darwin, led to religious impulses being secularised and sublimated in such phenomena as spiritualism. Interestingly some agnostics and scientists, most notably Alfred Wallace, credited as the co-discoverer with Darwin of the natural selection hypothesis, enthusiastically embraced spiritualism, which became popular in the last thirty years of the century.[113] Amongst the literature it produced was a book that promised to end resolutely any controversy over 'the interpretation of Scripture', W. F. Kirby's 1881 translation from the French of *The Four Gospels Explained by Their Writers; with an Appendix on the Ten Commandments*, which claims to record the gospel writers' communications direct from the spirit world.[114]

Spiritualism is one of the more obvious movements which offered to fill the spiritual vacuum felt by many after the assaults of Darwinian biology and biblical criticism. While science appears to have functioned as a substitute religion for some, art became something of a religion for the aesthetes of the last decade of the century. W. David Shaw draws a parallel between the reactionary 'move back into the sanctuary . . . associated with Tractarianism' and the 'later efforts of Pater and the aesthetes to restore to art a sense of purity and detachment'.[115] Walter Pater, a prize student and then colleague of Jowett's, finds in Plato a scripture for this new religion:

> When we remember Plato as the great lover, what the visible world was to him, what a large place the idea of Beauty, with its almost adequate realisation in that visible world, holds in his most abstract speculations as the clearest instance of the relation of the human mind to reality and truth, we might think that art also, the fine arts, would have been much for him; that the aesthetic element would be a significant one in his theory of morals and education. . . . Before him, you know, there had been no theorising about the beautiful, its place in life, and the like; and as a matter of fact he is the earliest critic of the fine arts. He anticipates the modern notion that art as such has no end but its own perfection, – 'art for art's sake.' . . . We have seen again that not in theory only, by the large place he assigns to our experiences regarding visible beauty in the formation of his doctrine of ideas, but that in the practical sphere also, this great fact of experience, the reality of beauty, has its importance with him. The loveliness of virtue as a harmony, the winning aspect of those 'images' of the absolute and unseen Temperance, Bravery, Justice, shed around us in the visible world for eyes that can see, the claim of the virtues as a visible representation by human persons and their acts of the eternal qualities of 'the eternal,' after all far out-weigh, as he thinks, the claim of mere utility. And accordingly, in education, all will begin and end in 'music,' in the promotion of qualities to which no truer name can be given than symmetry, aesthetic fitness, tone. Philosophy itself indeed, as he conceives it, is but the sympathetic appreciation of a kind of music in the very nature of things.[116]

This passage is from the beginning of a lecture on 'Plato's Aesthetics', which was published with other examples of Pater's Oxford lectures in *Plato and Platonism* (1893). The evidence of the extract suggests that the lecture it belongs to is something of a secular sermon. While Jowett diverted his energies from biblical hermeneutics into his interpretative work on Plato, his atheist friend Walter Pater conflates the two in his aestheticist sermon on Plato. The lecture begins, much as a sermon might, in a gesture which draws together his audience. It does this both by addressing them inclusively in the plural, and also by the eulogistic tone it establishes: 'When we remember Plato . . .' The individual that is mourned is, like the biblical figure of Christ, known to the congregation only through the written word. He is immediately endowed with a familiar character. This tone of complicity and familiarity is maintained later in the extract ('Before him, you know, . . .') and throughout the essay. There is also an echo of the biblical text of the Psalms, 'eyes have they, but they see not,'[117] in Pater's reference to 'those "images" of the absolute and unseen Temperance, Bravery, Justice, shed around us in the visible world for eyes that can see'.

While Hamilton, Mansel and the scientific agnostics were very influential in presenting the thesis that the idea of God is for the human mind unknowable, the experience by which the divine was, according to Coleridge, known through analogy persisted. Pater applies the implications of this insight to Plato, and in particular, to 'the large place he assigns to our experiences regarding visible beauty in the formation of his doctrine of ideas'. The transcendent Platonic Ideas or Forms are in this way largely dismissed in favour of their humanly perceptible analogies in the experience of 'visible beauty'. Instead of Plato's use of the example of beauty for the sake of the transcendent idea, we are left with beauty for its own sake, 'the modern notion that art as such has no end but its own perfection, – "art for art's sake."' Plato is in this way cast as a positivist[118] aesthete and his transcendent Forms are brought down to earth in the experiences of 'visible beauty', whilst still retaining their qualities of purity and aloofness. Religious aspirations of purity and transcendence are here, as in the 'The School of Giorgione' (1877), where he famously declares that '*All art constantly aspires towards the condition of music*',[119] identified with the abstract aesthetic form of music: 'Philosophy itself indeed, as he conceives it, is but the sympathetic appreciation of a kind of music in the very nature of things.' It is in these terms that, working within the confines of an age of agnosticism, aestheticism forms a kind of secular religion.

While Pater eventually became identified with a decadent *fin de siècle* crop of *fleurs du mal*, his Oxford education and teaching career were predicated upon establishment values which were considered fundamental to the character of its graduates, a group who were ear-marked for jobs in the running of the country and the colonies. The universities, largely as a consequence of a Royal Commission appointed in 1850 to reform them, assumed responsibility during the second half of the century for the formation of a Coleridgian 'clerisy', an intellectual and cultural elite, to take control of British public life. It was not until the 1850s that the major universities began to draw students on the basis of merit over money, and impose rigorous and standardised curricula and examinations. Thomas Hill Green, a student of Jowett's during the late

1850s, was one of the first of the students at Oxford that came from the middle classes. Increasing wealth and educational standards amongst this class, as well as the provision of generous scholarships based on examination performance, facilitated this movement, so that as a consequence the universities came to function largely as a training ground for the new middle-class intellectuals and professionals. Green was one of many university liberals devoted to the cause of broadening the franchise.[120]

A volume entitled *Essays On Reform*, containing essays on the reform of the House of Commons by a number of university liberals, provides an interesting and influential record of the state of British political culture thirty-five years after the 1832 Reform Act first extended the franchise to sections of the middle classes. The contribution by Leslie Stephen, 'On the Choice of Representatives by Popular Constituencies', directly attacks the old parliamentary school of aristocratic 'gentlemen': 'But Parliament is, after all, a place for transacting certain important national business, and not a school of deportment, or a society for the practice of rhetorical decorum.'[121] Stephen defines parliament in commonsense terms that are redolent with mercantile connotations, and in so doing asserts that it properly represents the interests of the middle classes, the Victorian nation of shopkeepers, over the old aristocrats. Classical orators such as Macaulay are dismissed as an anachronism, members of an obscure private 'society' parallel to the fops and dancing masters that presumably comprise the 'school of deportment'. This 'difference of form', of pretence and pomposity, that Stephen sees as marking the distinction 'between a legislature of gentlemen and one not of gentlemen' is the object of mockery earlier in the essay: 'There is such a thing as bullying in refined language, and telling lies, or receiving bribes, in accordance with all the usages of society. English statesmen have sometimes, it is said, blustered and browbeaten weak countries and afterwards truckled to powerful countries; if, in doing this, they have always used the language of gentlemen, that is a good thing so far as it goes, as doubtless of the two, it is better to have your nose pulled gracefully than awkwardly; but, for all that, the important fact is that your nose has been pulled.'[122] Stephen's use of simple and demotic language here underlines his middle-class suspicion of aristocratic ornament and embellishment. '[R]efined language' is regarded as a hypocritical effort to disguise the absurd and vulnerable physicality that 'gentlemen' share with all others of their species, the baseness which they make a pretence of having transcended. Stephen's straightforward and demotic use of language is representative of the 'platform' oratory which during the increasingly democratic Victorian period superseded classical political and religious oratory.

An analytical table appended to *Essays on Reform* records that Oxford University was at the time represented in the House of Commons by

136 graduates, twenty-six more than Cambridge, and 109 more than the third-place contender, Trinity College Dublin.[123] Oxford, especially Jowett's college, Balliol, functioned as something of a political seminary, teaching Classics and philosophy with special attention to moral and political issues. A series of lectures 'On the Principles of Political Obligation', which T. H. Green delivered in 1879–80 and which were published in 1888 (and in print until the 1960s), provides a good example of the way in which the study of philosophy was directed to specific social and political issues, providing a theoretical grounding for the practical responsibilities of politics and other parts of public life.

The lectures originally followed a series on Kantian moral philosophy and begin by surveying in some detail the philosophical theories of Spinoza, Hobbes, Locke, and Rousseau in their relation to the purpose Green sets himself of 'consider[ing] the moral function or object served by law, or by the system of rights and obligations which the state enforces, and in so doing to discover the true ground or justification for obedience to law'.[124] The quest of discovery is, however, limited to the audience or reader of the lectures. Green is quite certain about his own stance in relation to the question. The orientation to the question of political obligation that he offers his students is strongly polemical. His philosophical stance and teaching were directed against the moral implications of 'Comtism and materialism': 'against these,' he writes in 1864, 'I have been declaiming in a humble way for the last six years.'[125] His later lectures elaborate a political theory from his moral position of intentionalism or deontology, which in sharp contrast to Utilitarianism believes that it is the intentions that motivate acts, not their effects, which give them their moral value.

The *a priori* moral sense which Green theorises in his philosophy demands consistency in the manner prescribed by his Christian beliefs and, more particularly, by the Kantian Categorical Imperative: 'Act so that the maxim of thy will can always at the same time hold good as a principle of universal legislation.'[126] The basis of political obligation is accordingly traced to such a principle of will. Hence, for example, 'the polygamous husband' is condemned on the grounds of inconsistency as 'he requires a self-restraint from his wife which he does not put on himself, he is treating her uneqally.'[127] The Kantian imperative, like the Christian principle, 'Do unto others as you would be done by,' satisfies Green's idealist criteria for consistency and unity. Whereas Mill in his essay on the *Subjection of Women* draws analogies between the condition of women in marriage and slavery, Green sees there to be a necessary relationship between the two:

> Wherever slavery exists alongside of monogamy, on the one
> side people of the slave class are prevented from forming
> family ties, and the other side those people who are privileged

to marry, though they are confined to one wife, are constantly tempted to be false to the true monogamistic idea by the opportunity of using women as chattels to minister to their pleasures. The wife is thus no more than an institution, invested with certain dignities and privileges, for the continuation of the family; a continuation, which under pagan religions is considered necessary for the maintenance of certain ceremonies, and to which among ourselves an importance is attached wholly unconnected with the personal affection of the man for the wife. When slavery is abolished, and the title of all men and women equally to form families is established by law, the conception of the position of the wife necessarily rises.[128]

The free agency of human beings, according to the Kantian doctrine that Green develops upon, entails that they must be treated as ends in themselves, not instrumentally as means to an end, as is the case with women who are used by men 'as chattels to minister to their pleasures' and the wife who is regarded as 'no more than an institution'. Public life is conceived of here as the expression of the ideal moral nature of the free-willed agent. The manifestation of the good, its codification in law, occurs as the 'rise' of a 'conception'.

The Kantian enlightenment postulate of Green's political and social theory precludes him from positing essentialist differences between the genders. While affections are privileged here as natural between wife and husband, the conditions which attribute to them an inequality, such as the fetishisation of the wife as merely the reproductive 'institution', are referred to historical contingencies and placed in the comparative context of anthropology, whereby they disclose an affinity between the attitudes of 'pagan religions' and of Green's contemporaries, 'ourselves'.

'Green's role for the state is', according to Geoffrey Thomas, 'to provide conditions for the moral life in which every citizen can achieve self-realization.'[129] To apply different rules to some members of society on the basis of arbitrary and cultural distinctions is for Green unjustifiable. Yet, of course, the Victorian state was active in restricting the opportunities for self-realisation by women, most fundamentally in the failure to give women the suffrage. Indeed the highest representatives of the Victorian state, Queen Victoria and her long-serving Prime Minister William Gladstone, conducted a correspondence on the subject in 1870, when a bill for female suffrage was before the Parliament:

> The Queen feels so strongly upon this dangerous & unchristian & unnatural *cry* & movement of 'woman's rights,' – in wh[ich] she knows Mr. Gladstone *agrees*, (as he sent that excellent Pamphlett by a Lady) that she is most anxious that Mr. Gladstone & others sh[ou]ld take some steps to check this

alarming danger & to make whatever use they can of her name.

The peculiar subject position of the Queen ('The Queen is a woman herself – & knows what an anomaly her *own* position is')[130] is institutionalised in her prerogative of speaking of herself in the third person. Writing from this unique speaking position she almost naturally organises her discussion of the issue of gender inequality in terms of class and language, setting up a binary opposition between the vulgar street '*cry* of "woman's rights"' and the more discreet and decorous public expression of views on the subject, 'that excellent Pamphlett by a Lady'. The emphasis that Victoria places upon the '*cry*' is a sort of shrill shorthand for the conception she elaborates to another correspondent at this time of woman as 'the most hateful, heathen, and disgusting of human beings' should 'she [be] allowed to unsex herself'. The Queen exercises her royal prerogatives in the letter to Gladstone, endowing the pamphleteer with the title of 'Lady', and authorising the use of her name, the political 'transcendental signifier' of her age, to counter feminist attempts to undermine essentialist gender differences: 'God created men and women different – then let them remain each in their own position. Tennyson has some beautiful lines on the difference of men and women in *The Princess* . . .'[131]

Another bill for extending the vote to women was presented to parliament in 1892, the year in which Gladstone became Prime Minister for the fourth time. He argued that the bill, if successful, would place women out of their depth: 'She, not the individual woman, marked by special tastes, possessed of special gifts, but the woman as such, is by this change to be plenarily launched into the whirlpool of public life, such as it is in the nineteenth, and such as it is to be in the twentieth century.'[132] We can well imagine that Gladstone had Victoria in mind as the type for the atypical 'individual woman' who is able to deal with political power, the exception that proves his rule. Such a being is, in any case, distinguished from the generic 'woman as such'. The implication is that individuality is a masculine prerogative, as indeed it was, for it was only in the public sphere that specific vocational identities were allocated, whereas the private sphere of the home homogenised individual difference among women through the roles and names of wife and mother. Gladstone puts safety first: 'we have done nothing that plunges the woman as such into the turmoil of masculine life. My disposition is to do all for her which is free from that danger and reproach, but to take no step in advance until I am convinced of its safety.' The 'whirlpool of public life, . . . the turmoil of masculine life' is defined by a dynamism that, it is assumed, is anathema to the generic 'woman as such', who is thereby constructed as passive and so seen to require the paternalistic protection of the eighty-three-year-old Gladstone.

Writing culture

But civilization in itself is but a mixed good, if not far more a corrupting influence, the hectic of disease, not the bloom of health, and a nation so distinguished more fitly to be called a varnished than a polished people; where this civilization is not grounded in *cultivation*, in the harmonious developement of those qualities and faculties that characterize our *humanity*. We must be men in order to be citizens.

(S. T. Coleridge)[133]

Samuel Taylor Coleridge's last completed work, *On the Constitution of the Church and State according to the Idea of Each* (1830), demonstrates the crucial interconnections between philosophy, theology, historiography, and social and political theory in the formulation of ideas about culture and its dissemination through education in the nineteenth century. Anticipating Dickens's brilliant caricature of the *nouveaux riches* in the 'brannew' Veneerings, in his novel *Our Mutual Friend* (1864–65), Coleridge's distinction between a 'varnished' and a 'polished' people, between people who have achieved mere 'civilization' as opposed to those who have attained true 'cultivation', between material progress and moral culture, plays upon those middle-class anxieties about their cultural identity and legitimacy which form such a powerful motif of Victorian fiction.[134]

'Cultivation', or 'Culture' as it was to become in the lexicon of other nineteenth-century writers, most notably Matthew Arnold, emerged as an increasingly desirable commodity for the middle classes (Arnold's 'Philistines'), not only because of the 'polish' it conferred upon those whose class origins were less than impeccable, but also because of its perceived value as a bulwark against 'Anarchy'. In the aftermath of the French Revolution, and in the context of continuing political upheaval abroad and social instability, political reform and religious controversy at home, an ideal of culture which offered 'the harmonious developement of those qualities and faculties that characterize our *humanity*' offered reassurance to those of a more conservative bent. To counteract the pernicious effects of Liberalism and Democracy, a 'clerisy' of enlightened intellectuals should, in Coleridge's scheme, be responsible for the acculturation of the masses. But of course although, according to this 'ideology for the intelligentsia',[135] the activities of the clerisy are seen to benefit society as a whole, the clerisy are not, themselves, representative of society as a whole. If 'We must be men in order to be citizens', we must certainly be men in order to qualify as *bona fide* members of the clerisy, educated men who endorse a classical pedagogic ideal at that. The elitist assumptions of the theory of the clerisy and the culture it promotes as normative in fact work to emphasise cultural boundaries and to cement cultural difference.

The idea of the clerisy was a tenacious one in the nineteenth century, but the model of cultural authority it represents did not go uncontested. Writers of a more radical and democratic persuasion, such as John Stuart Mill and William Morris, argued for more equitable and inclusive definitions of culture. Moreover, alternative cultural paradigms – domestic cultures, female cultures, working-class cultures – which found their expression in the popular prose literature of the period, such as domestic manuals and magazines directed at female and working-class readerships, represented an affirmation of those less elevated activities of life from which 'Culture' as defined by the clerisy separated itself. The 'man of letters' may have seen himself as the principal purveyor of culture in the nineteenth century, and may have been represented as the voice of culture by later critical commentators on the period, but such alternative cultures are equally deserving of attention, not least because they constitute the potentially 'anarchic' forces against which hegemonic formulations of 'Culture' were defined, and against which society had to be defended.

For a self-made man of letters of humble social origins such as Carlyle there were good reasons, reasons of self-legitimation, for asserting the significance of his own intellectual and social role, as he did most explicitly in his lecture 'The Hero as Man of Letters'(1840). For Carlyle, the 'Man-of-Letters Hero must be regarded as our most important modern person':

> All this, of the importance and supreme importance of the Man of Letters in modern Society, and how the Press is to such a degree superseding the Pulpit, the Senate, the *Senatus Academicus* and much else, has been admitted for a good while; and recognised often enough, in late times, with a sort of sentimental triumph and wonderment. It seems to me, the Sentimental by and by will have to give place to the Practical. If Men of Letters *are* so incalculably influential, actually performing such work for us from age to age, and even from day to day, then I think we may conclude that Men of Letters will not always wander like unrecognised unregulated Ishmaelites among us![136]

Whereas Shelley had seen the poet as the unacknowledged legislator of the world, Carlyle casts the non-fiction prose writer in that role. An 'accident in society', who 'wanders like a wild Ishmaelite, in a world of which he is as the spiritual light, either the guidance or the misguidance',[137] the 'man of letters' nonetheless has a crucial vocation in that modern post-industrial society which Carlyle had described so memorably in his essay of 1829, *Signs of the Times*, as 'the Mechanical Age'. Carlyle saw his times as 'the Age of Machinery, in every outward and inward sense of that word.' Not only had mechanism taken over the methods of production, driving 'the living artisan . . . from his workshop, to make room for a speedier, inanimate one', and changing the social system, 'strangely altering the old relations, and increasing the distance between the rich and the poor'; it had gained control over 'the internal and spiritual also', 'our modes of thought and feeling':

> Men are grown mechanical in head and in heart, as well as
> in hand. They have lost faith in individual endeavour, and in
> natural force, of any kind. Not for internal perfection but for
> external combinations and arrangements, for institutions,
> constitutions, – for Mechanism of one sort or other, do they
> hope and struggle. Their whole efforts, attachments, opinions,
> turn on mechanism, and are of a mechanical character.[138]

It is the high calling of the 'man of letters' to be a clear-sighted critic of his times, and to restore faith in 'the imperishable dignity of man'; to respond positively to the changes brought about by progress, for

> this age also is advancing. Its very unrest, its ceaseless
> activity, its discontent contains matter of promise. Knowledge,
> education are opening the eyes of the humblest; are increasing
> the number of thinking minds without limit. This is as it
> should be; for not in turning back, not in resisting, but only
> in resolutely struggling forward, does our life consist.[139]

The 'times' to which Carlyle and Coleridge were responding in *Signs of the Times* and *On the Constitution of the Church and State* were, specifically, times of impending political, institutional and social reform, times when fears of the chaos and instability associated since the French Revolution with such reforms ran high. In the 1860s, in the face of a further extension of the franchise by the second Reform Act of 1867, Coleridge's idea of the clerisy and its function re-emerged in the writings of Matthew Arnold. In *Culture and Anarchy* (1869), Arnold addressed the fears of the upper classes now that a large proportion of working-class men had been given the vote, and suggested how a huge uneducated class might be taught how to participate in the running of the nation. The gist of its argument is that England exists in a state of 'Anarchy', not only in the open signs of working-class unrest but also in the more insidious creeds of middle-class laissez-faire Liberalism, 'doing as one likes', and he warns that this 'Anarchy' will only get worse if 'Culture' is not heeded:

The whole scope of the essay is to recommend culture as the great help out of our present difficulties; culture being a pursuit of our total perfection by means of getting to know, on all matters which most concern us, the best which has been thought and said in the world; and through this knowledge, turning a stream of fresh and free thought upon our stock notions and habits, which we now follow staunchly but mechanically, vainly imagining that there is a virtue in following them staunchly which makes up for the mischief of following them mechanically.[140]

Like Carlyle, Arnold registers the crisis of modernity through the metaphor of machinery in a way that underlines his sense of the connection between the political restlessness of mid-nineteenth-century England and the process of rapid industrialisation which had led to the expansion of a depressed working-class population:

Faith in machinery is, I said, our besetting danger; often in machinery most absurdly disproportioned to the end which this machinery, if it is to do any good at all, is to serve; but always in machinery, as if it had a value in and for itself. What is freedom but machinery? what is population but machinery? what is coal but machinery? what are railroads but machinery? what is wealth but machinery? what are, even, religious organisations but machinery?[141]

He deplores 'our bondage to machinery ... our proneness to value machinery as an end in itself, without looking beyond it to the end for which alone, in truth, it is valuable'.[142] Like Carlyle too he perceives an urgent need for 'men of letters', for a secularised version of Coleridge's clerisy, who alone, through the dissemination of 'culture', might release the modern world from its enslavement to and idolatry of machinery. In a later essay he would develop more fully his theory of an elitist 'remnant', and a State made up of the 'best self' of each class, that would counteract 'the unsoundness of the majority', which, 'if it is not withstood and remedied, must be their ruin.'[143] Here, that 'unsoundness' is suggested through the language he uses to invoke a violent, threatening, and monstrous working-class majority which, 'raw and half-developed, has long lain half-hidden amidst its poverty and squalor, and is now issuing from its hiding-place to assert an Englishman's heaven-born privilege of doing as he likes, and is beginning to perplex us by marching where it likes, meeting where it likes, bawling what it likes, breaking what it likes'.[144] In an unguarded passage in the first edition of *Culture and Anarchy*, 'sweetness and light' temporarily deserted him, and he recommended that the Hyde Park rioters should be dealt with by flogging the rank and file and hurling the ring-leaders from the Tarpeian Rock, but for the most part he puts forward 'Culture' as the most effective way to counter the 'Anarchy' which threatens to engulf civilised society. For 'Culture' promises to attain not only 'a *harmonious* perfection, developing all sides of our humanity', but also 'a *general* perfection, developing all parts of our society'.[145]

Arnold insists that 'the culture we recommend is, above all, an inward operation,' not to be confused with 'Mr. Bright's misconception of culture, as a smattering of Greek and Latin':[146]

> culture . . . places human perfection in an *internal* condition, in the growth and predominance of our humanity proper, as distinguished from our animality. It places it in the ever-increasing efficacy and in the general harmonious expansion of those gifts of thought and feeling, which make the peculiar dignity, wealth, and happiness of human nature . . . If culture, then, is a study of perfection, and of harmonious perfection, general perfection, and perfection which consists in becoming something rather than in having something, in an inward condition of the mind and spirit, not in an outward act of circumstances, – it is clear that culture, instead of being the frivolous and useless thing which Mr. Bright, and Mr. Frederic Harrison, and many other Liberals are apt to call it, has a very important function to fulfil for mankind. And this function is particularly important in our modern world, of which the whole civilisation is, to a much greater degree than the civilisation of Greece and Rome, mechanical and external, and tends constantly to become more so. But above all in our own country has culture a weighty part to perform, because here that mechanical character, which civilisation seems to take everywhere, is shown in the most eminent degree.[147]

Yet despite Arnold's historicist emphasis upon the particular context within which he writes, upon culture conceived as an 'internal condition' peculiarly adapted to handle the mechanistic nature of the modern condition, the cultural model he proposes is one which eschews both history and the modern in favour of a timeless cultural canon based on the literature of the classical golden age, one which indeed demands rather more than 'a smattering of Greek and Latin'. In Arnold's view, 'their commerce with the ancients appears to me to produce, in those who constantly practise it, a steadying and composing effect upon their judgment, not of literary works only, but of men and events in general.'[148] Although his work as an Inspector of Schools meant that he was more practically involved with the establishment of a state education system than any of his fellow spokesmen for the clerisy, and although he saw himself as an 'apostle of equality'[149] whose task it was to equip the masses to handle the new responsibilities conferred upon them by the march of democracy, he was the son of the classical historian Thomas Arnold of Rugby, and his education at that public school and afterwards at Oxford determined the kind of pedagogic ideals he held and the classical style he favoured. The emphasis on the importance of tradition and continuity at such institutions may have ensured that 'the best that has been thought and known in the world' was passed on from generation to generation, but it also ensured that the Maggie Tullivers and Jude Fawleys were excluded from their hallowed halls. Arnold's culture 'seeks to do away with classes; to make the best that has been thought and known in the world current everywhere',[150] but it is to his Nonconformist and Liberal enemies that he attributes the cry 'Let us all be in the same boat . . . open the Universities to everybody'.[151]

Arnold conducted his campaign against Liberalism, Philistinism, and the other enemies of 'Culture' in the periodical press, and this is reflected in the polemical journalistic style of works such as *Culture and Anarchy* and *Friendship's Garland* which, although eventually appearing in book form, were written as a series of articles over a period of time. Such texts constitute one side of an ongoing debate, the opposing side of which has been lost to the modern reader. They typically present not a polished, unified, logically structured argument, but rather one whose twists and turns, climaxes and challenges are reactive, determined by the critics with whom Arnold is always and everywhere engaging in a publicly waged dialogue.[152] The cut and thrust of his debating style is enlivened by brilliant conjuring tricks, whereby his opponents assume a textual life of their own as Nonconformists sipping tea while anarchy rages around them (one is reminded of Carlyle having tea with Geraldine Jewsbury while his wayward servant goes into labour in the next room), as hunting, shooting and fishing aristocrats, even as baying hounds themselves, thirsting for his blood: 'And here I think I see my enemies waiting for me with a hungry joy in their eyes. But I shall elude them.'[153]

In formulating his own educational philosophy in *The Idea of a University* (1852), John Henry Newman had pointed to the ascendancy of the periodical press as one of the chief threats to modern intellectual life, in its encouragement of 'the random theories and imposing sophistries and dashing paradoxes, which carry away half-formed and superficial intellects':

> Such parti-coloured ingenuities are indeed one of the chief evils of the day, and men of real talent are not slow to minister to them. An intellectual man, as the world now conceives of him, is one who is full of 'views' on all subjects of philosophy, on all matters of the day. It is almost thought a disgrace not to have a view at a moment's notice on any question from the

Personal Advent to the Choleras or Mesmerism. This is owing
in great measure to the necessities of periodical literature now
so much in request. Every quarter of a year, every month,
every day, there must be a supply, for the gratification of the
public, of new and luminous theories on the subjects of
religion, foreign politics, home politics, civil economy, finance,
trade, agriculture, emigration, and the colonies. Slavery, the
gold fields, German philosophy, the French Empire,
Wellington, Peel, Ireland, must all be practised on, day after
day, by what are called original thinkers. As the great man's
guest must produce his good stories or songs at the evening
banquet, as the platform orator exhibits his telling facts at mid-
day, so the journalist lies under the stern obligation of
extemporizing his lucid views, leading ideas, and nutshell
truths for the breakfast table. The very nature of periodical
literature, broken into small wholes, and demanded punctually
to an hour, involves the habit of his extempore philosophy.[154]

Newman is concerned not only that 'a demand for a reckless originality
of thought, and a sparkling plausibility of argument . . . a demand for
crude theory and unsound philosophy, rather than none at all' has been
created by the periodical press, but more importantly that 'The authority, which in former times was lodged in Universities, now resides in
very great measure in that literary world.'[155] Newman's aim, in the
discourses, occasional lectures and essays which were published together
as *The Idea of a University*, is to reassert the cultural authority of universities, and to argue for the importance of a liberal education in the
acquisition of 'real cultivation of mind'.[156]
   Although Newman speaks of the 'cruel slavery' of the journalist's lot
as one who has 'never indeed been in such circumstances myself, nor
in the temptations which they involve',[157] he was no stranger to public
debate; indeed, all his writings respond to works with which he dis-
agrees. In *The Idea of a University* he vigorously engages in topical
debates about what constitutes 'real cultivation of mind' and which form
of education is most calculated to achieve it. Arguing that the proper
function of universities was 'the diffusion and extension of knowledge
rather than the advancement' and that knowledge should be seen as an
end in itself, Newman explicitly attacks contemporary Utilitarian ideas
about university education which stressed the importance of applied
research, the expansion of the curriculum to include modern subjects,
and vocational training. Originally delivered in association with the
establishment of the Catholic University in Dublin, Newman's discourses are written from an explicitly sectarian perspective. But although
Newman's idea of a university has different religious affiliations from
Coleridge's idea of a clerisy and Arnold's idea of Culture, it rests upon

similarly idealist and elitist pedagogical assumptions and asserts like them the importance of maintaining the classical tradition. Newman's distrust of 'sparkling plausibility of argument' recalls Coleridge's contempt for varnish; while his dislike of the fragmentary nature of periodical writing 'broken into small wholes' reflects a predilection for a unified, harmonious organicism, for 'a wise and comprehensive view of things' and 'a connected view of the old with the new', that is characteristic of both Coleridge and Arnold. In his lecture 'Christianity and Letters' Newman describes the idea of civilisation as a process of growth and assimilation of culture:

> Looking, then, at the countries which surround the Mediterranean Sea as a whole, I see them to be, from time immemorial, the seat of an association of intellect and mind such as to deserve to be called the Intellect and Mind of the Human Kind. Starting as it does and advancing from certain centres, till their respective influences intersect and conflict, and then at length intermingle and combine, a common Thought has been generated, and a common Civilization defined and established.[158]

Like Coleridge and Arnold, Newman stresses, through the very rhythms of his prose, the continuity and harmony of 'Civilization', representing the past, present and future as a seamless web. He concedes that 'There are indeed great outlying portions of mankind which are not, perhaps never have been, included in this Human Society,' but these are dismissed as 'outlying portions and nothing else, fragmentary, unsociable, solitary, and unmeaning, protesting and revolting against the grand central formation of which I am speaking'.[159]

However, not all commentators on culture shared Newman's exclusive and conservative view of the march of civilisation. There were those who believed that those 'great outlying portions of mankind' were not beyond the pale, and who involved themselves enthusiastically in such initiatives as the Mechanics' Institutes, begun in 1823 in the light of Benthamite thinking, and the Working Men's Colleges which were formed in the middle of the century. William Morris, for instance – who became a Socialist, was actively involved in working-class educational initiatives, and attempted to develop a theory of culture which was inclusive of and relevant to the experiences of the majority working-class population – had little time for elitist formulations of culture. Although, like Newman and Arnold, he had studied at Oxford, he had little respect for his *alma mater* as a role-model for the modern university, seeing it rather as a bastion of privilege. As he wrote in a letter to the *Daily News* in 1885, 'The present theory of the use to which Oxford should be put appears to be that it should be used as a huge upper public school for fitting lads of the upper and middle class for their laborious future of living on other people's labour. For my part I do not think this a lofty conception of the function of a University.'[160] He is particularly disparaging of Arnold's Oxford-based view of 'culture':

> In the thirty years during which I have known Oxford more damage has been done to art (and therefore to literature) by Oxford 'culture' than centuries of professors could repair – for, indeed, it is irreparable. These coarse brutalities of 'light and leading' make education stink in the nostrils of thoughtful persons.[161]

Morris himself feels 'repulsion to the triumph of civilization', which he represents not in Newman's terms of a 'grand central formation', but rather as a vulgar, Whiggish desecration, 'all this filth of civilization':

> Apart from the desire to produce beautiful things, the leading passion of my life has been and is hatred of modern civilization. What shall I say of it now, when the words are put into my mouth, my hope of its destruction – what shall I say of its supplanting by Socialism?
> What shall I say concerning its mastery of and its waste of mechanical power, its commonwealth so poor, its enemies of the commonwealth so rich, its stupendous organization – for the misery of life! Its contempt of simple pleasures which everyone could enjoy but for its folly? Its eyeless vulgarity which has destroyed art, the one certain solace of labour? . . . The hope of the past times was gone, the struggles of mankind for many ages had produced nothing but this sordid, aimless, ugly confusion; the immediate future seemed to me likely to intensify all the present evils by sweeping away the last survivals of the days before the dull squalor of civilization had settled down on the world.

Again, Dickens's *Our Mutual Friend* provides a reference point for this impoverished dust-heap of a 'civilisation':

> Think of it! Was it all to end in a counting-house on the top of a cinder-heap, with Podsnap's drawing-room in the offing, and a Whig committee dealing out champagne to the rich and margarine to the poor in such convenient proportions as would make all men contented together, though the pleasure of the eyes was gone from the world, and the place of Homer was to be taken by Huxley? Yet, believe me, in my heart, when I really forced myself to look towards the future, that is what I

saw in it, and, as far as I could tell, scarce anyone seemed to think it worth while to struggle against such a consummation of civilization.[162]

But there were, Morris acknowledges, two who had struggled, who had engaged in 'open rebellion' against 'the measureless power of Whiggery' – Carlyle and Ruskin. Ruskin in particular, whom Morris describes as his 'master' before he became a Socialist, had inaugurated a quite different way of thinking about cultural issues, one which broke free from the idealist classical tradition and sought to root the idea of culture more firmly in history. For a man whose twin passions were 'the desire to produce beautiful things' and the 'hatred of modern civilization', Ruskin's conviction of the correlation between beautiful things and the health of the society that produces them, and his commitment, both theoretical and practical, to the democratisation of culture, were crucial formative influences.

In the introduction he wrote to the Kelmscott edition of Ruskin's essay 'The Nature of Gothic' (1892), from *The Stones of Venice*, volume II (1853), Morris described it as 'one of the very few necessary and inevitable utterances of the century', noting that 'the lesson Ruskin . . . teaches us, is that art is the expression of man's pleasure in labour'.[163] Four decades previously, the year after it was published, the essay had been reprinted as a pamphlet and distributed free of charge to all those attending courses at the newly opened Working Men's College. In 'The Nature of Gothic' it is precisely the culture of the Jude Fawleys that Ruskin celebrates when he invites his readers to compare the products of the machine age which surround them with the stonemasonry of a Gothic cathedral:

> And now, reader, look around this English room of yours, about which you have been proud so often, because the work of it was so good and strong, and the ornaments of it so finished. Examine again all those accurate mouldings, and perfect polishings, and unerring adjustments of the seasoned wood and tempered steel. Many a time you have exulted over them, and thought how great England was, because her slightest work was done so thoroughly. Alas! if read rightly, these perfectnesses are signs of a slavery in our England a thousand times more bitter and more degrading than that of the scourged African or helot Greek. Men may be beaten, chained, tormented, yoked like cattle, slaughtered like summer flies, and yet remain in one sense, and the best sense, free. But to smother their souls with them, to blight and hew into rotting pollards the suckling branches of their human intelligence, to make the flesh and skin which, after the

worm's work on it, is to see God, into leathern thongs to
yoke machinery with, – this is to be slave-masters indeed; and
there might be more freedom in England, though her feudal
lords' lightest words were worth men's lives, and though the
blood of the vexed husbandman dropped in the furrows of her
fields, than there is while the animation of her multitudes is
sent like fuel to feed the factory smoke, and the strength of
them is given daily to be wasted into the fineness of a web, or
racked into the exactness of a line.

And, on the other hand, go forth again to gaze upon the old
cathedral front, where you have smiled so often at the fantastic
ignorance of the old sculptors: examine once more those ugly
goblins, and formless monsters, and stern statues, anatomiless
and rigid; but do not mock at them, for they are signs of the
life and liberty of every workman who struck the stone; a
freedom of thought, and rank in scale of being, such as no
laws, no characters, no charities can secure; but which it must
be the first aim of all Europe at this day to regain for her
children.[164]

By contrast with Arnold, who sees the goal of culture as 'perfection', and
recommends classical culture as the model of such perfection, Ruskin
equates classical perfection, and modern attempts to emulate it, with
slavery. In his view, '*the demand for perfection is always a sign of a misunderstanding of the ends of art*', and, using architecture as his example, he
contends that 'no architecture can be truly noble which is *not* imperfect':

For since the architect, whom we will suppose capable of
doing all in perfection, cannot execute the whole with his own
hands, he must either make slaves of his workmen in the old
Greek, and present English fashion, and level his work to a
slave's capacities, which is to degrade it; or else he must take
his workmen as he finds them, and let them show their
weaknesses together with their strength, which will involve the
Gothic imperfection, but render the whole work as noble as
the intellect of the age can make it.[165]

Ruskin saw in Gothic imperfection a reflection and acknowledgement of the fallen state of humanity, and for this reason found Gothic
to be the most Christian of architectural schools. He also saw in the
humour and inventiveness and vitality of Gothic architecture an emblem
of a society in which the working man had more dignity and freedom, and took more delight in creative labour, than his counterparts in
ancient Greece or the Renaissance or nineteenth-century England. 'The
Nature of Gothic' is a paean to the culture of the working man. The

extraordinary intensity and reverence with which he describes the minutest details of buttresses, capitals, cornices and carvings honours the contribution made by even the humblest stonemason. The tones of Carlyle are heard, and the familiar metaphor of the machinery of modern life is invoked, but Ruskin's criticism is mediated, unlike either Carlyle's or Arnold's, through the aesthetic interpretation of Gothic and Renaissance architecture and of the very room in which the reader is presumed to sit. Ruskin was first and foremost an art historian and critic; however, he was concerned not merely with external forms and techniques but with the moral and ethical dimensions of art. He was committed to the view that there is a close moral relationship between art and the society that produces it. Hence, the aesthetic degradation into which modern Britain had fallen, as demonstrated in 'this room of yours', is linked by Ruskin to the practices and values of industrial capitalist society. He vigorously maintained throughout his life that

> the art of any country *is the exponent of its social and political
> virtues* . . . The art, or general productive and formative
> energy, of any country, is an exact exponent of its ethical life.
> You can have noble art only from noble persons, associated
> under laws fitted to their time and circumstances.[166]

Ruskin does not fight shy of pointing out the implications of this philosophy to his audience, even when it involves making a blunt appraisal of their own moral and cultural shortcomings. When he delivered his lecture entitled 'Traffic' at Bradford Town Hall in 1864, for instance, at the invitation of the townspeople who wished him to advise them on the style of architecture they should choose for their new Exchange building, his audience must have been somewhat taken aback by his opening remarks to the effect that 'I cannot speak, to purpose, of anything about which I do not care; and most simply and sorrowfully I have to tell you, in the outset, that I do *not* care about this Exchange of yours.' He explains to them 'frankly' that 'you cannot have good architecture merely by asking people's advice on occasion', because 'All good architecture is the expression of national life and character.'[167] He reminds them that this was his thesis in both *The Seven Lamps of Architecture* and *The Stones of Venice*, and now, he says, 'you ask me what style is best to build in, and how can I answer but . . . by another question – do you mean to build as Christians or as infidels?'[168] Here he must have touched his audience to the quick, striking at the very heart of their view of themselves as pious and God-fearing with the suggestion that they worshipped Mammon above all else:

> Now, we have, indeed, a nominal religion, to which we pay
> tithes of property and sevenths of time; but we have also a

practical and earnest religion, to which we devote nine-tenths
of our property, and six-sevenths of our time. And we dispute
a great deal about the nominal religion: but we are all
unanimous about this practical one; of which I think that you
will admit that the ruling goddess may be best generally
described as the 'Goddess of Getting-on,' or 'Britannia of the
Market.' . . . And all your great architectural works are, of
course, built to her. It is long since you built a great cathedral;
and how you would laugh at me if I proposed building a
cathedral on the top of one of these hills of yours, to make it
an Acropolis! But your railway mounds, vaster than the walls
of Babylon; your railroad stations, vaster than the temple of
Ephesus, and innumerable; your chimneys, how much more
mighty and costly than cathedral spires! your harbour-piers;
your warehouses; your exchanges! – all these are built to your
great Goddess of 'Getting-on'; and she has formed, and will
continue to form, your architecture, as long as you worship
her; and it is quite vain to ask me to tell you how to build to
her; you know far better than I.[169]

Then Ruskin, in a variation on his usual practice of reading actual architectural monuments, creates a fictional building that functions as a satiric
emblem of the spiritual condition of Victorian England:

I can only at present suggest decorating its frieze with pendant
purses; and making its pillars broad at the base, for the sticking
of bills. And in the innermost chambers of it there might be a
statue of Britannia of the Market, who may have, perhaps
advisably, a partridge for her crest, typical at once of her
courage in fighting for noble causes, and of her interest in
game; and round its neck, the inscription in golden letters,
'Perdix fovit quae non peperit.' Then, for her spear, she might
have a weaver's beam; and on her shield, instead of St
George's Cross, the Milanese boar, semi-fleeced, with the town
of Gennesaret proper, in the field; and the legend, 'In the best
market,' and her corslet, of leather, folded over her heart in
the shape of a purse, with thirty slits in it, for a piece of
money to go in at, on each day of the month. And I doubt
not but that people would come to see your exchange, and its
goddess, with applause.[170]

Ruskin's audience often comprised, as in this case, the very people
he scolded in his talks. For instance, at the time of the Art Treasures
Exhibition in 1857, Ruskin gave two long lectures in Manchester to an
audience composed largely of merchants and manufacturers, which he

opened with an uncompromising attack on the philosophy of laissez-faire, the 'let-alone' principle, as he called it, which was of course the ideology of those same northern Captains of Industry. His subject was, much to their surprise, not Italian *quattrocento* painting, or even art, but rather the political economy of art. Ruskin took it upon himself to instruct those present on the proper and most socially responsible use of wealth, and how it pertained to art.

When Ruskin published the four further essays on political economy which make up *Unto this Last* in the *Cornhill Magazine* in 1860, he said that they were 'reprobated' by most readers in a violent manner.[171] In these essays Ruskin rejects the notion of art as an isolated social phenomenon, and puts the labour of art in its broadest social, political, and economic context. His main argument is that human beings are not the 'covetous machines' they are represented as by 'political economy', and that working people could be motivated by 'social affection' if their living and working conditions were made more conducive to such emotions. He proposes specifically that workers be paid a guaranteed steady wage which is not subject to fluctuations in demand for their products. At present, he argues, 'the tendency of all modern mercantile operations is to throw both wages and trade into the form of a lottery, and to make the workman's pay depend on intermittent exertion, and the principal's profit on dexterously used chance.' It is the merchant-manufacturer's greedy opportunism and 'love of gambling', he implies, which is to blame for the delinquency of the workers: 'The masters cannot bear to let any opportunity of gain escape them, and frantically rush at every gap and breach in the walls of Fortune, raging to be rich, and affronting, with impatient covetousness, every risk of ruin, while the men prefer three days of violent labour, and three days of drunkenness, to six days of moderate work and wise rest.'[172] Ruskin reminds his well-heeled middle-class readers that their wealth depends upon the poverty of others, that the word 'rich' is a relative word 'implying its opposite "poor" as positively as the word "north" implies its opposite "south"':

> Men nearly always speak and write as if riches were absolute, and it were possible, by following certain scientific precepts, for everybody to be rich. Whereas riches are a power like that of electricity, acting only through inequalities or negations of itself. The force of the guinea you have in your pocket depends wholly on the default of a guinea in your neighbour's pocket. If he did not want it, it would be of no use to you; the degree of power it possesses depends accurately upon the need or desire he has for it, – and the art of making yourself rich, in the ordinary mercantile economist's sense, is therefore equally and necessarily the art of keeping your neighbour poor.[173]

Ruskin was, as he was the first to acknowledge, deeply indebted to Carlyle, whom he described, as Morris had described Ruskin, as his 'master'. 'I read [him] so constantly,' he wrote, 'that, without wilfully setting myself to imitate him, I find myself perpetually falling into his modes of expression.'[174] Ruskin was a much finer stylist than Carlyle. It was the brilliant rhetoric as much as the aesthetic theory of *Modern Painters* that captivated the contemporary reading public and was so warmly admired by other writers. Nevertheless their writing shares some notable stylistic features. Ruskin writes, like Carlyle, in a sermonising style, highly repetitive and hortatory, with an Evangelical ring to it. The preacher's tone complements the theme of damnation and salvation that runs through much of what he writes, and his work is dense with scriptural allusions. Like Carlyle, he assumes that biblical ethics are as applicable to economic and social issues as they are in every other sphere of human relations, and he challenges his middle-class audience to reconcile their ostensible religion with their industrial and commercial practices. Several of his works were originally delivered as lectures, but even those that were always intended for the printed page alone are characterised by a lecture style. Ruskin frequently appeals directly to his audience, sometimes as listener, sometimes as reader: 'My dear reader', 'I will tell you presently', 'I see that some of my readers look surprised at the expression', 'I can fancy your losing patience with me altogether just now', 'Would you not say', 'I assure you', 'And now, reader, look around this English room of yours', 'If you will tell me what you ultimately intend Bradford to be'. Like both Carlyle and Arnold, he conducts imaginary debates: 'I say you have despised Art! "What!" you again answer, "have we not Art exhibitions, miles long? and do we not pay thousands of pounds for single pictures?" '[175]

Another characteristic he shares with Carlyle is that he uses metaphors with a full sense of their rich cultural heritage,[176] in a way that is very different from the style of professional economists, and is also quite different from, say, Engels' kind of social criticism. Ruskin's social and economic writing, like his writing on art, resonates with scriptural allusions, but also with classical and other literary allusions. Mythic references have as natural a place in his political discussions as in his art criticism. Conflicting ideologies in contemporary economics are conceived in terms of archetypal mythical struggles: the Christian 'Sun of Justice' pitted against the archenemy Mammon, the Greek Apollo against Python the corrupter.[177] Such constant allusions to mythical and literary tradition lend his own views historical and moral authority.

A further rhetorical habit that recalls the prose styles of both Carlyle and Arnold is the constant definition and redefinition of key terms. Just as both Carlyle and Arnold make their redefinitions of 'machinery', for instance, into the lynchpin of an argument, so Ruskin gives us what he represents as the true meanings of the words 'value', 'wealth', and 'justice'. He proposes to give the reader the 'real' meaning of economic vocabulary by returning us to the original roots of the words. And so we are reminded that by the term 'mercantile economy' is meant the economy of 'merces' or of 'pay', and that the word 'value' is related to the word 'valiant'. By suggesting that he is getting back to a prior, 'truthful' form of language, he attempts to throw the technical definitions of economists into disrepute.

Ruskin was, also like Carlyle and Arnold, no socialist, for all that he had a significant influence on the young Morris and the fledgling British Labour Movement. His views on culture were considerably less elitist than Arnold's, and he often addressed the cultural needs of working people in his writing and lectures, arguing, for instance, in his lecture 'Of Kings' Treasuries', that 'valuable books should, in a civilized country, be within the reach of every one,' and that every city should have a public library.[178] As well as lecturing regularly at Working Men's Colleges, he published ninety-six open letters addressed 'to the Workmen and Labourers of Great Britain' as periodicals between 1871 and 1884, characteristically naming them obscurely as *Fors Clavigera*. Nevertheless he was a firm believer in the necessity, and indeed the desirability, of inequality, and in the maintenance of social hierarchy. 'If there be any one point insisted on throughout my works more frequently than another,' he wrote, 'that one point is the impossibility of Equality.'[179] His vision is of a paternalistic society, ruled by great men from above, his aim to show 'the eternal superiority of some men to others . . . and to show also the advisability of appointing such persons or person to guide, to lead, or on occasion even to compel and subdue, their inferiors according to their own better knowledge and wiser will'.[180]

As is clear from the analogies he draws, his societal model is a domestic and patriarchal one. The nation should function, in his view, like a well-run family: the manufacturer should treat his workers as he would his own son, or as he would an old family retainer. Ruskin's view of the role of women in this idealised domestic and societal paradigm is notorious among modern feminists,[181] and his delineation of the separate but complementary spheres of male and female influence in the companion essay to 'Of Kings' Treasuries', 'Of Queens' Gardens' (1865) has come to serve as the classic statement of the conservative Victorian sexual economy:

> Now their separate characters are briefly these. The man's
> power is active, progressive, defensive. He is eminently the
> doer, the creator, the discoverer, the defender. His intellect is
> for speculation and invention; his energy for adventure, for
> war, and for conquest wherever war is just, wherever conquest
> necessary. But the woman's power is for rule, not for battle, –
> and her intellect is not for invention or creation, but for sweet

ordering, arrangement, and decision. She sees the qualities of things, their claims, and their places. Her great function is Praise: she enters into no contest, but infallibly adjudges the crown of contest. By her office, and place, she is protected from all danger and temptation. The man, in his rough work in the open world, must encounter all peril and trial; – to him, therefore, must be the failure, the offence, the inevitable error: often he must be wounded, or subdued; often misled; and always hardened. But he guards the woman from all this; within his house, as ruled by her, unless she herself has sought it, need enter no danger, no temptation, no cause of error or offence. This is the true nature of home – it is the place of Peace; the shelter, not only from all injury, but from all terror, doubt, and division . . . so far as it is a sacred place, a vestal temple, a temple of the hearth watched over by Household Gods . . . so far it vindicates the name, and fulfils the praise, of Home.

And wherever a true wife comes, this home is always around her.[182]

This is, he asserts, 'the woman's true place and power', and it is through such a construction of femininity that the idea of the 'guiding function of the woman' is reconcilable with 'a true wifely subjection'.[183] To fulfil this lofty role, the woman must be 'incapable of error':

So far as she rules, all must be right, or nothing is. She must be enduringly, incorruptibly good; instinctively, infallibly wise – wise, not for self-development, but for self-renunciation: wise, not that she may set herself above her husband, but that she may never fail from his side: wise, not with the narrowness of insolent and loveless pride, but with the passionate gentleness of an infinitely variable, because infinitely applicable, modesty of service.[184]

In short, as the chivalrous manner and the idealised language of queenliness and vestal temples make clear, she must be, like Coventry Patmore's 'Angel in the House', a domestic goddess of the hearth. Herein lie her 'place' and her 'power', such as they are.

Ruskin helpfully goes on to answer the question 'What kind of education is to fit her for these?':

All such knowledge should be given her as may enable her to understand, and even to aid, the work of men: and yet it should be given, not as knowledge, – not as if it were, or could be, for her an object to know; but only to feel and to judge . . . she is to be taught somewhat to understand the nothingness of the proportion which that little world in which she lives and loves, bears to the world in which God lives and loves.[185]

A girl's education should be like a boy's, he argued, 'but quite differently directed':

> A woman, in any rank of life, ought to know whatever her husband is likely to know, but to know it in a different way. His command of it should be foundational and progressive; hers, general and accomplished for daily and helpful use . . . speaking broadly, a man ought to know any language or science he learns, thoroughly – while a woman ought to know the same language, or science, only so far as may enable her to sympathise in her husband's pleasures, and in those of his best friends.[186]

Ruskin's prescriptions about the proper nature and nurture of an essentially defined 'Woman' articulate a theory of womanhood which constituted the hegemonic gender ideology of the nineteenth century. The transition from the era of mercantile capitalism to that of industrial capitalism which took place between 1780 and 1830 saw the emergence of an industrial bourgeoisie which sought cultural and ideological as well as political and economic definition. Evangelicalism, the so-called 'religion of the household', was a crucial influence on the recodification of ideas about women which was so fundamental to the new bourgeois way of life.[187] The roots of Victorian domestic ideology are to be found in the writings of Evangelicals such as Hannah More, whose *Strictures on the Modern System of Female Education* (1799), for instance, asserted the importance of women's duties in the home and their power in the moral sphere. Over the ensuing decades, the Evangelical ideology of domesticity and dependence hardened into a prescriptive codification of gender roles, in which women assumed an ever more subordinate position. In the view of the liberal manufacturer W. R. Greg, for instance, writing in 1862, 'the natural duties and labours of wives and mothers' consisted in the main of 'completing, sweetening, and embellishing the existence of others'; and the concept of sexual difference which 'divid[ed]' and 'proportion[ed]' men and women into their separate public and private spheres, and which dictated marriage to be 'the despotic law of life', was sanctioned 'by the instincts which lie deepest, strongest, and most unanimously in the heart of humanity at large in all times and amid all people'.[188] And yet from Mary Wollstonecraft, whose *Vindication of the Rights of Woman* was published in 1792, onwards through the nineteenth century, the representation of such a view of 'Woman's' character and role as natural and universal had been opposed by those who believed it to be a historically specific social construction, and one which, moreover, had little to do with the actual social, political and legal position of women. William Thompson and Anna Wheeler, for instance, in their *Appeal of one half the human race, Women, against the pretensions of the other half, Men, to retain them in political, and thence in civil and domestic, slavery* (1825), presented a very different view of the domestic life of women from Ruskin's:

> Home, except on a few occasions, chiefly for the drillings of superstition to render her obedience more submissive, is the eternal prison-house of the wife: the husband paints it as the abode of calm bliss, but takes care to find, out-side of doors, for his own use, a species of bliss not quite so calm, but of a more varied and stimulating description. These are facts of such daily occurrence and notoriety, that to the multitudinous, unreflecting creatures, their victims, they pass by as the established order of nature.

The house, which is supposedly the woman's domain, is in fact, Thompson and Wheeler point out, '*his* house with everything in it; and of all fixtures the most abjectly his is his breeding machine, the wife'.[189] In 1846, at a time when 'The press has lately teemed with works treating of the condition, the destiny, the duties of women',[190] Anna Jameson published her essay '"Woman's Mission" and Woman's Position', in which she directly addresses 'the anomalous condition of woman in this Christian land of ours':

> I call it *anomalous*, because it inculcates one thing as the rule of right, and decrees another as the law of necessity. 'Woman's MISSION,' of which people can talk so well, and write so prettily, is incompatible with 'Woman's POSITION,' of which no one dares to think, much less to speak.[191]

Against 'the beautiful theory of the woman's existence, preached to her by moralists, sung to her by poets, till it has become the world's creed – and her own faith, even in the teeth of fact and experience!' she sets 'the real state of things', which, she demonstrates, 'is utterly at variance with [such truisms]; and they are but lying common-places at best.'[192]

The immediate context of Jameson's essay was the debate surrounding the Commissions of Enquiry and Government reports on the condition and employment of women and children in manufacturing towns and agricultural districts, and she first of all addresses the disjunction between the rhetoric that woman's 'sphere is *Home*, her vocation the

maternal' and the fact that many working-class women and their children are obliged to labour in the factory or the sweatshop or the field
'by a hard necessity'.[193] But she then goes on to point out that 'more
than two-thirds of [middle-class] women are now obliged to earn their
bread', and that such a woman

> may well think it a peculiar hardship, a cruel mockery, that
> while such an obligation is laid upon her, and the necessity and
> the severity of the labour increases every day, her capabilities
> are limited by law – or custom, strong as law; or prejudice,
> stronger than either, – to one or two departments, while,
> in every other, the door is shut against her. She is educated
> for one destiny, and another is inevitably before her. Her
> education instructs her to love and adorn her home – 'the
> woman's *proper* sphere,' – cultivates her affections, refines her
> sensibilities, gives her no higher aim but to please man, 'her
> protector;' – and allows her no other ambition than to become
> a good wife and mother. Thus prepared, or rather unprepared,
> her destiny sends her forth into the world to toil and endure
> as though she had nerves of iron; – she must learn to protect
> herself, or she is more likely to be the victim and prey of her
> 'protector, man,' – than his helpmate and companion. She
> cannot soothe his toils; for, like him, she must toil; to live,
> she must work, – but, by working, can she live?

Jameson eloquently states the case for those women who 'are destined
never to be either wives or mothers, though they have heard from their
infancy that such, by the appointment of God, is their vocation in this
world, and no other.' 'Such may be their vocation,' she avers, 'but such
is not their destiny.'[194] The essay ends with the plea, 'let her at least have
fair play.'[195]

   Cutting through the chivalrous language of angels and queens,
writers such as these present a more realistic picture of the position
of women in nineteenth-century England. In a paper published in 1868
bluntly entitled 'Criminals, idiots, women, and minors: is the classification sound?', Frances Power Cobbe points out the real company kept
by the heavenly household goddesses of Patmore's poetry and Ruskin's
prose, in terms of their actual legal status. Whilst the 'Woman Question'
had been the focus of keen public interest throughout the century, it
was in the 1860s, in the context of debates about extension of the
suffrage and the reform of laws which discriminated against women
(the first of the Matrimonial Causes Acts was passed in 1857, and the
first Married Women's Property Act in 1870), that both sides of this
most contentious of questions were most vigorously defended. John
Stuart Mill was elected to parliament in 1865 and in 1866 he introduced

the first bill for the enfranchisement of women. Although women's suffrage was not to be achieved for another fifty years, Mill's action inspired increased agitation for social, political and legal justice for women, and his essay *On the Subjection of Women*, written in 1861 and published in 1869, came to be regarded as a foundational work of feminism.

Mill's philosophical treatise on the position of women in contemporary England brings together ideas which had gained currency over a number of decades among those who contested the bourgeois ideology of the 'angel in the house'. In it, he explicitly takes issue with those who conceal the true oppression of women under a veil of chivalry:

> we are perpetually told that women are better than men, by
> those who are totally opposed to treating them as if they were
> as good; so that the saying has passed into a piece of tiresome
> cant, intended to put a complimentary face upon an injury,
> and resembling those celebrations of royal clemency which,
> according to Gulliver, the king of Lilliput always prefixed to
> his most sanguinary decrees.[196]

Women are declared by such writers to be morally superior to men, 'an empty compliment,' he contends, 'which must provoke a bitter smile from every woman of spirit, since there is no other situation in life in which it is the established order, and considered quite natural and suitable, that the better should obey the worse.'[197]

Mill points out that 'power holds a smoother language' in present-day England by comparison with the past,[198] and part of his purpose in the essay is to expose the ways in which language has been manipulated in the interests of ideology. And so whereas Ruskin's description of women's sphere is peppered with imperial imagery suggestive of their 'royal authority', their 'true queenly power', their 'queenly dominion', and the 'territories over which each of them reigned',[199] Mill emphasises the powerlessness of women, whom the law and custom render subject to men. While Ruskin, Patmore and others of the angels and queens school call upon Christianity and culture (the works of Shakespeare, Homer, Chaucer, Dante, Spenser, and so on) to legitimate their theory of woman's nature and function, and, as Jameson had put it, 'tell us one and all that the chief distinction between savage and civilized life, between Heathendom and Christendom, lies in the treatment and condition of the women; that by the position of the women in the scale of society we estimate the degree of civilization of that society,'[200] Mill contends that the treatment of women in nineteenth-century England resembles that of the most primitive pagan cultures in that it is based on 'the law of the strongest'.[201] Their state of enforced dependence is, he argues, 'the primitive state of slavery lasting on';[202] indeed, the legal position of women is in some respects even worse than that of the slave:

we are continually told that civilization and Christianity have restored to the woman her just rights. Meanwhile the wife is the actual bond-servant of her husband; no less so, as far as legal obligation goes, than slaves commonly so called. She vows a lifelong obedience to him at the altar, and is held to it all through her life by law . . . She can do no act whatever but by his permission, at least tacit. She can acquire no property but for him; the instant it becomes hers, even if by inheritance, it becomes *ipso facto* his. In this respect the wife's position under the common law of England is worse than that of slaves in the laws of many countries . . . I am far from pretending that wives are in general no better treated than slaves; but no slave is a slave to the same lengths, and in so full a sense of the word, as a wife is. Hardly any slave, except one immediately attached to the master's person, is a slave at all hours and all minutes; . . . Above all, a female slave has (in Christian countries) an admitted right, and is considered under a moral obligation, to refuse to her master the last familiarity. Not so the wife: however brutal a tyrant she may unfortunately be chained to – though she may know that he hates her, though it may be his daily pleasure to torture her, and though she may feel it impossible not to loathe him – he can claim from her and enforce the lowest degradation of a human being, that of being made the instrument of an animal function contrary to her inclinations.[203]

The comparison of women with slaves had been a common trope for defenders of women's rights ever since the appropriation of abolitionist rhetoric by women at the end of the previous century, but Mill is more explicit than most in calling attention to the sexual enslavement of married women to their husbands. Here the image of the angel is subverted even more radically; compelled by the law to endure rape within marriage, the wife is reduced from heavenly help-mate to 'the instrument of an animal function'. And if her status as wife is given no support by the law, neither is her status as mother: her children are 'by law *his* children. He alone has any legal rights over them. Not one act can she do towards or in relation to them, except by delegation from him. Even after he is dead she is not their legal guardian, unless he by will has made her so.'[204]

Having dismantled the idea that women have any real power, even as wives and mothers in the domestic realm over which they supposedly reign, Mill turns to the question of woman's nature, as so confidently defined by Ruskin and his school. 'Was there ever any domination which did not appear natural to those who possessed it?' he asks; 'everything which is usual appears natural'.[205] Anticipating the modern view of gender as a historically situated social construction, and playing with the words 'nature' and 'natural', Mill argues that 'What is now called the nature of women is an eminently artificial thing – the result of forced repression in some directions, unnatural stimulation in others . . . in the case of women, a hot-house and stove cultivation has always been carried on of some of the capabilities of their nature, for the benefit and pleasure of their masters.'[206] 'The masters of women', he contends, 'turned the whole force of education to effect their purpose,' which was to secure 'more than simple obedience', and it is their education which has kept women 'in so unnatural a state that their nature cannot but have been greatly distorted and disguised'.[207] Mill dismisses the supposedly essential mental differences said to exist between men and women as 'but the natural effect of the differences in their education and circumstances',[208] arguing that not only are women denied the education an opportunities accorded to men, but they are taught a different set of aspirations:

> All women are brought up from the very earliest years in the belief that their ideal of character is the very opposite to that of men; not self-will, and government by self-control, but submission, and yielding to the control of others. All the moralities tell them that it is the duty of women, and all the current sentimentalities that it is their nature, to live for others; to make complete abnegation of themselves, and to have no life but in their affections.[209]

For Mill, the 'gardens' over which Ruskin's 'queens' preside are all too clearly the product not of nature but of cultivation; the women themselves 'a kind of hothouse plants, shielded from the wholesome vicissitudes of air and temperature'.[210]

The profusion of prescriptive manuals for women on feminine manners and etiquette and domestic management testifies to the perspicacity of Mill's observations about the cultivation of femininity. That something supposedly so 'natural' should have to be so thoroughly taught is an irony that appears to have escaped writers such as Mrs Sarah Stickney Ellis, who wrote not only her famous series devoted to the women, mothers, wives, and daughters of England, but also other advice books and serials and fiction, all promoting the gender ideology of separate spheres and the need for women to be schooled in domesticity and subordination. According to Mrs Ellis, 'the place appointed [woman] by providence' is one of servitude. A 'woman of right feeling' should ask herself 'on first awaking to the avocations of the day':

> 'How shall I endeavour through this day to turn the time, the health, and the means permitted me to enjoy, to the best account? Is any one sick; I must visit their chamber without

delay, and try to give their apartment an air of comfort, by arranging such things as the wearied nurse may not have thought of. Is any one about to set off on a journey; I must see that the early meal is spread, or prepare it with my own hands, in order that the servant, who was working late last night, may profit by unbroken rest. Did I fail in what was kind or considerate to any of the family yesterday . . . Was any one exhausted by the last day's exertion . . . Or, if nothing extraordinary occurs to claim my attention, I will meet the family with a consciousness that, being the least engaged of any member of it, I am consequently the most at liberty to devote myself to the general good of the whole, by cultivating cheerful conversation, adapting myself to the prevailing tone of feeling, and leading those who are least happy, to think and speak of what will make them more so.'[211]

Her view is, in short, that 'the customs of English society have so constituted women the guardians of the comfort of their homes, that, like the Vestals of old, they cannot allow the lamp they cherish to be extinguished, or to fail for want of oil, without an equal share of degradation attaching to their names.'[212]

Writers such as Sarah Ellis were adept at maintaining a tension between subordination and power in their prescriptions for women.[213] Their works also ironically underline the precariousness of the gender order it was their business to sustain. Ellis's prescriptions for an idyllic companionate marriage based on the complementary virtues of protective manliness and compliant womanliness actually depended upon a rather negative view of marital behaviour.[214] She devotes a good deal of attention, for instance, to negotiating the tricky question of the properly submissive woman's 'management' of wayward or 'unreasonable' husbands as part of her domestic managerial responsibilities.

Another woman who made a career out of telling other women that they should not have careers was Isabella Beeton, whose *Book of Household Management* (1859–61) immediately made her into a household name. Like Sarah Ellis's work, Isabella Beeton's book unwittingly, it seems, underlines the internal contradictions and ironies of contemporary ideas about the nature of women and their domestic role. As in Sarah Ellis's books, there is a tension between the naturalisation of women's domestic role and the assumption that domestic skills have to be acquired, and must be taught by an expert in household management. Moreover, Mrs Beeton herself constantly defers to male authorities, peppering her prescriptions about proper womanly behaviour with quotations from Dr Johnson, Washington Irving, Lord Chatham, Bishop Hall, and others who testify to the fact that such duties and manners are divinely and providentially ordained. A further internal contradiction is that, whereas on the one hand it promotes the idea of an essential woman, Mrs Beeton's book in fact makes it clear that there are different kinds of women: there are mistresses and there are domestic servants, and their functions and duties are quite distinct. Nevertheless, because within the gender order the middle-class woman's role is one of servitude and subordination, because she is constructed as, in Sarah Ellis's words, a 'relative creature', economically dependent upon her 'master' who, in domestic terms, is chronically dependent upon her, there are clear parallels between the mistress and her servants.[215]

The ambiguities and tensions inherent within Mrs Beeton's immensely influential book are made clear when it is read against contemporary critiques of the condition of women, such as Nightingale's *Cassandra* and Mill's *On the Subjection of Women*. As Nightingale points out, although home is meant to be the woman's domain, her domestic activities are in fact highly regulated, and her power severely delimited, even within this her 'sphere'. Beeton's opening text from *Proverbs* reminds her readers that they must 'eat . . . not the bread of idleness',[216] and what follows demonstrates that what was designated as a place of peace for the man to return to following his labours in the world was, for the woman, a site of bustling activity in which she could find no peace. Nightingale observes that 'Women never have half an hour in all their lives (excepting before or after anybody is up in the house) that they can call their own, without fear of offending or of hurting someone.'[217] And they are obliged to busy themselves over trivialities. Nightingale's ironic comment that 'dinner is the great sacred ceremony of this day, the great sacrament' is echoed, without, irony, by Beeton's 'the next great event of the day . . . is "The Dinner".'[218] Nightingale explains the fact that 'Mrs A. . . . is not a Murillo' by 'a material difficulty, not a mental one':

> If she has a knife and fork in her hands for three hours of the day, she cannot have a pencil or brush . . . If she has a pen and ink in her hands during other three hours, writing answers for the penny post, again, she cannot have her pencil, and so *ad finitum* through life.[219]

Mill makes a similar point when he argues that the major reason 'why women remain behind men, even in the pursuits which are open to both of them' is that 'very few women have time for them.'[220]

It is easy to see how they would not have had time, had they followed Beeton's prescriptions about how the mistress of the house should spend her day. 'If the duties of a family do not sufficiently occupy the time of a mistress,' she advises, 'society should be formed of such a kind as will tend to the mutual interchange of general and interesting information.'[221] And yet the middle-class woman's social intercourse and her conversational subjects were the subject of rigid regulation:

After luncheon, morning calls and visits may be made and received. These may be divided under three heads: those of ceremony, friendship, and congratulation or condolence. Visits of ceremony, or courtesy . . . are uniformly required after dining at a friend's house, or after a ball, picnic, or any other party. These visits should be short, a stay of from fifteen to twenty minutes being quite sufficient. A lady paying a visit may remove her boa or neckerchief; but neither her shawl nor bonnet.

When other visitors are announced, it is well to retire as soon as possible, taking care to let it appear that their arrival is not the cause. When they are quietly seated, and the bustle of their entrance is over, rise from your chair, taking a kind leave of the hostess, and bowing politely to the guests. Should you call at an inconvenient time . . . retire as soon as possible, without, however, showing that you feel yourself an intruder . . .

In paying visits of friendship, it will not be so necessary to be guided by etiquette as in paying visits of ceremony; and if a lady be pressed by her friend to remove her shawl and bonnet, it can be done if it will not interfere with her subsequent arrangements. It is, however, requisite to call at suitable times, and to avoid staying too long, if your friend is engaged. The courtesies of society should ever be maintained, even in the domestic circle, and amongst the nearest friends. During these visits, the manners should be cosy and cheerful, and the subjects of conversation such as may be readily terminated. Serious discussions or arguments are to be altogether avoided.[222]

In short, women should not embark upon any conversation or any project which cannot be interrupted: 'the occupations of drawing, music, or reading should be suspended on the entrance of morning visitors'; the only activity which may be carried on in the drawing room under such circumstances is 'light needlework'. Nightingale is appalled by the lack of value placed on a woman's time that such social behaviour implies, and again her account provides an interesting gloss on Mrs Beeton's prescriptions:

It is a thing *so* accepted among women that they have nothing to do, that one woman has not the least scruple in saying to another, 'I will come and spend the morning with you.' And you would be thought quite surly and absurd, if you were to refuse it on the plea of occupation. Nay, it is thought a mark of amiability and affection, if you are 'on such terms' that you can 'come in' 'any morning you please.' . . .

Women have no means given them, whereby they *can* resist the 'claims of social life.' They are taught from their infancy upwards that it is wrong, ill-tempered, and a misunderstanding of 'woman's mission' (with a great M) if they do not allow themselves *willingly* to be interrupted at all hours.[223]

Ironically enough, having achieved fame in the Crimea, Nightingale herself was constructed as, in Harriet Martineau's words, a 'housewifely woman'. Moreover, such a misrepresentation was authorised by Nightingale's own writings on nursing, in that they everywhere invoke, exploit, and legitimate the militaristic strain inherent in the domestic ideology as articulated by writers such as Mrs Beeton, who begins her *Book of Household Management* with a comparison between the mistress of a house and 'the commander of an army.'[224]

As the examples of Florence Nightingale, Isabella Beeton, and Sarah Ellis demonstrate, the supposedly secure definitions of middle-class womanly and domestic ideals were in fact fraught with internal tensions and contradictions, and those texts which promoted the female culture of the home are frequently the sites of competing constructions of womanliness. The system of beliefs and institutions and practices which constituted middle-class Victorian gender ideology was neither fixed nor homogeneous but was rather, in Mary Poovey's words, 'both contested and always under construction; because it was always in the making, it was always open to revision, dispute, and the emergence of oppositional formulations'.[225] The periodical press, and particularly that portion of it addressed to female readers, played a significant role in this dynamic ideological formulation; indeed, a recent study of women's magazines suggests that 'the form of the magazine – open-ended, heterogeneous, fragmented – seems particularly appropriate to those whose object is the representation of femininity',[226] Mid-nineteenth-century magazines such as the *Englishwoman's Domestic Magazine*, edited and published by Samuel Beeton, figure in their pages the deeply contradictory nature of the bourgeois ideal of femininity and female culture: the Paris fashion plate, representing woman as social being and as object of desire, was accompanied by a dress-maker's paper pattern, which the thrifty and practical bourgeois housewife could make up, thereby combining the fashionable and the useful; fiction and gossip offered entertainment to a woman reader constructed as leisured, while recipes, household and gardening tips, and advice on the management of household finances gave practical information to one who took her domestic responsibilities seriously. The magazine's subtitle was 'An Illustrated Journal combining Practical Information, Instruction, and Amusement', and in an editorial preface of 1861, one year after the launch of a new series, Samuel Beeton congratulated himself on fulfilling the magazine's aim 'to inform our sisters what is the style and manner of the dress in vogue at the time of publication, what the fashionable and useful kind of needlework, and to add in every possible way, by imaginative and serious literature, and well-executed engravings, to the amusement and instruction of our reader'.[227]

Not least among the magazine's internal contradictions was the fact that it was edited by a man, one who, moreover, constructed his female readers as so entirely other to himself that he could find no language in which to speak to them:

> Where are the words to be found, and who, amongst all the great masters of style, could fitly mould those words into a sufficiently grateful form, to thank Sixty Thousand patronesses – Sixty Thousand of his fair countrywomen – for services invaluable? Shall we write our thanks in the pure Greek, or the bold Roman, or the pithy Saxon, or the lighter Anglo-Norman? Shall the expression of our gratitude be made in poetry or prose – in blank verse or in rhyme – closely or diffusely? For no one will doubt our powers. No one will dare to deny to him who has Sixty Thousand English-women-volunteers as a corps of trusty partisans – (think of that, ye Rifles!) – the ability to soar, at will, to the highest of Parnassus' heights, or return once again to the more accustomed Prosaic shores.[228]

Beeton's chivalrous hyperbole, flirtatious manner, and arch tone in his editorial prefaces and in the magazine's problem page, coyly titled 'The Englishwoman's Conversazione', suggest how unsettling even the public discourse of the woman's magazine was to the idea that women's culture was confined to the private sphere. His avuncular advice ridicules the very idea of women having an involvement, or even an interest, in public affairs:

> J. Purr. – Our correspondent, not a young lady, we think, is in a terrible fright about our going to war with France, or France going to war with us. She thinks, she says, if we have no objection, that the first is the best; by which we fancy she means that we had better go to war with France. Yes, that certainly would be the better plan; for no Englishman or Englishwoman would like to see Napoleon's Zouaves, and the Chasseurs de Vincennes, quartered in the pleasant cornfields of Sussex, or turning the Kentish hop-poles into tent-poles. And then, too, terrible question – most terrible of all questions – where would our ladies get, how could they get, when could

they get, that without which we are perfectly assured that no young maid, or middle-aged matron, could do without – the Paris fashions; especially now they have once seen them engraved, printed, and painted so beautifully in this magazine? No. Miss J. Purr (does she mean *j'ai peur*?), the force of fashion alone, we believe, and the immense interests connected with the ENGLISHWOMAN'S DOMESTIC MAGAZINE, would keep this nation from a war with France. This is in entire confidence; but we hereby give each of our readers permission to impart the secret to her husband, brother, or lover (yes), so that he may take it into account in his next operations on the Stock Exchange, and, as a return for the information, present her with a new silk dress (now the duty is off, they don't cost much) and a set of the eight volumes of the ENGLISHWOMAN'S DOMESTIC MAGAZINE already published.[229]

The obsession with fashion which Beeton here caricatures and indulges is condemned by John Stuart Mill as a symptom of women's deprivation of liberty: 'women's passion for personal beauty, and dress and display', he writes, is the product of a system in which women are allowed 'no existence of their own but what depends on others'.[230] Women's magazines were a medium for the production and consolidation of bourgeois gender ideology in Victorian England, but they, and the periodical press more broadly conceived, were also the forum for its contestation. The nineteenth century saw the democratisation of the periodical press, and one aspect of the development of a mass press and the growing tendency to address more specialised readerships was the differentiation of the female reader.[231] In the course of the century magazines were established which were directed at 'ladies' and 'gentlewomen', servants, mothers, girls engaged to be married, and, of course, feminists. The *English Woman's Journal* (1858–61), which later became the *English Woman's Review of Social and Industrial Questions* (1866–1910), although addressed specifically to women, resisted the ideology of gender-determined separate spheres, and fought vigorously for female suffrage and for equal education and employment opportunities. Moreover, the fact that a growing number of women, not content to remain on the cultural margins, began to be involved in a significant way in the more progressive mainstream periodicals, directed at a mixed readership, signified that women could contribute to the public cultural life of the nation. One such woman, Marian Evans, who undertook, albeit anonymously, the editorship of the *Westminster Review* in 1852, and regularly contributed to its pages, wrote an essay in 1852 on 'Woman in France: Madame de Sablé', in which she argues that the history and influence of this remarkable woman, who was only 'one in a firmament of feminine stars', 'has an important bearing on the culture of women in the present day':

> Women become superior in France by being admitted to a common fund of ideas, to common objects of interest with men; and this must ever be the condition at once of true womanly culture and of true social well-being. We have no faith in feminine conversazioni, where ladies are eloquent on Apollo and Mars; though we sympathize with the yearning activity of faculties which, deprived of their proper material, waste themselves in weaving fabrics out of cobwebs. Let the whole field of reality be laid open to woman as well as to man, and then that which is peculiar in her mental modification, instead of being, as it is now, a source of discord and repulsion between the sexes, will be found to be a necessary complement to the truth and beauty of life. Then we shall have the marriage of minds which alone can blend all the hues of thought and feeling in one lovely rainbow of promise for the harvest of human happiness.[232]

That it is impossible to imagine George Eliot (as Marian Evans was later to be known) sitting down along with Samuel Beeton's army of 60,000 'patronesses' to read his egregiously patronising prose clearly throws into question the idea that there was a homogeneous women's, or even mid-nineteenth-century middle-class English women's, culture. And just as there were many women's cultures, all in a state of process, in nineteenth-century England, so there were many broadly middle- and upper-class cultures, and many working-class cultures, which, fashion and manners aside, resisted the incursion of middle-class hegemony. Such cultural plurality was partly a function of the vast expansion and the diversity of the periodical press in the period, which was itself a product of improved printing technology and the gradual removal of the taxes on knowledge by the middle of the century. Whilst writers such as Coleridge and Arnold envisaged imposing 'Culture' on the masses from above, the development of an inexpensive popular press, together with an unprecedented expansion of literacy, created an arena for the debate of issues of cultural identity and for the articulation of minority cultures which problematises notions of the periodical press as the organ of a dominant middle-class ideology. The anarchic 'multitudinousness' of English cultural life, the fact that the critic 'feels himself to be speaking before a promiscuous multitude',[233] was a phenomenon of which Arnold disapproved, and yet it gave rise to a much more thoroughgoing and multi-faceted 'criticism of life' than his own unilaterally conceived Culture could encompass. It is to criticism, that crucial dimension of cultural activity, however it may be defined, that the final section is devoted.

Criticism

Who cares whether Mr. Ruskin's views on Turner are sound
or not? What does it matter? That mighty and majestic prose
of his, so fervid and so fiery coloured in its noble eloquence,
so rich in its elaborate symphonic music, so sure and certain,
at its best, in subtle choice of word and epithet, is at least as
great a work of art as any of those wonderful sunsets that
bleach or rot on their corrupted canvases in England's Gallery
. . . Who, again, cares whether Mr. Pater has put into the
portrait of Mona Lisa something that Leonardo never dreamed
of? The painter may have been merely the slave of an archaic
smile, as some have fancied, but whenever I pass into the cool
galleries of the Palace of the Louvre, and stand before that
strange figure 'set in its marble chair in that cirque of fantastic
rocks, as in some faint light under sea,' I murmur to myself,
'She is older than the rocks among which she sits . . .'
(Oscar Wilde)[234]

Oscar Wilde's brilliant essay 'The Critic as Artist', written in 1890,
provides a witty commentary on the theories and practices of criticism
in the nineteenth century. His celebration of 'criticism of the highest
kind' as an art form in itself, in that 'It treats the work of art simply as
a starting-point for a new creation,'[235] represents no single critic's theory,
and indeed significantly modifies the individual views of writers such as
Ruskin and Arnold, and yet 'The Critic as Artist' provides an effective
summation of what 'criticism' had come to mean by the end of the
century. Ruskin would have found Wilde's fictional spokesman Gilbert's
view that 'all art is, in its essence, immoral' outrageous, as he would the
aphoristic contentions that 'All artistic creation is absolutely subjective'
and 'the sphere of Art and the sphere of Ethics are absolutely distinct
and separate', and yet it is clear why Wilde found in his work a model
for 'the highest criticism', which is conceived as 'both creative and
independent', as 'the record of one's soul'.[236] Arnold's ideas about criticism are similarly invoked, subverted and reconfigured by Wilde. For
Gilbert, turning Arnold's famous catchphrase on its head, 'the primary
aim of the critic is to see the object as in itself it really is not'; the 'sole
aim' of the critic is 'to chronicle his own impressions'.[237] And yet Arnold's
view of 'the function of the critical spirit' in the nineteenth century is
appropriated and recast in Gilbert's formulation of 'the true man of
culture' as one who 'by fine scholarship and fastidious rejection has
made instinct self-conscious and intelligent, and can separate the work
that has distinction from the work that has it not', one who 'thus attains
to intellectual clarity, and, having learned "the best that is known and

thought in the world," lives – it is not fanciful to say so – with those who are the Immortals'.[238]

Wilde's essay pays homage to Arnold, Ruskin and Pater as individual voices that had a crucial formative influence on the development of criticism in his century, but it also recognises the importance of the periodical press. Wilde distinguishes between cultured critics of 'the higher class', who 'write for the sixpenny papers', and the 'ordinary journalist', who is described as 'giving us the opinions of the uneducated' and 'keep[ing] us in touch with the ignorance of the community',[239] reminding us that, just as Arnold's idea of 'Culture' was conceived as a response to the 'Anarchy' of political democracy, so, with the democratisation of the press, criticism was necessary for the cultural control of a vast and expanding newly-literate reading public. The exaggeratedly effete upper-class tones of Gilbert's sympathy for the 'poor reviewers' of second-rate three-volume novels who are 'apparently reduced to be the reporters of the police-court of literature, the chroniclers of the doing of the habitual criminals of art',[240] underline the imbrication of the literary review with the class dynamics of nineteenth-century society. Interestingly, novels are represented by Gilbert as the chief offenders, presumably because of their commonplace realism. As the genre most closely identified with the new more broadly-based and socially diverse reading public that came into being in the nineteenth century, the novel signified a new cultural force that had to be taken seriously if the reviews were to maintain and extend their own cultural authority.[241] It is significant that, although he insists upon the crucial role of criticism in contemporary nineteenth-century life, Wilde's Gilbert envisages the critic as one who retreats from the demands of the 'real world', who detaches himself from history; he predicts, indeed, that 'as civilisation progresses and we become more highly organised, the elect spirits of each age, the critical and cultured spirits, will grow less and less interested in actual life, and *will seek to gain their impressions almost entirely from what Art has touched.*'[242]

The modern view of what constitutes 'literature', and therefore what constitutes the proper object of criticism, began with Romantic reformulations of poetry and its role at the beginning of the nineteenth century. Wilde's paradoxical conception of criticism's leading role in the modern world, and yet detachment from 'actual life', may be said to stem from a contradiction inherent within Romanticism itself. For while in the hands of writers such as Blake and Shelley literature comes to function as a radical ideology, and indeed the imagination itself is politicised, there is also an insistence on the sovereignty and autonomy of the imagination, which is at odds with the notion that art is socially and politically engaged, that it is connected with history.[243]

Such tensions are apparent in the great manifesto of Romanticism which opens the nineteenth century, Wordsworth's Preface to *Lyrical*

Ballads (1800 and 1802). Wordsworth describes his 'principal object' in the poems there collected as having been 'to chuse incidents and situations from common life, and to relate or describe them, throughout, as far as was possible, in a selection of language really used by men; and, at the same time, to throw over them a certain colouring of imagination, whereby ordinary things should be presented to the mind in an unusual way'.[244] He disassociates himself from those 'Poets, who think that they are conferring honour upon themselves and their art in proportion as they separate themselves from the sympathies of men', and yet recommends that poetry be 'a selection of the language really spoken by men', a 'selection' which 'will entirely separate the composition from the vulgarity and meanness of ordinary life', and remove 'what would otherwise be painful or disgusting in the passion'.[245] The poet is represented, therefore, as both of the people and yet above them, one who can filter out the vulgarity and meanness and disgustingness leaving a purified 'ordinary' language and feeling. He is a *bona fide* spokesman for humanity, and yet he is separated from the commonality by virtue of his imaginative powers, having 'a greater knowledge of human nature, and a more comprehensive soul, than are supposed to be common among mankind'.[246]

The Romantics appropriated for their ideal of the poet qualities which have traditionally been ascribed to women: sensibility, tenderness, sympathy, moral insight, spontaneity, an ability to feel deeply.[247] Not only does the male Romantic poet usurp woman's famous capacity for empathy, intuition and powerful emotion (Keats's 'negative capability', Shelley's 'instinct and intuition of the poetical faculty', Wordsworth's 'spontaneous overflow of powerful feelings'), he even takes over her biological function in Shelley's representation of the work of art 'as a child in the mother's womb'.[248]

And yet it is important to point out that although feminine sensibilities and attributes were appropriated in Romantic poetics, poetry was not thereby feminised or marginalised. On the contrary, Wordsworth disapproved of books that 'Effeminately level down the truth/ To certain notions for the sake/ Of being understood at once.'[249] He advocated a 'manly' style for his exemplary poet, and both the poet and his audience are gendered male: he is 'a man speaking to men'.[250] Moreover, poetry was perceived not in purely aesthetic terms but as public discourse, and therefore belonging to the male domain, as the critic Francis Garden, drawing upon Wordsworth's formulation, makes clear: 'Call [poetry] a fine art as much as you will, – it is discourse, it is utterance; it is man speaking to man, man telling man his thoughts and feelings.'[251]

In the early part of the nineteenth century poetry was a powerful and masculinist mode of public discourse. At the turn of the century the botanist Erasmus Darwin was announcing his scientific discoveries in poetry, and the physicist Humphry Davy, a friend of Coleridge, often cast his thoughts on science and philosophy in poetic form. Although Coleridge distinguished poetry from science on the grounds that 'its *immediate* object [was] pleasure, not truth', science was nevertheless a legitimate subject for the poet who, 'described in *ideal* perfection, brings the whole soul of man into activity'.[252] Poetry, for Coleridge and Wordsworth, as for Blake and for the younger generation of Romantic poets, encompassed not only science but philosophy and politics. In fact poetry was perceived at the beginning of the century as arrogating to itself *all* forms of knowledge and their discourses. For Wordsworth, poetry is 'the breath and finer spirit of all knowledge: it is the impassioned expression which is in the countenance of all Science', while for Shelley 'It is at once the centre and circumference of knowledge; it is that which comprehends all science, and that to which all science must be referred. It is at the same time the root and blossom of all other systems of thought.'[253]

By contrast, the novel was associated with gothic sensationalism, domesticity, and sentimental romance, the domain of female writers and readers. The trope of female reading at the beginning of the nineteenth century, according to Ina Ferris, 'typically featured a passive, languorous body displaying itself on a sofa and neglecting domestic duties as it "devoured" the texts that fed its romantic and sexual fantasies'.[254] The rhetoric of gender in early nineteenth-century critical discourse on the novel tends to conflate the fictional text with its female readers. Ferris cites a review in 1820 of Amelia Opie's *Tales of the Heart*, which opens 'Novels, those dear delightful, condemned, yet irresistibly fascinating productions, boast no class of readers so numerous, no admirers so enthusiastic, as those still more fascinating beings, the young ladies of this fair island.'[255] She also points out how reviewers of the time 'transform texts into exemplary female bodies, either positive or negative', giving as an example John Wilson Croker's 1814 review of Fanny Burney's *The Wanderer*, which he describes as 'an old coquette who endeavours, by the wild tawdriness and laborious gaiety of her attire, to compensate for the loss of the natural charms of freshness, novelty, and youth'.[256] Novels were commonly thus figured as the corrupt and seductive loose women of literature, displacing what Coleridge called the 'correct and manly prose' of such 'masculine intellects' as Hooker, Bacon and Milton with a 'crumbly-friable' style, 'asthmatic', 'short-winded' and 'short-witted', which instils a 'habit of receiving pleasure without any exertion of thought, by the mere excitement of curiosity and sensibility'.[257] Needless to say, Coleridge held the view that 'Women are good novelists, but indifferent poets.'[258]

At the beginning of the century, then, the novel was gendered feminine and accorded little cultural status, whereas poetry was the most prestigious form of literature, perceived as a public discourse and a masculine preserve. However, by the latter part of the century these gender roles were reversed. The novel had found legitimation through the 'manly' fiction of writers such as Walter Scott, and had become the predominant literary form. The 'Silly Novels by Lady Novelists' pilloried by George Eliot in 1856 are absurd partly because they seem so outdated, as are the reviewers who exclaim 'in the choicest phraseology of puffery, that their pictures of life are brilliant, their characters well-drawn, their style fascinating, and their sentiments lofty', at the same time as they treat novelists of 'excellence' such as 'Harriet Martineau, Currer Bell, and Mrs Gaskell . . . as cavalierly as if they had been men.'[259] Meanwhile poetry was progressively marginalised, aestheticised, and feminised.[260] In a review of the first instalment of Coventry Patmore's *The Angel in the House*, written just a year before Eliot's 'Silly Novels . . .', poetry is explicitly associated with the domestic and with the kind of woman celebrated by the poem: '[Home] is a place of refuge from the storm and strife that is for ever going on in this competitive world. What should we do were it not for this happy haven [in] which . . . the grim brow grows smooth in the placid smile of love, poetry comes into the face that is furrowed with the hieroglyphs of business, and the shutup heart opens in the warmth of affection, and expands until it can embrace humanity in the arms of its love.'[261] No longer a forum for the public and masculinist discourses of science and politics, poetry was, by the end of the century, left under the banner of 'art for art's sake' to simply talk about itself. As Wilde observed in 'The Soul of Man under Socialism' (1890),

> In England, the arts that have escaped best are the arts in which the public take no interest. Poetry is an instance of what I mean. We have been able to have fine poetry in England because the public do not read it, and consequently do not influence it. The public like to insult poets because they are individual, but once they have insulted them, they leave them alone.[262]

One historical explanation for this radical decline in the status of poetry is that the cultural role of poetry, along with metaphysics (traditionally regarded as the 'queen' of the sciences), was being challenged by practical science, the findings of which were available to all social classes through the periodical press. By the middle of the century it was science and technological progress, not poetry, which had come to dominate the public imagination, providing the basis for utopian fantasies about the future, and the means of rationally and humanely organising society and dealing with its problems. Whereas Wordsworth and Shelley had perceived poetry to be integral to science and its proper expression, philosophers of science such as John Stuart Mill, writing in the 1830s, carefully distinguished between the spheres belonging to poetry and science, allocating emotional concerns to the former, and rationality and objective empirical experience to the latter. 'Whom, then, shall we call poets?', he asks, and, basing his idea of poetry on Wordsworth's 'emotion recollected in tranquillity', which had had such a profound effect on his own development, but neglecting Romanticism's wider claims for poetry, proposes 'Those who are so constituted, that emotions are the links of association by which their ideas, both sensuous and spiritual, are connected together.'[263] Mill does not go so far as his Utilitarian mentor Jeremy Bentham, who defined poetry as a pack of lies, but nor does he leave much room for it to participate in the public sphere or make truth claims about the world.

This was a matter of deep concern to John Ruskin, who coined the phrase 'pathetic fallacy' to describe the way in which the figurative language of poetry subjectivises experience and distorts the objective 'facts'. Taking as his example the lines from Charles Kingsley's *Alton Locke* (1850), 'They rowed her in across the rolling foam – /The cruel, crawling foam,' Ruskin objects that

> The foam is not cruel, neither does it crawl. The state of mind
> which attributes to it these characters of a living creature is one
> in which the reason is unhinged by grief. All violent feelings
> have the same effect. They produce in us a falseness in all
> our impressions of external things, which I would generally
> characterize as the 'pathetic fallacy.'[264]

Ruskin goes on to argue that although 'we are in the habit of considering this fallacy as eminently a character of poetical description, and the temper of mind in which we allow it, as one eminently poetical, because passionate', it is a 'falseness' that is not to be found in the work of 'the greatest poets'.[265] Although critics such as Roden Noel countered Ruskin's theory by asserting the validity of subjective experience against the current positivist scientific paradigm for knowledge,[266] the consensus among early to mid-Victorians was that pure scientific objectivity was the only grounds for truth. If, as Ruskin and others observed, poetry mixed subjective emotional states with descriptions of empirical facts, then it was guilty of a fatal confusion, a confusion which was associated early in the century with the feminine.

In Alfred Austin's view, the age was beset by all manner of 'feminine infirmities' – including its 'artificiality', its 'self-consciousness', its 'scepticism', its 'distracted aims' – and required a good dose of 'manly concentration' if it were to counteract 'the feminine, timorous, narrow, domesticated temper of the times', 'the feminine, narrow, domesticated, timorous Poetry of the Period', to produce 'great art'.[267] 'Feminine' is, all too clearly, a term of abuse. Austin, who would later succeed Tennyson as Poet Laureate, attacked Tennyson's 'feminine muse' which, he believed, made poetry the 'mere hand-maid' of women's 'interests, susceptibilities, and yearnings'. 'In these [days],' he wrote in 1870, 'as far as the faculty of the imagination and the objects on which it is exerted are concerned, we have, as novelists and poets, only women or men with womanly deficiencies, steeped in the feminine temper of the times, subdued to what they work in, and ringing such changes as can be rung on what . . . has well been called '"everlasting woman."''[268] Austin does not appear to distinguish between women and 'men with womanly deficiencies,' but another critic, Eric Robertson, in his 1883 study *English Poetesses*, detects 'a sexual distinction' between the poetical capabilities of the sexes 'lying in the very soul', although he actually appears to locate difference in her body, specifically her bosom and womb. He declares that the principal cause of woman's 'comparative lack of imagination' is that 'the springs of maternal feeling within her bosom are the secret of her life'. 'What woman,' he asks, 'would not have been Niobe rather than the artist who carved the Niobe?', and he announces 'children are the best poems Providence meant women to produce'. It is hardly surprising that, with encouragement like this, 'women have always been inferior to men as writers of poetry, and they always will be'.[269] According to another critic, R. H. Hutton, women have not produced great poetry because they are hopelessly superficial and fatally caught up in the humdrum of material existence: the poet 'must penetrate and battle for a time, nay even *live*, far beneath the surface of life, in order to create fine poetry', and women's imagination is 'not *separable*, as it were, in anything like the same degree [as that of men], from the visible surface and form of human existence'.[270] As such critical writing suggests, women were systematically excluded from the male discourse of poetry and yet at the same time were represented as the root cause of all that was wrong with contemporary literature.

Nineteenth-century critical vocabulary was, then, highly gendered. Not only poets and novelists, but the genres and sub-genres in which they wrote, the styles they affected, the language they used, the readers to whom they appealed were classified as masculine or feminine. Sexuality is the not-so-hidden agenda of many a putatively objective literary judgement. For instance Swinburne, who was attacked for his 'fleshly' concerns and his decadent and often quite explicit sexual references, is at times especially anxious to assert his healthy masculine credentials by marginalising some forms of poetry as feminine:

> with English versifiers now, the idyllic form is alone in fashion
> . . . We have idyls good and bad, ugly and pretty; idyls of the
> farm and the mill; idyls of the dining-room and the deanery;
> idyls of the gutter and the gibbet . . . The idyllic form is best
> for domestic and pastoral poetry. It is naturally on a lower
> level than that of tragic or lyric verse. Its gentle and maidenly

lips are somewhat narrow for the stream, and somewhat cold for the fire of song. It is very fit for the sole diet of girls; not very fit for the sole sustenance of man.[271]

'The office of adult art', he concludes, 'is neither puerile nor feminine, but virile.'[272] But Swinburne's protestations are treated with scorn by Alfred Austin who, always quick to spot a deviant, responds,

> Has Mr. Swinburne, acting up to his excellent theory, turned his back on the haunts of feminine muses, struck out a masculine strain, and wrung from strenuous chords nervous and extolling hymns worthy of men and gods? . . . his lyrics and ballads are [not] fit for the sole or even for part of the diet of girls. But what have men . . . – men brave, muscular, bold, upright, chivalrous – I will not say chaste, for that is scarcely a masculine quality . . . , but at any rate clean – . . . men daring, enduring, short of speech, and terrible in action – what have these to do with Mr. Swinburne's Venuses and Chastelards, his Anactorias and Faustines, his Dolores, his Sapphos, or his Hermaphroditus? . . . I do not say that they are not fair, much less that they are illegitimate, subjects for the poet's pen, but are they masculine? That is the question.[273]

Austin's conclusions about the role of the feminine in modern literature are unequivocal: 'We need not close our ear to the feminine note, but should not listen to it over much. The masculine note is necessarily dominant in life; and the note that is dominant in life should be dominant in literature and, most of all, in poetry.'[274]

Should it, though, be dominant in criticism? This was a matter of some debate in the nineteenth century, for arguably criticism legitimately required those 'feminine' attributes of sensibility and responsiveness which were considered so inappropriate to the highest art forms. However, even here R. H. Hutton, for instance, writing of Walter Pater and the 'cultus of impressionability', objects to the aesthetic critic's habit of 'recording every shade of namby-pamby tenderness in which his unreal passion for some rural beauty died away', and recommends that 'ordinary boys' would be better far 'hungering after the world of independent action for which they are not as yet mature enough, than to be tossing about on the ripple of small susceptibilities and emotions'.[275] W. H. Mallock was another who clearly preferred the manly tones of Matthew Arnold (parodied in his satirical *tour de force The New Republic* (1877) as Mr Luke) to the feminine cadences of Walter Pater, his Mr Rose, whose perverse sexual tastes are linked to his critical stance. Mr Rose, 'raising his eyebrows wearily, and sending his words floating down the table in a languid monotone', is given a thoroughly decadent script:

'I rather look upon life as a chamber, which we decorate as we
would decorate the chamber of the woman or the youth that
we love, tinting the walls of it with symphonies of subdued
colour, and filling it with works of fair form, and with
flowers, and with strange scents, and with instruments of
music . . . We have learned the weariness of creeds; and know
that for us the grave has no secrets. We have learned that the
aim of life is life; and what does successful life consist in?
Simply,' said Mr. Rose, speaking very slowly, and with a soft
solemnity, 'in the consciousness of exquisite living – in the
making our own each highest thrill of joy that the moment
offers us – be it some touch of colour on the sea or on the
mountains, the early dew in the crimson shadows of a rose,
the shining of a woman's limbs in clear water, or —— '
    Here unfortunately a sound of ''Sh' broke softly from
several mouths.[276]

As Mallock's parodic version of his style and views suggests, Pater's
own interests in art and sexuality strike a very different note from
Austin's. In the essay on Leonardo da Vinci which Wilde admired so
much, for instance, Pater observes that 'though he handles sacred subjects continually, he is the most profane of painters', nowhere more so
than in the painting of St John the Baptist in the Louvre, 'one of the few
naked figures Leonardo painted – whose delicate brown flesh and woman's hair no one would go out into the wilderness to seek, and whose
treacherous smile would have us understand something far beyond the
outward gesture or circumstance.'[277] This St John is as sexually ambiguous as he is morally ambiguous. Pater was fascinated by the painter's
sexual hybrids, by the 'face of doubtful sex'[278] which is a motif of his
work; indeed he uses such a face as the frontispiece to *Studies in the
History of the Renaissance* (1873).
    The fact that Yeats extracted Pater's famous description of the Mona
Lisa from this essay and reprinted it as a prose-poem to open his edition
of the *Oxford Book of Modern Verse* (1936) suggests that it was a different
kind of critical writing from Austin's in other ways too, in being exemplary of Wilde's ideal of criticism as itself a creative art. For Yeats, the
passage signalled the 'revolt against Victorianism', specifically against
the 'scientific and moral discursiveness' which were its besetting vices.
As a self-styled 'aesthetic critic', whose task is to delineate 'What is this
song or picture, this engaging personality presented in life or in a book
to *me*?', Pater had little time for the so-called scientific approach to
criticism of art historians such as Crowe and Cavalcaselle. In his essay
on Giorgione he comments on their work

    The accomplished science of the subject has come at last, and,
    as in other instances, has not made the past more real for us,

but assured us that we possess of it less than we seemed to
possess . . . now, in the 'New Vasari,' the great traditional
reputation, woven with so profuse demand on men's
admiration, has been scrutinised thread by thread; and what
remains of the most vivid and stimulating of Venetian masters,
a live flame, as it seems, in those shadowy times, has been
reduced almost to a name by his most recent critics.

In place of 'the real Giorgione and his authentic extant works' Pater
proposes a Giorgione perceived as 'a sort of personification of Venice',
and the 'vraie verité' of the painter is realised, by means of 'those more
liberal and durable impressions which . . . lie beyond, and must supplement, the narrower range of the strictly ascertained facts'.[279]

Pater was criticised by his contemporaries for failing to approach his
artistic and literary subjects 'by the true scientific method',[280] and yet he
himself frequently deployed the techniques and terminology of scientific
investigation to underwrite his own theory of impressionistic criticism.
Mischievously making use of Arnold to serve his own very different
purpose, he compares aesthetic criticism to the experimental methods
of physics and chemistry:

'to see the object as in itself it really is,' has been justly said to
be the aim of all true criticism whatever; and in aesthetic
criticism the first step towards seeing one's object as it really
is, is to know one's impression as it really is, to discriminate
it, to realise it distinctly. The objects with which aesthetic
criticism deals – music, poetry, artistic and accomplished forms
of human life – are indeed receptacles of so many powers or
forces: they possess, like the products of nature, so many
virtues or qualities. What is this song or picture, this engaging
personality presented in life or in a book, to *me*? What effect
does it really produce on me? Does it give me pleasure? and if
so, what sort or degree of pleasure? How is my nature
modified by its presence, and under its influence? The answers
to these questions are the original facts with which the
aesthetic critic has to do; and, as in the study of light, of
morals, of number, one must realise such primary data for
one's self, or not at all . . .

The aesthetic critic, then, regards all the objects with which
he has to do, all works of art, and the fairer forms of nature
and human life, as powers or forces producing pleasurable
sensations, each of a more or less peculiar or unique kind.
This influence he feels, and wishes to explain, by reducing it
to its elements . . . the function of the aesthetic critic is to
distinguish, to analyse, and separate from its adjuncts, the

virtue by which a picture, a landscape, a fair personality in
life or in a book, produces this special impression of beauty or
pleasure, to indicate what the source of that impression is, and
under what conditions it is experienced. His end is reached
when he has disengaged that virtue, and noted it, as a chemist
notes some natural element, for himself and others.[281]

Formalism and realism are subsumed into an all-embracing version of
affective criticism which is ironically itself made the subject of rigorous scientific analysis. Moreover, Pater's rejection of the possibility of
a truly objective knowledge is itself founded on a relativistic philosophy
which finds confirmation in evolutionary theory. But the subjectivism
which, for Pater, was a logical consequence of the fact that 'the idea
of development . . . is at last invading one by one, as the secret of
their explanation, all the products of the mind, the very mind itself,
the abstract reason; our certainty, for instance, that two and two make
four', remained a stumbling block for his critics. Reviewing *The Renaissance*, W. J. Stillman complains that he has learned 'not so much of the
theme as of Mr Pater himself', while Margaret Oliphant objects to the
fact that Pater finds in Botticelli's 'reverential, pathetic angel-faces, and
wistful, thoughtful Madonnas, a sentiment of dislike and repulsion from
the divine mystery placed among them' that was 'as alien to the spirit
of a medieval Italian, as it is perfectly consistent with that of a delicate
Oxford Don in the latter half of the nineteenth century'.[282]

But for Pater it is not only the impressions and sensations and personality of the viewer that are at issue in the aesthetic appreciation of
a work of art, but the expressive qualities of the work itself, and the
temperament of the artist represented therein. In his view, impersonality
in art was as impossible a concept as objectivity in criticism: 'The artist
will be felt; his subjectivity must and will colour the incidents, as his
very bodily eye *selects* the aspects of things.'[283] Moreover, this is something to be celebrated. By contrast with Ruskin's emphasis on 'truth to
nature' and his strictures against the 'pathetic fallacy', Pater seeks to
identify 'the seal on a man's work of what is most inward and peculiar
in his moods, and manner of apprehension'.[284] The very 'fleshliness' of
Dante Gabriel Rossetti's poetry that so offends Robert Buchanan is
what appeals to Pater, just as it is the very flagrancy of the poet's abuse
of the 'pathetic fallacy' that calls forth his highest praise:

With him, indeed, as in some revival of the old mythopoeic
age, common things – dawn, moon, night – are full of human
or personal expression, full of sentiment . . . with Rossetti
this sense of lifeless nature, after all, is translated to a higher
service, in which it does but incorporate itself with some phase
of strong emotion. Every one understands how this may

happen at critical moments of life, what a weirdly expressive soul may have crept, even in full noonday, into 'the white-flower'd elder-thicket,' when Godiva saw it 'gleam through the Gothic archways in the wall,' at the end of her terrible ride. To Rossetti it is so always, because to him life is a crisis at every moment.[285]

What to Austin would have been a sure indication that he was over-wrought and hysterical, and therefore, like Tennyson, irredeemably feminine, renders Rossetti, by the criteria of the aesthetic critic, 'an object of [a] peculiar kind of interest'.[286]

For Pater, as Wilde pointed out, criticism was an imaginative, creative activity, and he developed innovative prose forms, such as the 'Imaginary Portrait', in which to articulate his critical ideas. Although his luscious style seems quintessentially late nineteenth-century, he clearly inherits the Romantic sensibility of critics such as Coleridge, Lamb, Hazlitt and De Quincey, in whose essays on literature and art the modern distinction between critical and imaginative writing is not at issue. In their work, as in Pater's, subjectively determined aesthetic judgement is an inextricable part of the historical recovery of the writer or artist through their works. The artefact itself acts as a catalyst for the meeting of two personalities: that of the artist and that of the critic. A late nineteenth-century critic who shared Pater's commitment to impressionism, 'Vernon Lee' (the pen-name of Violet Paget), explained the fragmentary nature of her critical enterprise in a way that De Quincey, for instance, might have done: 'I have tried to understand only where my curiosity was awakened.'[287] De Quincey's wonderful essay 'On the Knocking at the Gate in *Macbeth*' (1823) arises from exactly such personal curiosity, and begins,

> From my boyish days I had always felt a great perplexity on one point in *Macbeth*. It was this: the knocking at the gate, which succeeds to the murder of Duncan, produced to my feelings an effect for which I never could account: the effect was – that it reflected back upon the murder a peculiar awfulness and a depth of solemnity: yet, however obstinately I endeavoured with my understanding to comprehend this, for many years I never could see *why* it should produce such an effect.[288]

Starting, then, with the effect upon himself of this episode, De Quincey goes on to explain how and why such an effect is achieved. His interest is in the character of Macbeth, and in how Shakespeare makes him live for us through such dramatic techniques – how 'the retiring of the human heart and the entrance of the fiendish heart was to be expressed and made sensible' – and his conclusion is that 'the further we press in our discoveries, the more we shall see proofs of design and self-supporting arrangement where the careless eye had seen nothing but accident!'[289] Interestingly 'Vernon Lee' was later to undertake a similarly close analysis of De Quincey's own writing in her essay 'The Syntax of De Quincey', in support of her thesis that 'The craft of the Writer consists . . . in manipulating the contents of his Reader's mind' through 'literary construction'.[290] In it she argues that there is a 'connection between the structure of a man's sentences and his more human characteristics; and that style, in so far as it is individual, is but a kind of gesture or gait, revealing with the faithfulness of an unconscious habit, the essential peculiarities of the Writer's temperament and modes of being'.[291] The 'something decidedly queer' that she detects in De Quincey's management of verbs becomes the basis for a brilliant exercise in 'literary psychology', in which his syntactical 'indifference to action', the 'nervelessness, of De Quincey's style', is related to 'the infirmity of the opiumeater's will'.[292]

One wonders whether Coleridge's prose style would have been judged by Lee to share De Quincey's characteristic stylistic 'infirmity'. The period in which Coleridge wrote and delivered the series of lectures on Shakespeare which generated such an extraordinary new wave of Shakespearean criticism amongst his contemporaries, marked a crisis in the history of his own opium addiction. But, his personal difficulties notwithstanding, the lectures were a great success, and may have been a catalyst for not only De Quincey's essays on the psychology of Shakespeare's stagecraft but also Lamb's on his plots, Hazlitt's lectures on his characters, and indirectly, therefore, Keats's informal epistolary criticism of his works. Coleridge himself implies a parallel between the importance and originality of his critical method and contemporary developments in the physical sciences by pointing out that his first course of lectures on Shakespeare was delivered in 'the same year in which Sir Humphry Davy, a fellow-lecturer, made his great revolutionary discoveries in chemistry'.[293] Informed by the ideas of German critics such as Friedrich Schlegel and philosophers such as Kant, the 'distinguishing feature' of whose philosophy he describes as that it 'treat[s] every subject in reference to the operation of the mental faculties to which it specially appertains',[294] Coleridge's lectures inaugurated a radical new development in English criticism by considering Shakespeare's plays as manifestations of his creative imagination. In line with his broader philosophical position, Coleridge was interested in the innate 'organic form' of Shakespearean drama, and in Shakespeare himself as 'a genial understanding directing self-consciously a power and an implicit wisdom deeper than consciousness'.[295] Perhaps the finest example of his method is to be found in his lecture on *Hamlet*. Here, as a report in the *Gazette* explained, he addresses the question of 'The seeming inconsistencies in the conduct and character of Hamlet [which] have long exercised the conjectural ingenuity of critics.' Rejecting the notion that these are a consequence of 'the capricious and irregular genius of Shakespeare' as 'vulgar' and 'indolent', Coleridge traces the character of Hamlet to 'Shakespeare's deep and accurate science in mental philosophy'.[296] Drawing upon personal experience, 'on the constitution of our own minds', and suggesting that Shakespeare's principal method of characterisation was '[to conceive] any one intellectual or moral faculty in morbid excess and then [to place] himself, thus mutilated and diseased, under given circumstances',[297] Coleridge reads Hamlet's character as a profound study in human nature:

> In Hamlet I conceive him to have wished to exemplify the moral necessity of a due balance between our attention to outward objects and our meditation on inward thoughts – a due balance between the real and the imaginary world. In Hamlet this balance does not exist – his thoughts, images, and fancy, [being] far more vivid than his perceptions, and his very perceptions, instantly passing thro' the medium of his contemplations, and acquiring as they pass a form and color not naturally their own. Hence great, enormous, intellectual activity, and a consequent proportionate aversion to real action, with all its symptoms and accompanying qualities.[298]

In Coleridge's critical writing the human mind, its qualities and behaviour, are continually represented as gendered.[299] Coleridge portrays Hamlet as suffering from an excess of 'masculine' intellect, but his creator, Shakespeare himself, as an androgynous fusion of 'masculine' and 'feminine' qualities:

> Shakespeare, no mere child of nature; no automaton of genius; no passive vehicle of inspiration possessed by the spirit, not possessing it; first studied patiently, meditated deeply, understood minutely, till knowledge become habitual and intuitive wedded itself to his habitual feelings, and at length gave birth to that stupendous power, by which he stands alone, with no equal or second in his own class.

Like Shelley, Coleridge arrogates to the male poet a birth-giving role, and like Keats he further feminises Shakespeare by stressing his capacity for 'negative capability': we are told that he 'darts himself forth, and passes into all the forms of human character and passion'; he 'becomes all things, yet for ever remaining himself'.[300] And yet, at the same time, Coleridge takes pains to differentiate Shakespeare's genius from the realm of the feminine by making it clear that it has the 'stupendous power' of a male child. His masculine credentials remain unsullied if his 'feminine' 'characterlessness' is represented as just one facet of his exemplary poetic 'universality'.[301]

Coleridge's anxieties about the gender of Shakespeare's genius are interestingly echoed in Walter Bagehot's 1853 essay on 'Shakespeare – The Man', in which Shakespeare is compared with Plato. Plato's writings are described as 'the intellect surveying and delineating intellectual characteristics', and therefore masculine; for, 'The mere intellect of a woman is a mere nothing. It originates nothing, it transmits nothing, it retains nothing'. By contrast, 'Shakespeare's being, like a woman's worked as a whole. He was capable of intellectual abstractedness, but commonly he was touched with the sense of earth.' Again he is represented as having an androgynous quality of 'thoughtful feeling'.[302] Like Coleridge, Bagehot is interested in 'the narrations of uneducated people' in Shakespeare, which, like the language of women, lack method. He cites Coleridge's 'nice criticism' that

> People of this sort are unable to look a long way in front of them and they wander from the right path. They get on too fast with one half, and then the other hopelessly lags. They can tell a story exactly as it is told to them (as an animal can go step by step where it has been before), but they can't calculate its bearings beforehand, or see how it is to be adapted to those to whom they are speaking, nor do they know how much they have thoroughly told and how much they have not.[303]

But Bagehot puts this observation to different use. Having noted disparagingly that 'Of course a metaphysician can account for it, and like S.T.C., assure you that if he had not observed it, he could have predicted it in a moment,' he himself points out that 'it is most likely that Shakespeare derived his acquaintance with it from the fact, from actual hearing, and not from what may be the juice, but is the slower process of metaphysical deduction'.[304] And so whereas Coleridge analyses the absence of method in the speech of Mistress Quickly as the product of 'an habitual submission of the understanding to mere events and images as such, and independent of any power of the mind to classify or appropriate them', Bagehot cites her narrative style as proof 'that Shakespeare had an enormous specific acquaintance with the common people.'[305]

Bagehot himself was somewhat contemptuous of 'the common people', and therefore, in political terms, resembled the conservative Coleridge more than the radical Romantic critic, William Hazlitt, who believed that women and other 'Uneducated people have most exuberance of invention, and the greatest freedom from prejudice,' and that 'Shakespear's was evidently an uneducated mind, both in the freshness of his imagination, and in the variety of his views.'[306] But in other respects Bagehot's pragmatic style of literary criticism (he decides on the basis of a close reading of his writing that Shakespeare was 'a judge of dogs', 'an out-of-door sporting man' who 'had been after a hare')[307] suggests that Hazlitt's Shakespearean criticism would have appealed to him much more than Coleridge's. It was not only their different political allegiances that distinguished Hazlitt and Coleridge as critics of Shakespeare, but their whole style of proceeding. Unlike Coleridge, who responds intellectually to the large philosophical ideas in Shakespeare's plays, rather than experientially to the individual poetic effects, Hazlitt grounds his criticism in 'well-founded particulars'.[308] Hence his interest in Shakespeare's characterisation lies less in the abstract general truths which fascinate Coleridge than in the particular details, in the fact that 'When he Conceived of a character, whether real or imaginary, he not only entered into all its thoughts and feelings, but seemed instantly, and as if by touching a secret spring, to be surrounded by all the same objects, "subject to the same skyey influences", the same local, outward, and unforseen accidents which would occur in reality.' He gives as an example a scene from *Hamlet*, and his discussion of it provides an effective contrast to Coleridge's method:

> Hamlet, in the scene with Rosencrans and Guildenstern, somewhat abruptly concludes his fine soliloquy on life by saying, 'Man delights not me, nor woman neither, though by your smiling you seem to say so.' Which is explained by their answer – 'My lord, we had no such stuff in our thoughts. But we smiled to think, if you delight not in man, what lenten entertainment the players shall receive from you, whom we met on the way': – as if while Hamlet was making this speech, his two old schoolfellows from Wittenberg had been really standing by, and he had seen them smiling by stealth, at the idea of the players crossing their minds. It is not 'a combination and a form' of words, a set speech or two, a preconcerted theory of a character, that will do this: but all the persons concerned must have been present in the poet's imagination, as at a kind of rehearsal; and whatever would have passed through their minds on the occasion, and have been observed by others, passed through his, and is made known to the reader.[309]

Hazlitt had a much greater sense of theatre than Coleridge, and a highly developed visual sense. He was, indeed, a talented painter, and not only did he bring his appreciation of the pictorial to the aid of literary criticism, but he also produced a substantial body of art criticism. Here too his emphasis is on the individual and the particular as opposed to the general and the ideal. In a series of articles for the journal *The Champion* in 1814 he mounted an attack on the Royal Academy and the kind of art it supported and promoted, basing his argument on a close critique of the principles upon which it was founded as expounded by Sir Joshua Reynolds in his *Discourses*. Against Reynolds' view that 'genius and invention are principally shewn in borrowing the ideas, and imitating the excellences of others', he argues for originality and asserts 'The imitation of nature is the great object of art.'[310] Against Reynolds' insistence upon the ideal, he maintains 'The concrete, and not the abstract, is the object of painting, and of all the works of imagination.'[311] In 1848 the members of the Pre-Raphaelite Brotherhood were to take a similar stand against the values of the Academy, basing their manifesto on the theories of John Ruskin, the first volume of whose *Modern Painters* had been published in 1843. Ruskin makes little reference to his predecessor, but he had read Hazlitt's art criticism, and would have found there many of his own most cherished principles, even if their tastes about particular artists differed; indeed, even where they did, their descriptions of certain works, such as Poussin's *Deluge*, which Hazlitt liked and Ruskin considered a 'monstrous abortion', are oddly similar.[312] Moreover, their tastes did converge in some important cases. Although Hazlitt admired Poussin and Claude, who compare so unfavourably with Turner in Ruskin's opinion, in 1817 he had described Turner as 'the ablest landscape painter now living', anticipating Ruskin's great defence by nearly three decades.

Both Hazlitt and Coleridge had an influence on the directions that were to be taken by later nineteenth-century critics of both literature and art, but, as was the case in many areas of intellectual life, criticism became noticeably more professionalised from the early 1840s onwards. Increasingly the criticism of art, in particular, became a subject of specialised knowledge rather than of amateur interest. The career of Anna Jameson, who has been described as 'the first professional English art historian',[313] provides an interesting example of the emergence of the specialist writer on art. Jameson published her first comments on art in 1826 in the form of an anonymous fictionalised account of her travels on the Continent, *Diary of an Ennuyée*. However, her early career as a professional writer was extraordinarily diverse. Among the works she produced, for instance, was an important study of Shakespeare's heroines, entitled *Characteristics of Women, Moral, Poetical and Historical* (1832), which is in the tradition of Hazlitt's character-orientated criticism of Shakespeare, but which because of its gender inflection represents a significant modification of the readings of Hazlitt, whom she describes as remarkable 'for his utter ignorance of women, generally and individually.'[314] Whilst it was fairly commonplace in the middle of the nineteenth century for Shakespeare's heroines to be celebrated as types of idealised womanhood – witness Ruskin's invocation of Shakespeare's exemplary women as authority for his own paean to 'Woman' in 'Of Queens' Gardens' – Jameson's work is exceptional in that she releases her heroines from male-determined plots in which marriage and death are the only destinies.[315] Even in this work the visual arts are present by analogy, as she describes Portia and Shylock as 'a magnificent beauty-breathing Titian by the side of a gorgeous Rembrandt' and Cordelia as an Italian Madonna, and as she paints in 'the gothic grandeur, the rich chiaroscuro, and deep-toned colours of Lady Macbeth'.[316]

However, although her interest in the visual arts is apparent in the publications of the first fifteen years of her writing career, from 1840 onwards she devoted herself seriously to a number of major art historical projects which mark a professional turn in her career, the most significant of which were her *Memoirs of the Early Italian Painters* (1845), *The Poetry of Sacred and Legendary Art* (1848), and *Legends of the Madonna* (1852). The former was modelled on the style of Vasari's *Lives of the Artists*, and contributed to the revival of interest in the Italian 'primitives' which was such a feature of the English art world of the 1840s. However, both the form and the subject matter of the latter two works were highly innovative; together with *Legends of the Monastic Orders* (1850) and the posthumously published *History of Our Lord* (1864), they constituted the first attempt by an English art historian at a comprehensive exposition of Christian iconography.

Her writings reached a popular audience – indeed, the French art historian A.-F. Rio believed that they had a greater effect than those of any of her contemporaries on the artistic education of the British public[317] – and they also influenced the work of numerous Victorian writers and artists, from George Eliot and the Brownings to Dante Gabriel Rossetti and even, it has been asserted, Ruskin, despite his disparaging comment in *Praeterita* that 'Mrs Jameson was absolutely without knowledge or instinct of painting (and had no sharpness of insight even for anything else); but she was candid and industrious, with a pleasant disposition to make the best of all she saw, and to say, compliantly that a picture was good, if anybody had ever said so before.'[318]

There are certainly parallels between Ruskin's and Jameson's writings on art. Both, for instance, were interested in early Italian art, and both were influenced by Rio's book on 'the poetry of Christian art'. But there were important differences between their respective ideas about art and objectives as art historians and critics. Whereas Jameson's was a relativist aesthetic founded on a belief in historical difference, and her aim was to facilitate an understanding of the artefacts of the past, Ruskin believed that there were absolute, transhistorical standards of beauty and art by which all art should be judged, and that modern painters should aspire to emulate the greatest art of the past.

The first volume of *Modern Painters*, which appeared in 1843, was by an anonymous Oxford graduate, but this work, together with *The Stones of Venice* (1851–53), was to establish Ruskin as the leading critic of his day and an authority on all matters aesthetic. The early volumes of *Modern Painters* (which ran to five volumes, the last of which was published in 1860) insist upon the faithful representation of the divinely inspired truths of nature in art and criticise landscape painting before Turner for failing to depict nature truthfully. 'Go to Nature in all singleness of heart,' he exhorted young artists, 'and walk with her laboriously and trustingly, having no other thoughts but how best to penetrate her meaning, and remember her instruction.'[319] It was a highly moralistic and prescriptive view of the status and function of art, based upon a religious reading of nature which was to be radically undermined by those scientists who were also in the 1840s and 1850s 'penetrating' nature's meaning. The artist is figured, in a way that is by now familiar to us, as androgynous, as capable of a masculine penetration of nature's secrets and also of feelings which are gendered feminine:

> The whole function of the artist in the world is to be a seeing and feeling creature; to be an instrument of such tenderness and sensitiveness, that no shadow, no hue, no line, no instantaneous and evanescent impression of the visual things around him, nor any of the emotions which they are capable of conveying to the spirit which has been given him, shall either be left unrecorded, or fade from the book of record . . . The work of his life is to be two-fold only; to see, to feel.[320]

Like Keats's negatively capable Shakespeare, Ruskin's ideal artist is construed as 'becom[ing] great when he becomes invisible'.[321] The play and power of the imagination 'depend altogether on our being able to forget ourselves and enter, like possessing spirits, into the bodies of things about us.'[322] Feminine self-abnegation combines with masculine possession of the bodies of things. Moreover, although he proposes that the artist become 'passive in sight, passive in utterance,'[323] what he recommends is, not a womanly passivity but a Wordsworthian 'wise passiveness' which tempers feminine impressionability with masculine wisdom. It is just such an androgynous ideal that he represents Turner as supremely achieving when he notes 'in these later subjects Nature herself was composing with him'.[324]

Modern Painters is, of course, much more than a set of prescriptions about what constitutes great art. As one of the finest stylists of the twentieth century, Virginia Woolf, remarked, 'Still, after sixty years or so, the style in which page after page of *Modern Painters* is written takes our breath away. We find ourselves marvelling at the words, as if all the fountains of the English language had been set playing in the sunlight for our pleasure.'[325] Ruskin paints a landscape with words as surely as ever Turner did with oils, and records a sublime poetic experience of the divinity of nature in prose as eloquently as Wordsworth did in verse:

It had been wild weather when I left Rome, and all across the
Campagna the clouds were sweeping in sulphurous blue, with
a clap of thunder or two, and breaking gleams of sun across
the Claudian aqueduct lighting up the infinity of its arches like
the bridge of chaos. But as I climbed the long slope of the
Alban Mount, the storm swept finally to the north, and the
noble outline of the domes of Albano, and graceful darkness of
its ilex grove, rose against pure streaks of alternate blue and
amber; the upper sky gradually flushing through the last
fragments of rain-cloud in deep palpitating azure, half aether
and half dew. The noonday sun came slanting down the rocky
slopes of La Riccia, and their masses of entangled and tall
foliage, whose autumnal tints were mixed with the wet
verdure of a thousand evergreens, were penetrated with it as
with rain. I cannot call it colour, it was conflagration. Purple,
and crimson, and scarlet, like the curtains of God's tabernacle,
the rejoicing trees sank into the valley in showers of light,
every separate leaf quivering with buoyant and burning life;
each, as it turned to reflect or to transmit the sunbeam, first a
torch and then an emerald. Far up into the recesses of the
valley, the green vistas arched like the hollows of mighty
waves of some crystalline sea, with the arbutus flowers dashed
along their flanks for foam, and silver flakes of orange spray
tossed into the air around them, breaking over the grey walls
of rock into a thousand separate stars, fading and kindling
alternately as the weak wind lifted and let them fall. Every
blade of grass burned like the golden floor of heaven, opening
in sudden gleams as the foliage broke and closed above it, as
sheet-lightning opens in a cloud at sunset; the motionless
masses of dark rock – dark though flushed with scarlet lichen,
casting their quiet shadows across its restless radiance, the
fountain underneath them filling its marble hollow with blue
mist and fitful sound; and over all, the multitudinous bars of
amber and rose, the sacred clouds that have no darkness, and
only exist to illumine, were seen in fathomless intervals
between the solemn and orbed repose of the stone pines,
passing to lose themselves in the last, white, blinding lustre of
the measureless line where the Campagna melted into the blaze
of the sea.[326]

At the end of this extraordinary passage, which with its 'rejoicing trees',
the 'restless radiance' of the rock face, and 'solemn . . . repose of the
stone pines' provides a marvellous counterpoint to his stern reprimands
against the use of the pathetic fallacy, Ruskin poses the simple question,
'Tell me who is likest this, Poussin or Turner?' As Ruskin has, with his

pen, painted for his reader a Turner, the question is a rhetorical one.[327] Ruskin adopts a similar strategy elsewhere in volume 1 of *Modern Painters*, painting a sublime, divinely suffused Alpine landscape, for example, after the manner of Turner, and then asking rhetorically 'tell me who has best delivered this His message unto men!'[328] His skill at summoning up the visual scene reminds us that Ruskin was himself an accomplished artist, but elsewhere he is the critic, describing Turner's actual canvases, even if he does treat the work of art, as Wilde observed, 'simply as a starting-point for a new creation,' as in his description of the *Slave Ship*:

> The noblest sea that Turner has ever painted, and, if so, the noblest certainly ever painted by man, is that of the *Slave Ship*, the chief Academy picture of the Exhibition of 1840. It is a sunset on the Atlantic, after prolonged storm; but the storm is partially lulled, and the torn and streaming rain-clouds are moving in scarlet lines to lose themselves in the hollow of the night. The whole surface of the sea included in the picture is divided into two ridges of enormous swell, not high, nor local, but a low broad heaving of the whole ocean, like the lifting of its bosom by deep-drawn breath after the torture of the storm. Between these two ridges the fire of the sunset falls along the trough of the sea, dyeing it with an awful but glorious light, the intense and lurid splendour which burns like gold, and bathes like blood. Along this fiery path and valley, the tossing waves by which the swell of the sea is restlessly divided, lift themselves in dark, indefinite, fantastic forms, each casting a faint and ghastly shadow behind it along the illumined foam. They do not rise everywhere, but three or four together in wild groups, fitfully and furiously, as the under strength of the swell compels or permits them; leaving between them treacherous spaces of level and whirling water, now lighted with green and lamp like fire, now flashing back the gold of the declining sun, now fearfully dyed from above with the undistinguishable images of the burning clouds, which fall upon them in flakes of crimson and scarlet, and give to the reckless waves the added motion of their own fiery flying. Purple and blue, the lurid shadows of the hollow breakers are cast upon the mist of night, which gathers cold and low, advancing like the shadow of death upon the guilty ship as it labours amidst the lightning of the sea, its thin masts written upon the sky in lines of blood, girded with condemnation in that fearful hue which signs the sky with horror, and mixes its flaming flood with the sunlight, and, cast far along the desolate heave of the sepulchral waves, incarnadines the multitudinous sea.[329]

In this sexually charged description of a stormy sea figured as a woman's body, 'lifting . . . its bosom by deep-drawn breath after the torture of the storm', and left bleeding by the passage of 'the guilty ship', the imagery of rape infuses the entire seascape with the crime signified by the ship, the traffic in slaves. It is an extraordinary rhetorical *tour de force*, in which the language utterly overpowers and controls the graphic image.

Both the highly wrought gothic style of the *Slave Ship* extract and the 'spontaneous overflow of powerful feeling' in response to nature's power recollected in the *La Riccia* passage demonstrate in different ways the affiliations of Ruskin's style with the Romantic tradition. In his emotional and spiritual sensitivity to the mystical power of the natural landscape he was profoundly influenced by Wordsworth; in his search for an organic unity which finds harmony in the infinite variety of the minutely particularised and constantly changing forms of nature he resembles Coleridge; the sensuousness of his language recalls Keats; his exaltation of the artist as a seer and of the creative power of the imagination is indebted to Romantic poetics; and the artists and writers he most admired, such as Turner and Byron, testify to his Romantic tastes. And yet Ruskin was critical of the introspection encouraged by Romanticism, and of its tendency to falsify nature through excess of feeling. Although he believed 'that the eye cannot rest on a material form, in a moment of depression or exultation, without communicating to that form a spirit and a life',[330] he did not wish to see objective truth overwhelmed and distorted by subjective impression. And yet it is the artist's response to nature that distinguishes art from science: 'Science studies the relations of things to each other: but art studies only their relations to man: and it requires of everything . . . only this, – what that thing is to the human heart.'[331] Art, like criticism, requires a balance between the objective, scientific, masculine fact and the subjective, feminine heart.

Ruskin's criticism of the English Romantic poets for seeing the world as a set of symbols whose function was to reveal the poet's psyche suggests that this balance was at best somewhat precarious. Interestingly Matthew Arnold, who waged a war against a similarly construed 'multitudinousness' by urging the necessity of seeing 'the object as in itself it really is', was also critical of 'the defect[s]' of English Romanticism.[332] Despite the reverence for Wordsworth which is so manifest in his poetry, Arnold accuses him of having 'plunged himself in the inward life', of having 'voluntarily cut himself off from the modern spirit'. His verdict on 'the English poetry of the first quarter of this century' is that 'with plenty of energy, plenty of creative force', it 'did not know enough'.[333] But as well as condemning the English Romantic poets for not having read enough books, Arnold castigates them for having read too much Shakespeare, whose work, in his view, has had a pernicious influence upon modern poetry. Among his great poetic abilities, Arnold explains,

Shakespeare had 'a special one of his own; a gift, namely, of happy, abundant, and ingenious expression, eminent and unrivalled', and it is this aspect of his writing which, to the neglect of all his other excellences as a poet, has proved to be the downfall of modern poetry:

> These other excellences were his fundamental excellences *as a poet*; what distinguishes the artist from the mere amateur, says Goethe, is *Architectonicè* in the highest sense; that power of execution, which creates, forms, and constitutes: not the profoundness of single thoughts, not the richness of imagery, not the abundance of illustration. But these attractive accessories of a poetical work being more easily seized than the spirit of the whole, and these accessories being possessed by Shakespeare in an unequalled degree, a young writer having recourse to Shakespeare as his model runs great risk of being vanquished and absorbed by them, and, in consequence, of reproducing, according to the measure of his power, these, and these alone. Of this preponderating quality of Shakespeare's genius, accordingly, almost the whole of modern English poetry has, it appears to me, felt the influence. To the exclusive attention on the part of his imitators to this it is in a great degree owing, that of the majority of modern poetical works the details alone are valuable, the composition worthless.

For 'clearness of arrangement, rigour of development, simplicity of style' he advises the modern poet to follow the 'purity of method' of the more austere, 'safer' classical authors.[334]

However, they should not expect to find such qualities in Francis Newman's 1856 translation of Homer's *Iliad*, which is the subject of an extended attack by Arnold on the grounds that it exemplifies the very 'eccentricity' and 'arbitrariness' that he finds so characteristic of English literature, by contrast with the literatures of France and Germany, of which, 'as of the intellect of Europe in general, the main effort, for now many years, has been a *critical* effort; the endeavour, in all branches of knowledge . . . to see the object as in itself it really is.'[335] The want of 'simple lucidity of mind'[336] that Arnold detects in Newman's translation appears to have been interpreted by Newman himself as a slight upon his masculinity, for he responded 'It is the fact, that scholars of fastidious refinement, but of a judgment which I think far more masculine than Mr. Arnold's, have passed a most encouraging sentence on large specimens of my translation.'[337] But the fact that Newman 'could boast how children and half-educated woman have extolled [his verses], how greedily a working man has inquired for them', only proves for Arnold 'that in our country a powerful misdirection of this kind is often more

likely to subjugate and pervert opinion, than to be checked and cor-
rected by it'.[338] The anarchic intellectual and moral tendencies of the age
are clearly associated in Arnold's mind with women and the uneducated
masses.

As his contemporary, the journalist R. H. Hutton, observed of Arnold,
'he regards the power of seeing things as they are as the monopoly of
a class; and indeed, arrived at as he arrived at it, it must always be the
monopoly of a class.' As such, in Hutton's opinion, Arnold's critical
views had little relevance to the general populace, whom he actually
despises:

> If you look for it, you may always find a way by which men
> with torpid minds may be stirred, *through* their conscience,
> into true moral and therefore also intellectual discriminations.
> But Mr. Arnold does not care for such a process. He prefers
> contemplating blankly the gulf between him and the uncultured
> people he pities. He exults in the intellectual paces which
> he displays before them, and to the beauty and delicately
> graduated variety of which they are simply blind. He is almost
> supercilious in his disdain for their clumsy and heavy tread.
> 'Let them that be filthy be filthy still,' is too accurate an
> expression of his grand unconcern. If we, the 'dim common
> populations,' get a blessing from Mr. Arnold at all, it will only
> be as Jacob obtained it from the angel who wrestled with him
> 'till the breaking of the day.' He has no spontaneous blessing
> to bestow on the class whose culture he despises; and as that
> culture begins to light up their sky he would only find a
> reason in it for leaving them, – 'let me go, for the day
> breaketh.'[339]

Shortly after the publication of Arnold's 'On Translating Homer,' Hutton
addressed the question of the function of criticism as defined therein in
a review in the *Spectator*:

> the only criticism which is really likely to be useful on the
> minor works of every-day literature is that which has been
> trained and disciplined in worthier studies. Here is the mistake
> of the cut-and-dried man of culture. He goes about with the
> secret of having learned to appreciate the 'grand style.' He has
> lived in Homer till he can recall the roll of that many-sounding
> sea . . . When first fortune compels him to deal with the daily
> literary efforts of ordinary Englishmen, he chooses such as are
> more or less connected with his real admirations . . . And no
> doubt it is a trial to men steeped in the culture of the noblest
> literature of the world, to appreciate fairly the ephemeral

productions of a busy generation. It seems beneath them, and the more they trample it beneath them, the less are they competent to detect its higher tendencies. But still the critic who allows this feeling to grow upon him abdicates his true office. Unless he can enter into the wants of his generation, he has no business to pretend to direct its thoughts.[340]

For Hutton, it is the newspaper critic who responds to the real cultural needs of 'ordinary Englishmen', rather than the 'intellectual angel' who pontificates from on high, that best serves the interests of English cultural life broadly conceived.

Arnold was, at the time when he produced his major critical works, Professor of Poetry at Oxford University, and therefore in a position to conduct a 'calm and leisurely intellectual survey'[341] of the cultural condition of England from his ivory tower. He was very conscious of the responsibilities of his position and felt that other members of the clerisy should be like-minded. Francis Newman's sins are hence compounded, for Arnold, by the fact that he holds the Chair of Latin at University College, London, and therefore speaks with the authority of a major academic institution. In the absence of a national Academy, such as France has, men like Newman had, according to Arnold, a particular responsibility to regulate the cultural life of England. Arnold attributes the cause of England's intellectual delinquency to the fact that literature is not there regarded as 'a living intellectual instrument', as it is in Europe – 'almost the last thing for which one would come to English literature is just that very thing which now Europe most desires – *criticism*' – and links this critical deficiency to the fact that it has no Academy:

> I think that in England, partly from the want of an Academy, partly from a national habit of intellect to which that want of an Academy is itself due, there exists too little of what I may call a public force of correct literary opinion, possessing within certain limits a clear sense of what is right and wrong, sound and unsound, and sharply recalling men of ability and learning from any flagrant misdirection of these their advantages.[342]

The solution to England's intellectual malaise, in Arnold's view, lies with 'criticism' and with the exercise and extension of 'the literary influence of academies'.[343]

The convergence of the perceived functions of criticism and of the academy in Arnold's cultural programme has not gone unnoticed by modern critics and theorists, and he has been either hailed or condemned for what all agree was his crucial role in the institutionalisation of literary studies within universities and in the development of 'English' as an academic discipline. Terry Eagleton, for instance, attributes the growth of English studies in the final decades of the nineteenth century to 'the failure of religion', and sees Arnold as a pivotal figure in the transferral to 'English' of the ideological power that religion had traditionally wielded.[344] Religion as well as literature had of course become the subject of criticism from various quarters in the nineteenth century, from evolutionary science to German biblical scholarship. Arnold too had turned his critical eye to the Christian religion in *Literature and Dogma* (1871–73) and *God and the Bible* (1875). In the latter, Arnold wrote, echoing Carlyle in *Sartor Resartus*: 'At the present moment two things about the Christian religion must surely be clear to anybody with eyes in his head. One is, that men cannot do without it: the other they cannot do with it as it is.'[345] He saw Christianity as it was currently conceived as being vulnerable to the Positivist tendencies of the times, and proposed to save what was important about it by demythologising it: stripping it of its theological foundations and its metaphysical and supernatural dimensions, and retaining only the spiritual experience and the moral truth which were empirically verifiable. In an essay of 1878 he predicts that the religion of the future will be

> a Catholicism purged, opening itself to the light and air,
> having the consciousness of its own poetry, freed from its
> sacerdotal despotism and freed from its pseudo-scientific
> apparatus of superannuated dogma. Its forms will be retained,
> as symbolizing with the force and charm of poetry a few
> cardinal facts and ideas.[346]

'The strongest part of our religion today,' he asserts, 'is its unconscious poetry,' and this being the case he imagines that 'most of what now passes with us for religion and philosophy will be replaced by poetry.'[347] Meanwhile, as Arnold's religion was starting to look more and more like poetry, his poetry, indeed his literature, his criticism, his culture, increasingly came to take over the traditional functions of religion. 'The right function of poetry', he averred, 'is to animate, to console, to rejoice – in one word, to *strengthen*'.[348] Its role is to interpret the moral world. 'Culture,' we are told, 'and science and literature are requisite, in the interest of religion itself'.[349] Indeed, 'culture goes beyond religion, as religion is generally conceived by us',[350] effectively replacing it as the arbiter of moral and spiritual values.

When Wilde's Gilbert announces in 1890 that 'It is to criticism that the future belongs,' and imagines an 'educational system' which would 'try and develop in the mind a more subtle quality of apprehension and discernment'[351] it is as if he foresees the rise of English from its unsteady beginnings in the Mechanics' Institutes and Working Men's Colleges to its triumphant establishment as the most morally serious of academic disciplines in the Cambridge of the 1930s. Arnold's emphasis on criticism as a moral activity involving the transmission of fundamental human values was to be refined and elaborated by the Leavises, but the roots of their own critical practice are clearly to be found in Arnold's dogmatic assertions of 'correct literary opinion', of what is 'right and wrong', 'sound and unsound'; in his cultural 'touchstones'; and in his ranking of writers, and erection of a canonical 'great tradition'. It is therefore somewhat ironic that the genre of literature in which Arnold himself excelled, non-fiction prose, should have been largely excluded from the literary canon which has dominated the study of English in the twentieth century and privileged the study of other genres. Arnold's critical prose might be seen to have unwittingly colluded in the creation of an English literary canon comprised of poetry, drama and fiction which effectively wrote out non-fiction prose, relegating it to 'background reading'. It is hoped that the present volume goes some way towards redressing this history of critical and pedagogical neglect by demonstrating the range and diversity of non-fiction prose in the nineteenth century and allowing it to take possession of the foreground.

Notes

1. William Wordsworth and S. T. Coleridge, *Lyrical Ballads – The Text of the 1798 Edition with the Additional 1800 Poems and the Prefaces*, edited by R. L. Brett and A. R. Jones, 2nd edn (London and New York, 1991), pp. 244–45.

2. Ibid, pp. 245–46.

3. The phrase is Benedict Anderson's. See his *Imagined Communities*, 2nd edn (London, 1991).

4. [R. K. Philp] *Enquire Within Upon Everything*, 63rd edn (London, n.d.), p. vii.

5. Ibid, p. 53.

6. Ibid, p. 74.

7. Ibid, pp. 156; 219; 260.

8. Ibid, p. iv.

9. Ibid, pp. 250; 61; 175; 337; 92; 49; 309; 69; 81; 232; 207; 329; 228.

10. *Mill on Bentham and Coleridge*, edited by F. R. Leavis (Cambridge, 1950), p. 104.

11. Many of which were invented in the latter half of the nineteenth century.

12. Thomas Carlyle, 'On History', in *Critical and Miscellaneous Essays*, I, 493–505 (p. 496). Cf. also 'On History Again' (1833): 'All Books . . . are in the long-run historical documents – as indeed all Speech itself is . . . History is not only the fittest study, but the only study, and includes all others whatsoever' (Ibid, II, 403–12 (p. 406)).

13. Cf. 'On History', where Carlyle distinguishes between the artisan as mechanistic and the artist as able to recognise the Romantic integrity of all experience and

thought: 'But the Artist in History may be distinguished from the Artisan in History; . . . men who labour mechanically in a department, without eye for the Whole. . . . ; and men who inform and ennoble the humblest department with an Idea of the Whole, and habitually know that only in the Whole is the Partial to be truly discerned' (Ibid, I, 500).

14. Mark Pattison, 'Tendencies of Religious Thought in England, 1688–1750', *Essays and Reviews*, 11th edn (London, 1863), p. 319.

15. William Paley, *Natural Theology*, 13th edn (London, 1810), p. 441.

16. Ibid, p. 543.

17. Ibid, pp. 456–59. The contrast with Darwin's later vision is, of course, very striking.

18. James Joyce, *Ulysses* (London, 1960), p. 379.

19. Paley, *Natural Theology*, p. 538.

20. Gillian Beer provides an enlightening commentary on the opening pages of Paley in *Darwin's Plots: Evolutionary Narrative in Darwin, George Eliot, and Nineteenth-Century Fiction* (London, 1983), pp. 83–84.

21. The eye, 'the examination of' which 'Sturmius held . . . was a cure for atheism' (*Natural Theology*, p. 53) is the main example of design discussed in chapter 3 of Paley's book.

22. See Paley's *Principles of Moral and Political Philosophy* (1785).

23. Paley, *Natural Theology*, pp. 466; 463. Paley, commenting upon the less felicitous aspects of nature, writes that 'the subject . . . of animals devouring one another, forms the chief, if not the only instance, in the works of the Deity, of an oeconomy, stamped by marks of design, in which the character of utility can be called in question' (p. 481).

24. Beer, *Darwin's Plots*, p. 40.

25. 'Introduction' to *Thomas Babington Macaulay: Selected Writings*, edited by John Clive and Thomas Pinney (Chicago, 1972), p. ix.

26. *The Works of Lord Macaulay*, edited by Lady Trevelyan, 8 vols (London, 1879), V, 122.

27. Rosemary Jann, *The Art and Science of Victorian History* (Columbus, Ohio, 1985), p. 73.

28. *The Works of Lord Macaulay*, V, 160.

29. Ibid, VII, 158.

30. J. M. Burrow, *A Liberal Descent: Victorian Historians and the English Past* (Cambridge, 1981), p. 88.

31. Quoted by George Watson, in *The English Ideology: Studies in the Language of Victorian Politics* (London, 1973), p. 124.

32. *The Works of Lord Macaulay*, V, 124.

33. Quoted from Trevelyan's *Life of Macaulay*, by Burrow, *A Liberal Descent*, p. 87.

34. *The Works of Lord Macaulay*, V, 157.

35. Ibid, p. 155.

36. *Macaulay: Selected Writings*, pp. 293–94.

37. *The Works of Lord Macaulay*, V, 155; 158. Macaulay illustrates his arguments in this essay with reference to details from Cervantes, Swift, Richardson, and Boswell.

38. Ibid, V, 154.

39. Ibid, p. 145.

40. Lewes, *A Biographical History of Philosophy*, Sir John Lubbock's Hundred Books (London, n.d. [1895]), pp. xv–xvi.

41. *Mill on Bentham and Coleridge*, p. 102.

42. Newman, for instance, appears to be content with a Lockean psychology, while Hamilton, and Mansel after him, follow upon the strain of Humean scepticism developed by Kant.

43. Lewes, *A Biographical History of Philosophy*, p. xix.

44. Ibid, p. xv.

45. *Mill on Bentham and Coleridge*, p. 111.

46. Ibid, p. 41.

47. Paley, *Natural Theology*, p. 491.

48. Ibid, p. 513. Similarly, biological diversity is regarded hierarchically, and, by resorting to the pseudo-scientific criteria of probability, is asserted as superior to an order founded on mutual equality: 'It is probable, that creation may be better replenished by sensitive beings of different sorts . . . by different orders of beings rising one above another in gradation, than by beings possessed of equal degrees of perfection' (p. 494).

49. *Mill on Bentham and Coleridge*, p. 95.

50. *Collected Works of John Stuart Mill*, edited by J. M. Robson *et al*, 33 vols (Toronto and London, 1963–91), vol. VIII, *A System of Logic Ratiocinative and Inductive*, edited by J. M. Robson (1974), p. 20.

51. *Mill on Bentham and Coleridge*, p. 50.

52. Quoted by Mill, ibid, p. 95.

53. Quoted by Mill, ibid, p. 96.

54. Quoted by Mill, ibid, p. 97.

55. Ibid, p. 98.

56. Quoted in David Oldroyd, *The Arch of Knowledge: An Introductory Study of the History of the Philosophy and Methodology of Science* (Sydney, 1986), p. 160.

57. *The Journals and Papers of Gerard Manley Hopkins*, edited by Humphry House and Graham Storey (Oxford, 1959), p. 120.

58. William Whewell, *The Philosophy of the Inductive Sciences*, 2nd edn, 2 vols (London, 1847), II, 36.

59. Hopkins, *Journals and Papers*, p. 118.

60. John Kenyon, *The History Men: The Historical Profession in England since the Renaissance* (Pittsburgh, 1984), pp. 113, 114.

61. Henry Thomas Buckle, 'Introduction', *The History of Civilization in England* (London, n.d.), p. 19.

62. Ibid, pp. 90–91.

63. Ibid, pp. 15–16.

64. Ibid, p. 18.

65. Wilde, *The Importance of Being Earnest*, in *Complete Works of Oscar Wilde*, Introduction by Vyvyan Holland (London and Glasgow, Collins, 1948), p. 373.

66. Buckle, *The History of Civilization in England*, p. 17.

67. Ibid, p. 88.

68. Cited in Genevieve Lloyd, *The Man of Reason: 'Male' and 'Female' in Western Philosophy* (London, 1984), pp. 11–12.

69. Buckle, *The History of Civilization in England*, p. 88.

70. Ibid, p. 87.

71. Carlyle's history of *The French Revolution*, for instance, articulates this sense of pessimism and degeneracy through the sustained metaphor of cannibalism: 'The lowest, least blessed fact one knows of, on which necessitous mortals have ever based themselves, seems to be the primitive one of Cannibalism: That I can devour Thee. What if such Primitive Fact were precisely the one we had with our improved methods to revert to, and begin anew from!' (*The French Revolution*, 2 vols (London, 1906), I, 44).

72. Walter Bagehot, *Physics and Politics: Or Thoughts on the Application of the Principles of 'Natural Selection' and 'Inheritance' to Political Society*, 8th edn (London, 1887), p. 201.

73. Ibid, p. 1.

74. Ibid, p. 2.

75. Ibid, p. 7.

76. Ibid, p. 8.

77. Ibid, p. 11.

78. Bagehot, 'The First Edinburgh Reviewers', in *Collected Works*, edited by N. St John Stevas, 15 vols (London, 1965–86), I, 308–41 (p. 311).

79. Bagehot, *Physics and Politics*, p. 204.

80. *The Collected Works of Walter Bagehot*, IV, 50–52.

81. Ibid, p. 52.

82. Alexander Bain, *The Senses and the Intellect*, 3rd edn (London, 1868), p. 3.

83. Mill, *A System of Logic*, p. 51.

84. *In Memoriam*, CXXIV.

85. Quoted from *Aids to Reflection* by Claude Welch, 'Samuel Taylor Coleridge', in *Nineteenth-Century Religious Thought in the West*, edited by N. Smart, J. Clayton, S. T. Katz and P. Sherry (Cambridge, 1985), vol. II, p. 16.

86. J. H. Newman, *An Essay in Aid of a Grammar of Assent* (London, 1870), p. 117.

87. S. T. Coleridge, *Biographia Literaria, or Biographical Sketches of My Literary Life and Opinions*, edited by James Engell and W. Jackson Bate, Bollingen Series, 2 vols (London, 1983), I, 304.

88. Newman, *Grammar of Assent*, p. 95.

89. Ibid, p. 99.

90. John Grote was the brother of the positivist historian of classical Greece, George Grote.

91. John Grote, *Exploratio Philosophica* [Part I] (Cambridge, 1865), p. 15.

92. W. David Shaw, *The Lucid Veil: Poetic Truth in the Victorian Age* (London, 1987), chapter 3.

93. Hence, for example, J. F. Ferrier's philosophy emphasises the fact that our perceptions are always 'framed' by the larger principle of personal consciousness. See Shaw, *The Lucid Veil*, pp. 48–53.

94. *Aids to Reflection*, Aphorism VII, *The Collected Works of Samuel Taylor Coleridge*, edited by K. Coburn and B. Winer, Bollingen Series, 75, in progress (London and Princeton, 1993), IX, 205; 206.

95. See Shaw, *The Lucid Veil*, pp. 150–52, 232–33.

96. Carlyle, *The French Revolution*, II, 390.

97. Carlyle, 'On History', *Critical and Miscellaneous Essays*, I, 496.

98. Ibid, p. 505.

99. Ibid, p. 500.

100. Carlyle, *The French Revolution*, II, 329.

101. Ibid, I, 344–45.

102. Ibid, I, 346.

103. Ibid, I, 347.

104. Ibid, I, 349.

105. Samuel Taylor Coleridge, *Confessions of an Inquiring Spirit* (London, 1840), p. 91.

106. Ibid, p. 1.

107. Welch, 'Samuel Taylor Coleridge', p. 15.

108. Benjamin Jowett, 'On the Interpretation of Scripture,' *Essays and Reviews*, p. 458. Cf. p. 455.

109. Ibid, pp. 450–51.

110. Ibid, p. 434. See also p. 495, 'Any passing phase of politics in art, or spurious philanthropy, may have a kind of Scriptural authority.'

111. Ibid, pp. 492–93.

112. Quoted in Leszek Kolakowski, *Main Currents of Marxism*, trans. P. S. Falla (Oxford, 1978), p. 129.

113. See chapter 10 of Friedrich Engels, *Dialectics of Nature* (London, 1940), pp. 297–310, and Alfred Wallace, *On Miracles and Modern Spiritualism* (London, 1875).

114. *The Four Gospels Explained by Their Writers; with an Appendix on the Ten Commandments*, edited by J. B. Roustaing, trans. W. F. Kirby, 3 vols (London, 1881). Interestingly the spirit-authors, editor and translator acknowledge 'the temporary usefulness of the errors resulting from the action of the human element in the production of the Gospels' (p. vii).

115. Shaw, *The Lucid Veil*, p. 119. See also pp. 153–57.

116. Walter Pater, *Plato and Platonism* (London, 1910), pp. 267–68.

117. Psalm 115: 6.

118. On Pater's use of the positivist George Grote's view of Plato in his lectures on the philosopher, see Frank Turner, *The Greek Heritage in Victorian Britain* (New Haven, Connecticut, 1981), pp. 406–14.

119. Walter Pater, *The Renaissance: Studies in Art and Poetry* (London, 1910), p. 135.

120. See Christopher Harvie, *The Lights of Liberalism: University Liberals and the Challenge of Democracy 1860–86* (London, 1976). Green's early public statements on the issue are discussed on pp. 116–18.

121. *Essays on Reform* (London, 1867), p. 88.

122. Ibid, p. 86.

123. Ibid, p. 328.

124. Ibid, p. 29.

125. R. L. Nettleship's 'Memoir' in *The Works of T. H. Green*, edited by R. L. Nettleship, 2nd edn, 3 vols (London, 1908–11), III, xli.

126. *Critique of Practical Reason*, 141, in *Kant's Critique of Practical Reason and Other Works on the Theory of Ethics*, trans. T. K. Abbott, 4th edn (London, 1889), p. 119.

127. T. H. Green, *Lectures on the Principles of Political Obligation* (London, 1931), p. 236.

128. Ibid, pp. 236–37.

129. Geoffrey Thomas, *The Moral Philosophy of T. H. Green* (Oxford, 1987), p. 362.

130. 'Queen Victoria to Mr. Gladstone', May 6, 1870. Philip Guedalla, *The Queen and Mr. Gladstone* (Garden City, N.Y., 1934), p. 271. This book is an edition of the correspondence between Victoria and Gladstone.

131. From a letter to Sir Theodore Martin, May 29, 1870. Quoted in Frank Hardie, *The Political Influence of Queen Victoria 1861–1901* (London, 1935), p. 140.

132. *Gladstone on woman suffrage* (London, National League for Opposing Woman Suffrage, [n.d.]), p. 2.

133. S. T. Coleridge, *On the Constitution of the Church and State, according to the Idea of Each; with aids towards a right judgement on the late Catholic Bill*, edited by John Barrell (London, 1972), pp. 33–34.

134. See, for instance, Dickens' *Great Expectations* and Gaskell's *North and South*, and Robin Gilmour's critical study *The Idea of the Gentleman in the Victorian Novel* (1981).

135. See Ben Knights, *The Idea of the Clerisy in the Nineteenth Century* (Cambridge, 1978), p. 7.

136. *The Works of Thomas Carlyle*, Centenary Edition, 30 vols (London, 1898), vol. V, *Heroes and Hero-Worship*, pp. 155, 165.

137. Ibid, p. 159.

138. Carlyle, 'Signs of the Times', *Critical and Miscellaneous Essays*, I, 473–74, 476.

139. Ibid, p. 83.

140. Matthew Arnold, *Culture and Anarchy*, edited by R. H. Super (Ann Arbor, Michigan, 1965), pp. 233–34.

141. Ibid, p. 96.

142. Ibid, p. 117.

143. See ibid, pp. 134–35, and 'Numbers; or The Majority and the Remnant', in *The Complete Prose Works of Matthew Arnold*, edited by R. H. Super, 11 vols (Ann Arbor, Michigan, 1960–77), X, 143ff.

144. Arnold, *Culture and Anarchy*, p. 143.

145. Ibid, p. 235.

146. Ibid, pp. 234, 99.

147. Ibid, pp. 94–95.

148. 'Preface to First Edition of *Poems*', in *The Complete Prose Works of Matthew Arnold*, I, 1–15 (p. 13).

149. Arnold, *Culture and Anarchy*, p. 113.

150. Ibid, p. 113.

151. Ibid, p. 240.

152. See *Matthew Arnold: Selected Prose*, edited by P. J. Keating (Harmondsworth, 1970), pp. 17–18.

153. Arnold, *Culture and Anarchy*, p. 124.

154. John Henry Newman, *The Idea of a University Defined and Illustrated* (London, 1923), p. xx.

155. Ibid, pp. xxi–xxii.

156. Ibid, p. xvi.

157. Ibid, p. xxi.

158. Ibid, p. 252.

159. Ibid, pp. 251–52.

160. Letter to the *Daily News*, 20 November 1885, *The Collected Letters of William Morris*, edited by Norman Kelvin, 2 vols (Princeton, 1984–87), II, 493.

161. Letter to *Pall Mall Gazette*, 1 November, 1886, ibid, II, 589–90.

162. Morris, 'How I Became a Socialist', in *Justice*, 16 June, 1894, *The Collected Works of William Morris*, 24 vols (London, 1910–15), XXIII, 277–81 (pp. 279–80).

163. Reprinted as an Appendix in *The Works of John Ruskin*, edited by E. T. Cook and Alexander Wedderburn, 39 vols (London, 1903–12), X, 460–62 (p. 460).

164. Ibid, X, 193–94.

165. Ibid, p. 202.

166. Ibid, XX, 39.

167. Ibid, XVIII, 433–34.

168. Ibid, p. 443.

169. Ibid, pp. 447–48.

170. Ibid, pp. 450–51.

171. Ibid, XVII, 17.

172. Ibid, pp. 35–36.

173. Ibid, p. 44.

174. See ibid, XIV, 288; XXIV, 347; XXXIV, 355; V, 427.

175. See, for instance, X, 193; XVI, 328, 335; XVIII, 88.

176. See Jeffrey L. Spear, *Dreams of an English Eden: Ruskin and his Tradition in Social Criticism* (New York, 1984).

177. See Raymond E. Fitch, *The Poison Sky: Myth and Apocalypse in Ruskin* (Athens, Ohio, and London, 1982), p. 457.

178. *The Works of John Ruskin*, XVIII, 33.

179. Ibid, XVII, 74.

180. Ibid.

181. Although see Jan Marsh's interesting article, '"Resolve to be a Great Paintress": Women Artists in Relation to Ruskin as Critic and Patron', *Nineteenth-Century Contexts*, 18, 2 (1994), 177–85, in which she remarks: 'I feel that the feminist quarrel with Ruskin has gone on long enough – or at least needs greater dissection' (p. 179).

182. *The Works of John Ruskin*, XVIII, 121–22.

183. Ibid, pp. 123, 121.

184. Ibid, p. 123.

185. Ibid, pp. 125–27.

186. Ibid, p. 128.

187. See Catherine Hall, *White, Male and Middle Class: Explorations in Feminism and History* (New York, 1992), pp. 75, 84. See also Nina Auerbach, *Woman and the Demon: The Life of a Victorian Myth* (Cambridge, Massachusetts, 1982), and Lynda Nead, *Myths of Sexuality: Representations of Women in Victorian Britain* (Oxford, 1988).

188. W. R. Greg, 'Why Are Women Redundant?', *National Review*, 14 (1862), 436, 438, 440.

189. William Thompson [and Anna Wheeler], *Appeal of one half the human race, Women, against the pretensions of the other half, Men, to retain them in political, and thence in civil and domestic, slavery* (London, 1825), pp. 79, 85. Ironically, 'one half' of the joint authors of this volume, Anna Wheeler, fails to make it onto the title page.

190. Jameson mentions Sarah Lewis's *Woman's Mission* (1839) and Marion Reid's *A Plea for Woman* (1843). Another important text of the period was Ann Lamb's *Can Women Regenerate Society?* (1844).

191. Anna Jameson, '"Woman's Mission" and Woman's Position', in *Memoirs and Essays Illustrative of Art, Literature, and Social Morals* (London, 1846), pp. 215, 218.

192. Ibid, pp. 217–18.

193. Ibid, p. 225.

194. Ibid, pp. 230–32.

195. Ibid, p. 247.

196. John Stuart Mill, *The Subjection of Women* (New York, 1986), p. 47.

197. Ibid, p. 82.

198. Ibid, p. 55.

199. *The Works of John Ruskin*, XVIII, 110–11, 139.

200. Jameson, '"Woman's Mission" and Woman's Position', p. 216.

201. Mill, *The Subjection of Women*, pp. 12–16.

202. Ibid, p. 11.

203. Ibid, pp. 36–37.

204. Ibid, p. 37.

205. Ibid, pp. 17, 18.

206. Ibid, p. 27.

207. Ibid, pp. 21, 62.

208. Ibid, p. 59.

209. Ibid, p. 21.

210. Ibid, p. 66.

211. Mrs [Sarah Stickney] Ellis, *The Women of England, their Social Duties and Domestic Habits* (London, c. 1840), pp. 33–34.

212. Ibid, p. 35.

213. See Leonore Davidoff and Catherine Hall, *Family Fortunes: Men and Women of the English Middle-Class, 1780–1850* (London, 1987), p. 183; on Sarah Ellis see pp. 180–85.

214. See A. James Hammerton, *Cruelty and Companionship: Conflict in Nineteenth-Century Married Life* (London and New York, 1992), pp. 76–78.

215. For a discussion of the housewife in relation to Marxist theories of the reproduction of labour power see Hall, *White, Male and Middle Class*, chapter 2, especially pp. 43–44, 52–53. See also Anita Levy, *Other Women: The Writing of Class, Race, and Gender, 1832–1898* (Princeton, N.J., 1991), chapter 1, on 'The Making of Domestic Culture'.

216. Mrs Isabella Beeton, *The Book of Household Management*. Originally published in 1859–61 in monthly supplements to S. O. Beeton's *The Englishwoman's Domestic Magazine*. First published by S. O. Beeton in 1861 as one volume. First edition facsimile (London, 1982), p. 1.

217. Florence Nightingale, *Cassandra and other selections from Suggestions for Thought*, edited by Mary Poovey (London, 1991), p. 213.

218. Ibid, p. 210; Beeton, *The Book of Household Management*, p. 11.

219. Nightingale, *Cassandra*, p. 210.

220. Mill, *The Subjection of Women*, p. 79.

221. Beeton, *The Book of Household Management*, p. 3.

222. Ibid, p. 10.

223. Nightingale, *Cassandra*, pp. 213–14.

224. Beeton, *The Book of Household Management*, p. 1. See Mary Poovey, *Uneven Developments: The Ideological Work of Gender in Mid-Victorian England* (London,

1989), pp. 166, 198. Chapter 6 offers a full discussion of 'the social construction of Florence Nightingale'.

225. Ibid, p. 3.

226. Ros Ballaster, Margaret Beetham, Elizabeth Frazer and Sandra Hebron, *Women's Worlds: Ideology, Femininity and the Woman's Magazine* (London, 1991), p. 7. See chapter 3 for a discussion of nineteenth-century women's magazines.

227. *The Englishwoman's Domestic Magazine*, New Series, 3 (1861), iii.

228. Ibid, 1 (1860), iii.

229. Ibid, 1 (1860), 48.

230. Mill, *The Subjection of Women*, p. 103.

231. See Ballaster et al, *Women's Worlds*, pp. 79, 2. On the female reader, see Kate Flint, *The Woman Reader, 1837–1914* (Oxford, 1993), and Sara Mills, ed., *Gendering the Reader* (New York and Hemel Hempstead, 1994).

232. George Eliot, 'Woman in France: Madame de Sablé', *Westminster Review* (October, 1854), reprinted in *George Eliot: Selected Essays, Poems and Other Writings*, edited by A. S. Byatt and Nicholas Warren (London, 1990), pp. 8–37 (pp. 36–37).

233. Arnold, 'The Literary Influence of Academies', *Prose Works*, III, 254–55.

234. Oscar Wilde, 'The Critic as Artist', in *Complete Works*, p. 1028.

235. Ibid, p. 1029.

236. Ibid, pp. 1044, 1045, 1048, 1026, 1027.

237. Ibid, pp. 1030, 1028.

238. Ibid, p. 1041.

239. Ibid, pp. 1022–48.

240. Ibid, p. 1022.

241. See Ina Ferris, 'From trope to code: The novel and the rhetoric of gender in nineteenth-century critical discourse', in *Rewriting the Victorians: theory, history, and the politics of gender*, edited by Linda M. Shires (New York and London, 1992), pp. 18–30 (p. 19).

242. Wilde, 'The Critic as Artist', *Complete Works*, p. 1034.

243. See Terry Eagleton, *Literary Theory: An Introduction* (Oxford, 1983), p. 20.

244. Wordsworth and Coleridge, *Lyrical Ballads – The Text of the 1798 Edition with the Additional 1800 Poems and the Prefaces*, edited by R. L. Brett and A. R. Jones, 2nd edn (London and New York, 1991), Preface of 1802, p. 244.

245. Ibid, pp. 245–46, 254, 256–57.

246. Ibid, p. 255.

247. Ibid, pp. 255–56. See Anne K. Mellor, *Romanticism and Gender* (New York and London, 1993), p. 23.

248. See Alan Richardson, 'Romanticism and the Colonization of the Feminine', in *Romanticism and Feminism*, edited by Anne K. Mellor, pp. 13–25; Percy Shelley, *A Defence of Poetry*, in *Shelley: Selected Poetry, Prose, and Letters*, edited by A. S. B. Glover (London, 1951), pp. 1023–55 (p. 1051).

249. Wordsworth, *The Prelude*, XII, 211–13.

250. Wordsworth and Coleridge, *Lyrical Ballads*, pp. 263, 255.

251. *Christian Remembrancer*, IV, N.S. (July, 1842), 42–58 (p. 49). Quoted by Isobel Armstrong, in her introduction to *Victorian Scrutinies: Reviews of Poetry 1830–1870* (London, 1972), p. 5. She comments, 'this might almost be called the classic Victorian position.'

252. Samuel Taylor Coleridge, *Biographia Literaria, or Biographical Sketches of My Literary Life and Opinions*, edited by James Engell and W. Jackson Bate, 2 vols (Princeton, 1983), II, 12, 15–16.

253. Wordsworth and Coleridge, *Lyrical Ballads*, p. 259; Shelley, *A Defence of Poetry*, pp. 1049–50.

254. Ina Ferris, 'From trope to code', p. 18.

255. *London Magazine* (1820), 178, quoted ibid, p. 23.

256. *Quarterly Review* (1814), 126, quoted ibid, p. 22.

257. Quoted in John Barrell, 'Masters of suspense: syntax and gender in Milton's sonnets', in *Poetry, language and politics* (Manchester, 1988), pp. 44–78 (p. 70).

258. S. T. Coleridge, *Lectures 1808–1819 on Literature*, edited by R. A. Foakes, 2 vols (Princeton and London, 1987), II, 193.

259. George Eliot, 'Silly Novels by Lady Novelists', *Westminster Review* (October, 1856), reprinted in *Selected Essays, Poems and Other Writings*, edited by A. S. Byatt and Nicholas Warren (London, 1990), pp. 140–63 (p. 161).

260. See Joseph Bristow's interesting discussion of this phenomenon in his introduction to *The Victorian Poet: Poetics and Persona* (London, New York, and Sydney, 1987).

261. *Eclectic Review* (May 1855), 551.

262. Wilde, *Complete Works*, p. 1091.

263. John Stuart Mill, 'Thoughts on Poetry and Its Varieties' (1833), in *The Collected Works of John Stuart Mill*, vol. I, *Autobiography and Literary Essays*, edited by John M. Robson and Jack Stillinger (Toronto and London, 1981), pp. 341–66 (p. 356).

264. *The Works of John Ruskin*, V, 205.

265. Ibid.

266. Roden Noel, 'On the Use of Metaphor and "Pathetic Fallacy" in Poetry', *Fortnightly Review* (1866).

267. Alfred Austin, 'Summary', in *The Poetry of the Period* (London, 1870), pp. 266, 273.

268. Alfred Austin, 'Mr. Swinburne', ibid, pp. 78–79, 96.

269. Eric S. Robertson, *English Poetesses: A Series of Critical Biographies, with Illustrative Extracts* (London, 1883), pp. xiii–xv.

270. [Richard Holt Hutton], 'Novels by the Authoress of "John Halifax"', *North British Review* (1858), 467.

271. Swinburne, 'Notes on Poems and Reviews', in *The Complete Works of Algernon Charles Swinburne*, edited by Sir Edmund Gosse and Thomas James Wise (New York, 1925, 1968), *Prose Works*, vol. VI, pp. 353–77 (pp. 371–72).

272. Ibid, p. 373.

273. Alfred Austin, 'Mr Swinburne', in *The Poetry of the Period*, pp. 85–86.

274. Alfred Austin, 'The Feminine Note in Literature', in *The Bridling of Pegasus* (London, 1910).

275. R. H. Hutton, 'The Cultus of Impressionability', reprinted in *A Victorian Spectator: Uncollected Writings of R. H. Hutton*, edited by Robert Tener and Malcolm Woodfield (Bristol, 1989), pp. 219–22 (pp. 221–22).

276. W. H. Mallock, *The New Republic: Culture, Faith and Philosophy in an English Country House*, edited by John Lucas (Leicester, 1975), pp. 27–28.

277. Walter Horatio Pater, 'Leonardo da Vinci', in *The Renaissance: Studies in Art and Poetry* (London, 1910), pp. 98–129 (pp. 118–19).

278. Ibid, p. 115.

279. 'The School of Giorgione', ibid, pp. 130–54 (pp. 143–44, 154).

280. [Emilia Pattison], unsigned review of *Studies in the History of the Renaissance, Westminster Review*, n.s. 43 (1873), 639–41.

281. Pater, 'Preface' to *The Renaissance*, pp. viii–x.

282. [W. J. Stillman], unsigned review of *Studies in the History of the Renaissance, Nation*, 17 (1873), 243–44; [Margaret Oliphant], unsigned review of *Studies in the History of the Renaissance, Blackwood's Magazine*, 114 (1873), 604–09.

283. Pater, review of the *Correspondence of Gustave Flaubert*, in *Uncollected Essays* (London, 1903), p. 108.

284. Pater, 'Luca Della Robbia', in *The Renaissance*, pp. 63–72 (p. 71).

285. Pater, 'Dante Gabriel Rossetti', in *Appreciations, with an Essay on Style* (London, 1910), pp. 205–28 (pp. 210–11).

286. Ibid, p. 205.

287. Vernon Lee, *Euphorion: being Studies of the Antique and the Mediaeval in the Renaissance*, 2 vols (London, 1884), 1, 8–9.

288. *De Quincey as Critic*, edited by John E. Jordan (London and Boston, 1973), pp. 240–44 (p. 240).

289. Ibid, pp. 243, 244.

290. Vernon Lee, *The Handling of Words and Other Studies in Literary Psychology* (London and New York, 1923), p. 1.

291. Ibid, p. 136.

292. Ibid, pp. 136, 141, 145.

293. S. T. Coleridge, *Shakespearean Criticism*, edited by T. M. Raysor, 2 vols (London, 1960), I, 17.

294. Ibid, II, 189.

295. Ibid, I, 198.

296. Ibid, II, 223.

297. Ibid, II, 223; I, 34.

298. Ibid, I, 34.

299. See Barrell, 'Masters of suspense', p. 66.

300. S. T. Coleridge, *Biographia Literaria*, II, 26–28. See Barrell, 'Masters of suspense', pp. 65–69, for an interesting discussion of this passage.

301. See Barrell, 'Masters of suspense', pp. 75–76.

302. Walter Bagehot, 'Shakespeare – The Man,' in *Literary Studies*, 2 vols (London and New York, 1911), pp. 112–53 (pp. 147–48).

303. Ibid, p. 129.

304. Ibid, pp. 129–30.

305. Coleridge, *The Friend*, edited by Barbara Rooke, 2 vols (London and Princeton, 1969) I, 451; Bagehot, 'Shakespeare – The Man', p. 131.

306. William Hazlitt, 'On the Ignorance of the Learned', in *The Complete Works of William Hazlitt*, edited by P. P. Howe, Centenary Edition, 21 vols (London and Toronto, 1931), VIII, 77.

307. Bagehot, 'Shakespeare – The Man', pp. 121, 116.

308. See R. S. White, *Keats as a Reader of Shakespeare* (London, 1987), p. 33. See also his editorial introduction to *Hazlitt's Criticism of Shakespeare: A Selection* (Lampeter, 1995), which locates Hazlitt's criticism as embedded in his radical political views and his lost vocation as a painter.

309. William Hazlitt, 'On Shakespeare and Milton', in *Lectures on the English Poets* (1818), *Complete Works*, V, 44–68 (pp. 48–49). See also his *Characters of Shakespeare's Plays* (1817), *Works*, IV, 165–361.

310. Hazlitt, *Complete Works*, XVIII, 64, 70.

311. Ibid, p. 78.

312. See Quentin Bell, *Ruskin* (London, 1963), p. 34.

313. Adele M. Holcomb, 'Anna Jameson: The First Professional English Art Historian', *Art History*, 6, 2, (1983), 171–87.

314. *Winter Studies and Summer Rambles in Canada*, 3 vols (London, 1838), I, 142–43. Quoted in Judith Johnston's fine study *Anna Jameson: Victorian, Feminist, Woman of Letters* (forthcoming, Aldershot, 1997), which has an excellent chapter on Jameson's criticism of Shakespeare.

315. See Nina Auerbach, *Woman and the Demon: The Life of a Victorian Myth* (Cambridge, Massachusetts, and London, 1982), p. 211,

316. Anna Jameson, *Characteristics of Women, Moral, Poetical and Historical*, 2 vols (London, 1832), I, 70; *Shakespeare's Heroines*, p. 378.

317. See Holcomb, 'Anna Jameson: The First Professional English Art Historian', p. 178.

318. *The Works of John Ruskin*, XXXV, 373. On Jameson's influences see Adele M. Holcomb, 'Anna Jameson (1794–1860): Sacred Art and Social Vision', in *Women as Interpreters of the Visual Arts, 1820–1979*, edited by Claire Richter Sherman, with Adele M. Holcomb (Westport, Connecticut and London, 1981).

319. *The Works of John Ruskin*, III, 624.

320. Ibid, VI, 49.

321. Ibid, III, 470.

322. See ibid, IV, 287; V, 125; and VI, 44.

323. Ibid, V, 125.

324. Ibid, XXXV, 310.

325. Virginia Woolf, *The Captain's Deathbed* (London, 1950), p. 50.

326. *The Works of John Ruskin*, III, 277–79.

327. See Quentin Bell, *Ruskin*, p. 27.

328. *The Works of John Ruskin*, III, 418–19.

329. Ibid, III, 571.

330. Ibid, IV, 72.

331. Ibid, XI, 48.

332. *The Letters of Matthew Arnold to Arthur Hugh Clough*, edited by Howard Foster Lowry (Oxford, 1932), p. 97; *On Translating Homer*, Lecture 2, in *The Complete Prose Works of Matthew Arnold*, I, 140; 'Heinrich Heine', in *Essays in Criticism, Complete Prose*, III, 122.

333. Arnold, 'The Function of Criticism at the Present Time', in *Essays in Criticism, Complete Prose*, III, 262; Arnold, Preface to First Edition of *Poems, Complete Prose*, I, 9–10.

334. Ibid, p. 12.

335. Arnold, 'On Translating Homer', Lecture 2, *Complete Prose*, I, 140.

336. Ibid, p. 141.

337. Footnote to 'On Translating Homer: Last Words'. Reply to Mr Newman, ibid, p. 172.

338. Ibid, p. 172.

339. R. H. Hutton, 'An Intellectual Angel', in *A Victorian Spectator: Uncollected Writings of R. H. Hutton*, edited by Tener and Woodfield, pp. 111–16 (pp. 114, 115–16).

340. Hutton, 'Mr. Grote on the Abuses of Newspaper Criticism', ibid, pp. 39–43 (pp. 42–43).

341. 'An Intellectual Angel', p. 114.

342. Arnold, 'On Translating Homer', Lecture 2, *Complete Works*, I, 140; 'On Translating Homer: Last Words', ibid, pp. 171–72.

343. See Arnold, 'The Literary Influence of Academies', *Complete Prose*, III, 232–57.

344. Terry Eagleton, *Literary Theory: An Introduction* (Oxford, 1983), pp. 22–25. See also his *The Function of Criticism, From 'The Spectator' to Post-Structuralism* (London, 1984), and Chris Baldick, *The Social Mission of English Criticism, 1848–1932* (Oxford, 1983).

345. Arnold, *Complete Prose*, VII, 378.

346. Ibid, VIII, 334.

347. Ibid, IX, 63, 161.

348. Ibid, VIII, 1.

349. Ibid, VI, 409.

350. Ibid, V, 94.

351. Wilde, *Complete Works*, pp. 1054–55.

Chronology

Date	Prose works	Other works	Historical/cultural events
1800	Davy *Researches, Chemical and Philosophical: chiefly concerning Nitrous Oxide and its Respiration* D. Wordsworth begins Grasmere Journal (–1803)	Edgeworth *Castle Rackrent* Wordsworth and Coleridge *Lyrical Ballads* 2nd edn. Burns *Works*	Union of Ireland with Britain Volta produces electrochemical generator Food riots Owen founds model factory at New Lanark
1801		Leigh Hunt *Juvenilia* Opie *Father and Daughter* Southey *Thalaba*	Pitt resigns Addington P.M. Danish fleet destroyed at Copenhagen Economic distress, high food prices
1802	Davy *Discourse Introductory to a Course of Lectures on Chemistry* *Edinburgh Review* founded *Cobbett's Political Register* founded Paley *Natural Theology*	Opie *Poems* Scott, ed. *Minstrelsy of the Scottish Border*	Peace of Amiens with France First Factory Act Society for Suppression of Vice formed Napoleon named Consul for life
1803	Godwin *Life of Chaucer* Lancaster *Improvements in Education*	Erasmus Darwin *The Temple of Nature* Jane Porter *Thaddeus of Warsaw*	War with France resumed British capture Delhi Caledonian Canal begun

Date	Prose works	Other works	Historical/cultural events
	Hayley *Life and Posthumous Writings of William Cowper*		Shrapnel invents timed bomb filled with shot
			Fulton demonstrates working steamship
			Irish patriot Robert Emmet executed
			France sells Louisiana to U.S.
1804		Blake *Jerusalem* *Milton*	Pitt returned P.M.
			Napoleon crowned hereditary emperor
		Edgeworth *Popular Tales*	Blake tried for treason
		Opie *Adeline Mowbray*	Britain declares war on Spain
			British and Foreign Bible Society formed
1805	Knight *Principles of Taste* *Eclectic Review* founded	Wordsworth *The Prelude* completed in ms Cary translation of Dante's *Inferno* Godwin *Fleetwood* Scott *The Lay of the Last Minstrel*	Britain, Austria and Russia join in Third Coalition Battle of Trafalgar Death of Nelson
1806	Lancaster *Plan for Educating Ten Thousand Poor Children* Inchbald ed. *The British Theatre* (–1809; 25 vols) Davy *On Some Chemical Agencies of Electricity*	Byron *Fugitive Pieces* Mary Robinson *The Poems* Moore *Epistles, Odes, and Other Poems*	Death of Pitt Death of Fox, Whig leader Grenville P.M. Napoleon closes Continental ports to British ships

Date	Prose works	Other works	Historical/cultural events
	Marcet *Conversations on Chemistry*	Owenson *Wild Irish Girl*	End of Holy Roman Empire
			First steam-operated textile mill opens in Manchester
1807	Hegel *Phenomenology of Mind*	Charles and Mary Lamb *Tales from Shakespeare*	Abolition of slave trade in British dominions
	Davy *On Some New Phenomena of Chemical Changes Produced by Electricity*	Bowdler, ed. *The Family Shakespeare*	Grenville resigns, Duke of Portland P.M.
		Byron *Hours of Idleness*	Russia signs Treaty of Tilsit, withdrawing from war with Napoleon
	Leigh Hunt *Critical Essays on the Performers of the London Theatres*	Crabbe *The Parish Register*	
		Charlotte Smith *Beachy Head*	France invades Portugal and Spain
1808	Dalton *A New System of Chemical Philosophy*	Goethe *Faust* (part I)	Spanish king deposed and Joseph Bonaparte installed as King of Spain
	Leigh Hunt edits *The Examiner*	Hemans *Poems*	British troops land in Portugal
		Hannah More *Coelebs in Search of a Wife*	Convention of Cintra allows French withdrawal
		Scott *Marmion*	Beginning of repeal of laws requiring death
		Jamieson *Dictionary of the Scottish Tongue*	penalty for minor crimes
1809	Coleridge *The Friend*	Byron *English Bards and Scotch Reviewers*	Motion for parliamentary reform defeated in House of Commons
	Quarterly Review founded	Edgeworth *Tales of Fashionable Life* (–1812)	Duke of Wellington commander-in-chief of British troops
	R. L. E. and M. Edgeworth *Professional Education*	C. and M. Lamb *Mrs Leicester's School*	Napoleon captures Vienna

Date	Prose works	Other works	Historical/cultural events
			Perceval P.M.
			Death of Thomas Paine
1810	W. Wordsworth 'Topographical Description of the Country of the Lakes' A. L. Barbauld *The British Novelists*	Crabbe *The Borough* Scott *Lady of the Lake* Brunton *Self-Control* P. B. Shelley *Zastrozzi* Anne Seward *Poetical Works*	Napoleon annexes Holland London riots in support of Burdett George III suffers from renewed bout of mental illness
1811	Ricardo *On the High Price of Bullion* Shelley and Hogg *The Necessity of Atheism* Hannah More *Practical Piety*	Austen *Sense and Sensibility* P. B. Shelley *St Irvyne*	George III declared insane, Prince of Wales installed as Prince Regent Luddite riots in Midlands Shelley expelled from Oxford Cobbett sentenced to two years gaol
1812	P. B. Shelley *A Letter to Lord Ellenborough*	Byron *Childe Harold's Pilgrimage*, cantos I and II Crabbe *Tales in Verse* Cary translation of Dante's *Purgatory* and *Paradise*	Frame-breaking Bill against Luddites Assassination of P.M. Spencer Perceval in House of Commons. Replaced by Lord Liverpool War declared with the U.S. Napoleon invades Russia
1813	Owen *A New View of Society*	Austen *Pride and Prejudice*	Wellington's victory at Vittoria

Date	Prose works	Other works	Historical/cultural events
		Byron *The Giaour*	Defeat of Napoleon at Leipzig
		M. R. Mitford *Narrative Poems on the Female Character*	Leigh Hunt imprisoned for libel on Prince Regent
		P. B. Shelley *Queen Mab*	Southey appointed Poet Laureate
		Scott *Rokeby*	East India Company monopoly in India ended
1814	Turner *England from the Norman Conquest to Edward I* *New Monthly Magazine* founded Malthus *Observations on the Effects of the Corn Laws*	Austen *Mansfield Park* Burney *The Wanderer* Scott *Waverley* Byron *The Corsair Lara* Wordsworth *The Excursion*	Abdication of Napoleon and exile to Elba Congress of Vienna End of war with U.S.A. Stephenson builds steam locomotive Edmund Kean's debut Covent Garden P. B. Shelley elopes with Mary Godwin
1815	A. W. Schlegel *A Course of Lectures on Dramatic Art and Literature* trans. J. Black Davy *On the Fire-Damp of Coal Mines, and on Methods of Lighting the Mines, so as to Prevent its Explosion*	Peacock *Headlong Hall* Scott *Guy Mannering Lord of the Isles* Byron *Hebrew Melodies* Leigh Hunt *The Descent of Liberty, a Mask* Wordsworth *The White Doe of Rylstone*	Napoleon escapes Elba, enters France Napoleon defeated at Battle of Waterloo Corn Law passed
1816	Cobbett *Political Register*	Austen *Emma*	Spa Fields riot, London

Date	Prose works	Other works	Historical/cultural events
	Coleridge *The Statesman's Manual* Marcet *Conversations on Political Economy*	Byron *Childe Harold's Pilgrimage*, III Coleridge *Christabel* *Kubla Khan* Scott *The Antiquary* P. B. Shelley *Alastor*	Riots in East Anglia and manufacturing districts Income tax abolished Elgin Marbles purchased by British Museum
1817	Coleridge *Biographia Literaria* Hazlitt *Characters of Shakespeare's Plays* *The Round Table* James Mill *The History of British India* *Blackwood's Edinburgh Magazine* founded Hone's radical paper, *Black Dwarf*, founded	Keats *Poems* Byron *Manfred* Godwin *Mandeville* Scott *Rob Roy* Edgeworth *Harrington* *Ormond*	Suspension of *habeas corpus* Suppression of democratic societies Trials of radical publisher William Hone Death of Princess Charlotte
1818	Henry Hallam *Europe during the Middle Ages* Hazlitt *Lectures on the English Poets* *A View of the English Stage* Davy *On the Safety Lamp for Coal Miners* Cobbett *A Year's Residence in the United States*	Austen *Northanger Abbey* *Persuasion* Mary Shelley *Frankenstein* Peacock *Nightmare Abbey* Ferrier *Marriage* Scott *Heart of Midlothian* Keats *Endymion* Byron *Childe Harold's Pilgrimage*, IV *Beppo*	Imprisonment of publisher Richard Carlile Defeat of Burdett's and Heron's motions for reform Vestries Act

Date	Prose works	Other works	Historical/cultural events
1819	Hazlitt *Lectures on the English Comic Writers* *Blackwood's Magazine* founded Marcet *Conversations on Natural Philosophy*	Byron *Don Juan*, cantos I and II Scott *Bride of Lammermoor* *Legend of Montrose* Crabbe *Tales of the Hall* Wordsworth *Peter Bell* P. B. Shelley 'The Masque of Anarchy' 'England in 1819' 'Song to the Men of England' Hone *The Political House that Jack Built*	Peterloo Massacre Cobbett returns from America with Paine's bones Passage of the Six Acts against radical activity William Parry's Arctic expedition Poor Relief Act
1820	*London Magazine* founded Godwin *Of Population* Hazlitt *Lectures on the Dramatic Literature of the Age of Shakespeare* Malthus *Principles of Political Economy* Lamb *Essays of Elia* D. Wordsworth *Journal of a Tour on the Continent*	Clare *Poems Descriptive of Rural Life* Keats *Lamia, Isabella, Eve of St Agnes, Hyperion, and Other Poems* Shelley *Prometheus Unbound* *The Cenci* Blake *Jerusalem* Mary Shelley *Matilda* (unpubd.) Scott *The Abbot* *Ivanhoe* *The Monastery* Elizabeth Barrett *The Battle of Marathon* Hone *The Man in the Moon*	Death of George III Accession of Regent as George IV 'Cato Street conspiracy' to assassinate government ministers Divorce trial of Queen Caroline and controversy over her attempts to claim her rights First iron steamship Sir Humphry Davy President of Royal Society

Date	Prose works	Other works	Historical/cultural events
1821	*Manchester Guardian* founded	Clare *The Village Minstrel*	Defeat of Durham's Reform Bill
	De Quincey *Confessions of an English Opium Eater*	P. B. Shelley *Epipsychidion* *Adonais*	Greek War of Independence begins
	Egan *Life in London*	Byron *Don Juan*, cantos III–V	
	James Mill *Elements of Political Economy*	L.E.L. (Laetitia Landon) *The Fate of Adelaide*	
	Lady Morgan *Italy*	Southey *A Vision of Judgement*	
	William E. Parry *Journal of a Voyage for the Discovery of a North-West Passage*	Beddoes *The Improvisatore*	
	P. B. Shelley 'A Defence of Poetry' (unpubd.)		
	H. Martineau 'Female Writers of Practical Divinity'		
	Clare *Sketches in the Life of John Clare*		
1822	*The Liberal* founded	P. B. Shelley *The Triumph of Life*	Sidmouth replaced by Peel as Home Secretary
	H. Martineau 'On Female Education'	Byron *The Vision of Judgement*	Suicide of Castlereagh; Canning becomes Foreign Secretary and Tory leader of House of Commons
	D. Wordsworth *Journal of My Second Tour in Scotland*	Rogers *Italy*	
		Beddoes *The Bride's Tragedy*	
		Digby *Broad Stone of Honour*	
1823	Ackermann produces the first of the Annuals, the *Forget-Me-Not*	Byron *Don Juan*, cantos VI–XIV	War between France and Spain

Date	Prose works	Other works	Historical/cultural events
	Hazlitt *Liber Amoris* *Characteristics*	M. Shelley *Valperga*	Byron in Greece as representative of London Philhellenes
	Lamb *Essays of Elia*	Felicia Hemans *The Vespers of Palermo* *The Siege of Valencia* *The Last Constantine*	
	Franklin *Narrative of a Journey to the Polar Sea*		
	Leigh Hunt *Ultra-Crepidarius*		
1824	*Westminster Review* founded	Byron *Don Juan*, cantos XV–XVI	Repeal of Combination Acts
	Godwin *History of the Commonwealth of England*	Hogg *Confessions of a Justified Sinner*	Opening of National Gallery
	Landor *Imaginary Conversations*, vols I–II	Scott *Redgauntlet*	London Institute inaugurated
		Carlyle translates Goethe's *Wilhelm Meister*	Charles X King of France
		M. R. Mitford *Our Villages* (–1832)	
		L.E.L. *The Improvisatrice*	
1825	Coleridge *Aids to Reflection*	Barbauld *Works*	Financial crisis
	Hazlitt *The Spirit of the Age* *Table Talk*	Hemans *The Forest Sanctuary* *Lays of Many Lands*	Catholic Relief Bill fails House of Lords
	Carlyle *Life of Schiller*	L.E.L. *The Troubadour*	Stockton and Darlington Railway
	James Mill *Essays on Government*	Scott *The Betrothed* *The Talisman*	
	Brougham *Observations on the Education of the People*		

Date	Prose works	Other works	Historical/cultural events
	Thompson and Wheeler *Appeal of One Half the Human Race . . .*		
1826	A. Jameson *Diary of an Ennuyée*	Elizabeth Barrett *An Essay on Mind, with Other Poems* Disraeli *Vivian Grey* (–1827) M. Shelley *The Last Man* Scott *Woodstock*	Russell's proposals on reform defeated Destruction of powerlooms by unemployed weavers Liverpool government falls; Canning P.M. Brougham founds Society for the Diffusion of Useful Knowledge
1827	Scott *Life of Napoleon*	Clare *The Shepherd's Calendar* Alfred and Charles Tennyson *Poems by Two Brothers* Keble *The Christian Year*	Greek independence won in Battle of Navarino Death of Canning; Wellington P.M. University of London founded
1828	Leigh Hunt *Lord Byron and Some of His Contemporaries* Tytler *History of Scotland* (–1843) Franklin *Journal of a Second Expedition to the Polar Sea* Parry *Narrative of an Attempt to Reach the North Pole* *Athenaeum* founded *Spectator* founded Hazlitt *Life of Napoleon Buonaparte*	Elliott *Corn Law Rhymes* Mitford *Rienzi* Bulwer *Pelham* Hemans *Records of Woman* Scott *The Fair Maid of Perth*	Repeal of Test and Corporation Acts Thomas Arnold becomes Head of Rugby School

Date	Prose works	Other works	Historical/cultural events
	D. Wordsworth *Journal of a Tour in the Isle of Man* Macaulay 'History'		
1829	James Mill *Analysis of the Human Mind* Marcet *Conversations on Vegetable Physiology*	Peacock *The Misfortunes of Elphin* Scott *Anne of Geierstein* Jerrold *Black-ey'd Susan*	Catholic Emancipation Metropolitan Police Act
1830	Cobbett *Rural Rides* Coleridge *On the Constitution of the Church and State* T. Moore *Life of Byron* *Fraser's Magazine* founded, ed. Maginn Hood's *Comic Almanac* founded Lyell *Principles of Geology* (1833) Carlyle 'On History' Davy *Consolations in Travel* Herschel *Preliminary Discourse on the Study of Natural Theology* Babbage *Reflections on the Decline of Science in England*	Tennyson *Poems, Chiefly Lyrical* Bulwer *Paul Clifford* Gore *Women as They Are* Hemans *Songs of the Affections* M. Shelley *The Fortunes of Perkin Warbeck*	Death of George IV; accession of William IV Wellington opposes reform; resigns: Grey administration comes in (Whig) July Revolutions in France Liverpool and Manchester Railway opened

Date	Prose works	Other works	Historical/cultural events
1831	Carlyle *Characteristics*	Disraeli *The Young Duke*	Reform Bill crisis
			BAAS founded
	Hegel *Lectures on the Philosophy of History*	Peacock *Crotchet Castle*	Faraday discovers electromagnetic induction
	A. Jameson *Memoirs of Celebrated Female Sovereigns*	Surtees *Jorrocks' Jaunts and Jollities* (–1834)	Darwin begins voyage of the *Beagle* (–1836)
	Somerville *Mechanism of the Heavens*		
1832	H. Martineau *Illustrations of Political Economy* (–1834)	Tennyson *Poems*	First Reform Act
			Durham University founded
	Carlyle 'Biography'	Walker *The Factory Lad*	Morse invents telegraph
	F. Trollope *Domestic Manners of the Americans*	Bulwer *Eugene Aram*	
		G. P. R. James *Henry Masterton*	
	Penny Magazine founded	Marryat *Peter Simple* (–1833)	
	Chambers's Journal founded	Disraeli *Contarini Fleming*	
	A. Jameson *Characteristics of Women*		
1833	Carlyle *Sartor Resartus* (–1834) 'On History Again'	R. Browning *Pauline*	Factory Act ('Children's Charter')
	Newman *et al* *Tracts for the Times* (–1837)	E. Barrett *Prometheus Bound, translated from Aeschylus and Miscellaneous Poems*	Oxford Movement begins
			First government grant for schools
	Keble *National Apostasy*	Newman 'Lead, Kindly Light'	
	T. Arnold *Principles of Church Reform*		

Date	Prose works	Other works	Historical/cultural events
	J. S. Mill 'What is Poetry?' *Penny Cyclopaedia* founded *Bridgewater Treatises* (–1836) Bulwer *England and the English* Macaulay 'Horace Walpole' P. Gaskell *The Manufacturing* *Population of England*		
1834	Somerville *On the Connexion of the* *Physical Sciences* Hallam *Essays and Remains* Martineau *Illustrations of Taxation* Newman *Parochial Sermons* (–1842)	Bulwer *Last Days of Pompeii* Ainsworth *Rookwood*	Abolition of slavery in British dominions Poor Law Amendment Act introduces workhouses Owen's Grand National Trades Union Tolpuddle Martyrs Melbourne P.M. (Whig) July; Peel P.M. (Tory) December Houses of Parliament burnt down
1835	D. F. Strauss *Das Leben Jesu* Tocqueville *Democracy in America*, I Macaulay 'Sir James Mackintosh' J. S. Mill Review of Tennyson's Poems Thirlwall *History of Greece* (–1844)	R. Browning *Paracelsus* Bulwer *Rienzi* C. Norton *The Wife and Woman's* *Reward*	Melbourne P.M. (Whig) April Municipal Corporations Act reforms English local government Fox Talbot's first photographs

Date	Prose works	Other works	Historical/cultural events
1836	Pugin *Contrasts* *Dublin Review* founded	Dickens *Sketches by Boz* *Pickwick Papers* (–1837) Marryat *Mr Midshipman Easy* R. Browning 'Porphyria's Lover' 'Johannes Agricola in Meditation' Keble, Newman *et al* *Lyra Apostolica*	First train in London (to Greenwich) Newspaper tax reduced London University given Royal Charter as examining body London Working Men's Association leads towards Chartism Botanic Society founded
1837	Carlyle *The History of the French Revolution* *Bentley's Miscellany* founded Macaulay 'Francis Bacon' H. Martineau *Society in America* Newman *The Prophetical Office of the Church* Ruskin *The Poetry of Architecture* (–1838) Barham *Ingoldsby Legends* Lockhart *Life of Sir Walter Scott* (–1838)	Dickens *Oliver Twist* Disraeli *Henrietta Temple* *Venetia* Thackeray *Yellowplush Correspondence* (–1838) R. Browning *Strafford*	Accession of Queen Victoria Barry begins work on the Reform Club Government School of Design set up Paper duty halved
1838	J. S. Mill 'Bentham' C. Hennell *An Inquiry Concerning the Origin of Christianity*	Dickens *Nicholas Nickleby* Bulwer *Alice, or the Mysteries*	Anti-Corn Law League founded 'People's Charter' issued by Chartists Brunel's *Great Western* crosses Atlantic

Date	Prose works	Other works	Historical/cultural events
	Mantell *The Wonders of Geology*		London–Birmingham railway completed
	Maurice *The Kingdom of Christ*		
	Newman, Keble, Pusey (eds) *Library of the Fathers of the Holy Catholic Church* (–1885)		
	T. Arnold *History of Rome* (–1843)		
	Macaulay 'Sir William Temple'		
	H. Martineau *A Retrospect of Western Travel*		
	A. Jameson *Winter Studies and Summer Rambles in Canada*		
1839	Carlyle *Chartism*	Martineau *Deerbrook*	Chartist riots
	Darwin *Voyage of the 'Beagle'*	Thackeray *Catherine* (–1840)	Anglo-Chinese Opium War
	Faraday *Experimental Researches in Electricity* (–1855)		Daguerre and Fox Talbot announce rival photographic processes
			Introduction of patents for gas cookers
	C. Norton *A Plain Letter to the Lord Chancellor on the Infants Custody Bill*		
	S. Ellis *The Women of England*		
1840	J. S. Mill 'Coleridge'	Dickens *Old Curiosity Shop* (–1841)	Marriage of Victoria and Albert
	Whewell *Philosophy of the Inductive Sciences*	Martineau *The Hour and the Man*	Penny Post introduced by Rowland Hill

Date	Prose works	Other works	Historical/cultural events
	Macaulay 'Lord Clive'	R. Browning *Sordello*	Houses of Parliament, by Barry and Pugin (–1852)
	Newman Sermon on 'Explicit and Implicit Reason'		Afghans surrender
	Thackeray *Paris Sketch Book*		Maoris yield sovereignty of New Zealand under Treaty of Waitangi
	Barham *Ingoldsby Legends* (–1847)		Anti-slavery convention held in London
	A. Jameson *Pictures of the Social Life of Germany*		
1841	Carlyle *On Heroes and Hero-Worship*	Dickens *Barnaby Rudge*	Peel P.M. (Tory)
	Newman *Tract XC The Tamworth Reading Room*	R. Browning *Pippa Passes*	Chemical Society founded London Library opened
	Macaulay 'Warren Hastings'		Governesses' Benevolent Institute
	Miller *The Old Red Sandstone*		
	Boucicault *London Assurance*		
	Punch founded		
	Dodd *Narrative of the Experience and Suffering of William Dodd, Factory Cripple*		
1842	Chadwick *Sanitary Condition of the Labouring Population of Great Britain*	Tennyson *Poems*	Mines Act Chartist riots after petition rejected
	Dickens *American Notes*	R. Browning *Dramatic Lyrics*	Mudie's Lending Library opened
	Macaulay 'Frederic the Great'	Macaulay *Lays of Ancient Rome*	Copyright Act
	Ashley 'Employment of		

Date	Prose works	Other works	Historical/cultural events
	Women and Children in Mines and Collieries'		
	˙Marcet *Conversations on the History of England* (–1844)		
1843	Carlyle *Past and Present*	Dickens *Christmas Carol* *Martin Chuzzlewit* (–1844)	Wordsworth Poet Laureate
	Ruskin *Modern Painters*, vol. I (–1860)		Ethnological Society founded
	J. S. Mill *System of Logic*		
	The *Economist* founded		
	Borrow *The Bible in Spain*		
	Macaulay *Essays, Critical and Historical*		
	Newman *Sermons Preached Before the University of Oxford*		
	A. Lovelace Translation and Commentary, *Sketch of the Analytical Engine Invented by Charles Babbage*		
1844	Chambers *Vestiges of the Natural History of Creation*	E. Barrett *Poems*	Factory Act limiting working hours for women and children
	Newman *et al* *Lives of the English Saints*	Barnes *Poems of Rural Life in the Dorset Dialect*	'Rochdale Pioneers': first Cooperative Society
	Keble *Praelectiones Academicae*	Patmore *Poems*	Ragged School Union
	North British Review founded	Dickens *The Chimes*	First public baths (Liverpool)

Date	Prose works	Other works	Historical/cultural events
	Finlay *Greece Under the Romans* Stanley *Life and Correspondence of Thomas Arnold* Kinglake *Eothen* Horne, ed. *A New Spirit of the Age*	Disraeli *Coningsby* Thackeray *Barry Lyndon* Yonge *Abbeychurch*	London YMCA First Joint Stock Act
1845	Carlyle *Oliver Cromwell's Letters and Speeches* De Quincey *Suspiria de Profundis* Engels *Die Lage der arbeitenden Klassen in England* Ford *Handbook for Travellers in Spain* M. Fuller *Women in the Nineteenth Century* Lewes *Biographical History of Philosophy* (−1846) Martineau *Letters on Mesmerism* Newman *Essay on the Development of Christian Doctrine* Warburton *The Crescent and the Cross* A. Jameson *Memoirs of the Early Italian Painters* E. Barrett and R. Browning begin correspondence	Disraeli *Sybil* R. Browning *Dramatic Romances and Lyrics* Jewsbury *Zoe* Thackeray *Diary of Jeames de la Pluche*	Newman's conversion to Roman Catholicism Irish potato famine (−1848) Sir John Franklin's expedition in search of the North-West Passage Maynooth grant for Irish education

Date	Prose works	Other works	Historical/cultural events
1846	Clough Letters to *The Balance* on political economy Grote *History of Greece* (–1856) (Horne) *Memoirs of a London Doll, Written by Herself* Ruskin *Modern Painters*, vol. II Strauss *Life of Jesus* (trans. George Eliot) Thackeray *Snobs of England* (–1847) *Notes of a Journey from Cornhill to Grand Cairo* *Daily News* founded A. Jameson *Memoirs and Essays Illustrative of Art, Literature, and Social Morals* Dickens *Pictures from Italy*	Bulwer *Lucretia* Dickens *Dombey and Son* (–1848) C., E. and A. Brontë *Poems* Keble *Lyra Innocentium* Lear *Book of Nonsense*	Repeal of Corn Laws (Peel) Russell P.M. (Whig) July Ether used as anaesthetic in operation Bohn's *Standard Library* begun Hakluyt Society founded to publish travel books Railway boom starts Electrical Telegraph Co. founded
1847	Clough *Consideration of Objections Against the Retrenchment Association* Helmholtz 'On the Conservation of Force [Energy]' Joule 'On the Mechanical Equivalent of Heat' Keble *Sermons* Thackeray *Mr Punch's Prize Novelists*	A. Brontë *Agnes Grey* C. Brontë *Jane Eyre* E. Brontë *Wuthering Heights* Tennyson *The Princess* Thackeray *Vanity Fair* Disraeli *Tancred*	10 Hours Factory Act Communist League founded J. Y. Simpson uses chloroform as general anaesthetic British Museum south front completed E. Blackwell first woman to attend medical school in the U.S.

Date	Prose works	Other works	Historical/cultural events
1848	Forster *Life and Adventures of Oliver Goldsmith* Martineau *Eastern Life, Prsent and Past* Marx and Engels *Communist Manifesto* Mill *Principles of Political Economy* Milnes, ed. *Life, Letters and Literary Remains of John Keats* A. Jameson *Sacred and Legendary Art* H. Ward *Five Years in Kaffirland* Somerville *Physical Geography*	A. Brontë *The Tenant of Wildfell Hall* Clough *The Bothie of Toper-na-Fuosich* Gaskell *Mary Barton* C. Kingsley *Yeast* Newman *Loss and Gain* Thackeray *Pendennis*	Revolutions in Europe Louis Napoleon President of France Cholera in England Public Health Act Failure of Chartist petition Rossetti, Millais and Hunt form Pre-Raphaelite Brotherhood Queen's College for Women founded in London
1849	Carlyle 'Occasional Discourse on the Nigger Question' Curzon *Visits to Monasteries in the Levant* Herschel *Outlines of Astronomy* Layard *Nineveh and its Remains* Macaulay *History of England from the Accession of James II* (–1861) Martineau *History of England*	C. Brontë *Shirley* Dickens *David Copperfield* (–1850) J. A. Froude *Nemesis of Faith* M. Arnold *The Strayed Reveller* Clough and Burbridge *Ambarvalia*	Rome proclaimed a republic under Mazzini, then taken by French Communist riots suppressed in Paris Disraeli becomes Conservative leader Bedford College for Women founded E. Blackwell qualifies as a doctor in U.S.

Date	Prose works	Other works	Historical/cultural events
	during the Thirty Years' Peace (–1850)		
	Mayhew *London Labour and the London Poor* (in *Morning Chronicle*) (–1850)		
	F. W. Newman *The Soul*		
	Ruskin *The Seven Lamps of Architecture*		
	Notes and Queries founded		
	The Lily founded by A. Bloomer		
1850	Carlyle *Latter-Day Pamphlets*	C. Kingsley *Alton Locke*	Public Libraries Act
	The Germ (Pre-Raphaelite journal) founded	Tennyson *In Memoriam A.H.H.*	Factory Act: 60-hour week for women and young persons
	Household Words founded and edited by Dickens	Wordsworth *The Prelude*	Miss Buss starts North London Collegiate School
	Merrivale *History of the Romans under the Empire*	E. Barrett Browning *Sonnets from the Portuguese* (in *Poems*)	Tennyson becomes Poet Laureate
	F. W. Newman *Phases of Faith*	R. Browning *Christmas Eve and Easter Day*	Wiseman made Cardinal; Roman Catholic hierarchy restored in England
	Beames *The Rookeries of London*	Jewsbury *Marian Withers* (–1851)	Butterfield's All Saints', Margaret Street (–1859)
	Leigh Hunt *Autobiography*		Natural Sciences Honours School set up at Oxford
1851	Carlyle *Life of John Sterling*	Gaskell *Cranford* (–1853)	Great Exhibition
	Fitzgerald *Euphranor: A Dialogue on Youth*	E. Barrett Browning *Casa Guidi Windows*	Natural Sciences Tripos set up at Cambridge

Date	Prose works	Other works	Historical/cultural events
	Newman *Lectures on the Present Position of Catholics in England* H. Spencer *Social Statics* Ruskin *The Stones of Venice*, vol. I (−1853) Trench *The Study of Words*	Meredith *Poems*	Owens College Manchester founded Louis Napoleon *coup d'état* Cubitt, King's Cross Station (−1852)
1852	R. Browning 'Shelley' Newman *University Education* (later *Idea of a University*) Nightingale begins *Cassandra* (−1859) Spencer 'The Development Hypothesis' 'Philosophy of Style' 'Theory of Population' A. Jameson *Legends of the Madonna* *Englishwoman's Domestic Magazine* published by Samuel Beeton	Dickens *Bleak House* (−1853) C. Kingsley *Hypatia* (−1853) Thackeray *Henry Esmond* M. Arnold *Empedocles on Etna and Other Poems* Tennyson *Ode on the Death of the Duke of Wellington*	Derby P.M. (Tory) February Wellington dies Aberdeen P.M. (Coalition) December Louis Napoleon proclaimed Emperor Department of Practical Art established Brunel and Wyatt, Paddington Station (−1854)
1853	Bagehot 'Shakespeare – The Individual' Froude 'England's Forgotten Worthies' H. Martineau translates *The Positive Philosophy of Auguste Comte*	C. Brontë *Villette* Gaskell *Ruth* Thackeray *The Newcomes* (−1855) Yonge *The Heir of Redclyffe*	Turkey declares war on Russia, Turkish fleet destroyed *Encyclopaedia Britannica*, 8th edition (−1860) Photographic Society set up Holman Hunt paints *The Light of the World*

Date	Prose works	Other works	Historical/cultural events
	F. D. Maurice *Theological Essays*	M. Arnold *Poems*	
	Thackeray *English Humourists of the Eighteenth Century*	Patmore *Tamerton Church-Tower and Other Poems*	
	Wallace *Travels on the Amazon and Rio Negro*		
1854	G. Eliot translates Feuerbach's *Essence of Christianity*	Dickens *Hard Times*	Crimean War starts (–1856)
	P. Gosse *Aquarium: An Unveiling of the Wonders of the Deep Sea*	Gaskell *North and South* (–1855)	Working Men's College, London, founded by Maurice
	Huxley 'On the Educational Value of the Natural History Sciences'	Patmore *The Angel in the House* (–1863)	University College, Dublin, founded
	H. Miller *My Schools and Schoolmasters*	Tennyson 'The Charge of the Light Brigade'	Pius IX makes Immaculate Conception an article of faith
	C. Norton *English Laws for Women in the Nineteenth Century*		Cheltenham Ladies' College founded
	H. Morley 'Ground in the Mill'		
	Dickens 'On Strike'		
1855	Bagehot 'The First Edinburgh Reviewers'	Dickens *Little Dorritt* (–1857)	Palmerston P.M. (Lib.)
	Burton *First Narrative of a Pilgrimage to El-Medinah and Meccah*	C. Kingsley *Westward Ho!*	Joint Stock Companies Act
		A. Trollope *The Warden*	Fall of Sebastopol
	Gatty *Parables from Nature* (–1871)	R. Browning *Men and Women*	Newspaper tax abolished

Date	Prose works	Other works	Historical/cultural events
	B. Leigh-Smith *Brief Summary of Laws Relating to Women*	Tennyson *Maud and Other Poems*	First Hoe rotary press in England
	Macaulay *History of England*, vols III–IV		Deane and Woodward begin Oxford Museum (–1859)
	Maurice *Learning and Working*		Livingstone discovers Victoria Falls
	Newman 'Who's to Blame?'		
	C. Norton *Letter to the Queen*		
	Daily Telegraph founded		
	Lewes *The Life and Works of Goethe*		
	Saturday Review founded		
	A. Jameson *Sisters of Charity: Catholic and Protestant*		
	Smiles *Life of George Stephenson*		
1856	Burton *First Footsteps in East Africa*	Newman *Callista*	Bessemer patents steel-making process
	J. A. Froude *History of England*, vols I and II (–1870)	C. Reade *It's Never Too Late to Mend*	Perkin discovers aniline dye
	B. Leigh-Smith *Women and Work*		
	Oxford and Cambridge Magazine		
	A. Jameson *The Communion of*		

Date	Prose works	Other works	Historical/cultural events
	Labour: Social Employments of Women		
	Müller 'Comparative Mythology'		
	G. Eliot 'Silly Novels by Lady Novelists'		
	Enquire Within Upon Everything		
1857	M. Arnold 'On the Modern Element in Literature'	C. Brontë *The Professor*	Indian Mutiny (–1859)
	H. T. Buckle *History of Civilization in England*, vol. I (–1861)	G. Eliot *Scenes of Clerical Life*	Matrimonial Causes Act
		Hughes *Tom Brown's Schooldays*	Manchester Art Treasures Exhibition
	Gaskell *The Life of Charlotte Brontë*	Thackeray *The Virginians*	Oxford Union frescoes painted by Rossetti, Morris and Burne-Jones
	P. Gosse *Omphalos*	A. Trollope *Barchester Towers*	Arnold Professor of Poetry at Oxford
	Livingstone *Missionary Travels and Researches in South Africa*	E. Barrett Browning *Aurora Leigh*	Neanderthal Man discovered in Germany
	H. Miller *The Testimony of the Rocks*		National Association for the Promotion of Social Science formed
	Ruskin *The Political Economy of Art*		
1858	Carlyle *Frederick the Great*, vols I–II (–1865)	Ballantyne *The Coral Island*	Derby P.M. (Tory)
	Gladstone *Studies on Homer*	Farrar *Eric; or, Little by Little*	Brunel's *Great Eastern* launched
	The English Woman's Journal founded	Macdonald *Phantastes*	Powers of East India Company transferred to the Crown

Date	Prose works	Other works	Historical/cultural events
		A. Trollope *Dr Thorne*	Jewish Disabilities Act
			Property qualification for M.P.s abolished
		Clough *Amours de Voyage*	
			Fenian Brotherhood founded in Ireland
		Morris *The Defence of Guinevere and Other Poems*	
			Darwin and Wallace deliver joint paper on evolution
			Ruskin's 'unconversion' in Turin
1859	*All the Year Round*, founded and edited by Dickens	Collins *Woman in White*	Palmerston P.M. (Whig-Lib.)
		Dickens *Tale of Two Cities*	Franco-Austrian War (–1861)
	Englishwoman's Journal founded	G. Eliot *Adam Bede*	Foreign Office begun in Italian Renaissance style
	Macmillan's Magazine	Meredith *Ordeal of Richard Feverel*	First oil well drilled in USA
	Arnold *England and the Italian Question*		
	Bagehot 'Parliamentary Reform'	A. Trollope *The Bertrams*	
	I. Beeton *Book of Household Management*	Fitzgerald *Rubaiyat of Omar Khayyam*	
	Darwin *On the Origin of Species by Means of Natural Selection*	Tennyson *Idylls of the King* (–1885)	
	Masson *Life of John Milton*		
	J. S. Mill *On Liberty*		
	Nightingale *Notes on Hospitals* *Notes on Nursing* *Cassandra*		

Date	Prose works	Other works	Historical/cultural events
	Ruskin *The Two Paths* *Elements of Drawing* Smiles *Self-Help*		
1860	Bradlaugh founds *National Reformer* Burton *Lake Regions of Central Africa* *Cornhill Magazine* founded, ed. Thackeray E. Davies *Letters to Daily Newspaper* *Essays and Reviews* Faraday *Various Forces of Matter* Ruskin *Unto this Last* Spencer *System of Synthetic Philosophy* (–1896)	Dickens *Great Expectations* (–1861) G. Eliot *The Mill on the Floss* Trollope *Framley Parsonage*	Italian unification Huxley-Wilberforce debate at the Oxford BAAS meeting Discovery of the source of the Nile Scott, St Pancras Station Society for Promoting Employment of Women founded Nightingale Training School opened
1861	M. Arnold (H *Translating Home*) 'Democracy' Colenso *Commentary on Romans* Faraday *Six Lectures on the Chemical History of a Candle* Maine *Ancient Law* J. S. Mill *Utilitarianism*	G. Eliot *Silas Marner* Hughes *Tom Brown at Oxford* C. Reade *The Cloister and the Hearth* Thackeray *Adventures of Philip* (–1862) Trollope *Orley Farm* (–1862)	American Civil War (–1865) Death of Prince Albert Emancipation of serfs in Russia Victor Emmanuel King of Italy Lowe's Revised Code: payment by results in grants to schools Post Office Savings Bank opened

Date	Prose works	Other works	Historical/cultural events
	Considerations on Representative Government Muller *Science of Languages* (–1864) Spedding *The Letters and the Life of Francis Bacon* Spencer *Education* Smiles *Lives of the Engineers* (–1862) Williams *Literary Women of England*	Wood *East Lynne* D. G. Rossetti trans. *Early Italian Poets together with Dante's Vita Nuova* Palgrave *Golden Treasury of Songs and Lyrics* Baker *Hymns Ancient and Modern*	Morris and Company founded Paper tax abolished Female Middle Class Emigration Society founded
1862	M. Arnold *On Translating Homer: Last Words* Butler 'Darwin on the Origin of Species: A Dialogue' Colenso *The Pentateuch Examined* (–1879) Kelvin *On the Age of the Sun's Heat* Yonge, ed. *Biographies of Good Women* J. Kavanagh, ed. *Women of Letters* W. R. Greg 'Why Are Women Redundant?'	G. Eliot *Romola* C. Rossetti *Goblin Market* A. Trollope *The Small House at Allingham* E. Barrett Browning *Last Poems* Meredith *Modern Love*	*Alabama* built at Birkenhead for Confederates Bismarck Prussian premier Lancashire cotton famine Companies Act: limited liability
1863	Butler *A First Year in Canterbury Settlement*	Gaskell *Sylvia's Lovers* *Cousin Phyllis* (–1864)	Anthropological Society formed

Date	Prose works	Other works	Historical/cultural events
	'Darwin Among the Machines'	C. Kingsley The Water-Babies	Cambridge Local Exams opened to girls
	Gardiner History of England from the accession of James I (–1882)	Oliphant The Rector and the Doctor's Family Salem Chapel	Metropolitan Line opened Scott's Albert Memorial (–1872)
	Gilchrist Life of William Blake	C. Reade Hard Cash	
	Huxley Man's Place in Nature		
	Kinglake The Invasion of the Crimea (–1887)		
	Lyell The Antiquity of Man		
	Renan Life of Jesus		
	Speke Journal of the Discovery of the Source of the Nile		
	Taine History of English Literature		
	Tyndall Heat as a Mode of Motion		
	W. Reade Savage Africa		
	Victoria Magazine founded		
1864	Bagehot 'Wordsworth, Tennyson, and Browning or Pure Ornate, and Grotesque Art in English Poetry' Newman Apologia Pro Vita Sua	Dickens Our Mutual Friend (–1865) Gaskell Wives and Daughters (–1866) Le Fanu Uncle Silas	International Working Men's Association founded in London Octavia Hill starts work on slums Clerk Maxwell describes hypothetically electro-magnetic radiation

Date	Prose works	Other works	Historical/cultural events
	Pater writes 'Diaphaneitè'	A. Trollope *Can You Forgive Her?* (–1865)	First Contagious Diseases Act
	Spencer *Principles of Biology* (–1867)	R. Browning *Dramatis Personae*	Pasteur invents 'pasteurisation'
	The Month founded	Tennyson *Idylls of the Hearth* (later *Enoch Arden*)	
	A. Jameson *The History of Our Lord*	Hawker *Quest of the Sangraal*	
1865	M. Arnold *Essays in Criticism*, first series	Carroll *Alice's Adventures in Wonderland*	Russell P.M. (Whig-Lib.)
	Butler *Evidence for the Resurrection*	C. Kingsley *Hereward the Wake*	Lincoln assassinated Lister introduces antiseptic surgery
	Hopkins writes 'On the Origin of Beauty: A Platonic Dialogue'	Yonge *The Clever Woman of the Family*	Slavery abolished in U.S.A.
	Lecky *History of the Rise and Influence of the Spirit of Rationalism in Europe*	Clough *Dipsychus* Newman *The Dream of Gerontius*	Eyre suppresses revolt in Jamaica Booth founds Salvation Army
	Livingstone *The Zambesi and its Tributaries*	Swinburne *Atalanta in Calydon*	Elizabeth Garrett Anderson gains medical licence
	J. Lubbock *Prehistoric Times*		Taunton Commission into Education includes girls' schools
	J. F. McLennan *Primitive Marriage*		Kensington Society formed
	W. G. Palgrave *Personal Narrative of the Year's Journey through Central and Eastern Arabia*		
	Ruskin *Sesame and Lilies*		

Date	Prose works	Other works	Historical/cultural events
	Seeley *Ecce Homo*		
	Argosy founded, ed. Mrs Henry Wood		
	Fortnightly Review founded		
	Pall Mall Gazette founded		
	Smiles *Lives of Boulton and* *Watt*		
	J. Grote *Exploratio Philosophica*, I		
1866	Carlyle *Inaugural Lecture at* *Edinburgh: On the* *Choice of Books* *Contemporary Review* founded Dallas *The Gay Science* E. Davies *The Higher Education of* *Women* Hopkins starts writing *Journal* Pater 'Coleridge' Ruskin *Crown of Wild Olive* *The Englishwoman's* *Review* founded	G. Eliot *Felix Holt the Radical* Meredith *Vittoria* Oliphant *Mrs Marjoribanks* Trollope *The Claverings* (–1867) *The Last Chronicle of* *Barset* (–1867) C. Rossetti *The Prince's Progress* *and Other Poems* Swinburne *Poems and Ballads*, first series	Derby P.M. (Tory) Fenians active in Ireland Elizabeth Garrett opens dispensary for women Dr Barnado starts children's homes Work starts on London underground railway Second Contagious Diseases Act First petition to Parliament for female suffrage Mendel discovers laws of heredity Nobel discovers dynamite
1867	M. Arnold *On the Study of Celtic* *Literature* Bagehot *The English Constitution*	A. Trollope *Phineas Finn* (–1869) M. Arnold *New Poems*	Second Reform Act Typewriter invented Henry Irving on the London stage

Date	Prose works	Other works	Historical/cultural events
	Carlyle *Shooting Niagara: And After?*	Morris *The Life and Death of Jason*	Council for Promoting Higher Education for Women founded
	Freeman *History of the Norman Conquest* (–1876)	Swinburne *Song of Italy*	National Society for Women's Suffrage founded
	Marx *Das Kapital*, I (trans. 1887)		Factory Act Lister describes antiseptic surgery in *The Lancet*
	Pater 'Winckelmann'		Albert Hall begun (–1871)
	Ruskin *Time and Tide*		
	Sidgwick 'Prophet of Culture'		
1868	Huxley 'Liberal Education and Where to Find It' 'On the Physical Basis of Life'	Collins *The Moonstone* Trollope *He Knew he was Right*	Disraeli P.M. (Tory) February Gladstone P.M. (Lib.) December
	Pater 'Poems of William Morris'	R. Browning *The Ring and the Book*	Public executions abolished
	Swinburne *William Blake: A Critical Essay*	G. Eliot *The Spanish Gypsy* Morris *The Earthly Paradise*	British Trades Union Congress formed
	The Revolution newspaper founded by Stanton and Anthony	Newman *Verses on Various Occasions*	
	F. Power Cobbe 'Criminals, idiots, women, and minors: is the classification sound?'	L. M. Alcott *Little Women*	
	Queen Victoria *Leaves from the Journal of our Life in the Highlands, from 1848–1861*		

Date	Prose works	Other works	Historical/cultural events
1869	M. Arnold *Culture and Anarchy* *St Paul and Protestantism*	L. M. Alcott *Good Wives*	Girton College, Cambridge, founded
	J. Butler *Women's Work and Culture*	Blackmore *Lorna Doone* Collins *Man and Wife* (–1870)	Suez Canal opened Mendeleev's periodic table of the elements
	Galton *Hereditary Genius*	M. Arnold *Collected Poems*	Metaphysical Society formed
	Lecky *History of European Morals*	Clough *Poems and Prose Remains*	Third Contagious Diseases Act Ladies' National
	J. S. Mill *On the Subjection of Women*	Tennyson *Holy Grail and Other Poems*	Association Against Contagious Diseases Acts formed
	Ruskin *The Queen of the Air*		
	A. R. Wallace *The Malay Archipelago*		
	Graphic Magazine founded		
	Nature founded		
	Martineau *Biographical Sketches, 1852–1868*		
	Somerville *On Molecular and Microscopic Science*		
1870	Austin *The Poetry of the Period*	Dickens *Edwin Drood*	Franco-Prussian War (–1871)
	Huxley *Lay Sermons*	Disraeli *Lothair*	Papal infallibility declared
	Lubbock *The Origin of Civilisation*	Meredith *Adventures of Harry Richmond* (–1871)	Forster's Education Act English Literature made a subject in
	Newman *A Grammar of Assent*	D. G. Rossetti *Poems*	elementary schools Married Women's Property Act gives

Date	Prose works	Other works	Historical/cultural events
	Spencer *Principles of Psychology* (–1872)		wives rights over own earnings
			Devonshire Commission on Scientific Education
			Civil Service opened to competitive examination
1871	M. Arnold *Friendship's Garland*	Bulwer *The Coming Race*	Trade unions legalised
	Buchanan 'The Fleshly School of Poetry'	Carroll *Through the Looking-Glass*	Religious tests abolished at Oxford, Cambridge and Durham
	J. Butler *Constitution Violated*	G. Eliot *Middlemarch* (–1872)	Anthropological Institute formed
	Darwin *The Descent of Man*	Hardy *Desperate Remedies*	Army Reform Acts
	D. G. Rossetti 'Stealthy School of Criticism'	Trollope *The Eustace Diamonds* (–1873)	Royal Commission on Contagious Diseases Paris Commune set up and suppressed
	Ruskin *Fors Clavigera* (–1884)	Lear *Nonsense Songs and Verses*	Stanley finds Livingstone
	Tylor *Primitive Culture*	Swinburne *Songs Before Sunrise*	Anne Clough starts house of residence at Cambridge (Newnham College in 1876)
	Stephen *The Playground of Europe*		
1872	Bagehot *Physics and Politics*	Butler *Erewhon*	(Secret) Ballot Act
	Darwin *The Expression of the Emotions in Man*	Hardy *Under the Greenwood Tree* *A Pair of Blue Eyes* (–1873)	Edison perfects electric telegraph Girls' Public Day School Trust established
	Forster *Life of Dickens* (–1874)	R. Browning *Fifine at the Fair*	
	Nietzsche *The Birth of Tragedy*	Morris *Love is Enough*	

Date	Prose works	Other works	Historical/cultural events
	W. Reade *The Martyrdom of Man*	Tennyson *Gareth and Lynette*	
	Ruskin *Munera Pulveris*		
	Stanley *How I found Livingstone*		
1873	M. Arnold *Literature and Dogma*	Collins *The New Magdalen*	Cavendish Laboratory set up in Cambridge
	Hopkins writes lecture notes on 'Rhetoric'	A. Trollope *Phineas Redux* (–1874)	
	Maurice *The Friendship of Books*	R. Browning *Red Cotton Night-Cap Country*	
	Clerk Maxwell *Electricity and Magnetism*	Dobson *Vignettes in Rhyme*	
	J. S. Mill *Autobiography*		
	Newman *The Idea of a University Defined and Illustrated*		
	Pater *Studies in the History of the Renaissance*		
	Stephen *Essays in Freethinking and Plainspeaking*		
	M. Somerville *Personal Recollections*		
	Sara Coleridge *Recollections of the Early Life*		
1874	Galton *English Men of Science: Their Nature and Nurture*	Hardy *Far from the Madding Crowd*	Disraeli P.M. (Tory) Factory Act
	Green *Short History of the English People*	Meredith *Beauchamp's Career* (–1875)	Paris – First Impressionist Exhibition

Date	Prose works	Other works	Historical/cultural events
	Lewes *Problems of Life and Mind* (–1879)	A. Trollope *The Way We Live Now* (–1875)	Moody and Sankey lead Evangelical revival in Britain
	J. S. Mill *Three Essays on Religion*	Thomson *The City of Dreadful Night*	London School of Economics opened to women
	Morley *On Compromise*		Strike of agricultural workers
	Sedgwick *The Methods of Ethics*		Women's Provident and Protective League founded
	Stephen *Hours in a Library* (–1879)		London School of Medicine for Women founded
	W. Stubbs *Constitutional History of England* (–1878)		
	Tyndall 'Address' to the Belfast BAAS		
1875	M. Arnold *God and the Bible*	Hardy *The Hand of Ethelberta* (–1876)	Britain buys major holding of Suez Canal shares
	Carlyle *The Early Kings of Norway*	A. Trollope *The Prime Minister* (–1876)	Theosophical Society founded
	Creighton *History of Rome*	Hopkins writes *The Wreck of the Deutschland*	France becomes a Republic
	Symonds *Renaissance in Italy* (–1898)		Public Health Act
1876	Bradley *Ethical Studies*	G. Eliot *Daniel Deronda*	Bell patents telephone
	Spencer *Principles of Sociology* (–1896)	Carroll *The Hunting of the Snark*	Edison invents phonograph
	Stephen *English Thought in the 18th Century*	Morris *Sigurd the Volsung*	Victoria proclaimed Empress of India Bulgarian atrocities

Date	Prose works	Other works	Historical/cultural events
	Trevelyan *Life and Letters of Lord Macaulay*	Tennyson *Harold*	Otto invents four-stroke internal-combustion engine
	Darwin *Recollections of the Development of my Mind and Character*		Disraeli becomes Earl of Beaconsfield
			Royal Commission on Factories and Workshops
			Mind founded
1877	Arnold *Last Essays on Church and Religion*	Mallock *The New Republic*	Bradlaugh–Besant trial
		Sewell *Black Beauty*	Delane editor of the *Times*
	Finlay *History of Greece from its Conquest by the Romans*	Patmore *The Unknown Eros and Other Poems*	Russo-Turkish War
			Grosvenor Gallery opens
	Martineau *Autobiography*		Morris, Webb and Faulkner found Society for Protection of Ancient Buildings
	Meredith *On the Idea of Comedy Nineteenth Century* founded		Praxiteles' *Hermes* found at Olympia
			Universities of Oxford and Cambridge Act
	A. Besant *The Gospel of Atheism My Path to Atheism*		M. Grey Training College for Women founded
1878	*English Men of Letters* series begun, ed. Morley	Hardy *Return of the Native*	Salvation Army re-established
		Mallock *The New Paul and Virginia*	Paris Exhibition
	Lecky *History of England in the Eighteenth Century*		Ruskin–Whistler libel trial
	Pater 'Child in the House'		F. M. Brown begins decoration of Manchester Town Hall
	Smiles *George Moore: Merchant and Philanthropist*		National and Union Training School founded
			London University admits women

Date	Prose works	Other works	Historical/cultural events
1879	M. Arnold *Mixed Essays* A. Bebel *Woman and Socialism* Butler *Evolution, Old and New* J. S. Mill 'Chapters on Socialism' Morris 'Art of the People' Spencer *Principles of Ethics* (−1893) T. H. Green lectures 'On the Principles of Political Obligation' (−1880, published 1888) Stevenson *Travels with a Donkey* *Cambridge Review* founded *The Boys' Own Paper* founded	G. Eliot *Impressions of Theophrastus Such* Meredith *The Egoist* A. Trollope *The Duke's Children* (−1880) R. Browning *Dramatic Idylls*, first series	Electric light bulb invented Afghan and Zulu wars Ayrton addresses British Association on 'Electricity as a Motive Power' Somerville Hall and Lady Margaret Hall founded at Oxford Invention of the Mensinga Diaphragm
1880	M. Arnold 'The Study of Poetry' Hopkins writes notes on the *Spiritual Exercises* Huxley 'Science and Culture' 'Vernon Lee' *Studies of the Eighteenth Century in Italy*	Gissing *Workers in the Dawn* Hardy *The Trumpet-Major* *A Laodicean* (−1881) Shorthouse *John Inglesant* A. Trollope *Dr Wortle's School* R. Browning *Dramatic Idyls*, second series Tennyson *Ballads*, etc.	Gladstone P.M. (Lib.) Bradlaugh MP refuses to swear on the Bible Elementary school made compulsory Manchester University founded Metaphysical Society disbanded

Date	Prose works	Other works	Historical/cultural events
1881	Butler *Alps and Sanctuaries* Carlyle *Reminiscences* Morris 'Pattern-designing'	W. Hale White *Autobiography of Mark Rutherford* Stevenson *Treasure Island* (–1882) C. Rossetti 'Monna Innominata' in *Pageant and Other Poems* D. G. Rossetti *Ballads and Sonnets* Wilde *Poems*	First Anglo-Boer War Browning Society founded Cambridge degrees open to women *Habeas corpus* suspended in Ireland Gladstone's Irish Land Act Natural History Museum, South Kensington Hyndman forms Marxist Democratic Federation Gilbert and Sullivan's *Patience*
1882	M. Arnold 'A Word about America' Creighton *History of the Papacy* J. A. Froude *Carlyle: The First Forty Years* Stephen undertakes editorship of *Dictionary of National Biography* Thomson (Lord Kelvin) *Mathematical and Physical Papers*	Hardy *Two on a Tower* Stevenson *New Arabian Nights* Swinburne *Tristram of Lyonesse*	Married Women's Property Act gives women separate rights Phoenix Park murders Society for Psychical Research founded International Gas and Electricity Exhibition
1883	J. W. Carlyle *Letters and Memorials*, prepared by T. Carlyle, ed. by Froude Morris 'Art, Wealth and Riches'	Henty *Under Drake's Flag* Moore *A Modern Lover* Stevenson *The Black Arrow*	Women's Cooperative Guild founded Royal College of Music founded

Date	Prose works	Other works	Historical/cultural events
	Seeley *The Expansion of England* A. Trollope *Autobiography* Nietzsche *Thus Spoke Zarathustra*	Meredith *Poems and Lyrics of the Joy of Earth*	
1884	J. A. Froude *Carlyle: Life in London* H. James *The Art of Fiction* Morris 'Art and Socialism' Ruskin *The Storm-Cloud of the Nineteenth Century* Smiles *Men of Invention and Industry* Spencer *The Man versus the State* Engels *Origin of the Family* 'Vernon Lee' *Euphorion* M. Kingsley *Charles Kingsley: His Letters and Memorials of his Life*	Gissing *The Unclassed* Ward *Miss Bretherton* Tennyson *Becket* *Revised Version of Old Testament* 'Vernon Lee' *Miss Brown: A Novel*	Third Reform Act Fabian Society formed Berlin Conference of European Powers on the future of Africa *Oxford English Dictionary* ed. Murray (−1928)
1885	M. Arnold 'A Word More about America' *Commonweal* founded Cross *George Eliot's Life as Related in her Letters and Journals*	Haggard *King Solomon's Mines* Meredith *Diana of the Crossways* Moore *A Mummer's Life*	Salisbury P.M. (Lib.) Fall of Khartoum Daimler invents internal combustion engine Criminal Law Amendment Act

Date	Prose works	Other works	Historical/cultural events
	Dictionary of National Biography, I ed. Stephen	Pater *Marius the Epicurean*	Starley's 'Rover' safety bicycle invented
	Pattison *Memoirs*	'Rutherford' (White) *Mark Rutherford's Deliverance*	
	Ruskin *Praeterita* (–1889)	Hopkins writes 'Terrible Sonnets'	
	Whistler *Ten O'Clock Lecture*	Ingelow *Poems*	
	M. Davitt *Leaves from a Prison Diary*	Morris *Pilgrims of Hope*	
	A. Besant *Autobiographical Sketches*	Tennyson *Tiresias and Other Poems*	
1886	Dowden *Life of Percy Bysshe Shelley*	Gissing *Demos*	Repeal of Contagious Diseases Acts
	Morris *A Dream of John Ball* (–1887)	Haggard *She*	Trafalgar Square riots
	Nietzsche *Beyond Good and Evil*	Hardy *The Mayor of Casterbridge* *The Woodlanders* (–1887)	Gladstone P.M. (Lib.) February Salisbury P.M. (Tory) August
		Moore *A Drama in Muslin*	St Hugh's Hall, Oxford, founded
		Stevenson *Dr Jekyll and Mr Hyde* *Kidnapped*	Severn Tunnel built Millais' *Bubbles* bought for £2,200 to advertise Pears' soap
		Kipling *Departmental Ditties*	
		Tennyson *Locksley Hall Sixty Years After*	
		'Corelli' *A Romance of Two Worlds*	
1887	C. Darwin *Autobiography*	Doyle *A Study in Scarlet*	Queen Victoria's Golden Jubilee

Date	Prose works	Other works	Historical/cultural events
	Pater *Imaginary Portraits*	Gissing *Thyrza*	Independent Labour Party founded
		Haggard *Allan Quartermain*	Zululand annexed
		Jefferies *Amaryllis at the Fair*	Rational Dress Campaign
		'Rutherford' *The Revolution in Tanner's Lane*	Arts and Crafts Exhibition Society founded
		R. Browning *Parleyings with Certain People of Importance in their Day*	
		Meredith *Ballads and Poems of Tragic Life*	
1888	M. Arnold *Essays in Criticism,* second series 'Civilization in the United States'	Gissing *A Life's Morning*	Accession of Kaiser Wilhelm II
		Hardy *Wessex Tales*	Local Government Act
	Doughty *Travels in Arabia Deserta*	Kipling *Plain Tales from the Hills*	Kodak box camera invented by Eastman
	Huxley 'The Struggle for Existence'	Stevenson *The Master of Ballantrae* (–1889)	Dunlop's pneumatic tyre
	Morris *A Dream of John Ball*	Ward *Robert Elsmere*	Hertz demonstrates 'wireless' transmission of electro-magnetic energy
		Wilde *The Happy Prince and Other Tales*	
1889	C. Booth *Life and Labour of the People,* vol. I (–1903)	Gissing *The Nether World*	London dock strike
		Jerome *Three Men in a Boat*	Eiffel Tower
	Huxley 'Agnosticism and Christianity'	E. B. Browning *Poetical Works*	International Congress of Psychology, Paris
			Prevention of Cruelty to Children Act

Date	Prose works	Other works	Historical/cultural events
	Nietzsche *Twilight of the Idols*	R. Browning *Asolando*	Women's Trade Union League
	Pater *Appreciations*	Swinburne *Poems and Ballads*, third series	Board of Education established
	Shaw *Fabian Essays*	Yeats *The Wanderings of Oisin*	First public electricity supply, London
	A. Besant *Why I Became a Theosophist*		
1890	W. Booth *In Darkest England*	Gissing *The Emancipated*	Housing of the Working Classes Act
	Frazer *The Golden Bough* (–1915)	Kipling *Soldiers Three*	International anti-slavery conference in Brussels
	W. James *Principles of Psychology*	Meredith *One of Our Conquerors* (–1891)	Rhodes P.M. of Cape Colony
	Stanley *In Darkest Africa*	Morris *News from Nowhere*	First electric underground railway starts operating in London
	'Walter' *My Secret Life*	Wilde *The Picture of Dorian Gray*	Forth Bridge opened
	Whistler *The Gentle Art of Making Enemies*	Austin *English Lyrics*	Morris founds Kelmscott Press
	Woman founded	Doyle *The Sign of Four*	Tennyson records 'Blow, bugle, blow', 'The Charge of the Light Brigade', 'Come into the garden, Maud' on wax cylinders
	Maxwell *Scientific Papers*	Dickinson *Poems*	
			Fall of Parnell
1891	Hutton *Cardinal Newman*	Wilde *A House of Pomegranates* *Lord Savile's Crime and Other Stories*	Construction of Trans-Siberian Railway begun
	Wilde 'The Soul of Man Under Socialism' *Intentions*	Gissing *New Grub Street*	International Copyright Law
	Strand Magazine founded		

Date	Prose works	Other works	Historical/cultural events
	R. W. Church *History of the Oxford Movement* Moore *Impressions and Opinions*	Hardy *Tess of the d'Urbervilles* Ibsen *Hedda Gabler*	
1892	Saintsbury *Miscellaneous Essays*	Doyle *The Adventures of Sherlock Holmes* Gissing *Born in Exile* Hardy *The Well-Beloved* Ward *The History of David Grieve* Wilde *Lady Windermere's Fan*	Gladstone P.M. (Lib.) Keir Hardie first Labour MP Diesel patents internal-combustion engine First automatic telephone switchboard introduced
1893	Pater *Plato and Platonism* The *Studio* founded J. A. Froude *Life and Letters of Erasmus: Lectures at Oxford* (−1894) A. Besant *Autobiography* F. H. Bradley *Appearance and Reality* Symonds *Life of Michelangelo Buonarroti* *Walt Whitman*	Gissing *The Odd Women* 'Corelli' *Barabbas: A Dream of the World's Tragedy* Wilde *A Woman of No Importance* Λ. Meynell *Poems* Yeats *The Celtic Twilight*	Royal commission on Employment of Labour Independent Labour Party formed Commons pass, Lords reject Second Irish Home Rule Bill Art Nouveau appears in Europe Benz constructs his 4-wheel car Ford builds his first car
1894	Hutton *Contemporary Thought and Thinkers* *Woman's Signal* founded	Gissing *In the Year of Jubilee* Hardy *Jude the Obscure* (−1895)	Dreyfus trial in Paris Gladstone resigns, Lord Rosebery P.M. (Lib.)

Date	Prose works	Other works	Historical/cultural events
	The Yellow Book launched	Moore *Esther Waters*	Inheritance tax introduced
	Smiles *Josiah Wedgewood*	Ward *Marcella*	Lumière brothers invent cinematograph
	Mayer *Women of Letters*	'Egerton' *Keynotes and Discords*	
	F. Power Cobbe *Life of Frances Power Cobbe*	Kipling *The Jungle Book*	
	S. and B. Webb *History of Trade Unionism*	G. and W. Grossmith *Diary of a Nobody*	
	Swinburne *Studies in Prose and Poetry*	Shaw *Arms and the Man*	
	Thomson (Kelvin) *The Molecular Tactics of a Crystal*		
1895	'Vernon Lee' *Renaissance Fancies and Studies*	Gissing *Eve's Ransom*	Wilde tried and imprisoned for homosexual offences
	Balfour *Foundations of Belief*	'Corelli' *The Sorrows of Satan*	Lord Salisbury (Tory) P.M.
	Seeley *Growth of British Policy*	Meredith *The Amazing Marriage*	Röntgen discovers x-ray
	Freud *Studies in Hysteria*	Wilde *An Ideal Husband* *The Importance of Being Earnest*	Marconi invents wireless telegraphy
		Wells *The Time Machine*	London School of Economics founded
		Conrad *Almayer's Folly*	First Promenade Concert arranged by Robert Newman, conductor Henry J. Wood
		Moore *The Celibates*	
		Yeats *Poems*	

Date	Prose works	Other works	Historical/cultural events
1896	A. Besant *Why I am a Socialist* Wilde begins *De Profundis* (published 1905) *The Savoy* published Jan.–Dec. F. Darwin *Life and Letters of Charles Darwin* Saintsbury *History of Nineteenth-Century Literature* *Daily Mail* begins publication A. Meynell *The Colour of Life, and Other Essays*	'Corelli' *The Mighty Atom* Dowson *Verses* Housman *A Shropshire Lad*	Wilde's *Salome* performed in Paris by Bernhardt Kelmscott *Chaucer* published First modern Olympic Games held in Athens
1897	M. Kingsley *Travels in West Africa* Oliphant *Annals of a Publishing House* H. Ellis *Studies in the Psychology of Sex* (–1928) *Sexual Inversion* S. and B. Webb *Industrial Democracy*	Gissing *The Whirlpool* Stoker *Dracula* Conrad *Nigger of the 'Narcissus'*	Queen Victoria's Diamond Jubilee Workmen's Compensation Act Marconi founds Wireless Telegraph Co. Ramsay discovers helium
1898	C. P. Gilman *Women and Economics* Saintsbury *Short History of English Literature* L. Stephen *Studies of a Biographer* Gissing *Charles Dickens*	Hardy *Wessex Poems* Wilde *The Ballad of Reading Gaol* James *The Turn of the Screw*	Irish Local Government Act M. and Mme Curie discover radium Zeppelin builds airship Paris Metro opens Spanish-American War

Date	Prose works	Other works	Historical/cultural events
1899	M. Kingsley *West African Studies*	Gissing *The Crown of Life*	Boer War (–1902)
	Oliphant *Autobiography and Letters*	Conrad *Heart of Darkness*	First free milk for poor mothers
	Symons *The Symbolist Movement in Literature*	Yeats *The Wind Among the Reeds*	First woman member of the Institute of Electrical Engineers
	Chamberlain *Foundations of the Nineteenth Century*		Board of Education and London Borough Councils created
	A. Meynell *John Ruskin*		International Women's Congress held in London
			Irish Literary Theatre
1900	Freud *Interpretation of Dreams*	'Corelli' *Boy*	Labour Party founded
	Saintsbury *History of Criticism*	Conrad *Lord Jim*	Manufacture of electric cookers and irons
		Shaw *Three Plays for Puritans*	China: Boxer Rebellion
			Planck's quantum theory

General Bibliographies

Note: Each section is arranged alphabetically. Place of publication is London unless otherwise stated.

(i) Nineteenth-century prose: bibliographies, reference guides, critical studies

Butrym, A. J., ed. *Essays on the Essay: Redefining the Genre* (Athens, Georgia, 1989). (Revisionist volume on the genre of the prose essay.)

Delaura, D. J., ed. *Victorian Prose: a Guide to Research* (New York, 1973). (Still-useful MLA guide, despite its cut-off date of 1971.)

Gaull, M. *English Romanticism: The Human Context* (1988). (Voluminous compendium containing brief idea summaries of Romantic prose writers.)

Landow, G. P. *Elegant Jeremiahs: The Sage from Carlyle to Mailer* (Ithaca, N.Y., 1986). (On how Victorian non-fiction prose has come to be accepted and discussed as 'literature'.)

Levine, G. and W. Madden, eds *The Art of Victorian Prose* (New York, London and Toronto, 1968). (Crosses generic boundaries and argues for an aesthetic of non-fiction prose.)

Levine, G. 'Victorian Studies', in Greenblatt, S. and G. Gunn, eds, *Redrawing the Boundaries: The Transformation of English and American Literary Studies* (New York, 1992), pp. 130–53. (Excellent account of recent critical revisioning of Victorian Studies.)

Levine, R. A., ed. *The Victorian Experience: The Prose Writers* (Athens, Ohio, 1982). (Essays on the major prose writers by well-known scholars.)

Madden, L. and D. Dixon *The Nineteenth-Century Periodical Press in Britain: A Bibliography of Modern Studies, 1901–1971* (Toronto, 1976).

Propas, S. W. *Victorian Studies: A Research Guide* (New York, 1992). (Attempts to re-map the area of Victorian Studies.)

Small, I. 'Recent Work on Nineteenth-Century Prose: "Oeuvre", Genre or Discourse', *Prose Studies*, 10 (1987), 42–50.

Thesing, W. B. *Dictionary of Literary Biography*, vol. 55 (*Victorian Prose Writers Before 1867*) and vol. 57 (*Victorian Prose Writers After 1867*) (Detroit, 1987). (Collection of biographical and critical essays on fifty-eight prose writers, only five of whom are women.)

Turner, P. *English Literature 1832–1890 Excluding the Novel* (1989). (Authoritative overview, with chapters on science, travel, history, and various forms of non-fiction.)

Vann, J. D. and R. T. Van Arsdel, eds *Victorian Periodicals: A Guide to Research* (1978).

Vinson, J., ed. *The Victorian Period* (1983). (Essays and bibliographical surveys, with a cut-off date of 1978.)

Wilson, H. W. and D. L. Hoeveler *English Prose and Criticism in the Nineteenth Century: A Guide to Information Sources* (Detroit, 1979). (Uneven selective guide, including bibliographies of twelve Romantic and twenty-two Victorian prose writers.)

Wolff, M., et al *The Waterloo Directory of Victorian Periodicals, 1824–1900: Phase I* (Waterloo, Ontario, 1977).

(ii) Scientific writing

Abir-am, P. and D. Outram, eds *Uneasy Careers and Intimate Lives: Women in Science, 1789–1979* (New York, N.J., 1987).

Alaya, F. 'Victorian Science and the "Genius" of Woman', *Journal of the History of Ideas*, 38 (1977), 261–80.

Annals of Scholarship, 4, 1 (1986), Special Number on Science and Literature.

Barber, L. *The Heyday of Natural History 1820–1870* (1980). (A lively introduction to the early Victorian fascination with the natural world and the intellectual issues it raised.)

Beer, G. *Darwin's Plots: Evolutionary Narrative in Darwin, George Eliot, and Nineteenth-Century Fiction* (1983). (Groundbreaking study of the fictive language and structures of evolutionary science and the relation of Darwin's writing to Victorian narrative.)

Beer, G. 'Parable, Professionalisation, and Literary Allusion in Victorian Scientific Writing', *AUMLA*, 74 (1990), 48–68.

Beer, G. 'Translation or Transformation?: The Relations of Literature and Science', *Notes and Records of the Royal Society of London*, 44 (1990), 81–99.

Benjamin, M., ed. *Science and Sensibility: Gender and Scientific Enquiry, 1780–1945* (Oxford, 1991). (On 'the scientific construction of gender and the gendered construction of science in the nineteenth century'.)

Bowler, P. J. *Evolution: The History of an Idea* (Berkeley, California, 1984). (Standard account.)

Brantlinger, P., ed. *Energy and Entropy: Science and Culture in Victorian Britain: Essays from Victorian Studies* (Bloomington, Indiana, 1989). (Thirteen essays, in which Darwin, Chambers and Huxley figure prominently.)

Brock, W. H. 'British Science Periodicals and Culture: 1820–1850', *Victorian Periodicals Review*, 21, 2 (1988), 47–55.

Brush, S. G. *The Temperature of History* (New York, 1978). (On thermodynamics.)

Burrow, J. W. *Evolution and Society: A Study in Victorian Social Theory* (Cambridge, 1966). (On the influence of evolution on anthropology and other historical sciences.)

Cannon, S. F. *Science in Culture: The Early Victorian Period* (New York, 1978). (Explores various scientific circles and their views.)

Cardwell, D. S. L. *The Organisation of Science in England* (1957, 1972). (On the development of science as a profession.)

Chapple, J. A. V. *Science and Literature in the Nineteenth Century* (1986). (An introduction to the field through commentary on extracts from a variety of sciences.)

Cooter, R. *The Cultural Meaning of Popular Science: Phrenology and the Organisation of Consent in Nineteenth-Century Britain* (Cambridge, 1984). (Ambitious and comprehensive.)

Cosslett, T. *The 'Scientific Movement' and Victorian Literature* (Brighton, 1982). (Explores the imaginative implications of science for Victorian writers.)

Cosslett, T., ed. *Science and Religion in the Nineteenth Century* (Cambridge, 1984).

(Extracts from the evolutionary controversy with a helpful introduction and notes.)

Cunningham, A. and N. Jardine, eds *Romanticism and the Sciences* (Cambridge, 1990). (Excellent collection of essays.)

Dale, P. A. *In Pursuit of a Scientific Culture: Science, Art, and Society in the Victorian Age* (Madison, Wisconsin, 1989). (On scientific positivism.)

Faas, E. *Retreat into the Mind: Victorian Poetry and the Rise of Psychiatry* (Princeton, N.J., 1988). (Exhaustive study of the early development of mental science and its relationship to contemporary culture.)

Gillispie, C. C. *Genesis and Geology* (New York, 1959). (On geology and its impact on religious belief.)

Gooday, G. 'Nature in the Laboratory: Domestication and Discipline with the Microscope in Victorian Life Science', *British Journal for the History of Science*, 24, 3 (1991), 307–41.

Gould, S. J. *Time's Arrow, Time's Cycle* (Cambridge, Massachusetts, and London, 1987). (On the implications of geology for the Victorian sense of time.)

Inkster, I. and J. Morell, eds *Metropolis and Province: Science in British Culture, 1780–1850* (1983). (On science and scientific culture in Britain during its early period of industrialisation and urbanisation.)

Jacobus, M. and E. F. Keller, eds *Body/Politics: Women and the Discourses of Science* (1990). (Includes essays on nineteenth-century science.)

Jacyna, L. S. 'The Physiology of Mind, the Unity of Nature, and the Moral Order in Victorian Thought', *The British Journal for the History of Science*, 14 (1981), 109–32. (On the physiology of mind and its cultural implications.)

Jordanova, L. *Sexual Visions: Images of Gender in Science and Medicine between the Eighteenth and Twentieth Centuries* (Madison, Wisconsin, 1989). (Important history of the idea of 'nature', the processes through which 'naturalisation' takes place, and the scientific and social construction of gender.)

Jordanova, L. and R. Porter, eds *Images of the Earth: Essays in the History of the Environmental Sciences* (Chalfont St. Giles, 1979.)

Jordanova, L. J., ed. *Languages of Nature: Critical Essays on Science and Literature* (1986). (On the discourses of science in the eighteenth and nineteenth centuries.)

Kargon, R. H. *Science in Victorian Manchester: Enterprise and Expertise* (Baltimore and London, 1977). (On the development of provincial science.)

Knight, D. *The Age of Science: The Scientific World-view in the Nineteenth Century* (Oxford, 1986). (Authoritative history of some areas of British science in the period, accessible to non-specialists.)

Knight, D. M. *Natural Science Books in English 1600–1900* (1972).

Knoepflmacher, U. C. and G. B. Tennyson, eds *Nature and the Victorian Imagination* (Berkeley, California, and Los Angeles, 1977). (Twenty-five essays demonstrating the discursive relations among disciplines.)

Kohn, D. ed. *The Darwinian Heritage* (Princeton, N.J., 1985).

Levine, G., ed. *Realism and Representation: Essays on the Problem of Realism in Relation to Science, Literature, and Culture* (Madison, Wisconsin, 1993).

Levine, G. and A. Rauch, eds *One Culture: Essays in Science and Literature* (Madison, Wisconsin, 1987). (Essays by distinguished scholars on the relation of science, history and literature.)

Locke, D. *Science as Writing* (New Haven, Connecticut, 1992). (Stimulating study of the rhetoric of scientific writing.)

Merrill, L. *The Romance of Victorian Natural History* (Oxford, 1989). (Popular writing on natural history and collecting.)

Metz, N. A. 'Science in *Household Words*: "The Poetic . . . Passed into our Common Life"', *Victorian Periodicals Newsletter*, 11 (1978), 121–33.

Moore, J. R., ed. *History, Humanity and Evolution: Essays for John C. Greene* (Cambridge, 1989). (Interesting collection, prefaced by a lively interview.)

Morton, P. *The Vital Science: Biology and the Literary Imagination, 1860–1900* (1984). (Important and original study, setting Darwin in the context of lesser known evolutionary thinkers and writers.)

Moscucci, O. *The Science of Woman: Gynaecology and Gender in England, 1800–1929* (Cambridge, 1990). (Valuable study of the development of medicine in relation to women's health issues in the period.)

Paradis, J. and T. Postlewait, eds *Victorian Science and Victorian Values: Literary Perspectives* (New Brunswick, N.J., 1985). (Collection of essays on the discursive interplay within disciplines.)

Peterfreund, S., ed. *Literature and Science: Theory and Practice* (Boston, 1990).

Phillips, P. *The Scientific Lady: A Social History of Women's Scientific Interests, 1520–1918* (1990).

Porter, R. and G. S. Rousseau, eds *The Ferment of Knowledge: Studies in the Historiography of Science* (New York, 1980).

Russett, C. E. *Sexual Science: The Victorian Construction of Womanhood* (Cambridge, Massachusetts, 1989). (On scientific discourses in late nineteenth-century England.)

Shatzberg, W., R. Waite and J. Johnson, eds *The Relations of Literature and Science: An Annotated Bibliography of Scholarship 1880–1980* (New York, 1987).

Shuttleworth, S. and J. Christie, eds *Nature Transfigured: Science and Literature, 1700–1900* (Manchester, 1989). (Detailed case studies of particular moments when literature was informed by scientific ideas.)

Simons, H. W., ed. *Rhetoric in the Human Sciences* (1989).

Turner, F. M. *Between Science and Religion: The Reaction to Scientific Naturalism in Late Victorian England* (New Haven, Connecticut, 1974). (Explores the development of a post-Darwinian scientific ideology.)

Turner, M. A. *Mechanism and the Novel: Science in the Narrative Process* (Cambridge, 1993). (On the tradition of mechanistic science as derived from Newton, and its impact on scientific writing and fiction.)

Woodring, C. *Nature into Art: Cultural Transformations in Nineteenth-Century Britain* (Cambridge, Massachusetts, 1989). (Comprehensive, compellingly written history of the idea of nature, exploring the relations between science and literature in the period.)

Young, R. M. 'Natural Theology, Victorian Periodicals and the Fragmentation of a Common Context', in *Darwin's Metaphor* (Cambridge, 1981).

Zappan, J. P. 'Scientific Rhetoric in the Nineteenth and Early Twentieth Centuries: Herbert Spencer, Thomas H. Huxley, and John Dewey', in C. Bazerman, ed. *Textual Dynamics of the Professions: Historical and Contemporary Studies of Writing in Professional Communities* (Madison, Wisconsin, 1991), pp. 145–67.

(iii) Travel and exploration literature

Barrell, J. 'Death on the Nile: Fantasy and the Literature of Tourism 1840–1860', *Essays in Criticism*, 41 (1991), 97–127.

Birkett, D. *Spinsters Abroad: Victorian Lady Explorers* (Oxford and New York, 1989). (Good introductory survey of twenty lady explorers.)

Bongie, C. *Exotic Memories: Literature, Colonialism, and the Fin de Siècle* (Stanford, Connecticut, 1991).

Brantlinger, P. *Rule of Darkness: British Literature and Imperialism, 1830–1914*

(Ithaca, N.Y., and London, 1988). (Wide-ranging study of imperialist ideology in the Victorian and Edwardian period, particularly valuable on the myth of the 'Dark Continent'.)

Buzard, J. *The Beaten Track: European Tourism, Literature, and the Ways to 'Culture' 1800–1918* (New York, 1993).

Chaudhuri, N. and M. Strobel, eds *Western Women and Imperialism: Complicity and Resistance* (Bloomington and Indianapolis, 1992).

Conrad, P. *Imagining America* (1980).

David, D. *Rule Britannia: Women, Empire, and Victorian Writing* (Ithaca, N.Y., 1996).

Eldridge, C. C. *Victorian Imperialism* (1978). (Useful short history of events and issues.)

Foster, S. *Across New Worlds: Nineteenth-Century Women Travellers and their Writings* (New York and London, 1990).

Frawley, M. H. 'Fair Amazons Abroad: The Social Construction of the Victorian Adventuress', *Annals of Scholarship*, 7 (1990), 501–22.

Frawley, M. H. 'Desert Places/Gendered Spaces: Victorian Women in the Middle East', *Nineteenth-Century Contexts*, 15 (1991), 49–64.

Hamalian, L., ed. *Ladies on the Loose: Women Travellers of the Eighteenth and Nineteenth Centuries* (New York, 1981).

Hibbert, C. *Africa Explored: Europeans in the Dark Continent, 1769–1880* (1982).

Howard, C. and J. H. Plumb, eds *West African Explorers* (Oxford, 1951).

Hyam, R. *Empire and Sexuality: The British Experience* (Manchester, 1990). (Uneven.)

Kroller, E. M. 'First Impressions: Rhetorical Strategies in Travel Writing by Victorian Women', *Ariel*, 21 (1990), 87–99.

Lackey, K. 'Eighteenth-Century Aesthetic Theory and the Nineteenth-Century Traveler in Trans-Allegheny America: F. Trollope, Dickens, Irving and Parkman', *American Studies*, 32 (1991), 33–48.

Lorimer, D. *Colour, Class and the Victorians: English Attitudes to the Negro in Mid-Nineteenth Century* (Leicester, 1978).

Lorimer, D. 'Theoretical Racism in Late Victorian Anthropology, 1870–1900', *Victorian Studies*, 31 (1988), 405–30. (History of the Anthropological Institute and of its journal.)

Mclynn, F. *Hearts of Darkness: The European Exploration of Africa* (London, 1993).

Melman, B. *Women's Orients: English Women and the Middle East, 1718–1918* (1992).

Mills, S. *Discourses of Difference: An Analysis of Women's Travel Writing and Colonialism* (London and New York, 1991). (On women as agents within the colonial context.)

Moyles, R. G. and D. Owram, *Imperial Dreams and Colonial Realities: British News of Canada 1880–1914* (Toronto, 1988).

Pratt, M. L. *Imperial Eyes: Travel Writing and Transculturation* (London and New York, 1992). (An important, subtly argued, historically grounded study of the complex interrelation of race, class, and gender issues in eighteenth- and nineteenth-century travel literature.)

Robertson, D. 'Mid-Victorians Amongst the Alps', in U. C. Knoepflmacher and G. B. Tennyson, eds, *Nature and the Victorian Imagination* (Berkeley, California, 1977), pp. 113–36.

Robinson, J. *Wayward Women: A Guide to Women Travellers* (Oxford, 1990).

Said, E. *Orientalism: Western Concepts of the Orient* (New York, 1978). (Immensely influential study of the West's imagination of the East.)

Shattock, J. 'Travel Writing Victorian and Modern: A Review of Recent Research', *Prose Studies*, 5 (1982), 151–64.

Spurr, D. *The Rhetoric of Empire: Colonial Discourse in Journalism, Travel Writing, and Imperial Administration* (Durham and London, 1993). (An introduction to modern European colonial discourse.)

Stafford, B. M. *Voyage into Substance: Art, Science, Nature, and the Illustrated Travel Account, 1760–1840* (Cambridge, Massachusetts, 1984).

Stevenson, C. B. *Victorian Women Travel Writers in Africa* (Boston, 1982).

Stevenson, C. B. 'Female Anger and African Politics: The Case of Two Victorian "Lady Travellers"', *Turn-of-the-Century Woman*, 2 (1985), 7–117.

Stocking, G. *Victorian Anthropology* (New York and London, 1987). (A rich, ambitious, erudite but entertaining study of the emerging discipline of anthropology, particularly the impact upon it of Darwin.)

Thornton, R. 'Narrative Ethnography in Africa, 1850–1920', *Man*, 18 (1983).

Tidrick, K. *Empire and the English Character* (1990).

Tinling, M. *Women into the Unknown: A Sourcebook on Women Explorers and Travelers* (New York, 1989).

Vaughan, J. *The English Guide Book, c. 1780–1870: An Illustrated History* (Newton Abbot, 1974).

Wheelwright, J. *Amazons and Military Maids* (1989).

(iv) Social reportage

Briggs, A. *Victorian Cities* (Harmondsworth, 1963).

Davies, G. 'Foreign Bodies: Images of the London Working Class at the End of the Nineteenth Century', *Literature and History*, 14 (1988), 64–80.

Dyos, H. J. and M. Wolff, eds *The Victorian City: Images and Realities*, 2 vols, (1973). (Thirty-eight essays on London and provincial cities.)

Feldman, D. and G. S. Jones, eds *Metropolis – London: Histories and Representations since 1800* (1989). (Uneven collection of essays in urban history.)

Himmelfarb, G. *The Idea of Poverty in the Early Industrial Age* (1984). (Important study of a central idea in modern culture written by a distinguished scholar.)

Inglis, K. S. *Churches and the Working Classes in Victorian England* (1963).

Jones, G. S. *Outcast London: A Study in the Relationship Between Classes in Victorian Society* (Oxford, 1971).

Keating, P., ed. *Into Unknown England, 1866–1913: Selections from the Social Explorers* (Manchester, 1976). (Useful selection of primary texts, with lucid introduction.)

Lepenies, W. *Between Literature and Science: The Rise of Sociology*, translated by R. J. Hollingdale (Cambridge, 1988).

Macdonald, S. P. '"Population Thinking" in Victorian Science and Literature', *Mosaic*, 17, 4 (1984), 35–51.

Mackenzie, D. A. *Statistics in Britain, 1865–1930: The Social Construction of Scientific Knowledge* (Edinburgh, 1981).

Metz, N. A. 'Discovering a World of Suffering: Fiction and the Rhetoric of Sanitary Reform, 1840–1860', *Nineteenth-Century Contexts*, 15 (1991), 65–81.

Parker, J. *Women and Welfare: Ten Victorian Women in Public Social Service* (Basingstoke, 1988).

Poovey, M. 'Domesticity and Class Formation: Chadwick's 1842 Sanitary Report', in D. Simpson, ed., *Subject to History: Ideology, Class, Gender* (Ithaca, N.Y., 1991), pp. 65–83.

Poovey, M. 'Figures of Arithmetic, Figures of Speech: The Discourse of Statistics in the 1830s', *Critical Inquiry* (1992–93), 256–76.

Porter, T. *The Rise of Statistical Thinking, 1820–1900* (Princeton, N.J., 1986). (A major study.)

Schwarzbach, F. S. '"Beyond Words": Exploring the Literature of Urban Exploration', *Proteus*, 6, 1 (1989), 22–31.

Shelston, A. and D., eds *The Industrial City: 1820–1870* (1989). (Intelligent editorial comment on a range of prose texts.)

Stigler, S. M. *The History of Statistics: The Measurement of Uncertainty before 1900* (Cambridge, Massachusetts, 1986). (Impressive study of the early history of the discipline.)

Thernstrom S. and R. Jennet, eds *Nineteenth-Century Cities: Essays in the New Urban History* (New Haven, Connecticut, 1969).

(v) Biography, Autobiography, Journals, Letters

Amigoni, D. 'Life Histories and the Cultural Politics of Historical Knowing: *The Dictionary of National Biography* and the late Nineteenth-Century Political Field', in S. Dex, ed. *Life and Work History Analyses: Qualitative and Quantitative Developments* (1991), pp. 144–66.

Amigoni, D. *Victorian Biography: Intellectuals and the Ordering of Discourse* (Brighton, 1993). (Examines biography in relation to the emerging master-narratives 'literature' and 'history' in Victorian academic culture.)

Bell, S. G. and M. Yalom, eds *Revealing Lives: Autobiography, Biography, and Gender* (Albany, N.Y., 1990). (Demonstrates the varieties of approach that characterise the debates on the role of gender in constructing life-history.)

Benstock, S., ed. *The Private Self: Theory and Practice of Women's Autobiographical Writings* (Chapel Hill, N.C., 1988). (Wide-ranging and useful collection of feminist essays.)

Bree, G. 'Autogynography', *The Southern Review*, 22, 2 (1986), 223–30.

Brodzki, B. and C. Schenk *Life/Lines. Theorizing Women's Autobiography* (Ithaca, N.Y., 1988). (Focuses on issues of gender, ethnicity, class, and culture in the understanding of a women's auto/biographical tradition.)

Buckley, J. H. 'Toward Early-Modern Autobiography: The Roles of Oscar Wilde, George Moore, Edmund Gosse, and Henry James', in R. Kiely and J. Hildebidle, eds *Modernism Reconsidered* (Cambridge, Massachusetts, 1983).

Buckley, J. H., *The Turning Key: Autobiography and the Subjective Impulse since 1800* (Cambridge, Massachusetts, and London, 1984). (A short all-male survey.)

Burnett, J., ed. *Useful Toil: Autobiographies of Working People from the 1820s to the 1920s* (1974).

Cafarelli, A. W. *Prose in the Age of Poets: Romanticism and Biographical Narrative from Johnson to De Quincey* (1990). (Wide-ranging study, with significant chapters on Hazlitt and De Quincey).

Cardinal, R. 'Unlocking the Diary', *Comparative Criticism*, 12 (1990), 71–87.

Cockshut, A. O. J. *Truth to Life: The Art of Biography in the Nineteenth Century* (1974). (Focuses on religious aspects of biographies of great men.)

Cockshut, A. O. J. *The Art of Autobiography in 19th and 20th Century England* (New Haven, Connecticut, 1984). (Emphasises representation of childhood in autobiography.)

Corbett, M. J. *Representing Femininity: Middle-Class Subjectivity in Victorian and Edwardian Women's Autobiography* (New York, 1992). (On the 'experience of gender' and its manifestations in middle-class female life-narrative.)

Costello, J. 'Taking the "Woman" out of Women's Autobiography: The Perils and Potentials of Theorizing Female Subjectivities', *diacritics*, 21 (1991), 123–34.

Dawson, C. *Prophets of Past Time: Seven British Autobiographers, 1880–1914* (1988). (Discusses W. H. White, G. Tyrell, S. Butler, E. Gosse, G. Moore, F. M. Ford, and W. B. Yeats.)

Fleishman, A. *Figures of Autobiography: The Language of Self-Writing in Victorian and Modern England* (Berkeley, California, and London, 1983). (On how the language of autobiography is always mediated, a reworking of stories told by others.)

Gagnier, R. *Subjectivities: A History of Self-Representation in Britain, 1832–1920* (New York and Oxford, 1991). (A major interdisciplinary study, that draws on a full range of working-class autobiographical texts, and historicises hegemonic middle-class subjectivity.)

Gelpi, B. C. 'The Innocent I: Dickens' Influence on Victorian Autobiography', in J. H. Buckley, ed. *The Worlds of Victorian Fiction* (Cambridge, Massachusetts, 1975), pp. 57–71.

Gristwood, S. *Recording Angels: The Secret World of Women's Diaries* (1988).

Hart, F. R. 'Boswell and the Romantics: A Chapter in the History of Biographical Theory', *ELH*, 27 (1960), 44–65.

Henderson, H. *The Victorian Self: Autobiography and Biblical Narrative* (Ithaca, N.Y., and London, 1989). (On the fate of typologically patterned autobiography in an age when providential history is under threat.)

Hogan, R. 'Engendered Autobiographies: The Diary as a Feminine Form', *Prose Studies*, 14 (1991), 95–107.

Iles, T., ed. *All Sides of the Subject: Women and Biography* (New York and London, 1992).

Jay, P. *Being in the Text: Self Representation from Wordsworth to Roland Barthes* (Ithaca, N.Y., 1984). (On strategies of self-representation, and the concepts behind them.)

Jelinek, E. C., ed. *Women's Autobiography: Essays in Criticism* (Bloomington, Indiana, and London, 1980). (Early feminist collection on the poetics of autobiography.)

Landow, G. P., ed. *Approaches to Victorian Autobiography* (Athens, Ohio, 1979). (Useful collection, with an excellent introduction.)

Lang, C. 'Autobiography in the Aftermath of Romanticism', *diacritics*, 12 (1982), 2–16.

Loesberg, J. *Fictions of Consciousness: Mill, Newman, and the Reading of Victorian Prose* (New Brunswick, N.J., and London, 1986). (Reconstructs intellectual context which motivated Mill's *Autobiography* and Newman's *Apologia*.)

Machann, C. 'The Function of Illness and Disability in Three Victorian Biographies', *A/B: Auto/Biography Studies*, 6, 1 (1991), 26–32.

Maitzen, R. '"This Feminine Preserve": Historical Biographies by Victorian Women', *Victorian Studies*, 38, 3 (1995), 371–93. (On Agnes Strickland, Hannah Lawrence, Julia Kavanagh and other female biographers.)

Nadel, I. B. *Biography: Fiction, Fact and Form* (1984). (On the professionalisation and institutionalisation of biography in the nineteenth century.)

Nussbaum, F. *The Autobiographical Subject* (1989).

Olney, J., ed. *Autobiography: Essays Theoretical and Critical* (Princeton, N.J., 1980).

Olney, J. *Studies in Autobiography* (Oxford, 1988).

Peterson, L. H. *Victorian Autobiography: The Tradition of Self-Interpretation* (New Haven, Connecticut, and London, 1986). (Literary and historical reading of the genre of spiritual autobiography.)

Priestley, P., ed. *Victorian Prison Lives: English Prison Biography 1830–1914* (1985).

Raoul, V. 'Women and Diaries: Gender and Genre', *Mosaic* 22/23 (1989), 57–65.

Reed, J. W. *English Biography in the Early Nineteenth Century: 1801–1838* (New Haven, Connecticut, 1966).

Sanders, V. *The Private Lives of Victorian Women: Autobiography in Nineteenth-Century England* (New York, 1989). (Well-researched study of middle-class professional women autobiographers.)

Shelston, A. *Biography* (1977). (A useful short introduction to the genre.)

Smith, S. *A Poetics of Women's Autobiography: Marginality and the Fictions of Self-Representation* (Bloomington, Indiana, 1987).

Spengemann, W. C. *The Forms of Autobiography: Episodes in the History of a Literary Genre* (New Haven, Connecticut, 1980).

Stanley, L. 'Moments of Writing: Is There a Feminist Auto/biography?', *Gender and History*, 2, 1 (1990), 58–67.

Stanton, D., ed. *The Female Autograph* (New York, 1984).

Stull, H. I. *The Evolution of the Autobiography from 1770–1850: A Comparative Study and Analysis* (New York, 1985).

Swindells, J. *Victorian Writing and Working Women: The Other Side of Silence* (1986). (On the relationship between class, gender, and literary professionalism. Focuses on working-class female autobiography.)

Vincent, D. *Bread, Knowledge, and Freedom: A Study of Nineteenth-Century Working Class Autobiography* (1981). (A major work.)

Women's Studies, 20, 1 (1992). Special Number on Autobiography.

(vi) Discourses of culture

Adams, J. E. *Dandies and Desert Saints: Styles of Victorian Manhood* (Ithaca, N.Y., 1995). (A cultural history of masculine identity in Victorian literature from Carlyle to Wilde, drawing on feminist and queer theory.)

Aers, D., J. Cook and D. Punter *Romanticism and Ideology: Studies in English Writing, 1765–1830* (1981). (On the social relations of Romantic writing from Blake to Hazlitt.)

Altick, R. D. *The English Common Reader: A Social History of the Mass Reading Public, 1800–1900* (Chicago and London, 1957)./(Standard work.)

Altick, R. D. *Victorian People and Ideas* (New York, 1973). (Survey of Victorian life and thought.)

Aspinall, A. *Politics and the Press, c. 1780–1850* (1949).

Auerbach, N. *Woman and the Demon: The Life of a Victorian Myth* (Cambridge, Massachusetts, and London, 1982). (Important feminist historicist study of Victorian culture.)

Bainbridge, C., ed. *100 Years of Journalism: Social Aspects of the Press* (1984).

Baldick, C. *The Social Mission of English Criticism: 1848–1932* (Oxford, 1983). (Traces the Victorian roots of Leavisite criticism.)

Ballaster, R., M. Beetham, E. Frazer and S. Hebron, *Women's Worlds: Ideology, Femininity and the Woman's Magazine* (1991). (Includes useful discussions and bibliography of nineteenth-century women's magazines.)

Bann, S. *The Clothing of Clio: A Study of the Representation of History in Nineteenth-Century Britain and France* (Cambridge, 1984). (Deploys the techniques of rhetorical analysis to discover a 'historical poetics'.)

Barrell, J. *The Political Theory of Painting from Reynolds to Hazlitt* (New Haven, Connecticut, 1986). (Considers the interaction of aesthetic and political theory).

Bebbington, D. W. *Evangelicalism in Modern Britain: A History from the 1730s to the 1980s* (1989). (Challenging survey.)

Beetham, M. *A Magazine of Her Own? Domesticity and Desire in the Woman's Magazine 1800–1914* (London and New York, 1996).

Bentley, M. *The Climax of Liberal Politics: British Liberalism in Theory and Practice 1868–1918* (1987).

Binfield, C. *So Down to Prayers: Studies in English Nonconformity* (1977). (A series of case studies.)

Blake, R. *The Conservative Party from Peel to Thatcher* (1985). (Good introduction.)

Bowler, P. J. *The Invention of Progress: The Victorians and the Past* (Oxford, 1989). (Relates theories of evolution to the other historical sciences and to contemporary ideas of progress.)

Bradley, I. *The Call to Seriousness* (1976). (The impact of Evangelicalism on Victorian life.)

Brake, L. *Subjugated Knowledge: Journalism, Gender and Literature in the Nineteenth Century* (Basingstoke, 1994).

Brake, L., A. Jones and L. Madden, eds *Investigating Victorian Journalism* (1990). (Brings together the fields of literary history, journalism studies, and history.)

Brantlinger, P. *The Spirit of Reform: British Literature and Politics, 1832–1867* (Cambridge, Massachusetts, and London, 1977).

Brown, L. *Victorian News and Newspapers* (Oxford, 1985). (Insightful and disciplined; concentrates on the period 1860–1890.)

Budd, S. *Varieties of Unbelief: Atheists and Agnostics in English Society 1850–1960* (1977).

Bullen, J. B. *The Myth of the Renaissance in Nineteenth-Century Writing* (Oxford, 1994). (Wide-ranging scholarly study.)

Burrow, J. W. *A Liberal Descent: Victorian Historians and the English Past* (Cambridge, 1981). (Analysis of the 'Whig' school of historiography.)

Butler, L. St. J. *Victorian Doubts: Literary and Cultural Discourses* (New York and London, 1990). (Detailed traditional study.)

Butler, M. *Romantics, Rebels, and Reactionaries: English Literature and Its Background, 1760–1830* (Oxford and New York, 1982). (Important study that challenges naive identifications of political and literary revolutions.)

Caine, B. *Victorian Feminists* (Oxford and New York, 1992). (Scholarly contextual readings of the lives and works of Emily Davies, Frances Power Cobbe, Josephine Butler and Millicent Garrett Fawcett.)

Campbell, C. *The Romantic Ethic and the Spirit of Modern Consumerism* (Oxford, 1987).

Canary, R. H. and H. Kozicki, eds *The Writing of History: Literary Form and Historical Understanding* (Madison, Wisconsin, 1978).

Chadwick, O. *The Victorian Church*, 2nd edn, 2 vols *Ecclesiastical History of England*, ed. by J. D. Dickinson, vols VII–VIII (1970). (The standard history, this magisterial but highly readable account focuses on the Church of England.)

Chadwick, O. *The Secularisation of the European Mind in the Nineteenth Century* (Cambridge, 1975). (Authoritative.)

Chai, L. *Aestheticism: The Religion of Art in Post-Romantic Literature* (New York, 1990). (Interesting new readings of Pater and Wilde.)

Chapman, R. *The Victorian Debate: English Literature and Society, 1832–1901* (1968). (Wide-ranging.)

Chapman, R. *The Sense of the Past in Victorian Literature* (London and Sydney, 1986). (Examines literary representations of different periods from the national past.)

Clive, J. 'The Use of the Past in Victorian England', *Salmagundi*, 68–69 (1985–86), 48–65.

Clive, J. *Not by Fact Alone: Essays on the Writing and Reading of History* (1990). (Insightful essays by a distinguished historian of Victorian England.)

Clubbe, J. and J. Meckier, eds *Victorian Perspectives* (1989). (Important collection of essays by distinguished scholars.)

Collini, S., D. Winch and J. Burrow *That Noble Science of Politics* (Cambridge, 1983).

Colls, R. and P. Dodd, eds *Englishness: Politics and Culture 1880–1920* (1986).

Crosby, C. *The Ends of History: Victorians and 'the Woman Question'* (1991). (On the nineteenth-century conceptualisation of history.)

Cross, N. *The Common Writer: Life in Nineteenth-Century Grub Street* (Cambridge, 1985). (Fascinating history of authorship and culture, based on the archives of the Royal Literary Fund.)

Culler, A. D. *The Victorian Mirror of History* (New Haven, Connecticut, and London, 1985). (Explores different conceptions and uses of history in the period.)

Dale, P. A. *The Victorian Critic and the Idea of History: Carlyle, Arnold, Pater* (Cambridge, Massachusetts, 1977).

David, D. *Intellectual Women and Victorian Patriarchy: Harriet Martineau, Elizabeth Barrett Browning and George Eliot* (Ithaca, N.Y., 1987). (Theorised and historicised study of literary women within patriarchy.)

Davidoff, L. and C. Hall *Family Fortunes: Men and Women of the English Middle-Class, 1780–1850* (1987). (A major study.)

Delaura, D. J. *Hebrew and Hellene in Victorian England: Newman, Arnold and Pater* (Austen, Texas, 1969). (Important scholarly study of intertextuality and the development of a cultural tradition.)

Dellamora, R. *Masculine Desire: The Sexual Politics of Victorian Aestheticism* (Chapel Hill, N.C., and London, 1990). (Wide-ranging study of the history of masculine desire as a literary topic.)

Eagleton, T. *The Function of Criticism: from the 'Spectator' to Post-Structuralism* (1984). (Brief study of the history and contradictions of the modern critical endeavour.)

Ellegard, A. *The Readership of the Periodical Press in Mid-Victorian Britain* (Göteborg, 1957).

Ellison, J. *Delicate Subjects: Romanticism, Gender, and the Ethics of Understanding* (Ithaca, N.Y., 1990). (Sophisticated argument, referring to Schleiermacher, Coleridge, and Fuller.)

Epstein Nord, D. *Walking the Victorian Streets: Women, Representation, and the City* (Ithaca, N.Y., and London, 1995).

Feuchtwanger, E. J. *Democracy and Empire: Britain 1865–1914* (1985). (On the practical politics of reform.)

Forster, M. *Significant Sisters: the Grassroots of Active Feminism, 1839–1939* (1984). (Discusses the lives of eight prominent feminists.)

Fraser, H. *Beauty and Belief: Aesthetics and Religion in Victorian Literature* (Cambridge, 1986). (From the Oxford Movement to Aestheticism.)

Fraser, H. *The Victorians and Renaissance Italy* (Oxford, 1992). (On the construction of the Renaissance in Victorian art and writing.)

Gallagher, C. *The Industrial Reformation of English Fiction, 1832–1867* (Chicago, 1985). (Traces the impact of industrialism as an intellectual development on major philosophical and social issues of the period and on Victorian narrative.)

Gallagher, C. and T. Laqueur, eds *The Making of the Modern Body: Sexuality and Society in the Nineteenth Century* (Berkeley, California, 1987). (Essays from the journal *Representations* on the centrality of the body in nineteenth-century debates.)

Gay, P. *The Bourgeois Experience: Victoria to Freud* (New York, 1984). (An important study.)

Gilbert, A. D. *Religion and Society in Industrial England: Church, Chapel and Social*

Change, 1740–1914 (1976). (On the interaction between the Church of England and Evangelicalism.)

Gilbert, S. M. and S. Gubar *The Madwoman in the Attic: The Woman Writer and the Nineteenth-Century Literary Imagination* (New Haven, Connecticut, and London, 1979). (Major first-wave feminist reconfiguration of the canon.)

Gorham, D. *The Victorian Girl and the Feminine Ideal* (1982).

Gross, J. *The Rise and Fall of the Man of Letters: Aspects of English Literary Life since 1800* (1969).

Hall, C. *White, Male and Middle Class: Explorations in Feminism and History* (New York, 1992). (Fine study of the intersections of gender and class.)

Hammerton, A. J. *Cruelty and Companionship: Conflict in Nineteenth-Century Married Life* (London and New York, 1992). (Challenges notions of the Victorian domestic idyll.)

Helsinger, E., R. Sheets and W. Veeder, eds *Woman Question: Society and Literature in Britain and America*, 3 vols (New York, 1983). (Informed commentary on a wide interdisciplinary range of topics.)

Herbert, C. *Culture and Anomie: Ethnographic Imagination in the Nineteenth Century* (Chicago, 1991). (On the historical roots of the culture concept.)

Heyck, T. W. *The Transformation of Intellectual Life in Victorian England* (1982). (On the development of a specialised intellectual class.)

Himmelfarb, G. *Victorian Minds* (1968). (Lively and readable.)

Hollis, P., ed. *Women in Public: the Women's Movement 1850–1900* (1979). (Documents from the women's movement.)

Holloway, J. *The Victorian Sage: Studies in Argument* (1953). (On Carlyle, Disraeli, George Eliot, Newman, Matthew Arnold, and Hardy.)

Homans, M. *Bearing the Word: Women Writers and Poetic Identity* (Princeton, N.J., 1980). (On 'what it meant for a woman to write in the nineteenth century'.)

Houghton, W. E. *The Victorian Frame of Mind, 1830–1870* (1957). (Still useful survey of predominant attitudes, but suggests a coherence which has been contested by more recent studies.)

Jann, R. *The Art and Science of Victorian History* (Columbus, Ohio, 1986).

Jay, E., ed. *The Evangelical and Oxford Movements* (Cambridge, 1983). (Essays illustrating aspects of both movements.)

Jenkyns, R. *The Victorians and Ancient Greece* (Oxford, 1980). (On the cultural manifestations of Victorian Hellenism.)

Klancher, J. *The Making of English Reading Audiences, 1790–1832* (Madison, Wisconsin, 1987). (Wide-ranging account of the place of Romantic literature in relation to newly emergent readerships.)

Knights, B. *The Idea of the Clerisy in the Nineteenth Century* (Cambridge, 1978). (Traces the development of an important nineteenth-century cultural concept.)

Langland, E. *Nobody's Angels: Middle-Class Women and Domestic Ideology in Victorian Culture* (Ithaca, N.Y., 1995). (Compares the position of real women with their status as household angels.)

Latane, D. E. 'The Birth of the Author in the Victorian Archive', *Victorian Periodicals Review*, 22, 3 (1989), 109–17.

Lee, A. *The Origins of the Popular Press* (1976).

Le Quesne, A. L., *et al Victorian Thinkers: Carlyle, Ruskin, Arnold, Morris* (Oxford, 1993).

Lerner, L., ed. *The Context of English Literature: The Victorians* (1978). (Introductory essays on literature, society, and art.)

Levine, P. '"The Humanising Influences of Afternoon Tea"', *Victorian Studies*, 34 (1990), 293–306. (On Victorian feminist periodicals.)

Levine, P. *Victorian Feminism 1850–1900* (1987). (On feminist activists and their organisational structures.)

Levy, A. *Other Women: The Writing of Class, Race, and Gender, 1832–1898* (Princeton, N.J., 1991). (Analyses the discourses of early sociologists, anthropologists and psychologists.)

Lightman, B. *The Origins of Agnosticism: Victorian Unbelief and the Limits of Knowledge* (Baltimore, 1987).

McCalman, I. *Radical Underworld: Prophets, Revolutionaries and pornographers in London, 1795–1840* (1989). (An important reassessment of early nineteenth-century radical culture.)

McFarland, T. *Romantic Cruxes: The English Essayists and the Spirit of the Age* (Oxford, 1987).

McGann, J. J., ed. *Historical Studies and Literary Criticism* (Madison, Wisconsin, 1985). (Essays on the political circumstance of literature.)

McGowan, J. P. *Representation and Revelation: Victorian Realism from Carlyle to Yeats* (Columbia, Missouri, 1986).

Manning, P. J. *Reading Romantics: Texts and Contexts* (New York, 1990).

Mellor, A. K., ed. *Romanticism and Feminism* (Bloomington, Indiana, 1988). (Both modern feminist critiques of Romanticism and historical investigation of Romantic feminism.)

Mermin, D. *Godiva's Ride: Women of Letters in England, 1830–1880* (Bloomington and Indianapolis, 1993). (On the professional female writer.)

Mitchell, S. *The Fallen Angel: Chastity, Class and Women's Reading, 1835–1880* (Bowling Green, Ohio, 1981).

Morgan, T. E., ed. *Victorian Sages and Cultural Discourse: Renegotiating Gender and Power* (New Brunswick, N.J., 1990). (Important collection of essays on sage writing as discourse.)

Morse, D. *High Victorian Culture* (New York, 1993). (Uneven study of the first four decades of Victoria's reign.)

Nash, D. *Secularism, Art, and Freedom* (Leicester, London, New York, 1992). (On the Secular movement, 1850–1890).

Newsome, D. *The Parting of Friends* (1966). (Good introduction to the Oxford Movement.)

Orel, H. *Victorian Literary Critics: G. H. Lewes, Walter Bagehot, R. H. Hutton, Leslie Stephen, Andrew Lang, George Saintsbury, and Edmund Gosse* (1984).

Owen, A. *The Darkened Room: Women, Power, and Spiritualism in Late Victorian England* (1989). (Probes the meaning of spiritualist practices and beliefs within the larger context of Victorian culture.)

Palmegiano, E. M. *Women and British Periodicals 1832–76* (Toronto, 1976).

Parsons, G., ed. *Religion in Victorian Britain*, 4 vols (Manchester, 1988). (An excellent introduction to all aspects of religious belief and practice.)

Perkins, H. *The Rise of Professional Society: England Since 1880* (1989). (On the sociology of the professional classes.)

Poovey, M. *Uneven Developments: The Ideological Work of Gender in Mid-Victorian England* (1989). (An important and innovative account of how gender is constructed in Victorian culture.)

Prickett, S. *Romanticism and Religion: The Tradition of Coleridge amd Wordsworth in the Victorian Church* (Cambridge, 1976). (Influential study in the history of ideas.)

Psomiades, 'Beauty's Body: Gender Ideology and British Aestheticism', *Victorian Studies*, 36 (1992), 31–52.

Pykett, L. 'Reading the Periodical Press: Text and Context', *Victorian Periodicals Review*, 22, 3 (1989), 101–9.

Reardon, B. M. G. *From Coleridge to Gore: A Century of Religious Thought in Britain* (1971). (Useful standard survey.)

Rendall, J., ed. *Equal or Different: Women's Politics 1800–1914* (Oxford, 1987).

Richards, T. *The Commodity Culture of Victorian England: Advertising and Spectacle 1851–1914* (1990). (Draws on theories of mass culture and spectacle.)

Royle, E. *Radicals, Secularists, and Republicans: Popular Freethought in Britain, 1866–1915* (Manchester, 1980).

Shanley, M. L. *Feminism, Marriage, and the Law in Victorian England, 1850–1895* (Princeton, N.J., 1989). (Detailed and comprehensive study.)

Shattock, J. 'Nineteenth Century Periodicals Research Then and Now', *Prose Studies,* 10 (1987), 27–30.

Shattock, J. *Politics and Reviewers: The 'Edinburgh' and the 'Quarterly' in the Early Victorian Age* (1989).

Shattock, J. and M. Wolff, eds *The Victorian Periodical Press: Samplings and Soundings* (Leicester and Toronto, 1982). (Useful collection of essays.)

Shaw, W. D. *Victorians and Mystery: Crisis of Representation* (1990). (On Victorian epistemology and language about the 'mysteries' of science, faith, and fiction.)

Sherman, C. R. with A. M. Holcomb, eds *Women as Interpreters of the Visual Arts, 1820–1979* (Westport, Connecticut, and London, 1981). (Includes essays on nineteenth-century English women art critics.)

Shevelov, K. *Women and Print Culture: The Construction of Femininity in the Early Periodical* (1989).

Shires, L., ed. *Re-Writing the Victorians: Theory, History, and the Politics of Gender* (1992). (Revisionist essays.)

Showalter, E. *The Female Malady: Women, Madness and English Culture, 1830–1980* (1987).

Sigsworth, E. M., ed. *In Search of Victorian Values: Aspects of Nineteenth-Century Thought and Society* (Manchester, 1988). (Attempts to reclaim Victorian values in all their complexity, in the context of their appropriation by Thatcherism.)

Siskin, C. *The Historicity of Romantic Discourse* (New York, 1988). (An analysis of 'the discursive power of English Romanticism'.)

Small, I. *Conditions for Criticism: Authority, Knowledge and Literature in the Late Nineteenth Century* (Oxford, 1990). (Argues for the interdependence of criticism with other fields of thought.)

Smout, T. C., ed. *Victorian Values: A Joint Symposium of the Royal Society of Edinburgh and the British Academy* (Oxford, 1992).

Sullivan, A., ed. *British Literary Magazines: The Victorian and Edwardian Age, 1837–1913* (Westport, Connecticut, and London, 1983).

Thomas, W. E. S. *The Philosophic Radicals* (Oxford, 1979). (On Utilitarianism as a movement.)

Thompson, E. P. *The Making of the English Working Class* (1963). (A major classic.)

Turner, F. M. *The Greek Heritage in Victorian England* (New Haven, Connecticut, 1981). (On the intellectual formulations of Victorian Hellenism.)

Turner, F. M. *Contesting Cultural Authority: Essays in Victorian Intellectual Life* (Cambridge, 1993). (Essays in cultural history by a distinguished scholar.)

Vann, J. D. and R. T. Van Arsdel *Victorian Periodicals and Victorian Society* (Aldershot, 1994).

Vicinus, M., ed. *Suffer and Be Still: Women in the Victorian Age* (1972). (A wide range of essays from scholars in different disciplines.)

Vicinus, M., ed. *A Widening Sphere: Changing Roles of Victorian Women* (Bloomington, Indiana, and London, 1977). (Essays on how women were confined by the ideology of 'separate spheres' and how they challenged it.)

Vincent, D. *Literacy and Popular Culture: England 1750–1914* (Cambridge, 1989). (First-rate, original study.)

Vincent, J. *The Formation of the Liberal Party 1857–68* (1966). (Good introduction.)

Watson, G. *The English Ideology* (1973). (On Victorian liberalism and its literary connections.)

Webb, R. K. *The British Working Class Reader, 1790–1848: Literacy and Social Tension* (1955).

Weeks, J. *Sex, Politics and Society: The Regulation of Sexuality Since 1800* (2nd edn, 1989).

Wheeler, M. *Death and the Future Life in Victorian Literature and Theology* (Cambridge, New York, Melbourne, 1990). (Wide-ranging literary-historical study.)

White, C. L. *Women's Magazines 1693–1968* (1970).

White, H. *Metahistory: The Historical Imagination in Nineteenth-Century Europe* (Baltimore, 1973). (An 'analysis of the deep structure of the historical imagination'.)

Williams, R. *Culture and Society, 1780–1950* (Harmondsworth, 1958). (Indispensable classic on the history of ideas of culture in relation to social change.)

Wolfreys, J. *Being English: Narratives, Idioms, and Performances of National Identity from Coleridge to Trollope* (Albany, N.Y., 1994). (On ideas of national identity in nineteenth-century England.)

Individual Authors

Notes on biography, major works and criticism. Each entry is divided into three sections:

Outline of author's life and literary career.

Selected modern editions of prose works, biographies and letters. Place of publication is London unless otherwise stated.

Selected critical works on non-fiction prose, etc. Listed alphabetically by author. Place of publication is London unless otherwise stated.

ARNOLD, Matthew (1822–88), born at Laleham-on-Thames, was the eldest son of Mary (Penrose) and Thomas Arnold, liberal theologian and Headmaster of Rugby School, and godson of John Keble, one of the founders of the Oxford Movement. He was educated at Winchester, Rugby, and Balliol College, Oxford. He was elected to an Oriel Fellowship in 1845, but became Private Secretary to Lord Lansdowne in 1847, and then an Inspector of Schools just prior to his marriage to Lucy Wightman in 1851. He worked in this area until his retirement in 1886, always retaining close ties with Oxford, however, where he was Professor of Poetry from 1857 to 1867. Arnold began his literary career as a poet, publishing *The Strayed Reveller* in 1849 and *Poems* in 1853. His Preface to the 1853 volume was his first essay in literary criticism, and constituted an important statement of the critical principles he was to formulate in his Oxford lectures and maintain throughout his life. 'The Function of Criticism at the Present Time', published as the introductory essay to his first collection of *Essays in Criticism* (1865), argued for the vital role of the 'critical spirit' in the modern world, a theme he elaborated in *Culture and Anarchy*, published in 1869 amidst the fierce political debates surrounding the Second Reform Act of 1867. In the 1870s he entered the religious debates surrounding the 'Higher Criticism' of the Bible, publishing *St Paul and Protestantism* (1870), *Literature and Dogma* (1873), and *God and the Bible* (1875). Following a lecture tour to the United States, he wrote *Discourses in America* (1885). At the end of his life he returned to literary matters, writing on Wordsworth, Byron, Keats and Gray for the Second Series of *Essays in Criticism* (1888).

> *The Complete Prose Works of Matthew Arnold*, edited by R. H. Super, 11 vols (Ann Arbor, Michigan, 1960–77).
> P. Honan, *Matthew Arnold: A Life* (1981).

> See: K. Allott, ed., *Matthew Arnold* (1975). (Essays covering all areas of Arnold's work.)
> R. ApRoberts, *Arnold and God* (Berkeley, California, 1983).
> W. E. Buckler, *Matthew Arnold's Prose: Three Essays in Literary Enlargement* (New York, 1983).

S. Collini, *Arnold* (Oxford, 1988). (Short introduction.)

C. Dawson and J. Pfordresher, eds, *Matthew Arnold, Prose Writings: The Critical Heritage* (1979).

R. Giddings, ed., *Matthew Arnold: Between Two Worlds* (1986).

J. C. Livingston, *Arnold and Christianity* (South Carolina, 1986).

C. Machann and F. D. Burt, eds, *Matthew Arnold in his Time and Ours: Centenary Essays* (Charlottesville, Virginia, 1988).

I. B. Nadel, 'Textual Criticism and Non-Fictional Prose: The Case of Matthew Arnold', *University of Toronto Quarterly*, 58 (1988–89), 263–74.

D. G. Riede, *Matthew Arnold and the Betrayal of Language* (Charlottesville, Virginia, 1988).

L. Trilling, *Matthew Arnold* (2nd edn, 1949). (A major study, still important.)

BAGEHOT, Walter (1826–77), born in Langport, Somerset, was the son of a Unitarian banker and Anglican mother, and educated at local schools and University College London. After graduation in 1848 he studied for the Bar but, although called in 1852, chose to return to Langport to join the family bank. Bagehot and R. H. Hutton had become friends as undergraduates, and in 1855 they founded the Unitarian *National Review*. In 1857 he began writing for the *Economist*. He married the owner's daughter in 1858, and became editor in 1860, a position he held until his death. A leading figure in Victorian journalism, his own main spheres of interest were politics and literature. *The English Constitution* first appeared as a series of articles for the *Fortnightly Review* (1865–67); *Physics and Politics or thoughts on the application of the principles of 'natural selection' and 'inheritance' to political society* was published in 1872; and *Lombard Street: a description of the Money Market* in 1873. His literary critical writings, collected in *Literary Studies* (3 vols, 1879–95), include some particularly acute essays on contemporary writers.

Collected Works, edited by N. St John-Stevas, 15 vols (1965–86).
Literary Studies, Everyman edition, 2 vols (1911).
The English Constitution, introduction by R. H. S. Crossman (1963).
N. St John-Stevas, *Walter Bagehot: A Study of his Life and Thought* (1959).

See: J. Burrow, S. Collini, and D. Winch, *That Noble Science of Politics* (Cambridge, 1983).

G. Himmelfarb, *Victorian Minds* (1968).

W. E. Houghton, 'Periodical Literature and the Articulate Classes', in J. Shattock and M. Wolff, eds, *The Victorian Periodical Press: Samplings and Soundings* (Leicester and Toronto, 1982), pp. 3–27.

H. Orel, *Victorian Literary Critics: George Henry Lewes, Walter Bagehot, Richard Holt Hutton, Leslie Stephen, Andrew Lang, George Saintsbury and Edmund Gosse* (1984).

C. H. Sisson, *The Case of Walter Bagehot* (1972).

BEETON, Isabella Mary (1836–65), born Isabella Mayson in London, was the eldest of a family of twenty-one. She was brought up at Epsom, where her step-father, Henry Dorling, was clerk to the racecourse. Following her education in Heidelberg, she returned to England and married the publisher Samuel Beeton. Shortly after, at the age of twenty-one, she began compiling the *Book of Household Management* for which she was to become famed. It first appeared in 1859 in monthly parts as a supplement to the

Englishwoman's Domestic Magazine, edited by her husband, and was published as a single volume in 1861. Isabella Beeton died of puerperal fever after the birth of her fourth child in 1865 at the age of twenty-eight.

> H. M. Hyde, *Mr and Mrs Beeton* (1951).
> N. Spain, *Mrs Beeton and her Husband* (1948).

> See: C. Clausen, 'How to Join the Middle Classes with the Help of Dr Smiles and Mrs Beeton', *The American Scholar* 62 (1993), 403–18.

BESANT, Annie (1847–1933), born in London, was the only daughter of Emily (Morris) and William Wood, a businessman and scholar. She was educated by evangelist Ellen Marryat, with whom she travelled to the Continent in 1863. She married Frank Besant, a clergyman, in 1867 and gave birth to a son and daughter; however, following a religious crisis, she left her husband in 1873. She met the freethought activist Charles Bradlaugh in the following year, and began lecturing and writing for the National Secular Society, publishing *The Gospel of Atheism* and *My Path to Atheism* in 1877. In 1877 also, she and Bradlaugh were prosecuted for publishing Knowlton's pamphlet on contraception. Her loss of custody of both her children in 1879 was in large part due to such subversive activities. From 1883 to 1888 Annie Besant was the General Editor and Science Correspondent of *Our Corner*, and published her important lectures on social issues in the magazine. In 1885 she became a Socialist and joined the Fabian Society, and in 1888 led the first strike of London match-girls. She published *Why I am Socialist* in 1896. In 1889 she wrote about her other main commitment in *Why I Became a Theosophist*, and in 1907 became President of the Theosophical Society. Having first visited India in 1893, she later made it her home, and thereafter devoted herself to the nationalist cause.

> *A Selection of the Social and Political Pamphlets of Annie Besant*, with Preface and Notes by John Saville (New York, 1970).
> R. Dinnage, *Annie Besant* (Harmondsworth and New York, 1986).
> R. Manvell, *The Trial of Annie Besant and Charles Bradlaugh* (1976).
> A. H. Nethercot, *The First Five Lives of Annie Besant* (Chicago, 1960).

> See: T. L. Broughton, 'Women's Autobiography: The Self at Stake?', *Prose Studies*, 14 (1991), 76–94.
> S. Chandrasekhar, *A Dirty Filthy Book: The Writings of Charles Knowlton and Annie Besant on Reproductive Physiology and Birth Control, and an Account of the Bradlaugh–Besant Trial* (Berkeley, California, 1981).

BOOTH, Charles (1840–1916), born in Liverpool, made himself wealthy through the foundation of some factories and the Booth Steamship Company. Although interested in radical theories and movements in his youth, he maintained a conservative belief in 'laissez-faire' throughout his life. He was affiliated to no political or religious organisation. In 1875 he moved with his wife Mary to London, where, sceptical of reports of widespread poverty, he began his monumental inquiry into the condition and occupations of the people of London, whose object was to show 'the numerical relation which poverty, misery and depravity bear to regular earnings and comparative comfort, and to describe the general conditions under which each class lives'. His survey was to take seventeen years to accomplish, and revealed that the problem was even worse than had been feared. The first part, *Labour and Life of the People*, appeared in 1889, and the complete seventeen-volume *Life and Labour of the People of London* from 1891 to 1903. He was initially aided in his work by his wife's cousin, Beatrice Webb, who writes about him in her autobiography *My Apprenticeship* (1926), and credits him with the introduction of the Old Age Pensions Act of 1908.

> M. Booth, *Charles Booth, a Memoir* (1918).
> B. Norman-Butler, *Victorian Aspirations: The Life and Labour of Charles and Mary Booth* (1972).

> See: D. Englander, 'Booth's Jews: the presentation of Jews and Judaism in *Life and Labour of the People in London*', *Victorian Studies*, 32 (1989), 551–71.
> R. O'Day, 'Interviews and Investigations: Charles Booth and the making of the Religious Influences Survey', *History*, 74 (1989), 361–77.
> R. O'Day, 'Retrieved Riches: Charles Booth's *Life and Labour of the People in London*', *History Today*, 39 (1989), 29–35.
> R. O'Day and D. Englander, *Mr Charles Booth's Inquiry: Life and Labour of the People in London Reconsidered* (London and Rio Grande, Ohio, 1993).

BUCKLE, Henry Thomas (1821–62), born in Lee, but brought up in London, was the son of Jane (Middleton), a devoted mother and strong Calvinist, and Thomas Henry Buckle, a Tory ship-owner. A delicate child, Henry was educated mainly at home, before entering his father's business. After his father's sudden death in 1840, he went travelling on the Continent with his mother and sister, and returned a freethinker and a radical. Financially independent, and having discovered the joy of learning on his travels, he committed himself to serious study, beginning with a course in medieval history. In 1857 he published the first volume of his *History of Civilization in England*, a book which took him fifteen years to write and which was to establish his reputation as a leading historian of civilisation. In the following year he delivered a lecture at the Royal Institution on 'The Influence of Women on the Progress of Knowledge'. Buckle's health was much affected by his mother's death in 1859, and by the death of a favourite nephew later in the same year, and delayed progress on the second volume of his *History*, which he nevertheless published in 1861. In October 1861 he went travelling in the Middle East, taking with him the two eldest sons of his friends Henry Huth and his wife, the younger of whom was eventually to write his biography. During the trip Buckle was infected with typhoid fever and died in Damascus.

> *On Scotland and the Scottish Intellect*, edited by H. J. Hanham (Chicago, 1970).
> *The Miscellaneous and Posthumous Works of Henry Thomas Buckle*, edited with a biographical notice by Helen Taylor, 3 vols (1872).
> A. H. Huth, *The Life and Writings of Henry Thomas Buckle*, 2 vols (1880).
> G. St Aubyn, *A Victorian Eminence: the Life and Works of Henry Thomas Buckle* (1958).

> See: J. P. Kenyon, *The History Men: The Historical Profession in England since the Renaissance* (1983).
> J. M. Robertson, *Buckle and his Critics* (1895).

CARLYLE, Jane Baillie Welsh (1801–66), born in Haddington, East Lothian, was the only child of Grace (Welsh) and Dr John Welsh and was educated at Haddington School from the age of four. In 1826 she married Thomas Carlyle, and in 1828 they moved to the remote farmhouse of Craigenputtock, where they lived for six years before moving to London in 1834, settling at 5 Cheyne Row, Chelsea. She was a great support to her husband, both intellectually and emotionally, as he established his reputation as a spiritual leader and social prophet, despite her own poor health. In his posthumously published *Reminiscences* he acknowledged her contribution to his own success, and expressed deep remorse for the demands he had made on her. Jane Carlyle herself wrote voluminously, but in the form of letters and memoirs, rather than for publication, although in 1883 some of her letters were published by J. A. Froude.

> *Jane Welsh Carlyle: Letters to her Family*, edited by Leonard Huxley (1924).
> *The Collected Letters of Thomas and Jane Welsh Carlyle*, edited by C. R. Sanders and K. J. Fielding, 16 vols (Durham, N. C., and Edinburgh, 1970–).
> *I too am Here: Selections from the Letters of Jane Welsh Carlyle*, edited by A. and M. M. Simpson (Cambridge, 1977).
> J. S. Collis, *The Carlyles* (1971).
> L. and E. Hanson, *Life of Jane Welsh Carlyle* (1952).
> N. B. Morrison, *True Minds: The Marriage of Thomas and Jane Carlyle* (1974).

> See: Aileen Christianson, 'Rewriting Herself: Jane Welsh-Carlyle's Letters', *Scotlands*, 2 (1994), 47–52.
> A. Christianson, 'Jane Welsh Carlyle and her Friendships with Women in the 1840s', *Prose Studies*, 10 (1987), 283–95.
> A. Christianson, 'Jane Welsh Carlyle's Private Writing Career', in D. Gifford and D. Porter, eds, *McMillan's History of Scottish Women's Literature* (Edinburgh, forthcoming).
> N. Clarke, *Ambitious Heights: Writing, Friendship, Love: The Jewsbury Sisters, Felicia Hemans, and Jane Welsh Carlyle* (1990).
> E. Hardwick, 'Amateurs: Dorothy Wordsworth and Jane Carlyle', *New York Review of Books*, 30 Nov., 1972, 3–4.
> S. Hileman, 'Autobiographical Narrative in the Letters of Jane Carlyle', *A/B: Auto/Biography Studies*, 4, 2 (1988), 107–17,

CARLYLE, Thomas (1795–1881), born in Ecclefechan, Dumfriesshire, was the son of a stonemason, and educated at Annan Academy and Edinburgh University. Abandoning plans to enter, first, the ministry, then the law, he turned to literature, and began to establish a reputation as a German specialist in the 1820s with his translation of *Wilhelm Meister's Apprenticeship* (1824), his *Life of Schiller* (1825), and his four-volume anthology of *German Romance* (1827). Following his marriage to Jane Welsh in 1826 he wrote numerous important articles on contemporary subjects, including 'Signs for the Times' (1829) and 'Characteristics' (1831), for the *Edinburgh Review*, as well as *Sartor Resartus* (1833–34), which recounts the spiritual crisis of his youth and its resolution. The publication of this last in book form in 1838, together with *The History of the French Revolution* (1837) confirmed his reputation and, now living in London, he became a leading figure in the debates about contemporary social issues which dominated the 1840s, denouncing the evils of the post-industrial 'mechanical age' in *Chartism* (1839) and *Past and Present* (1843), and advocating leadership and heroism in *On Heroes, Hero-Worship, and the Heroic in History* (1841). He was to become increasingly conservative in the 1850s and 1860s, the violent hostility of his response to the 1867 Reform Act in 'Shooting Niagara' revealing the extent of his disaffection from the principles of political democracy. His biographies of John Sterling (1851) and Frederick the Great (6 vols, 1858–65), and his own autobiographical *Reminiscences* (published posthumously in 1881), are the most enduring, and endearing, works of these years.

Works: Centenary Edition, edited by H. D. Traill, 30 vols (New York and London, 1896–99).

The Collected Letters of Thomas and Jane Welsh Carlyle, edited by C. R. Sanders and K. J. Fielding, in progress (Durham, N. C., and Edinburgh, 1970–).

Sartor Resartus, edited by K. McSweeney and P. Sabor (Oxford, 1987).

The French Revolution, edited by K. J. Fielding and D. Sorensen (Oxford, 1989).

J. A. Froude, *Thomas Carlyle: A History of the First Forty Years of his Life, 1795–1835*, 2 vols (1882) and *Thomas Carlyle: A History of his Life in London, 1843–1881*, 2 vols (1884). Available in an abridged *Life of Carlyle*, edited by J. Clubbe (1979). (The first and still the best biography.)

F. Kaplan, *Thomas Carlyle: A Biography* (Cambridge, 1983).

See: R. Ashton, *The German Idea: Four English Writers and the Reception of German Thought 1800–1860* (Cambridge, 1980).

G. Beer, 'Carlylean Transports', in *Arguing with the Past: Essays in Narrative from Woolf to Sidney* (1989).

T. Broughton, 'The Froude-Carlyle Controversy, Biography and the Victorian Man of Letters: Married Life – as a Literary Problem', *Victorian Studies*, 38, 4, (Summer 1995), 551–85.

J. Clubbe, ed., *Carlyle and his Contemporaries* (Durham, N. C., 1976).

M. Cummings, *A Disimprisoned Epic: Form and Vision in Carlyle's French Revolution* (Philadelphia, 1988).

P. A. Dale, '*Sartor Resartus* and the Inverse Sublime: The Art of Humorous Destruction', in M. W. Bloomfield, ed., *Allegory, Myth, and Symbol* (Cambridge, Massachusetts, 1981), pp. 293–312.

H. Feinberg, 'Carlyle and Mill: Style as the Shape of Content', *Victorians Institute Journal*, 17 (1989), 77–85.

E. L. Gilbert, 'Rescuing Reality: Carlyle, Froude, and Biographical Truth-Telling', *Victorian Studies*, 34 (1991), 295 314.

W. V. Harris 'Interpretive Historicism: *Signs of the Times* and *Culture and Anarchy* in their Contexts', *Nineteenth-Century Literature*, 44 (1990), 411–64.

J. Hillis Miller, '"Hieroglyphical Truth" in *Sartor Resartus*: Carlyle and the Language of Parable', in J. Clubbe and J. Meckier, eds *Victorian Perspectives: Six Essays* (Newark, N.J., 1989), pp. 1–20.

Jann, R. *The Art and Science of Victorian History* (Columbus, Ohio, 1985).

A. L. Le Quesne, *Carlyle* (Oxford, 1982). (Useful short introduction.)

C. Persak, 'Rhetoric in Praise of Silence: The Ideology of Carlyle's Paradox', *Rhetoric Society Quarterly*, 21, 1 (1991), 38–52.

J. D. Rosenberg, *Carlyle and the Burden of History* (Oxford, 1985). (Fine study of *The French Revolution*.)

J. D. Rosenberg, 'Carlyle and Historical Narration', *The Carlyle Annual*, 10 (1989), 14–20.

C. de L. Ryals, 'Carlyle's *The French Revolution*: A True Fiction',
ELH, 54 (1987), 925–40.

R. L. Tarr, *Thomas Carlyle: A Descriptive Bibliography* (Pittsburgh,
1989).

G. B. Tennyson, *Sartor Called Resartus* (Princeton, N.J., 1965). (On
the genesis, structure, and style of *Sartor*.)

D. J. Trela 'Froude on the Carlyles: The Victorian Debate over
Biography', in K. Ottesen, ed. *Victorian Scandals: Representations of
Gender and Class* (Athens, Ohio, 1992), pp. 180–206.

C. R. Vanden Bossche, *Carlyle and the Search for Authority*
(Columbus, Ohio, 1991).

COBBETT, William (1763–1835), born in Farnham, Surrey, was of peasant
origin. Largely self-educated, he ran away from home at the age of ten or
eleven to work in Kew Gardens, then later as a clerk in London. He
enlisted as a soldier and served in New Brunswick from 1784 to 1791. He
obtained his discharge and, back in England, and married to Anne (Nancy)
Reid, whom he had met in America, brought an action of corruption and
peculation against some of his former officers. In 1792, to avoid counter-
charges by the military establishment, he was obliged to retire first to
France and then to America, where he became, under the pseudonym
'Peter Porcupine', an influential political journalist in support of the
Washington administration. A libel action brought against him in 1800
forced him to return to England, where he became an anti-Radical
journalist, founding and writing *Cobbett's Political Register* in 1802.
However, his views changed, and by 1804 he was writing in support of
the Radical cause. He was imprisoned for two years in Newgate Prison for
seditious libel, after which he fled to America, where he farmed and wrote,
as he was again to do upon his return to England. He was a prolific and
diverse writer, publishing works ranging from practical primers and
handbooks for the literate poor, to a *History of the Protestant 'Reformation' in
England and Ireland* (1824). His best-known work, *Rural Rides* (1830), a
collection of reflections on his travels through rural England which had
begun to appear in the *Political Register* in 1821, is an acute work of social
criticism. Cobbett was elected MP for Oldham in the reformed Parliament
of 1832.

> *The Autobiography of William Cobbett: The Progress of a Plough-boy to
> a Seat in Parliament*, edited by W Reitzel (1967),
> G Spater, *William Cobbett. The Poor Man's Friend*, 2 vols
> (Cambridge, 1982).

See: F. G. A. M. Aarts, 'William Cobbett: Radical, Reactionary and Poor
Man's Grammarian', *Neophilologus*, 70, 4 (1986), 603–14.

J. R. Andrews, 'The Rhetorical Birth of a Political Pamphleteer:
William Cobbett's "Observations on Priestley's emigration"', in
T. W. Benson and L. Perry, eds, *American Rhetoric: Context and
Criticism* (Carbondale, Illinois, 1989), pp. 201–20.

I. Dyck, *William Cobbett and Rural Popular Culture* (Cambridge,
1992). (An important reassessment.)

K. Gilmartin, '"Victims of Argument, Slaves of Fact": Hunt,
Hazlitt, Cobbett and the Literature of Opposition', *The
Wordsworth Circle*, 21, 3 (1990), 90–96.

D. Green, *Great Cobbett: The Noblest Agitator* (Oxford, 1985).

L. Lemrow, 'William Cobbett's Journalism for the Lower Orders',
Victorian Periodicals Review, 15, 1 (1982), 11–20.

L. Mattrass, *William Cobbett: The Politics of Style* (Cambridge, 1995).

J. Sambrook, *William Cobbett* (1973). (Life and letters.)

A. J. Sambrook, 'Cobbett and the French Revolution', *Yearbook of English Studies*, 19 (1989), 231–42.

K. W. Schweizer and R. Klein, 'The Progress of William Cobbett, 1800–1806', *Durham University Journal*, 81, 2 (1989), 221–27.

R. Williams, *Cobbett* (Oxford, 1983).

COLERIDGE, Samuel Taylor (1772–1834), was the youngest son of the vicar of Ottery St Mary in Devon, and was himself intended for the Church. He was educated at Christ's Hospital and Jesus College, Cambridge, where, despite his academic brilliance, he failed to take his degree. His youthful radicalism manifested itself in an enthusiasm for French Revolutionary politics, and in a proposed scheme, devised with his undergraduate friend Robert Southey, to set up a commune, or 'Pantisocracy', in New England. The only lasting outcome of this plan was Coleridge's marriage to Sara Fricker in 1795, which was itself to founder a decade later. His first poems appeared in the *Morning Chronicle* in 1794, and his first volume, *Poetry on Various Subjects*, was published in 1796. He contemplated entering the Unitarian ministry at this period, and edited a radical Christian journal, *The Watchman*, which ran for ten issues. Moving to Nether Stowey on the edge of the Quantock hills in Somerset, Coleridge developed a close and creative friendship with Dorothy and William Wordsworth, who were then living two miles away at Alfoxden, and wrote some of his greatest poems. In 1798 Coleridge and Wordsworth published a selection of their work as the experimental volume *Lyrical Ballads*. Disenchanted with the course taken by events in France, Coleridge went to Germany to study Kant, Schiller and Schelling in 1798–99, and shortly after his return to England, following a period of journalism in London, settled with his family near the Wordsworths in Keswick in the Lake District in 1800. His marriage had begun to fail by this time, a process hastened and confirmed when he fell in love with Sara Hutchinson, whose sister Mary married Wordsworth in 1802. During this period his opium use, which had begun in the previous decade, hardened into dependency. In 1808 he delivered the first of many series of lectures on poetry at the Royal Institution, attracting large and distinguished audiences. At the end of that year he joined the Wordsworths at Grasmere, where, over the ensuing eighteen months, he produced *The Friend*, a 'literary, moral, and political weekly paper' designed to educate the English in post-Kantian idealism, which ran for twenty-eight issues from 1809–10. 1810 saw a crisis in his relationship with both the Wordsworths and Sara Hutchinson, and Coleridge moved to London, where he lectured and wrote despite his deep personal distress and failure of health. After a physical and mental breakdown in 1813, and a period of medical treatment and convalescence, during which he still found time to write one of his most important works, *Biographia Literaria*, in 1816 he found refuge in the Highgate home of the young surgeon Dr James Gillman, where he was to settle for the rest of his life. Described by Carlyle as 'the Sage of Highgate', he presided over a circle of old friends and younger disciples, and wrote the great prose texts on social and religious issues of his final decades: the two *Lay Sermons* of 1816 and 1817; a three-volume edition of *The Friend*, including a 'Treatise on Method' (1818); *Aids to Reflection* (1825); and his last major publication, *On the Constitution of the Church and State* (1830).

> *The Collected Works of Samuel Taylor Coleridge*, edited by K. Coburn and B. Winer, Bollingen Series 75, in progress (London and Princeton, N.J., 1969–).

The Notebooks of Samuel Taylor Coleridge, edited by K. Coburn *et al*,
in progress (New York, 1957–)

Coleridge on Shakespeare: The Text of the Lectures of 1811–12, edited
by R. A. Foakes (1971).

Collected Letters of Samuel Taylor Coleridge, edited by E. L. Griggs, 6
vols (Oxford, 1956–71).

W. Hazlitt, 'On My First Acquaintance with Poets' (1823).

W. J. Bate, *Coleridge* (1968).

See: W. C. Anderson, 'The Dramatization of Thought in Coleridge's
Prose', *Prose Studies*, 6, 3 (1983), 264–73.

R. Ashton, *The German Idea: Four English Writers and the Reception of
German Thought 1800–1860* (Cambridge, 1980). (Useful on the
intellectual context.)

H. D. Baker, 'Landscape as Textual Practice in Coleridge's
Notebooks', *ELH*, 59 (1992), 651–70.

J. Beer, 'Coleridge as Critic', *Prose Studies*, 13 (1990), 4–17.

F. Burwick, ed., *Coleridge's* Biographia Literaria: *Text and Meaning*
(Columbus, Ohio, 1990).

A. S. Byatt, *Unruly Times: Wordsworth and Coleridge in their Time*
(1989).

S. Bygrave, *Coleridge and the Self: Romantic Egotism* (Basingstoke,
1986).

J. A. Carlson, *In the Theatre of Romanticism: Coleridge, Nationalism,
Women* (Cambridge, 1994).

J. Christiansen, *Coleridge's Blessed Machine of Language* (Ithaca, N.Y.,
1981). (Illuminates the significance of Coleridge's fragmentary
discourse.)

D. Coleman, *Coleridge and* The Friend (Oxford, 1988). (Excellent
close study.)

T. Corrigan, *Coleridge, Language, and Criticism* (Athens, Georgia,
1982).

G. Davidson, *Coleridge's Career* (1990).

M. Edmundson, 'Vital Intimations: Wordsworth, Coleridge, and the
Promise of Criticism', *South Atlantic Quarterly*, 91 (1992), 739–64.

J. Ellison, 'The Daughter of Logic, Coleridge's *Essays on the
Principles of Method*', *Prose Studies*, 12 (1989), 224–39.

A. C. Goodson, *Verbal Imagination: Coleridge and the Language of
Modern Criticism* (Oxford, 1988).

P. Hamilton, *Coleridge's Poetics* (Oxford, 1983). (Intelligent, subtle
study.)

R. Holmes, *Coleridge* (Oxford, 1982).

P. J. Kitson and T. N. Corns, eds, *Coleridge and the Armoury of the
Human Mind: Essays in his Prose Writings* (1991). (First published as
a special number of *Prose Studies*, 13, 3 (1990).)

T. H. Levere, *Poetry Realised in Nature: Samuel Taylor Coleridge and
Early Nineteenth-Century Science* (Cambridge, 1981). (Interesting on
the cross-fertilisation of ideas.)

J. Morrow, *Coleridge's Political Thought: Property, Morality and the
Limits of Traditional Discourse* (1990).

D. H. Reiman, 'Coleridge and the Art of Equivocation', *Studies in
Romanticism*, 25 (1986), 125–50.

N. Roe, *Wordsworth and Coleridge: The Radical Years* (Oxford, 1988).

S. Vine, 'To "make a bull": Autobiography, Idealism and Writing in
Coleridge's *Biographia Literaria*', *Prose Studies*, 13 (1990), 99–114.

I. Wylie, *Young Coleridge and the Philosophers of Nature* (Oxford, 1989).

CULLWICK, Hannah (1833–1909), born in Shifnal, Shropshire, was the daughter of a housemaid and a saddler. She went into service in 1841 at the age of eight, and in 1854 moved to London, where she met Arthur Munby, an upper-middle-class poet and barrister. He encouraged her to keep a diary for his benefit, recording all the details of her daily drudgery, and she did so for the next two decades. Following an eighteen-year secret courtship, the couple were married in 1873; however, refusing the role of 'lady', Hannah preferred to live as Munby's servant. Although they were together for fifty-four years, their relationship was only made public when Munby's will was published in 1910.

> *The Diaries of Hannah Cullwick, Victorian Maidservant*, edited by Liz Stanley (1984).
> D. Hudson, *Munby, Man of Two Worlds: The Life and Diaries of Arthur J. Munby, 1828–1910* (1972).

> See: L. Davidoff, 'Class and Gender in Victorian England: The Diaries of Arthur J. Munby and Hannah Cullwick', *Feminist Studies*, 5, 1 (1979), 86–141. (Sophisticated analysis.)
> S. Green, 'Making a Marginal Text Central in the Undergraduate Literature Course: The case of Hannah Cullwick's Diaries', *College Literature*, 18 (1991), 132–37.
> L. Stanley, 'Biography as Microscope or Kaleidoscope? The Case of "Power" in Hannah Cullwick's Relationship with Arthur Munby', *Women's Studies International Forum*, 10, 1 (1987), 19–31.

DARWIN, Charles (1809–82), born in Shrewsbury, was the son of a doctor and grandson of the evolutionist poet Erasmus Darwin. He was educated locally and at Edinburgh University and Cambridge University where, having abandoned plans for careers first in medicine and then in the Church, he became interested in biology. The Professor of Botany, J. S. Henslow, secured him the post of naturalist to HMS Beagle, which left England in 1831 for a scientific survey of the coast of South America. Darwin spent the next five years circumnavigating the world, gathering the evidence for the theories which were later to make his reputation. On his return he published the results of his work on coral reefs and volcanic islands, and an account of his journey in *The Voyage of the 'Beagle'* (1839), but his hypothesis on evolution by natural selection, based on his observation of species mutation in the Galapagos Islands, remained in draft form, until he discovered that Alfred Russell Wallace had independently arrived at the same conclusions. They presented a joint paper to the Linnaean Society, and in 1859 Darwin published *On the Origin of Species by Means of Natural Selection*. Darwin was similarly reticent about spelling out the implications of the theory of evolution for mankind, and it was not until twelve years later, in 1871, that he published *The Descent of Man*. He spent the final decades of his life with his family in semi-retirement at his home at Down House in Kent, engaged in less momentous botanical studies on topics such as orchids and vegetable mould.

> *The Origin of Species*, edited by J. W. Burrow (Harmondsworth, 1968). (Lucid introduction.)
> *Charles Darwin's Beagle Diary*, edited by R. D. Keynes (Cambridge, 1988).

Charles Darwin: On Evolution, edited by T. F. Glick and D. Kohn (Lancaster, 1996).

The Collected Papers of Charles Darwin, edited by P. H. Barrett, 2 vols (Chicago, 1977).

C. Darwin and T. H. Huxley, *Autobiographies*, edited by G. de Beer (Oxford, 1974).

The Correspondence of Charles Darwin, edited by F. Burckhardt, S. Smith, *et al.*, 9 vols to date (Cambridge, 1985–).

A. Desmond and J. Moore, *Darwin* (1991). (A full and scholarly biography.)

See: D. Amigoni and J. Wallace, eds, *Charles Darwin's* The Origin of Species: *New Interdisciplinary Essays* (Manchester, 1995).

P. Barrish, 'Accumulating Variation: Darwin's *On the Origin of Species* and Contemporary Literary and Cultural Theory', *Victorian Contexts*, 34, 4 (1991), 431–54.

G. Beer, *Darwin's Plots: Evolutionary Narrative in Darwin, George Eliot, and Nineteenth-Century Fiction* (1983). (Dazzling analysis of Darwin's narrative.)

G. Beer, '"The Face of Nature": Anthropomorphic Elements in the Language of *The Origin of Species*', in L. J. Jordanova, ed., *Languages of Nature: Critical Essays on Science and Literature* (New Brunswick, N.J., 1986), pp. 207–43.

L. S. Bergmann, 'Reshaping the Roles of Man, God, and Nature: Darwin's Rhetoric in *On the Origin of Species*', in J. W. Slade and J. Yaross, eds, *Beyond the Two Cultures: Essays in Science, Technology, and Literature* (Ames, Iowa, 1990), pp. 79–98.

P. J. Bowler, *Charles Darwin: The Man and his Influence* (Oxford, 1990).

J. A. Campbell, 'Scientific Discovery and Rhetorical Invention: The Path to Darwin's Origin', in H. W. Simons, ed. *The Rhetorical Turn: Invention and Persuasion in the Conduct of Inquiry* (Chicago, 1990), pp. 58–90.

J. A. Campbell, 'Scientific Revolution and the Grammar of Culture: The Case of Darwin's *Origin*', *The Quarterly Journal of Speech*, 72, 4 (1986), 351–76.

D. C. Dennett, *Darwin's Dangerous Idea: Evolution and the Meanings of Life* (1995).

J. R. Durant, ed., *Darwinism and Divinity: Essays on Evolution and Religious Belief* (Oxford, 1985).

A. Ellegard, *Darwin and the General Reader: The Reception of Darwin's Theory of Evolution in the British Periodical Press, 1859–1872* (Chicago, 1990).

A. G. Gross, '*The Origin of Species*: Evolutionary Taxonomy as an Example of the Rhetoric of Science', in H. W. Simons, ed., *The Rhetorical Turn: Invention and Persuasion in the Conduct of Inquiry* (Chicago, 1990), pp. 91–115.

R. J. Halliday, *Darwinism, Biology and Race* (Warwick, 1990).

J. Howard, *Darwin* (1982). (Short introduction.)

D. Kohn, ed., *The Darwinian Heritage* (Princeton, N.J., 1985).

G. Levine, 'Charles Darwin's Reluctant Revolution', *South Atlantic Quarterly*, 91 (1992), 525–55.

P. Morton, *The Vital Science: Biology and the Literary Imagination 1860–1900* (1984). (An important study.)

J. Rachels, *Created from Animals: The Moral Implications of Darwinism* (Oxford, 1990).

R. J. Richards, *Darwinism and the Emergence of Evolutionary Theories of Mind and Behavior* (Chicago, 1987).

M. Ruse, *The Darwinian Paradigm: Essays on its History, Philosophy, and Religious Implications* (1989).

R. B. Yeazell, 'Nature's Courtship Plot in Darwin and Ellis', *The Yale Journal of Criticism*, 2, 2 (1989), 33–53.

DAVY, Humphry (1778–1829), born in Penzance, Cornwall, was the son of Robert Davy, a wood-carver of good family who pursued his craft for pleasure, and Grace (Millett), also of an old family, who had been brought up by the eminent surgeon John Tonkin after the death of her parents. Humphry Davy's childhood was spent partly with his parents at Varfell, the family estate in Ludgvan, and partly with Tonkin, who arranged his education at the Penzance Grammar School, and later with the Rev. Dr Cardew at Truro. His interest in poetry and in experimental science developed at an early age, the latter fostered by a Quaker saddler named Robert Dunkin. After his father's death in 1794, Davy was apprenticed to the Penzance surgeon John Bingham Borlase where, in the apothecary's dispensary, he became a chemist. He quickly developed a reputation, and in 1798 was offered the position of laboratory superintendent at Dr Beddoes' newly established 'Pneumatic Institution'. It was during this period that he met Coleridge and Southey. He began to publish the results of his research on heat and light in 1799, and shortly after published his research on nitrous oxide and its respiration. When the Royal Institution was founded in London, Davy was appointed as Director of the chemical laboratory and Lecturer in Chemistry, and delivered the first of his tremendously popular series of lectures in 1801. He was made Professor in the following year, and elected to a Fellowship of the Royal Society in 1803. His fame spread to Europe following the Bakerian Lecture of 1807 where he explained all his experiments and discoveries in electricity before the Royal Society. He continued his researches in electro-chemical science to great international acclaim, and was knighted in 1812, in the same year marrying the heiress Jane Apreece. In 1815 he began to develop a safety lamp for coal-miners. He was created a baronet in 1818. In 1820 he was elected to succeed Sir Joseph Banks as President of the Royal Society, a position which he resigned in 1827 due to poor health.

The Collected Works of Sir Humphry Davy, edited by J. Davy, 9 vols (1839–40). Vol I is John Davy's *Memoirs of the Life of Sir Humphry Davy*.

J. A. Paris, *The Life of Sir Humphry Davy*, 2 vols (1831).

A. Treneer, *The Mercurial Chemist: A Life of Sir Humphry Davy* (1963).

See: S. Forgan, ed., *Science and the Sons of Genius: Studies on Humphry Davy* (1980)

C. Lawrence, 'The Power and the Glory: Humphry Davy and Romanticism', in A. Cunningham and N. Jardine, eds, *Romanticism and the Sciences* (Cambridge, 1990), pp. 213–27. (Useful, contextualising account.)

C. A. Russell, *Sir Humphry Davy* (Bletchley, 1972). (Clear Open University study guide.)

DE QUINCEY, Thomas (1785–1859, born in Manchester, was the second son of a linen merchant, who died in 1793, and an Evangelical mother, an associate of Hannah More. He was educated at schools in Bath and

Winkfield, and finally at Manchester Grammar School, from which he
absconded in 1802, living in destitution in Wales and London until he was
reconciled with his mother and guardians in 1803. In the same year he
went to Worcester College, Oxford, where, despite his reputation as an
outstanding classicist, he did not present himself for his final examinations.
In 1806 he came of age, but soon spent his modest inheritance, mainly on
books, and for much of the rest of his life was to live in straitened
circumstances. Having met Coleridge and Wordsworth, whom he had
admired for many years, he moved up to the Lake District and settled at
Dove Cottage when William and Dorothy Wordsworth moved to Allan
Bank. The friendship between them deteriorated, however, as De
Quincey's opium use, begun in 1804, became habitual and as he persisted
in his affair with Margaret Simpson, the daughter of a local farmer, whom
he married in 1817. They were to have eight children, and, having by this
time exhausted his private means, De Quincey had to work hard as a
journalist to support his family. From 1821 to 1824 he wrote mainly for
The London Magazine, where *Confessions of an English Opium Eater* first
appeared in 1821, bringing him immediate notoriety and recognition. For
the next 30 years he earned a precarious living, mainly in Edinburgh, by
his articles and reviews on a remarkable range of subjects, most of which
appeared in *Blackwood's* and later in *Tait's Edinburgh Magazine*, where he
published his *Recollections of the Lakes and the Lake Poets* (1834–39), which
was to complete his estrangement from the Wordsworth family. Despite
his tremendous productivity, De Quincey never earned enough to achieve
financial security; he was imprisoned for debt in 1832, forced into
bankruptcy in 1833, and frequently suffered humiliation and harassment at
the hands of his creditors.

> *Confessions of an English Opium-Eater, and other writings*, edited by
>   G. Lindop (Oxford, 1985).
> *Recollections of the Lakes and the Lake Poets*, edited by D. Wright
>   (Harmondsworth, 1970).
> *De Quincey as Critic*, edited by J. E. Jordan (1973).
> *Selected Essays on Rhetoric*, edited by F. Barwick (Carbondale,
>   Illinois, and Edinburgh, 1967).
> G. Lindop, *The Opium-Eater: A Life of Thomas De Quincey* (1981).
>   (Sympathetic biography, compellingly written.)
> R. Woof, *Thomas De Quincey 1785–1859* (Grasmere, 1985).

See: J. Barrell, *The Infection of Thomas De Quincey: A Psychopathology of
      Imperialism* (New Haven, Connecticut, 1991). (Reads De
      Quincey's work as a complex Freudian case-study.)
   E. Baxter, *De Quincey's Art of Autobiography* (Edinburgh, 1990).
      (Intelligent study.)
   J. Black, *The Aesthetics of Murder: A Study in Romantic Literature and
      Contemporary Culture* (Baltimore, 1991). (A cultural history of
      murder focused on readings of De Quincey's essays 'On Murder'.)
   A. W. Cafarelli, 'De Quincey and Wordsworthian narrative', *Studies
      in Romanticism*, 28 (1989), 121–47.
   R. Caseby, *The Opium-Eating Editor: Thomas De Quincey and the
      Westmorland Gazette* (Kendal, 1985).
   J. Coates, 'Aspects of De Quincey's "High Tory" Prose in Theory
      and Practice', *Durham University Journal*, 53, 175–85.
   W. T. Covino, 'Thomas De Quincey in a Revisionist History of
      Rhetoric', *Pre/Text: A Journal of Rhetorical Theory*, 4, 2 (1983),
      121–36.

A. Digwaney and L. Needham, '"A Sort of Previous Lubrication" :
De Quincey's Preface to *Confessions of an English Opium Eater*',
The Quarterly Journal of Speech, 71, 4 (1985), 457–69.

N. Leask, '"Murdering One's Double": De Quincey's *Confessions of
an English Opium Eater* and S. T. Coleridge's *Biographia Literaria*',
Prose Studies, 13 (1990), 78–98.

A. Leighton, 'De Quincey and Women', in S. Copley and J. Whale,
eds, *Beyond Romanticism: New Approaches to Texts and Contexts
1780–1830* (1992), pp. 160–77.

G. Lindop, *The Works of Thomas De Quincey* (1994).

J. McDonagh, 'Writings on the Mind: Thomas De Quincey and the
Importance of the Palimpsest in Nineteenth-Century Thought',
Prose Studies, 10 (1987), 207–24.

J. McDonagh, 'Do or Die: Problems of Agency and Gender in the
Aesthetics of Murder', *Genders*, 5 (1989), 120–34.

J. McDonagh, 'Opium and the Imperial Imagination', in
P. W. Martin and R. Jarvis, eds, *Reviewing Romanticism* (1992).

T. McFarland, *Romantic Cruxes: The English Essayists and the Spirit of
the Age* (Oxford, 1987).

J. Hillis Miller, *The Disappearance of God: Five Nineteenth-Century
Writers* (Cambridge, Massachusetts, 1963).

M. Russett, 'Wordsworth's Gothic Interpreter: De Quincey
Personifies "We Are Seven"', *Studies in Romanticism*, 30 (1991),
345–65.

R. L. Snyder, ed., *Thomas De Quincey: Centenary Studies* (Norman,
Oklahoma, 1985).

J. Wilner, 'Autobiography and Addiction: The Case of De Quincey',
Genre, 14, 4 (1981), 493–503.

J. C. Whale, *Thomas De Quincey's Reluctant Autobiography* (1984).

ENGELS, Friedrich (1820–95), the son of a wealthy cotton manufacturer in
Barmen, in the Rhineland, reacted against his family's whole ethos and
became a communist by the time he was twenty. He left for England in
1842 to supervise his father's business in Manchester, making his first
personal contact with Karl Marx en route. He stayed there for two years,
writing the *Condition of the Working Class in England* from 1844–45, the
first book to deal with the working class as a whole and to offer a general
analysis of the evolution of industrial capitalism and of the social and
political impact of industrialisation. It was published in Leipzig in 1845,
with a preface and dedication (in English 'to the working classes of Great
Britain', and was published in English in 1887 (American edition) and 1892
(British edition). Engels collaborated with Marx, who settled in London in
1849, in writing *The German Ideology* (1845–46, but not published until
1932), the *Communist Manifesto* (1848) and *Das Kapital*, the third volume of
which he completed after Marx's death.

The Condition of the Working Class in England, edited by
E. Hobsbawm (St Albans, 1969).

W. O. Henderson, *The Life of Friedrich Engels* (2 vols, 1976).

See: M. E. Blanchard, *In Search of the City: Engels, Baudelaire, Rimbaud*
(Saratoga, N.Y., 1985).

T. Carver, *Engels* (Oxford, 1981).

GREEN, Thomas Hill (1836–82), the youngest of four children of Valentine
Green, the Rector of Birkin, Yorkshire, and his first wife, was born and

brought up in Birkin. After his mother's death when he was one, he was educated by his father until he was sent to Rugby at the age of fourteen. In 1855 he entered Balliol College, Oxford, where he was taught by Benjamin Jowett, and in 1860, following graduation, became a Fellow himself. His intellectual interests ranged widely across ancient and modern history, politics, literature and theology, but he was principally a philosopher, bringing his idealist principles to bear on his religious and political position. His religious views were such that he was reluctant to take orders, although he signed the Thirty-Nine Articles upon taking his M.A. degree. After beginning work on a translation of F. C. Baur's *History of the Christian Church* and an edition of Aristotle's *Ethics*, he was appointed Assistant Commissioner to the Royal Commission on Middle-Class Schools, a position which occupied him through 1865 and 1866. In 1866 he was appointed to a teaching position at Balliol, and became increasingly influential in both the College and the University, lecturing on Aristotle and the early Greek philosophers as well as on seventeenth- and eighteenth-century English thought, and distinguishing himself as the leading exponent of German Idealist thought. In 1871 he married Charlotte Symonds, the sister of his friend John Addington Symonds. He published a new edition of Hume's works in 1874–75, and was elected to the Whyte Professorship of Moral Philosophy in 1878, a position he held until 1882, the year of his death from heart disease. His lectures form the substance of his unfinished *Prolegomena to Ethics*, which was edited and published posthumously by A. C. Bradley in 1883.

> *The Works of T. H. Green*, edited by R. L. Nettleship, 3 vols (1885–88).

> See: I. M. Greengarten, *Thomas Hill Green and the Development of Liberal-Democratic Thought* (Toronto, 1981).
> P. P. Nicholson, *The Political Philosophy of the British Idealists: Selected Studies* (Cambridge, New York, etc., 1990). (Focuses on Green.)
> M. Richter, *The Politics of Conscience: T. H. Green and His Age* (1964).
> G. Thomas, *The Moral Philosophy of T. H. Green* (Oxford, 1987).
> A. Vincent, ed., *The Philosophy of T. H. Green* (1986).

HAZLITT, William (1778–1830), born at Maidstone, Kent, was the son of a Unitarian minister. After a period in America, most of his youth was spent in the village of Wem, near Shrewsbury, where he was educated mainly by his father, a man of strong liberal views. He was intended for the ministry, but abandoned his studies at the Unitarian College at Hackney with a view to becoming a painter. Through his father he met Coleridge, and through him Wordsworth, whose *Lyrical Ballads* he greatly admired, and although he continued to paint he determined on a career as a writer. He was a prolific critic, journalist, essayist and lecturer, whose sympathies were always on the radical side – which was later to bring him into conflict with Coleridge and Wordsworth. He was an ardent republican and strong supporter of the French Revolution and Napoleon. He was also deeply concerned about social ills at home. Always a polymath, his earlier writings are mainly in the area of political journalism, but by about 1810 his interests had shifted to philosophy, and by 1812 to literary criticism. He wrote regularly for the *Morning Chronicle, The Champion*, Leigh Hunt's *Examiner* and the *Edinburgh Review*. His *Characters of Shakespeare* appeared in 1817, to be swiftly followed by a book of essays written with Leigh

Hunt, *The Round Table* (1817), his *View of the English Stage* (1818), his *Lectures on the English Poets* (1818), and *Lectures on the English Comic Writers* (1819). 1819 also saw the publication of his *Political Essays*, on the conditions of the poor, and the beginning of a destructive love affair with Sarah Walker, his landlord's daughter. In 1822 he divorced his wife Sarah Stoddard, whom he had married in 1808, and in 1823, after Sarah Walker left him, published *Liber Amoris*, a painful account of the whole affair. He was arrested for debt at this time. In 1824 he married Isabella Bridgewater, and travelled in Europe, collecting material for his projected *Life of Napoleon*, which was published in 1828–30.

> *The Complete Works of William Hazlitt*, edited by P. P. Howe, Centenary Edition, 21 vols (1930–34).
> *Hazlitt's Criticism of Shakespeare: A Selection*, edited by R. S. White (Lampeter, 1995).
> *The Letters of William Hazlitt*, edited by H. M. Sikes (1979).
> S. Jones, *Hazlitt: A Life: from Winterslow to Frith Street* (Oxford, 1989). (Meticulously researched account of Hazlitt as a 'realist romantic idealist'.)

See: W. P. Albrecht, 'Structure in Two of Hazlitt's Essays', *Studies in Romanticism*, 21 (1982), 181–90.
F. D. Anderson and A. A. King, 'Hazlitt as a Critic of Parliamentary Speaking', *The Quarterly Journal of Speech*, 67 (1981), 47–56.
J. Bate, *Shakespearean Constitutions* (Oxford, 1989). (Includes a stimulating account of Hazlitt's Shakespearean criticism.)
D. Bromwich, *Hazlitt: The Mind of a Critic* (New York and Oxford, 1983).
S. Dentith, *A Rhetoric of the Real* (Hemel Hempstead, 1990). (Contains an interesting chapter on Hazlitt.)
N. Enright, 'William Hazlitt and his "Familiar Style"', in A. J. Butrym, ed., *Essays on the Essay: Redefining the Genre* (Athens, Georgia, 1989), pp. 116–25.
J. Haefner, '"The soul speaking in the face": Hazlitt's Concept of Character', *Studies in English Literature 1500–1900*, 24 (1984), 655–70.
J. Haefner, 'Rhetoric and Art: George Campbell, William Hazlitt, and "Gusto"', *Charles Lamb Bulletin*, 63 (1988), 234–43.
S. Jones, 'First Flight: Image and Theme in a Hazlitt Essay', *Prose Studies*, 8 (1985), 35–47.
J. Kinnaird, *William Hazlitt: Critic of Power* (New York, 1978).
R. Levin, 'Hazlitt on *Henry V*, and the Appropriation of Shakespeare', *Shakespeare Quarterly*, 35 (1984), 134–41.
T. McFarland, *Romantic Cruxes: The English Essayists and the Spirit of the Age* (Oxford, 1987).
J. Mulvihill, 'Hazlitt on Parliamentary Eloquence', *Prose Studies*, 12 (1989), 132–46.
J. Mulvihill, 'Hazlitt and "First Principles"', *Studies in Romanticism*, 29 (1990), 241–55.
R. Park, *Hazlitt and the Spirit of the Age: Abstraction and Critical Theory* (Oxford, 1971).
M. Ward, 'Preparing for the National Gallery: The Art Criticism of William Hazlitt and P. G. Patmore', *Victorian Periodicals Review*, 23, 3 (1990), 104–10.
J. Whale, 'Hazlitt on Burke: The Ambivalent position of a Radical Essayist', *Studies in Romanticism*, 25 (1986), 465–81.

HUTTON, Richard Holt (1826–97), born in Leeds, was the third son and fifth child of the Unitarian minister Dr Joseph Hutton. In 1835 the family moved to London, where Richard attended first the school connected with University College, London (which had been established for the benefit of dissenters and other non-Anglicans, who were excluded from Oxford and Cambridge), then the College itself. He studied mathematics, natural philosophy, Latin and Greek, in all of which he excelled, and graduated in 1845. Abandoning his plans for a career in the law, he decided to take up the Unitarian ministry, and entered Manchester New College in 1847. James Martineau and John James Taylor were his mentors. In 1849 he was appointed Vice-Principal and Chaplain of University Hall, and the following year he taught at a school in Manchester. He married Anne Mary Roscoe in 1851, and in the same year was invited to help edit the Unitarian weekly newspaper the *Inquirer*. He was forced to resign when he contracted an inflammation of the lungs in the following year. He and his wife went to Barbados in an attempt to cure his illness, but caught yellow fever soon after their arrival, from which Mary died within two months. On his return to England, Hutton turned to editing as his profession. From 1853–55 he edited the *Inquirer* and the Unitarian quarterly the *Prospective Review*. In 1855 he helped found the *National Review*, which he co-edited with his friend Walter Bageot until 1862, and from 1857 to 1861 he was literary editor of the *Economist*. He married Eliza Roscoe, Mary's cousin, in 1858, by which time he was tending towards Anglicanism. From 1861 until his death he was joint editor, with Meredith White Townsend, of the *Spectator*, which, under their control, became the most influential of the British weeklies. His works include the two-volume *Essays Theological and Literary* (1871), the volume on Scott for the English Men of Letters series, an edition, in three volumes, of Walter Bagehot's writings (1879–81), a book on Newman (1891), a two-volume collection of his articles from the *Spectator, Contemporary Thought and Thinkers* (1894), and the posthumously published *Aspects of Religious and Scientific Thought* (1899).

> *A Victorian Spectator: Uncollected Writings of R. H. Hutton*, edited by R. Tener and M. Woodfield (Bristol, 1989).

> See: M. Woodfield, *R. H. Hutton: Critic and Theologian: the Writings on Newman, Arnold, Tennyson, Wordsworth, and George Eliot* (Oxford, 1986).
> M. Woodfield, 'Victorian Weekly Reviews and Reviewing after 1860: R. H. Hutton and the *Spectator*', *Yearbook of English Studies*, 16 (1986), 74–91.

JAMESON, Anna Brownell (1794–1860), born in Dublin, was the eldest of the five daughters of Denis Brownell Murphy, Irish miniature painter, and his English wife. The family moved to England in 1798 and settled in London, where Anna was educated at home. She became a governess at the age of sixteen, an experience which was to be mined in her writings, beginning with her first publication *A Lady's Diary* (1825, republished as *Diary of an Ennuyée* in 1826), which is the fictional travel-autobiography of a young governess. She married Robert Jameson, a lawyer, in 1825, but the union was not a happy one and they parted in 1829, when he was appointed puisne judge to Dominica. Anna went to Germany for the first time in that year, sparking a life-long love of German art and literature which was strengthened by her close friendship with Ottilie von Goethe. She wrote a number of popular historical and literary critical works in the early 1830s, all with a female slant, such as *Memoirs of Celebrated Female Sovereigns* (1831) and her lively study of Shakespeare's heroines, *Characteristics of Women* (1832), establishing herself as a professional writer. Robert Jameson went to Canada in 1836 to take up the position of Vice-Chancellor of Upper Canada, and Anna briefly joined him in Toronto for the purpose of helping him gain a promotion and of formally separating and sorting out their affairs, and then travelled in Canada, before returning to London, where she published *Winter Studies and Summer Rambles in Canada* (1838). Charged with the responsibility of financially supporting her parents and sisters, she wrote prolifically, and across a diverse field. She published *Pictures of the Social Life of Germany* in 1840, and contributed articles on a range of topics to the periodical press, including her celebrated report on the findings of the Commission on the Employment of Children of 1843. *Memoirs and Essays Illustrative of Art, Literature, and Social Morals* appeared in 1846. Although *Diary of an Ennuyée* had included some art criticism, it was in the 1840s that she began working seriously in the area in which she was to find most acclaim. She wrote handbooks to British art collections, *Memoirs of the Early Italian Painters* (1845), and arguably her most important work, *Sacred and Legendary Art* (2 vols, 1848), the beginning of a series which was to run to five volumes and included *Legends of the Madonna, as Represented in the Fine Arts* (1852). From 1851 she had a Civil List pension, but continued to live in straitened circumstances, which did not improve upon her husband's death in 1854 as she was omitted from his will. Her own personal experiences sharpened her sense of the dilemmas and contradictions of '"Woman's Mission" and Woman's Position', to borrow the terms of one of her own essays, and she wrote and lectured on feminist issues in her later years. Her influential lectures were published as *Sisters of Charity: Catholic and Protestant* (1855) and *The Communion of Labour: Social Employments of Women* (1856), and she helped found the *English Woman's Journal* with Bessie Parkes. Her last work, completed by her friend and fellow art historian Elizabeth Eastlake, was *The History of Our Lord*. Published posthumously in 1864, it was the final volume of the series *Sacred and Legendary Art*.

Clara Thomas, *Love and Work Enough: The Life of Anna Jameson* (1967).

See: H. M. Buss, 'Anna Jameson's *Winter Rambles and Summer Studies in Canada* as Epistolary Dijournal', in M. Kadar, ed., *Essays on Life Writing: From Genre to Literary Practice* (Toronto, 1992), pp. 42–60.

B. Friewald, '"Femininely Speaking": Anna Jameson's *Winter Studies and Summer Rambles in Canada*', in S. Neuman et al, *Amazing Space: Writing Canadian Women's Writing* (Edmonton, 1986), pp. 61–73.

T. M. F. Gerry, '"I am translated": Anna Jameson's Sketches and *Winter Studies and Summer Rambles in Canada*', *Journal of Canadian Studies*, 25 (1990–91), 34–49.

A. M. Holcomb, 'Anna Jameson: Sacred Art and Social Vision', in C. R. Sherman and A. Holcomb, eds, *Women and Interpreters of the Visual Arts, 1820–1979* (Westport, Connecticut, 1981), pp. 93–121. (Good introduction to Jameson's art criticism.)

A. M. Holcomb, 'Anna Jameson: The First Professional English Art Historian', *Art History*, 6 (1983), 171–87.

J. Johnston, *Anna Jameson: Victorian, Feminist, Woman of Letters* (Aldershot, 1997). (First full critical assessment of the full range of Jameson's writings.)

P. Nestor, *Female Friendships and Communities* (1985).

JOWETT, Benjamin (1817–93), born at Camberwell, was educated at St Paul's School, elected to a Scholarship at Balliol College, Oxford, in 1835, and to a Fellowship in 1838. Tutor of Balliol College from 1842 to 1870, when he was elected Master, and member of the Commission enquiring into admission by examination into the Indian Civil Service in 1853, he was appointed to the Regius Chair of Greek in 1855 on the recommendation of Lord Palmerston. A Broad Churchman, he outraged Tractarian opinion with his *Commentary on the Epistles of St Paul to the Thessalonians, Galatians, and Romans* (1855), and came near to being charged with heresy because of his controversial contribution, an essay on the interpretation of Scripture, to *Essays and Reviews* (1860). He successfully promoted the Act that abolished religious tests for university degrees in 1871. Renowned as a brilliant teacher, he published edited translations of the *Dialogues* of Plato (1871), Thucydides (1881), and Aristotle's *Poetics* (1885). He was appointed Vice-Chancellor of Oxford University 1882–86.

> E. Abbott and L. Campbell, *The Life and Letters of Benjamin Jowett, M.A.*, 2 vols (1897).

> See: P. Hinchliff, 'Ethics, Evolution and Biblical Criticism in the Thought of Benjamin Jowett and John William Colenso', *The Journal of Ecclesiastical History*, 37 (1986), 91–110.

KINGSLEY, Mary Henrietta (1862–1900), born in Islington, London, was the only daughter of Mary (Bailey) and Dr George Henry Kingsley. Brought up in Cambridge, she was more or less self-educated, and for years looked after her invalid mother during her father's absence abroad. Her parents' deaths in 1893 meant that she was suddenly free to travel, and she quickly made up for lost time, sailing first to the Canaries and then to West Africa, where she travelled from Freetown to Luanda, collecting fish, insects, and data on tribal religions and customs. After a second journey to West Africa, during which she climbed Mount Cameroon, she returned to England and wrote *Travels in West Africa* (1897) and *West African Studies* (1899), establishing herself as a leading spokesperson on colonial affairs. She returned to Africa in 1900 as a nurse and journalist during the Boer War, and died there after contracting typhus whilst nursing prisoners of war. The African Society was founded in 1901 in her memory.

> K. Frank, *A Voyager Out: The Life of Mary Kingsley* (Boston, 1986) (Useful, if uncritical biography.)

> See: D. Birkett, 'West Africa's Mary Kingsley', *History Today*, 37 (1987), 10–16.

> D. Birkett, *Spinsters Abroad: Victorian Lady Explorers* (Oxford, 1989).

> D. Birkett, *Mary Kingsley: Imperial Adventuress* (1992).

> D. Birkett and J. Wheelwright, '"How Could She?": Unpalatable Facts and Feminist Heroines', *Gender and History*, 2, 1 (1990), 49–57. (Addresses some of the problems facing modern feminists reading Victorian women writers such as Kingsley.)

> A. Blunt, *Travel, Gender and Imperialism: Mary Kingsley and West Africa* (New York, 1994).

> J. Flint, 'Mary Kingsley: A Reassessment', *Journal of African History*, 4 (1963), 95–104.

> E.-M. Kroller, 'First Impressions: Rhetorical Strategies in Travel-Writing by Victorian Women', *Ariel*, 21 (1990), 87–99.

> M. L. Pratt, *Imperial Eyes: Travel Writing and Transculturation* (1992). (Includes an excellent brief discussion of Kingsley.)

LIVINGSTONE, David (1813–73), born at Blantyre, Lanarkshire, was the second son of Agnes (Hunter) and Neil Livingstone, a tailor, then small tea-dealer, and was brought up in a religious household. At the age of ten he was sent to work in the local cotton factory where his grandfather, father and uncles had all worked in the past, but studied prodigiously at night school and at home, becoming learned in the Classics and, particularly, in botany, zoology, and geology. Having resolved to be a missionary, he decided he needed medical training and, at the age of nineteen, whilst working as a cotton-spinner, he studied at Anderson College and Glasgow University. He joined the London Missionary Society, and continued his medical and scientific studies in London, gaining his degree from Glasgow University in 1840. After his ordination as a missionary, he set sail for the Cape of Good Hope, whence he embarked on a 700-mile journey into the interior, the first of several expeditions which were to make him the most celebrated Victorian explorer. In 1844 he married Mary Moffat, who joined him on his missionary travels, and was to bear five children. In the course of his journeys over the next few years, Livingstone 'discovered' (for Europeans) Lake Ngami, and the River Zambesi at Sesheke. Having sent his wife and children back to England, he embarked from Cape Town on a dangerous expedition across the African continent which was to take four years, during which time he suffered numerous prolonged attacks of fever and dysentery. He returned to London in 1856, where he received a hero's welcome. In 1857 he published *Missionary Travels*, which sold phenomenally well, and made Livingstone's fortune. Much of his money was spent on further expeditions, during one of which, in 1862, his wife died of fever. In 1865 he published his *Narrative of an Expedition to the Zambesi and its Tributaries, and of the Discovery of the Lakes Shirwa and Nyassa, 1858–1864*, and in the same year set off again for Africa with the duel objective of exploring Nyasaland and locating the source of the Nile. It was during this expedition, in 1871, that the famous encounter with H. M. Stanley, who had been sent by the proprietor of the *New York Herald* to find him, took place, and later, in 1873, that Livingstone died.

> *Livingstone's African Journal, 1853–1856*, edited by I. Schapera, 2 vols (1963).
> J. S. Robertson, *The Life of David Livingstone, the Great Missionary Explorer* (1884).
> H. M. Stanley, *How I found Livingstone: Travels, Adventures and Discoveries in Central Africa including four months' residence with Dr Livingstone* (n.d.)
> T. Jeal, *Livingstone* (1973).

> See: B. Allen, 'David Livingstone and the Imperial Imagination', *Nineteenth-Century Prose*, 19, 1 (1991), 16–25.
> D. O. Helly, *Livingstone's Legacy: Horace Waller and Victorian Mythmaking* (Athens, Ohio, 1987).
> C. Northcott, *David Livingstone: his Triumph, Decline and Fall* (Guildford, 1973).
> B. Pachai, ed., *Livingstone: Man of Africa: Memorial Essays, 1873–1973* (Harlow, 1973).
> *David Livingstone and the Victorian Encounter with Africa*, Exhibition Catalogue, National Portrait Gallery (London, 1996).

MACAULAY, Thomas Babington (1800–59), born in Leicestershire, grew up in a prosperous Evangelical family. Educated at boarding school under the Reverend Matthew Preston, he entered Trinity College, Cambridge in

1818, where he twice won the Chancellor's Medal for poetry and won a prize for his essay on William III. He was elected a Fellow of Trinity in 1824, and was called to the Bar in 1826. Meanwhile, he had begun to make his mark as a journalist with his contributions to *Knight's Quarterly Magazine* of 1823–4 and a series of review essays for the Whig *Edinburgh Review* beginning in 1825, which brought him to the attention of Lord Lansdowne. Sponsored by Lansdowne, he was elected M.P. for the pocket borough of Calne in 1830. After its abolition following the Reform Act, he was elected M.P. for Leeds, but retired from the House of Commons in the following year to become the legal member on the Governor-General's Supreme Council for India, a position he held until 1838. Whilst in India, Macaulay helped initiate educational and penal reform, and wrote his essay on Bacon (1837) and most of *The Lays of Ancient Rome* (1842). Upon his return to Britain, he became M.P. for Edinburgh in 1839, and served as Secretary-at-War in the Melbourne administration. He continued to write for the *Edinburgh Review* until 1844, and in 1843 the first collected edition of his *Critical and Historical Essays* was published. The first two volumes of his *History of England from the Accession of James II* were published in 1848, and were an immediate success. Having suffered electoral defeat at Edinburgh in 1847, Macaulay became Lord Rector of the University of Glasgow in 1848, and devoted himself to writing. He regained his seat in 1852, and over the next four years wrote five biographies for the *Encyclopaedia Britannica*. He published his *Speeches* in 1853, and in 1855 volumes 3 and 4 of *The History of England*. In the following year he resigned from the House of Commons and became Baron Macaulay in 1857. The final volume of the *History* was published posthumously in 1861 by his sister Hannah, who had married Charles Trevelyan in 1834.

Letters of Thomas Babington Macaulay, edited by T. Pinney, 6 vols (1974–81).

The History of England, edited and abridged by H. Trevor-Roper (Harmondsworth, 1979).

G. O. Trevelyan, *The Life and Letters of Lord Macaulay* (2 vols, 1876; 1 vol., Oxford, 1978).

See: J. W. Burrow, *A Liberal Descent: Victorian Historians and the English Past* (Cambridge, 1981).

J. Clive, *Thomas Babington Macaulay: The Shaping of the Historian* (1973). (On the biographical roots of Macaulay's historiography.)

W. A. Davis, '"This Is My Theory". Macaulay on Periodical Style', *Victorian Periodicals Review*, 20 (1987), 12–22.

P. Gay, *Style in History* (1975).

R. Jann, *The Art and Science of Victorian History* (Columbus, Ohio, 1985).

G. Levine, *The Boundaries of Fiction: Carlyle, Macaulay, Newman* (Princeton, N.J., 1968).

W. A. Madden, 'Macaulay's Style', in G. Levine and W. A. Madden, eds, *The Art of Victorian Prose* (New York, 1968), pp. 127–53.

J. Millgate, *Macaulay* (1973). (Good introduction.)

M. Phillips, 'Macaulay, Scott, and the Literary Challenge to Historiography', *Journal of the History of Ideas*, 50 (1989), 117–33.

MARTINEAU, Harriet (1802–76), born in Norwich, was the sixth of eight children of Elizabeth (Rankin) and Thomas Martineau, a cloth manufacturer descended from the Huguenots. In her *Autobiography* she depicts an unhappy childhood. Physically infirm, she suffered from deafness, and was educated at home by her Unitarian parents, at a local school, and at a Bristol boarding school. In her twenties she was a regular contributor to the *Monthly Repository*, writing articles on religion and women's issues (such as 'Female Writers of Practical Divinity' (1821) and 'On Female Education' (1822)), and, following the failure of the family firm in 1829, she began to write professionally in order to support her family. Her series of popularising didactic stories *Illustrations of Political Economy* (9 vols, 1832–34) established her reputation, and she moved to London. After travelling in America from 1834–36 she published *Society in America* (1837), which was followed by her novels *Deerbrook*, in 1839, and *The Hour and the Man* in 1841. By this time she had lost her faith and become interested in mesmerism and, following a serious illness which she believed to have been cured by mesmerism, she wrote a letter on the subject in 1844 to the *Athenaeum* which caused a furore. In 1845 she designed and built a house in Ambleside in the Lake District, where she spent the rest of her life. She continued to publish prolifically, producing an abridged translation of Comte's *Philosophie Positive* (1853), contributing articles to the London *Daily News* in the 1850s and 1860s in support of divorce reform and the repeal of the Contagious Diseases Acts, writing for the *Edinburgh Review* and *Household Words*, and preparing numerous biographical sketches, as well as her own *Autobiography* (1877), which was published posthumously by her friend Maria Weston Chapman.

> *Society in America*, edited and abridged by S. M. Liset (New York, 1962).
> *Harriet Martineau on Women*, edited by G. G. Yates (New Brunswick, N.J., 1985). (A useful selection.)
> *Harriet Martineau: Selected Letters*, edited by V. Sanders (New York and Oxford, 1990).
> R. K. Webb, *Harriet Martineau: A Radical Victorian* (New York and London, 1960). (Places Martineau in relation to Victorian radicalism.)
> V. Wheatley, *The Life and Work of Harriet Martineau* (1957).

See: J. Barrell, 'Death on the Nile: Fantasy and the Literature of Tourism, 1840–1860', *Essays in Criticism*, 41 (1991), 97–127.
D. David, *Intellectual Women and Victorian Patriarchy: Harriet Martineau, Elizabeth Barrett Browning, George Eliot* (1987).
M. H. Frawley, 'Desert Places/Gendered Spaces: Victorian Women in the Middle East', *Nineteenth-Century Contexts*, 15 (1991), 49–64.
M. H. Frawley, 'Harriet Martineau in America: Gender and the Discourse of Sociology', *Victorian Newsletter*, 81 (1992), 13–20.
S. Hoecker-Drysdale, *Harriet Martineau: First Woman Sociologist* (Oxford, 1992).
S. Hunter, *Harriet Martineau: The Poetics of Moralism* (Aldershot, 1995). (Argues that her religious life and her invention of a public role were inseparable.)
P. Marks, 'Harriet Martineau: Fraser's "Maid of (Dis)Honour"', *Victorian Periodicals Review*, 19 (1986), 28–34.
L. H. Peterson, 'Harriet Martineau's *Household Education*: Revising the Feminine Tradition', *Bucknell Review*, 34, 2 (1990), 183–94.
L. H. Peterson, 'Harriet Martineau: Masculine Discourse, Female Sage', in T. E. Morgan, ed., *Victorian Sages and Cultural Discourse: Renegotiating Gender and Power* (New Brunswick, N.J., 1990), pp. 171–86.

V. Sanders, *Reason Over Passion: Harriet Martineau and the Victorian Novel* (Hemel Hempstead, 1986). (Intelligent discussion.)

G. Thomas, *Harriet Martineau* (Boston, Massachusetts, 1985). (General introduction.)

MAYHEW, Henry (1812–87), born in London, one of seventeen children, was the son of an attorney, Joshua Dorset Joseph Mayhew. He ran away from Westminster School, and went to sea, travelling to Calcutta before returning to London and becoming articled to his father. After three years of the law, he turned to literature, publishing the weekly periodical *Figaro in London* with Gilbert à Beckett in the 1830s, and starting the journal *The Thief*. He also began his career as a dramatist at this time: his farces *The Wandering Minstrel* and *But However* were performed in the West End in 1834 and 1838 respectively. He continued to write dramatic and fictional texts over the following decades, but his principal effort was directed at his journalism. He was one of the originators, and for a brief period, one of the editors, of *Punch* in 1841; and he was one of the first, and the best-known, of the philanthropic journalists who were to bring the plight of London's poor to public attention in the middle of the century. Beginning with a series of articles in the *Morning Chronicle*, collected in two volumes in 1851, Mayhew over the next decade conducted the research which was eventually to be published as *London Labour and the London Poor* in 1865. Meanwhile he had travelled and lived in Germany for a period, and wrote books on German topography (1856 and 1858), German life and manners (1864), and *The Boyhood of Martin Luther* (1865); as well as numerous minor works on diverse subjects, from education to science. In his final years he wrote *Young Benjamin Franklin* (1870), started another periodical, *Only Once a Year*, and in 1871 wrote a report on working men's clubs.

> *The Unknown Mayhew: Selections from the* Morning Chronicle, edited by E. P. Thompson and Eileen Yeo (1971). (A useful selection with excellent introductory essays.)

See: C. Gallagher, 'The Body Versus the Social Body in the Works of Thomas Malthus and Henry Mayhew', *Representations*, 14 (1986), 83–106.

C. Herbert, 'Rat Worship and Taboo in Mayhew's London', *Representations*, 23 (1988), 1–24.

G. Himmelfarb, *The Idea of Poverty: England in the Early Industrial Age* (1984).

A Humphreys, *Travels into the Poor Man's Country: The Work of Henry Mayhew* (Athens, Georgia, 1977).

N. A. Metz, 'Mayhew's Book of Lists', *University of Hartford Studies in Literature*, 14 (1982), 41–49.

E. P. Thompson, 'The Political Education of Henry Mayhew', *Victorian Studies*, 11, 1 (1967), 43–62.

G. Woodcock, 'Henry Mayhew and the Undiscovered Country of the Poor', *Sewanee Review*, 92 (1984), 556–73.

MILL, John Stuart (1806–73), born in London, was the eldest son of the Utilitarian James Mill, who, famously, subjected him to an experimental education at home whereby he learnt Greek at the age of three. As a young man, Mill was involved in numerous Radical causes. In 1823, at the age of seventeen, he spent one night in confinement for distributing pamphlets advocating birth control, and in the same year he followed his father into the East India Company, where he was appointed as a clerk. He was to work there until 1858, eventually being promoted to the position of Chief Examiner that his father had held. In 1826–27, he experienced a mental crisis, or depressive breakdown, which he later ascribes in his *Autobiography* (1873) to the excessive cultivation of his intellect at the expense of his feelings. In 1830 he met and fell in love with Harriet Taylor, whom he was eventually to marry in 1851 following her husband's death in 1849. In 1835 he founded the *London and Westminster Review*, which he edited until 1840. After his father's death in 1836 he entered into a period of reassessment of his Benthamite inheritance, publishing his essay on Bentham in 1840, *A System of Logic* in 1843, *Principles of Political Economy* in 1848, and *Utilitarianism* in 1863. The libertarian principles espoused in *On Liberty* (1859), published after the death of his wife, and dedicated to her, are directed particularly at the 'woman question' in *On the Subjection of Women* (1869), and he made use of his three years as Liberal M.P. for Westminster (1865–68) to fight for women's suffrage. Although his attempted amendment of the 1867 Reform Bill was unsuccessful, it focused support for women's rights. His other main political platform, proportional representation, is argued for in *Considerations on Representative Government* (1861). After his death in Avignon, where he was buried with his wife, his *Autobiography, Three Essays in Religion*, and *Chapters on Socialism* were published posthumously by his step-daughter, Harriet Taylor.

Collected Works, edited by J. M. Robson, *et al.*, 33 vols (Toronto and London, 1963–91).

The Subjection of Women, by J. S. Mill.

Enfranchisement of Women, by Harriet Taylor Mill, edited by K. Soper (1983).

Autobiography, edited by J. Stillinger (New York, 1969).

M. St J. Packe, *The Life of John Stuart Mill* (1954).

See: S. H. Aiken, 'Scripture and Poetic Discourse in *The Subjection of Women*', PMLA, 98 (1983), 353–73.

F. R. Berger, *Happiness, Justice, and Freedom: The Moral and Political Philosophy of John Stuart Mill* (Berkeley, California, 1984).

J. H. Buckley, 'John Stuart Mill's "True" Autobiography', *Studies in the Literary Imagination*, 23 (1990), 223–31.

J. Carlisle, *John Stuart Mill and the Writing of Character* (Athens, Georgia, 1991). (On the relationship between psychological and intellectual matters in Mill's life and writing.)

H. Feinberg, 'Carlyle and Mill: Style as the Shape of Content', *Victorian Institute Journal*, 17 (1989), 77–85.

F. W. Garforth, *Educative Democracy: John Stuart Mill on Education in Society* (Oxford, 1980).

M. Green, 'Sympathy and the Social Value of Poetry: J. S. Mill's Literary Essays', *University of Toronto Quarterly*, 60 (1991), 452–68.

G. Himmelfarb, *On Liberty and Liberalism: the Case of John Stuart Mill* (New York, 1974). (Provocative approach to a classic text.)

A. S. Kahan, *Aristocratic Liberalism: the Social and Political Thought of Jacob Burckhardt, John Stuart Mill and Alexis de Tocqueville* (New York, 1992).

G. C. Kerner, *Three Philosophical Moralists: Mill, Kant, and Sartre: An Introduction to Ethics* (Oxford, 1990).

B. Kinzer, A. P. Robson, and J. M. Robson, *A Moralist In and Out of Parliament: John Stuart Mill at Westminster, 1865–1868* (Toronto, Buffalo, and London, 1992). (Detailed account of Mill's years in Parliament.)

M. Laine, *Bibliography of Works on John Stuart Mill* (Toronto, 1982).

M. Laine, ed., *A Cultivated Mind: Essays on J. S. Mill presented to John M. Robson* (Toronto, Buffalo, and London, 1991). (*Festschrift* for the general editor of the *Collected Works*; most of the contributors are distinguished scholars.)

J. Loesberg, *Fictions of Consciousness: Mill, Newman, and the Reading of Victorian Prose* (New Brunswick, N.J., 1986). (Contextualises Mill's *Autobiography*.)

J. M. Robson, *The Improvement of Mankind: the Social and Political Thought of John Stuart Mill* (Toronto and London, 1968).

A. Ryan, *The Philosophy of John Stuart Mill* (1970; 2nd edn 1987). (Authoritative study by a leading political philosopher.)

A. Ryan, *J. S. Mill* (1975). (Useful survey.)

J. Shaddock, 'The Anarchic "I": John Stuart Mill's *Autobiography*', *Mid-Hudson Language Studies*, 12 (1989), 54–61.

J. Skorupski, *John Stuart Mill* (1989).

W. Thomas, *Mill* (Oxford, 1985). (Good short introduction.)

M. Warner, 'Philosophical Autobiography: St Augustine and John Stuart Mill', in A. P. Griffiths, ed., *Philosophy and Literature* (Cambridge, 1984), pp. 189–210.

MORRIS, William (1834–96), born in Walthamstow, was the eldest son of a wealthy stockbroker. He was brought up in the Essex countryside, and educated at Marlborough and Exeter College, Oxford, where he met Edward Burne-Jones, whose enthusiasm for medievalism, for Ruskin, and for Pre-Raphaelitism he shared. Rossetti enlisted both aspiring young artists to help paint murals in the new Oxford Union, and Morris abandoned his original plans for a career in the Church for a career in art. His father had died in 1847, and when he came of age Morris inherited a large unearned income. He was articled to the London architect Street in 1856, and in 1859 married Jane Burden, who had sat as a model for the Union frescoes, and was to become the most famous of Pre-Raphaelite faces through Rossetti's portraits. The couple settled in the Red House at Bexley Heath, an early 'vernacular' building designed for him by Philip Webb, and had two daughters. In 1861 Morris founded the firm of Morris, Marshall, Faulkner & Co., which was to produce distinctive furniture, stained glass, tiles, wallpaper and fabrics. *The Defence of Guenevere* (1858) and *The Earthly Paradise* (1868–71) established his reputation as a poet. He was offered, and rejected, first the Oxford Professorship of Poetry in succession to Arnold, then the Poet Laureateship in succession to Tennyson. In 1878 he moved to Kelmscott Manor in Oxfordshire. He became increasingly politically active. In 1877, he wrote a manifesto 'To the Working-Men of England'. In 1883 he became a Socialist, and was one of the founders of the Socialist League in 1884. He subsidised and edited the journal *The Commonweal*. His political philosophy informs his utopian romances *A Dream of John Ball* (1886) and *News from Nowhere* (1890). Until his death he pursued his aesthetic interests at the same time as his political commitments, playing a key role in the foundation of the Arts and Crafts Exhibition Society in 1887, and setting up the Kelmscott Press in 1890 to produce illustrated editions of classic texts. The Kelmscott *Chaucer*, illustrated by Burne-Jones, was published in 1896, the year of Morris's death.

Collected Works, 24 vols (1910–15; reprinted 1966, 1992).
Political Writings of William Morris, edited by A. L. Morton (1973).
The Unpublished Lectures of William Morris, edited by E. D. LeMire (Detroit, Michigan, 1969).

A. Briggs, ed., *William Morris: Selected Writings and Designs* (Harmondsworth, 1962; reprinted 1984).
The Collected Letters of William Morris, edited by N. Kelvin, 2 vols (Princeton, N.J., 1984–87).
J. W. Mackail, *The Life of William Morris*, 2 vols (1899).
P. Henderson, *William Morris: His Life, Work, and Friends* (1967), (Well-illustrated general biography.)
J. Lindsay, *William Morris: His Life and Work* (1975). (Detailed, lengthy study, focusing on Morris's Marxism.)
P. Faulkner, *Against the Age: An Introduction to William Morris* (1980). (Concise, informative literary biography).
F. MacCarthy, *William Morris: A Life for Our Time* (1994).

See: F. S. Boos and C. G. Silver, eds. *Socialism and the Literary Artistry of William Morris* (Columbia, Missouri, 1990).
J. McGann, '"A Thing to Mind": The Materialist Aesthetic of William Morris', *Huntington Library Quarterly*, 55, 1 (1992), 55–74.
P. Stansky, *William Morris* (Oxford, 1983). (Brief overview of Morris's achievement.)
E. P. Thompson, *William Morris: Romantic to Revolutionary* (New York, 1977). (A major study of Morris's intellectual and political development.)

NEWMAN, John Henry (1801–90), born in London, was the son of an Evangelical banker. He was educated at Ealing School where, at the age of fifteen, he had what he later described as 'an interior conversion', and then at Trinity College, Oxford. In 1822 he won a Fellowship at Oriel College, and from 1833 to 1841 was the most charismatic of the leaders of the Oxford Movement, writing a number of the ninety *Tracts for the Times* that gave the Tractarians their name, which explored the 'Catholic' inheritance of Anglican belief and worship. After a long and painful struggle, Newman was converted to Roman Catholicism in 1845. He published two works which offered theological and personal justification for his change of heart: *An Essay on the Development of Christian Doctrine* (1845) and, following Charles Kingsley's public accusations against himself and his Church, the *Apologia Pro Vita Sua* (1864). As a Roman Catholic Newman was looked upon with suspicion at first and given little support from Rome. Nevertheless, he founded the Birmingham Oratory, and subsequently set up the Catholic University in Dublin, out of which came his series of lectures on liberal education *The Idea of a University* (1859). Amongst his many literary and theological writings may be counted his two novels, *Loss and Gain* (1848) and *Callista: A Sketch of the Third Century* (1856), *The Dream of Gerontius* (1856), and *An Essay in Aid of a Grammar of Assent* (1870). He was made a Cardinal in 1879.

Apologia Pro Vita Sua, edited by M. J. Svaglic (Oxford, 1967).
An Essay on the Development of Christian Doctrine, edited by J. M. Cameron (Harmondsworth, 1974).
The Idea of a University, edited by I. T. Ker (Oxford, 1976).
Sermons, 1824–1843, vol. I, edited by P. Murray (Oxford, 1991).
The Letters and Diaries of John Henry Newman, edited by C. S. Dessain, T. Gornall and I. T. Ker, 31 vols (1961–78).
W. Ward, *The Life of John Henry Cardinal Newman*, 2 vols (1912).
M. Trevor, *Newman*, 2 vols (1962). (Standard modern biography.)
B. Martin, *John Henry Newman: His Life and Work* (1982).
I. T. Ker, *John Henry Newman: a Biography* (Oxford, 1988). (Valuable in tracing Newman's intellectual development.)

D. Newsome, *Convert Cardinals: John Henry Newman and Henry Edward Manning* (1993).

See: E. Block, ed., *Critical Essays on John Henry Newman* (Victoria, British Columbia, 1992). (On biographical and aesthetic issues in Newman studies.)

J. Britt, *John Henry Newman's Rhetoric: Becoming a Discriminating Reader* (New York, 1991).

O. S. Buckton, '"An unnatural state": Gender, "Perversion", and Newman's *Apologia Pro Vita Sua*', *Victorian Studies*, 35 (1992), 359–83.

J. Carroll, 'Arnold, Newman, and Cultural Salvation', *Victorian Poetry*, 26 (1988), 163–78.

O. Chadwick, *Newman* (Oxford, 1983). (Excellent brief study.)

J. Coats, John Henry Newman's 'Tamworth Reading Room': Adjusting Rhetorical Approaches for the Periodical Press', *Victorian Periodicals Review*, 24, 4 (1991), 173–80.

A. J. Crowley, 'The Performance of the Grammar: Reading and Writing Newman's Narrative of Assent', *Renascence*, 43 (1990–91), 137–58.

A. D. Culler, *Imperial Intellect: A Study of Newman's Educational Ideal* (New Haven, Connecticut, 1955). (On *The Idea of a University*.)

C. S. Dessain, *John Henry Newman* (1966, 1971). (Good short introduction.)

S. Gilley, *Newman and his Age* (1990).

G. H. Goodwin, 'Keble and Newman: Tractarian Aesthetics and the Romantic Tradition', *Victorian Studies*, 30 (1987), 475–94.

D. Goslee, 'Rhetoric as Confusion in Newman's Parochial Sermons', *Modern Language Quarterly*, 48 (1987), 339–63.

W. Jost, *Rhetorical Thought in John Henry Newman* (Columbia, Missouri, 1989).

I. Ker and A. G. Hill, eds, *Newman After a Hundred Years* (Oxford, 1990).

J. Loesberg, *Fictions of Consciousness: Mill, Newman, and the Reading of Victorian Prose* (New Brunswick, N.J., 1986). (Contextualises the writing of the *Apologia*.)

G. Magill, ed., *Discourse and Context: An Interdisciplinary Study of John Henry Newman* (Carbondale and Edwardsville, Illinois, 1993). (On the interdisciplinary implications of his thought.)

S. Thomas, *Newman and Heresy: The Anglican Years* (Cambridge, 1991).

M. Woodfield, 'Knowing without Telling: Newman and the Resistance to Narrative', *Renascence*, 43 (1990–91), 61–80.

NIGHTINGALE, Florence (1820–1910), born in Florence, was the daughter of Frances (Smith) and William Edward Nightingale, a country gentleman. Educated at home, she had a 'call from God' at the age of 16 to work for humanity, but found there was little scope for women to engage in meaningful social activity within the constraints of a middle-class home, as she powerfully articulated in *Casssandra*, written in 1852. Against the wishes of her parents she spent three months nursing with the Protestant Deaconesses at Kaiserswerth on the Rhine in 1851, and two years later became Superintendent of the Hospital for Gentlewomen in London. Her opportunities to effect hospital and nursing reform in this position prepared her for the task ahead of her when, after the outbreak of the Crimean War, she led a group of nurses to Turkey, and discovered the dire state of hospital administration there. Charged with preparing the Report of the Royal Commission on the Sanitary State of the Army, Nightingale worked herself into a state of exhaustion and following her collapse in 1857 retired from public life. Nevertheless she continued to exercise extraordinary influence from her invalid bed, continuing to supervise the Report, initiating the subsequent Royal Commission on the Sanitary State of the Indian Army, 1859–63, overseeing the foundation of the Nightingale School for Nurses at St Thomas's Hospital in 1860, and involving herself in the reform of the War Office.

> *Cassandra and Other Selections from Suggestions for Thought*, edited by Mary Poovey (1991).
>
> *Ever Yours, Florence Nightingale: Selected Letters*, edited by M. Vicinus and B. Nergaard (1989). (Judicious selection that covers the main concerns of Nightingale's life and illuminates her internal spiritual struggles as a young women.)
>
> C. Woodham-Smith, *Florence Nightingale, 1820–1910* (1950). (Standard life.)
>
> See: J. Barrell, 'Death on the Nile: Fantasy and the Literature of Tourism, 1840–1860', *Essays in Criticism*, 41 (1991), 97–127. (Includes discussion of Nightingale's *Letters from Egypt*.)
>
> N. Boyd, *Josephine Butler, Octavia Hill, Florence Nightingale: Three Victorian Women who Changed their World* (1982).
>
> C. Kahane, 'The Aesthetic Politics of Rage', *Literature: Literature Interpretation Theory*, 3, 1 (1991), 19–31.
>
> G. P. Landow, 'Aggressive (Re)interpretations of the Female Sage: Florence Nightingale's *Casssandra*', in T. E. Morgan, ed., *Victorian Sages and Cultural Discourse: Renegotiating Gender and Power* (New Brunswick, N.J., 1990), pp. 32–45. (On negotiations of gender and genre in *Cassandra*.)
>
> M. Poovey, *Uneven Developments: The Ideological Work of Gender in Mid-Victorian England* (Chicago, 1988). (Important chapter on Nightingale.)
>
> E. L. Pugh, 'Florence Nightingale and J. S. Mill Debate Women's Rights', *Journal of British Studies*, 21, 2 (1982), 118–38.
>
> E. Showalter, 'Florence Nightingale's Feminist Complaint: Women, Religion, and *Suggestions for Thought*', *Signs: Journal of Women in Culture and Society*, 6, 3 (1981), 395–412. (Early revisionary study.)
>
> E. Showalter, 'Miranda and Cassandra: The Discourse of the Feminist Intellectual', in F. Howe, ed., *Tradition and the Talents of Women* (Urbana, Illinois, 1991), pp. 313–27.

NORTON, Caroline Elizabeth Sarah (1808–77), born in London, was the daughter of the Scottish novelist Henrietta Sheridan, *née* Callender, and Tom Sheridan, son of the playwright R. B. Sheridan and grandson of Francis Sheridan. Following the loss of the family fortune in 1809, her parents went to the Cape, leaving Caroline and her siblings to be brought up by aunts in Scotland from 1813 onwards. Caroline was sent to school in Surrey in 1817, where she met George Norton, whom she married in 1827. Having written poems and stories since childhood, she began to write professionally, publishing her first volumes of poetry in 1829 and 1830, two stories, *The Wife and Woman's Reward* together in 1835, and a long narrative poem *A Voice from the Factories* in 1836. She became editor of a court magazine in 1831, then of the *English Annual* from 1834–38. She also moved in the highest political circles as a close friend of Lord Melbourne and other senior Whig ministers. In 1836, her marriage, which had been deteriorating for some time, broke down irrevocably when her husband accused her publicly of adultery with Lord Melbourne, marking the beginning of a long campaign to regain access to her three sons and rights to her own income. Her pamphlet *A Plain Letter to the Lord Chancellor on the Infants Custody Bill* influenced the passing of the Bill in 1839, and her *English Laws for Women in the Nineteenth Century* (1854) and *A Letter to the Queen on Lord Cranworth's Marriage and Divorce Bill* (1855) supported the Divorce Bill and the Married Women's Property Bill. These polemical pamphlets, like some of her stories and novels (such as *The Wife* and *The Woman's Reward*, and *Lost and Saved* (1863)) are based on her own personal experiences. She continued to write novels, as well as stories, poems, and songs for the periodical press until her death, which took place shortly after her marriage to Sir William Stirling Maxwell.

> *Selected Writings of Caroline Norton*, edited by J. O. Hoge and
> J. Marcus (Delmar, N.J., 1978).
> A. Acland, *Caroline Norton* (1948).
> A. Chedzoy, *A Scandalous Woman: The Story of Caroline Norton* (1992).

> See: D. E. Casper, 'Caroline Norton: Her Writings', *Bulletin of Bibliography*, 40, 2 (1983), 113–16.
> M. M. Clarke, 'William Thackeray's Fiction and Caroline Norton's Biography: Narrative Matrix of Feminist Legal Reform', *Dickens Studies Annual: Essays on Victorian Fiction*, 18 (1989), 337–51.
> M. Forster, *Significant Sisters: The Grassroots of Active Feminism 1839–1939* (New York, 1984). (Includes a fair assessment of Norton's achievement.)
> M. Poovey, *Uneven Developments: The Ideological Work of Gender in Mid-Victorian England* (Chicago, 1988). (Contains an important historicised discussion of Norton's writing.)

PALEY, William (1743–1805), born at Peterborough, was the eldest child of Elizabeth (Clapham) and William Paley, headmaster of Giggleswick Grammar School. Educated at his father's school and Christ's College, Cambridge, he was elected Fellow of his college in 1766 and ordained priest in 1767. Over the next few years he lectured at the University and preached at Whitewell, until he was presented to the rectory of Musgrave, Cumberland, in 1775. He married Jane Hewitt in the following year, and in 1777 resigned Musgrave in favour of two parishes, Dalston and Appleby. He became Archdeacon of Carlisle in 1782. His earlier lectures at Cambridge were expanded into a book, the *Principles of Morals and Political Philosophy* (1785), which was immediately adopted as a text-book at Cambridge. In 1785 Paley became Chancellor of the diocese, and in the period 1789–92 was an active supporter of abolitionism. In 1791 his wife died, leaving him with eight children. He published steadily, but did not repeat his earlier success until 1794, when *Evidences of Christianity* first appeared, bringing him rich preferment within the Church. *Natural Theology; or Evidence of the Existence and Attributes of the Deity collected from the Appearances of Nature* was published in 1802, and was into its twentieth edition by 1820.

> G. W. Meadley, *Memoirs of William Paley, D.D.* (1809; 2nd enlarged edn. 1810).

See: M. Francis, 'Naturalism and William Paley', *History of European Ideas*, 10, 2 (1989), 203–20.

M. Fuchs, 'The Violence of a Meek Divine: Some Aspects of William Paley's Social Views', *Cycnos*, 6 (1990), 77–85.

PATER, Walter Horatio (1839–94), born in London, was the son of a surgeon who was formerly Roman Catholic, and who died when he was three. He was educated in Enfield and at King's School, Canterbury, then at Queen's College Oxford, 1858–62. He was elected to a Fellowship at Brasenose in 1864, and lived quietly in Oxford with his sisters, although he soon developed a reputation as an impressionistic critic of artists and writers. His first collection of essays, *Studies in the History of the Renaissance*, appeared in 1873, its controversial 'Conclusion' – advocating the need to live intensely, for the moment's sake, in a world defined by flux – establishing him as the father of British aestheticism. He resigned his tutorship in 1883, but not his Fellowship, and moved to London. His most characteristic and innovative writing took the form of the critical essay, and he published another collection, *Appreciations*, in 1889, but he also wrote a novel, *Marius the Epicurean: His Sensations and Ideas* (1885), a philosophical study, *Plato and Platonism* (1893), and a collection of *Imaginary Portraits* (1887). He returned to Oxford in 1893, shortly before his death.

Works, 10 vols (1910; reprinted 1967).
The Renaissance, edited by A. Phillips (Oxford, 1986).
Letters of Walter Pater, edited by L. Evans (Oxford, 1970).
M. Levey, *The Case of Walter Pater* (1978). (On the man and his work).

See: L. Brake, 'Aesthetics in the Affray: Pater's *Appreciations, with an Essay on Style*', in S. Regan, ed., *The Politics of Pleasure: Aesthetics and Cultural Theory* (Buckingham, 1992), pp. 59–86.

W. E. Buckler, 'The Poetics of Pater's Prose: *The Child in the House*', *Victorian Poetry*, 23 (1985), 281–88.

R. Dellamora, 'An Essay in Sexual Liberation, Victorian Style: Walter Pater's "Two Early French Stories"', in S. Kellogg, ed., *Literary Visions of Homosexuality* (New York, 1983), pp. 139–50.

T. S. Eliot, 'Arnold and Pater', in *Selected Essays* (1951). (Influential essay, from a Modernist and Anglo-Catholic perspective.)

L. Higgins, 'Concluding or Occluding Gestures: How Appropriate is Pater's "Conclusion" to *The Renaissance*?', *Dalhousie Review*, 69 (1989), 349–56.

G. Hough, *The Last Romantics* (1949). (Still important early study.)

W. Iser, *Walter Pater: The Aesthetic Moment*, trans. D. H. Wilson (Cambridge, 1987). (Important study by a leading reception theorist.)

G. Monsman, *Walter Pater* (1977). (Introduction to the life and works.)

G. Monsman, *Walter Pater's Art of Autobiography* (New Haven, Connecticut, 1980). (On the autobiographical in Pater's writing.)

C. Williams, *Transfigured World: Walter Pater's Aesthetic Historicism* (Ithaca, N.Y., 1989). (Intelligent study.)

RUSKIN, John (1819–1900), born in London, was the only child of Margaret (Cox), a strict Evangelical, and John James Ruskin, a successful wine-merchant and a keen art-lover. He was educated privately before entering Christ Church, Oxford, in 1836, where he won the Newdigate Prize for Poetry in 1839. In 1843, the year after his graduation, he published

the first volume of *Modern Painters*, in which he defends the work of
J. M. W. Turner, whom he had first met in 1840. During his first visit to
Italy without his parents he developed an enthusiasm for the Italian
'Primitives', which is articulated in volume 2 of *Modern Painters*. In 1848 he
married Euphemia (Effie) Gray, although the marriage was to be annulled
seven years later on the grounds of non-consummation. Ruskin published
The Seven Lamps of Architecture in 1849 following a tour of Normandy and
its Gothic architecture, and *The Stones of Venice* (1851, 1853) in celebration
of Venetian Gothic. By this time he had publicly championed the Pre-
Raphaelite painters, who had emerged in 1848 and claimed to paint
according to Ruskinian principles. *Modern Painters* volumes 3 and 4 were
published in 1856 and volume 5 in 1860. In 1858 he met the nine-year-old
Rose La Touche, with whom he fell in love, initiating another disastrous
relationship which was to end with her insanity and death in 1875 and the
onset of his own madness. In 1858 too he lost his Evangelical faith. With
the completion of *Modern Painters* Ruskin turned his attention to social
issues, beginning with four articles attacking political economy in the
Cornhill, which were published together in 1862 as *Unto this Last*. In 1863
he published *Munera Pulveris*, outlining some positive strategies for
economic and social reform, and in 1871 he began writing *Fors Clavigera*,
an intermittent series of public letters to 'the workmen and labourers of
Great Britain'. However, he did not abandon art altogether; indeed, in
1869 he became the first Slade Professor of Fine Art at Oxford, a position
which he resigned in 1878 following his symbolic defeat in the Whistler
libel trial and the first of the seven mental breakdowns which were to
cloud his later years. In 1885 he began publishing his autobiography,
Praeterita, which was brought to a premature conclusion by his final
breakdown in 1889, the year before his death.

The Works of John Ruskin, edited by E. T. Cook and
    A. Wedderburn, Library Edition, 39 vols (1903–12).
J. D. Hunt, *The Wider Sea: A Life of John Ruskin* (1982).
T. Hilton, *John Ruskin: The Early Years, 1819–1859* (New Haven,
    Connecticut, 1985). (First in projected two-volume biography)

See: P. D. Anthony, *John Ruskin's Labour: A Study of Ruskin's Social
    Theory* (Cambridge, 1983).
    L. M. Austin, '*Praeterita*: in the act of rebellion', *Modern Language
    Quarterly*, 48 (1987), 42–58.
    L. M. Austin, *The Practical Ruskin: Economics and Audience in the Late
    Work* (Baltimore, 1991).
    D. Birch, *Ruskin's Myths* (Oxford, 1988). (Fine scholarly study.)
    M. W. Brooks, *John Ruskin and Victorian Architecture* (London and
    New Brunswick, N.J., 1986).
    M. A. Caws, 'Ruskin's Rage and Ours: The Dramatic Style',
    Browning Institute Studies, 18 (1990), 33–53.
    A. B. Crowder, 'Ruskin's Past-and-Present Rhetoric in *Modern
    Painters*', *Victorians Institute Journal*, 10 (1981–82), 69–88.
    S. Emerson, *Ruskin: The Genesis of Invention* (Cambridge, 1993).
    C. S. Finley, 'Scott, Ruskin, and the Landscape of Autobiography',
    Studies in Romanticism, 26 (1987), 549–72.
    C. S. Finley, *Nature's Covenant: Figures of Landscape in Ruskin*
    (Pennsylvania, 1992).
    R. Hewison, *John Ruskin: The Argument of the Eye* (1976).
    (Important study of Ruskin's aesthetics.)
    R. Hewison, ed., *New Approaches to Ruskin: Thirteen Essays* (1981).

W. S. Johnson, 'Style in Ruskin and Ruskin on Style', *Victorian Newsletter*, 59 (1981), 1–6.

G. P. Landow, *Ruskin* (1985). (Short introductory study.)

C. Machann, 'John Ruskin's Style', *Language and Literature*, 8 (1983), 33–53.

J. Hillis Miller, '*Praeterita* and the Pathetic Fallacy', in J. J. McGann, ed., *Victorian Connections* (Charlottesville, Virginia, 1989), pp. 172–78.

J. D. Rosenberg, *The Darkening Glass: A Portrait of Ruskin's Genius* (New York, 1961). (Pioneering modern study.)

P. Sawyer, 'Ruskin and the Matriarchal Logos', in T. E. Morgan, ed., *Victorian Sages and Cultural Discourse: Renegotiating Gender and Power* (New Brunswick, N.J., 1990), pp. 129–41.

J. L. Spear, *Dreams of an English Eden: Ruskin and his Tradition in Social Criticism* (New York, 1984).

M. Wheeler and N. Whiteley, eds, *The Lamp of Memory: Ruskin, Tradition and Architecture* (Manchester, 1992). (Excellent collection of essays.)

M. Wheeler, ed., *Ruskin and Environment: The Storm-Cloud of the Nineteenth Century* (Manchester, 1995). (Wide-ranging volume.)

G. Wihl, *Ruskin and the Rhetoric of Infallibility* (New Haven, Connecticut, 1985).

WILDE, Oscar Fingal O'Flahertie Wills (1854–1900), born in Dublin, was the son of Jane Francesca (Elgee) – the writer 'Speranza' – and the Irish surgeon Sir William Wilde. He studied Classics at Trinity College Dublin, then at Magdalen College, Oxford, where he was awarded First Class Honours and won the Newdigate Prize for Poetry in 1878 and established his reputation as an aesthete. He published his first volume of poems in 1881, the year in which Gilbert and Sullivan's *Patience* satirised and made famous his aesthetic pose, and in the following year he went on a lecture tour to the United States. In 1884 he married Constance Lloyd, and from 1887 to 1889 was editor of *The Woman's World*. In 1888 he published a volume of fairy stories, *The Happy Prince and other tales*, written for his sons. His only novel, *The Picture of Dorian Gray*, appeared in *Lippincott's Magazine* in 1890, and in 1891 he published *The Soul of Man Under Socialism, Intentions, A House of Pomegranates*, and *Lord Savile's Crime and Other Stories*. In 1892 *Lady Windermere's Fan* brought theatrical success, which was consolidated by *A Woman of No Importance* (1893), *An Ideal Husband* (1895), and *The Importance of Being Earnest* (1895). *Salome*, written in French, was performed in Paris by Bernhardt in 1896 (having been refused a licence in England), and published in 1894 in an English translation by Lord Alfred Douglas and with illustrations by Beardsley. Douglas's father, the Marquis of Queensbury, disapproved of his son's relationship with the feted playwright and publicly insulted Wilde in 1895, thereby beginning the chain of events which was to lead to Wilde's trial and two-year imprisonment for homosexual offences. Whilst in prison Wilde wrote a bitterly reproachful letter of self-justification to Douglas, which was published in part in 1905 as *De Profundis*. After his release, bankrupt and disgraced, Wilde went to live in France, where he wrote *The Ballad of Reading Gaol* (1898). He died in Paris.

Complete Works of Oscar Wilde, introduced by Vyvyan Holland (1966). *The Artist as Critic: Critical Writings of Oscar Wilde*, edited by R. Ellmann (1970).

Letters, edited by R. Hart-Davis (1962).
The Uncollected Oscar Wilde, edited by John Wyse Jackson (1991).
Oscar Wilde's Oxford Notebooks: A Portrait of Mind in the Making,
    edited by P. E. Smith and M. S. Helfand (New York, 1989).
R. Ellmann, *Oscar Wilde* (1987). (Authoritative biography).
M. Knox, *Oscar Wilde: A Long and Lovely Suicide* (New Haven,
    Connecticut and London, 1994). (Provocative Freudian
    psychoanalytic biography.)

See: P. F. Behrendt, *Oscar Wilde: Eros and Aesthetics* (New York, 1991).
        (Sees Wilde's homosexuality as the inspiration of his finest work.)
     R. Ellmann, ed., *Oscar Wilde: A Collection of Critical Essays* (New
        York, 1969).
     R. Gagnier, *Idylls of the Marketplace: Oscar Wilde and the Victorian
        Public* (Aldershot, 1987).
     R. Gagnier, ed., *Critical Essays on Oscar Wilde* (New York, 1991).
        (Essays from a wide range of critical approaches).
     N. Kohl, *Oscar Wilde: The Works of a Conformist Rebel*, trans.
        D. H. Wilson (Cambridge, 1989).
     P. Raby, *Oscar Wilde* (Cambridge, 1988).
     A. Sinfield, *The Wilde Century: Effeminacy, Oscar Wilde and the Queer
        Moment* (1994).

WORDSWORTH, Dorothy (1771–1855), born in Cumberland, was the daughter
    of Ann (Cookson) and John Wordsworth. After her mother's death in
    1778, she was separated from her beloved brothers and brought up by
    uncongenial relations. Reunited with her brother William in 1894, she
    devoted the next thirty-five years tirelessly to supporting his poetic
    vocation and to looking after him and, later, upon his marriage, his family.
    Although she herself wrote some poetry it is as a diarist that she excels.
    Her journals, kept at Alfoxden and in Germany, in 1798, and at Grasmere,
    from 1800–3, her happiest years, when she and William lived alone, are
    her finest work. She also wrote narratives of tours in Scotland and Europe
    (1803, 1820, 1822). Following a serious illness in 1829 she suffered from
    arteriosclerosis and premature senility.

            The Journals of Dorothy Wordsworth, ed. E. de Selincourt (1941). (The
                only edition to aim at completeness.)
            The Journals of Dorothy Wordsworth, introduction by H. Darbishire
                (2nd edn, edited by M. Moorman, Oxford, 1971).
            The Grasmere Journals, edited by P. Woof (Oxford, 1991).
            Dorothy Wordsworth: Selections from the Journals, edited by
                P. Hamilton (1992). (Lucid introduction.)
            The Letters of William and Dorothy Wordsworth, edited by
                E. de Selincourt, 8 vols (2nd edn, Oxford, 1967–93).
            R. Gittings and J. Manton, *Dorothy Wordsworth* (1985).

    See: E. Gunn, *A Passion for the Particular: Dorothy Wordsworth: A Portrait*
            (1981).
         M. Homans, *Women Writers and Poetic Identity: Dorothy Wordsworth,
            Emily Brontë, and Emily Dickinson* (Princeton, N.J., 1980).
            (Important study.)
         S. M. Levin, *Dorothy Wordsworth and Romanticism* (New Brunswick,
            N.J., 1987).
         A. K. Mellor, *Romanticism and Gender* (New York and London,
            1993).

J. Simons, *Diaries and Journals of Literary Women from Fanny Burney to Virginia Woolf* (1990). (Intelligent discussion.)

P. Woof, 'Dorothy Wordsworth and the Pleasures of Recognition: An Approach to the Travel Journals', *The Wordsworth Circle*, 22, 3 (1991), 150–65.

P. Woof, 'Dorothy Wordsworth's Grasmere Journals: the patterns and pressures of composition', in R. Brinkley and K. Hanley, eds, *Romantic Revisions* (Cambridge, 1992), pp. 169–90.

Index

Note: Bold numbers refer to the section on Individual Authors